First Innings.

How Out.	Name of Bowler.	Runs.
Ct Alexander	Bannerman	8 6
Bowled	Palmer	1 5 2
Bowled	Bannerman	5 5
Bowled	Alexander	2 8
Ct Bonner	Alexander	5 2
Bowled	Bannerman	2 3
Ct Boyle	Moule	4 2
not out		1 1
Ct Bannerman	Moule	0
Bowled	Moule	0
Run out		2
		8
		1 1
		· 0
	Total of First Innings	4 2 0

| 3 for 4 0 4 | 7 for 4 1 0 | 8 for 4 1 0 | 9 for 4 1 3 | 10 for 6 2 0 |

Second Innings

W. G. GRACE

W. G. GRACE
A Life

SIMON RAE

faber and faber

First published in Great Britain in 1998
by Faber and Faber Limited
3 Queen Square London WC1N 3AU

Photoset by Parker Typesetting Service, Leicester
Printed in England by Clays Ltd, St Ives plc

A CIP record for this book
is available from the British Library

ISBN 0–571–17855–3

2 4 6 8 10 9 7 5 3

To the Memory of Geoffrey Rippon

CONTENTS

ILLUSTRATIONS

Plates 1–6, 8, 10, 13, 14, 16, 17, 22, 25, 27, 28, 29: Roger Mann Collection. Plate 7: Mortlock Library of Southern Australiana, State Library of South Australia, Adelaide. Plate 9: Bearne's (Auctioneers), Exeter. Plates 12, 21, 30: David Frith Collection. Plates 15, 23: Rick Smith Collection. Plate 18: The Robert Opie Collection, Museum of Advertising and Packaging, Gloucester. Plate 24: Tony Sheldon Collection. Plate 26: Roy Barratt.

ENDPAPERS: Scoresheets of the first Test Match played in England, in September 1880. Grace scored his first Test century (*front*) but was outscored by one run by Billy Murdoch (*back*). (Surrey County Cricket Picture Library)

PREFACE

W. G. Grace was unquestionably the dominant personality in Victorian cricket. Some saw him as a classic case of arrested development, a perpetual schoolboy. Certainly he could act the part, as snapshots of him irritating a decidedly unamused Lord Hawke and the Kent captain, J. R. Mason, at the Hastings Festival in 1901, graphically demonstrate (see Plate 25). This is the W.G. of a hundred well-loved anecdotes – irrepressible, child-like, larger than life – and the excuse many writers have taken to produce a caricature rather than a character. For A. Thomson, 'the outsize opulence of his personality made him akin to Mr Pickwick or the jolly Ghost of Christmas Present or Tristram Shandy's Uncle Toby . . . or the great Sir John Falstaff . . . G. K. Chesterton once said that Pickwick was the true English fairy and W.G., that bulky sprite, was a prodigious Puck in a truly English midsummer day's dream.'[1] In this fairy-tale world, Grace 'was king, and though he was a merry monarch rather than an absolute one, his reign was never challenged.'[2]

C. B. Fry, who had the advantage of knowing and playing with Grace, was also reminded of the original merry monarch, but was unequivocal about which aspects of Henry VIII he had in mind. 'Except for his real friends W.G. had a formidable eye and a beetling brow; . . . he knew who he was and who you were, and he possessed when it came to it, an Olympian dignity.'[3] In fact, Grace had what all kings have, power, and the story of his life is largely the story of the exercise of that power.

Perhaps a distinction needs to be made between influence, which Grace unquestionably had, and the daunting personal power that Fry identified. The timing of Grace's emergence onto the scene in the mid-1860s happened to give him an enormous say in the future of the game, which hung in the balance between, on the one hand, a demoralized MCC and the few amateur-controlled counties and, on the other, the northern professionals who, with their Packer-like touring teams, had the makings of an alternative structure wholly independent of Lord's. Grace was the pivotal figure in this power-struggle. With his explosive talent, he was the man the crowds wanted to see, and they would have followed him into either camp. In throwing in his lot with the MCC, he effectively headed off a schism which could have seen the amateur and professional elements drift apart, and handed the control of the game back to the Lord's establishment.

He demanded nothing in return except to be allowed to flout that establishment's most sacred tenet, amateurism. Grace made far more money from the game than any of the professionals, and although this led to controversy that blew up periodically throughout his career, there was nothing anyone could do about it. This was the pattern of his life. He used his power to get what he wanted, and given his imperviousness to criticism, it has to be said he was remarkably successful.

In addition to causing much friction during his lifetime, Grace's 'shamateurism' has drawn reproof from later writers. Benny Green wonders aloud what Grace thought of the 'nonsense' of the amateur–professional divide, and chides him for not renouncing his amateur status and putting paid 'once and for all to the hypocrisy of a two-tiered social structure in the game which was to endure for a hundred years'.[4]

The reason why such a course was unthinkable lies with Grace's family and upbringing. Coming from a fairly humble provincial background, Grace straddled the class lines, but his father, Dr Henry Mills Grace, had no doubts as to the family's rightful place in Victorian society. For any son of his to have played openly as a professional would have been anathema to him. His death in 1871 came at a crucial stage in Grace's life, and it is arguable that he would not have adopted such a blatantly semi-professional lifestyle as he did during the 1870s had his father still been alive. Just how much money Grace made in this period is difficult to determine, but in extrapolating from the known facts, I have shown that cricket provided him with a comfortable living while he was qualifying to become a doctor.

Apart from his mother, Martha Grace, and his uncle, Alfred Pocock, who between them took an impassioned interest in his development as a player, the other formative influence in his life was his elder brother, Edward Mills Grace (E.M.). E.M. was seven years his senior, and a brilliant cricketer in his own right. He set a high standard for his younger brother, who trailed in his wake for many years before finally overhauling him. The intense rivalry between the two – indeed, the fiercely competitive atmosphere generated by five excessively keen if variously talented siblings – is the at the root of Grace's extraordinarily combative character.

Grace's ability to assert himself received a huge boost when he shot up in height as a teenager. He ultimately reached six foot two, and with his enormous beard and the weight he put on in his late twenties, he became a truly imposing physical presence. Unfortuately this went with a violent temper, and there were too many occasions on which he was provoked to actual violence (and was once extremely lucky to avoid ending up in court on a charge of assault). For the man who came to personify cricket, Grace's behaviour often fell woefully short of acceptable standards, and accusations of sharp practice, trickery, intransigence and bullying ring down the years.

Nowhere were the howls of protest louder than Australia, where Grace was twice welcomed as a hero and twice seen off on the boat home with a sense of relief. With the exception of Douglas Jardine, he is the most unpopular England captain ever to tour down under. This makes his two tours (1873–4 and 1891–2) of particular interest. Never was he subjected to such close scrutiny, and never – as he questioned umpires' decisions, appealed for catches that he knew were not out, threatened to come to blows with officials, and ran a piratical course through his contractual agreements – was his character shown up in such a bad light. The Australians encountered similar behaviour from him when they came to England. In 1878 he more or less kidnapped a player from their dressing room at Lord's, and at the Oval in 1882 he so incensed the entire team, and specifically the Demon, Frederick Spofforth, that England suffered a devastating retribution. There is a strong case for saying that Grace was inadvertently responsible for the creation of the whole Ashes saga.

But for all his lack of judgement in the heat of the moment, Grace had the best interests of the game at heart, and did an enormous amount to promote Anglo-Australian cricket. He played a more vital role in setting up the first ever Test on English soil in 1880 than he has normally been given credit for, and even though past his cricketing prime, he established the competitive tone over the next two decades. If sport is war without the shooting, Grace was cricket's natural warlord, and though his antics sometimes appalled them, the Australians kept coming back with wave after wave of superlative bowlers to try their skills against him. Spofforth and Boyle, Turner and Ferris, Trumble, Giffen, Noble, Jones – his was the wicket they sought above all others. And when the smoke of battle rolled away, there were few grudges. In later years Grace became the best of friends with men like Billy Murdoch and Spofforth, and is mentioned with affectionate admiration in the memoirs of others. For all his faults,

Grace was a difficult man to dislike for long, and for the vast majority of his contemporaries, playing with him was a privilege. George Beldam, the brilliant sports photographer, spoke for many when he wrote: 'To play under him was to worship him . . . To know him was to love him.'[5]

Stories of his kindness are legion, and though in money matters he was penny sharp, he was not mean – in 1895 he insisted on giving Alfred Shaw the gate money from his benefit match at Lord's to compensate the great Notts bowler for the disaster of his own benefit match earlier in the season. His medical skills were often disparaged, but as a humble GP in Bristol he won the confidence and affection of his patients, and many of the poorest testified to his generosity in neglecting to send bills they could ill afford to pay. He was especially fond of children, and they were obviously fascinated by him. In 1995 his grand-daughter, Primrose Worthington, told Cliff Morgan on *Sport on 4* how she remembered sitting on his lap as a little girl, plaiting his beard. Grace was a demanding father, perhaps too demanding in the case of his eldest son, who bore his world-famous initials, but he was undeniably devoted to his family, and experienced the agony of so many Victorian parents when he lost two of his four children as young adults.

He had become a legend long before the end of his playing career, but though he could walk with kings – he strolled with two future monarchs – he never lost the common touch, and would readily shake hands with complete strangers if they had the courage to approach him in the street. For all the adulation he attracted, he remained, according to the editor of *Wisden*, the most natural and unspoiled of men. 'Whenever and wherever one met him he was always the same. There was not the smallest trace of affectation about him . . . No man who ever won such world-wide fame could have been more modest in speaking of his own doings.'[6]

His achievements speak for themselves: 54,896 first-class runs (boosted by his phenomenal scoring in minor cricket to over 100,000 runs in all), and 2,876 wickets. And yet, because of their Victorian provenance, his figures do not seem to carry as much conviction as one would expect. The question I have been most frequently asked while engaged on this book is: Just how good was W.G.? Perhaps the abandonment of England's first Test against the West Indies in January 1998 can help put his performances in perspective. As a leader in the *Guardian* pointed out, in Grace's day, 'Tests were routinely played on awful pitches and batsmen just had to cope – W.G. Grace was famous for the way he dealt with shooters.'[7] The Lord's wicket of the 1860s and 1870s was far worse than Sabina Park, and if the bowlers weren't as fast as Ambrose and Walsh, they were certainly quick enough to kill, as the death of George Summer in 1870 proved. In his teens Grace was hitting centuries when fifty was the summit of most batsmen's ambition, and by the time the wickets had improved in the 1890s and Ranjitsinhji, Fry, Abel and Hayward were vying to break the records he had established, old-stagers reflected that had Grace then been in his prime, the bowlers would simply never have got him out.

The truth is, 150 years after his birth W. G. Grace remains, deservedly, the best-known cricketer in the history of the game.

*

This book had its origins in a radio programme I wrote and presented for Radio 4 in 1995. *Not at Dorking* took its title came from a remark attributed to the Surrey stonewaller Harry Jupp, when he was bowled first ball in a benefit match in his home town. 'Ain't you going out, Juppy?' the opposing captain plaintively enquired. 'Not at Dorking,' replied Jupp, busily putting the bails back on. Grace, who played a lot of cricket with Jupp in the 1860s and 70s, was similarly reluctant to leave the crease, and although the programme was not exclusively about him, he naturally became a leading character. A cast of professional actors was supplemented by Christopher Martin-Jenkins and David Lloyd, who played themselves, and gave a very convincing performance commentating on Grace's last great innings at the Oval in 1906 while staring out from the BBC commentary box over the empty acres of Edgbaston. My thanks to them and the rest of a versatile team, and to the producer, Viv Beeby.

Among those who heard *Not at Dorking* was Matthew Evans, the Chairman of Faber and Faber, who put my vague thoughts of exploring Grace and his period further into sharp focus by inviting me to submit a proposal for a biography. I am extremely grateful to him for that initial spur and the commission that followed. I am also indebted to my editor, Julian Loose, and his assistant, Luke Vinten, for their support, encouragement and invaluable criticism. I should also mention Daniel Balado-Lopez, who undertook the demanding task of copy-editing the manuscript. My thanks go to them, and to everyone else involved in the production and promotion of this book.

I would like to thank John Whitworth, Janice Thomson, Ian Smith and Lachlan Mackinnon for their valuable suggestions during the manuscript's progress. I am particularly grateful to David Kynaston, who generously volunteered to read each chapter as I wrote it, and gave me the benefit of his expertise, not only on W.G. and nineteenth-century cricket, but on the wider historical background, saving me from innumerable howlers (though, needless to say, the errors that remain are entirely my responsibility).

All biographers are indebted to those who precede them. By and large, Grace has been well served. In addition to the four books which bear his name as author, Methven Brownlee's biography of 1887 gives an intimate, if uncritical, portrait of him as he appeared to his contemporaries. The *Memorial Biography* of 1919 is, I think, unique in drawing on the recollections of so many contributors, and remains an invaluable source to this day. Bernard Darwin's personal memoir of 1934 vividly evokes Grace in his later years, while, for all its tendency to hagiography, A. A. Thomson's *The Great Cricketer* (1957) is an entertaining and ultimately moving book. No survey, however brief, should overlook Neville Cardus's persuasive essays on both the man and his period, and C. L. R. James's seminal work *Beyond a Boundary* (1963), which was (in part) an attempt to place W.G. and the game he championed at the centre of Victorian culture. Eric Midwinter's *W. G. Grace: His Life and Times* (1981) successfully set Grace in his social context, while, most recently, Robert Low turned the spotlight back onto Grace the cricketer in *W.G.* (1997).

I have also gained illumination from a number of other publications concentrating on different aspects of Grace's life and career. In 1989 the Downend Local History Society published Peris Jones's extensive research into the family background, and *Gentlemen and Players* is the most thorough account of the early years that I know of. David Kynaston's *W.G.'s Birthday Party* (1991) is a masterly celebration of Grace's 1898 Jubilee Match, and those who took part in it. Derek West's three scholarly volumes issued by Darf Publishers are essential reading for anyone interested in the background to W.G.'s cricketing life, and *The Players* (1988) by Ric Sissons is another major contribution to the history of Victorian cricket. David Rayvern Allen's anthology *Cricket with Grace* (1990) brings together many fugitive pieces, and I also found much of interest in *Bat & Pad* (1984), edited by Pat Mullins and Philip Derriman, and *Cradle Days* (1989), a collection of the cricket writings of T. P. Horan ('Felix'), edited by Pat Mullins and Brian Crowley. In *W.G. at Kadina* (1994) Bernard Whimpress produced an exemplary monograph on the most shameful episode of Grace's career, and I am also grateful to him for allowing me to read his unpublished thesis on the strained relations between Grace and his Australian hosts. *W.G. Down Under* by Rick Smith and Ron Williams gives a complete account of both Grace tours, while Rick Smith's *ABC Guide to Australian Test Cricketers* proved a highly useful reference work.

I found myself consulting Sir Pelham Warner's *Gentlemen v. Players* with great regularity, and Bill Frindall's *The Wisden Book of Test Cricket* was similarly never far from the top of the volumes heaped around my desk. I am also very grateful to Bill Frindall for compiling the Statistical Survey, and for outlining the controversy surrounding Grace's record. While accepting the arguments for retaining the traditional figures, I have, perhaps inconsistently, used Derek Lodge's volume published by the Association of Cricket Statisticians for Grace's season-by-season aggregates and averages, and take this opportunity to acknowledge this invaluable resource. As far as Grace's minor cricket is concerned, I have relied upon Neville Weston's meticulously researched summary, published in a limited edition of fifty in 1973. At last, in this 150th anniversary year, the two halves of Grace's career will be united in the covers of one book: J. R. Webber has produced the definitive match-by-match account of Grace's performances in both first-class and minor cricket, *The Chronicle of W.G.*, to be published by the Association of Cricket Statisticians. While I regret not having had access to this treasure trove of nearly 1,000 pages, I am grateful to its compiler for some useful hints and sound advice. For modern monetary equivalents I have used the conversion table at the back of Richard Roberts's *Schroders: Merchants and Bankers* (MacMillan 1992).

I have been greatly helped by a number of cricket archivists, librarians and museum curators, in both the United Kingdom and Australia, and would like to thank the following for their courtesy and kindness: Stephen Green and his assistant Michael Wolton at Lord's; Peter Wynne-Thomas at Trent Bridge, Bert Avery at the County Ground, Bristol, Geoff Hancock at the Oval, and Malcolm Lorimer, Don Ambrose and Keith Hayhurst at Old Trafford; John Wood at the Library of the New South Wales Cricket Association, Sydney, Bernard Whimpress at the Adelaide Oval, and Ross Peacock, David Studham and Jena Pullman at the Melbourne Cricket Ground.

I have also benefited from the generosity of several private collectors. Roger Mann opened his great collection to me and worked tirelessly to supply my requests for photographs; David Frith sent photocopies of his Grace letters along with a selection of photographs; Malcolm Lorimer showed me some of Neville Weston's scrapbooks; Rick Smith gave me a copy of George Arthur's scrapbook covering Grace's tour of 1873–4, along with much other valuable material, including a couple of rare photographs. Roy Barratt and Tony Sheldon also contributed valuable prints. My thanks to all of them. I would also like to thank Brian Bearne for allowing me access to Grace's collection of cricket books that his firm auctioned in Exeter in 1996. I was given every assistance by Robin Barlow and Richard Bearne to take the fullest advantage of this unique opportunity, and I am extremely grateful to them. Anton Bantock, of the Malago Society, generously loaned me Nora Peache's diary.

A number of people have shared their family reminiscences of W.G. with me: Julian Lawton Smith, Peggy Gruber, Robert Gretton, Richard Matthews. I am particularly grateful to Colonel G. F. Grace, the grandson of E. M. Grace, for allowing me to listen to an audio cassette he had made of his father's (Edgar Mervyn Grace's) recollections of W.G., and to Dr Richard Bernard for showing me round the various family sites in Downend, and discussing his great-great-uncle's medical career with me. It was with great sadness that I heard of Dr Bernard's death as the book was nearing completion. Ken and Anne Clarke generously shared the fruits of their meticulous research into Grace's servant Harriet Fowler, and I am happy to acknowledge the help they have given me in passing on census returns, death certificates and other painstakingly acquired material. Dr Peter Toghill displayed a similar generosity in giving me the benefit of his extensive knowledge of Grace's medical training.

I am also indebted to the secretaries, librarians or archivists of the following institutions for their prompt and full reponses to enquiries: The Royal Archive, Windsor; The Royal College of Surgeons of England; The Royal College of Physicians of Edinburgh; The General Medical Council; The University Library, Aberdeen; The Central Library, Aberdeen.

I did the bulk of my research in the British Library, and was fortunate to experience both the fading splendour of the old British Museum Reading Room and the chaste opulence of Colin St John Wilson's new St Pancras building. The staff maintained a high level of efficiency and courtesy throughout what must have been an enormously stressful period and I am grateful for all the help I have received from them. I would also like to thank the staffs of the other libraries I visited: The Bodleian Library, Oxford; Grimsby Reference Library; Hull Central Library; The

Mitchell Library, Glasgow; Bristol Central Library; Manchester Central Library; The London Library; Devizes Library; Chippenham Library; and the British Library's Newspaper Division, Colindale. In Australia I used the state libraries of New South Wales, Victoria and South Australia, as well as the town libraries of Ballarat (NSW) and Launceston (Tasmania).

The hospitality I met with on my Australian trip was quite overwhelming and I would like to thank the following for making my stay as enjoyable as it was productive: Holly Davis and Noek Witzard, Penny and Roger Fenton, Jack Pollard, Richard Cashman, Alfred James, Charles and Audrey Nicholson, Angus Trumble, Simon Trumble, Robert Trumble, Fiona Gruber and Mark Williams, Martin Flanagan, Rick and Leanne Smith.

I would also like to thank the following for their special contributions to the project: Hilary Fields set up innumerable contacts as well as producing some invaluable research material; Norman Isaacs trawled Colindale in an attempt to track down what now appears to be apocryphal German war propaganda arising from W.G.'s death; and Jill Grey helped with some late supplementary research. Will Commery was my guide to Elmer's End Cemetery and the Crystal Palace; David Inshaw was my photographer and beard consultant; Eric Norris quickly helped me build up a working library of Grace texts; Chris Greenwood, Peter Howard and Chris West between them fielded various computing disasters; and my agent, Michael Thomas, has been a similarly powerful force for sanity.

Others who have helped in one way or another are: Mike Adams, Dr Stephen Bailey (Director of Physical Education, Winchester College), Jo Batchelor, Mark Bland, Richard Boston, Daphne Bryant, David Buxton, Gerry Byrne, John Caperon, Wendy Cope, John Cordingley, Oliver Cyriax, Joan Eastwood, Matthew Engel, Trevor Enifer of the Crystal Palace Foundation, Janet Gruber, Penny Gruber, Roger Hamilton, Sophie Hannah, Frank Keating, John King, John Kirkaldy, Owen Kyffin, Alistair Lawrence, Jack Long, Tony Lurcock, Sue Maconie, Christopher Martin, Brian Pearce, Nick Pearson, Gerard Siggins, Martin Smith, Poppy Szaybo, Anne Taylor, Ray Taylor, Richard Taylor, Bill Wallis, Pat and John Winser, Kit Wright, Richard Wright. My thanks to all of them.

All writers demand tolerance and understanding from those closest to them. I have received both in abundance from my mother, Jill Rae, whose great generosity also removed the additional burden of financial worry in the closing stages. Janice Thomson was exposed to dangerous levels of freshly gleaned information over long periods of time, but came through the ordeal with her temper intact, and at a crucial moment boosted morale with the gift of a splendid pub sign featuring Grace himself. My daughter, Albertine Rae, has been forbearance personified. I am deeply grateful to each of them; without their support I would not have completed this book in time for W.G.'s 150th birthday.

S. R.
Devizes – Hackney
January 1996 – February 1998

ONE

Oᴺᴇ of W. G. Grace's grandfathers was a butler; one of his sons became an admiral. Grace, like his father and his four brothers, trained as a doctor. Though he did not go to public school or either of the ancient universities, he made sure his eldest son did. This steadily rising curve from relative obscurity to moderate eminence may seem insignificant beside Grace's spectacular leap to enduring and world-wide fame, but it was of great importance to him. As a towering figure on the stage of Victorian England, he was rivalled in terms of public recognition only by the Queen herself and William Ewart Gladstone, but he remained, to a remarkable degree, an ordinary representative of Middle England.

He was born and brought up a West Countryman, and never lost the slight burr of a Gloucestershire accent. Bristol, where he spent his years in general practice, was a major port and a bustling commercial centre, participating fully in the unprecedented economic expansion of the Victorian period, but the surrounding countryside, where he spent his formative years, remained locked in the timeless agricultural cycle celebrated in the novels of Thomas Hardy. Unimpressed – and certainly unintimidated – by metropolitan sophistication, Grace conducted his life with a countryman's canniness according to a dependable, and unquestioned, provincial code of hard work and thrift.

Typical of his class and true to his regional origins, Grace was undoubtedly also the creation of his family. Some great men appear like cuckoos in the nest, having nothing in common with their parents or siblings. Grace is inseparable from his background, and his success was grounded in a tight-knit family network whose support, values, training, code of discipline and internal rivalries underpinned his personality. It was a hard school, but it generated huge self-confidence. The family was fiercely protective of its own, pulling together instinctively in the face of any external challenge. Grace's home provided a bastion against the outside world, and a forcing house for his immense talents. What he learned in this family environment sustained and governed him throughout his life, and his career developed in accordance with the path laid down for him. His strengths and weaknesses were family strengths and weaknesses. His greatness, it might be said, was simply an exaggeration of his Graceness.

*

Little is known about Grace's paternal grandfather, Henry Grace, and the facts that exist are mainly derived from a court case in which he was posthumously cast in the role of villainous family retainer. Thirty years after his death he was remembered as 'a great coarse, potbellied, unwieldy man, wholly deficient . . . in the Grace of God'.[1] This vicious portrait is hardly reliable, however. It was part of the testimony of Thomas Provis, who, like the far more notorious Tichborne Claimant after him, concocted a false identity and laid claim to a great inheritance. Provis's intended victims were the Smyth family of Ashton Court, Bristol.

The case was heard at Gloucester Crown Court in August 1853. Provis appeared as the plaintiff under his alias, Sir Richard Smyth, and presented a 'last will and testament' that had turned up conveniently in an old family servant's trunk. This document purported to prove that he was the legitimate, if unacknowledged, son of Sir Hugh Smyth, who had died in 1825. In it the deceased baronet explains how he came to accept his long-lost heir:

From the circumstances of a family nature, this boy was brought up in private, and through the rascallity [sic] of my butler, Grace, under whose especial charge my son was, he left England clandestinely in the year 1813, and I had been assured by Grace that my son had died abroad, but at the death of Grace I became possessed of doubts of my son's demise. Now under the impression that my son had died I made a will in the year 1814. That will I now abrogate, annul and sett asside [sic], by this last will and testament, and by the document do acknowledge Richard Hugh Smyth my legitimate son and heir.[2]

This was a persuasive piece of evidence, if genuine. But as Sir Frederick Thesiger, acting for the Smyth family, pointed out, the only thing it unquestionably proved was that in the later stages of his life, Sir Hugh had developed the same spelling foibles as his supposed son. To the great amusement of the court, a brief spelling test exposed the plaintiff's ingrained preference for double consonants. Indeed, so effective was Thesiger's conduct of the case generally that Provis's position collapsed on the third day of the trial and he was bounced into an ignominious confession of perjury and fraud.

One of the many witnesses called was Elizabeth Grace, Henry Grace's widow. Although well into her seventies, she made the effort to travel to Gloucester, and the evidence she gave supplies the bulk of what is known about her and her husband.

Elizabeth Mills, as she was before her marriage, was the personal maid of Margaret Wilson (daughter of the Bishop of Bristol), who married Hugh Smyth in 1797. Elizabeth soon followed her mistress into matrimony when she met Henry Grace in 1800 and it was through her that Grace came to be employed, in 1801, at Ashton Court. (This scotched Provis's claim that Henry Grace had taken charge of him as an infant in 1797.)

As has been pointed out in previous accounts of the case, Elizabeth Grace's evidence completely cleared her husband and contributed to Provis's downfall, but the surprising fact is that she appeared not for the Smyth family, but for the plaintiff. 'Sir Richard' had been in the Bristol area for some years prior to the court case, testing the water and building up support. He masqueraded as an educationalist (and claimed amongst other things to have shared a study with the great Thomas Arnold at Winchester). It was in this capacity that Elizabeth Grace had met him, as she had been running her own small school in Bristol for many years. 'Sir Richard' developed the acquaintance, seeing how useful Mrs Grace could be to him, and doubtless hinting that he would be generous to his friends if he won his case. She agreed to be interviewed by his solicitor and came to court prepared to testify that the new will was in Sir Hugh's handwriting. However, when the implications of Provis's position became apparent, she beat a hasty retreat, claiming, 'I cannot see any writing.' In a rather candid aside later, she lamented, 'I was never told, if I came to speak for the plaintiff, it was for a forger and I should be imprisoned.'[3] There was no danger of that, but Thesiger subjected her to a rigorous cross-examination which revealed the details of her early life.

The Graces had started a family soon after their marriage, and Elizabeth moved out of Ashton Court to set up home in Bristol. Henry later took out a lease on the house for his own lifetime and that of his daughter, Anne, who was born in 1805. His wages, which were fifteen shillings a week in 1804, proved inadequate, and in 1808, fewer than three weeks before she was due to give birth again, Elizabeth took the drastic step of advertising for pupils in the local papers. She announced the opening of a school for girls under twelve years of age, at her own home, offering board and tuition for eighteen guineas per annum. Her son, Henry Mills Grace, was born on 22 February 1808.

After living apart for several years, Elizabeth and her husband formally separated in 1819. Two years later Henry Grace died, leaving Elizabeth nothing but the lease on the house. She never remarried, and spent the rest of her long life struggling to provide for herself and her children. In addition to Anne, she had two other daughters, Elizabeth and Mary. They remain shadowy figures. The likelihood is that after helping in their mother's school they left home to become governesses, or slipped quietly into the anonymity of marriage.

Life offered very different prospects for Henry Mills. Surrounded by adoring females from the beginning, and the focus of his mother's ambitions, he was to escape the genteel poverty in which he was raised and make dramatic progress up the social ladder by joining the medical profession. The process of becoming a doctor was a difficult one for someone from a poor background. The Royal College of Physicians recruited its members almost exclusively from Oxford and Cambridge, and had little interest in widening the social catchment of the profession. Pressure for change came from the Royal College of Surgeons, which by the 1830s had about 200 fellows and 8,000 licentiates. Third in the jealously guarded medical hierarchy was the Society of Apothecaries. It was their desire to raise their members' standing above that of common tradesmen through a rigorous examination system which made a great contribution to improving standards in the first half of the century. The society required five years' apprenticeship before examination, and developed the custom of 'walking the hospitals' as useful work experience.

This at least would weed out those who fainted at the sight of blood. Hospitals in those days were not for the squeamish. Watching someone having a leg sawn off with no palliative other than a glass of laudanum and a rag on which to bite was guaranteed to weed out those who hadn't the stomach for it. All five Grace brothers followed in their father's footsteps through the bloodied sawdust. Though not without compassion, they were not a sentimental family.

With London taking the lead, hospitals began to organize schools of their own to take the place of the unregulated apprenticeship system. The men they turned out were relatively well educated and well trained, though socially beneath the physicians and surgeons. By about 1830 the term 'general practitioner' came into use.

This is what Henry Mills Grace aspired to be, though as there was no Medical School in Bristol until 1833, he must have worked towards his examinations as a local surgeon's apprentice before finishing his training at St Thomas's and Guy's in London. He certainly worked hard. His son records that he used to play cricket on the Clifton Downs 'between the hours of five and eight in the morning', because that was the only time he could get off.[4]

Although there was no legal requirement for a doctor to be qualified until the Medical Act of 1858, Henry Mills Grace gained his LSA (Licentiate of the Apothecaries Company) in 1829 and MRCS (Member of the Royal College of Surgeons) in 1830. He set great store by his qualifications, an attitude he passed on to his sons. When he applied to the Westerleigh Parish Vestry committee in 1832 for the post of parish surgeon, he emphasized that he 'would not presume to propose myself were I not legally qualified'.[5]

*

In 1830, Henry Mills Grace faced the new decade with the hard-won title of 'Doctor' and every prospect of a rewarding career ahead of him. He was an energetic, well-favoured man of five foot ten inches, devoted to outdoor pursuits. Cricket absorbed what spare time he could find in the summer, and in winter he followed the hounds. Although not possessed of a good fortune, he had his health and his profession, and was now clearly in want of a wife.

He found her in the home of one of Bristol's most prominent, not to say eccentric, citizens, George Pocock. Pocock, like Henry's mother, was in the education business, running his own school – or, rather, 'Academy' – at Prospect Place. His prospectus spoke encouragingly of the 'airiness and extent of the premises', and described a 'system of education . . . calculated chiefly for men of business'. This included 'penmanship, in all its hands, elocution, arithmetic, mensuration illustrated by globes, accompanied by a general view of the commercial world'.[6]

As viewed from Prospect Place, the commercial world must have appeared full of promise. Bristol was a prosperous city and the country's second port. A gazetteer of the time gave this thumbnail sketch: 'Bristol is a seaport, and county of itself, its chief trade is with the West Indies, its manufactures are the sugar refinery, earthenware, soap, and hats; has 18 churches, a cathedral, guildhall, custom-house, and exchange . . . Steam packets to Dublin, Cork, Waterford, Liverpool, Carmarthen, Haverford-west, Swansea, Newport, Chepstow, Ilfracombe, and Tenby.'[7] And the city's communications were soon to be extended by the engineering genius of the age, Isambard Kingdom Brunel, the rising star of the Great Western Railway.

With boarders paying twenty-five guineas a year and day pupils four, the Academy was a success. A measure of Pocock's worldly wealth can be gleaned from a public audit he printed in 1820 to establish his credentials as a leading supporter of the Methodist community. He had been, he said,

the primary cause under God of raising not less than ten entirely new societies, and eight new chapels, for the erection of some of which he advanced the whole amount, £900 on one, £600 on another, and £300 on a third; [he had contributed] liberally towards the erection of every chapel in the kingdom whenever applied to, and that without a solitary exception; . . . giving £60 toward the erection of St Philip's Chapel in this city; [and] lending various sums of money to Trustees of chapels in almost every direction; [while] aiding the funds for the Methodist poor, several of whom are and have been for years the regular pensioners of himself and his wife . . .[8]

This catalogue of charitable activity appeared in Pocock's opening broadside in a vitriolic pamphlet war with the city's Methodist establishment. The fundamental issue was authority and power. Pocock was an active and energetic man of progressive ideas, and his ambitions to improve the lot of his fellow man were by no means limited to teaching the sons of tradesmen the basics of mensuration. He wanted to extend the benefits of education and religious instruction to those on the fringes of society, and if they would not come to chapel to hear the Word, he would take the Word to them. In addition to its port and other commercial interests, Bristol was also an important mining area. The miners eked out a pitiable existence in slovenly villages or squatter camps, with no provision for schooling or worship. Pocock's scheme involved travelling round the mining districts and preaching from a tent. The project was a notable success. The colliers were even persuaded to subscribe a pittance towards some basic education for their children. The number of tent preachers rose.

Unhappily, Pocock's good results, combined with his insistence on keeping the reins of the operation in his own hands, provoked jealousy among the Bristol brethren, and in scenes that could have been lifted from *Silas Marner*, and which foreshadowed some of his grandsons' battles, Pocock and his supporters were called to account, roundly stigmatized, and finally 'excluded'.

Displaying the robust passion for self-justification which became a pronounced family trait, Pocock retaliated. He had the organ he had donated to his local chapel removed. Further fuel was added to an already blazing fire by the appearance of 'The Methodist Pill', a defamatory satire on the hypocrisy of Pocock's opponents ('the Pill is an excellent discovery for enabling the Preachers' Wives and Daughters to follow the fashions of the World, and the Preachers to study Politics, instead of Religion, for on the Sunday morning this Pill will cast a sanctimonious smirk on the former, and will work miracles on the latter').[9] Despite Pocock's denials that the noxious pamphlet emanated from his Academy, a couple of the brethren paid a visit to the printer, as a result of which they were able to denounce two of Pocock's sons, George Pocock junior and John, as the perpetrators.

Undeflected by this embarrassing filial support, Pocock signed off with a third pamphlet, 'Facts without a Veil' (1820), in which he defended the stance he and his allies had taken and roundly condemned the 'fabric of Methodist Government [which] is tottering on every side, and must eventually fall, unless the disgusting haughtiness of several lordly Preachers be speedily humbled'.[10] The rupture with the Bristol brethren was total and irreparable. History does not relate what happened to the organ.

Pocock retired inside the walls of his Academy for a while, but the timetable's unvarying treadmill could not keep him satisfied for long. Through experimenting with his pupils' kites on 'the breezy eminences of Clifton and Durdham Downs' he stumbled upon a radical new form of transport.

The story of how he developed his kite-drawn carriage is told at exuberant length in his book *The Aeropleustic Art* (1827). Parts of this make chilling reading for anyone concerned with the development of English cricket. First Pocock launched his third son, Alfred, on a kite-drawn sledge. This was whisked away by the wind 'with a velocity so great, that all attempts to overtake it were quite fruitless'. The Downs in those days were pitted with quarries and the future coach of England's greatest cricketer whistled over the lip of one of these, landing '(as it happened) in perfect safety'. Pocock's confidence in his inventions, and his casual attitude to his children's safety, are demonstrated even more clearly in his next experiment, which involved flight. He proudly records that he allowed his daughter, Martha, 'the daring honour' of being '*the* first Aeropleust', and gaily launched W. G. Grace's mother-to-be into the sky, strapped into a chair attached to an array of huge kites.[11] In one version of the story, Martha was actually sailed across the Clifton Gorge, but Pocock himself, never one to play down the heroics of any member of his family, makes no such claim.

Despite Martha's inaugural flight, kites could not mount a serious challenge to the hot air balloon which the Montgolfier brothers had pioneered in the 1780s. Pocock, however, persisted with his kite-carriage, or 'charvolant' as he called it. Most of the stories about this bizarre experiment have to be treated with suspicion, but it seems Pocock first road-tested his invention in 1822, taking his family from Bristol to Marlborough at speeds of between sixteen and twenty miles an hour, and scandalizing onlookers by allowing his daughters their turn to steer. A more ambitious trip to London in 1827 is said to have caused a sensation in the capital, and the following year it is claimed that George IV demanded to inspect the 'charvolant' personally at Ascot in June, but newspaper accounts of the race meeting are silent on the subject, and the Royal Archive at Windsor has no record of any such encounter.[12] Nevertheless, there does seem to have been something of a craze for kite-riding among the young men of Bristol at this time, and Henry Mills Grace was one of them, and this is presumably how he met Martha. By the autumn of 1831 a date had been set for the wedding.

Unfortunately it coincided with the worst riot in the city's history. The whole country was in a volatile state after the House of Lords' rejection of the second Reform Bill. Sporadic window-smashing in London was followed by more serious disturbances in the Midlands, but by far the worst trouble flared up in Bristol. The immediate cause was the visit of the city's recorder, Sir Charles Wetherell. Wetherell was heartily disliked for his anti-Reform position, and when he arrived on Saturday, 29 October, he was met by large and hostile crowds who stoned his carriage enthusiastically all the way to the Guildhall. By the time he was bustled on to the Mansion House for a formal dinner, the situation was getting out of control. Despite a personal appeal by the mayor, who showed great courage throughout, the crowd would not be placated, and soon rioters broke into the ground floor of the building, seizing among other things Wetherell's portmanteau. The sight of his linen being ripped to shreds by a jeering mob was enough to persuade him to beat a retreat, and he escaped over the roofs disguised, it was said, in women's clothing.

Although the recorder escaped with his skin, the city did not get off so lightly. Mindful, no doubt, of the embarrassing carnage of the Peterloo massacre only a dozen years earlier, the commanding officer of the military force on hand deployed his men with great restraint, and at no little personal risk rode about through the mêlée pleading with the crowds to disperse. They would not, and the rest of the weekend was given over to an orgy of looting and destruction. Sunday was particularly bad, with a ragged army tramping in from the outlying districts led, according to several sources, by those same marginalized miners to whom Pocock had addressed his tent ministry.

The mob broke into the prisons and laid siege to the bishop's palace on College Green. Then, as though ticking off the buildings on the gazetteer's list, they burnt down the Customs House and several warehouses, from one of which issued a stream of burning rum 'filling the gutters so fast that the drains could not carry it off'. A 'hedge of fire' ignited across a street and several women who ran its terrifying gauntlet were set alight and were only saved by the alacrity of a detachment of sailors who wrestled them to the ground and rolled them about until the flames were extinguished. Floodgates were opened and bridges wantonly destroyed. And through the town, bands of young men lurched from house to house demanding 'drink or blood'.[13] Pocock and his family must have spent an agonizing night looking out over the ravaged city, wondering where the next plume of flame and smoke would spring up, and whether they would hear the heavy blows of a cudgel on the door.

By Monday the whirlwind had blown itself out, but the city presented a dismal spectacle:

Morning dawned on such a scene as had never before been witnessed in this place. The flames, it is true, were subsiding, but the appearance of Queen square was appalling in the extreme. Numerous buildings were reduced to a heap of smoking ruins, and others were . . . falling in; while around, in various parts, lay several of the rioters, in the last stage of senseless intoxication, and with countenances more resembling fiends than men.[14]

Pocock's Academy had survived unscathed (unlike a number of other schools that appeared in the lengthy newspaper lists of businesses destroyed). Estimates of the damage ranged from £200,000 to £2 million; casualties were put at twelve dead and ninety-four wounded. Tuesday and Wednesday saw inquests on some of the charred and mutilated remains, and on Thursday, 3 November, Henry Mills Grace and Martha Pocock were married in St Michael's Church, just around the corner from Prospect Place. The church was described by a contemporary as 'a vicious combination of Grecian and Gothic architecture', but it seems unlikely that, with much of the city beyond its walls reduced to smouldering rubble, either bride or groom would have been unduly worried by its 'architectural absurdities'.[15]

TWO

Henry Grace had already decided where he would practise his profession, and, leaving Bristol to bury the dead and start rebuilding, he and Martha 'settled down in Downend, Gloucestershire, where they lived for the rest of their lives'.[1] Although today subsumed into the urban sprawl of Bristol, Downend in 1831 was a distinct village surrounded by countryside. The Graces' first home was Downend House, North Street, an unexceptional Georgian building with creeper partially covering the façade and two cedar trees in the front garden. When the house was sold after the Great War, the estate agent advertised this 'old-world Period House where the late W. G. Grace, the Famous Cricketer, was born' as having six bedrooms, a cloakroom, a bathroom and three reception rooms.[2] It sounds spacious, but as their family increased, it gradually began to seem less so.

Like any other community in England, Downend was rigidly stratified in terms of class. There were a handful of powerful and wealthy inhabitants like the Caves of Cleve Hill, who were Bristol bankers and Merchant Venturers, and Robert Lewis of Cleve Lodge, whose estate included property in Wales. Such people would, in all but the most extreme emergency, call on their Bristol physicians for medical attention. There was a small middle-class contingent centred on the vicar and the vicarage, and below them a jealously calibrated scale of tradesmen, servants and artisans engaged in cottage industries like pin-making or candle-making. Below them were the bedraggled ranks of labourers and farm-workers. Times were difficult in the 1830s, and even more so in the 1840s when the 'Condition of England' became a major concern with politicians, novelists and social commentators alike. Whatever its eventual benefits, the Reform Act which was finally passed in 1832 did nothing in the short term to alleviate the endemic poverty of the lower classes.

With the prosperity of the High Victorian period still some way off, a young doctor dependent on the fees of his patients had to work hard to make ends meet. Henry Grace would ride for miles at a moment's notice to visit the sick. The roads were poor, and treacherous at night, and a man on horseback or thrown about in a gig had no protection from the weather. Like the sons he fathered, Dr Grace was exceptionally tough, and he needed to be.

His first son, Henry, was born on 31 January 1833, followed by Annie in 1834. The early years at Downend were taxing as Dr Grace strove to establish himself, and Martha adapted to her role as mother and mistress of the household. But no matter how busy they were, they kept up with the family in Bristol, and would almost certainly have found time to visit Clifton during a momentous week in August 1836, when the British Association for Advancement of Science held its first conference there. The nation's leading 'philosophers', as scientists were then known, gathered for a week of lectures and demonstrations which were enthusiastically attended by the local inhabitants. Among the many peripheral attractions on offer, *The Times* reported, 'Mr Pocock will exhibit his kite-carriage daily on Durdham-down'.[3]

The kite-carriage was, however, upstaged by the dramatic events at the Clifton Gorge where Isambard Kingdom Brunel attempted to establish a fixed link between the two sides as the first stage of his magnificent suspension bridge. This attracted enormous public interest, which intensified when, half-way through the week, a hawser drawing the first solid bar across to the Clifton side gave way. Miraculously no one was killed, but the bar was seriously damaged. The accident was a severe set-back, 'but Mr Brunel immediately set a great number of hands to work, and feels confident he shall have the bar in its place, uniting these stupendous rocks, on Saturday morning'.[4] That confidence was justified, and on Saturday, 27 August 1836 the bar was in place and the foundation stone laid. The Downs were thronged with people, and the river below was filled with jostling boats. A trumpet blast and cheers from crowds on both sides of the gorge announced that Brunel's great project was truly under way. George Pocock saluted the efforts of a fellow visionary with a sky message reading 'Success to the Undertaking', though surprisingly his banner was suspended not from kites but from balloons.

Such high days and holidays would have been few and far between – a village celebration of the coronation of the new young Queen in June 1837 certainly, but there can have been little else to disrupt the hard-working routine as Henry and Martha devoted themselves to their responsibilities. They were to have nine children in all – the same as

Victoria and Albert – and in every respect they were the typical Victorian family.

With more mouths to feed, Dr Grace sought ways of increasing his income. The neighbouring parish of Mangotsfield was at the heart of Bristol's mining area, and, tapping perhaps the old Smyth connection, Henry Grace became surgeon to the collieries of Sir John Smyth & Co., the most important of the Coalpit Heath mines. The lot of the miners had barely improved since the days of George Pocock's tent mission, and in Bristol, as elsewhere, boys were still sent underground despite the Factory Act of 1833 which had outlawed the employment of children under the age of nine. Pressure from Lord Shaftesbury and others eventually resulted in a Commission of Inquiry into the State of Children in Employment, and a government commissioner, Elijah Waring, arrived in south Gloucestershire in 1841. Henry Grace was one of the doctors Waring interviewed, and he came across as 'an intelligent practitioner [and] a gentleman of benevolent and considerate feelings'. However, he towed the company line on the dangers of mining and told Waring that accidents 'were generally the result of carelessness on the part of the miner, in not supporting the roof with proper caution'.[5]

He may have reviewed his confidence in the mines' safety standards when he was called to a terrible accident in 1845. Five men died at one of the Soundwell collieries when a rope snapped at the end of a shift. There was only one survivor, and the terrible fall had left him with an arm 'broken to pieces and his head and back cut in several places'. Dr Grace had the unenviable task of amputating the ruined limb, while his patient, conscious throughout, stoically smoked his pipe. A local rope-maker told the inquest: 'I never saw rope . . . in such a bad condition in my life. I have seen better rope brought to my yard as old junk.'[6]

In addition to his work for the collieries, Dr Grace served as parish doctor, and, after 1848, as Medical Officer for the Mangotsfield Guardians of the Poor, with responsibility for Mangotsfield, Staple Hill and Downend. He was also a consultant at the nearby lunatic asylum, known locally as Mason's Madhouse, and in 1848 was involved in a case against its owner, Dr Joseph Bompas, on the charge of admitting patients without the proper certificates signed by two doctors. An inquiry was held, but the charges were not substantiated. At some stage his medical responsibilities were further increased when he was appointed Surgeon to the Royal Gloucestershire Hussars, a position of sufficient importance to be inscribed on his tombstone.

On top of his duties as a doctor, he added to his workload by becoming the local registrar, recording the births, deaths and marriages of the parish, and, from 1841, overseeing the census returns. He liked to involve his family in his activities as much as he could, and over the years anyone available was conscripted as an enumerator. Dr Grace exemplified the Victorian values of hard work, ambition and public service, and it is a mark of his success as a father that he instilled the same virtues in his sons.

*

Dr Grace's best-known legacy to his sons was, of course, his love of cricket (though he was also a keen huntsman, following the Duke of Beaufort's hounds during the winter months). The most detailed account of how cricket came to dominate life at Downend comes in the two volumes of memoirs written by W.G. – *Cricket* (1891) and *'W.G.' Cricketing Reminiscences and Personal Recollections* (1899). Although they were both ghosted, Grace took enormous pains over them, and they certainly tell the story as he wanted it told. He was meticulous as far as facts and figures were concerned, and between them the two books provide an accurate, if unanalytical, record of the cricket of his time and his personal achievements. Though they remain selectively silent on the controversies that dogged his career, there is no reason to doubt their reliability as far as the early years are concerned. The portrait of Dr Grace that emerges from their pages is a loving and appreciative one.

According to W.G., it appears that it was his eldest brother, Henry, who was mainly responsible for the resurgence of their father's interest in the game. There was no team in the village, and Dr Grace had to be content with 'running into Bristol now and again, to look at the matches of the Clifton and Bristol clubs'. However, when Henry was sent away to school as an eight-year-old, he became besotted with the game, and 'every time he came home he would talk of nothing but cricket. My father realised that he would be compelled sooner or later to create time to help him, if he desired to keep in touch with him physically as well as mentally. He was strong in the belief that if you want to educate and influence a boy thoroughly it is as important to play with him as to work with him.' Dr Grace decided to make a cricket pitch in the garden. 'It was not much of a pitch, nor was it full size; but it was sufficient to teach the rudiments of the game.'[7] That was the start of the family regime of practice and coaching that was to bear such astonishing fruit in the years to come.

Not content with providing practice in the garden, and perhaps feeling that he still had some life as a player left in him, Dr Grace decided to establish a cricket club in the locality. Downend was not large enough to support a club on its own, so he brought in the neighbouring villages which collectively formed the Mangotsfield Cricket Club. The best place to play was a nearby common called Rodway Hill. As its name suggests, it was by no means flat, so once again Dr Grace took the lead in making a new cricket pitch. He had a most useful ally in his brother-in-law, Alfred Pocock, the youngest of Martha's brothers. Although he had been living at the St Michael's Hill Academy when his father died in 1843 (he is the witness on George Pocock's death certificate), Alfred had not followed his elder brother, the scurrilous pamphleteer, into the family education business. In the census of 1861, his occupation is given as 'Lithographic Artist'. The fact that he was staying at Downend when the census was taken is not surprising. He was very close to his sister, got on extremely well with his brother-in-law, and made the twelve-mile round trip from his home on the other side of Bristol two or three times a week.

The two men who founded the Downend cricketing dynasty were only average players themselves. Alfred Pocock did not take up the game until he was was twenty-three, though he had the advantage of being a 'first-class racquet player'. It was perhaps this late start and the need to apply himself consciously to acquire the basics of the game that made him such a good coach. Dr Grace was an obstinate right-hand bat, though he bowled and threw with his left. Although he lacked the natural skills of his famous sons, he brought to his game an abundance of energy, enthusiasm and determination. He was also a forceful personality with the power to bend others to his will – an instinctive empire-builder. In 1846 he persuaded the neighbouring West Gloucestershire Cricket Club to amalgamate with the Mangotsfield Club, whose unpromising name passed into oblivion. The control of the new club, however, passed swiftly into Dr Grace's hands. On the field he was supported by Alfred, and two of Martha's nephews who came down from London for their summer holidays, William Rees and George Gilbert. And of course his own sons swelled the ranks as soon as they were considered old enough. The West Gloucestershire Club was the launch-pad for three of the greatest careers in nineteenth-century cricket, but once it ceased to be a useful vehicle for the family's ambitions, it was allowed to die. It played its last match in 1867, the year after Fred, the youngest of the Test-class triumvirate, made his first-class debut.

As Henry and Martha became an established feature of Downend life, the family grew in the approved fashion. Fanny was born in 1838, Alfred in 1840. Edward Mills, known throughout his adult life by his initials, E.M., was born on 28 November 1841, followed by Alice in 1845 and Elizabeth Blanche in 1846. The year 1848 was troubled by revolutions on the continent and sporadic Chartist outbreaks at home, but the Graces were more concerned with Martha's eighth pregnancy. With seven children as well as servants to accommodate, the house was crowded, and there is a family tradition that Martha moved into the nearby midwife's home, Clematis Cottage, for her confinement. Whether this happened or not, she gave birth to her fourth son on her own birthday, 18 July, and on 8 August, with his cricketing cousin William Rees as godfather, the baby was baptized William Gilbert. Of the two Christian names he received, Gilbert was the one favoured by his family and close friends, though his mother apparently called him Willie. The rest of the world would know him by his initials, and a range of titles from the Champion to the Old Man, derived in awe and affection from his unique position in the game he made his own.

*

Although he would have known Downend House throughout his childhood, Gilbert can have had no memories of actually living there. In 1850, with another baby expected (George Frederick), Dr Grace decided to move. The new house was called The Chesnuts ('the dropping of the centre "t" in "Chestnuts" is an etymological freak sanctioned by custom').[8] It wasn't a big move, as the new house was only a couple of hundred yards away, on the other side of the street.

Downend House still stands, albeit in a rather drab, anonymous condition, its front garden lost to a busy main road, but The Chesnuts has not survived. It was knocked down in the 1930s to make way for a cinema that was never built, and the site is now occupied by a Somerfield supermarket. A contemporary description of the lost building reads: 'Standing with its back to the high-road, "The Chesnuts" is embowered in fine old chestnut-trees (from which the house derives its name) . . . and the avenue leading up to the house from the lodge, though short, is exceedingly picturesque.'[9] The lodge doubled as Dr Grace's surgery and boarding accommodation for several young medical students over the years. The property's distinguishing feature as far as the Grace boys were concerned was the orchard. Now the supermarket's car park, in the 1850s it became an extraordinary forcing house for cricketing talent.

Aided by Henry, already embarked on his medical studies, and the faithful Uncle Pocock, Dr Grace set about creating his third cricket pitch, assaulting the apple trees with Gladstonian vigour and then mowing and rolling the grass until it was fit to play on. 'The orchard was about eighty yards in length . . . On the left of it was a high wall; on the right, Mr Cave's wood and a deep quarry full of water.' This pioneering work of 1851 was supplemented by other members of the family. E.M., in particular, devoted much time to improving the wicket as he grew older, and W.G. commented, 'I cannot remember when it was not in a condition worthy of a first-rate club.' The best thing about it, though, was its situation: 'we had only to step out of the house and begin to play, and that to a medical family whose duties took them so far from home was a priceless boon'.[10]

Well within W.G.'s own lifetime, something of an Arcadian myth grew up around the family cricket practice, with sisters, not to mention Martha herself, gamely bowling at the boys, and the three dogs – Don, Ponto and Noble – gambolling about fielding the ball and barking disapprovingly at E.M.'s cross-batted slogs into the quarry. At the centre of it all, whirling his bat like Excalibur removed effortlessly from the stone, stands the infant Champion himself. Grace was at some pains to dispel the wilder flights of fancy, denying, for instance, that his sisters ever did more than look on and occasionally throw the ball back if it was hit in their direction. As for his own talents, he dismissed the notion that he was 'born a cricketer': 'I believe that cricketers are made by coaching and practice, and that nerve, eyesight, physique and patience, although necessary, would not be of much use alone.' He allowed, however, that 'Hereditary instinct is helpful, because it would be absurd to deny that successful cricketers often run in families.' But Grace tended to back nurture over nature:

I was born in the atmosphere of cricket. My father, who was a keen sportsman, was full of enthusiasm for the game, while my mother took even more interest in all that concerned cricket and cricketers. When I was not much taller than a wicket, I used to wonder what were the hard cuts, leg hits, and long drives, about which my father and brothers were constantly talking. As far back as I can remember cricket was a common theme of conversation at home.[11]

Unlike his father, who was very much the focus of attention as a child, Gilbert was a relatively minor character in a large and busy household. The 1851 census shows that in addition to the family – and a visitor, Martha's niece Catherine Gilbert – there was a domestic staff comprising a lady's maid, a cook, a parlourmaid and a nursemaid. Living in the lodge above Dr Grace's surgery were Henry Grace junior, another medical student, Stephen Langley and an errand-boy, William Harris of Mangotsfield.

Alfred and E.M. were not included in the census; they were away at school – Goodenough House in Ealing, run by Martha's brother-in-law, George Gilbert. Alfred was eleven and E.M. ten, so their two-and-a-half-year-old brother would have been of little interest to them when they were home in the holidays. Henry, now eighteen, probably had a cheery word for him when their paths crossed, but as a hard-working medical student would have had little time to stop and play, while Dr Grace was as frenetically busy as ever. Fred was still a baby, which meant not only that he was too young to be a companion, but also that he attracted a disproportionate share of Martha's maternal attention. Immediately above Gilbert in the family hierarchy were his two sisters, Alice and Blanche. In 1851 they were six and five respectively, and though they may have doted on the infant Fred, it is probably fair to assume that they had a lot more in common with each other than with an importunate toddler. It would be overstating the case to suggest that Gilbert was in any way neglected as a young child, but he must nevertheless have been somewhat isolated within the family structure before Fred came on stream as a serviceable younger brother, and this may have been one of the roots of the shyness he displayed in his teens and as a young man.

This state of affairs did not last long. Gilbert was soon inducted into the 'rudiments' of the family obsession, and as soon as Fred was up and running, 'we played about the garden in a rough and ready way, and used to make the nurses bowl to us'. Gilbert soon graduated from this kindergarten cricket to something nearer the real thing:

I used to chalk a wicket on a wall and get a stable-boy and one or two youngsters from the village to join me. So I got some sort of practice – sometimes with a broom-handle instead of a bat . . . I consider that a great deal of my quickness of eye is due to the fact that the boys with whom I played bowled a very large proportion of fast underhand 'daisy cutters' which used to jump about in a most erratic way, and needed a lot of watching.[12]

There are parallels here with Bradman's endless games with a golf ball and a stump behind the wash-house in Bowral. But while Bradman honed his hand-to-eye co-ordination in virtual isolation, Grace's early and continuing experience of cricket was emphatically social: 'My father, my brother Henry, and my uncle Pocock practised at every spare moment, and we youngsters fielded for them from the time we could run about.'¹³ At a moment the scene could be set: Dr Grace at the crease; Uncle Pocock, still warm from his morning walk, preparing to bowl; Henry taking a break from his anatomy books, crouched behind the wicket; E.M. and Alfred poised to race the dogs to field the ball; and the much smaller Gilbert waiting at a safe distance, hoping it would be hit in his direction.

This was W.G.'s template for the game throughout his life. Where possible, wherever he lived, he had a practice net in the garden, and the season started with the first crocuses of March, however inclement the weather, and carried on well into autumn. But although deeply serious, cricket was never a quiet game when played by the Graces. It was a noisy, boisterous, intensely focused activity, generating a great deal of excited controversy, and what the Victorians called 'chaff', a rather pointed teasing that ensured the competitive edge was never absent for an instant. This was not necessarily to other people's taste, but Grace never played cricket any other way. Whether he was taking part in a Test match or a game on the village green, he was always totally involved, highly vocal and fiercely combative.

There were other legacies from these vitally important formative years. Watching his father stripped to his waistcoat for a few balls between visits to patients showed him that enthusiasm took precedence over formality. It also demonstrated that there was no upper age limit for a cricketer. Dr Grace played on right through his middle age, and W.G. played first-class cricket until his sixtieth year, and was still opening the batting for England at fifty. With his father's example before him, it would never have occurred to him that there was any incongruity involved.

Other attitudes became deeply ingrained from an early age. Having to field for long periods with the scant reward of a few balls at the end of the session ('a quarter of an hour's innings for the grown-ups and five minutes for the small ones')¹⁴ taught him the extreme value of being at the wicket. Few cricketers have shown as much raw appetite for batting as W.G. So many of his centuries were big centuries; so many developed into double centuries (indeed, his first first-class century was a double, and a ground record into the bargain). E.M. was another whose reluctance to leave the crease became legendary,* and he too had toiled long and hard

* At school, when given out lbw by general acclamation, he took a leaf out of his grandfather Pocock's book and took the stumps with him.

as a junior member of the cricket academy before being allowed parity with the men.

Where E.M. and W.G. learned different lessons was in matters of technique. E.M. was always a hitter. With a very good eye, and perhaps a need to draw attention away from his elder brother, Henry, he would happily cross-bat straight balls over the wall into the quarry. Uncle Pocock attributed this dangerous, if exhilarating, approach to the fact that E.M. had been started with too big a bat, but the habit was too strong to be rectified, so he turned his attention to Gilbert. Grace readily acknowledged the debt he owed to his uncle: 'Nothing pleased him so much as watching a correct style of play; and he would bowl willingly for hours to a promising youngster, and was delighted to see him punish an indifferent ball. He bowled roundarm, medium pace, could break both ways, and was very straight. I have known him hit a single stump six times in twenty balls, and he was not satisfied unless he did it.' 'His bowling was not fast enough to frighten us, but straight and accurate enough to enable us to learn the first principles of batting; viz., good defence', and he made sure that Gilbert had 'a bat to suit my strength'.[15] Pocock's training was patient and meticulous:

he would show me how to hold the bat so as to use it freely; give me guard according to the side of the wicket he bowled; place my feet in the proper position, and impress on me the need to stand upright. For months, for years I might say, I had to be content with simply stopping the ball, happy if I could keep it away from the wicket.

'Keep your left shoulder well forward, and get over the ball,' he kept drumming into our heads; 'until you do that, you will never do any good. And keep your eye fixed on the bowler, and never lose sight of the ball from the time it leaves his hand. There must be no playing or hitting wildly.'

I did all that – in my own mind – as conscientiously and persistently as any boy works at anything he loves; but somehow I could not make the progress I longed for. Too soon would come a ball on the blind spot, and I was beaten. I should like to be able to say that I had no difficulty in learning, and that proficiency came to me much easier than it comes to other boys. The reverse is the truth. I had to work as hard at learning cricket as I ever worked at my profession, or anything else. Very quickly I learned that there was no royal road there, and that if I wanted to be a good cricketer I must persevere. I was fortunate in having a good tutor, and a strong gift of perseverence; that is as much as I can say to students of the game.[16]

For the cricket-mad boys the cricket pitch in the orchard was a source of inexhaustible delight, and their parents also found 'a great charm in the new arrangement, for it kept the entire family together. Rarely did we practise without my mother being present as an onlooker.'[17] But there was nothing cosy about this family closeness. Grace's cricket was fostered in an atmosphere of intense sibling rivalry. Given the age differences between the boys, eight years between Henry and E.M. and another seven between E.M. and W.G., great efforts were required to bridge the gap. E.M managed to overhaul Henry, a capable but by no means outstanding club cricketer, during W.G.'s childhood. Gilbert had a far harder task in catching up with E.M. It took him until he was seventeen.

In the meantime, he had his childhood to get through like anyone else. By all accounts he led a fairly carefree existence at Downend. He was allowed to roam freely, and lived the life of a country boy, with its bird's-nesting and stone throwing. (He was a great believer in the importance of stone throwing, and in later life blamed the decline in English fielding on the falling numbers of country-bred boys who strengthened their arms by pitching stones at birds in the fields.) Like Tom Brown, he was given to 'fraternizing with all the village boys, with whom he made expeditions all round the neighbourhood'. And like his fictional namesake created by Richmal Crompton, he had his own gang with whom he regularly got into scrapes. On one occasion they were chased by a bull. Gilbert was carrying a stout cudgel, 'and, being fearless and quick, he gave the bull a "welt" on the nose that fairly staggered and stopped him'.[18]

He appeared in a less heroic light on another expedition, when he was allowed the use of a gun for some hare shooting. He shot a fox instead and fell into deep disgrace with his father, who maintained that anyone who could shoot a fox 'would commit almost any crime'. Gilbert was apparently under a cloud of parental disapproval for several days.[19] Even more unpopular, at least with his sisters, was his habit of catching snakes, which he would smuggle into the house, only for them to escape, triggering arias of screaming when discovered. There are no accounts of Dr Grace's disciplinary methods, but to judge from the photographs of him in stern middle age, it seems unlikely that he had much difficulty keeping his sons in check.

Over even the most carefree childhood the long shadow of the school gates must fall. Grace was a notoriously unscholarly man, who almost never voluntarily read anything in later life (which makes his persistence with his medical training all the more heroic). Details of his education are skimpy, but he started at Miss Trotman's dame school in the village and was then entrusted to 'a Mr Curtis of Winterbourne'. Later, as a day-boy he attended the Dickensian-sounding Rudgway House School, run by a Mr Malpas, until he was fourteen. One of the masters, David Bernard, was a friend of the family and had fallen in love with Alice. In true *Just William* style, Gilbert extracted maximum advantage from this happy turn of events, coming to an understanding that any marbles his future brother-in-law confiscated should come to him. According to his first biographer, Gilbert was the undisputed 'champion at marbles, on one occasion clearing out the school'.[20] Throughout his life, whatever he played – cricket, cards, croquet, golf or bowls – Grace played to win, and he never minded taking advantage of anything that improved his chances.

THREE

As the 1850s got under way, Dr Grace must have looked with some satisfaction on the little world he dominated. His eldest son was well on the way to becoming a qualified doctor, his next two boys were growing up strong and active, and the two young ones were showing a healthy interest in his ruling passion; if Annie remained unmarried, there was still time, Fanny was growing up into a useful companion for Martha, and Alice and Blanche were presentable little girls who looked set fair to follow their appointed path to matrimony and motherhood. Beyond The Chesnuts' boundaries, the cricket club he had called into being had burgeoned, swallowing its nearest rival and giving him almost total control of the game in the locality. But that was by no means the summit of his ambition. Looking into the future, he saw no reason why Gloucestershire should not eventually boast a county side to compete with the likes of Surrey, Kent and Nottinghamshire. It would take time, but he certainly had the dedication to make his dream a reality. As a first step in raising interest and testing the cricketing strength of the Bristol area, he decided to arrange a fixture with the All England XI.

Founded in 1846 by the Nottinghamshire slow bowler and father of Trent Bridge, William Clarke, the All England XI, or AEE, was the first and most famous of a number of professional touring teams which travelled the country playing local sides against the odds. This meant taking the field against numerically stronger sides, usually of twenty-two and often reinforced with one or two professionals as 'given men'. Games against the odds may seem bizarre to modern eyes, and like the equally alien (and equally popular) single-wicket encounters, they did not survive the nineteenth century.* At the time Clarke started his enterprise, cricket was largely confined to London and the south-east, with Yorkshire and Nottingham the main centres away from the metropolitan area. Clarke

* Single-wicket matches were so called because only one player batted at a time. They could be between equal teams of anything up to six a side, or cast as 'odds' matches, with five or six professionals taking on eleven or twelve opponents.

capitalized on the growing interest in the game away from its traditional heartlands, and offered to take cricket wherever there was a demand for it. Within a few seasons he had created something quite new, a travelling cricket circus of the best professional players which was wholly independent of Lord's or any other established authority.

Kerry Packer's nineteenth-century precursor was a character. During a match he allowed himself only a cigar and a bottle of soda at lunch, but was reputed to be able to polish off a whole goose for dinner. He had lost an eye playing fives, which limited his effectiveness as a batsman, but his under-arm bowling was deadly. Clarke was one of those cricketers who matures with age, and he produced his best cricket after the age of forty. He was rightly proud of the AEE, and paints a rosy picture of his drive to take cricket to all four corners of the kingdom:

These matches bring all classes together; men of all shades congregate, folks of all ages meet, if they can't join in the game, they can take delight in seeing their relations or friends excelling others. The wealthy and great derive advantage from them as well as those inferior in station: they have an opportunity of seeing that there is good sense as well as good dispositions amongst their poorer neighbours, while these gain by mixing in better society an improvement in manners and morals.[1]

The suggestion of disinterested missionary intent overlooks the hard commercial motive behind Clarke's experiment. As Grace remarks bluntly in *Cricket*, the Eleven was 'conducted on business principles', and very lucrative it could be too. Clarke's basic rate was sixty-five pounds down for the team's appearance, and at the end of a match he would conduct an old-fashioned army pay parade, calling up the players one by one. He would also call out the sums he was paying them: 'Four pounds for you', or 'Three pounds for you', or 'Fifty shillings for you', depending on performance and seniority. 'Then, with a smile of profound satisfaction, the manager shovelled the remaining coins into his trouser pockets, adding, *"and thirty-seven pounds for me!"*'[2] There were other ways of dividing the cake, and sometimes Clarke would take the risk of staging a game himself, paying for the hire of the ground and keeping the gate money. Catering was also an important part of the equation, and many of the matches were staged by publicans. But however the deal was struck, the battered old hat-box from which Clarke was inseparable was invariably heavier at the conclusion of the match.

Wherever the Eleven went – and they went most places, helped by the expanding rail network – they were liberally fêted as the star attraction. Richard Daft, an AEE regular, looked back fondly on their matches as 'the pleasantest I ever took part in, for in all cases we were made much of by the supporters of the teams we played against, who generally did everything in their power to make us comfortable'.[3]

Confident that Bristol could put on as good a show as any other provincial backwater, Dr Grace wrote to Clarke and secured a fixture with the AEE in 1854. As the British and French armies were gathering at Gallipoli for their campaign in the Crimea, Gloucestershire's most energetic cricket generalissimo once more marshalled his resources and set to work on a patch of ground behind the Full Moon Hotel, North Street, Bristol. The five-year-old Gilbert was driven over to see the pitch 'which my father's gardener and several other men were preparing. It was originally a ridge and furrow field, and had been specially re-laid in the previous autumn. The pitch was first-rate, but the rest of the ground was rough and uneven.'[4] On grounds commandeered for a one-off match the changing facilities were non-existent, but even regular venues rarely had pavilions. Instead, tents were erected, both for the players to change in and for any sort of catering. Sanitation was rudimentary.

The match was played over three days – 22, 23 and 24 June – and Gilbert sat with his mother in her pony trap. 'I don't remember much about the cricket, but I recollect that some of the England team played in top hats.'[5] The modern eye would have been caught by much more than the headwear. The classical uniformity of white shirt and white flannels was still some years off and teams wore a variety of colourful shirts and sashes. The two great Nottinghamshire bowlers J. C. Shaw and Fred Morley wore white and black striped shirts and would have looked more like Newcastle United footballers than cricketers, while the legendary Alfred Shaw sported 'a checked shirt of large pattern and dark hue'.[6] The All England 'strip' consisted of red dots on a white background. Footwear was equally variable, with men taking the field in 'black boots or shoes, [before] brown boots were worn, until everyone by degrees took to wearing white ones'.[7] And until the sweater was invented, fielders kept themselves warm with tight-fitting flannel jackets, which, according to Dickens in *The Pickwick Papers*, made them look like 'amateur stone-masons'.

There was certainly an air of Dickensian comicality about the game itself as a great horde of men and boys issued onto the field and arranged themselves around the wicket. For a number of years *Lillywhite's*

Companion used to print a diagram with the fielding positions for a twenty-two, with such tantalizing possibilities as 'Deep Cover No.1', 'Middle Wicket', 'Long Off No.2', 'Sharp Long Leg', 'Half Leg', 'Short Leg Short', 'Short Leg Square' and 'Deep Long Slip' (the last line of defence, behind even 'Long Stop'). Batting in the midst of this forest of fielders was a claustrophobic experience. Grace was to play an enormous amount of cricket against the odds and reckoned that it helped him develop his precision in placing the ball as well as refining his judgement of a run. Without those skills, a batsman could become totally becalmed, unless he resorted to the only alternative, which was to have a heave and hope to clear the outfield. There were no boundaries and every hit had to be run out. A really weighty blow could result in five, six, seven or even more runs.

Bowling had reached the mid-way point in its evolution from under-arm to over-arm and was mainly round-arm, though the various bowling styles overlapped. The old-fashioned fast under-arm 'trundler', who could generate surprising pace but relied mainly on brute force and the vagaries of the pitch, could still be found, though they were gradually giving way to bowlers of a more scientific approach. Accuracy, whatever the style, was at a premium. As Clarke said, batsmen were often used to receiving only 'one straight ball in the over', so any bowler who could keep a half-decent line was guaranteed success. The over was four balls, though many were increased by wides. Indeed, with wicket-keeping in its infancy (a long-stop was regarded as obligatory until the great Australian, John McCarthy Blackham, revolutionized the keeper's art), extras often proved a more reliable source of runs than the bat.

Batting had not accommodated itself to round-arm bowling particularly well. In the period following its introduction (1828–61) the volume of runs scored declined. Roland Bowen calculated that there were 'only five season averages over 30', and Fuller Pilch alone managed an average of over thirty-five in 1834 and 1835.[8] Fifty was regarded as a substantial innings, and centuries were exceptionally rare. Batsmen usually fell into one of two schools. Many simply devoted themselves to survival, hovering watchfully over the crease and stabbing down on the ball as it shot towards them. Others would hit out, knowing that one opportunistic slog could produce more runs than half their timid brethren could show for an hour's poking about. In Clarke's experience batsmen 'are most inclined to play back'. Given the uncertain surfaces on which they played, and the low regard for 'odious padding', that is hardly surprising.

Of course the most common score among the twenty-two in an odds match was 0.* In the West Gloucestershire match against All England, both Dr Grace and the twenty-one-year-old Henry scored ducks, though Uncle Pocock managed 3. West Gloucestershire scored 43 – which was exactly what George Parr made. Parr, the 'Lion of the North', was the leading professional batsman of the day, and Clarke's eventual successor as player-manager of the AEE. The Gloucestershire men had an equally disappointing second innings. They were routed by Clarke, Caffyn and Willsher, and the professionals were comfortable winners by 149 runs. But it was by no means an ignominious defeat. As Grace commented with mature hindsight, 'It is doubtful whether nine men out of the eleven could have been excelled.'[9]

Nothing daunted, Dr Grace invited Clarke to bring the All England team down again in 1855. Clarke did not play on that occasion. He was having trouble with his eyesight and suffering generally from ill health – he died the following year. Although the result was an even heavier defeat, W.G. recalled more of the game: 'In the first innings my brother Henry was top scorer with 13, and in the second my father with 16. Uncle Pocock made 15. There were no other double figures reached by the West Gloucestershiremen, who made 48 in the first innings and 78 in the second.'[10] Their second-innings score was matched exactly by the remarkably named Julius Caesar, a diminutive and neurotic man, but an aggressive bat, and one of the earliest to use the pull shot.

That would have been of particular interest to the fourteen-year-old E.M., who, along with Alfred, had been excused school for three days to play in the match. Alfred made a pair; E.M. managed only 1 and 3, but his courageous fielding at long-stop impressed everybody, including William Clarke, who gave him a presentation bat as a reward. 'It was,' says W.G., 'a great thing then to have a bat given you by one of the All England players.'[11] Gilbert had a moment of reflected glory when he was allowed to carry the bat home in triumph.

*

Clarke's generosity did not stop at giving E.M. a bat. The previous year he had spent some time talking to Martha Grace. He must have

---

* Edward Pooley, the England wicket-keeper, exploited this statistical commonplace when touring New Zealand in 1876–7, betting that he could predict each player's individual score in an odds match. The fracas that ensued when he put down nought for all of them resulted in his going directly to jail, not collecting his winnings, and missing the boat back to Australia for the first ever Test match.

exchanged pleasantries with dozens of cricketers' wives as he made his way around the country, but Martha Grace was special. Richard Daft said she 'knew ten times as much about cricket as any lady he ever knew'[12] and Clarke obviously appreciated her interest in the game. As a token of his respect he brought her a little book, *Cricket Notes* by William Bolland, to which he himself had contributed an appendix of 'Practical Hints'. It became a family heirloom, which eventually came down to W.G. He had it on his desk when compiling *Cricket* and quoted the inscription:

> PRESENTED TO MRS GRACE
> BY WILLIAM CLARKE,
> SECRETARY, ALL-ENGLAND ELEVEN[13]

It is a fascinating volume, because its two authors, united within one set of covers, were the leading representatives of the two halves of the cricket world. While Clarke was the dominant figure in the professional game, William Bolland was president of the first and most prestigious wandering amateur club, I Zingari. I Zingari (the name derives from the Italian *zingaro*, meaning 'gypsy', to signal the club's nomadic bent) was founded in 1845, the year before the AEE, to provide continuing top-quality cricket for public school and university men, and like the AEE it was prepared to travel widely for its fixtures, though it soon adopted Lord's as an unofficial home base. But although the two clubs played the same game, that was about as much as they did have in common. IZ, as it was known, was the preserve of the upper crust (including even royalty; the Prince of Wales played a few matches and attended many more as a spectator), and the standard bearer of the amateur game, while the AEE, as its detractors emphasized, played solely for '£ s d'.

Grace says that the book was treasured and read avidly 'by the younger members of the family', probably concentrating initially on Clarke's practical tips. 'Never try to pull a straight ball across you. There are many chances against you if you do. For you have only the width of the ball to hit at, while it may chance to rise suddenly or turn out of its course . . .'[14] might have been written specifically with E.M. in mind, while Gilbert's difficulties with the blind spot were addressed with reassuring straightforwardness: 'Never let the ball get you in two minds, if you do it will cause you to play half way.'[15] Clarke also made more general points about the conduct of the game: 'How unjust it is to an Umpire, when he has given his best opinion on some nice point (such as the ball grazing a man's bat or glove), for the batsman to go away and say he was not out and so create a bad feeling. I said before there are some (and they ought to know better) who never are out, unless the bowler makes the middle stump turn a summerset.'[16] This proved a lesson the Graces found particularly hard to absorb.

When they turned to the front of the book, they would have found much of interest in William Bolland's more expansive depictions of the game they were so desperately keen to play. While other boys were marching at the head of armies or chopping ogres down to size, Gilbert was introduced to the enchantments of Lord's and the heroic deeds of the previous generation of cricketing giants, such as Alfred Mynn, the Lion of Kent, and his fellow Kent stalwart Fuller Pilch, 'that host in himself, that model of combined power and grace . . . the most safe, powerful, and *intentional* hitter that ever lived'.[17] (Pilch had only just retired, and he continued his involvement with the game as an umpire. He certainly stood in a match at Canterbury made memorable by E.M., and in all probability he saw W.G. play too, though Grace makes no mention of meeting him.)

Perhaps the passages in Bolland that sank deepest into Gilbert's consciousness concerned the Gentlemen v. Players match which had produced an almost unbroken string of victories for the professionals. Bolland blew hot and cold about the possibility of halting this depressing trend:

[W]hat a Player can accomplish, a Gentleman can accomplish – why not? We admit the great advantages under which eleven Players meet eleven Gentlemen annually. Year by year they continue in constant practice – they have the opportunity of watching the batting of the men they are to oppose. They cannot be absent from Lord's – it is their profession for the time to be at Cricket. They bowl in practice, and discover errors of which they afterwards have an opportunity of taking advantage. But look at the reverse of the picture – equally capable of excellence, as we have said, the Gentlemen have one great drawback – incessant change. They have no regular eleven.[18]

And he concludes, 'Let the Gentlemen always remember their inferiority, arising from causes before stated; individually there may be an approach to equality; collectively the Players should be superior.'[19] In a few short years Grace was to stand that gloomy prognostication on its head, and claim a great deal more than 'an approach to equality' with the professionals.

FOUR

ALTHOUGH the AEE played a Bristol and District Twenty-Two the following year (1856), there would be no further involvement for members of the Grace family until Gilbert himself was old enough to play against the Eleven nine years later. Dr Grace had taken a measure of the cricketing strength at his disposal and was prepared to bide his time.

Meanwhile there was much local club cricket to be played along with incessant practice sessions in the orchard. In all things Dr Grace led by example, and one match, which earned a place in the family annals, demonstrated both his views on how the game should be played and the stubbornness, not to say cussedness, which became a Grace hallmark.

Henry and Uncle Pocock had played for Bristol against a weak Thornbury side, who were beaten easily. The Thornbury captain, Mr Williams, 'a player of University reputation', was piqued at the outcome and, despite the onset of autumn, offered to play a return match for a stake of twenty-five pounds. When he heard this, Dr Grace denounced it as daylight robbery, and further declared he would allow no member of the family 'to take part in any match which is played for money, as it is introducing a form of gambling into the game, which is wrong and must do harm to it'.[1] He then announced that he would turn out for Thornbury.

The game fell on a cold day in October, and the Bristol team was obviously only interested in the pecuniary aspect of the affair. Indeed, they wouldn't play until they had seen the colour of the Thornbury team's money. Mr Williams produced his team's twenty-five pounds, but when the same was required of the Bristol captain, he had to admit he hadn't got it. Dr Grace's invective was a good deal sharper than the chill wind that was blowing flecks of snow across the ground, and soon the Bristol team, including Henry and Uncle Pocock, were ignominiously emptying their pockets and pooling their watches.

Honour satisfied, Dr Grace and Mr Williams then opened the batting for Thornbury against the bowling of Henry and Uncle Pocock. While

Williams made 45 'in brilliant fashion', the doctor staunchly defended his wicket, accumulating twelve out of the opening partnership of sixty. The rest of the inexperienced batting order fell away disastrously and only another fifteen runs were added, but Dr Grace carried his bat for 17. W.G. continues the story:

With the exception of my father, there was not one of the Thornbury lot who had ever been known to bowl, and it was thought the match would be over by 5 o'clock. It was over earlier than that.

My father bowled the first over, and a good one it was; not a run scored off it. Laughing was general when Mr Williams commenced at the other end. He fell back on the old, old resource when everything else has failed – underhand grubs! There was not quite so much laughing at the end of the over, when he had clean-bowled one man, and the scoring-sheet was still blank.

Snow had fallen during the day, and the wicket cut up badly. My father bowled as steadily and patiently as he had batted; and Mr Williams slung in his grubs, and got a wicket nearly every other over. The match was all over by 4.45, and Bristol had scored something less than 50 runs.

The Bristol team was a laughing stock, but it was even worse for Henry and Uncle Pocock. They 'were chaffed unmercifully' when they got back to Downend, 'and it was many a long day day before they heard the last of that match'.[2]

W.G. obviously loved this quixotic episode – he gives it three pages in *Cricket*, rather more space than his second Australian tour gets in *Reminiscences* – and his admiration for his father shines through every line of it (though he passes no comment on the prohibition against betting on the game). In addition to exposing the dangers of hubris on the cricket field, it illustrates the intense competition between members of the family. Although they would unite as one against a common foe, no quarter was asked or given when they found themselves on opposite teams. W.G.'s rivalry with E.M. would provide the clearest example of this, but that was still some way ahead. At the end of the 1850s, E.M. was a phenomenon carrying all before him, while Gilbert was just a little boy hoping desperately to improve enough simply to be worthy to walk onto the same pitch.

His chance came in 1857, on 19 July, the day after his ninth birthday. He played for West Gloucestershire, of course, and their opponents were Bedminster. The match took place on Rodway Hill. Even with his father, brothers and uncle around him, this was a nerve-racking occasion, and Martha must have felt particularly anxious as she watched him walk to the wicket for the first time. Today a boy of nine playing in an adult game would be given an easy one to get off the mark. Whether or not Gilbert benefited from such a gesture, he managed to score three runs in this first innings, and was not out into the bargain. It was a satisfactory start, but he came down to earth in the two other matches he played that season. These were both against Clifton, and in his three innings he managed only a single.

The next year he had seven innings, and managed a total of seventeen runs (with one not out). The most dramatic game was memorable not for its cricket but for the violent incident that brought it to an untimely close. The match was between West Gloucestershire and Redland and took place in July, ten days after Gilbert's tenth birthday. It started badly when an obstreperous drunk took possession of the pitch. When peaceful persuasion failed, Alfred, the family's pugilist (though by no means the only one useful with his fists), was detailed to try force. After a brief exchange of blows, the intruder retired hurt and the match began. It had reached an interesting stage later in the afternoon when it was once more disrupted. The original nuisance returned, supported this time by a posse of like-minded roughs. Alfred stepped forward to do battle once more, but single combat was superseded when the invaders lit upon 'a convenient heap of stones'. Not for the last time members of the Grace family found themselves under attack by a hostile mob. 'For a while West Gloucestershire and Redland, fighting side by side, had rather the worst of the contest; but, charging shoulder to shoulder with stumps and bats, they drove the crowd from the heap of stones, and assumed the offensive.' What Grace described as 'a lively state of affairs' prevailed for the next half hour, during which Dr Grace rode off and fetched a magistrate to read the Riot Act. 'Fortunately . . . so extreme a measure was unnecessary, and the opposition collapsed; but the match had to be abandoned.'[3] Gilbert was presumably kept well out of the way of the flying stones, but he would have learned a lesson about standing your ground and meeting force with force.

The fracas did not make the newspapers, but it would hardly have stood out in the catalogue of outrages covered in the following day's *Western Daily Press*, which included accounts of a Westbury man 'dreadfully beaten and kicked on the night of Wedmore Fair', an old man attacked on Bedminster Down by two ruffians 'who stole up behind him and filled his eyes with mud' before relieving him of four pounds, and a 'Horrible Attempted Murder' in which the seventeen-year-old vicar's daughter was subjected to a frenzied knife attack not 300 yards from her father's vicarage. They were lawless times.[4]

1859 was a miserable year. Gilbert had twelve innings (three not out) and scored a mere twelve runs; 'Heart-rending!' Methven Brownlee remarks in a facetious running commentary on these early failures. In the light of what was to come, these initial disappointments could be treated as an amusing false start, and no doubt the mature W.G. enjoyed the joke himself. But it was no laughing matter at the time, and he must have known some bleak moments as he contemplated his abject lack of success. On the evidence of his first three seasons there was no reason to believe that he would become even a competent club cricketer. All the while E.M. was going from strength to strength, attracting universal plaudits for his electric fielding and his devastating batting. In one game, an inter-club match at Clifton, W.G. and E.M. were on opposing sides. The elder brother showed no mercy: W. G. Grace bowled E. M. Grace, 0.

But Gilbert refused to give up. Next year, 1860, he was out in the orchard in March as usual, listening to Uncle Pocock, trying to keep his bat straight, and fixing those sharp-sighted eyes on every ball bowled to him, as determined as ever to prove himself. And at last he did. In a match which in his own words marked 'an epoch in my cricket career',[5] he scored his first fifty. It was a two-day mid-week game against Clifton starting on Thursday, 19 July, the day after his twelfth birthday. E.M. scored 150, commended by the *Western Daily Press* for 'being obtained without his giving a single chance'.[6] Uncle Pocock played correctly for 44, so when Gilbert went in at number eight he faced an already demoralized attack. But that is not to take anything away from his performance. He batted 'very patiently and correctly'[7] to the close of play for 36 not out. This was easily his highest score in adult cricket to date, and his father, who sat through the innings with his pads on waiting to go in after him, was overjoyed. Both parents 'were very proud next day when I carried my score on to 51'. As to his own reaction, 'I don't think my greatest efforts have ever given me more pleasure than that first big innings.'[8] His was the second highest score, and it helped boost the West Gloucestershire total to an impressive 381, though the wicket was so good that Clifton saved the game quite easily.

Given his triumph in the Clifton match, it is surprising that Gilbert played only four innings in 1860, which yielded a total of eighty-two runs at a commendable average of 20.50. These are the figures given by Neville Weston in his *W. G. Grace The Great Cricketer: A Statistical*

Record of His Performances in Minor Cricket, and it is of course possible there were other matches which escaped this meticulous chronicler.

1861 did not show any significant improvement – eighteen innings (five not out) for 102 runs – though this was the year when Gilbert, following as usual in E.M.'s footsteps, first became involved with the Lansdown Cricket Club in Bath. Founded in the 1820s, Lansdown CC was the premier club in the area, and could almost claim to be the MCC of the West Country. It attracted the top university players and boasted fixtures against Oxford University and the MCC. Dr Grace had managed to get matches against the club, but they were very one-sided affairs. In one the West Gloucestershire side was terrorized by the Etonian Walter Marcon, whose under-arm deliveries were faster than anything they had ever seen, and in a game in 1847 they had been dismissed for the derisory total of six runs. Thinking that if they couldn't beat Lansdown, they might as well join them, Dr Grace and Alfred Pocock went over to Bath and became members, starting a family connection that lasted the rest of the century. E.M. played his first match for Lansdown in 1857 at the age of sixteen, and now Gilbert, in his thirteenth year, made two appearances for the club, both away games. Against Frenchay on 5 July he made 13 not out, and later in the month he scored 14 not out and took a catch at Knole Park. Lansdown won both games comfortably.

Gilbert also played against Lansdown for West Gloucestershire, and on 8 August he stepped out for the first time onto their magnificent ground at Sydenham Field. This was described by the *Bath Chronicle* as 'admirably adapted to cricket, [while] the scenery it commands is gladdening and panoramic. On the one hand, fields swell upwards, wave upon wave, until the view is bounded by a dark line of hills; on the other, the city rises in a series of terraces, cut in masses of verdurous foliage.'[9] Gilbert would have had a fair amount of time to enjoy the view, as he made only 8 and 4 not out. However, the match was a triumph for West Gloucestershire: Lansdown lost on first innings by 100 runs.

Gilbert was now 'very tall for [his] age, and could get well over the ball'. His height and increased strength also helped his bowling. Uncle Pocock had sensibly started him bowling at eighteen yards rather than the full twenty-two, and 'a good length was the principle point drilled into our heads'. Gilbert 'pegged away very perseveringly' and was finally 'paid the compliment of being considered the forlorn hope when the regular bowlers of the club had failed'.[10] As with his batting, he made a quiet beginning as a bowler, capturing a modest three wickets in 1861.

His performances in 1862 were much better. The tally of wickets went up to twenty-two, and in nineteen innings (five not out), he scored 298 runs. This was the year Dr Grace made his first attempt at raising a county side, and 'what was undoubtedly the first match of Gloucestershire County was played at Clifton . . . under the title of The Gentlemen of Gloucestershire v. Devonshire'.[11] Gloucestershire won a crushing victory by an innings and seventy-seven runs. 'We did not lay claim to first-class form; but . . . we naturally considered that we were not far from it.' Grace didn't play – 'I was not considered good enough' – but he was picked for the return, 'the first important match I played in', and scored 18.[12] He is also credited with 24 not out against Corsham (who fielded twenty-two), and 34 not out and 35 not out, both against Lansdown, for Clifton and Bedminster respectively.

As all keen young cricketers with time on their hands discover, availability, especially at short notice, is a great aid to selection, and from this time on Gilbert followed his elder brothers in playing wherever a game was offered. The fact that he was getting games for other clubs shows that he was building up something of a local reputation, if only as the promising younger brother of the notorious E.M.

E.M. was now the best-known cricketer in the Bristol area, though his willingness to heave balls from outside the off-stump across to leg upset purists and bowlers alike. 'Many of the foremost players of the day found their bowling treated in a high-handed manner to which they were entirely unaccustomed, so that often they lost first their length, then their nerve, and finally their temper.'[13] He made his mark on the wider national stage when he played for South Wales against the MCC & Ground at Lord's. The '& Ground' signified the presence of a professional element in the MCC's amateur ranks – on this occasion, the famous groundstaff bowlers George Wootton and James Grundy. Professionals were the 'other ranks' of cricket: their names appeared in the scoresheet unadorned by initials or title, they had separate and inferior changing rooms, and were generally treated as second-class citizens. But senior professionals, like experienced NCOs, could expect a measure of respect from the younger amateurs. Wootton and Grundy were very senior pros, and pretty set in their ways. It would be fair to say they did not take to E.M. He was obviously a ringer (possibly a paid one) with no obvious qualifications to play for the South Wales team, and his attitude to batting was insupportable. There were certain unwritten rules in cricket, and a clearly defined range of shots to which a batsman was expected to keep. If the ball was straight it should be played straight; to play across the line was like potting an opponent's ball in billiards. It simply wasn't done. E.M. seemed unaware of these conventions and carved his way to a carefree 118. At one point, after he had pulled yet another ball from the off to square leg, Grundy could restrain himself no longer: *'That's* not cricket,' he protested. 'But it's four,' came the exasperating rejoinder.[14]*

E.M. was a positive dynamo on the cricket field. At the crease he was 'a cat on hot bricks'[15] and his restless aggression never let the bowlers settle. His bowling, an aggravating mix of round-arm and under-hand lobs, was a force to be reckoned with too. And at some stage in his teens he made the transition from long-stop to point, where he stood suicidally close, poised 'like an old-fashioned sprinter about to start a race'[16] and unflinchingly taking catches off the hardest hits. He became universally acknowledged as the finest fielder ever seen in that position, and his intimidating presence accounted for innumerable wickets over the years. *Scores and Biographies*** described him as 'overflowing with cricket at every pore, full of lusty life, cheerily gay, with energy inexhaustible'.[17]

His breakthrough into first-class cricket came at Canterbury Cricket Week in August 1862. Canterbury Week was the first cricket festival, and the prototype for those that sprang up elsewhere. It was a social occasion, with the St Lawrence ground, then as now, ringed with tents and resplendent with flags and bunting. The cricket was supplemented by a variety of theatrical entertainments put on by the Old Stagers in the evenings, and the whole atmosphere was one of relaxed conviviality. For some years Dr Grace and Martha had made the Canterbury pilgrimage. The Doctor could now afford more leisure and was always keen to extend his network of cricketing connections. On hearing that the visiting teams, the All England Eleven and the MCC, were short of players, he suggested sending for E.M. A telegram was despatched and E.M. hurried down, fresh from scoring an undefeated double century in a club match at Knole Park, to play in the first match for the AEE. In his first first-class innings he was out for a duck (setting a precedent followed by his two younger brothers). This no doubt gave Wootton and Grundy, who were

---

* Once, when a similarly outraged bowler asked George Parr, 'Where did that ball pitch?' he replied, 'In the hedge, I think.' (Quoted in Tony Lewis's *Double Century – The Story of MCC and Cricket* (London, 1987), pp. 107–8.)

** Arthur Haygarth and Frederick Lillywhite's multi-volume compilation covering nearly all important matches from 1746 to 1878.

both playing for the All England Eleven, some quiet satisfaction, but E.M. was back to his objectionable best in the second innings, when he made his maiden fifty. His 56 was particularly impressive since there was only one other double-figure score in the innings. But that was as nothing compared to what came next.

E.M. was not at this stage a member of the MCC, a fact that wouldn't have troubled him in the slightest, but his inclusion in their team for the second match of the week sparked a serious controversy. When the Kent captain, Mr South Norton, discovered E.M. had been picked, he protested strongly, supported by the rest of his side. The MCC captain, R. A. Fitzgerald (who became Secretary of the club the following year), stood firm, and E.M. certainly did not offer to withdraw. The match was only saved by the intervention of W. de Chair Baker, the Manager of the Week.

The Kent team took the field, but 'unwillingly . . . and under protest'.[18] Some men might have felt inhibited by having caused such bad feeling in what was, after all, a friendly festival match. Not E.M. Watched by Fuller Pilch, who was umpiring, he took five wickets in the first innings. Then, exhibiting all the sensitivity of a Norse berserker, he massacred the Kent bowling, hitting 192 not out, the highest first-class score ever seen on the St Lawrence ground. Nor had he finished. Rubbing handfuls of salt into the hosts' wounds, he proceeded to take all ten of Kent's second-innings wickets. (It was in fact a twelve-a-side match, but one of the Kent team was absent in the second innings.) South Norton was so incensed that he never played at Canterbury again, and there were mutterings in the MCC as well. Lord Harris, later the doyen both of Lord's and St Lawrence, sided retrospectively with the mutterers: '[T]he MCC, before all clubs, should be specially scrupulous in playing only *bona-fide* members.'[19]

Unconcerned by all the attendant brouhaha, the Grace party returned home celebrating their all-conquering hero's triumph. Even as Kent members were smoothing down their ruffled feathers, E.M. shot to the pinnacle of fame as the most talented amateur all-rounder of the day. This was not the last time the St Lawrence ground would see record-breaking performances by a member of the Grace family, but no one then could have guessed that E.M.'s success would in turn be overshadowed by his younger brother, who was struggling so painfully to put two consecutive scores together in local club cricket.

In fact, Gilbert's chances of making any mark in cricket, or indeed life, were put in severe jeopardy that winter when he was struck down by an attack of pneumonia. Before the discovery of antibiotics, pneumonia was potentially fatal, and it seems that Gilbert's life was almost despaired of. However, his father's medical expertise and his mother's and sisters' watchful nursing, aided, no doubt, by a strong dose of Grace wilfulness, pulled him through. His illness seems to have been a turning point in his physical development. He emerged from his sick bed with a renewed zest for life and astonished everybody by suddenly growing much taller. He shot up towards his final height of six foot two inches which lifted him easily above the rest of the family, none of whom topped six feet. Whether there was any connection between the pneumonia and this sudden growth is uncertain. It might simply have been a coincidental 'pubertal spurt'. It certainly had an enormous influence on his life.*

His new stature had an immediate impact on his standing in the family hierarchy. Frank Sulloway, cartographer of the rocky terrain of sibling relationships, remarks that 'prudent laterborn strategies include acquiescing to first born demands'[20] and Brownlee notes of Gilbert that 'a certain submission to the elder brother was never refused, *while he had physical as well as moral weight to enforce it*' (my italics).[21] But with added height and commensurate strength, W.G. could dispense with prudence, and turn his back on deference. One incident, recorded by Brownlee, overturned the status quo once and for all: 'Disputing, as brothers will do, and forgetful for the moment of the sacred right, he picked up his elder brother, carried him inside, and deposited him on some wet or hot spot, we forget which. The revolution was complete so far as he was concerned, and cherished institutions received a shock that was felt throughout the family. W.G. was considered beyond the pale of argument, and was left alone for the future.'[22] On the verge of manhood, Gilbert had asserted his independence, and throughout the rest of his life he countenanced precious few challenges to his sovereign will.

---

* One little-known legacy of his illness was the conviction that it had cost him one of his lungs. Arthur Porritt, his ghost-writer for *Reminiscences*, recalls that when he questioned this, Grace became extremely angry and called in his wife to corroborate it (*The Best I Remember*, p. 34). Medical opinion today is as sceptical as Porritt, but Grace apparently maintained this belief throughout a career of superabundant physical activity.

FIVE

THE year 1863 saw some important changes in Gilbert's life. In the aftermath of his illness, his father decided to remove him from school, and he continued his education at home. One of those charged with supervising his studies was the Reverend John Walter Dann, a graduate of Trinity College, Dublin, who came to Downend as curate at the parish church in 1866. His reward for the patient hours he spent with Gilbert and his books was the hand of one of his pupil's sisters, and he married Blanche in 1869.

As far as cricket was concerned, 1863 was a landmark year. Grace says it was 'really the beginning of my serious cricket, for then I played in most of the West Gloucestershire matches. In 19 innings I made 350 runs, not against schoolboys, but against the best gentlemen cricketers of that time, many of them Varsity men and capital players.'[1] The West Gloucestershire club was at its peak, and although his cousins William Rees and George Gilbert had dropped out, 'E.M. was a host in himself; Henry, Alfred, and my uncle as good as they had ever been',[2] while W.G., with Fred hard on his heels, improved all the time. Gilbert also turned out for Clifton, Lansdown, Redcliff, Knole Park, Frenchay and Stapleton, and the runs he scored for them pushed up his aggregate to 673 (in forty-two innings, six of them not out). Fittingly, his best score was for West Gloucestershire – 86 against Clifton – and he also made a 74, another fifty, three forties and two thirties. He was coming of age as a cricketer.

It took him a while to shake the last of the sick-room out of his system, and he made a tentative start to the season, playing in two of Clifton's warm-up games on Durdham Down in May – not getting a bat in either of them. He then had the thrill of being picked, along with E.M. and Henry, for a Twenty-two of Lansdown against the All England Eleven at Sydenham Field. Unhappily, he bagged a pair, caught twice off Chris Tinley's artful lobs (a disappointment passed over in silence in both *Cricket* and *Reminiscences*). E.M. produced the innings of the match, 73 out of a total of 189 in the first innings. Henry only got 3, but proved his worth as a bowler. A collapse typical of odds matches saw Lansdown dismissed for 57 in their second innings (E.M. again top scorer, but this time with only 9). The professionals did not find batting any easier and won a tight match by three wickets.

Sydenham Field was not a lucky ground for Gilbert in 1863. When he returned in August, playing for Clifton, he came up against E.M. representing Lansdown. The outcome was even worse than the Clifton inter-club match in 1859: E.M. dismissed him for nought *twice*, lbw in the first innings, clean-bowled in the second. He would have known better than to expect a single to get off the mark.* 'The fact that he was bowling against his younger brother, who was only 15 years old, made no difference to [E.M.], who all through his life played without the least sentiment; he was never known to play otherwise than cricket in the strictest sense; he gave no favours and expected none.'³

Gilbert had a chance to redeem himself when the AEE returned to the West Country to play the Bristol and District XXII at the end of August. He had earned his place with a 52 not out for the Gentlemen of Gloucestershire v. Gentlemen of Somerset at Bath. E.M., who was captain, may have regarded his younger brother as his personal rabbit, but he still considered him worthy of a place in the twenty-two. Gilbert was by some way the youngest member of the team. A contemporary recalls him as 'a lanky, loose-limbed youth with fuzzy hair already beginning to show on the sides of his face . . . he had the rugged physiognomy characteristic of the Graces, which made them look more like farmers than doctors, and he was full of life and vim'.⁴

On William Clarke's death, George Parr had taken over as the game's leading impresario. He was having an undistinguished season in 1863, and in fact hardly played after July. He didn't play in the match on Durdham Down but his All England XI was up to full strength, and included the fast bowling pair Jackson and Tarrant. John Jackson, of Nottinghamshire, was six feet tall and weighed fifteen stone. His nickname was 'Old Foghorn' because every time he took a wicket he pulled his handkerchief out and blew his nose. This happened quite often. He was also known as 'The Demon' because he was frighteningly fast and belligerent with it. (In the rare event of a batsman standing up to him

---

* In his entire career Grace collected only four pairs, all in minor matches, the last in 1870. On each occasion only one bowler was responsible, so E.M. had a place on a very select roll of honour. (1916 *Wisden*, p. 117.)

he deployed a potentially lethal beamer.) He was more than a match for most first-class batsmen and far too good for the lesser fry. At Uppingham, he once bowled six men in seven balls. George Tarrant, by contrast, was a surprisingly small man, but made up for his lack of stature by bowling with such ferocity that he earned the title 'Tear 'em Tarrant'. He was also a noted pugilist and George Parr's minder. (On one occasion Parr swung the first blow in a fight then calmly called up Tarrant to finish the business.) Tarrant bowled round the wicket, and his approach to the crease was electrifying: 'He was all over the place like a flash of lightning, never sparing himself, and frightening timid batsmen. He was the terror of twenty-twos when he played for the All-England Eleven, some of his long-hops bounding over their heads, causing them to change colour and funk at the next straight one.'[5] These two were a fearful prospect for grown men, let alone a boy of fifteen, and Grace was understandably nervous.

He was down to bat ten, and it can't have helped his nerves when the wicket which would have brought him to the crease fell on the stroke of lunch. However, he received succour from an unexpected source. Tarrant, for all his ferocious reputation, was a kindly soul, and he took Grace aside during the lunch interval to bowl to him. He got a poor return for his generosity. On arriving at the wicket after lunch, Grace promptly hit him out of the attack. 'Whether I had got my eye in during the luncheon hour, or whether he was kind enough to send me down one or two loose balls by way of encouragement, I don't know; but I knocked him about so freely that he was taken off, and Tinley went on with underhands.'[6] This should have set alarm bells ringing, but it didn't. Flushed with his triumph over Tarrant, Gilbert decided to exact revenge for his pair at Sydenham Field. He hit the slow bowler's first ball away towards the scoring tent, but then over-reached himself trying to repeat the shot and was clean-bowled. But he had made his mark with a highly creditable 32.

Not only did this make him 'quite a hero for the rest of the season', it helped materially to bring about a famous victory. With E.M.'s 37 and two other scores of over thirty, the home team made a very respectable 212. Then, showing the same variety as at Canterbury, E.M. got the professionals on the run and they were forced to follow on. Although that denied Gilbert the chance to bat again, his active participation was not over. In the All England second innings, the Yorkshire batsman Ned Stephenson started to dig in. E.M. called up his younger brother with the instruction: 'Pitch him one or two well up, and I'll go and catch him in the long field.' Gilbert did exactly that. 'Stephenson hit the very first ball straight to E.M., who never dropped a catch in those days.'[7] Bristol and District XXII ran out winners by an innings and twenty runs, to Dr Grace's great joy. With E.M.'s continuing form and Gilbert's startling improvement, he could at last see the nucleus of a first-class team emerging.

At some time in 1860 or 1861, Martha Grace had written to George Parr commending E.M. as 'a splendid hitter and most excellent catch' (adding that she had 'another son, now twelve years of age, who will in time be a much better player than his brother because his back stroke is sounder, and he always plays with a straight bat').[8] Whatever influence that may have had, E.M.'s batting at Canterbury the previous year, followed by his performances in 1863, obviously created a favourable impression, and Parr invited him to join his tour to Australia and New Zealand over the winter. This was something of a gamble, both on Parr's part and on E.M.'s. There had been two previous overseas tours, one to North America in 1859 which Parr had led, and H. H. Stephenson's to Australia in 1861–2. Both had been all-professional affairs. E.M. would be the only amateur on this third expedition, and the first to go abroad with an English team. But he was a cricketer before he was a Gentleman, and his forceful, outgoing personality (not to mention his medical skills) made him an attractive proposition as a travelling companion on the long and potentially dangerous trip. As though to underline his qualifications, E.M. scored 112 (out of 193) for Fourteen Gentlemen of the South against a scratch side of 'Eleven Players' in his last innings of the season, which brought his average up to an exceptional 40. When he went to Australia he was, according to his biographer F. S. Ashley-Cooper, 'the most talked-of player living'.[9]

*

The 1860s were a watershed for English cricket. Grace himself called it cricket's 'most critical period', and it witnessed a crucial power struggle for the control and direction of the game (though the parties to this conflict had much in common with Matthew Arnold's ignorant armies clashing by night). At the start of the 1860s, the professionals were in a position to mount a serious challenge to the Lord's establishment; by the seventies, the balance of power had swung firmly and irreversibly back to the amateur citadel. The single most important factor in this turn-around was the emergence of Grace himself as a player of unprecedented ability, and his decision to nail his colours to the MCC mast.

When the decade opened Lord's was in the doldrums. Interest in cricket at St John's Wood had been declining for some time, and though the great matches, the Varsity match and the Eton–Harrow match still brought in the crowds, few turned up to watch 'Scratch teams of amateurs' pitted against the club strengthened by a couple of groundstaff bowlers. Edward Rutter, a committee member in the 1870s, recalled Lord's as an inhospitable place with 'no stands or fixed seats of any kind, nothing but the small old pavilion and a line of loose benches running part of the way round the ground [which] in most matches presented rather a dreary scene. To anyone but the Committee . . . it was becoming evident that the Club was in danger of losing its influence . . . But the Committee were deplorably lethargic and out of date.'[10] R. A. Fitzgerald became Secretary in 1863 and worked tirelessly to change the prevailing culture. But he faced an uphill struggle. In the country as a whole, amateur commitment to the first-class game was half-hearted at best. For most, cricket was simply part of the year-long round of social and sporting pleasures, of no more intrinsic importance than racing, shooting or hunting. Come the Glorious Twelfth, anyone with the means disappeared off to the Scottish grouse moors. Lord's shut down completely in August, a tradition that lasted until 1867.

Good-quality nomadic cricket held greater attractions for some than the more arduous three-day county game. Alfred Lubbock, just out of Eton in the early 1860s, was frequently asked to play for Kent, but 'rather preferred one-day West Kent, I.Z., or MCC matches'.[11] The problem continued into the 1870s. Surrey was badly plagued by amateurs picking their games and refusing to travel north to play the top professional sides, Nottinghamshire and Yorkshire. In Frederick Gale's forthright view, 'the reign of the amateurs ruined the county'.[12] The amateur ethos allowed for natural talent, but was hostile to undue application and extreme forms of competition. Anthony Trollope made the point tellingly in his *British Sports and Pastimes*: 'To play Billiards is the amusement of a gentlemen; to play Billiards pre-eminently well is the life's work of a man who, in learning to do so, can hardly have continued to be a gentlemen in the best sense of the word.'[13]

At a lower level the game enjoyed a boom in popularity. A plethora of new clubs sprang up, but the improvement of playing standards was not necessarily their main concern. Some cricket historians, falling for the propaganda of *Tom Brown's Schooldays* (1857), have seen the mid-century expansion of cricket as part of the wholesome spread of muscular Christianity. In real life, high-minded proponents of spiritual service through selfless sporting endeavour were in a minority compared to those who simply saw cricket as one of life's pleasures.

The 1860s (like the 1960s) saw a new generation enjoying the fruits of their parents' growing prosperity. Cricket attracted moneyed young men with a hedonistic approach to life, and provided an opportunity for various forms of exhibitionism. The Oxford Harlequins, for instance, disported themselves in caps and shirts 'quartered brown, blue, and red, with a broad stripe of the same colours down their trousers'.[14] R. A. Fitzgerald, writing as 'Quid', fired a satiric broadside at young Splasher, 'a decided dandy' who leaves one club and forms another in order to carry out 'the pet object of his ambition by investing his new club in a fiery shirt and sanguineous hose'. Splasher lures other members from his old club, especially those 'with good calves, [who] were tickled by the notion of the knickerbockers' and the prospect of showing off their legs to any members of the opposite sex among the spectators.[15] There is rather more Flashman than Tom Brown here, and those with the best interests of the game at heart were concerned that the amateurs' prominent position was in danger of being frittered away. Lord Harris, an ardent advocate of county cricket, and the man mainly responsible for the resurgence of Kent (which was reconstituted under his presidency in 1870), was another keen reformer, but he felt 'as one preaching in the wilderness' when he tried to challenge attitudes that had become ingrained during the 1860s: 'I remember at an MCC dinner being almost laughed at for a vehement exhortation to the Gentlemen to give up their country-house cricket, and support their Counties.'[16]

Cricket, like the times themselves, was on the move. The whole country was restless with the desire for change, which, on the larger stage, culminated in the passing of the second Reform Bill in 1867. Some of this democratic ferment permeated the world of cricket, and in 1863 the right of Lord's to dominate the game was challenged when a 'Cricket Parliament' was proposed in the columns of the *Sporting Life*. The agitation continued for two years, and the MCC was pilloried as autocratic and out of touch. 'It was argued that when the MCC took upon itself the responsibility of being lawgiver for cricket the game was confined to a few of the Southern counties, and that as cricket had gradually extended to the North and was becoming popular all over the country, the *regime* of the MCC ought to come to an end. To legislate for the vast cricket-playing community was . . . too great a task for a single

44

club.' Instead an assembly was proposed, made up of 'practical and business men from every part of the United Kingdom' who could speak for their respective constituencies. Looking back, Grace dismissed it as 'nothing but an attack upon the Marylebone Club', which, 'happily for cricket', came to nothing.[17] Although the attempted constitutional coup failed, the North–South, 'Us and Them' divide remained, and the regional rebellion was carried on by means of a haphazard guerrilla war pursued by the professionals from their northern strongholds. With clearer aims, better leadership and, above all, with the right allies, this could well have succeeded in wresting power away from Lord's.

Working men had been paid for their cricketing skills since the previous century, but in the Hambledon heyday of the 1770s and 1780s, the players were bound to the game's rich patrons by near-feudal ties. Lumpy Stevens, whose habit of sending balls through the old two-stick wicket was responsible for the introduction of the middle stump, was employed as one of Lord Tankerville's gardeners, the third Duke of Dorset employed three of England's best cricketers on his estates, and Sir Horatio Mann was not above poaching players to work on his rolling acres and bolster his own eleven.[18] When cricket's centre of gravity moved from Broad-Halfpenny Down to London, the White Conduit Club and, finally, the Marylebone Cricket Club, demand for professional services increased. By 1806 there was a sufficient pool of professionals for a strong team to be selected for the inaugural Gentlemen v. Players match at Thomas Lord's original ground in Dorset Square. Lord himself had been a ground bowler with the White Conduit Club before becoming the world's most famous cricket ground manager. But there were few escape routes for the majority of his fellow professionals, and as a class they remained subservient to the clubs that employed them.

The position began to change in the 1840s with the drift of the population away from the land into the towns. The new urban populations needed recreation, especially after the introduction of half-day holidays on Saturday. As the game took root among the working class, there were more openings for professionals, and with better employment opportunities there was a greater prospect of independence. Ric Sissons, the historian of the professional cricketer, also cites the growth of Chartism as a boost to working-class confidence, pointing out that Nottinghamshire, a Chartist stronghold, was the 'epicentre of professional cricket'.[19] And it was there that William Clarke started his All England Eleven.

Clarke's self-appointed task of taking his team all over England was made easier by two important developments: the expansion of the railway system and the introduction of the penny post. At the same time, cricket began to receive a fuller coverage in such papers as *Bell's Life*, which helped to generate more interest in the game and, in turn, more demand for Clarke's particular brand of it – and, by extension, for the services of professionals in general, as groundsmen, ground bowlers, coaches and umpires. So successful was Clarke's enterprise that he received three times more requests for visits by his team than he could meet. There was clearly room for more than one professional touring team, and when Clarke's avaricious ways provoked a split in the AEE ranks, a splinter group under the leadership of John Wisden formed the United All England Eleven (UAEE) in 1852 to challenge his monopoly. Other imitators followed, though many were short-lived.

This upsurge of cricket was part of a wider development of sport. The Football Association was founded in 1863, the Amateur Athletic Club followed in 1866, and the Rugby Football Union in 1871. As C. L. R. James noted, 'All of a sudden, everyone wanted organized sports and games.'[20] The number of professional cricketers that could expect to make some sort of living continued to grow, and the game provided a possible, if uncertain, ladder to lower middle-class respectability and beyond. Some professionals emulated William Clarke and became cricketing entrepreneurs. George Parr, Alfred Shaw and Arthur Shrewsbury all made handsome profits from arranging overseas tours. Professionals who went abroad usually took a stock of cricket equipment to sell, and some, like the Lillywhite clan, developed the sale and manufacture of sporting goods into a thriving business for the home market. The most successful cricketer-businessman was probably the Nottinghamshire professional William Gunn, founder of Gunn & Moore, who left an estate worth nearly £60,000 when he died in 1921.

But if the financial gap between amateur and professional was beginning to narrow, the social divide became, if anything, deeper. At Hambledon the unbridgeable social distinctions were irrelevant once the ball was cracking stockinged shins and nipping blood out of bare knuckles, and the aristrocratic leaders of the game were as happy rubbing shoulders with their cricketing equals as they were debating horse-flesh with their grooms. But the Victorians, with their wearisome snobbery, constructed a system of virtual class apartheid, which was rigorously maintained. While the amateurs travelled first-class and put up at the best hotels, and then submitted large expenses claims to cover the bills, the professionals, who had to pay their way out of their wage packets, travelled third-class and made do with indifferent lodgings. If the weather was fine they would sometimes save money by sleeping rough in a local park. These were not men with whom the amateurs felt they could mix socially. Lord Harris expresses the unquestioned assumptions of his own class when he remarks: 'In the great matches of the sixties one does not find many amateurs playing for either All England or the United All England, and not much wonder, perhaps; there would have been no companionship at all touring the country with either of those professional teams.'[21]

Despite their lowly status, the professionals had nonetheless gradually increased their leverage on the game. Clarke himself clashed with the MCC in 1854, refusing to release his stars, or 'cracks' as they were known in contemporary slang, for the Gentlemen v. Players match. The Lord's authorities might bluster but they were effectually powerless. As Kerry Packer demonstrated over a hundred years later, money proves stronger than appeals to ancient loyalties. As the Packer affair also showed, some accommodation can normally be reached once the proverbial dead bodies have been cleared away. Whatever their suspicions of the all-professional sides, the MCC decided it would be better to have them inside the stockade than out, and on Whit Monday, 1 June 1857, Lord's hosted the first of a series of All England v. United All England matches that continued until 1869. The fixture was a stronger attraction than the Gentlemen v. Players because the two sides were more evenly matched, and huge crowds attended. As well as providing one of the high spots of the season, AEE v. UAEE matches raised money for the Cricketers' Fund Friendly Society, which aimed to provide the professionals with some insurance cover for injury and limited pension provision.

Although they were given reluctant recognition by the Lord's authorities, the travelling elevens attracted vitriolic criticism from die-hard traditionalists. Anthony Trollope, in the preface to *British Sports and Pastimes*, fulminated against the 'arrogance and extravagance of the professionals', and regarded 'the so-called England Elevens, which go caravaning about the country playing against two bowlers and twenty duffers for the benefit of some enterprising publican' as 'the monster nuisance of the day'.[22] Arthur Haygarth punctuated *Scores and Biographies* with gibes at the professionals' unreliability, bickering and overriding interest in gate money. And Fitzgerald, writing in 1866, struck the same note, deploring the 'growing evil, that professional cricket is lapsing into £ s. d. Matches are nowadays becoming speculative, and the cricketer's hand is not more often in the pocket than his eye is on the gate.'[23] While acknowledging Clarke's pioneering missionary work he now questioned the value of the system he established. But the fact was that the travelling elevens' fixtures attracted the crowds. Fitzgerald might appeal to the public to boycott what he dismissed as 'the *Pot-house* class of matches', but it was a futile gesture. The professionals had seized the commercial high ground and there was no reason why they should relinquish it. As Fitzgerald admitted, 'by banding together, instead of being distributed throughout the country, [the professionals] have taken all the plums and left us generally to get on as well as we can with the dough'.[24] The only way to retrieve the situation was for the amateurs to rouse themselves, and Fitzgerald issued a ringing call to arms:

It is high time for the gentlemen cricketers of England to assert their position, not only as patrons of the game, but as performers. We think that cricket would recover much of its 'tone' if there was a more general fusion of the gentleman with the professional element . . . Let not cricket descend to the inferior grade of a gladiatorial exhibition – the trained combatant and the pampered spectator. Let the amateur go hand-in-hand with the professional, but with one object in view – the maintenance of our game on its original principle.[25]

*

In joining George Parr's tour to Australia in 1863–4, E.M. was anticipating Fitzgerald's call for 'fusion'. His experience bore out some of Lord Harris's doubts about the possibility of 'companionship' between an amateur and professionals, and to begin with his presence in the team caused friction. In his account of the trip he wrote: 'My position with the eleven had been somewhat difficult. It required no extraordinary penetration to see that any little occurrence might raise bad feeling, and at first one or two had almost looked out occasions to try to quarrel.' However, this did not last, and E.M. was soon accepted for who and what he was, and indeed made some genuine friendships. He decided to stay on for a few weeks at the end of the tour, and when he saw the rest of the team off, 'two or three shook hands with me with tears glittering in their eyes'.[26]

The most intriguing aspect of the tour is E.M.'s relationship with George Parr. Parr was a powerful figure, and the natural leader of the professionals had they been able to forget their differences and unite in a common cause. The success of the AEE and the UAEE had proved that there was a healthy market for the professionals' brand of cricket, and in initiating overseas tours, the professionals had also stumbled upon the path leading to the most important development of the century – international Test cricket, with its potentially huge audience and revenues. There seems no reason to doubt that the professionals, with unity and vision, could have established an alternative structure for the game, as Rugby League did when it broke with Rugby Union. The future was there for the taking. There was one major factor that time had not yet revealed, but if Parr had formed an alliance with E.M., and through him with W.G., the course of cricket history could have been radically different. However, it was not to be. E.M. gives no indication that he and Parr became particularly intimate or that Parr made any suggestion that he should abandon his proposed medical career and throw in his lot with the AEE. The opportunity passed, in all probability unnoticed by either of them.

The team sailed in Brunel's famous steamer, the *Great Britain*, and the voyage out took sixty-one days. E.M. proved the value of having a medical student in the party, counselling Julius Caesar on his gout and pulling a tooth for Tarrant. When they reached Melbourne they found freak rainfalls had produced the worst flooding anyone could remember. But they were given a rousing reception and amongst the public demonstrations of goodwill, E.M. was reunited with a familiar face – George Gilbert, 'looking jolly and well, with his moustache and beard'. He had emigrated some time before and now had three children. He was keeping up his cricket and had recently scored a century.[27] After the rains the Melbourne Cricket Ground was soft, but the match against Twenty-two of Victoria went ahead, watched by an estimated 40,000. It was a draw.

The Australians had made some advances since H. H. Stephenson's trip the previous year, but Parr's side proved too strong for them and went through the tour winning ten matches with six drawn. All the games were against the odds, and the programme was enlivened by a number of single-wicket matches in which E.M. played, often with Tarrant or Jackson as partner.

E.M. found much to praise in Australia. There was 'less ignorance, less superstition, and more enterprise among the million of Australians than among the same number taken indiscriminately at home or from any other part of the world. No nation was ever founded under such auspicious circumstances.'[28] It was, in fact, a 'golden land' and, E.M. went on, 'I have no reason to believe that there were hidden beneath this glittering surface those festering sores – poverty, ignorance, and injustice, which are corroding the vitals of so many older states.'[29] In addition, he revelled in the climate. E.M. 'more than most men, loved sunshine'.[30]

But, as his younger brothers were to discover ten years later, not everything was perfect in this antipodean paradise. Travel, by land or sea, was physically exhausting and on occasion positively dangerous. On one trip round the coast the tourists were involved in a collision, and though their ship was not badly damaged Parr, who had a pathological fear of drowning, nearly went out of his mind, while Tarrant suffered a panic attack and had to be manhandled out of a lifeboat being launched to rescue passengers from the other ship which was going down fast. E.M. celebrated his return to dry land by challenging any six local players to a single-wicket match. He was undefeated on 106 at the end of the day.

Taken as a whole, however, the tour was not a great personal success for him. He was hampered by injury – he developed a painful whitlow on one of his fingers – and failed to produce the scintillating form he had been showing for the last two seasons in England. He finished fifth in the tourists' batting averages with a disappointing aggregate of 269 runs at 13.9. Although he was to produce some brilliant performances in the years to come, he would never recapture his position in the English game. Worse, he was supplanted by his younger brother. Ashley-Cooper states the case baldly: 'when [E.M.] left England he was the greatest player in the world, but soon after his return he found himself surpassed by W.G.'[31]

*

E.M.'s decision to stay on in Australia after the rest of the team sailed for home in April 1864 meant he missed the first half of the English season, and as his brother records, 'his absence . . . gave me my first opportunity to play in a really big match. My brother Henry and I were invited to join in the annual tour of the South Wales team. I do not know what was my qualification for playing for South Wales, but we didn't trouble much about qualification in those days.'[32]

Gilbert had already been asked to play for the rump of the All England Eleven against XIV of Lansdown over at Bath earlier in the season. He acquitted himself well with an innings of 15 which ended when 'an unfortunate mistake of [John] Lillywhite's resulted in a run out'.[33] Now he was to see the wider world for the first time. He travelled up to London with Henry on the Great Western Railway with its seven-foot track, its spacious carriages resplendent in the company livery of chocolate and cream, and the enforced ten-minute stop at Swindon, where passengers were routinely fleeced in the most palatial refreshment rooms in provincial England. They then sped on to London at sixty miles an hour, nearly twice as fast as any other railway, and finally disembarked at Paddington.

The tour involved three matches – against the Gentlemen of Surrey at the Oval, the Gentlemen of Sussex on the Hove ground, Brighton, and MCC at Lord's. Henry could only commit himself to the Oval match, but Gilbert was down for the first two games. E.M. was expected back any day, and it was hoped he could take Henry's place at Brighton, and then play in the MCC match. However, the Grace battle-plan hit problems almost as soon as Henry and Gilbert arrived at the Oval.

They had both changed and were ready to start the match against the Surrey amateurs when the South Wales captain, John Lloyd, approached Henry and asked whether he would mind Gilbert dropping out of the Sussex match as 'he had the offer of a very good player, and he believed their opponents were exceptionally strong'.[34] Henry did mind very much, and said so forcefully. Gilbert had been invited to play in both games, and he would play in both – or not at all. And if he didn't play, neither would Henry, and if Henry didn't play, none of the Graces would ever play for the South Wales Club again. Gilbert's name went back on the team sheet for Brighton.

The Oval wicket was one of the best in the country, and proved one of the most productive for W.G. in the years ahead. On his first appearance he showed promise of what was to come with a competent 38 in his second innings to follow his disappointing 5 in the first. (Henry scored 11 and 49.) He also took four wickets in the Surrey Gentlemen's first innings.

Despite this encouraging start, Gilbert was not entirely happy on the next leg of the tour. He was a boy away from home for the first time, and if, as the evidence suggests, Henry had to return to Bristol, he would have travelled down to Brighton in the company of strangers. Like any cricket touring team, the Welshmen were out to enjoy themselves, and there would have been the usual banter and horseplay, from which Gilbert – 'quiet and shy in manner', in marked contrast to the ebullient E.M.[35] – would have been excluded. His Gloucestershire accent (which he never lost) may have been a source of not entirely innocent amusement, and the fact that he was playing at the behest of his elder brother would not have made the situation any easier. In manhood he developed as tough a hide as anyone, but at Brighton he was clearly lonely and in need of moral support. He admits as much in *Reminiscences* when he gives a rare insight into his feelings as he looked forward to E.M.'s return: 'I desired it eagerly, if only to give me heart. His ringing voice and cheery tones would have been invaluable to me.' But, despite a promising paragraph in the press in which he was inexplicably described as the 'Rev. E. M. Grace', E.M. did not make it in time.[36] This left the South Wales team a man short, which was ironic after the unpleasantness at the Oval, and put particular onus on W.G. to uphold the family honour.

He did so, triumphantly. Going in at three, he scored 170 without giving a chance, and to prove that this was no flash in the pan he ran up 56 not out in the second innings. *John Lillywhite's Cricketer's Companion* recorded that 'Mr J[ohn] Lloyd was partnered by Mr W. G. Grace (the younger brother of the celebrated cricketer), and they were not parted until the score stood at 207 (or 188 runs had been added). Mr Lloyd left for 82, a well-played innings; but young Mr Grace did not leave until he had scored 170 runs, pronounced to be "the finest innings played last season (up to that period, July 15th) on the Brighton Ground".' Indeed, the *Companion* went further, hailing Grace's performance as 'one of the greatest batting feats of the great batting season of 1864'.[37]

It was a magnificent achievement, for which John Lloyd presented him with a suitably inscribed bat. Centuries were far rarer than they became – Frederick Lillywhite's *Guide to Cricketers* (1865)* lists just seventy-six 'Scores of 100 or more made since 1850 in first-class matches', and only six of these, including W.G.'s, were over 150. Even though it was subsequently denied first-class status, 170 remains a hugely impressive

---

* The bibliographical cat's-cradle perpetrated by the Lillywhite family takes some untangling. Frederick (son of Frederick William Lillywhite, the great Sussex bowler) started his *Guide to Cricketers* in 1848; his brother, John, started his *Cricketer's Companion* (known as 'Green Lilly' on account of its cover) in 1865. After two years' fruitless rivalry, they amalgamated, the *Companion* 'incorporating' the *Guide*. In 1872 their cousin, James Lillywhite junior, started his *Cricketers' Annual*, with its distinctive red cover ('Red Lilly'). A further period of competition ensued, which ended with another amalgamation in 1880. *John and James Lillywhite's Cricketer's Companion*, which still incorporated the *Guide*, survived until 1883 when James announced he was 'now sole proprietor'. After 1885 the *Companion* was incorporated with the *Annual*, which continued until 1900.

score, and it says at least as much for Grace's stamina as for his concentration that he batted so long. Alfred Lubbock recalled that in those days, 'When a batsman had got a hundred . . . he had generally had enough of it, as boundaries were the exception, not the rule, and everything was run out, so much that players would often get out on purpose.'[38] W.G.'s star quality was established beyond doubt, and he looked back on Brighton as a turning point. Identifying his 'entire absence of nervousness' as a major factor in his success, he remarked that after the Brighton match, 'I cannot remember ever again being really nervous, although on many occasions I have felt anxious to do well. I thus started with a great advantage over most batsmen, and to add to this I feel sure I was helped by my determination to get the better of the bowler before he began to get the better of me.'[39] Grace had what all great players have, the big-match temperament.

He was naturally invited to remain in the team for the match against the MCC, and to cap an unimaginably successful trip, Grace made his debut at Lord's against the MCC on 22 July, four days after his sixteenth birthday.

Lord's in 1864 was 'practically a country ground, it being almost open country northwards and westwards. An old-fashioned tavern, with trees in front, was the hostelry, and the pavilion was somewhat of a rustic kind, with a shrubbery in front. The tennis court was the only other building on the ground.'[40] Apart from hits to the pavilion, everything had to be run out (boundaries were only introduced after a spectator was hurt in a collision with one A. N. Hornby), and all-run fives were not uncommon. There was even a nine scored in 1856. On the other hand, hard hits against the tennis court wall (later demolished to make way for the Mound Stand) bounced back into play, often limiting the batsman to a single. The scorers sat elevated on their 'perch' with 'no shelter or covering of any description'.[41] But a new scorebox and telegraph were erected the following year. In 1864 the scoreboard dating from 1846 gave the total, number of wickets and the last man's score, and on big match days Frederick Lillywhite would put up his printing tent and run off scorecards.

However, the aspect of Lord's that mattered most to the players was the wicket. It was terrible. W.G. recalls 'the creases were not chalked out, but were actually cut out of the turf one inch deep, and about one inch wide. As matches were being frequently played, and no pains were taken to fill up the holes, it is quite easy to imagine what a terrible condition the turf presented.' It was perfectly possible to 'pick up a handful of small pieces of gravel'[42] from the wicket, and Frederick Gale vividly evoked its dangers when he wrote:

Had I been a wicket-keeper or batsman at Lord's I should have liked (*plus* my gloves and pads) to have worn a single-stick mask, a Life Guardsman's cuirass, and a tin stomach-warmer. The wicket reminded me of a middle-aged gentleman's head of hair, when the middle-aged gentleman, to conceal the baldness of his crown, applies a pair of wet brushes to some favourite long locks and brushes them across the top of his head . . . The place where the ball pitched was covered with rough grass wetted and rolled down. It never had been, and never could be, good turf.[43]

The effects were predictably unpredictable: 'It was no uncommon occurrence in those days to see, out of an over of four balls, three shoot, and the other bump right over the batsman's head.'[44] Although some returfing was undertaken and a 'ground-keeper' employed, improvement was slow. It was not until the death of George Summers in 1870 that the problem was taken seriously.

Quite why the square was in such a poor state is a mystery. Thomas Lord had twice had to change the site of his cricket ground, and on both occasions he had gone to the trouble of having the turf transferred, so he at least appreciated its importance. The subsequent neglect was attributable in part to the innate conservatism that prevailed at Lord's. When a mowing machine appeared in the 1830s, one senior member immediately 'summoned some navvies . . . and gave peremptory orders for instantaneous destruction of the infernal machine'.[45] It certainly wasn't a question of money, because the MCC had just embarked on a huge round of expenditure. They renewed the lease for ninety-nine years (and in 1866 raised a mortgage to buy the freehold for £18,000), and plans were afoot to extend the pavilion and improve facilities generally. Somehow the state of the square was overlooked. It made little difference to W.G.. Lord's soon became one of his favourite grounds, and his ability to overcome the vagaries of the wickets was a cause of admiring astonishment.

By now E.M. was safely back in England, and he opened the batting for the South Wales team. However, the long voyage and lack of practice told, and he was out for a duck. Gilbert, batting at four, beat that by exactly fifty. It was a portentous debut, though there were few to witness it, the attendance, according to *The Times*, 'being very scanty'.[46] When the MCC batted the two brothers did the bulk of the bowling, E.M. taking four wickets, Gilbert one. Both failed in the second innings, a dismal procession of 79 all out, and the match was left unfinished with the MCC in a strong position. Later in July, they again turned out for South Wales, against I Zingari at Lord's. They opened together, E.M. scoring 55 and W.G. 34 in the first innings, and 18 and 47 respectively in the second. I Zingari won a close match by three wickets.

The Grace brothers were never invited to join I Zingari. They were regarded by many as provincial upstarts whose amateur credentials would not bear close examination. Not only were they widely believed to make money out of the game, but their whole approach was seen as over-zealous. They were, in Trollope's formulation, simply too good to be regarded as gentlemen 'in the best sense of the word'. Failure to penetrate one of the inner sanctums of the cricket establishment is unlikely to have bothered W.G., and it did not prevent his sporting the IZ colours on occasion. In 1895 he even posed for a portrait wearing the club blazer.[47]

At the end of the season W.G. could look back with immense satisfaction at his first steps beyond club cricket. The distinction between first-class and non-first-class matches was not as clear-cut in the 1860s as it later became. Grace calls the matches he played for the South Wales Club in 1864 first-class, although they are not included in the figures compiled by Ashley-Cooper (see Appendix, page 497). However, they remain impressive, by any standards, for a boy in his sixteenth year. 'In first class matches I scored 402 runs for seven innings, average 57; and at the end of the season I had an aggregate of 1079. I had played well enough to merit an opinion from John Lillywhite's Companion, in its summary for the season: "Mr. W. G. Grace promises to be a good bat: bowls very fairly."'[48] During the course of his long career W.G. grew inured to the superlatives lavished on him, but at the outset it was understandably different. That edition of Lillywhite's was in his library of cricket books and the tops of both the pages recording the Brighton innings are firmly folded down and the relevant paragraphs proudly marked. The pale green cover is signed with his strong signature, underneath which is written 'To be returned', heavily underlined.

The *Companion*'s coverage of the early years of Grace's career charts graphically the turn-around in the relative positions of E.M. and W.G. References to W.G. as the 'younger brother of the celebrated cricketer' dried up very quickly. In 1866 W.G. advanced in Lillywhite's estimation to 'A very good bat, and bowls well', but E.M. still held the senior position with two and a half lines of enthusiastic endorsement: 'A tremendous hitter; has made wonderful scores; bowls both round-arm, a moderate pace, and "lobs", and an excellent field anywhere.' By 1867 W.G. has overtaken him with four lines: 'A magnificent batsman, with defensive and hitting powers second to none . . .' The following year, W.G.'s encomium gets into its sixth line with two 'magnificents', one 'marvellous' and one 'a host in himself'. The 1869 edition gives W.G. six full lines and crowns him with 'the title of the best all-round player in England'. By 1870 he is into a seventh line and 'Generally admitted to be the most wonderful cricketer that ever handled a bat.'[49]

*

The Lillywhite monopoly on cricket publishing did not go unchallenged. In 1864 John Wisden brought out his first *Cricketers' Almanack*, though it can hardly have looked much of a rival to the long-established *Guide*. The cricketers' Bible made an engagingly uncertain start. Clearly influenced by the great omnium gatherum *Old Moore's Almanack*, Wisden supplemented his fairly skimpy cricket coverage with a hotch-potch of miscellaneous information – the dates of the Crusades, the battles of the Wars of the Roses, a summary of the trial of Charles I, and, perhaps more suitable for a quiz in the pavilion on a wet afternoon, the winners of the Derby, the Oaks and the St Leger. Filling his pages with more relevant material was not going to be a problem in the years ahead as W.G.'s deeds demanded more and more of his space.

Grace's first year in senior cricket also coincided with the last crucial development that paved the way for the emergence of the modern game: the legalization of over-arm bowling. This had long been coming, though it generated high passions. (It had been one of the main demands of those pressing for a Cricket Parliament.) Law X, which defined a fair delivery as one bowled from no higher than the shoulder, had long been breached with impunity, but in 1862 John Lillywhite brought the matter to a head by no-balling the main proponent of over-arm bowling, Ned Willsher, in a match at the Oval between England and Surrey. Willsher was one of nine professionals playing for England, and they all walked off, leaving two rather bemused amateurs to follow in their wake. The Surrey authorities tried to persuade Lillywhite to relent, and when he wouldn't, replaced him to allow the match to continue. But his very public stand made it inevitable that the law would be changed, and in June 1864 all reference to the height of the hand was dropped.

The political fall-out from Lillywhite's action was considerable. Eight of the professionals in the England team were from the north, and they convinced themselves they were victims of a southern plot. Relations between Nottinghamshire and Surrey, which had been bad for some time, worsened dramatically, widening to a clear-cut north–south schism. Although the Surrey–Nottinghamshire match took place as planned in July 1864, the northern professionals boycotted both the England v. Surrey and North v. South fixtures later in the season. The latter match was a farce as a strong South XI won a crushing victory over a makeshift team. At the end of the disappointing first day's play, the South team issued a strong protest and declared they would not honour the return match at Newmarket (in October!), and this was the end of the North–South fixture for some years. It was replaced by the unsatisfactory North of the Thames v. South of the Thames series.

A more significant effect, so far as Grace was to be concerned, was the founding of a new professional touring team, the United South Eleven, based, as its name indicated, on a regional footing. Using the language of the American Civil War, at that time producing record levels of carnage on the battlefield, *Scores and Biographies* noted that the United South was 'formed at first entirely from "secessionists" from the All England and United All England Elevens, principally the latter body.' The cricket nation was thus polarized, with players north and south 'attending entirely to their own interests, regardless of the welfare of the "noble game"'.[50] As Grace remarks in *Cricket*, after 1864 'the All-England and United Elevens were seen very little in the south'.[51]

While the professionals were consolidating their divisions, the establishment's model of the game was strengthened by the formation of both Middlesex and Lancashire County Cricket Clubs. Though there was as yet no official championship, an informal champion county could usually be identified, though as the leading counties did not always play each other, a universal consensus was not always possible. In 1864 there could be no dispute: Surrey led the way with eight wins and only one defeat in fourteen matches.

It was still Dr Grace's ambition to bring a Gloucestershire team into the lists, and 1864 provided him with fresh grounds for optimism, as a third son, G.F., began to make a name for himself in local cricket. Fred 'did not play with so straight a bat . . . but, for his age, he was much more resolute in his hitting, and in the field showed something of the dash and certainty which characterised him in that branch of the game in after years'.[52] With three formidable talents to deploy it would not be long before the Doctor was in a position to startle the cricket world considerably.

SIX

GRACE's first important match of the 1865 season was for Eighteen of the Lansdown Club against the United All England at Bath on 8, 9 and 10 June. Undeterred by the thought of his impending medical exams, E.M. accepted the responsibility of captaining the Lansdown team, and was obviously spurred to great things by the odds being offered around the ground. '[T]he betting was 3 to 1 in favour of the England XI and there were side bets of £100 to £1 and £5 to 1/- that E.M. would not score a hundred.'[1] Having possibly done a little business with the bookies, E.M. went out and belted a vigorous 121 (including a hit into the river). W.G. scored 11 and Henry 8 in the Lansdown total of 299, and between them the three Grace brothers took every single England wicket to fall, as the professionals were tumbled out for 99 and 87, going down by an innings and 113 runs.

Despite the calibre of the players involved, this did not count as a first-class fixture. Grace had to wait till the match between Gentlemen of the South and Players of the South at the Oval on 22 and 23 June for his first-class debut. And just as E.M. had done three years before at Canterbury, W.G. started with a duck. He was sent in at three ('a compliment which I keenly felt I had not justified')[2] and faced the all-rounder George Bennett. Bennett's bowling was 'very slow, flighted high in the air and most deceptive'.[3] Grace eyed the open spaces of the long field. Throughout his life he was susceptible to an early rush of blood, and he succumbed on this occasion: 'W. G. Grace, Esq., st. Stephenson, b. Bennett, 0'. 'Chagrined' was the word he employed in *Cricket* to describe his feelings,[4] but that must have been an understatement. At least E.M. wasn't there to pass judgement. He had pulled out of the game with a boil on his face that shut up one eye.[5]

Grace made up for his batting failure with a striking performance with the ball. Bowling throughout both innings (with I. D. Walker) he took thirteen wickets for eighty-four runs. His list of victims is impressive: Harry Jupp (twice); both John and James Lillywhite; T. Lockyer (twice);

H. H. Stephenson and Julius Caesar (twice). It was a remarkable debut, as *Scores and Biographies* recognized: 'Mr W. G. Grace bowled very effectively, and his extreme youth (but 16!) must be taken into consideration.'[6]

Although the start of his career coincided with the legalization of over-arm bowling, he had been coached under the old dispensation, and he never developed a modern side-on action with a high delivery. His bowling was described as 'a kind of slinging and his pace was fast medium. He had not then acquired any of his subsequent craftiness with the ball. He used to bowl straight on the wicket, trusting to the ground to do the rest – as it used to do in the sixties.'[7] For variation he would 'now and then [put] in a slower one'.[8] This uncomplicated approach was widespread. Kortright, the great amateur fast bowler of the next generation, recalled: 'Personally, I didn't worry a great deal about how I held the ball in relation to the seam as long as I got a firm grip on it, and I think most of my contemporaries felt the same.'[9] In the days before swing, fast bowlers often rubbed the ball in the dirt to get a better purchase, though there is no record of anyone actually keeping a supply handy in his pocket.

Grace was an extremely sharp fielder to his own bowling. 'Few bowlers could cover such a wide range of field and he never feared and rarely missed a hot return.'[10] Indeed, his fielding generally made a big impact, impressing one witness 'if anything more than his batting or bowling, for he was a beautiful thrower. He could run like a deer and had a very safe pair of hands. As a saver of runs he was unsurpassed.' But for all his instinctive fluency of movement on the field of play, the rare photographs of him at this stage show an awkward, self-conscious figure, 'a loose-limbed lean boy [who] looked older than he was . . . [I]ndications of the beard which subsequently distinguished him through life were even then apparent.'[11]

This was the youth who made his first appearance in the fixture that he would dominat for the next three decades: Gentlemen v. Players. In the pre-Test era, selection for either team was the highest recognition a cricketer could aspire to. To be picked, as Grace was, a fortnight before his seventeenth birthday was remarkable, though he was not the only debutant of note. Richard Humphrey, Harry Jupp and the great Alfred Shaw all made their first appearance for the Players in the same match, which was played at the Oval on 3, 4 and 5 July. Grace, going in at eight, made 23 (bowled Shaw) and 12 not out. He had, however, been picked primarily as a bowler, and more than earned his place with seven wickets from seventy-five (four-ball) overs (4 for 65 and 3 for 60). The Players still won – they had never lost to the Gentlemen on the Surrey ground – but they would have taken note of the newcomer as one to watch.

In the return a week later, the Gentlemen brought their disastrous sequence of nineteen matches without a win to a close, triumphing in the game at Lord's for the first time in twelve years. The two architects of victory were E.M., who took eleven wickets in the match, and B. B. Cooper who scored a fine 70. Cooper also stumped Parr, making his last appearance for the Players, when the Lion of the North was looking dangerous on 60. E.M. thought Gilbert was put in too low at the Oval, and had him promoted so they could open together. Unfortunately this brotherly good turn backfired when Gilbert was run out for 3. In the second innings they established a better understanding, and W.G. helped to accumulate the seventy-seven required for victory with a breezy 34. This, according to eye-witnesses, included a huge hit through a bedroom window of the old tavern, but the shot was subsequently claimed by E.M., and is credited to him in Ashley-Cooper's biography, with the added detail that the landlord 'was facetiously advised to frame the broken pane, and make an heirloom of it'.[12]

E.M. and Gilbert next played together at Islington where Middlesex first raised their standard on a ten-acre ground at the north-east corner of the Cattle Market (before moving to Prince's and finally Lord's). The match, between the Gentlemen of England and the Gentlemen of Middlesex, coincided with Grace's seventeenth birthday and he narrowly missed winning a presentation bat as an extra birthday present when he was dismissed two short of his fifty. He made 34 in the second innings, but was overshadowed by E.M. who scored 111 to help the Gentlemen of England to a win by four wickets. The Islington ground showed its superiority to Lord's as a playing surface, yielding a total of 822 runs for thirty-six wickets over the three days.

The brothers returned to London at the end of July, joining the South Wales team for one match of their cricket tour, v. I Zingari at Lord's. They more or less monopolized the fixture, and if a point is sought where E.M. and W.G. reached cricketing parity before the seesaw finally abandoned the horizontal, this may well have been it. Over the course of the game they matched each other almost run for run, ball for ball and wicket for wicket. W.G. failed in the first innings (0) but scored 85 in the second. E.M. scored 89 in the first innings and failed in the second (13).

They shared the bowling throughout, with exactly the same number of deliveries in the first innings (152), from which E.M. took 5 for 73 and W.G. 5 for 59. In the second innings, E.M. pulled ahead taking 7 for 56 to W.G.'s 3 for 41, but W.G. had the edge in catches, taking five in the match (three off E.M.) while E.M. took one (off W.G.). The other players were reduced to mere onlookers, as the two brothers battled it out as keenly, and no doubt as volubly, as they would have done in the orchard back at Downend. I Zingari lost by 104 runs, and can't have been overjoyed at being beaten by a couple of bumptious Bristolians masquerading as Welshmen.

Nearer the end of the season E.M. represented another side for whom he had no very obvious qualifications – the Gentlemen of Surrey – and nearly provoked a riot. The match, for the benefit of the Surrey ground bowlers, was against the United South, and the trouble came when E.M. got rid of an unbudgeable Harry Jupp with an example of the delivery immortalized by Conan Doyle in 'The Story of Spedegue's Dropper'. After only one or two sighters, E.M. managed to land a steepling lob right on the bails. Jupp was livid, and the Oval crowd showed their support by invading the pitch. The Surrey Gentlemen armed themselves with stumps and formed a defensive square in the time-honoured fashion. Violence was averted, and E.M. carried on blithely through the rest of the match, scoring two fifties and claiming two more presentation bats (which brought his total to seventy-five).

E.M. never minded whose nose he put out of joint, and was impossible to intimidate, either with a cricket ball or by any other means. His conduct throughout his life was characterized by a bristling independence. Once, on the way to the wicket, he was served with a subpoena to appear in a breach of promise case. He coolly handed it to the umpire and hit seventy before reading it.[13] When in later years his conduct as coroner was censured (the possibility that cricket interfered with the exercise of his duties came into the charges, and it is certainly part of the apocryphal record that he once gave instructions that a corpse should be put on ice until the end of play) he defended himself adroitly and had no qualms about crossing swords with the Home Secretary. He provided a powerful role model for W.G., who in adult life would prove every bit as determined to be his own man and have his own way.

E.M. missed the South Wales match against the Gentlemen of Surrey (leaving W.G. to take 8 for 72 in the home team's one innings), but the two were back in harness together at the Oval towards the end of August, representing an England XI against the full Surrey XI. They opened the batting for England, putting on eighty. E.M. made 44, W.G. 35. Surrey collapsed in their first innings, but made a better fist of things in their second, reaching the safety of 216 for 6 by the end of the game. Despite his recent successes, W.G. didn't bowl a single over.

It was a minor oversight. In an astonishingly short time Grace had established himself as a more-than-useful all-rounder with huge potential. In his first season in first-class cricket he had played five matches, scored 189 at an average of 27, taken twenty wickets at 13.40, and been picked for both the Gentlemen and an England XI. On the basis of that promising beginning he can have looked forward with nothing but unbridled optimism.

*

Grace started the 1866 season in May by travelling up to Oxford, accompanied by his mother and Fred, who was making his first-class debut. The two brothers, aged seventeen and fifteen, were playing for a hastily collected Gentlemen of England team standing in at short notice for Buckinghamshire who couldn't raise a side. It was not one of the family's finest occasions. W.G. failed with the bat (2 and 0), and Fred followed in his and E.M.'s footsteps by beginning his first-class career with a duck. The undergraduates won at a gallop by ten wickets. E. S. Carter, who later took Holy Orders, was playing in the match (and clean-bowled Fred in both innings). He remembered W.G. being caught at short leg off a 'half-cock' shot and returning to the players' tent to face his mother. She was reported to have said, 'Willie, Willie, haven't I told you over and over again how to play that ball?' Grace breakfasted with Carter the following morning in his rooms at Worcester College, and the future cleric tried his best to interest him in becoming an undergraduate. 'We walked round and round the beautiful garden after breakfast, talking over the possibility: but he was sure that his father would not sacrifice the time from his study for the medical profession. So it turned out, and the great W.G. was lost to Oxford.'[14]

Grace immediately returned to Bristol and another scholastic encounter. He ran up 150 not out against Clifton College, playing for Clifton, and he continued in tutorial vein when he accompanied the Lansdown Club to Winchester and scored a hundred runs (34, 75) against the college.

At the beginning of June he was given a hard assignment himself when E.M. passed on the job of captaining Eighteen Colts of Nottingham and

Sheffield against the AEE at Sheffield. Why E.M. dropped out isn't known, but as a newly qualified doctor he was perhaps finding it necessary to make compromises between his professional calling and his cricketing commitments. How widely publicized this substitution was is not clear. Perhaps the Graces simply sprung the change on the organizers without any warning. When a local paper exposed the high level of expenses paid to the Colts' amateur captain, they cited E.M. as the (unworthy) recipient. E.M. promptly sued. (There was clearly some doubt as to which Grace they had got. The *Sheffield and Rotherham Independent* sat on the fence, referring to 'W. E. Grace'.)[15]

Although W.G. had captained sides before, this was the first time in an important match. To lead a side of ambitious young cricketers he had never met before against the country's professional elite was a daunting task, especially away from home on alien territory. Neither Bristol nor London could have prepared him for Sheffield, and when he got there he felt he had 'got to the world's end'.[16] (Years later, the Australian bowler Hugh Trumble suffered a similar culture shock, declaring 'the smoke from the factories is horrible, and they say the big factories always bank their fires when the visiting side goes in to bat'.)[17]

Grace arrived in Sheffield at a particularly difficult time. The country was in turmoil after Gladstone's failure to get his Reform Bill through Parliament, and confidence had been rocked by the failure of a major bank on 'Black Friday' which triggered a string of bankruptcies. In the north the general uncertainty was increased by the volatility of industrial relations. A series of strikes and lock-outs was already generating outbreaks of civil disorder, and several cases of intimidation were going through the courts. In the autumn the nation would be shocked by the 'Sheffield Outrages' in which the level of violence escalated to the point where a black-leg's house was blown up with dynamite. Even the AEE got caught up in the prevailing press hostility to organized labour. One of the local papers quoted approvingly an article in the *Field* deploring the fact that the professionals 'already consider themselves as "corporations", with some kind of "vested rights"; [and] that they are much more difficult to manage than they were'.[18]

This was not an ideal stage for a seventeen-year-old southern amateur (widely believed to be taking money for his services) to make his first appearance in the lead role. Nor was the venue calculated to raise the spirits. The Hyde Park ground was on a high hill, and after an interminable ride to the top, Grace found an exposed playing area with facilities 'of the most primitive description'.[19] Everything pointed to a very testing two days. Even the weather was unfriendly, and the start of the match was delayed by rain until 1.30. George Parr had won the toss and when the AEE batted, the Colts were handicapped by the wet ground, which prevented the bowlers getting a foothold. The wicket itself, however, was good and the AEE took full advantage of the conditions to reach 183 for 8 by the close of play. Grace let his team-mates do most of the bowling, though he came on for a brief spell, sending down three consecutive maidens.

It had seemed doubtful whether there would be enough time to finish the game, but on the second morning J. C. Shaw and George Atkinson brushed the Colts aside for 84. Tinley wasn't even needed, though he caught Grace off Shaw for 9. The Colts followed on, ninety-nine runs behind. Wickets continued to fall regularly, but Grace dug in, determined to salvage something from the débâcle. This made the professionals restless. They were all eager to get the game over as quickly as possible, collect their money and leave Sheffield behind them. And they had no hesitation in communicating their feelings. 'They begged me to get out,' he recorded in *Reminiscences*,[20] and he was obviously under a great deal of pressure to comply. It would have made sense. The match was as good as lost. Like them, he had a train to catch, so he would be doing himself a good turn, at the same time as obliging men whom he had worshipped as heroes from afar, and who were, in many cases, also personal friends and companions of his brother. But he refused to budge. Over after over he stuck it out, deaf to pleas and abuse alike. He eventually fell to Shaw, who toiled for thirty-seven overs, taking 7 for 27, and made his way back to the sparse comforts of the changing tent applauded by the small crowd. He made 36 out of the Colts' total of 91 (leaving the AEE winners by an innings and eight runs). Only two other members of the team scraped into double figures. Grace may not have made any friends among the professionals, but he left no one in any doubt that he could be quite as cussed as E.M. In all the hundreds of matches in which he played, the Sheffield Colts game hardly stands out, yet it was an important test of character which he undoubtedly passed.

Whether or not he was looking forward to meeting Parr and his men on more familiar turf, he did not have the opportunity, as this year the northern boycott of the Gentlemen–Players match extended to Lord's as well as the Oval. Even without the northern cracks, it was a closely fought contest. W.G. failed with the bat, but bowled nearly a hundred overs, taking 4 for 72 in the professionals' first innings (E.M. took 6 for 25). Despite a small first-innings lead, the Gentlemen could not press home the advantage, losing by thirty-eight runs. Although he again did little as a batsman, W.G. played an influential part in the Gentlemen's win at the Oval, taking 7 for 51 as the Players collapsed to 106 all out.

In the middle of July, after a farcically one-sided North–South match which the South won by an innings, E.M. and W.G. returned home to join forces with their three other brothers for a local match between West Gloucestershire and Knole Park at Almondsbury. Uncle Pocock was also playing, and Dr Grace senior was present, possibly standing as umpire. A rare early photograph (see Plate 3) shows the West Gloucestershire team grouped against the trunk of a massive oak tree in the Knole Park grounds. With his cricketing sons ranked around him, Dr Grace in his top hat sits in the centre looking into the distance as though contemplating the truth in the age-old commonplace about little acorns. W.G. gazes steadily at the camera. The beard is not yet established, though his sideburns straggle down to meet untidily at his chin, and there is a discernible moustache. He wears a light-coloured cap and brown boots. Henry sports a striped shirt and a square beard beneath a clean-shaven mouth. E.M., aquiline and darkly handsome, looks like a Victorian Anthony Sher, while Alfred wears a hugely baggy cap and a full beard. Fred sits in the front row. Not yet old enough at fifteen for facial hair, he nevertheless appears a young man rather than a boy. He has the same intense look as W.G. His hands, loosely clasped between his knees, seem abnormally large. No one smiles much in Victorian photography – the exposure time was too long – but the West Gloucestershire team look a particularly determined and formidable group.

They were certainly too much for the home side, and the main interest in the game lay in the competition between the Graces to get a bowl. Having top-scored with 66, E.M. took seven wickets in the Knole Park first innings and looked set to win the match on his own. But Henry intervened and he and Fred took over, bowling West Gloucestershire to victory by an innings and thirty-four runs.

One of the less prominent members of the West Gloucestershire team was Rowland Brotherhood. He could certainly tell the Graces a thing or two about family sides, as he was one of the eleven brothers who sometimes turned out as the Brotherhood XI. But of course, the brotherhood that counted in the West Country was the Grace clan. They played the game as hard at club level as they did in first-class games, and E.M. in particular was a terror to the local sides. The ferocity of his batting was frightening, and on small grounds much of the afternoon could be spent retrieving the ball from neighbouring fields. W.G. records that in the 1860s 'it was more than once seriously proposed that he should not be allowed to play'.[21] They couldn't stop him, and when, in later years, he became The Coroner, they wouldn't even dare to try.

More often than not the local cricketers found the full might of the Graces ranged against them, but from time to time the brothers appeared on opposite sides, usually with dramatic results. On one occasion (September 1864) W.G. agreed to play for Henry's village Hanham against a neighbouring hamlet, Bitton. They were just leaving Downend when E.M. cadged a lift, throwing his cricket bag into the carriage 'in case they happened to be one short'. Surprisingly they fell for this ruse; E.M. had in fact been recruited by Bitton. On a wet track he took most of the wickets for his adoptive club, who were left just ten to win the match. E.M. announced that he would knock the runs off with a couple of blows – and was bowled by a shooter for a duck. The rest of the team followed in quick succession, many of them having to change back hurriedly into their cricket gear. Apart from three byes, 'only one man scored at all'. With W.G. taking six wickets, Hanham bowled Bitton out for 6, and won by three runs. Henry and W.G. had what must have been a very long last laugh.[22] In another match, Henry and E.M. were on the opposite side to W.G., who hit a ball to the boundary where it was caught. He claimed the catch was taken over the boundary. Henry and E.M. were vehement it was fair. The unhappy umpire was caught in the conflicting force fields of three very powerful personalities, but in the end acceded to Henry's peremptory command, 'Be a man and give him out.' The finger went up reluctantly, and W.G. made his even more reluctant way back to the changing tent. Grace's view of E.M.'s judgement was summed up by his remark on a similar occasion when he told an umpire, 'Take no notice of *him*. It's when I appeal that it's out.'[23]

E.M. and W.G. were back on the same side for the England–Surrey match at the Oval, which started on 30 July. Once more, the Northern stars refused to play, 'preferring', as *Scores and Biographies* tartly put it, 'the Twenty-two matches as being more lucrative'. When Jupp snapped up E.M. for 9 off Humphrey, Surrey might have considered they had an even chance. They were soon disabused. W.G. went in five and after a slightly hesitant couple of overs got into his stride. He was not out at stumps, and the following day he carried on an innings which was 'steadily played as well as finely hit' to reach 224 not out when the innings closed. It was not only his maiden first-class century, but was by some way the highest first-class score at the Oval, and the crowd gave him a tumultuous reception. The cheering could be heard far beyond the walls of the ground. Grace made just under half the England total of 521, and in his one innings 'more runs off the bat than Surrey did in their twenty-two'.[24] A total of 431 runs was scored while he was at the wicket, and as they would all have been run out, he must, over the two days, have covered around 9,000 yards in short sprints.

Which makes what followed all the more extraordinary. Far from being exhausted, Grace had another arena in which he wanted to demonstrate his explosive physical powers. There was a meeting of the newly formed National Olympian Association at the Crystal Palace and Grace had put his name down for the 440 yards hurdles, presumably before he received the invitation to play for England. The Oval match took precedence, of course, but when the opportunity arose, Grace had the cheek to ask permission to take part in the race. It says much for the easy-going nature of the game in the 1860s that the England captain, V. E. Walker, allowed him leave of absence. Perhaps Walker's own jaunty fifty down the order had put him in an indulgent mood. (Grace was honest enough in *The History of a Hundred Centuries* to admit that his own response as captain to a similar request would have been unprintable.)[25]

So while the England team was taking the field at the start of the Surrey innings, Grace was rattling in a cab across south London to the Crystal Palace. There, resplendent in his singlet and gaily coloured running knickerbockers, he won the 440 yards hurdle race in a time of one minute ten seconds over twenty hurdles.[26] Not until C. B. Fry nonchalantly put aside his cigar and claimed the world record long jump three decades later would a cricketer display such athletic prowess.

*

Grace's unique pre-eminence as a cricketer has tended to obscure the fact that he was also an all-round athlete of the highest calibre. Just as his cricket was fostered by the family nursery at Downend, so his competitive running came out of a boyhood trying to keep up with his elder brothers, specifically E.M. They used to take part in athletics meetings at the Zoological Gardens in Clifton, and their rivalry was extreme. In 1866 they had a battle of Steve Ovett–Sebastian Coe proportions in the sprints. E.M. was generally reckoned to be the faster by a head over 100 yards, but on this occasion Gilbert beat him, largely by 'beating the pistol'.[27] This was another example of all being fair in the love–hate relationship between siblings. E.M. was left seething and wound himself up to a competitive fury for the 200 yards, which was Gilbert's preferred distance. He ran as he had never run before, beating W.G. into second place. Honour was satisfied, but E.M. was still livid and in W.G.'s recollection 'wouldn't speak to me after this for a time'.[28]

Grace's style was effective but hardly elegant. 'When I came out at sixteen I was unmercifully chaffed at the way I threw my legs and arms about, but I persevered . . .'[29] He was generally the star of the Clifton meetings: in 1866 he was awarded a gold medal for all-round proficiency, and on another occasion when he went up to collect his trophies from the mayor of Bristol, the band suddenly struck up 'See the conquering hero comes'. The mayor consoled the other competitors with the reflection that 'he will grow old and stiff some day'.[30]

Just as they travelled round the Bristol area playing cricket, so the Grace brothers would compete in any local athletics meeting they could get to. In 1870 W.G. went to the Bedminster Cricket Club Sports and won the 100 yards, came second in the 220 yards hurdles, won the quarter-mile hurdles and finished third in the 440. And once cricket began taking him to London on a regular basis, he started running in the capital as well. In a London Athletic Club meeting in 1867 he won the 200 yards hurdles, and went on to win at least a dozen more hurdles races at the highest level. C. E. Green remembered his 'lolloping style with a tremendous stride', and saw him at a sports meeting at Blackheath in 1868, attired in 'salmon coloured running drawers', winning the 100 yards, the quarter mile and the hurdles.[31] *Scores and Biographies* included a paragraph on Grace as 'a pedestrian', and recorded that in handicap races he was never beaten 'from the scratch', adding that by the end of 1869 he had won 'no less than seventy cups or prizes'. In those days athletics meetings were often hosted by cricket clubs, and it was natural that throwing the cricket ball should be included as one of the events. He is credited with a throw of 122 yards at Eastbourne, and on another occasion he threw a ball 109 yards one way and 105 yards back.[32]

Grace's athletic career did not last beyond the 1860s. His gradual increase in weight brought his hurdling days to an end, and eventually even stopped him riding with the hounds because there was no horse strong enough to lift him over the hedges. But there was no let-up in strenuous physical exercise. In a revealing paragraph in *Cricket*, he talks about how he and E.M. maintained their fitness during the off season:

We were known to be fond of hunting, shooting, and fishing, as well as cricketing. Immediately we laid down the bat, we took up the gun or rod . . . I find a day's shooting or fishing, or a run with the harriers or beagles, of great use during the winter months, and I take care to have plenty of walking. In the months of February and March I begin to prepare for the season, increasing the amount of exercise, and by the beginning of May I feel fit enough to face the cricketing season.[33]

His physical stamina lasted virtually to the end of his life, and well into his sixties he was capable of exhausting men half his age with his regime of non-stop activity.

*

When he returned to the Oval after his triumph on the race track, Grace found that the England team had kept a tight grip on the game, which they duly won by an innings and 296. While extolling Grace's personal contribution, *Scores and Biographies* commented, 'it was now absurd for Surrey or any other *single* county to continue playing against All England'. An England side did play Middlesex the following year but the match proved equally one-sided and the experiment was abandoned. It wasn't until 1877 that it was revived, when the county taking on the rest of the country was Gloucestershire.

At the beginning of August, E.M. and W.G. both played for the the United South for the first time. Their opponents were drawn from that other great cricketing family, the Walkers, and the game took place on Walker's ground, Southgate. E.M. only appeared a couple of times for the USEE, but W.G. and Fred were to become regulars. W.G. began his long, and lucrative, involvement by scoring 0 and 2.

There was a strong Grace presence at Canterbury for what turned out to be a wet and windy Cricket Week. In addition to E.M. and W.G., Fred went too in the hope of picking up a game. He was lucky. George Bennett was late, and Fred stepped into the breach for the South of the Thames against the North of the Thames. The first appearance of the 'Three Graces' on the St Lawrence ground was not a glorious one. As the compiler of the history of the Canterbury Cricket Week rather smugly notes, 'In their first innings they made 9 between them' (E.M. 8, W.G. 0, G.F. 1).[34] Fred made 3 not out in his second innings, but had a happier game for the Gentlemen of the South v. I Zingari, scoring 3 and 17. E.M. had a wretched few days with the bat on the ground which had seen his greatest triumph, but W.G. showed some family form with 30 and 50 against IZ, and between them the two senior brothers destroyed the I Zingari batting as they had the previous year.

W.G. was not eligible to play in the third match, MCC v. Gentlemen of Kent, but he took part in the Clifton Cricket Week when he got home. He had two innings and scored 157 and 78, which kept his eye in for his last first-class appearance of the season, for the Gentlemen of the South against the Players of the South at the Oval. The start of the match was delayed while the last places in the amateurs' team were filled. Even when it did get under way, the Gentlemen had to take the field with a couple of substitutes. This lackadaisical approach to punctuality was endemic among amateurs, and drew forth regular reproaches from the sporting press.

Grace didn't mind if others missed the boat; it simply left him with more to do. He now embarked on another marathon bowling stint, and, starting with Jupp, whom he dismissed without needing to resort to his brother's under-hand methods, he steadily worked his way through the Players' batting line-up in a spell of forty-eight overs. Apart from George Griffith, reckoned the hardest hitter before C. I. Thornton, who struck out vigorously and was unlucky to be stranded on 97, none of the players made much headway against him, and he finished with 7 for 92 in an all-out total of 207. On the second day W.G. went in at number five and produced another stunning performance for the Oval crowd, though it was probably appreciated less by the Surrey players who had fielded through the first one a month before. If anything his domination was more complete. Certainly his percentage of his side's total increased. Out of 297, Grace hit 173, and he scored those out of only 240 runs made while he was at the crease. The next highest innings was 44.

It was an innings of great power – such power, in fact, that he broke his bat. To mark his double century for England, the Oval authorities had given him a presentation bat, complete with silver plate, and this he now called for. There had been no time to knock it in, but careless of the consequences Grace was soon blazing away, hitting James Lillywhite for two all-run sixes. As the professionals watched him sprinting up and down the wicket, with the silver plate on his bat glinting in the sunshine, they must have sensed that they were witnessing the transformation of the game as they knew it. Nothing was ever going to be quite the same again.

Rain on the third morning washed out any hope of a result, and the pros could put their feet up in the comforting knowledge that they were being paid for doing nothing. W.G. splashed off to Paddington and home to prepare for his last fling of the season, the West Gloucestershire tour of the Welsh Borders, where they would play a series of matches against the odds. This reunited him with E.M. and the two set off to wreak havoc among the cannon fodder. Against Ross and District they took forty wickets between them, but at Monmouth there was a departure from the script. E.M. and W.G. were actually at the wicket at the start of the West Gloucestershire innings when the Monmouth captain asked if they minded playing with a ball that had been used for a few overs and was 'slightly soiled'. After his performance at the Oval, W.G. must have felt confident of hitting a hundred off a turnip, but E.M. made a scene and 'insisted upon the rules of the game being observed'. This meant someone had to be despatched into the town to buy a new ball. An embarrassing interlude followed as the two batsmen, the two umpires and the twenty-two men of Monmouth and District stood around idly in the late summer sunshine. E.M.'s martinet demeanour would have discouraged levity, but perhaps the atmosphere was lightened by a bit of communal humming. Time passed. The distant church bells marked the quarter. E.M. fretted. A new cricket ball wasn't that much to ask, surely? At last the man returned from town. The new ball was produced, and probably held quite close to E.M.'s nose for his personal inspection, before being passed to the bowler. The fielders wandered back to their places. W.G. resumed his stance. The umpire called 'Play!', up ran the bowler, down came the first delivery, and off went the bails. Grace would get used to the outbursts of raucous rejoicing provoked by the fall of his wicket, but this must have been one of his more humiliating departures from the crease – for which, no doubt, he held E.M. largely responsible.

There was embarrassment of a more sombre complexion in the next match at Hereford, when E.M.'s commitment to 'the rules of the game' appeared in a different light. The Hereford umpire, who has come down to us unadorned by Christian name or title simply as Craggs, gave E.M. out. E.M. said he wasn't out, that he wasn't going out, and that Craggs wasn't fit to officiate and should be replaced. Craggs stood by his decision; the Hereford team stood by Craggs. Irritable force met immovable object. Impasse. As the historian of Herefordshire cricket observed, 'there seemed every prospect of the match coming to a premature and unpleasant termination', before mildly noting that 'the universal law of cricket and good manners is that an umpire's decision shall be final'. E.M. knew that as well as anybody. All the Graces did, and as a general principle they respected it. They just happened to have an unshakeable conviction that they knew better, and that in their case the umpire should defer to them. On this occasion, in the face of over-whelming and unbulliable odds, E.M. calmed down sufficiently to storm off to the changing tent and the match proceeded. The steadfast Twenty-two of Hereford and District won by forty-three runs.[35]

When he finally returned to Downend to unpack his cricket bag for the last time, W.G. could look back on a triumphant season. In his eight first-class matches (thirteen innings) he had scored 581 runs at the extraordinarily high average of 52.81 with two large undefeated centuries, and his thirty-one wickets cost 15.58 each. *Lillywhite's Companion*, giving averages for the first time, reflected the contemporary confusion over what constituted first-class status by adding further matches to produce a total of 640 runs at 42.10. With the exception of HRH the Prince of Wales, who was given pride of place at the head of the table (a courtesy which did him no favours – two innings, two runs for an average of one), all the batsmen were listed in alphabetical order, so the disparity between 'Grace, E.M.' (fourteen innings, 241 runs, average 17) and 'Grace, W.G.' was impossible to overlook.

*

The next year, 1867, was a bad one for English cricket, and a bad year for Grace. Although the MCC was pressing ahead with the modernization of Lord's – 1867 saw the opening of the grandstand with refreshment bars and 'suitable' lavatories – the politics of the game was anything but forward-looking. Attitudes in the professional ranks hardened to such an extent that the matches between North and South and the two All England XIs had to be cancelled. The MCC was powerless to effect a truce, but expressed its displeasure by declaring 'it is no longer desirable to extend the patronage of the Marylebone Cricket Club to the Cricketers' Fund exclusively; but a fund has now been formed which shall be called "The Marylebone Profesional Fund", which shall have for its object the support of the professional players who during their career shall have conducted themselves to the entire satisfaction of the Committee of the M.C.C.'[36] Grace's personal tribulations were sym-pathetically catalogued by *Sporting Life*:

[F]rom May 10 to June Mr W. G. Grace was laid up through a sprained ankle; from July 10 until August 10 scarlet fever laid him low; and on August 26, when fielding for England v Surrey and Sussex the forefinger of his right hand was split open: and as if this was not enough, when out with his gun on 'St Partridge's Day' the wound reopened, and thus was this fine cricketer not only prevented from participating in some of the best matches of the season, but from hitting up his leeway in September. . .[37]

In the four first-class matches in which he could play there was no repetition of the achievements of the previous year. He had only six innings, and accumulated 154 at 30.80. His highest score was 75, for England v. Middlesex at Lord's in June. On a vicious wicket at the same venue in July, which produced a dismally low-scoring match, he made 18 (out of 87) for the Gentlemen v. Players, and in the second innings saw the Gentlemen home with 37 not out. He was batting with Alfred Lubbock as the fifty-five required were knocked off, and Lubbock recalled: 'W.G. amused me a good deal while we were in. He always called me "Allfred," [sic] and he kept saying, "Steady, Allfred," "Don't be in a hurry, Allfred," and all that sort of thing; while I meanwhile kept admonishing him with, "Steady, Gilbert," and "Well played, G.," as the Players were bowling up all they knew.'[38]

Grace also bowled up all he knew, taking eleven wickets in the match, and 8 for 25 in the Players' second innings to seize victory. Lubbock remembered his bowling as well as his batting, without giving any great insight why his 'modest medium pace' should have exerted such a malign spell over the professionals, beyond saying it appeared 'to puzzle them entirely'. This puzzlement was widely shared. Grace took thirty-nine wickets in his abbreviated season, at an average of 7.51, and had now taken ninety first-class wickets at 10.38, which compared well with his great professional contemporaries. Alfred Shaw, for instance, had a career average of 12.12.

*

1868 made up for the disappointments of 1867. For one thing, the weather was perfect, indeed 'abnormally hot'. A schoolboy, E. F. S. Tylecote, set the tone for the season by scoring 404 not out in a house match at Clifton College in May. It took him eight afternoons, and established a record for the highest individual innings in any sort of cricket.

Grace played in only seven first-class matches, starting at Lord's in June, when he was included in an England side against the MCC &

Ground. On another indifferent wicket he stood head and shoulders above everyone else, making 29 out of 96 and 66 out of 179 to help his side home by ninety-two runs late on the second day. Fred also played for England, making his debut at Lord's at seventeen, while E.M. was on the MCC team and his 27 was the second highest score in their first innings of 106. (J. R. Webber has established that this was the only time W.G. and E.M. played against each other in first-class cricket. Remarkably the match seems to have passed off without incident.) The South of the Thames v. North of the Thames match was finished in a single day, thanks to another poor Lord's wicket and Grace's bowling. He took 11 for 66 to help win the game by nine wickets.

The next match at Lord's on 12 and 13 June was between the MCC and the first ever touring team from Australia, the 'Aboriginal Blacks of Australia, with C. Lawrence', as they appear in *Scores and Biographies*. Charles Lawrence (who had toured with H. H. Stephenson's team in 1862 and stayed on) and Tom Wills, an Australian educated at Rugby and a Cambridge blue, had coached an Aborigine cricket team which first toured the country at home before making the long voyage to England.* The Aborigines were an exotic attraction, and the demonstrations of spear and boomerang throwing with which they rounded off their matches pandered to the public taste for hybrid entertainments. However, unlike the troupes of clown cricketers whose farcical travesties were enjoying a brief vogue, the Aborigines were serious sportsmen. The MCC accorded the visitors great respect, putting out a socially distinguished team against them which included an earl, a viscount and a lieutenant-colonel. The Aborigines, in their individual coloured sashes (to help identify them), competed on equal terms until they collapsed disastrously in their second innings.

Grace was not then a member of MCC, or he might have made a historic match even more notable. There is no record that he played against the Aborigines, or even saw them play, but the consensus of opinion seemed to be that they were 'about equal to third-class English teams; . . . it was generally admitted that two players, Mullagh and Cuzens, showed very good all-round form'.[39] *Wisden* records that Grace joined the Aborigines in their 'athletic sports' at the Oval, and that 'in three successive attempts, [he] threw the cricket ball 116, 117, and 118 yards'.[40] He does not, however, mention this anywhere himself.

* Wills did not accompany them on tour. He was a drinker and was held partly responsible through negligence for the number of fatalities among the Aborigines during the first year.

75

On 25 and 26 June Gloucestershire followed in the Aborigines' footsteps to Lord's where the MCC found the emergent cricketers of the West Country more of a handful, losing to them by 134 runs. E.M. was top scorer with 65, backed up by T. G. Matthews (27 and 32) and W.G. (24 and 13). Fred was also playing, but failed with the bat. He didn't get much of a bowl either, though he took two catches off W.G. as his elder brothers dismissed the MCC for 69 and 91. Although the match was not granted first-class status, it strengthened Gloucestershire's claims to be admitted into the charmed circle.

W.G. returned to Lord's once more within the week to represent the Gentlemen against the Players, and produced one of his most commanding performances. The wicket was a disgrace, quite bare in places, and it proved fast and erratic. A long-stop was *de rigueur*, as good-length balls sometimes shot over the wicket-keeper's head. Grace went in at three (after E.M. had been run out for 1) and faced the might of Wootton, Silcock, Willsher, Grundy and James Lillywhite. B. B. Cooper stayed with him for a while and scored a respectable 28. No one else got into double figures. But as wickets fell, Grace determinedly dug out the shooters, dodged the lifters or took them on his chest, and hit anything loose with impressive power. It must have seemed as though there were two games going on at the same time: at one end, the succession of amateurs prodded, poked and departed; at the other, Grace cracked the ball away through the field with absolute authority. Out of a total of 201 he made 134 not out, and there's no knowing how many more he would have scored had he not run out of partners. In his own assessment, it was 'one of the finest innings I have ever played'.[41] Even more than his two great innings at the Oval the previous year, it stamped him as a talent apart. He then opened the bowling for the Gentlemen and took 6 for 50 as the professionals were dismissed for 115, and 4 for 31 when they followed on. Only when they had been dismissed for the second time, for 116, did he rest, forgoing a second knock. (E.M. saw the Gentlemen home with 22 not out.) W.G. had won the most important match of the season virtually on his own.

With the northern professionals still refusing to play at the Oval, the return was an even more one-sided affair. The Gentlemen's crushing victory was due largely to I. D. Walker's 165, though Grace chipped in with 6 for 55 in the Players' first innings of 126. As he reflected happily, 'at last the happy time had come when the Gentlemen could hold their own in these contests'.[42]

Grace had a quiet July, returning to the Oval at the end of the month for Gentlemen of the South v. Players of the South. The Players got some sort of revenge for their defeat in the two main encounters, and although W.G. scored 55 in his first innings, he was bowled for a duck by Ned Willsher in his second. The professionals also seem to have found some sort of answer to his bowling, as he toiled away for sixty-six overs taking 2 for 139. Not that lack of success diminished his enthusiasm for bowling. C. E. Green remembers the captain I. D. Walker discussing the possibility of a change: 'W.G., who was bowling from the pavilion end, said quite seriously, "I tell you what, I'll go on at the other end." It never occurred to him for a moment that he himself should be taken off!'[43]

In August he went down to Canterbury for the Cricket Week and a game between South of the Thames and North of the Thames. In contrast to Lord's the St Lawrence wicket was a batsman's dream, and this year was playing better than ever. The match, which North of the Thames won, produced 1,018 runs and three centuries. Grace scored two of them – 130 and 102. No one had scored a century in each innings since 1817, when William Lambert made 107 not out and 157 for Sussex against Epsom at Lord's. (E.M. continued his poor Canterbury form with 13 and 0.)

Still ineligible for the MCC, Grace left to play United South against the Walker's XV at Southgate. His 68, supported by the guileful slows of James Southerton, was the basis of a ten-wicket win. However, when they went on to play a Twenty-two of Worcestershire, the weight of numbers proved too great, and they lost by fifty-seven runs. Grace was bowled twice by the given man, William McIntyre, for 11 and 16.

Without a county to play for, Grace still had relatively little first-class cricket, but as he would throughout his career, he filled the gaps in his diary with minor matches. These divided into two categories: professional engagements against the odds, for which he was paid, and local club matches in the Bristol area, though whether he expected an appearance fee for these is uncertain. He was always a formidable recruit, whatever his terms, and this year scored 111 (out of 177) for Bedminster against Lansdown, and 210 for Clifton against the Civil Service. He rounded off his first-class season playing for England against Surrey and Middlesex combined at the Oval on 17, 18 and 19 August. This was Julius Caesar's benefit, and as usual Grace pulled out all the stops, scoring 24 out of 115 and 19 out of 79 and taking 7 for 28 and 5 for 67, though he could not prevent the two London counties stealing home by a single wicket.

After the set-back of 1867, he again averaged over fifty in first-class matches, his 588 runs coming at 65.33, while his forty-four wickets cost only 14.52 each. He was now indisputably the cricketer of the age, the Champion.

*

However, though he was a giant in the world of sport, there was no suggestion that this should have any bearing on his career. It remained unquestioned that he would follow his father and brothers into the medical profession. In addition to the overtures from Oxford, there were rumours that Grace was considering taking a place at Caius College, Cambridge, which had a long medical tradition. This created 'a lot of excitement amongst the cricket set at Cambridge', but in the end it came to nothing. When asked in later life whether it had been a serious possibility, W.G. replied, 'Yes, I really came very near doing so.'[44] He certainly would have gone had his father allowed it. Though he had no desire to ape the airs of the more exquisite amateurs he met when playing I Zingari, for instance, he may have felt that three years at an Oxbridge college would smooth some of his rough corners and give him the social confidence he lacked. And he would have enjoyed making his mark in the Varsity match. In the end Dr Grace's caution, and the size of his income, determined that it should remain a fantasy. On 7 October 1868 William Gilbert Grace enrolled at the Bristol Medical School, becoming a pupil of Mr Tibbits. He is listed fifth out of six in a 'Class of General Perpetual Students', and as it took him eleven years to qualify the title was peculiarly apt.

In addition to his lectures, Grace got some practical experience helping his father. This aspect of his training did not always go smoothly. On one occasion he attended a patient with typhoid fever, and gave him a prescription. Dr Grace made a call later in the day and found the man's condition had worsened. He examined the medicine Gilbert had given him and threw the bottle out of the window, saying, 'Damn the stupid fool!'[45] In fact, there was little medical science could offer in the face of the disease. After cholera, typhoid fever was one of the period's greatest killers. Much later in life Grace would receive an awful reminder of its terrifying power to strike down the unlikeliest victim without warning or remission.

*

At the start of the 1869 season Grace was elected a member of the MCC. He was proposed by T. Burgoyne, the Treasurer, and seconded by

78

R. A. Fitzgerald, the Secretary, who recognized how vital it was to claim him for the club and the interests it represented. He was already the greatest attraction cricket had ever known, drawing huge crowds wherever he played. Had he thrown in his lot with the professionals, the cricket world would have shifted on its axis once and for all. As it was, the MCC regained its authority over the game by 'hanging onto W.G.'s shirt-tails'.[46]

With Grace on side, the threat posed by the professionals was never likely to amount to much, though their squabbles remained a constant irritant. The North–South divide remained as rancorous as ever and attempts to heal the breach foundered on George Parr's stubbornness. Although the North–South match was resumed, Parr found a new bone of contention in the Cricketers' Fund, voting against its continuation because it bound the northern professionals in with the southern players. The northern professionals still attracted the criticism of those outraged by any show of independence. Fred Gale, who wrote under the fitting pen-name the 'Old Buffer', accused them of 'prostituting cricket in the North by playing . . . gate-matches against pigmies' and jeered at the 'cheap laurels' earned by those who preferred playing for the All England team instead of representing the Players against the Gentlemen at Lord's.[47] But in fact the power of the northern professionals was already waning. The future of the game rested in the hands of the MCC's newest member, and although Grace brought about a revolution in cricket, he was by nature a conservative, and his influence reinforced the status quo to such an extent that it remained unchallenged within his lifetime, and indeed long after his death.

Grace proved a loyal and tireless servant of the MCC, albeit on his own terms. His background made it almost inevitable that he rejected the radical option of turning professional. Although the Grace family was happy to fraternize with the professionals, and probably had more in common with the likes of George Parr than with those who flocked to Lord's in their finery for the Varsity or Eton–Harrow match, there was no doubt which side of the great divide they were on. Dr Grace had struggled hard to rise from his humble origins; his sons were to be gentlemen, and they would therefore play as amateurs, however flagrantly their personal circumstances required them to breach the amateur code. Grace expressed his views on the MCC with characteristic robustness in *Reminiscences*:

My own personal feeling is that the laws and regulations of cricket generally could not have been entrusted to better hands than those of the MCC. The club has always set a high standard to the cricket world, and has never refused to consider reasonable suggestions from responsible cricketers. It has acted with the impartiality of the High Court of Appeal, and has always safeguarded the best interests of the game, without unduly interfering with the rights and liberties of cricketers, individually or collectively. In cricket the classical maxim that he governs best who governs least applies as completely as it does in national life. A judicious conservatism – born of a dread of change which is not improvement – has always guided the counsels of the MCC, and if it had done nothing else than successfully resist some of the ridiculous proposals which have from time to time been noisily advocated, it would have done splendid service to our national game. If the MCC had listened to the agitations which have been sprung upon it during the last thirty years there would have been continual alteration of the rules, and finality or fixity would have been impossible. Legislative tinkering would have been fatal to cricket, and the MCC had, I think, shown its wisdom by throwing its influence against precipitate action.[48]

*

Predictably enough, Grace repaid the club's confidence in him by making a century on his debut against Oxford University in May. The next highest score after his 117 was 37 by one of the groundstaff. Grace says little about the match beyond commenting on the cold weather and the state of the wicket ('good'). Interestingly, he also states that it was 'my first appearance at Oxford', conveniently forgetting the rather less successful trip three years previously.[49]

The Gentlemen beat the Players in both their matches, though Grace's contribution was relatively modest. By now, though, his mere presence gave his side an edge. If he failed with the bat, as he did twice for MCC v. Lancashire on a typical Lord's snake-pit in July, he would make amends with the ball (in the Lancashire second innings, Grace's analysis was 27.3 overs, nineteen maidens, six wickets for ten runs; the highest team score in the game was 67). If he failed in his first innings, the bowling side could normally look forward to a long day in the field second time round.

He really came good in July, when he scored four of the six centuries he recorded during the season. The first was for the MCC against Surrey at the Oval on 1 and 2 July. After his two previous massive scores at the Oval, 138 might be seen as a relative let-off, but in the paltry MCC total of 215 it was another disproportionately large contribution, and he followed it up with 6 for 70 to ensure victory by nine wickets.

Nottinghamshire provided tougher opposition, but Grace was equal to the challenge, scoring 48 out of 112 in the MCC's first innings. Then, in response to Richard Daft's patient 103 for the visitors, he made 121 out of 210, though even that proved insufficient to save the match.

Then it was back to the Oval for Gentlemen of the South v. Players of the South. The groundsman had produced a perfect wicket and the Players took full advantage of it. Jupp and Pooley opened with a stand of 142 and the total reached 475. Grace bowled some sixty-three overs. The Players' innings closed mid-way through the second day's play, and despite his lengthy bowling stint, W.G. eagerly buckled on his pads and went out to open with B. B. Cooper. Grace says that for three and three-quarter hours they 'defied' the bowlers. 'Flayed' might have been more accurate. They failed by a run to double the Players' opening stand, and their 283 remained a first-class record for many years. They were not separated until the Players resorted to Mantle 'who was by far the worst bowler on the field'.[50] Momentarily lost in contemplation of the opportunities for plunder, Grace hit back a return catch, and six balls later Cooper also succumbed. Grace scored 180, including two sixes, one five and ten fours. Cooper made 101. The *Telegraph* gives a portrait of Grace in this innings:

The characteristic of Mr Grace's play was that he knew exactly where every ball he hit would go. Just the strength required was expended and no more . . . Watching most other men – even good players – your main object is to see how they will defend themselves against the bowling; watching Mr Gilbert Grace, you can hardly help feeling as though the batsman were himself the assailant. You want to know, not how he will keep up his stumps, but where he will choose to hit. On Friday last he chose to hit all over the ground; and he did it! Young men, however, are never satisfied, and so, for the sake of a little variety, he sent the ball into the nearest street.[51]

It was this performance that prompted Tom Emmett, Yorkshire's rising star, to remark: 'It's all very well against this South Country bowling; let him come up to Sheffield against me and George.' 'George' was George Freeman, whom Grace came to rate as highly as any he ever faced. Grace duly went up to Sheffield to play in the North–South match at the end of July, and George Freeman duly bowled him out. Unfortunately from the North's point of view, he had scored 122 in the first innings before it happened. And the 122 came out of a total of 173, with B. B. Cooper's 23 the only other double-figure score. It was the decisive innings in a low-scoring match which the South won comfortably. This was the first time Grace had faced Freeman, and he was impressed. Not, however, as impressed as Emmett was. When he was asked what he thought of Grace, having seen him on home territory, he ruefully admitted that he was 'a non-such', adding, with feeling, 'he ought to be made to play with a littler bat'.[52] That was a thought shared, but never quite so well expressed, by dozens of bowlers over the years to come. J. C. Shaw was another bowler whose equanimity was tested over the years. He was playing in the North–South return match at Canterbury and registered a notable success when he bowled W.G. for a duck in the first innings. But he toiled long and hard in the second as Grace made 96. The Kent bowlers were taken to task in the next match, when Grace became the first batsman to score a century before lunch in an important fixture. He made 116 for MCC, going on to 127 after the interval.

What was it about Grace that made him so good, that raised him so far above his contemporaries? C. B. Fry put that question to Alfred Shaw, who claimed the distinction of heading the list of bowlers who had dismissed the Champion most often (forty-nine times). The Nottingham-shire professional, who was arguably the most accurate bowler of his day, gave his considered response: 'Well, he was big with a long reach, he watched her close and he was very correct.'[53]

The foundation of his batting was certainly his faultless defence. As his mother had suggested to George Parr, W.G. would make a better batsman even than E.M. because he could play back as well as forward (and, though she was too diplomatic to mention this in her letter, he played straight). But the wickets he played on – especially the notorious Lord's square – were such that the unexpected was always likely to happen. Club batsmen today retire to the pavilion shaking their heads at the injustice of a malign universe when a ball keeps a little low. In the 1860s you could watch one ball go over your head (and over the wicket-keeper's) while the next might not leave the ground. The shooter was simply a fact of life that had to be dealt with. To play the shooter a batsman needed a hawk's eye and lightning reactions. C. L. R. James, combining personal experience, theoretical insight and historical imagination, has a fascinating passage on playing the ball that never leaves the ground:

Before we reached the second eleven we played on dirt pitches, and there was always the problem of the dead shooter. Some of us learned to play it. As soon as, playing back, you lost sight of the ball on the rise, you dug your bat deep down behind where you stood so that it sloped towards the bowler. More than that, you could see the shooting off-break and calculate where to dig down. But to play this stroke, which we had to play twice every three overs or so, you could not take the right foot across the wickets. If you did you could not possibly get the bat down in time, you would hit your own foot more often than not. I am convinced that it was the right foot stationary or taken straight back which allowed W.G. Grace to play the four shooters in succession for which the crowd rose to him at Lord's in the days of treacherous wickets.[54]

Grace was emphatic that the right foot should be planted outside the leg-stump, and strongly recommended that the left should not cover any part of the wicket either. His stance was completed by 'holding the bat in what is called the pendulum fashion, which tends to facility of movement, without diminishing in the slightest degree the batsman's power of defence. I await the attack of the bowler with the top of the handle of my bat just above my waist, and the bottom of the blade almost on a level with the centre of the middle stump.' The weapon poised so ominously to strike was, by modern standards, light. 'Personally,' he wrote, 'I play with a bat weighing about 2 lb. 5 oz., which . . . is heavy enough for anybody.' Although he was a thunderous driver, he was also a great cutter, and, as he says, 'I never saw a good cutter use a heavy bat.'[55]

If keeping out shooters was one essential skill in the 1860s and 1870s, keeping down lifters was another. Grace's soundness against the sharply rising ball was just one of the many things that impressed the Australians on his first tour in 1873–4: 'Mr Grace frequently played balls down that rose breast high in a way that surprised the [local players] who were accustomed to see their own men bob their heads and let such go by.'[56] When Grace came into the first-class game it was dominated by a 'generation of slinging, erratic, physically dangerous fast-bowlers'.[57] In the view of one veteran of the period, 'He killed professional fast bowling; for years they were almost afraid to bowl within his reach.'[58] As John Arlott points out, 'in the fixture lists of those days, with so many matches like Gentlemen v Players, so many more by MCC at first-class level than now, North v South – and even Smokers v Non-smokers . . . the better bowlers had to encounter "The Champion" perhaps a dozen times a season.'[59] Through 'trial, error and punishment' hard lessons were learned, and bowling evolved to recognize length as more valuable than sheer speed.

Grace's remorseless subjugation of the fast men was rooted in power, confidence, concentration and great physical courage. Astonishingly, according to E. H. D. Sewell, who played with him at the Crystal Palace, Grace never wore a box.[60] Although versions of the 'abdominal protector' had been available since 1851 many leading batsmen, including Grace, Ranji, Trumper and Fry, apparently preferred to bat without one. Nevertheless Neville Cardus suggests that Grace did not believe this basic form of protection was wholly superfluous. When A. C. M. Croome came into the Gloucestershire side against Surrey, W.G. insisted that he couldn't face Tom Richardson without one. However, when the cumbersome wire construction Croome found at short notice started producing audible clangs, W.G. went down the wicket and said, 'I told you to get a box, not a musical box.'[61] As a true Victorian, Grace naturally makes no specific reference to the matter in print, but in his advice to young cricketers he is clearly on the side of common sense: 'Take every precaution to protect the body when batting. Do not face fast bowling without leg-guards, and do not dispense with batting gloves.'[62] It seems likely that even if he usually batted without one, he still carried a box around in his cricket bag.

In dealing with deviation off the wicket, Grace set little store by watching the bowler's hand, preferring 'to watch the ball, and not to anticipate events'.[63] It is sometimes said that he was not fully tested as a batsman as he retired before the great googly revolution – though he saw enough of the innovation in 1907 to acknowledge the problems it posed, and it is impossible to believe that he would not have found ways of solving them. He certainly faced and overcame every other sort of bowling. The modern distinction between cut and spin did not become current until the end of the era, but every bowler, even the fastest, would attempt to put some 'break' on the ball, and if bowlers were less sophisticated than they became, it was only because the wickets did so much of the work for them.

Grace could be vulnerable against slow bowling, especially early in his innings, and was often caught in the deep or stumped before he was set. Though slightly more restrained than E.M., he was by instinct an attacking batsmen, and if he judged the ball was there to be hit, he would go after it, whatever the state of the game. Sydney Pardon, the editor of *Wisden*, wrote: 'He was, in the main, quite orthodox in style, his bat being as perfectly straight as Fuller Pilch's, but he greatly enlarged the domain of orthodoxy, playing a far more aggressive and punishing game than any of the classic batsmen who came before him.'[64] Lord Harris also compared Grace with Fuller Pilch: 'The great feature of Fuller's batting was his forward play, he used a bat with a short handle and abnormally long pod, so that, whilst he could smother the ball, and drive and play to leg, he could not cut: whereas W.G. could hit all round [and] used every known stroke, except the draw which had become all but obsolete'. He also 'introduced what was then a novel stroke . . . viz: the push to leg with a straight bat off the straight ball, and his mastery of this stroke was so great that he could place the ball with great success clear of short leg and even two short legs.'[65] Grace very seldom left the ball and, thanks to his high back-lift, the impact when he made contact was considerable. Lord Russell, speaking at Lord's in July 1879 when Grace was presented with his first national testimonial, underlined this weight of stroke: 'In playing a ball, Mr Grace put[s] every muscle into it from the sole of his foot to the crown of his head.'[66] Grace often joked that he didn't like defensive strokes because you 'only got three for them', and it was this unremitting emphasis on scoring runs that put the bowlers under so much pressure.

Grace also had huge reserves of concentration. For hour after hour his mind never lost its intense focus. And there was no relaxation when he reached three figures; a mere hundred was never enough. His temperament, too, was perfectly suited to making big scores. When Stuart Wortley painted the famous portrait of him at the wicket at Lord's he was impressed by how relaxed Grace was in his stance, and asked, 'But, Dr Grace, would you stand as easily if the game were in a tight place?' He replied, 'Certainly, because, after all, I should only be facing the next ball.'[67]

By the end of the 1860s the combination of technique and temperament had made him the most complete batsman ever seen. As *Scores and Biographies* acknowledged, 'he is the glory and the pride of English cricketers, having long and justly too earned for himself the title of "the champion", which has been held (it is believed) by no one else except by the late Mr Alfred Mynn.'[68] At some stage an admirer made Grace the fitting present of a pair of Alfred Mynn's pads. They were tanned a dark yellow with age, and he seems to have worn them fairly regularly for a time before finally donating them to the museum at Lord's.

In the last season of an eventful decade Grace passed a thousand runs in first-class cricket for the first time. In fifteen matches he scored 1,320 runs at 52.86. One newspaper, grappling with a problem that would exercise journalists for the next thirty years, drew a comparision with the leading racehorse of the day: 'batting so triumphantly superior to all kinds of bowling brought against it has never been witnessed in our generation. Not merely is Mr Gilbert Grace the best batsman in England: it is the old story of the race – "Eclipse" first; the rest nowhere.'[69] As so often, the incomparable batting tended to overshadow the bowling, but he took seventy-three wickets in the season (at 16.28), thus giving notice that the undreamed-of double – a thousand runs and a hundred wickets – was in his sights.

The cricket world had entered the Age of Grace.

SEVEN

THE MCC'S May meeting in 1870 set the tone for cricket's new era. Perhaps the most important announcement was that 'the differences amongst the players have been healed', and so, once again, 'the best cricketers of the kingdom' would be on show at Lord's. The North and South match would be played on Whit Monday (for the benefit of the MCC Fund), and the United North and United South would meet each other in July for the Cricketers' Fund. The outlook was promising: 'The Club has at length passed through its most critical epoch. The large expenditure which has necessarily been incurred is now at an end . . . All the buildings on the premises have been put in thorough repair. The ground has not only been renovated, but is now extended to its natural limits.'[1] Tragedy in June would show there was no room for complacency over the most important – and neglected – part of Lord's, the wicket, but clearly the game's leading club had set itself on the appropriate footing for the demands of the modern period. Membership continued to rise and now stood at around 1,300, and the ground improvements meant that the general public would be encouraged to attend in greater numbers and would be better served when they came. The cricket economy, to judge by the developments at Headquarters, was booming.

There was, however, no fanfare in the nation's leading newspaper to welcome the opening of the cricket season. *The Times* devoted far more space to 'The Two Young Men in Women's Clothes' (one 'dressed in a white satin dress with tulle and pink roses') who infiltrated the Boat Race crowds, causing, apparently, more offence than amusement.[2] It chose to overlook entirely Grace's first appearance at Lord's, in the Left-hand v. Right-hand match, confining its 'Sporting Intelligence' to the Chester races, and his second match, MCC v. Surrey at the Oval, was only covered perfunctorily. His 49 out of a total of 153 was not deemed worthy of notice, though his 5 for 37 off twenty-seven overs on 17 May was mentioned in despatches.[3]

The year was remembered by Grace as 'one of my best'. The weather was kind and 'wickets were dry and fast'. W.G. was still improving: 'My defence had grown stronger, and my hitting powers had improved also.' He scored 'at a great pace', though as with previous seasons, it took him a while to find his best form.[4] Indeed, in a warm-up match for Bedminster against the Great Western Railway Company, he collected the last of his four pairs, dismissed on both occasions by John Thomas Laverick, a forgeman whose cricket career ended when his hand was 'crushed by a steam hammer'.[5]

Once again he went up to Oxford for the MCC match in May. The university was still buzzing after a group of rowdy undergraduates had 'abstracted' some ancient pieces of sculpture from the Christ Church library and burnt them in the middle of Peckwater Quad.[6] No doubt Grace was regaled with the lurid details, but a late night of port and gossip had no effect on his performance on the field of play. In the MCC's first innings he scored a brisk fifty that included two extraordinary shots – 'a cut for seven and another for five'.[7] Wootton and Shaw quickly wrapped up the university's second innings, and Grace then produced an authoritative innings of 73 not out to win the game comfortably for the MCC by six wickets.

He faced a more exacting trial in his next match for MCC. This was against Yorkshire at Lord's and he was confronted by Emmett and Freeman on the usual nightmare of a wicket. So bad was it that neither side made a hundred in its first innings. In the second, Grace made a stand with C. E. Green against the ferocious assault of the two Yorkshire fast bowlers. Emmett was making his first appearance at Lord's. In the thumbnail sketch it accorded to each debutant, *Scores and Biographies* described him as 'a high, fast, left, round-armed bowler, with a sweeping delivery, and a break back from the off'.[8] But this was only half the story. Emmett was a true eccentric and no description of him was complete without mentioning his 'extraordinary antics . . . his quaint appearance, and erratic recklessness'. When he first went on to bowl he almost invariably started with two or three wides, 'not doubtful wides, but thoroughly out-and-out unquestionable, glaring wides'. But he also had 'one impossible ball – it pitched between the batsman's leg and the wicket, and breaking towards the off would just displace the bails'. Grace admitted that even he found this unplayable, but consoled himself with the thought that it 'would beat any batsman on earth'. In Grace's assessment, Emmett 'was at once one of the most popular and proficient professional cricketers of his time', and he clearly had great affection for him.[9]

But however likeable, Emmett still had the fast bowler's usual allocation of aggression. George Freeman was even more dangerous. Grace told Pelham Warner, 'When he hit you on the thigh it hurt. The ball seemed to sizzle into your leg, so much spin did he get on her.'[10] On this occasion both batsmen were 'cruelly battered about'. After his innings Grace's legs resembled beaten steaks, and nearly fifty years later, Green wrote, 'to this day I carry a mark on my chest where I was struck by a very fast rising ball from Freeman'.[11] Freeman himself recalled the ordeal with something approaching awe: 'Tom Emmett and I have often said it was a marvel the doctor was not either maimed or unnerved for the rest of his days or killed outright. I often think of his pluck when I watch a modern batsman scared if a medium-paced ball hits him on the hand; he should have seen our expresses flying about his ribs, shoulder and head in 1870.' Emmett told an interviewer that he did not believe 'W.G. had a square inch of sound flesh on his body after that innings'.[12] When Emmett finally got him out, he had scored 66. The rest of the team managed ninety-five runs between them, and the match was lost by one wicket.

There were a number of close finishes at Lord's that year. The most famous was the Varsity match in which F. C. Cobden took the last three Oxford wickets in the last over to snatch a spectacular victory for the Light Blues by two runs. Grace may have felt a pang of envy, though of course, his presence in one side or the other would have upset the fine balance between them. His university ambitions would have to wait until he had a son of his own.

In the meantime his father's dream of establishing Gloucestershire as a first-class county was at last realized, though the situation was complicated by the existence of a rival club, the Cheltenham and Gloucestershire Cricket Club, which had been founded in 1863 and had Lord Fitzhardinge as its president. Cheltenham and Gloucestershire CC probably had first-class aspirations, but clearly Dr Grace had the stronger hand, and the club that emerged was the one he built around the powerhouse of his three cricketing sons. There remains some confusion as to exactly when the Gloucestershire County Cricket Club officially came into existence. Its centenary was celebrated in 1970, but the constitutional trappings were not in place until 1871, when the Duke of Beaufort took office as president and Lord Fitzhardinge became a vice-president. The Cheltenham and Gloucester abandoned the unequal struggle and was wound up in March 1871. The new county joined

Surrey, Sussex, Yorkshire, Nottinghamshire, Middlesex, Lancashire and Kent to constitute what was known as 'the Octarchy', though there were other counties on the fringes with claims to be considered first-class. Derbyshire County Cricket Club was also founded in 1870, but took some time to gain first-class recognition and departed from the top table in 1887, before being readmitted in 1894, while Cambridgeshire, once a cricketing stronghold, finally relinquished its first-class status in 1871.

As a dress rehearsal Gloucestershire played Glamorgan at Bristol in May, and overwhelmed them thanks to an innings of 197 by W.G. Gloucestershire made 418, and bowled out their visitors for 104 and 46. In June they played their first first-class match against seasoned opponents Surrey. The game was something of a throwback to earlier times as it was staged on the unenclosed expanse of Durdham Down. The playing area was simply marked out by flags and no gate could be collected. Tents were erected, a band hired, and the spectators who drove, rode or walked up from Bristol in their thousands formed a ring, with the better-off watching from the comfort of their carriages. It was, of course, a family occasion. The three Graces were playing and E.M. was captain, but even so, Surrey, with a strong core of professionals including Jupp, H. H. Stephenson and Southerton, were the fancied team. Gloucestershire batted first, with W.G. and E.M. opening. W.G.'s 26 was the highest in a disappointing total of 106, and the visitors gained a first-innings lead of twenty-eight. When W.G. succumbed to Southerton for 25 in the second innings, it looked as though the favourites were almost home and dry. However, although Southerton worked his way through the rest of the team, taking 9 for 67, runs also accrued as Gloucestershire climbed to 167 all out. When it came to the fourth innings, Surrey collapsed dramatically to the bowling of W.G. and Fred (who bowled throughout). Although Jupp clung on stubbornly, ever on the look-out for some fiendish bit of legerdemain from E.M., and carried his bat for the game's highest score of 50 not out, Surrey were dismissed for 88 and Gloucestershire won their first county match by fifty-one runs.

After this spectacular triumph, Grace returned to London for the reinstated North v. South game. This was Parr's last appearance at Lord's (at the age of forty-four) and he made a characteristic 41. Grace himself had a quiet match, and without his lead the South underperformed. The northern players probably felt they had something to prove, and ran out winners by six wickets.

Grace was in better form when he made his first century for the United

South (115) against Twenty-two of Sleaford, who had Roger Iddison as their given man. As usual Grace made no concessions to his opponents, whatever their standard, as one of the Sleaford team found to his cost. W.G. records the incident in *Cricket*:

He was fielding at short-leg to Iddison's lob-bowling, and was standing a little in front, about twelve yards from the wicket. Iddison would have him closer in, and eventually he was placed four yards nearer. I did not say anything at the time, but could not help thinking the position would have to be abandoned before Fred and I had finished batting.

Iddison pitched the first or second ball of the over a little too far up, and I stepped out and hit it on the full pitch. It went straight to the unfortunate fieldsman, hit him on the ankle, and then travelled far enough to enable us to run four.

The fielder put a brave face on it – 'He was a rare plucked one, and never winced' – but at the end of the over when he retreated to the outfield, 'and thought no one was looking, he began to rub vigorously. We saw little of him next day, and I believe he was laid up for some time afterwards.' The moral Grace draws is a cricketing one: 'I think it cured Iddison of placing a man so near when bowling lobs', while the injured fielder learned that the Hippocratic oath was suspended when Grace was at the wicket.[13]

That cricket can be a mortally dangerous game was tragically emphasized in Grace's next match. This was MCC v. Nottinghamshire, played at Lord's on 13, 14 and 15 June, and it will always be remembered for the accident that caused the death of George Summers. The game was played in the usual relaxed and friendly spirit. Due to late arrivals, the MCC team took the field with *four* substitutes,[14] and when V. E. Walker dislocated a finger early in the Nottinghamshire first innings, Richard Daft, the visitors' captain, allowed a substitute to take his place for the rest of the match, though this was 'technically, a breach of the rules'[15] and was widely criticized in the sporting press. The card indicates a relatively high-scoring game between two well-matched sides. Nottinghamshire scored 267, of which Daft made 117. Grace, who never liked to be outshone by anyone, equalled Daft's score exactly, carrying his bat through the MCC's first innings of 183. Having failed by four runs to avoid the (obligatory) follow-on, and despite the loss of Grace for a duck, the MCC set up an interesting final day with a total of 240.

It was on the third morning that disaster struck. George Summers, who had scored 41 in the Nottinghamshire first innings, came in at number three. The first ball he received, from Jack Platts, lifted and struck him on the temple. Summers collapsed at the wicket, and on this occasion Grace's medical instincts came into play immediately. He was quickly kneeling over the felled batsman, taking his pulse and listening for his heartbeat. Summers came round, and although he was obviously too shaken to continue batting, he was not thought to be in any serious danger. No one suspected he had fractured his skull, and though he obviously should have been sent to hospital as a precautionary measure, he spent the rest of the day sitting about in the sun, and then travelled back to Nottinghamshire by train, which 'shook him terribly'.[16] Four days later, to everyone's immense shock, he died. Platts was a genuine fast bowler striving to make an impression on his debut at Lord's. Grace said that he suffered great 'mental distraction'[17] over Summers, and exonerated him from blame, asserting that 'the ball did not bump higher than many I had to play in the same match'.[18] Richard Daft, the next man in, took a different view, and in protest at what he saw as intimidatory bowling, came to the wicket with his head swathed in towels secured by a scarf. 'The first delivery he received was a hair-raising bouncer', and Daft addressed Platts 'with a few choice observations expressed in the Anglo-Saxon vernacular'.[19]

George Summers was a popular young man, and his death struck a chord among the nation's followers of sport, and was felt particularly in his home county. The MCC paid for his gravestone on which was inscribed: 'This Tablet is erected to the Memory of George Summers by the Marylebone Cricket Club, to mark their sense of his qualities as a cricketer, and to testify their regret at the untimely accident on Lord's ground, which cut short a career so full of promise, June 19th, 1870, in the 26th year of his age.' It cost thirty pounds, which, many may have reflected, might have been better spent ensuring a less lethal wicket in the first place. Although they made no admission of liability, the Lord's authorities were sufficiently jolted by the incident to turn their attention, at last, to the state of the square, and from this time on a heavy roller was used to pacify it. The match, for those involved in it, would inevitably be overshadowed by the tragedy they had witnessed. Whether Grace ever reproached himself for not having insisted on Summers being taken to hospital cannot be determined. As a twenty-two-year-old medical student he perhaps did not feel in a position to dictate to a man senior in age and apparently recovered sufficiently to make his own decisions.

Grace witnessed only one other fatal accident on the cricket field, 'that of a poor boy at Harrow':

I was invited by Lord Bessborough to go down with him . . . to give the schoolboys some practice, and I always think that both he and I were indirectly the cause of this fatality, although it was one of a character that could not be foreseen. While another game was going on we were hitting catches to some of the boys, and the unfortunate boy who was killed was standing as umpire. I think he was looking round watching us, when a ball was hit to leg, and struck the poor boy with such force that he gave one gasp and then expired. I am glad to say that in this case also, the players, who were the indirect cause of the boy's death, were in no way to blame.[20]

Grace followed the Nottinghamshire match with a game for the United South against Eighteen of Manchester Broughton. The Broughton Club was a keen rival to Old Trafford, though its approach was rather different. There was little or no distinction between amateurs and professionals, members and the public, and Broughton realized the importance of staging attractive matches and inviting the players that people wanted to see. Grace and the United South team were an annual attraction throughout the 1870s, and the fixture was always very well attended. Although Grace was the main draw, he only scored 15 (though he did take six wickets in the Broughton first innings). Fred, whose involvement with the United South was growing all the time, scored a fifty.

Grace's next match involved a return to the two-tier class structure on which Lord's was founded. MCC & Ground v. Cambridge was intended as a practice match before the Varsity match, but degenerated into farce when the 'Ground' component, Wootton and Biddulph, were batting for the MCC. The appearance at the wicket of two of the Lord's workhorses provoked the undergraduates into an exhibition of juvenile silliness. C. I. 'Buns' Thornton bowled 'grubs' while 'Mr Yardley adopted the somewhat novel style of bowling one ball with the right hand and another with the left.'[21] The two professionals took full advantage of this patronizing larkiness and put on a stand of 120.

Grace was looking through the other end of the class telescope in his next match at Lord's. He and Fred were the only amateurs playing when the United North beat the United South by an innings. The brothers then travelled with the United South team to the Earl of Stamford's seat, Enville Hall, for a fixture against I Zingari, who must have looked askance at their presence in a team of seasoned professionals. But however little regard he had for the conventions, Grace was the reason 30,000 people flocked to the ground over the three days.

Grace was unambiguously back in the amateur fold for the Gentlemen v. Players match at the Oval. In the first innings he was dismissed cheaply by Southerton (who was making his first appearance for the Players at the age of forty-two), but in the second innings he once again treated the Oval crowd to a double century – 215 out of 513. This included an on-drive for *eight*, three fives and fourteen fours, and was the first double century ever scored in a Gentleman–Players match. (Fred, making his debut for the Gentlemen, bagged a pair.)

After the tame draw at the Oval, the more sporting wicket at Lord's was expected to produce a result. Against the background of a rather more serious conflict on the continent where France and Germany's sabre-rattling finally tipped over into war, the two sides reconvened at St John's Wood to do battle once more. The first day of the match, 18 July, was W.G.'s twenty-second birthday, and, as it happened, the day Pope Pius IX declared himself infallible.[22] Grace underlined his own near infallibility with an astonishing 109 out of 187. The next highest score was 22, and no one else on either side could begin to master the conditions. The Gentlemen's first innings disintegrated ludicrously when Tom Hayward senior was put on as a forlorn hope. He took a hat-trick of W.G., C. K. Francis and Fred as the last five wickets fell for nine runs, and put the Players back in the game. Southerton and Farrands ran through the Gentlemen on the second day, dismissing them for 87. The Players were within twenty-four of their target at seven o'clock, the agreed closing time, but as the light was still good it was agreed to play the match out. In a tense climax, the professionals' tail-enders crept to within four runs of victory before the last man put up an easy catch on the stroke of 7.30.

Grace's high scoring continued through the summer heatwave. He made 84 for MCC against Surrey, and carried on harrying the Surrey bowlers with a century that helped Gloucestershire complete an auspicious double when they played the return match at the Oval. He produced an even more brilliant performance for Gloucestershire at Lord's at the start of August, scoring 172 (out of 276) against a weak MCC side to maintain the county's one hundred per cent record. He added little to his Canterbury Week honours board, 46 in the MCC–Kent match being his best effort. Not that he would have minded: 'In those days, we . . . play[ed] cricket for

94

pleasure and not for records, of which we thought very little. Our first consideration was to have a good game, and we did not mind very much whether we won or lost, so long as the cricket was enjoyable.'[23] His approach to festival cricket is clear from *The Times* match report of the MCC v. Kent game (12 August): 'Willsher led off the bowling at the city wicket; the first ball Mr Grace played, from the second he realized four runs, but from the third he was caught from a lofty hit.' The disappointed crowd had the consolation of seeing I. C. Thornton hit an on-drive in Kent's second innings 'which pitched in the centre of the next field at a distance of, as near as could be reckoned, 132 yards'.[24]

Leaving Canterbury's canvas pavilions, perhaps with a catchy tune from the Old Stagers' theatricals still going round in his head, Grace travelled north to Beeston to represent the Gentleman of the South against the Gentlemen of the North. Grace had never played in Nottinghamshire before, and there were huge crowds to see him. They only saw him bowl on the first day as the Gentlemen of the North won the toss and batted. In high temperatures, he toiled away to take 6 for 89 in forty-six overs. Not out over night, he began the second day with what he himself classed as 'a brilliant 77'[25] but was for once completely overshadowed by those coming after him. I. D. Walker scored 179 and Fred went even better with 189 not out, his maiden first-class century. The two were in for six hours, and the next man, George Strachan, sat patiently with his pads on for the duration, only to be out second ball when he finally got to the wicket. The match petered out as a draw, but the spectators had seen a fine exhibition of amateur batting.

Grace played in two more first-class matches without conspicuous success (in the last, at Dewsbury, the North crushed the South by an innings and 154 runs), but crammed in as much non-first-class cricket as he could, mainly for the United South. The standard of some of these matches was poor. At Scarborough W.G.'s 13 was the highest score in the United South's dismal total of 44, and they lost to Twenty-two of Scarborough by the bizarre-sounding margin of twenty-one wickets. For Twenty-two of Worcestershire against the United North, Grace scored 74 out of 114. 'I got out when the score stood 96 for seventeen wickets, my last nine partners having all failed to score a single run.'[26]

In positively his last match at the end of September he played for E.M.'s Eleven v. Twenty-two of Thornbury. The game was attended by 'no less than twenty-three of the Grace family'[27] and E.M. seized the

95

opportunity to remind all and sundry of a few home truths. All five brothers were playing, although Alfred is recorded as 'absent' on the scoresheet. Perhaps he grew tired of the massacre. The hapless Twenty-two started surprisingly well, dismissing E.M.'s team for 93, of which W.G. and Fred scored eighty-three. They then dutifully processed to and from the wicket, mown down by E.M. and Henry for fifty. Not satisfied with that, E.M. insisted on the second innings. Back onto the field went the Twenty-two and back to the wicket strode E.M. and W.G. W.G. soon departed for 12. Fred came in and hit another 40, but after that E.M. had the stage to himself. The score passed 100 and mounted steadily to 200, then, ludicrously, to 300 as E.M. smote the flagging bowling with the fury of an Old Testament prophet. He might have lost the title of champion batsman in the eyes of the nation, but here with the family gathered as witnesses, he had the chance to prove that he could still bat his illustrious brother into the shade, and had no qualms about sacrificing his own club members on the altar of his pride. When stumps were finally drawn E.M. was left triumphant on 211 not out.

But nothing he visited upon the mute inglorious footsoldiers of local cricket could modify by a decimal point W.G.'s unprecedented figures for the season. For the Gentlemen against the Players he averaged 85.25; Gloucestershire's two first-class fixtures yielded an average of 64.66; and he headed the overall first-class averages with 1,808 runs at 54.78. He had also taken fifty wickets at 15.70.

*

As wine connoisseurs debate the competing excellences of vintages, so the cricket enthusiasts can argue which was W.G.'s 'greatest' season. In any such discussion, 1871 will feature prominently. He started in dazzling form, with four centuries and a 98 in his first seven innings. Three of the centuries were large – 181 (MCC v. Surrey), 178 (South v. North) and 162 (Gentlemen of England v. Cambridge University). And so it went on. His 189 out of 310 for Single v. Married at Lord's (Willsher's benefit match) was compiled on a wicket made treacherous by rain. It took him fifteen minutes to get off the mark, but then he scored at a cracking pace. Harry Perkins (who followed Fitzgerald as MCC Secretary) wrote later: 'I have often been asked which was the finest innings I ever saw W.G. play. My answer is always the same: July 10, 1871, Single v. Married, 189 not out, total score 310. Rain stopped play at frequent intervals, the wicket at times was apparently unplayable. I think on the last occasion that this question was put to me, W.G. was appealed to in my presence and confirmed my judgment.'[28] *

The first over or two offered the bowler his best chance. In fact first ball was best, as J. C. Shaw demonstrated in the North v. South match at the Oval at the end of July. This was H. H. Stephenson's benefit match and he must have been just as disappointed as Grace when Shaw's appeal rang round the ground as the spectators were still finding their seats and settling down. This was not one of those occasions when the umpire could be swayed by the argument that the crowd had come to see the Champion bat and not the bowler bowl, and John Lillywhite, who was officiating, had little hesitation in sending Grace on his way. W.G. was mortified and apologized profusely to Stephenson. However, he made amends in the second innings, which started on the afternoon of the second day. 'After the first over or two I began to hit at a rare pace, and I paid particular attention to J. C. Shaw. At the close of the day's play my score was 142 not out, and only two wickets had fallen for 195.'[29] Grace, Stephenson and the crowd went to bed happy, and returned for an equally felicitous day the next morning. Shaw finally took Grace's wicket for the second time in the match, but not before his score had risen to 268. This was his highest first-class innings to date, and a new ground record for the Oval. It had taken him 320 minutes, and demonstrated his absolute mastery of the best professional bowling the North could put out. It was probably after this match that Shaw made his famous remark: 'I puts the ball where I likes, and he puts it where he likes.'

History was soon to repeat itself. A Gentlemen v. Players match had been arranged for John Lillywhite's benefit on the old Hove ground, Brighton, where Grace scored his first century in senior cricket in 1864. It was shortly to be lost to development, and he was no doubt intent on bidding it a suitable farewell. Lillywhite, too, was expecting great things. In the event, he was to find out exactly how Stephenson had felt in his benefit match. This time Grace survived two balls before Shaw sent his off-stump cartwheeling. The crestfallen batsman returned to the pavilion, with no great hopes that he could retrieve the situation second time around. But Lillywhite refused to be defeatist, and pressing two sovereigns into his hand said, 'Pay me a sixpence back for every run you make in the second innings.' It was, Grace said, 'the greatest compliment

* This was not Grace's definitive assessment. In *Reminiscences* he gives the palm to his innings against Yorkshire at Cheltenham in August 1876, and there were, of course, many other candidates.

I have ever had paid to my batting skill'.[30] It also proved an expensive one. When Fred joined him at 35 for 1, the two brothers added 240 in two and a half hours. It probably seemed longer than that to the fielding side.

They ran the Players ragged. Fred scored a chanceless and very aggressive 98. W.G. went on past the three-figure mark: 'At the end of the day's play, the total was 353 for three wickets; my score being 200 not out.' In the excitement of reaching his second double century of the season, he had forgotten all about the bet. Lillywhite hadn't and dunned him for 'five pounds on account' almost before his tumultuous reception had died down. W.G. paid up with good grace, but told Lillywhite if he didn't let him off the rest of the bet, 'I shall knock down my wicket first over tomorrow.'[31] Lillywhite consented, though he lost little by it as Grace scored only another seventeen runs on the third morning.

Any player would obviously want Grace to appear in his benefit match, and would think a chit for 'expenses' a small price to pay for his presence. Grace always played when he could, and wrote, 'No part of my cricket experience has given me more pleasure than my batting success in benefit matches. I always hoped to do something extraordinary on those occasions; and . . . I nearly always accomplished it.'[32] His relations with the pros underwent some ups and downs, especially on tour, but as his career with the United South showed, he had no objection to playing with them, though relations were always conducted strictly on his terms. As Tony Lewis put it, his unique status was such that 'he could run with the amateurs and hunt with the professionals'.[33] The professionals knew better than anyone just how good he was – 'He was worth any two of us,' one admitted[34] – and their view of him seems to have been one of resigned awe, with little hint of jealousy or resentment. Grace was no prima donna. Despite being so obviously in a class of his own, he was astonishingly modest, and generous in his appreciation of others' achievements. He could be autocratic and overbearing; he could lose his temper; he could be unfair; but he never adopted the patrician airs of a Lord Harris or Archie MacLaren; never lost the common touch.

As his domination over the game increased, and his career went on and on, seemingly without end, his relationship with the professionals naturally altered. Those who were playing at the outset began to drop out, and a new generation came forward. For them he was already a living legend, though not necessarily one it was easy to live with. But for all the awe he inspired, and the exasperation he caused, he was a difficult man to dislike, let alone hate. Playing with him, despite the occasional flashpoints, was on the whole a privilege, and the professionals were proud of their association with him.

As an example of the passing of the generations, George Parr played his last match at Trent Bridge in May. Surprisingly, neither he nor any one else had ever scored a century on the ground. This changed in August, when Grace accompanied the Gloucestershire team to Nottingham. The two counties had met for the first time at the beginning of the month, and the newcomers, fielding a team of eleven amateurs against the Nottinghamshire professionals, had had the better of the drawn game. W.G. (78) and E.M. (65) put on over a hundred for the first wicket which, according to *Scores and Biographies*, had never been done against Nottinghamshire before.[35] W.G. had also scored 55 in his second innings.

The interest in Nottingham sparked by Grace's arrival was ovewhelming. The mill hands poured out of the factories, and many bets were laid that he would break the ground's duck and reach three figures. Those backing the Champion looked onto a good thing as he sailed past his fifty and seemed to be coasting to his target, but his old adversary, Jem Shaw, had other ideas, having him caught for 79 (out of a total of 147). Grace seems to have been about the only one on the ground who wasn't aware of the situation. When Daft said to him, 'You ought to have made a hundred, it's never been done in a first-class match on this ground,' he replied, 'Why didn't you tell me before and I'd have done it. Never mind, I'll do it next innings.'[36] Sure enough he did: 116, again just over half his side's total of 217. The Nottingham crowd had the best of everything, as they also had the satisfaction of seeing Gloucestershire going down to their first first-class defeat.

It was often said that Grace provided half the bricks in the cricket pavilions of England. He could certainly claim some responsibility for the decision to build the one at Trent Bridge, as an extract from an early history of the Nottinghamshire club makes clear: 'The season was remarkable for introducing to the Nottingham public Mr W. G. Grace . . . The attendance at the match was very large, no less than £437 1s 8d. being taken, and the result was that the Committee began to consider and decide upon the desirability of erecting a Pavilion on the south side of the ground. This was subsequently carried out at a cost of about £1500.'[37] That page in Grace's own copy of the book is heavily turned down, probably to mark the reference to his century, but he would also have been interested in the gate figure. He had an extremely acute idea of his own worth, and decades before sports stars put their financial affairs in the hands of agents, he drove an extremely hard bargain.

Money was becoming increasingly important as the game expanded. Although unquestioningly committed to the amateur ethos on the field of play, cricket's administrators and policy makers were becoming more attuned to the commercial dimension. In 1871 Parliament introduced the first bank holidays, and more working men were getting Saturday afternoons off. Lord's introduced turnstiles – 'Those unerring tell-tales' – and so, 'for the first time an authentic return for the great matches was obtainable'.[38] The crowds were there and willing to come. If, to keep the turnstiles clicking, a blind eye had to be turned to 'shamateurism' in the ranks of the Gentlemen, then so be it.

It was a wonderful year for cricket and a wonderful year for Grace. He scored 2,739 runs in twenty-five first-class matches at an astounding average of 78.25, and made an unprecedented ten centuries. This was the first time any batsman had scored two thousand runs in a season, and as C. L. R. James noted, it was as though someone scored 5,000 runs in a domestic season today. As an indication of how far above his contemporaries he was, the next highest average was Richard Daft's 39, which would itself have been regarded as remarkable only a few years earlier. Grace also took seventy-nine wickets at 17.02. The double was coming ever closer.

It was a wonderful year, too, for Dr Grace. Everything he had striven for was reaching fruition. His three cricketing sons were renowned throughout the country, and the county club he had brought into existence was going from strength to strength. Gloucestershire played five fixtures in 1871, defeating the MCC at Lord's and twice thrashing Surrey by an innings (the second match, at Clifton, being memorable for a magnificent double century by T. G. Matthews). The Nottinghamshire bowling had proved too much for everyone except W.G. at Trent Bridge, but the county had had the better of the drawn match at Clifton. The future promised almost limitless possibilities.

But Henry Mills Grace was not to see it. In December he insisted on riding out with the hounds, despite having a heavy cold, and then compounded matters by sitting up all night with a patient. His decline was alarmingly swift and he died two days before Christmas, a few weeks short of his sixty-third birthday. Dr Grace was the rock on which his close-knit family was founded, and the most important influence on his sons. He was central to their lives and the shock of his death was extreme. When Matthew Arnold lost the father who had so dominated the first twenty years of his life, he felt his 'sole source of *information* was gone'.[39] Grace must have experienced a similar sense of abrupt dispossession. Though he was now fully adult, he had not fully matured; he had conquered the cricketing world, but was not necessarily master of himself. Martha, of course, remained to give unstinting support and some measure of guidance, and he could always turn to Henry for advice on his medical training. But his father's untimely death deprived him of the restraining hand of someone with natural and unquestioned authority over him. It was a bitter end to a brilliant year.

EIGHT

For all his hard work, Dr Grace did not die a wealthy man. He left enough for Martha to continue to live in the family home, but there was no large inheritance for his sons. Henry, Alfred and E.M. had all qualified and were set up in their respective practices, but W.G. was in the early stages of his training, and Fred would only begin his in the autumn of 1872.

As medical students, W.G. and Fred had their fees to find, and books and equipment to pay for, quite apart from their ordinary living expenses. Their winters were taken up with their studies, and in the summer they were playing cricket. Notionally their amateur status precluded their earning any money from the game, which left them with no visible means of financial support. In fact, they were generally recognized to be semi-professionals, and set about maximizing their profits in a thoroughly businesslike way. This provoked frequent comment in the press and caused the authorities intermittent embarrassment, though none, so far as can be judged, to either of them. Grace played on imperturbably through the squalls of controversy, while defending his amateur status vigorously whenever it was questioned.*

How much money he made out of cricket is hard to say. No documentary evidence of Grace's financial dealings with promoters in the United Kingdom during the early years of his career has come to light (the story is different with his two Australian tours), but there are pointers. In 1872 Grace took the United South Eleven to Scotland for the first time. In fact he made two trips a week apart, to Edinburgh and Glasgow. There was great curiosity to see him north of the border, and the Scots were rather less squeamish than the English about the financial realities. The historian of Scottish cricket quotes one of those involved as saying, 'It takes a lot of money to bring Grace down.'[1]

---

* Grace was not the first amateur to take money for playing. According to Roland Bowen (*Cricket – A History of its Growth and Development*, p. 112), 'it was not out of line with the behaviour of other celebrated amateur cricketers before him, and for a long way back, in one form or another'.

The procedure for hiring a team of first-class cricketers was well established. Having identified a gap in the first-class fixture list, the team manager offered a list of possible players and negotiated a deal with the promoters, paying the players a flat fee and pocketing the surplus. Correspondence in the minutes of the Clydesdale Club, Glasgow, shows the system in operation, albeit a little later in the century. Louis Hall, the ex-Yorkshire player, was sounded out about bringing a team to play the club. He replied:

At present I have no matches fixed for Scotland & on looking thro' the May fixtures, I am afraid unless you had it on the 6, 7, 8th May, or earlier, I should not be able to give you a fairly representative team.

If I brought a first class team North for one match, I am afraid I could not do it for less than £100, 3 days. I find Yorkshire, Lancashire, Derbyshire, Leicestershire are all at liberty on these dates . . .[2]

W.G. must have written any number of similar letters during the 1870s, and probably demanded the same sort of fee (£100 in 1872 being worth rather more than £3,000 in today's terms). The professionals who played for the United South were paid no more than five pounds each which left fifty-five pounds' (or well over £1,500) profit on each match. W.G. would certainly have taken the larger share of this, and if he took two thirds to Fred's one third, that would have given him something in the region of £1,000 (in today's terms) for each USEE match.

This provides the basis for a rough assessment of his earnings. His involvement with the United South started modestly: he played six matches in 1870 and 1871, and five in 1872. But in 1873 he played sixteen games, and for the next five seasons he averaged around ten appearances, which would have brought in between £10,000 and £15,000 in our terms. It may have been considerably more. In addition, he would have negotiated appearance fees with all the other teams for whom he played in odds matches. And on top of that, there were his 'expenses' for first-class matches. Evidence that emerged embarrassingly at the end of the decade indicated that he expected fifteen pounds when he played for Gloucestershire, and he is generally reckoned to have received twenty for appearing in the Gentlemen v. Players matches and similar important fixtures at Lord's and the other major venues. He averaged just under twenty-five first-class matches a season through the 1870s, which would yield between £400 and £500 a year (£12,000 to £15,000 today). Coupled with his take from the United South and other appearance fees, it is probably fair to say that he made a minimum of £30,000 a year out of domestic cricket in today's terms during the 1870s, and in addition he made two highly profitable overseas tours. Though this is small beer compared to the vast incomes contemporary sports stars receive, it is clear that Grace made a comfortable living out of cricket – and, despite playing as an amateur, earned far more than any of the professionals.

The news that Grace was coming to Scotland created a great deal of interest. Methven Brownlee – who later moved to Bristol, befriended Grace and wrote his biography – remembered how the visit caused a 'great flutter and expectation in cricket circles all over Scotland'. The AEE had been making regular trips north for some years, 'but we had never seen Grace, and how we had talked and dreamed about him'.[3] The United South's first match was against Twenty-two of the Carlton and Edinburgh Clubs on 23, 24 and 25 May. Ironically Grace was completely outshone by one of the local batsmen, J. M. Cotterill, who racked up 95 out of 154 in the Twenty-two's second innings. This included the truly Grace-like feat of scoring eighty-three runs while his partners accounted for just seven on the second day. He hit four drives out of the ground, and was caught by Fred off Southerton trying to produce another one to bring up his century. The United South made 60 and 107, Grace's contributions being 8 and 17, and a tidy tally of wickets can't have been much consolation to him as the Eleven were routed by sixty-four runs.

By the time he returned to Scotland a week later, he had atoned for his failures at Edinburgh with a match-winning century for the MCC at Lord's, and an estimated 7,000 flocked to Holyrood Park in Glasgow with '"Grace! Grace!" . . . in every mouth'.[4] They had to be patient, though, as first it rained and then the Glasgow Twenty-two batted. As he often did in odds matches, Grace held himself back till the second day in order to be seen by the maximum number of spectators (and boost the gate money). Unhappily his innings, when it came, was brief. He had scored fourteen when he drove fiercely at the Clydesdale fast bowler Andrew McAllister. A fielder at long-off who was just finishing a conversation with a friend suddenly saw the ball plummeting towards him, rushed in to meet it, and caught it. Things got worse. The wicket was wet, and McAllister exploited the conditions admirably, taking 7 for 17 and leaving the cream of the south's professional cricketers with the derisory total of 49 (Fred scored the only other double-figure score – 10).

Grace was never happy with failure. But there was more than just pride at stake; this was a business venture, and the Scots wanted value for their money. In the second innings they got it. When McAllister was quizzed by those who missed the day's play, he told them ruefully: 'I did my best, but . . . the ground wasn't big enough.'[5] Grace scored 112 with 'six drives out of the ground for 6 each'.[6] One of the sixes landed in a passing cab. Another drive hit the girlfriend of one of the Scottish players. At lunchtime he moved her to what he considered a safer vantage point, though his choice of square leg shows a touching innocence as to the range of W.G.'s strokes, and during the afternoon she was hit a second time. She did not reappear on the third day. There were only two other double-figure scores (12 and 29) in the United South innings, and they lost the match by six wickets. But that hardly mattered. Grace had produced the performance the crowds had come to see, and ensured there would be further invitations to bring sides north of the border.

Grace was always open to other offers. For instance, he turned out for Melton Mowbray as the given man in their Twenty-two against the AEE. He kept wicket, something he enjoyed, and would once do, *in extremis*, in a Test match. Even in this unaccustomed role, his star quality was unmistakable. He hared after a ball deflected behind the wicket and ran out one of the Eleven dawdling for his third run with a direct hit on the stumps. Wherever he played the crowds came to watch him, and his willingness to travel anywhere in the country meant he was seen by vast numbers of people who would not have been able or willing to travel to the metropolitan centres. No one before him had been anything like as accessible to the public, and with every season his fame and his popularity increased.

*

Grace enjoyed exhibition matches (and depended on them for much of his income), but the first-class game always had first call. The summer of 1872 was wet, and Grace missed the end of the season when he went on tour with R. A. Fitzgerald's team to Canada and the United States early in August, but he nevertheless remained well ahead of the field, scoring 1,485 runs at an average of 57.11, and taking fifty-six wickets at 12.1.

He was largely instrumental in helping the South to exact revenge for the North's recent victories. To make up for the matches lost over recent seasons, the two sides met three times before the end of May. The first match was at the newly opened Prince's ground at Han's Place, Kensington. This was the brainchild of the Prince brothers, who converted an old market garden into what they hoped would be a fashionable rival even to Lord's. They certainly produced 'a very fine ground . . . together with an asphalte [sic] skating-rink for wheel-skating'. The Princes knew little about cricket, but were keen to cash in on its growing popularity. They were also eager to attract the the social élite, and the tone was set by the patronage of the Prince of Wales, who would bring other members of the royal family to watch games between I Zingari and the Household Brigade. Alfred Lubbock, who was on the committee, recalls, 'at most of the matches a whole bevy of duchesses and dowagers came down nominally to see the cricket; but, as a rule, they sat with their backs to the game, watching their daughters skating on the asphalte, in happy ignorance . . . that a good hit might at any time catch them full in the small of the back'.[7] For the benefit of the unattentive spectator, a band played throughout most of the game, and was a higher priority than the cricketers. When a ball was hit into the bandstand, one of the brothers went out and asked the batsman to be more careful in future.

For all its inattentive dowagers, the Prince's ground provided consistently good wickets during its brief existence, and on his first appearance there on 16 May Grace scored 87 out of 186 for the South, but the rain came and the match had to be abandoned. The South won the two matches that were finished, and Grace contributed scores of 65 (out of 134), 31 (out of 95) and 37 (out of 86). And he continued taking the sword to the North's bowling when he scored 101 and 43 not out – 'hit in a crushing, heart-breaking manner'[8] at virtually a run a minute – in the MCC's eight-wicket win over Yorkshire on 27 and 28 May.

While he could despatch the fastest bowling on any sort of wicket, Grace showed some vulnerability against the slows. It was Roger Iddison with his lobs that claimed his wicket in the Yorkshire match, and James Southerton, the Surrey spinner, now began a conspicuously successful run against him. A recent addition to the growing volume of verse on W.G., 'A Lay at Lord's', had referred to the great man smiling 'at all Southerton's striving'. But now it was Southerton who was smiling, dismissing him twice in the game between Surrey and the MCC at Lord's. This was one of those matches which seem hardly credible to modern eyes. Indeed, it was extraordinary in its own time. Incessant rain delayed the start from Monday to the Tuesday, and even with a tarpaulin laid over the wicket there was no effective protection for the playing surface. Grace was given out lbw – by, as he remembered with asperity, 'our own umpire, Royston'[9] – and that triggered as abject a collapse as the annals of first-class cricket can show. With seven wickets lost without a run scored, an all-out total of nought was a strong possibility. This exciting scenario was spoilt by a few lusty blows from a tail-ender, on whose dismissal the scoreboard read: Total 8; Wickets 9; Last man 8. The last pair doubled that, but even on a minefield of a wicket 16 was not a defensible score. The whole innings lasted no more than forty-four minutes. Surrey were skittled out for 49, but kept their nerve and won the match by five wickets. They also won a nail-bitingly close match against Gloucestershire three weeks later by a single wicket. Again, Southerton claimed Grace's wicket twice, clean-bowling him both times. Then, availing himself of the relaxed qualification rules, which allowed a player to represent a county on grounds either of birth or residence, he followed the Gloucestershire team down to Hove and dismissed Grace again for Sussex. (In the list of bowlers who got his wicket the most times, Southerton shares fourth place with thirty-one successes.)

June was a quiet month for Grace. Only two fifties broke an uncharacteristic sequence of single-figure scores, but if the Players assembling for the two back-to-back fixtures against the Gentlemen were secretly thinking that he might have burnt himself out, they were in for a sad disappointment. The Gentlemen won both games handsomely. Grace's scores were 77 (out of 177) and 112 (out of 214) at Lord's, and 117 in his only innings at the Oval. And he hadn't finished with the northern pros either, because he capped those performances with 170 playing for 'England' against Nottinghamshire and Yorkshire combined at Lord's in early July. He went from strength to strength, and reminded those captains who had inexplicably declined to bowl him for much of the season that he remained a potent wicket-taker. He took twelve wickets in the return match against Surrey at Cheltenham (which Gloucestershire won by an innings); he had another five-wicket haul (which included Fred) when he played for MCC against the South; and then returned to the Oval to give the North's bowlers some more punishment.

This was the beginning of one of those purple patches which left his contemporaries awestruck. Starting on 25 July, he scored 114 in his only innings in the South v. North match (George Griffith's benefit) before the largest crowd of the season. The reason he didn't get a second innings was that he took eleven wickets, and with under sixty to win he let someone else have a bat. While the public were absorbing the news that Morton Stanley had finally tracked down Livingstone in darkest Africa,

Grace made another expedition to the heart of the industrial north for Gloucestershire's match against Yorkshire at Sheffield and scored 150. He also returned bowling figures of 8 for 33 and 7 for 46. In a six-day period he had scored 264 runs in two innings – out of a total of 589 from the bat – and taken twenty-six wickets. He also took five catches. From Sheffield the Gloucestershire side travelled south to Nottingham, where Grace wound down with 67 and 7 for 162 during a mammoth bowling stint of eighty-nine overs, as Nottinghamshire piled up a huge total of 489.

The match ended on the Saturday (3 August) and Grace headed for the railway station to catch the train back to Bristol. The statistics of the travelling Grace put in to play cricket would be as extraordinary as those of his runs and wickets. Week after week for forty summers he spent uncomfortable hours looking out over the fields and backyards of England. In addition to the delays and discomforts of Victorian rail travel, there was no small risk to life and limb. The competing railway companies, eager to shave every last penny of expenditure, constantly compromised their safety standards. The contemporary press is filled with hair-raising accounts of derailments, collisions and near misses. On the last day of the Nottinghamshire–Gloucestershire match at Trent Bridge there was an accident on the Lancashire and Yorkshire Railway just outside Manchester. Four people were killed and the line was closed for a day.[10] Accidents were such a feature of the times that *Punch* suggested medical students should forsake the dissecting table for the railway cuttings.[11] Although Grace followed that advice to the letter, there is no record of his ever gaining supplementary clinical experience at the site of a crash.

Grace threw his cricket bag into a railway compartment one more time when he went down to Canterbury for yet another North–South encounter at the start of the Cricket Week. With Fitzgerald's tour party due to sail for North America on the Thursday, this was an engagement he should have declined, and he probably wished he had when the first day (August Bank Holiday) was completely washed out. The game did get under way on the Tuesday, but Grace made only 15 and dropped a sitter at mid-off.[12] For once his mind seems not to have been on the job in hand, as his thoughts turned to the long and potentially hazardous voyage ahead. The Canterbury crowds were further short-changed when he missed the last day's play to start on his journey to Liverpool. (In his absence the North won a lacklustre game by an innings.)

Grace went home to Downend to pack and say goodbye to his mother and the rest of the family, before making his way up to Liverpool to meet the other members of the team on Thursday, 8 August. Cricket had taken him to most areas of England, and up to Scotland, but sailing across the Atlantic to Canada and America was travel on a different scale. It was Grace's first big touring adventure, and it was to be by far the happiest.

NINE

THE 1872 tour of North America was another step in Grace's accelerated climb towards world-wide recognition and a further demonstration of his unprecedented popular appeal. As far as the trip's sponsors were concerned, his presence was an absolute requirement, and wherever the team went he was the focus of attention. The standard of cricket was in the main ludicrously low, but what mattered was that it provided a stage on which the Champion could perform. Fitzgerald wrote a light-hearted account of the team's triumphs and disasters called *Wickets in the West; or The Twelve in America*, of which Grace is the undoubted star. He is referred to on virtually every page by one of his many mock-heroic titles: 'Leviathan', 'The Mammoth', 'Gilbert the Great'. The book even has a portrait of him embossed in gold on its red cloth cover above a facsimile of his signature.

Grace was delighted with it when it came out the following year, and it was one of the very few volumes in his personal collection that shows signs of having been read avidly all the way through. Thumbprints stain the corners of pages and there are bold pencil marks down the margins alongside descriptions of his various exploits. The tour was a high point of his early years, and he retained fond memories of it throughout his life. In the drawing room of his last home he gave pride of place to a 'Set of photos Canadian Cricket Team (1872) in gilt frame'[1] and looking back on the trip in *Reminiscences* he called it 'a prolonged and happy picnic'.[2] It was his last period of freedom from the domestic, cricketing and professional responsibilities, and under Fitzgerald's fatherly eye he could relax, be himself, play up to his serio-comic role as the world's cricketing prodigy, and enjoy himself.

*

Fitzgerald was not the first to take a team out to Canada and the United States. The first English cricket tour anywhere was George Parr's all-professional expedition to North America in 1859; Ned Willsher followed in his footsteps nine years later, again with an all-professional squad. Fitzgerald was breaking new ground by choosing a side of amateurs, though as so often, the distinction was purely one of social class. The Twelve were as well remunerated as any professional touring team. *Scores and Biographies* states categorically that, in addition to having all their expenses, including travel, covered, 'For each match each gentleman cricketer received from their opponents 600 dollars in gold.'[3] Fitzgerald, who as MCC Secretary was the arbiter of amateur status, clearly saw no contradiction in the arrangements and vehemently defended his men (all of whom were MCC members and therefore Gentlemen by definition) when they came in for criticism on their return.

The first feelers had been put out by the Canadians in 1871, but Grace had been unable or unwilling to go, so the trip was deferred for a year. Once Grace had agreed to tour, Fitzgerald had little difficulty in raising the rest of the team, but was then plunged into despair by late cancellations. 'Mr Thornton saw a picture in a shop-window of a ship in distress'[4] and three days before they were due to sail two of the Walker brothers pulled out. Fitzgerald's frantic last-minute recruiting drive proved successful, and the team finally comprised Fitzgerald himself, Grace, Alfred and Edgar Lubbock, A. N. 'Monky' Hornby, the Hon. George Harris, Arthur Appleby, W. H. Hadow, C. J. Ottaway, C. K. Francis, Francis Pickering and W. M. Rose. The professional, Frank Farrands, accompanied them as umpire, and, one suspects, as baggage-master and general factotum. The team photograph (see Plate 5) shows a group of privileged young men in relaxed and expansive mood. The two great beards – Fitzgerald's even fuller than W.G.'s – dominate the portrait, but the rest of the team were not without distinction, as a reporter in Montreal observed:

In personal appearance there is nothing about any of [them] which would be called strikingly English. Fitzgerald, Rose, and Pickering are only of medium height, the remainder averaging about 5ft. 11in. Grace is a six-footer, with a full black beard. Ottaway, on the contrary, has no hirsute adornment, while the moustachettes of Pickering and Harris are in the incipient mood. Hadow would be called the handsome man, Edgar Lubbock the homely one . . . George Harris will be Lord Harris if he survives his father. He appears a very sensible and clever fellow. Hornby is a light-weight, active and jolly. Appleby and Alfred Lubbock are finely built, and have strong handsome features. All the men are well adapted to captivate the ladies . . .[5]

Quite apart from their eligibility as bachelors, Fitzgerald's team included some formidable cricketers. Apart from Grace, both Harris and Hornby were future England captains. Alfred Lubbock and C. J. Ottaway had, like Harris, been outstanding batsmen at Eton. Ottaway, a true sporting all-rounder, was still at Oxford and, in addition to cricket, represented the university at soccer, rackets, running and royal tennis. Hadow and Appleby had made appearances for the Gentlemen, Appleby providing a rare instance of an amateur fast bowler. Fitzgerald himself was not a great cricketer, but his personality dominated the trip:

Whether it was the magnificence of his swagger, the luxuriance of his beard, the fun that rolled out from him so easily, or the power of swiping, I do not know, but as regards each he could not escape notice. He was a power in the land in those days, as indeed the Secretary of the MCC should always be, and in addition he introduced a vein of joviality into the matches he played in which the spectators were as well able to enjoy as the players.[6]

After a farewell lunch given by the local cricketing fraternity, they joined their ship, the SS *Sarmatian*. Among their fellow passengers were a hundred children from one of the London orphanages, who were being sent out to 'a land of new life and promise'. That evening they were drawn up on deck, led through some ragged singing and lectured on the kindness that was being done to them, with a final exhortation 'never to forget that they were English boys and English girls'. 'There was,' Fitzgerald added, 'a half-lost look about many' as they took their last farewell of the country of their birth.[7] Unlike the rest of the touring party, for whom 'these hapless waifs and strays' provided a fleeting reminder of a nether world none would ever have to visit, Grace would spend most of his working life among the poor. In the great ship of Victorian society, Grace was naturally keen to secure a place for himself and his family in the first-class accommodation, but he would become intimately familiar with the cramped and unsanitary conditions that prevailed on the lower decks.

For now, though, he had to acclimatize to his new circumstances. It was his first time away from home for an extended period and it was his first time at sea. And in terms of class, too, he was in uncharted waters. He had, of course, played with most, if not all, of his fellow tourists over the recent seasons, but his social background was very different. Just as E.M. had been the odd man out among the professionals on Parr's Australian tour, so W.G. stood out among Fitzgerald's Old Harrovians and Old Etonians. He could have been made to feel it, but he wasn't. This was partly because his star status lifted him above the invisible, but all too tangible, demarcation lines Victorian snobbery guarded so jealously. For the younger men of the party he was a sporting hero and they could all bask in a degree of reflected glory. But they obviously warmed to him personally. In particular, George Harris, who had worshipped him from afar as a boy at Eton, now found him a very congenial companion. He later recalled 'the kindly, sympathetic consideration which characterized [Grace's] comradeship', adding that 'the tour commenced and cemented a friendship between us which I value at the highest'.[8]

What first brought them together was the misery of sea-sickness. They were not the only sufferers, but Grace remembers they were the worst affected. 'We both made up our minds that if the captain would only lower a boat for us we would try to get back to Old England again.'[9] They were happily unaware of the violent weather rampaging up and down the Canadian seaboard. The central tower of the Parliament building in Ottawa was struck, a church in Quebec burnt down, and the steamship *Vicksburg* was blown ashore while navigating the St Lawrence.[10] They only learned about the storms when they reached their destination, and they were blessed with calm seas for the crossing. Grace and Harris eventually found their sea legs and once their stomachs had settled started to take a healthy interest in the ship's provisions ('breakfast at 8.30 a.m., lunch at 12, dine at 4, tea at 7, and grog at 9 p.m').[11] They idled away the time with such pursuits as Shovelboard and Ringing the Peg – 'an innocent amusement,' Fitzgerald noted, '[that] has the charm of occupying the body without distressing the mind. It consists of throwing rings of rope at an erect peg, you make the game what you like, and if you don't like, you let it slide.' One of the alternatives, pursued by an indeterminate number of the team, was competing for the attentions of the few young women on board.[12]

After a week they saw icebergs and then 'several objects very like whales, and pronounced to be such'.[13] Tell-tale seaweed followed, and they had their first sight of land. The ship passed through the Straits of Belle Isle, and entered 'the placid waters of the St Lawrence'.[14] There were few other boats, but everyone pressed to the rail to look at the wreck of the *Vicksburg*. When the epic grandeur of the scenery eventually palled, whist 'set in with violence'[15] – a comment vigorously marked in Grace's copy of Fitzgerald's book, indicating his enthusiastic presence at the card-tables.

They finally docked at Quebec on 17 August, 'after making the fastest passage of the year (2656 miles in nine days one and half hours) and one that has seldom been beaten since'.[16] But it was late (10.30 p.m.) so the Twelve had only time to celebrate their arrival, making the 'night hideous with their outburst of joy at finding themselves once more on land' before returning to the ship for their last night on board. Fitzgerald lay awake, revolving 'in his mind the various chances of the game, but he fell asleep at last like his less thoughtful comrades, and dreamed that W.G. was not out, 1000, he couldn't tell where, but he awoke refreshed'.[17]

The euphoria of arrival was dampened when they found that although their hosts were there to greet them, no accommodation had been booked. The hotels were crowded, and those with rooms free proved unsatisfactory. In the end, the team were given beds at the Stadacona Club or billeted in private houses. They spent the day sightseeing, and the following evening they were invited by Lord Dufferin, the Governor of Canada, to a banquet at the Citadel. Whether they had too much to drink, or were simply overtaken by an excess of adventurousness, Grace, Fitzgerald, Pickering and Ottaway suddenly decided, despite the lateness of the hour, to set off on a shooting and fishing expedition into the bush. This particular hunt by night nearly came to grief several times, as the track was appalling and the driver ('cheerful if unintelligible') seemed to have little idea of where he was going. When he drove the trap against a fallen tree-trunk unseen in the darkness, Ottaway narrowly escaped scalping. They finally arrived at a crude hunting lodge where they took an early breakfast and then split up. Grace and Fitzgerald chose the river while Pickering and Ottaway opted to shoot.

They were in the real wilds. 'The solitude of the bush is indescribable,' Fitzgerald wrote. 'The strange noises proceed more from inanimate nature than living beings. An aged tree falls, or a bough cracks, a cascade breaks into distant echoes, but no joyous carol of bird is heard, no hurried flight of wild fowl or pigeon.'[18] W.G. had never caught a trout with a fly rod in his life before but quickly developed the knack, and found it as easy as running up a big score at the Oval. 'As soon as the fly touched the water the fish dashed greedily at it, and we hauled them in as rapidly as could be.' The first century partnership of the tour was achieved by noon – 130 trout ('most of them small, but now and again running to about a pound'). The others had been less successful, having bagged only 'one unfortunate small bird which was scarcely worth [the] powder', before being chased off a private plot of land by 'an indignant and stalwart virago' waving a stick.[19] The return journey was even more frightening than the night drive as they could now see the perils to which they were exposed, but they survived, and eventually bowled into the Stadacona Club late in the afternoon, tired, dirty, and very hungry. They had missed the formalities of a champagne luncheon, but made a belated assault on a side of beef and the few remaining bottles.

Cricket at Quebec had died with the departure of the garrison, but the tourists agreed to put on a public practice session for those curious to see the old game once more. After being up all night and out in the bush all day, the hunting party still had enough energy to turn out on the Esplanade Field. It might have been better if Grace had retired to his room, because he hit the ball hard to Hadow who put his finger out trying to catch it.

That evening they set off for Montreal on the night train. In the rush, the trout that had been packed specially in ice got left behind. Consolation was at hand. The chairman of the railway company had given them his personal carriage, a luxurious saloon with its own bar. The line was popularly known as the 'Grand Drunk', and it certainly lived up to its reputation as the Twelve were plied unstintingly with 'champagne and other sedatives'.[20] They arrived at Montreal at seven in the morning on 21 August and booked in at the St Lawrence Hall Hotel. This was a huge edifice with a front of 3,000 feet along St James Street opposite the French Cathedral, with banks and the post office conveniently near by. Despite the fact that he had barely had an hour's uninterrupted sleep for two nights, Grace joined the rest of the team as they went to explore. The heat was oppressive (ninety-two degrees in the shade), but they soldiered on until they found the cricket ground in Catherine Street. It was a singularly ill-favoured site. Not only was it a disconcerting shape ('three-cornered')[21] but it was in 'a deplorable condition'. It had been used as a rubbish tip, and the surface was pitted and uneven. 'Luckily, some heavy thunderstorms improved the wicket, and by dint of hard work it was made fit to play upon, though it was bad enough in all conscience.'[22]

They had another practice session, no less disastrous than the first. Grace struck a towering shot into a neighbouring garden. They lost the ball, but W.G. was given a large melon by the admiring gardener. With a typically sharp eye for relative values, Grace noted that melons were plentiful and a great deal cheaper than cricket balls in Montreal. Then Francis was struck senseless by a blow to the temple, and Fitzgerald called a halt 'before anybody was killed'.[23]

The start of the match the next day was held up by more thunderstorms. The weather and the fact that it was the holiday season and many families were out of town resulted in a disappointingly small crowd, but the Montreal Twenty-two added some brightness to the scene with their coloured outfits. Fitzgerald won the toss and sent in W.G. and Ottaway. The locals were clearly no match for the tourists, but the dubious wicket made batting difficult, and in Fitzgerald's view the bowling was 'remarkably good'. W.G. played freely and rode his luck while Ottaway defended patiently. They put on a hundred together, and after Ottaway was out Grace sailed on with some majestic hits. He looked set for a century when a surprising and involuntary intervention cut him short on 81. 'Nobody would have guessed that a stout Gentleman with a pipe in his mouth, and of the name of Benjamin, would have put the *coup de grâce* to the Leviathan. He did. W.G. cut a very hot one into the abdominal regions of Mr B; it stuck there, and the lucky Benjamin bounded into the air, and was carried in triumph by his comrades round the wickets.'[24] Fitzgerald's Pickwickian note was carried over into the evening festivities – a 'Banquet to the Gentlemen of England' – at which Grace made the first of his famous Canadian addresses. Fitzgerald described the inaugural effort:

The speech of the evening was W.G.'s. It had been looked forward to with impatience, not to say a tinge of envy, by the Eleven. He replied to the toast of the 'Champion Batsman of Cricketdom'. He said, 'Gentlemen, I beg to thank you for the honour you have done me; I never saw better bowling than I have seen today, and I hope to see as good wherever I go.' The speech took longer to deliver than you might imagine from its brevity, but it was greeted with applause from all who were in a proper position to hear it.[25]

Grace probably conceived this form of words as the way to stay on his feet for the shortest possible time without causing offence, but its reception revealed unsuspected comic potential, and as the tour went on the formula became a firm favourite. To the immense delight of his fellow tourists, Grace repeated the first speech word for word, simply substituting an alternative for 'bowling' as appropriate. In later years when called upon to speak he would sometimes say, 'I think I must give them one of my Canadian speeches.' It was quite a night, and some of the team struggled to make it to the ground on time in the morning. Fitzgerald himself is down in the scoresheet as 'unwell, o'. It hardly mattered, as the match dwindled into one-sided futility with the tourists reaching an unassailable 255 and then dismissing the locals for 48 and 67. Rose's under-arm lobs mesmerized them, while W.G.'s huge presence at point intimidated them. Rose took thirty-three wickets in all, and nought was the most popular score. The local press took an enthusiastic if ill-informed interest in the proceedings, and naturally Grace was the object of closest scrutiny:

Mr Grace is a large-framed, loose-jointed man, and you would say that his gait is a trifle awkward and shambling, but when he goes into the field you see that he is quick-sighted, sure-handed, and light-footed as the rest. He always goes in first, and to see him tap the ball gently to the off for one, draw it to the on for two, pound it to the limits for four, drive it beyond the most distant long leg for six, looks as easy as rolling off a log.[26]

The Twelve were news wherever they went, and throughout the tour they were shadowed by a couple of hard-drinking journalists:

We called them Stiff and Strong. Stiff knew all about the game, and followed it closely, except when under the invigorating influence of too many cocktails. Strong knew nothing of cricket, and, although also a too ardent admirer of an 'eye-opener', trusted to Stiff's weak moments to be able to crib his remarks on the game. If Stiff left his book while he retired to the refreshment tent for a minute, or indulged in forty winks, Strong was down on his notes like a shot, and his paper next morning was full of Stiff's best things in Strong's best style.[27]

From Montreal the Twelve went on to Ottawa for another one-sided match, and more lionizing. Although the standard of hospitality was high, the hotels proved unfriendly and potentially dangerous places where the bar never shut and no one ever answered the service bell. On one occasion W.G. was woken at about 2.30 by an altercation from the saloon. He went down and found Farrands hotly disputing a bar-fly's claim to have scored fifty off Freeman. 'Farrands would not listen to this assertion, and bluntly told the man that Freeman would knock him, bat and all, right through the wickets in a couple of overs.' The stand-off was moving rapidly to blows when Grace stepped in, and 'poured oil on the troubled waters' so effectively that when he retired to bed he left the two men drinking happily together.[28]

The ground at Ottawa was in better shape than the one in Montreal, and a much larger crowd turned out to watch. Grace was under the weather – 'enfeebled by internal disorders' according to Fitzgerald,[29] suffering 'a severe attack of British cholera' in Brownlee's version.[30] Being dragged out of bed to settle bar-room disputes in the small hours can't have helped his condition. However, he still scored 73, albeit with a runner. It took him ninety-one overs, and included several chances. He was eventually bowled by a daisy-cutter. Rose's lobs and Appleby's left-arm lifters duly despatched the locals, Appleby returning the astonishing figures of twelve wickets for three runs. 'From motives of humanity' he was not allowed to bowl in the second innings. Even so, the Twenty-two managed only 49 as opposed to 43, giving the tourists victory by an innings and 110 runs.

The inevitable banquet took place in a leaky marquee. One of the items on the menu was haunch of bear, which Grace gamely tried, but found 'It was quite impossible to get one's teeth through it, and though the taste for bear may perhaps be cultivated, like the taste for olives, I fought shy of the delicacy ever afterwards.'[31] When it came to his speech, he singled out the quality of the ground for special praise.

The Twelve spent long enough in Ottawa to be taken down the Slides by some of the local beauties, a wet but intimate experience according to Fitzgerald: 'a lady clinging to each arm tightly, or if nervous yourself, clinging to a waist not loth to be pressed, a raft and rushing of water, a sudden dip, a stifled scream, a wild hurrah from a bridge, under which you slide, a succession of the above sensations in less time than you can say your prayers, a gradual unclinging and unfastening of waists, and the danger is done'.[32] Grace thought it 'exciting work for the first time, and makes a pleasant diversion, but it is a pastime of which one soon tires'.[33] There was also 'an impromptu hop' in the hotel that was 'kept up with spirit till 4 a.m.'.[34]

From Ottawa they sailed up Lake Ontario to Toronto, where everything was an improvement on what had gone before – even down to the provision of towels and soap in the pavilion. The interest in the cricket was keener, with a stand erected for 2,000 spectators, and the ground was excellent. The match against the local Twenty-two started on Monday, 2 September, and for the third time Fitzgerald won the toss and sent W.G. and Ottaway in to open the innings. For the third time Grace demonstrated his powers of application, and this time did reach his century. He was in a light-hearted mood and teased the crowd with a ploy he would use to bait the Australians – the pretend walk towards the pavilion when a bump ball was caught. Fitzgerald noted that 'A general cheer was succeeded by a hollow groan, when it was seen that the great man had no intention to leave his wicket; it was the old kid – first bound catch to point.'[35] He gave some genuine chances, but all were dropped, and he hit five sixes, breaking his bat in the process. When he was finally dismissed, he had scored 142 out of 241. '[A]gainst a smart 22, barring a few accidents, [it] was a great performance' in Fitzgerald's estimation.[36]

On the second day the Twelve took their total to 319. The sun blazed down and the heat was 'inimical to strict cricket'.[37] Such was the easy-going atmosphere that on resuming after lunch only seven of the team appeared, the rest having been seduced away, their captain stated, by 'some hospitable friend'.[38] Nothing, however, distracted Grace from cricket. Despite the hours he had spent at the crease, he was beginning to chafe at not being given a bowl. For reasons best known to himself, Fitzgerald had no regard for his bowling. Grace was never backwards in coming forwards and had been getting tired of the preference given to Rose's innocuous lobs. He now persuaded his sceptical captain that he 'could diddle them out just as cheaply'.[39] This may have been his first experiment with the slower style of bowling to which he turned later in his career. On this occasion it was not a success, and Fitzgerald recorded with satisfaction that his efforts were 'severely punished'.[40]

Large crowds attended every day, 'including most of the fair sex of the neighbourhood',[41] and the team's popularity was even greater off the field. There was a reception at the Royal Canadian Yacht Club at which W.G. delivered his third speech ('batting'), and a dance where his performance caught the eye of a local reporter: 'Mr Grace, who must now be known by sight to more people in England than Mr Gladstone himself, was especially noticeable for the skill and agility of his movements.'[42] He was getting pretty well known in Canada too, and was often stopped in the street by working men or backwoodsmen who wanted to shake his hand. Fitzgerald wrote that he and some of his team were disconcerted by the easy democracy of social relations:

It was at first almost strange to us, Englishmen with our insular prejudices of caste or superior education, to be greeted, as we were, in the familiar, but not vulgar manner of our brothers in Canada ... At first our hand did not instinctively press the kindly fist held out to us. The sympathetic chord is not struck at the first touch. The hard crust of old English prejudice does not crumble without a struggle in the operation. But it did crumble ere we left the Dominion.[43]

Before they left Toronto they went on a grand excursion by train and lake steamer. The day culminated in a dinner and dance at Allandale, a romantically secluded up-country station where 'in the intervals of dancing, promenades on the platform were taken; and perhaps a railway station never witnessed so many flirtations'.[44] They got back to Toronto at two in the morning.

At the end of the week they played a scratch game of eleven a side, with Fitzgerald and Grace picking teams from the combined forces of the tour party and members of the Toronto Club. It was another extremely hot day, and the ground was invaded by 'myriads of bright butterflies' floating in the breeze. In keeping with the holiday mood, Grace advanced down the wicket second ball and was stumped. In the second innings he held himself back – at the request, it was rumoured, of 'a deputation of ladies'.[45] He had hit twenty-seven in seven vigorous blows, including a six out of the ground, when 'just [as] I was well set, and scoring freely, my opponents, who thought they had had enough of me for that day, bribed the umpire to give me out lbw, and I retired discomforted, much to their amusement and my own disgust'.[46] Perhaps this was a gentle hint not to take the game too seriously, but his natural competitiveness was irrepressible, and he took seven cheap wickets when Fitzgerald's XI went in to chase 123. They were all out for 63. The large crowd besieged the pavilion cheering the players and demanding speeches. When the team went to the theatre in the evening, the band struck up 'Rule Britannia', and the house gave them a standing ovation. (And at some stage during the week an admirer offered Grace a bear cub to take home, but he reluctantly declined the gift.)

They then travelled on to the old barracks town of London, which was a disappointment after Toronto. Their hotel was dreadful – 'starvation and flies formed the menu'[47] – and the whole place seemed to be tainted with paraffin. Fitzgerald commented: 'Oil is cheap, not to say nasty; we had long been acquainted with its marvellous properties, we had detected it in every room and smelt it in every passage from Quebec to London. It was brought home to us here, or rather we were brought home to its home. The bread tasted of oil, the beer was impregnated with oil, the ice was oily, the attendants were oily.' The hotel even lacked a serviceable bathroom, and the players were recommended to try the sulphur baths. These were oily too – and 'extremely cold' – so they walked about the streets unwashed and unimpressed at London's attempts to ape its great namesake: 'The Thames is not a magnificent river . . . Westminster Bridge is not a gorgeous structure. We passed St Paul's Cathedral on our return to the hotel. We were not tempted to linger in its precincts.'[48]

The ground, at the old barracks, was no improvement on the town itself. The wicket was so well camouflaged that they walked over it without noticing. Fitzgerald won the toss (as he did on every occasion in Canada) and elected to bat. He had given Ottaway, Appleby and Francis 'leave to spend the Sabbath in the same pew with three of the loveliest ladies of Toronto'[49] on the strict understanding that they would be in London for the start of play. They weren't, so Hornby stood in for Ottaway as Grace's opening partner. The wicket was 'dead from thunder showers',[50] and the bowling straight and fast with a liberal supply of shooters. Grace made 31 and the rest of the team managed only a further fifty-eight runs between them. The Londoners trooped in and out for 55.

That night there was the most terrific thunderstorm. Fitzgerald wrote: 'It broke in a deluge of rain, accompanied by lightning, which defies description. Sheets of electric light illumined the dark sky, revealing vistas of the surrounding forest, and forming a display of the elements at war, such as is never witnessed in Europe.'[51] There was a reception and ball for the visitors, but Grace cried off. Perhaps he was still suffering from his earlier illness, or simply didn't fancy exposing himself to the elements. He would certainly have been hard pressed to find anything praiseworthy to drop into his famous speech. (Fitzgerald recorded that the barracks where lunch was served were so dilapidated that 'the rats and vermin had long since left them, as much too comfortless'.)[52]

His rest showed benefits the next day when he scored easily the highest innings of the match, 76 out of the 130 made while he was at the crease. The Twelve (all of whom were playing) made a respectable 161, which was far too much for the home side. However, despite Fitzgerald's desire to get the match over, they only took ten of the twenty-one wickets required in the remainder of the second day's play, and had to return to the ground to mop up the rest in the morning. When the game ended there was time for a brief croquet tournament. Grace partnered Fitzgerald, and they played the local lady champions, whom they ungallantly beat, though 'not without a good struggle'. In the other match, Alfred Lubbock and Harris narrowly beat 'two young ladies just out of the schoolroom'.[53]

They left London with relief, bound for Hamilton, their final stop on the Canadian leg of the tour. For once Grace failed, scoring only 17. When Hamilton batted Rose was once more the chief agent of destruction, his eyes sparkling 'with an unwonted glare behind his crystals'.[54] The locals were caught like rabbits in headlights, collapsing to an all-out total of 86. They then followed on and soon found themselves 24 for 7.

At this point the game descended into farce. The tourists wanted to finish the match early so as to get an extra day at the Niagara Falls. The Hamilton team agreed to play on, though the light was failing rapidly. 'At 5.55 ten wickets were down for 43 runs . . . [and] the moon now rose,' Fitzgerald wrote. The fielders were reduced to crouching, or in some cases actually lying down, to get a sight of the ball, while the batsmen could steal runs with impunity. The crowd couldn't see either, so pressed in closer and closer, 'encroaching considerably upon the wickets'. At 6.25 eighteen wickets were down for sixty. The last wicket proved hard to get, and Grace lobbied successfully to bowl. He had no compunction in sending down 'an uncompromising sneak' to bring the match to an end. 'It was skittles rather than cricket, and was only jusitified by the necessities of the case,' concluded the captain.[55]

When they got to the Falls, the whole team, apart from Rose, went through the Cave of Winds, and endured a series of drenchings and buffetings clad in felt sandals and thick flannel suits. There was also time for a less interactive appreciation of the scenery. One of the few photographs from the tour is of 'A Group Taken at Niagara Falls'. Four unidentified men stand at the back looking as though they might be about to break into song, while W.G. and C. K. Francis occupy the foreground with three immaculately coiffured young ladies. W.G. lies full-length staring levelly at the camera, while the girl immediately beside turns away, though her hand lies close to his shoulder. Was he as indifferent to his companion as he seems? W.G. gives no hint, remarking flatly: 'The photograph hangs in my room as I write, and conjures up many happy reminiscences of our Niagara experiences.'[56]

Grace clearly did not number among these a party the Twelve threw to repay some of the hospitality they had received. Few of their Canadian guests could attend at such short notice, and they were forced to issue invitations on the American side of the Falls. The proceedings began uneasily. The hotel ballroom was large, and the hosts' hearts 'sank on entering it; a solemn row of strangers lined the walls, enlivened only by an occasional eye-glass raised inquiringly as one after another the Twelve appeared'. The ice was eventually broken, and with the aid of 'a capital band, a little life was soon set going'. Once more there were opportunities for dalliance, 'and the neighbourhood of the Falls led to moonlight rambles'.[57] W.G.'s memories do not extend to moonlight rambles; indeed he seems to have been relieved that the arrival of the Sabbath brought the night to an early close: 'unfortunately – or as some of us thought very fortunately – . . . [the] dancing had to stop at midnight'.[58]

On 16 September the Twelve took their last look at the Falls and after travelling overnight arrived at Albany at seven a.m. before sailing down the Hudson to New York. They put up at the Brevort House, the best hotel in town, where, Fitzgerald noted, 'You can rub along . . . just comfortably, but not extravagantly, on the small matter of £3 per day, your rooms will be palatial, the attendance perfect. Dinners equal to anything in Paris.'[59]

Their first match involved a ferry crossing to New Jersey where they were to play Twenty-two of the St George's Club. The Hoboken ground was 'approached by unfinished streets, and surrounded by "carcases" of houses in an advanced stage of non-completion',[60] but a fair crowd turned up to see play start at noon. Fitzgerald lost his first toss on the tour and the New Yorkers batted. They did no better than the Canadians against Rose and Appleby and were all out shortly after lunch for 66.

Grace and Ottaway opened as usual. W.G. was described in the local press as 'a monarch in his might', and lived up to his billing by twice hitting the ball out of the ground, ending the day undefeated on 67 out of an unbroken stand of 102. Both openers were out early the following morning, but the rest of the team raised the total to 249. Grace talked his way into seeing whether he 'could get the St George's men out even quicker than Rose',[61] and this time he could. 'It was a complete slaughter of the innocents' according to a local press report. 'The fact is, Grace frightened them. They thought they saw some unknown and fatal influence in his bowling, and they simply played right into his hands.'[62] The innings lasted an hour and twenty minutes and produced forty-four runs. Grace took 11 for 26, Appleby 9 for 18. The match was rounded off with the obligatory banquet at the Travellers' Club, and Grace gave his fifth speech of the tour: 'Gentlemen, I have to thank you for the honour you have done me. I have never tasted better oysters than I have tasted here to-day, and I hope I shall get as good wherever I go.'[63]

The following evening the team explored New York's gaslit night-spots, the Halls of Light. These were gin palaces, Fitzgerald found, with scantily clad waitresses masquerading as 'nymphs in no garb of a later date than the palmy days of Lais of Corinth . . . Their looks are not seductive, nor does the spirit you imbibe aid the charm. We thought we might be prejudiced by the first hall we entered, so we tried several others, but with the same unpleasant result. There is no want of decorum, and nothing to offend a Quaker beyond a dearth of beauty . . . You are provoked without provocation. You are disgusted in your delight.' New

York's dangerous reputation was confirmed when they were told at one establishment that there had been a shooting two nights before. '[T]he amiable man behind the counter, with his sleeves tucked up, shot a man through the heart' when he tried to force his way in after closing time. 'Verdict, Served him right, and accepted by all who knew New York intimately.'[64]

The team moved on from New York to play the most important match of the tour against Twenty-Two of Philadelphia. Philadelphia was the heartland of American cricket, and huge crowds thronged to the German Town Cricket Club. 'The road might have been to the Epsom Downs on the morning of the Derby. The railroad was a continuous train,' wrote the captain.[65] The specially erected grandstand rapidly filled. A band played. The weather was perfect.

Fitzgerald lost the toss and the Twenty-two batted. Once again, Appleby proved too fast and Rose too tempting, but Grace also managed to get in on the act with what Fitzgerald described disparagingly as his 'high-and-home-easy' style. He was effective too, taking 9 for 22 in the Philadelphians' total of 68. The Englishmen then came up against the pick of the bowlers they met on the tour. Grace's assessment of them was generous: 'Newhall, who was a right-hand fast bowler, was one of the best . . . I ever played against; whilst Mead, a medium pace left-hander, kept up a wonderfully good length.' When Newhall bowled Grace for 14 the crowd responded vociferously: 'I have heard many a great shout go up in various parts of the globe at my dismissal, but I never remember anything quite equal to the wild roar that greeted my downfall on this occasion.'[66] The two Americans bowled through the innings, dismissing the Twelve for 105. The Philadelphian second innings took the same course as their first, though this time Grace replaced Rose entirely and bowled throughout with Appleby. The game was watched with intense and partisan interest. The ladies in the grandstand shrieked whenever a wicket fell, and the whole crowd cheered every single run as gradually the deficit was knocked off and the home team inched into the lead. In the end they made 74, Appleby taking 8 for 24 and Grace 11 for 46.

The Philadelphians had done well to set the tourists a target, albeit a small one of 33. The ground was packed again the following morning to see Grace and Ottaway walk out to the middle shortly after noon. The wicket had 'worn tolerably well', but two days' play had given it a 'rough edge, which was much in favour of fast bowling'. Grace gave his opinion that 'the few runs would take some getting'.[67] And so it proved. He got off the mark with a single in Newhall's first over, but lost Ottaway to a fast delivery that sent his middle stump flying. Hornby made one good hit for three to leg, but was then snapped up at short leg. That brought Alfred Lubbock out to join Grace with the score on 8 for 2. Apart from a few high-risk short singles, the runs almost dried up. 'Ball after ball was sent down, which we could do nothing beyond playing, and maiden over followed maiden over in unbroken monotony.' After three quarters of an hour the run total was fifteen. 'The wicket was crumbling, and getting worse and worse. Newhall's bowling rose dangerously, and Mead, as usual, kept up a splendid length.' First Lubbock went, and then Grace himself was caught in the slips. He had batted just under an hour and scored seven runs. 'This is about the slowest pace at which I ever remember scoring,' he remarked. His fall again provoked wild jubilation. Hats and parasols were flung into the air and the cheering and applause accompanied him all the way back to the pavilion. At 18 for 4 and with the great man gone, the Americans sensed a real chance of an astonishing victory.[68]

Hadow and Harris calmed the visitors' nerves with a steady partnership, and appeared to be steering them to a comfortable victory when, with the score on 29, Harris slashed at a lifter from Newhall and was caught at cover-point for 'a most valuable 9'. Two more wickets fell on 29 and the tension mounted unbearably. Grace recalled:

The excitement, which had been growing intenser every moment, was now extraordinary. The atmosphere was electrical. I never remember seeing a team or a crowd of spectators more excited. They were in rhapsodies, and could scarcely keep still. The quietude amid which each ball was bowled was almost deathly, and no wonder, for thirteen successive maiden overs had been bowled and not a run had been secured for half an hour, during which time three wickets had fallen.[69]

Edgar Lubbock was not expected to lay a bat on Newhall, but he broke the deadlock with a leg-bye to bring up the thirty. His partner was Appleby, who now produced the stroke of the day, a full-blooded off-drive which sped through the packed field all the way to the boundary, and the visitors were home by a whisker. Grace was greatly impressed with the fight the Americans had put up, and Lord Harris remembered the game as one of the best he ever played in. He also noted that Fitzgerald's team was the only English side in forty years to win against the odds in Philadelphia, making the performance 'very high class'.[70]

Rather less high-class were Fitzgerald's travel arrangements at the conclusion of the match. The fixture had been added to the programme after the tour had started and he had taken a calculated gamble that they could finish it in two days. When it ran into the third day their schedule was derailed, and they had to hurry away to catch the train to Boston, cutting short the usual pleasantries. This 'apparent' discourtesy left their hosts understandably offended. They upset the Bostonians as well, turning up a day late after a nightmare of missed connections. Their planned visit to Harvard was cancelled, and as the steamer was due to sail from Quebec in a couple of days' time, the Boston match was reduced to a one-day fixture. Fitzgerald had some business to conduct and made a diplomatic withdrawal, leaving Grace in charge.

It was a thankless task. The weather had broken and heavy rain had made the cricket ground unfit for play. As a result, the fixture was moved to the baseball ground. Between twenty and thirty bags of sawdust had to be used around the playing area, and even then, Grace recalled, 'some of the fieldsmen stood ankle deep in sawdust and slush'.[71] The Bostonians batted first and were dismissed for 51. When Fitzgerald came back from town he was astonished to find that the tourists' score stood at 39 for 8, of which Grace had made 26. This included two towering hits out of the ground for which he was only credited four. The rest of the team were obviously on their last legs, but Grace drove them on, and after they gained exact parity on first innings, the home team's second innings started at 3.30. Grace opened the bowling with Appleby and took 13 for 35 as the Twenty-two were dismissed for 44. Grace failed when he batted a second time, and wickets fell at an alarming rate. At 11 for 5 'the light was now darkness'. Fitzgerald

consulted the umpires as to continuing, but on discovering that only ten minutes more play was at stake, went in himself, remained two overs, and finally received a full pitch on the big toe, which, for all he knew, from all he saw, might with equal pleasure have been landed on his nose. It was the last ball bowled in the American tour. The Umpire cried time, the [batsmen] carried their bats back to the dark room, where their comrades were huddled together, and in darkness and in damp was brought to a close the last match of the series . . . [with] the honours, if any, strictly divided.[72]

After a last night of banqueting and speechmaking the Twelve left Boston for Quebec early on the morning of 27 September. Their final journey on the Grand Drunk remained in Grace's memory for two things

– the glorious colours of the Fall, and, as the route took them through the Prohibition state of Maine, 'the curious experience of being absolutely unable to get, for love or money, anything stronger by way of refreshment than thick soup, washed down with weak tea and indifferent coffee'.[73] They sailed from Quebec the same day, and docked at Liverpool on 8 October.

*

The tour had been a great success, from both a social and a cricketing point of view. Fitzgerald was the first to concede that the standard had not been high, but remarked that 'it is no slight handicap to match any eleven, on indifferent grounds, against a Twenty-two. The Canadian teams were certainly weak in batting, but their bowling was always good.' The ease of their victories in seven out of the eight matches was 'of course largely due to the never-failing bat of W. G. Grace'. Fitzgerald records his aggregate as 540 runs at an average of 49.1; the next highest was Alfred Lubbock with 146 runs, and the next best average was Appleby's 16.4. And despite Fitzgerald's blind spot regarding his bowling, Grace was the third most successful bowler after Appleby and Rose with sixty-six wickets at under five apiece. As to the missionary effects of the trip, Fitzgerald foresaw the inevitable decline of cricket in the face of baseball in America, but had higher hopes for Canada, while acknowledging that 'No Canadian is likely to become a second W.G. if he lives to be a hundred and plays till past four score.'[74]

For Grace it had been a pleasurable and a formative experience, giving him a taste of celebrity that continued even after he had packed his cricket bag at the end of the day's play. At the same time he enjoyed mixing with men of his own age but from a more privileged background, and the friendships that developed over cocktails on the Grand Drunk lasted the rest of his life. The relationship with George Harris, who inherited his father's title shortly after their return, was of particular significance. By the end of the decade, Lord Harris had risen to a position of pre-eminence in the MCC hierarchy. Harris became a great stickler for the conventional proprieties, and there was much in Grace's subsequent career to which he might have been expected to take exception. But he remained staunchly loyal to Grace, whom he undoubtedly regarded as 'One of Us'.

In fact there was a foretaste of future controversies when the tourists got back to England. Instead of being welcomed home with honour, they returned to face a groundswell of criticism. Grace, it was claimed, had been hawked around like a circus animal in exchange for a free holiday, and the whole team had been guilty of exploiting their hosts and infringing their amateur status. Fitzgerald was quick to reply, publishing a lengthy letter in *Bell's Life* which he reprinted at the end of *Wickets in the West*. Grace, he said, was 'a phenomenon in the game',[75] whose every appearance drew vast and excited crowds. There was no shame attached to providing the Canadians with the chance of seeing him, while at the same time taking the opportunity to breathe new life into their moribund domestic game. Fitzgerald vigorously denied that the project had 'originated in any spirit of speculation'[76] and dismissed accusations that the Twelve had displayed 'an inordinate desire to banquet and carouse at the expense of the "poor dependency"' as 'offensive to the Canadian hosts, [and] unjust to the English guests'.[77] In fact, he claimed robustly, '[N]othing could contribute more to a good understanding between the inhabitants of both countries than a visit of gentlemen, on pleasure bent and on information bound.'[78] Grace showed no interest in the row in which he featured so prominently; the final pages of his copy of *Wickets in the West* are left untouched by his pencil. By the time Fitzgerald's book was published, he had more important things to think about. At some point over the winter he had become engaged to be married.

Very little is known about Grace's personal life, but the few shreds of evidence suggest that, in contrast to the outgoing E.M., who in the course of an ardent lifetime married four times, W.G. was rather shy with women. One reason for this was almost certainly his voice, which for so large and so obviously virile a man was remarkably high-pitched. According to descendants of the girl in question, Grace once had a proposal of marriage rejected 'because of his high, squeaky voice',[79] and if that was the case it is hardly surprising that he was inhibited by self-consciousness. It is certainly clear from accounts of the Canadian tour that he was not one of the members of the team who took advantage of the more relaxed Canadian mores governing relations between the sexes. However, watching his companions flirting at close quarters may have convinced him that the business wasn't so impossibly difficult after all, but whether or not that was the spur, some time after his return he plucked up courage to propose, and was accepted.

His fiancée was Agnes Nichols Day, the nineteen-year-old daughter of one of the Grace cousins, William Day. Day was a lithographer, or 'publisher' as he put it in the 1871 census return, living in Brompton. That census lists nine other children and only one resident servant, suggesting one of the chaotically overcrowded households so beloved of Dickens making a determined show of respectability on rather limited means. A great deal of the domestic chores and minding of the younger children would have fallen to the elder daughters, and whatever the personal attractions of shy, loud, high-voiced, cricket-obsessed cousin Gilbert, marriage clearly presented Agnes with an appealing escape route. What she can't have guessed when she accepted him was that she would spend her honeymoon 12,000 miles from home courtesy of a consortium of businessmen associated with the Melbourne Cricket Club.

TEN

EIGHTEEN-seventy-three was a momentous year for Grace. He played a prodigious amount of cricket, and despite the weather, which was both bitterly cold and very wet, he had one of his greatest all-round seasons. He also got married, and in the autumn took a cricket team out to Australia.

John Lillywhite's Cricketers' Companion commented, 'The only cricketer that has ever earned the title of Champion, year after year finds him holding his own in undisputed pre-eminence, and there is no British sport or pastime in which one performer so entirely eclipses all the best efforts of other votaries.'[1] It was in deference to his unique standing that some of the matches in which he played were granted first-class status to allow him the first double of 2,000 runs and 100 wickets. Revisionist statisticians have reduced the totals to 1,805 runs and 75 wickets, but it was still a vintage year, in which, in all kinds of cricket, he topped 3,000 runs.

At twenty-four, he was the monarch of all he surveyed, and his belief in the divine right of kings was made clear to all. Before the season opened he showed his inflexibility in a row with Nottinghamshire. He had promised the Yorkshire professional Joseph Rowbotham to play in his benefit match at the beginning of the last week in July, but when Nottinghamshire proposed the same dates for their match with Gloucestershire, Grace agreed, thinking it would save a journey to play at Trent Bridge first and then go on to Sheffield afterwards. This, however, spelt disaster for Rowbotham, who travelled down from Yorkshire to beg Grace to reconsider. The professional's diplomatic mission succeeded, and Grace wrote to Nottinghamshire demanding that they change the Gloucestershire fixture back to the original dates. This they were understandably reluctant to do, but Grace was adamant, and wrote a final ultimatum on 2 April:

I have thought the matter well over and am come to this conclusion: you must give way for Rowbotham's benefit match. You may think I am using a strong expression in saying 'must' but I think it is just to him as he had these dates, 28th, 29th and 30th, given him by the Yorkshire Committee two or three months ago. If you will do this, you will greatly oblige me; if not, the only thing I can do is to say that I shall not play at Nottingham.

I gave you my word that Gloucestershire would play on the 28th, not then knowing it would make a difference to Rowbotham's benefit. If you like to play Notts v. Gloucester without any of the Graces, do by all means. Now, I am sorry to write like this, but I can assure you that I think you ought to give in. Rowbotham has been to see me and has explained to me that Thursdays and Fridays are the worst days in the week for a benefit match in Sheffield. Please write me an answer as soon as you get this as I want it settled.

Yours truly, W. G. Grace[2]

The peremptory tone was typical, as was the threat of a total family boycott (the same tactic Henry had used at the Oval in 1864). Nor was there the slightest acknowledgement that the whole problem was of his making in the first place. Once he had made up his mind, that was it. Business would be conducted on his terms, or not at all – even if it meant jeopardizing an important county match (just how important would only appear at the end of the season). It must have been a difficult decision, given the amount of gate money Grace would generate, but the Nottinghamshire committee refused to be brow-beaten, and the fixture was cancelled.

Grace's high-handedness had further repercussions. He had not only treated the Nottinghamshire committee with scant courtesy, he had also gone over the heads of his own committee, and not surprisingly some members objected. As always, the family closed ranks, with E.M. holding the party line against all comers. As a passage, later deleted, in the Gloucestershire Committee Minutes Book indicates, this caused some 'angry conversation of not too polite a nature (as the Reverend J. Greene disputed the correctness of the notes taken by the Secretary of the Committee Meeting March 20 saying that his memory was superior to the black and white testimony of the Secretary)'. Feelings ran so high that a subsequent meeting was boycotted by the entire committee. E.M. laconically recorded: 'Present: E.M.Grace, and that's all.'[3]

While E.M. faced down internal dissent at home, Grace acted as the county's representative in the wider world. Pressure had been mounting for some time to put county cricket on a more regulated footing. There was no officially sanctioned or supervised county championship; indeed the concept of a 'champion county' was the creation of the sporting press and specialist publications like *Wisden* and the two Lillywhite almanacks. The title was awarded on a crude system of subtracting losses from wins, but as the counties did not play a uniform number of matches, this was hardly satisfactory. With more county cricket being played, and the public becoming increasingly interested in the first-class game as opposed to odds matches against the AEE and other professional Elevens, there was an urgent need for reform.

The man who took the initiative was Charles Alcock. He was not only the Surrey Secretary, but also the Secretary of the Football Association. He had been the driving force behind the establishment of the FA Cup (first played the previous year, with the final at the Oval), and saw how important it was for sporting institutions to keep up with the times. One of the requirements for any competitive structure involving teams was a set of rules governing qualification, and in April he called a meeting at the Oval to revise the existing, ineffectual, regulations. Hitherto, a player had been allowed to represent both his county of birth *and* county of residence. The country's best slow bowler, James Southerton, turned out for Sussex and Surrey season after season, and though few others emulated him, it was obviously a loop-hole that needed to be closed. The new rule, for which Grace cast Gloucestershire's vote, stipulated that players would have to choose at the beginning of each season which county they would play for. In addition 'a *bona fide* residence of two years'[4] was laid down for both amateurs and professionals (a rule Grace was happy to accept, though equally happy to circumvent when it suited him).

The MCC at this stage saw the championship 'as nothing to do with them',[5] but they were not averse to cashing in on the burgeoning enthusiasm for inter-county cricket, and now came up with a forward-looking proposal, the Champion County Knock-out competition, in which all matches were to be played at Lord's. As it happened, there was only one match. Kent routed a Sussex team intimidated by the fast bowling of George Edward Coles operating on another lethal Lord's pitch, and the knock-out idea fell from favour for nearly a hundred years. Grace was certainly against it. This was probably because it had serious implications for the itinerant Elevens. As *Lillywhite's Companion* pointed out, professionals 'would not be able to make any definite arrangements at the beginning of the season without the risk of their being entirely upset by the result of the first round'.[6] The thought of having the smooth running of the United South programme disrupted in this way was enough to keep Grace and Gloucestershire out of the new competition, thus almost certainly guaranteeing its failure.

*

The Gloucestershire season started in May with what became a traditional encounter between the county eleven and a side of twenty-two Colts. The Colts did surprisingly well, scoring 132 and 134, while the seniors in their one innings mustered only 98, of which W.G. and E.M. made 24 and 22 respectively. Grace had another warm-up game, for the MCC against Hertfordshire at Chorleywood, and got his eye in with an innings of 47. He then went to Thame for the first of the United South's fixtures, against Twenty-Two of South Oxfordshire. The home team had taken the precaution of getting in four given men, which weighted the odds too heavily, and they won by 111 runs.

This unremarkable game is perhaps most noteworthy on account of the admission charges. Entry to a cricket ground normally cost sixpence; the promoters of the Thame match put it up to a shilling. The Prince brothers were also prepared to test the elasticity of demand by charging a shilling for Grace's first first-class game of the season, South v. North. The gamble paid off, and large crowds flocked in to see him score 68 in the second innings. The match was played for the benefit of the Cricketers' Fund, and *Scores and Biographies* gives an interesting breakdown of the monies involved. Total expenses were £135 (roughly £4,500 at 1998 values), £66 for the Northern Eleven and £40 for the South. The umpires were paid £4 each, the scorers shared £2, the telegraph man got ten shillings, while the money-takers and gatemen shared £7 10s. The police presence cost £3 and £1 17s 6d was spent on posters, with another five shillings going on stationery and postage. The balls cost £1 10s. The gate receipts were £276 (or around £10,000 in today's terms) and the fund benefited to the tune of £159 11s 11d.[7]

These figures show the sort of money generated by a match in which Grace was playing, and this season he exploited his earnings capacity with the United South to the full. He played sixteen matches for them, which given the amount of travelling involved speaks volumes for his stamina as well as his eye for the main chance. Although James Lillywhite continued as Secretary, W.G. and Fred virtually took over the team. W.G. was the star, but Fred probably had as much if not more to do with running the side. He hardly ever missed a match, and sometimes captained it in his brother's absence. Indeed, it was on occasion referred to as G. F. Grace's United South of England XI.

The 1870s were the twilight years of the travelling Elevens, and competition for fixtures increased. In Grace the United South obviously held the trump card, and they rapidly abandoned any pretence of regional affiliation, roaming far and wide into the traditional heartlands of the AEE and UAEE. The professionals who made up the United South team were happy to be dragged along in the Grace brothers' wake. They had to travel long distances, put up with indifferent accommodation and play on dubious wickets, but they did not have to over-exert themselves in the actual matches. W.G. and Fred were incapable of playing a game of pat-a-cake without straining every sinew to win it, and on the cricket field never relaxed for an instant. The pros were simply the supporting cast, content to go through the motions for a little extra money in their pockets.

At the end of May they went up to Edinburgh. On paper a team containing not only W.G. and Fred, but Richard Humphrey, Harry Jupp, Ned Pooley and James Lillywhite, looked strong enough to handle a local Eighteen. On the pitch it was a different story, and the crowds that packed into the Grange ground saw them dismissed for 90 and 60. Only Grace's two scores of 36 and 22 saved them from defeat and they scraped home by just sixteen runs, well within the allocated time.

With the match finishing early, they were forced to start another one. Grace remained good value to the end, opening his shoulders and hitting a rapid 47. This included three giant sixes, one of which was lofted to the left of the pavilion and must have seemed bound for the castle itself towering over long-on's shoulder. It was estimated to have carried 140 yards. Humphrey (29) and Jupp (23) made more modest contributions to a total of 166 before the usual turkey-shoot began. The Eighteen had made 33 for 9 by the time a halt was called and cabs rattled away to Waverley station for the long ride south.

The match ended on Saturday, 24 May. Whether he went home to Downend, or straight to London, Grace would have spent at least ten hours in a train. He then had Sunday in which to recuperate before turning up at Lord's to play for the MCC against Yorkshire on Monday (26 May). This was a short-lived affair on a rain-affected wicket, and the MCC won after an hour's play on the second morning. On Thursday Grace was half-way back up to Edinburgh again for a United South game against Eighteen of Darlington. Both he and Humphrey scored fifties, but Darlington won by thirty-one runs. The game ran its course over three days – 29, 30 and 31 May – and Grace was back at Lord's on Whit

Monday (2 June) for Wootton's benefit match, the return between North and South. There was a crowd of around 7,000 on the first day, but they had to wait until late in the afternoon to see Grace at the wicket. Their patience was rewarded with an explosive little cameo. W.G. opened with Jupp and between them they hit twelve runs from Alfred Shaw's first over and ten from Rylott's, and had taken the score to fifty in twenty-five minutes when Grace holed out for 37.

He knew the crowds came to see him demolish bowling attacks, and in benefit matches especially he was prepared to take risks to satisfy them. But with only one fifty from five first-class games, it was time to remind everyone of his true capabilities. On his return to Prince's for Gentlemen of the South v. Players of the North, he scored a peerless 145 out of 237. *The Times* noted his return to form: 'The batting of Mr WG Grace was the chief feature of the second day's play. He was at the wickets nearly four hours and a half . . . without giving a chance save that which was taken.'[8] The professional bowlers ranged against him were Alfred Shaw, J. C. Shaw, Alan Hill, William McIntyre and Tom Emmett, and they were far too good for the others. E.M. made 26 and the next highest score was Ottaway's 17. (Fred made a duck, caught and bowled Emmett.) Grace was last man out, and therefore ran all the 237 runs scored. In the second innings he failed, and the rest of the team went down like dominoes. Chasing 174 to win, they were all out for 62.

Gloucestershire's championship season started in the second week of June with a victory over Surrey at the Oval. Grace led from the front, putting on 156 with E.M. at better than a run a minute to lay the foundation for a total of 290. Fred then took five wickets as Surrey were dismissed for 131, and only Jupp's stubborn 83 in their second innings helped set Gloucestershire a target, but they made the required 135 for the loss of five wickets.

On the first afternoon of the match – Monday, 9 June – Alcock convened another meeting of the county representatives to finalize qualification rules. E.M and W.G. attended for Gloucestershire. The two principles established at the first meeting – that no cricketer should play for more than one county, and that players could choose between their county of birth and residence – were confirmed. Then, whether out of conviction or as a conciliatory gesture, Grace seconded a Nottinghamshire amendment that broadened the residence qualification to allow a cricketer 'to play for the county in which his family home is, so long as it remains open to him as an occasional residence'.[9] The proposals were forwarded to Lord's and adopted at a meeting of the MCC on 1 July.

One of the first cricketers affected by the new qualification rules was George Strachan, a useful all-rounder and brilliant fielder, who, faced with the choice between Gloucestershire and Surrey, opted for the latter, whom he later captained. Another player who would change allegiance was Grace's cousin, Walter Raleigh Gilbert. He started his career with Middlesex, but later moved to Gloucestershire. At nineteen he was already making a name for himself as 'a most excellent, steady batsman'.[10] He was also a brilliant out-fielder and an occasional bowler of slow round-arm. Grace, who had a good eye for young talent, and was naturally well disposed towards a member of the family, invited him to join the United South.

Gilbert made his debut for the team when he joined a short northern tour slotted into a twelve-day gap in W.G.'s first-class schedule. The first match was in Manchester against Broughton, and it clashed with a county game between Lancashire and Surrey at Old Trafford. This might have proved problematic for the Surrey wicket-keeper, Pooley, but he had just been suspended after what *Scores and Biographies* called 'an unfortunate dispute',[11] which may have involved 'laying a bet against his own side'.[12] The Surrey committee was sufficiently outraged to declare that he should not play for the United South until reinstated in the county side. Neither he nor Grace took a blind bit of notice, and he played at Broughton, executing a smart stumping off W.G.'s bowling to dismiss the home team's best batsman.

The crowds, which turned their back on Old Trafford in order to see the Champion, witnessed an exciting match, though Grace made only 4 in his first innings. The scores were close – Broughton 131, United South 149. W.G. and Fred took most of the wickets in the second innings, in which Broughton scraped to 98, and then Grace scored 45 to steer his side home by five wickets. As always, more was wanted, and it was agreed to play out the rest of the innings. The United South's professionals showed what they thought of overtime: the last five wickets fell for six runs.

Picking up reinforcements from the Surrey team that had been playing at Old Trafford, they crossed the Pennines to play Eighteen of Bradford. However, even with Humphrey, Jupp and Southerton restored to the side, they came close to humiliation. Bradford's given men were Alan Hill and George Ulyett, known as 'Happy Jack'. Ulyett bowled Grace for 2, and the whole of the side was skittled out for 30. The wicket was so bad that it was changed by agreement after the first innings. Even so, it was hardly what was expected of top professional cricketers, as Grace in all probability pointed out forcefully before their second innings. Typically he led the way with 27 and cousin Gilbert proved his worth with 47, while James Lillywhite hit an invaluable not out half century going in at number nine. They still lost – by nine wickets – but some credibility had been restored.

On returning south for the season's great matches, Grace hit a run of form that was impressive even by his own high standards. He went first to the Oval (where any remarks about fraternizing with the pariah Pooley doubtless fell on determinedly deaf ears) to play for Gentlemen of the South v. Players of the South. He was up against several of the men with whom he had just been playing – Jupp, Humphrey, Lillywhite, Southerton – and took the opportunity to remind them of the superior class that was guaranteeing a useful supplement to their wages. He scored 134 (including a cut and a drive for five apiece) out of only 185 made while he was at the crease, and with Fred contributing an aggressive 74 not out, the professionals were left facing a total of 339, which proved far beyond them.

That was the prelude to the three Gentlemen v. Players matches staged between 30 June and 18 July. The first was at Lord's. On a day 'by no means favourable to cricket'[13] Grace scored 163 (out of 315) including an all-run on-drive for seven. The Gentlemen won by an innings and fifty-five runs in two days. The second was at the Oval. Grace scored 158 (out of 330). The Gentlemen won by an innings and eleven runs in two days. W.G. also took 7 for 65 in the Players' second innings and four catches in the match. The third was at Prince's. Grace let the professionals off with a modest 70, but A. N. Hornby took up the baton as century-maker with 104, while Fred brought the family contribution to over three figures with 63 out of a total of 313. As though to make up for his relative failure with the bat, Grace opened the bowling for the Gentlemen, taking three of the four wickets to fall before stumps, and finishing with 5 for 62 in the first innings. When the Players followed on, Fred took six wickets to clinch the Gentlemen's third victory, by an innings and fifty-four runs. It was a fitting way to mark Grace's twenty-fifth birthday. In the three matches he had scored 391 runs at an average of 130 – or 42 per cent of his side's runs from the bat. He had had one outrageous stroke of luck during this demonstration of unprecedented mastery. In the Oval match he hit the second ball he received from Emmett firmly onto his stumps. The bails stayed put, and he compounded the bowler's grief by hitting his next three overs for twenty-five.

There had been another, more serious, check to W.G.'s royal progress over the period of the three Gentlemen–Players matches. In the gap between the games at Prince's and the Oval (7, 8 and 9 July), Grace took a United South side to Leicester and was bowled for a duck by a journeyman professional called Fred Randon. The rest of the United South team, who had probably been anticipating an undemanding day in the vicinity of the beer tent, were hustled out in quick succession for 76. Grace worked off his feelings with a long spell of bowling which brought him 9 for 70. When he batted a second time he began warily, obviously intent on exacting retribution. However, after scoring just eight runs, he let another delivery from Randon through his famed defence.* Fred made 53, but got little support, and the team registered another defeat.

The United South's next match took them further north to play Twenty-two of Wakefield, strengthened by Greenwood, Lockwood and the long-suffering Emmett, who must have enjoyed the Randon story. There was to be no repeat. Grace scored 20 and the highest score of the match, 51, which secured victory by eight wickets.

At the beginning of the third week of July, Grace returned to Lord's for a reunion of Fitzgerald's tourists. It had been hoped that a Canadian team would come over to play them, but when this fell through a match against an MCC XV with Rylott was arranged. As an odds match it should not have counted as first-class, but for Grace – and for no one else playing on either side – it did count, and the century he scored was added to his growing tally of three-figure scores (see Appendix, page 499). *The Times* was unimpressed, declaring the game devoid of interest, though it produced some excellent cricket and a marvellously exciting finish. The MCC team had some talented cricketers, including Fred, who opened the bowling for them. Fred played more cricket with his brother than anybody, and very rarely played against him. When he did, he found it no easier going than anyone else. On this occasion he came off second best, as W.G. set the pace in an opening stand of 117 with his old partner Ottaway, before going on to reach 152. Fred's figures were 2 for 96.

The rest of the match produced high drama with a touch of low farce

* Randon did get some deserved recognition. He played twice for Leicestershire against the MCC later in the season, taking twenty wickets in the two games, and the following year was employed as a ground bowler at Lord's.

138

reminiscent of the Canadian trip. After reducing the MCC to 82 for 10, the tourists let the number thirteen, F. Tillyard Esq., hit 92 and suddenly found their anticipated first-innings lead whittled down to sixty-one. When they batted again, Ottaway was 'absent (unwell)'; Grace failed, and a flurry of wickets followed. Alfred Lubbock was hauled out of the tennis court to shore up the innings with Fitzgerald, who was so lame he had to have Lord Harris as a runner. That came to a predictably sorry end when Harris set off for a suicidal single, but not before the total had reached a respectable 139, setting the MCC a target of just over 200. Appleby reproduced his tour form and ripped out the top order, but the MCC rallied and with the last man, Rylott, at the crease got surprisingly close. In the end the tourists won, but only by a margin of twenty-four in a game that produced 1,036 runs.

Grace's festival of high scoring continued in his next match. The northern professionals must have cursed the fixture list that pitted the North against the South once more at the Oval. Did the great man never tire? The answer was the largest of his season's six centuries, 192 not out, during which he ran all of the 311 runs of the South's innings. He was twice dropped before fifty and again on 143, but apart from these lapses he batted with Olympian authority, hitting seven fives, eight fours, fifteen threes, sixteen twos and forty-eight singles in an innings of five hours in hot sunshine. The heat was so great that Ephraim Lockwood got sunstroke and had to go home. Tom Emmett slaved away with only the scant consolation of bowling Fred. The South won by an innings and fifty-eight runs, W.G. taking the last two wickets in a spell of 4 for 20 in the North's second innings. This 'very hollow victory'[14] took just two days, and on the third day the two sides staged a meaningless exhibition match for the sake of the Oval coffers. Needless to say, Grace both bowled and batted with gusto. There really was no limit to his appetite for the game.

It was now time for the controversial benefit match at Sheffield, and Grace must have been as pleased as Rowbotham at the vast numbers that thronged through the Bramall Lane gates: 12,000 packed the ground on the first day (Monday), followed by 7,000 and 4,000 on the Tuesday and Wednesday, 'one of the greatest demonstrations' of Grace's popularity.[15] Emmett wasn't playing. There was, perhaps, only so much flesh and blood could take. He was well out of it. To the delight of the crowd, encroaching 'within thirty yards of the wicket'[16] at some points, Grace progressed easily to his fifty, and looked a safe bet for another century when Ulyett had him caught for 79. Yorkshire were skittled out for 113, the beneficiary succumbing contentedly to W.G. Although they performed better in their second innings, they were never in the hunt, and Gloucestershire took the game by six wickets, while Rowbotham could rejoice in a wonderfully successful benefit.

There was a week's respite for the northern bowlers during which W.G. and Fred took part in an extraordinary match between MCC and Surrey. Fred mysteriously turned out for Surrey (so much for the new qualification rules) and thus came up against W.G. for the second time in a month. This time Grace had him stumped as one of his three victims in Surrey's second innings, and Fred provided more ammunition for brotherly chaff when he dropped a catch on the boundary that allowed W.G. and the number eleven to sneak home by a single wicket chasing the tiny total of 55.

Most of the usual cast reassembled at Canterbury for the fourth match of the season between North and South. For once Grace failed to score a century, dismissed on 98. And after all the fruitless overs he'd sent down at the Champion during the previous few weeks, Tom Emmett was the lucky bowler. But the South still scored 369, and won by seven wickets.

The North had batted first, and during their innings W.G. indulged in a little festival pantomime. At the fall of a wicket he borrowed the not out batsman's bat and got Lord Harris to bowl to him. This was technically a violation of Law 47 which stated that 'when one of the strikers shall have been put out the use of the bat shall not be allowed to *any* person until the next striker shall come in'. But then Grace was not 'any person', and neither was Lord Harris. In the years ahead he would become the most dominant figure in the MCC since Lord Frederick Beauclerk. This harmless schoolboy diversion called forth surprisingly weighty reproofs from the press. *The Times* called it 'a ridiculous sort of by play', saying it could not be 'too severely reprehended, as it is not only bad as an example, but in open violation of the laws of the Marylebone Club'.[17] The *Sporting Life* was even more vehement, reporting that the Canterbury Week Secretary, Mr de Chair Baker, who was no stranger to controversy involving members of the Grace family, had 'expressed his entire disapprobation of such a proceeding, and regretted that the classic ground of St Lawrence should have been disgraced in such a manner'.[18] Mr Baker obviously failed to convey his disapprobation strongly enough because Grace repeated 'his objectionable practice' the next day. The *Sporting Life* again condemned him:

As a member of the Marylebone Club, and coming prominently before the public as perhaps the first cricketer of the day, Mr Gilbert Grace should be the last person to violate the laws of cricket, and in their interests, and for the sake of cricketers in general, who may easily be led away by bad example, we trust he will never be so forgetful and so deliberate in breaking them. In Australia, in particular, we hope he will be careful to avoid such practices.[19]

Grace took no notice, and continued to enjoy the week very much on his own terms. He dominated the next match, Gentlemen of MCC v. Kent, though less with the bat (1 and 57) than with the ball. This was a twelve-a-side match, and in Kent's first innings he took 5 for 55 and then replicated E.M.'s feat of 1862 by taking ten wickets in their second innings. His analysis read: 46.1–15–92–10. He continued bowling well when Gloucestershire resumed their county programme. He took 4 for 88 against Yorkshire at Clifton, and though he failed with the bat, Fred made a magnificent 165 and E.M. hit 64 in a daunting total of 404. Tom Emmett obviously decided that batting was a more rewarding occupation than bowling, and hit out for a defiant century. For once the tables were turned as he slogged Grace's bowling around the ground, but the Champion got him in the end, and the home team won by five wickets.

From Clifton, W.G. went down to Portsmouth where he scored 49 for the United South against Twenty-two of East Hampshire. E.M., whose responsibilities now only allowed him to play Saturday club cricket between county games, spent a merciless afternoon amassing 259 not out in a hundred minutes for Thornbury. The two brothers were reunited for the second Clifton match, the return against Surrey. They opened together on a dull, unpleasant morning, and W.G. may have had to stroke a rare smile away into his beard when the terror of the local clubs was bamboozled by Southerton into hitting his wicket for a duck. In an unlikely coincidence, Grace followed suit, hitting the wicket so hard that he 'knocked a stump clean out of the ground'.[20] He had, however, scored 48 before it happened, and in the second innings he produced a majestic display of 160 not out. William Caffyn, who had played in the first match Grace ever watched back in 1854, was making his last appearance for Surrey, and ended his first-class career caught Fred, bowled W.G. for 25. The Surrey game was drawn, and so was the last match against Sussex at Cheltenham. E.M. and W.G. put on 113 for the first wicket, and Frank Townsend followed that with a century, but rain prevented a finish. Gloucestershire finished the season unbeaten, with four wins. As

Nottinghamshire had won five matches and lost one, the two counties came out joint champions. Grace's peremptory behaviour at the start of the season had, it turned out, scotched the championship decider. His only comment in *Reminiscences* is that 'The Gloucestershire team consisted entirely of amateurs, while the Nottingham Eleven was composed of professionals.'[21]

While the Nottinghamshire professionals were scraping the mud from their boots and putting their pads away for the winter, Gloucestershire's indefatigable amateur was embarking on one last expedition with the United South. At the beginning of September they were at Lincoln where they won by 122 runs, with W.G. and Fred scoring 71 and 41 and Southerton completely mesmerizing the local Twenty-two. The USEE then travelled nearly five hundred miles to Inverness, where it was no surprise to find the 'wicket almost unplayable'.[22] The match was abandoned without a result. W.G.'s enthusiasm was undiminished, if uninfectious. While the professionals mooched around in the mud doing the bare minimum, he top-scored in the United South's only completed innings with 36 out of 79, and snapped up eight catches at point when the Twenty-two of Northern Scotland batted.

This Scottish adventure was set up by Fred, who had been registered as a medical student at Aberdeen the previous year. Their next match took them to Aberdeen itself to play Twenty-Two of the Scottish North Eastern Counties. The weather was kinder than in Inverness, and although it was cold with the occasional shower, there was a good crowd. The band of the Royal Aberdeenshire Highlanders was also present to add to the atmosphere. The United South batted first, and the home side filed onto the field looking more like a rugby team than cricketers in their new shirts of black, blue and yellow stripes. His way to the boundary cut off by this colourful picket line, Grace opted for the aerial route. After a few sighters he 'stepped out to one of Craig's balls, and picking it up in his usual style, drove it right out of the ground for six'.[23] This was what the spectators had come to see, but it was risky. Jupp, Humphrey and Gilbert collected three runs between them trying the same approach, and Grace himself, after a couple of chances, was finally well caught for 28. Fred hit the top score of 30 in similar vein, but the side was dismissed for 96 on the first day.

The Twenty-two had overhauled this by stumps, ending the day on 100 for 12, and the following morning they reached 135. Trailing by thirty-nine, the visitors needed a good start, but first Jupp and then Grace himself fell early to good catches off Craig. Humphrey made 32, including a six into the neighbouring turnip field, but only Gilbert (21) and Fred (22) gave much support, and they were all out for 102, leaving the Scots sixty-four to win. They were made to work hard for it, and on the third morning of the match, under the watchful eye of W.G. at point, lost wicket after wicket while the telegraph appeared to stand still. At 45 for 13 it looked anybody's match. In the end they scraped home by six wickets. It was a fine achievement, though the *Aberdeen Journal* got a little carried away in describing Grace's band of mercenaries as 'the best Eleven of England'. As usual when a game ended early, more cricket was demanded. Grace obliged and hit up a few runs, but when he was out he packed his bags and headed for the station, leaving the rest of the side to go through the motions until time ran out. Presumably he slipped away early in order to spend the Sunday with Agnes, who must, by now, have realized what she was letting herself in for.

However Grace spent his Sunday, on Monday morning (15 September) he was in Northampton to lead his travel-weary troops against a local Eighteen. There wasn't much of a battle on the pitch, but Grace got into a fight off it. The United South batted first, and Grace was not out at lunch, after which rain set in. According to the local paper, 'Play was not again resumed till half past four'.[24] A shooting gallery had been set up just outside the ground, and Grace went off to while away the idle hours. At some stage the rain must have stopped, and one of the bystanders, a builder from the town, obviously thought the game should be resumed. He came up to Grace and enquired officiously, 'Why don't you go and play cricket, keeping the crowd waiting like you are doing?' In the heated exchange that ensued he struck W.G. in the face, cutting it with his ring. While not exactly offering the other cheek, Grace disentangled himself without retaliating, but when Fred saw the blood and asked who had hit him, he indicated 'that cad over there against the entrance'. Fred said, 'If you don't go and give him a good hiding, I shall,' so Grace strode across and laid into him 'with sledge-hammer blows', blacking both his eyes. He then went out on to the field to resume his innings as though nothing had happened, to loud applause from the crowd.[25] The incident was kept quiet at the time, though the *Northampton Herald* made a reference to injuries inflicted on spectators as the players practised. The full details only came to light this century when an eye-witness sent an account of the fight to the local paper.

The actual cricket was rather less dramatic. Once again the United

South's batting relied almost entirely on the two brothers. Grace scored 45 out of 102 in the first innings, and Fred made 44 not out in the second in which the rest of the side managed only forty-two more runs between them. The Eighteen knocked off the small deficit, winning the match by fifteen wickets. The game was again held up 'for some considerable time' over the lunch interval on the third day when Grace held a meeting for the seven professionals who had agreed to tour Australia with him. They met the Australian agent and signed the articles of agreement covering the terms of their service. Among those who signed was the Northamptonshire given man, Martin McIntyre, a fast bowler like his brother, William. He had taken a number of wickets in the match in progress and also hit the top score of 30 in the Eighteen's first innings.

Though autumn was now setting in, Grace was not finished with the United South yet. Their next endurance test was a three-day match in Dublin against Twenty-two of the Leinster Club on 18, 19 and 20 September. Most of the professionals had clearly reached the end of their tether by this stage, and only Grace and Fred, supported by Southerton and Lillywhite, produced any worthwhile cricket. W.G. scored 36 out of 95 and 40 out of 159, while Fred top-scored with 54. The Dubliners batted with great application to reach a total of 212. James Lillywhite bowled 164 balls for sixty-four runs and Southerton 285 balls for eighty-one. The home side was less successful in their second innings, and although chasing a total of only 43 to win, were in dire straits at 13 for 6 when time ran out.

There was one last revenue-raising fixture. This was at least back on home territory. On 22, 23 and 24 September they played Twenty-two of the New Cross Albion Club in south London. Grace made a fine 91 out of 211, and then, after Lillywhite and Southerton had bowled the locals out for 73, joined forces with Fred to bowl them out again for 99. As the game finished early, a single-wicket match was arranged for the third day. Releasing the rest of the side, who may well have been on the point of packing their bags and going home anyway, Grace teamed up with cousin Gilbert and Henry Charlwood against twelve of the local team. W.G. made four out of the six runs scored and then took nine wickets for eight runs in 117 deliveries when the Twelve had their innings. However pointless the exercise, he always tried.

The United South's record was not a particularly glorious one. According to *Lillywhite's Companion*, they played fifteen matches, won five, lost seven and drew three. The *Companion* credits Grace with 825 runs at an average of 26.19. (These figures include the 47 he scored in the second game against the Gentlemen of Edinburgh in May, but unaccountably leave out the fixture at Bradford in June which again required a supplementary exhibition match. Grace batted three times, raising his aggregate to 926 runs.) Fred followed him with 451 runs at 18.1, and Gilbert was third with 229 at 14.5. There were only three more averages in double figures. The United South's bowling was more impressive. James Lillywhite took 165 wickets at 6.57, Southerton 93 at 5.17, Grace 91 at 6.28 and Fred 57 at 7.2.[26] It is significant that W.G. and Fred, who had most to gain financially, were the only members of the team, apart from the two professional bowlers, who really pulled their weight. Grace clearly had difficulties in motivating the rest of the team. As the Australian tour was to prove, man-management was not his strong suit.

He still had one last engagement. Right at the end of September, he took a W. G. Grace XI down to Gravesend to play a benefit match for George Bennett. He was bowled by Willsher for 2 in the first innings, but made amends in the second with a characteristic 69 not out. He also had the distinction of dismissing two Lords – Lord Clifton and Lord Harris – in his spell of 5 for 33. Harris had a wretched game. He was barracked for dropping a catch and thereafter 'hooted and hissed if he made the slightest mistake'.[27] The match, which the visitors won by seven wickets, ended on 27 September, leaving Grace just under a month to make the final arrangements for the Australian tour – and get married.

ELEVEN

THE idea of getting Grace to go to Australia had been floated early in 1872 when the Melbourne Cricket Club wrote to him to find out what his terms might be. Grace's demand for a personal fee of £1,500 'startled' the Melbourne committee, as well it might. Today's equivalent would be about £50,000, and for a contemporary yardstick, the Lord's gate receipts for 1872 came to £3,047 8s.[1] This unheard-of figure also dampened the enthusiasm of the South Australia Cricket Association, which had shown an initial interest.[2] The Australians decided they could not afford Grace, and yet it would have been absurd to bring out a team without him. The plan was shelved.

But the need for a tour became more pressing. It was ten years since Parr's side had made the trip, and the Australian domestic game required some outside stimulation. Once again Grace was approached; once again he replied that he was willing to come. His personal fee remained £1,500, but his life had become more complicated with his engagement to be married in the autumn. Characteristically he turned this potential problem to his advantage. As he complacently puts it in his *Reminiscences*, 'The future Mrs Grace . . . consented to our marriage taking place a few weeks before the date of departure for Australia, so that the tour might be regarded as an extension of our honeymoon.'[3] And who should pay for the honeymoon? Those who wanted him to come to Australia. The tour promoters, a syndicate of Melbourne Cricket Club members, found him no more flexible than anyone else did, and eventually agreed to cover travel costs and expenses for himself and Agnes – in addition, of course, to the original £1,500. The future Mrs Grace probably didn't take much persuading, if indeed she was given any choice in the matter at all. A first-class trip to Australia was an exciting prospect, especially as it would provide a rare opportunity to spend an extended period with a husband whose lifestyle was obviously going to keep him away from home for a sizeable proportion of every year for the foreseeable future.

Grace had the whole season in which to recruit his tour party, but he encountered the usual frustrations. He had 'great hopes' of persuading William Yardley and A. N. Hornby to make the trip, but they dropped out. As for the leading professionals, 'I invited Tom Emmett and Alfred Shaw to include themselves in my combination, but neither could comply with my request.'[4] This bland statement makes no suggestion as to why they turned him down, but the answer is pretty straightforward. Despite his own princely fee, the terms he was offering were niggardly. The professionals would get a basic £150, plus twenty pounds' spending money, 'to play in 14 Cricket matches at such times and places as the said William Gilbert Grace shall from time to time direct'. The Articles of Agreement also stipulated that each player

hereby agrees during such period as foresaid to place himself under the entire disposal and directions of the said William Gilbert Grace and to obey all his orders and to play in each of the aforesaid 14 Cricket matches if required by the said William Gilbert Grace so to do and the said Cricketer hereby agrees with the said William Gilbert Grace that he will not play in any other Cricket match or Cricket matches than those authorized by the said William Gilbert Grace or engage in any other pursuit without the consent in writing of the said William Gilbert Grace first obtained until the fourteen matches have been played.

In return,

The said William Gilbert Grace hereby agrees to provide for the said Cricketer a free second class passage to Australia and back to England by one of the Peninsular and Oriental Steam Company's Vessels and to provide Hotel accommodation and to pay all travelling and other expenses during the said engagement except wines spirits and other liquors but hereby agrees to pay the said Cricketer the sum of £20 towards his expenses as for wines spirits and other liquors . . .[5]

Grace was a great man for the small print.

Possibly to W.G.'s relief, the tempestuous Pooley also found the terms unacceptable, so the wicket-keeping duties fell to his friend and Gloucestershire wicket-keeper, Arthur Bush. Although the process made him 'heartweary',[6] Grace finally mustered eleven intrepid cricketers who agreed to follow him through thick and thin: Fred, Walter Gilbert, J. A. Bush, F. H. Boult, Arthur Greenwood, Richard Humphrey, Harry Jupp, James Lillywhite, Martin McIntyre, William Oscroft and James Southerton. Including Grace himself there were five amateurs (all from Gloucestershire apart from Gilbert, who later joined the family shire) and seven professionals. This was the first mixed touring team, and the divide, which opened when the professionals disappeared into the second-class cabins on the lower decks, would provide a constant source of friction throughout the tour.

It was obviously a risk to take only twelve players for a trip scheduled to last three months, but Grace and the promoters were keen to produce the maximum profit. It would be hard work for all of them, especially the bowlers, Lillywhite and the forty-six-year-old Southerton. But the greatest burden, of course, fell on Grace himself. Not only was he required to play in all the matches, but in the absence of a manager he had to bear the full responsibility for the day-to-day running of the tour, from travel arrangements to public relations.

But before Grace set sail into the unknown, he had to embark on another uncertain venture – marriage. By modern standards, the Victorians enjoyed almost total freedom from press intrusion. Just as Grace's public brawl at Northampton was kept out of the papers, so his wedding, despite his fame, was not perceived as newsworthy at all. There was simply an announcement in the Marriages column of *The Times*:

On 9th Oct., at the Church of St Matthias', West Brompton, by the Rev. John Dann, M.A., brother-in-law of the bridegroom, assisted by the Rev S. C. Haines, M.A., Vicar, and the Rev. A. J. N. Macdonald, WILLIAM GILBERT GRACE, fourth son of the late Henry Mills Grace, M.R.C.S. LOND., of Downend, Gloucestershire, to AGNES NICHOLLS DAY, daughter of William Day, 19 Coherne-road, S.W. No cards.[7]

Arthur Bush was best man. Grace obviously regarded him as a safe pair of hands.

There was little notice taken of the coming tour either, and Grace was allowed to complete his preparations without being pestered by the press. Instead of getting down to furnishing their first home, the newly-weds had to set about shopping and packing for a honeymoon on the other side of the globe. The Australian sunshine must have seemed particularly desirable as the English autumn turned malicious. Howling winds and drenching rain made their last few days dismal, and boded ill for a bad sailor like Grace.

On Wednesday, 22 October the Graces travelled down to South-ampton from London accompanied by a group of cricketing acquaintances, including Charles Alcock. They were met by 'a party of Gloucestershire friends, consisting of my mother, Mrs Gilbert, Colonel

Bush (Mr J.A. Bush's father), and my old schoolfellow, Jack Lloyd . . .'[8] E.M. was too busy to attend the farewell dinner, but no doubt sent appropriate good wishes.

On the following morning – Thursday, 23 October – before the team sailed, they were entertained to breakfast by the captain of their ship, the P&O liner the *Mirzapore*. Replying to the toast, 'The Australian Twelve – a pleasant voyage and a safe return', Grace said that they 'had a duty to perform to maintain the honour of English cricket, and to uphold the high character of English cricketers'.[9] They then repaired to the dock and were taken out to the ship. It was some time before anyone noticed that they were a man short. Harry Jupp had a marked partiality for alcohol and had overslept, but Alcock was equal to the crisis and, descending a rope ladder 'at some personal risk', jumped into a small boat and made for the shore. He was not having a Surrey player letting the side down, and bundled the bleary-eyed opening batsman 'into the tug with the mails'.[10]

Having avoided losing a key player at the outset, the tourists settled down to the long voyage. This was 'an even more formidable undertaking in the seventies than it is now,' Grace wrote twenty years later. 'We were fifty-two days on shipboard before we reached Australia.'[11] Grace filled some of the interminable hours by keeping a diary. Where the original manuscript ended up is something of a mystery, but several secondary sources quote from it, and Brownlee obviously had access to it when he wrote his biography of Grace. James Southerton also kept a diary (now preserved at Trent Bridge), and there were detailed accounts of the tour in both Lillywhite almanacks the following year. Fred is usually credited with the one in *John Lillywhite's Companion*, while presumably James Lillywhite wrote the report in his own *Annual*. Grace was hardly a rival to Boswell, but his brief jottings do give a pointer to how he was feeling. As on the Atlantic crossing the year before, he suffered badly from sea-sickness:

October 24th. – Not at all right; never turned out – sympathy below.
25th. – Dinner on deck; beginning to crawl.

They negotiated the Bay of Biscay without suffering the anticipated horrors, and marked their arrival at Gibraltar with modest celebrations: '[Oct] 27th. piano on deck; small dance.' The worst still lay before them. They ran into a terrible storm in the Mediterranean – torrential rain, thunder and lightning, followed by gale force winds. '[T]wo or three hundred plates and saucers smashed', Grace noted grimly. They reached the haven of Malta on Saturday, 1 November and attended a reception at the United Service Club. Grace perked up: 'On board ship again. Leap-frog and boxing; nearly killed one of the team!'[12]

At Alexandria, the British Consul tried to persuade them to play a cricket match, but Grace had developed a strong aversion to the Egyptian port and had no desire to risk being stranded there. Everyone was eager to see the Suez Canal, which had been opened just four years earlier, but it turned out to be a disappointment. '[I]n those days ships did not use search-lights, and could consequently only steam through the Canal by daylight – pulling up at night till dawn.' As a result their 'progress through the canal was tediously slow, and we soon got tired of the monotonous stretches of sand which meet the eye on both sides.'[13]

Grace was bored. Not even the luxury of a first-class cabin and the joys of young married love could alleviate the tedium of enforced physical inactivity. There was nothing to shoot. The puerile deck games soon palled, and everyone suddenly remembered unfinished letters home when he appeared hopefully dangling his boxing gloves. Still, he contrived to drop a line over the side to tempt the sluggish fish.

The rest of the team were affected too. It was a dangerous time, when tempers were short and idleness provoked mischief. There was an unpleasant incident involving another passenger, an unprepossessing Scot, who had been very sea-sick for most of the voyage. He was much fussed over by some of the female passengers, but his misinterpretation of their motives resulted in a humiliation which in turn led to his retiring to his cabin and playing his bagpipes dolefully through the long airless nights. Patience finally ran out, and, Brownlee reported, 'one of the team . . . seized the largest water-jug, poured the contents through an opening, and drenched the little man'. He took it badly, and catching Fred smiling, said, 'Mr Grace, you are no gentleman!' This was a mistake. '[B]acked by the real offender, Fred gave him till sunset to apologise – or take a thrashing. He looked at sky, and sea; into human eyes, but could see neither sympathy nor help.' After a long and lonely day the unhappy man duly apologized.[14]

Apart from baiting fellow passengers, the amateur members of the team also amused themselves by pursuing the various women on board. 'There was witching moonlight about this time and music, dancing, and quiet walking and talking with the fair sex became prevalent. Tennyson, Longfellow, and Shelley were committed in the morning to be whispered to willing ears and throbbing hearts in the evening.'[15] With Agnes by his side, Grace had no need of poetry. He preferred cards. But here again his intense competitiveness soon came up against the law of diminishing returns. After a few pocket-emptying rounds of whist, Grace found himself shuffling the pack on his own.

The ship's progress was painfully slow. They ran into fog. Then the captain took the ship 'the wrong side of a buoy' and they were 'stuck in the mud [for] the best part of the day'. Eventually they passed through the canal and the voyage picked up momentum once more. They reached Galle Harbour on the southern coast of Ceylon on 23 November. There they had to 'tranship' to the *Nubia*, 'a smaller steamer, with which we were not at first prepossessed, but which took us safely and comfortably to Melbourne.'[16] They made their first landing at King George's Sound, Western Australia, on 8 December, and went on shore for a few hours while the ship was coaling.

Grace's first act on Australian soil was to narrowly miss decapitating his cousin with a boomerang. It was the start of an eventful three months.

TWELVE

THE boomerang incident occurred on the local cricket ground where the Englishmen were welcomed by a group of Aborigines who put on a display of 'native sports' for them. Always prepared to have a go, W.G. tried his hand with a boomerang, 'but failed again and again'. He then got it right and the weapon suddenly 'flew away down the . . . ground, fell a few yards in front of one of the players, took a second flight with increased velocity, and just missed the head of one of the members of the team. It was a narrow escape, as another foot would have involved an inquest.'[1] Having avoided the attentions of the local coroner, Walter Gilbert must have welcomed the brief cricket practice that followed. Grace was marginally less dangerous with a bat in his hand. Martin McIntyre even managed to bowl him for the first time in his career.

It took them six more days to reach Melbourne, but they made good time and arrived earlier than expected. A reception committee of dignitaries, along with leading figures in Victorian cricket, hurried onto a steamer and met the *Nubia* before she docked. Grace's distinctive figure was immediately recognized at the rail. They gave three cheers, which the tourists returned with gusto. Once ashore, Mr McArthur, president of the Melbourne Cricket Club, offered the Graces his carriage, and the rest of the team went by coach-and-four to the Port Phillip Hotel. A large crowd turned out, eager to see the heroes they had been reading about in the papers for weeks. They were not disappointed. The cricketers were reported to be 'in fine fettle' and 'the champion himself looks splendidly, and is a fine strapping muscular young Englishman; and McIntyre, the fast bowler of the team, is also a good specimen of strength and activity'.[2] However, the Port Phillip represented the parting of the ways for these two examples of English manhood, McIntyre going on with his fellow professionals to less salubrious quarters at the White Hart. This produced widespread comment in the press: 'In the colonies I have always been led to believe that the cricket-field levels all social distinctions, but in England . . . a line is drawn between gentlemen and professionals, and in many cases the latter are made to feel their social position somewhat acutely.' Rumours of 'some unpleasantness' between the two camps quickly spread.[3]

Not that the Australians were without their own problems, as the English contingent would see for themselves that afternoon. After lunch Grace and Agnes were driven to the South Melbourne ground where the home team was playing the Melbourne Cricket Club in the Challenge Cup Final. The game was held up while W.G. and the other tourists were formally welcomed in front of the pavilion amid excited cheering from around the ground. Grace made a brief speech, but urged that play should continue so that he could see what they would be up against when they met Victoria in a fortnight's time. As the visitors settled down to watch the game, one of the local officials commented proudly on the the good humour of the spectators and praised their impartiality and sportsmanship, a remark he was soon to regret.

Among those taking part in the final were two men with whom Grace would have much to do in the future. One was John Conway, the South Melbourne captain; the other was Billy Midwinter, a large-framed man of over six feet who had been born in the Forest of Dean before being brought out to Australia as a child. Grace could not have known he was looking at a fellow countryman, let alone a future member of his own county team, but he would have been impressed with Midwinter's batting when he opened the innings for South Melbourne as they set out to get the 150 they needed to win the cup. He was shaping well for a good score when he was run out. More wickets followed, including a dubious lbw off the old Surrey medium-pacer Sam Cosstick, who was now the Melbourne CC professional.

Betting was still rife in Australian cricket and a great deal of money was resting on the outcome of the match. The South Melbourne supporters' good humour and impartiality came under increasing pressure as their team got to within twenty runs of the target with two wickets standing. Tension was rising steadily when there was a close call for a run out. The batsman, Albert Major, was deemed to have made his ground. Gibson, the Melbourne captain and wicket-keeper, threw the ball down in disgust, but rapidly retrieved it when Major wandered out of his ground to get his breath back and confer with his partner. Whipping the bails off a second time, Gibson appealed again, and the umpire, clearly intimidated, gave Major out.

All hell broke loose. Stones rained onto the pitch closely followed by sections of the crowd, determined that the batsman should be reinstated. Play was suspended, and the only hope for a resumption was an agreement between the captains. Conway wouldn't go on without Major, Gibson wouldn't allow him back to the crease, and the game was abandoned amid scenes of chaos. It needed a police escort to get the visiting Melbourne team out of the ground, and even then they were chased down the road by a mob of 'roughs and larrikins who followed them . . . hooting and pelting them'. The incident caused a huge stir, and the visitors were invited to arbitrate. Grace was reluctantly dragged into the controversy, and his mouthpiece was the cricketing cleric Revd Walter Fellows (brother of Harvey Fellows the fast under-arm bowler), who informed the *Australasian*: 'I have talked the matter over with Mr W. G. Grace, and we are unanimous in our opinion that the decision of the umpire is final, and that Mr Major was out . . .' For good measure, Grace added, 'I quite agree with Mr Fellows.' Other members of the touring party took a different line. Southerton thought the ball was clearly dead and that it was 'sharp practice' on Gibson's part to have made a second run-out appeal.[4] It was by no means the last divergence of opinion on the trip.

The riot at the South Melbourne ground had further ramifications. The players for the Victorian team would largely be chosen from the ranks of the two feuding clubs, and the fracas poisoned the selection process. The animosity between Conway and Gibson was such that when they met on the street they nearly came to blows with their umbrellas and were only separated by the friends they were with. One local paper remarked, 'these assaults are becoming rather too common, and unless the leading clubs take some action to effectually repress them, cricketers will have to go down to practice armed with bowie knives and revolvers'.[5]

Meanwhile, the English party were settling in and looking around them. Melbourne was an exciting city, riding high in its roller-coaster cycle of boom and bust. Money poured in from the goldfields, and Victoria's capital was confidently emerging from the shadow of its great rival, Sydney. A journalist pointed to the city's building programme as a barometer of its prosperity: 'The warehouses are bigger and the dwellings more comfortable than those which would have contented us in old days. Visitors to Sydney used to return surprised at the number of handsome houses, standing in well-kept grounds, unlike any to be found near Melbourne. Now we see mansions of the same kind rising in our own suburbs.'[6] Extravagance was the hallmark of 'Marvellous Melbourne', and that extended to its hospitality. The Englishmen, struggling to find their land legs after their long voyage, were inundated with invitations. On the Tuesday after their arrival they were given a champagne reception by the mayor, and then moved on from the town hall to go and drink more champagne at a party thrown by one of the city's leading wool merchants. According to the *Australasian*, only the Graces, Boult and Gilbert showed up for practice that afternoon.

The facilities at the Melbourne Cricket Ground were poor. Grace was worried at the lack of preparations for the big match only a few days ahead, and was appalled when the groundsman told him, 'we'll select a pitch and put the roller on it on the morning of the match, and that will be all right'. This was not good enough for Grace, and in one of his few diplomatic successes of the tour, he persuaded the Club authorities to allow him a hand in the preparations. Years later he wrote, 'I take upon myself the credit of having shown the Australians how to prepare a wicket.'[7]

The practice sessions were open to the public. There was a widely believed rumour that Grace had backed himself to get through the tour without being bowled. In a betting culture like Melbourne's, this could only heighten interest in the champion, and there was always a crowd several deep around his net. In Australia, as in England, anyone was permitted to have a bowl at the stars, and the story of how a slight saturnine stranger from New South Wales ran up and scattered the great man's stumps is still confidently repeated to this day. The source of this tale was the protagonist himself, Frederick Robert Spofforth:

I had a lark with the Old Man at the nets. In those days, though I stood six feet three inches, I only weighed ten stone six. But I could bowl faster than any man in the world. W.G. was at the nets at Melbourne and I lolled up two or three balls in a funny slow way. Two or three of those round asked: 'What's the matter with you, Spoff?' I replied: 'I am going to have a rise out of that W.G.' Suddenly I sent him down one of my very fastest. He lifted his bat half up in his characteristic way, but down went his off stump, and he called out in his quick fashion when not liking anything: 'Where did that come from? Who bowled that?' But I slipped away, having done my job.[8]

The details are all convincing, especially Grace's querulous 'Who bowled that?', but, for all its artistic authenticity, the story isn't true. At the time Spofforth was on holiday in Tasmania with his brother, and the cricket historian Ric Finlay has established that they were on the island 'for the whole period from 18 December 1873 to 12 January 1874'.[9] There is no evidence that Spofforth made the lengthy and costly crossing to Melbourne to unleash his legendary delivery.

Harry Boyle, who would soon become Spofforth's great partner in destruction, certainly was there and perhaps his account of his first sight of W.G. was the inspiration for Spofforth's venture into historical fiction. Boyle, however, did not bowl at Grace, but merely stood stroking his beard and watching. He is said to have remarked, 'If I could get a ball in between his leg and the wicket, I could get him,' which suggests he was thinking of exploiting Grace's trademark push off his legs to mid-wicket. Boyle was a dangerous bowler with a growing reputation and a big following in his home town of Bendigo. It is quite likely that he would have backed himself to spoil Grace's bet that he would never be bowled on the tour.

Whether or not Grace ever did make such a wager, he certainly seems to have given a more tangible hostage to fortune regarding the whole team's performance. In his last letter to the promoters before leaving England, he wrote; 'I am proud to say that I have succeeded in getting together a very strong tream, and if we lose a single match, all I can say is that your teams of 22 must be a good deal stronger than we play in England.' This appeared in the *Australasian* on 22 November 1873, and was widely reprinted in the Australian press.

Reporters were, of course, impatient to make their own assessments of the man and his players, and their interest quickened when the tourists moved out of the nets for a practice in the middle. Grace lived up to expectations, but they were not particularly impressed by the rest of the batting. Southerton's bowling, however, made a distinct impression: '[He] put in the ball with wonderful precision, always dead on the wicket and breaking from both sides.'[10] There was no suggestion that the English players were finding it hard to acclimatize. Indeed, their preparations seemed to be going far better than the local team's. The Victorian practice sessions were conducted in 'a very desultory manner'[11] and several of the players simply refused to attend. The keenest students of form, the bookmakers, made the English team 3/1 favourites to win the match.

The build-up to the match caused great excitement. 'Grace and his team have formed almost the only topic of conversation. Column on column has been devoted to the subject in each of the morning papers. On the railway, in the streets, in the 'buses – everywhere, in fact – nothing else has been talked about except cricket.'[12] There were even calls for the two teams to compete on an equal footing, though they came to nothing. The match, starting on Boxing Day, would be between the All England Eleven and Eighteen of Victoria.

*

But first there was Christmas – an Australian Christmas, 'in which ice-pails are substituted for yule logs and fern leaves for holly. Plum-puddings and pantomimes appear simultaneously in London and Melbourne; but, having conceded so much to custom, we are free to find recreation more appropriate to our Midsummer holydays [sic]'.[13] W.G.'s chosen recreation was shooting. Whether Agnes regarded that as appropriate or not, Grace left her in the hotel and went out into the country in the hope, as he wrote in his diary, 'of bagging some kangaroos, though no such luck'.[14]

Roaming the outback in search of elusive marsupials was probably better preparation for the match than over-indulging in Melbourne, and it seems highly likely that several of the team were nursing hangovers when they arrived at the Melbourne Cricket Ground on the morning of 26 December. The home side had graver problems. The season of peace and goodwill had not brought a resolution to the feud between the rival camps of Melbourne cricketers, and although the Victorian side had finally been picked, there was still no captain. The start of play was delayed while this was thrashed out in the dressing room. The result of the conclave was that George Robertson, a Tasmanian who had won a cricket blue at Oxford, was elected as the compromise candidate.

Robertson began well by winning the toss, and shortly after noon Grace led his team out to wild applause from the estimated 10,000-strong crowd. This number grew during the day, so that by mid-afternoon there were nearly 20,000 spectators in the ground. There might have been even more but for the weather, which was cold with a sharp southerly wind blowing all day 'accompanied by clouds of dust'. These were not ideal conditions in which to bowl. Furthermore, after Grace's intervention, the wicket proved first-rate. Southerton thought it 'splendid . . . not to be surpassed in England, except by having more grass on it'.[15] The Victorians' batting was also better than expected. B. B. Cooper, with whom Grace had put on 283 at the Oval in 1869, was one of several English exiles who had helped raise Australian standards, and now he steered the Victorians safely through the first session for the loss of only three wickets. The score was a very healthy 83 at lunch.

While a band entertained the crowd with selections from Verdi, Strauss and Donizetti, the players, officials and guests repaired to a large marquee to enjoy an excellent spread at the promoters' expense. Afterwards there were the inevitable toasts – 'The Queen' and 'The Governor' (who was present, along with several leading political figures) – followed by speeches. Grace, of course, was required to speak on all such occasions, and as captain of the team could not get by with the simple formula that had served him so well in Canada. In addition to the usual pleasantries, he made what seemed the magnanimous offer to play out the game if a result could not be reached in the three days. This was a tacit admission that his bowlers were proving drastically less effective than he had anticipated. As Fred put it in his report for *Lillywhite's Companion*, 'The professionals could not bowl a bit.'[16]

Things were no better after lunch. In fact they got worse, and Grace showed signs of losing his temper when Humphrey missed an easy chance to run out Cooper. The batsman enjoyed his second life, bringing up the 150 with an authoritative cut off McIntyre. When the total reached 170, Grace called the team around him for what one report called 'a consultation' to try to inject a bit of urgency into the proceedings, and shortly after took matters into his own hands, going on to bowl with Fred at the other end. It was Fred who got the breakthrough, inducing Cooper to tread on his stumps sixteen runs short of his century. More wickets fell, including Midwinter's to a catch behind that the batsman was clearly unhappy with. But the tourists had belatedly taken control, and at close of play the Victorians had lost ten wickets for 245. Grace admitted that he had been surprised by their performance, which, he said, 'was equal to the batting of the best county team in England'.[17]

The following morning (Saturday) started badly. One of the amateurs insisted on driving the carriage taking them to the ground, got too close to the kerb, and overturned the vehicle. The local press reported that Arthur Bush was responsible, but Brownlee says it was Fred, who 'plied the whip . . . too freely', inducing the horse to bolt. Fred steered the beast into the wooden railings beside the road 'and the old horse replied by kicking the carriage to pieces and levelling twelve feet of the fence'.[18] Perhaps Bush shouldered the blame to protect the younger man. Whoever the reckless driver was, it was an embarrassing incident, and although no one was hurt they were all badly shaken up. Grace's aggravation was increased when Greenwood, Humphrey and McIntyre also contrived to be late and he had to ask Robertson for substitutes.

These irritations gave an extra edge to his play, and he rattled through the Victorian tail, at one point taking five wickets without conceding a run, to finish with 10 for 58. With the benefit of hindsight, he cursed himself for not bowling earlier. The Victorian total of 266 was far higher than anyone had believed possible, and it would take a huge score from W.G. to save the game, let alone win it. The England innings started at twenty to one, and 'Cheer after cheer rose from every corner of the densely packed ring of spectators, as the towering form of the champion cricketer of the world appeared in the field, and when the assembled Eighteen gave their cheer for the captain, there was one united outburst of applause, which was heard in Jolimont, in Richmond, and faintly in far off South Yarra.'[19]

This extraordinary reception was almost followed by a catastrophic anti-climax. Jupp dabbed the opening delivery behind the stumps, and Grace set off for a suicidal single. He was saved only by a bad misfield. He then settled down to play himself in against the bowling of Sam Cosstick and F. E. Allan, a tall left-hander of some pace who bowled wearing a cap. Whenever he took a wicket he would fling it into the air, and his success in the Melbourne area was such that he was known as 'the bowler of the century'. Perhaps to show that the batsman of the century was more than a match for any local hero with pretensions to greatness, Grace knocked Allan about more or less at will, much to the amusement of the crowd.

He was not at his absolute best, though, and missed a number of balls down the legside. He also snicked a ball from Allan to the wicket-keeper, but Boult, who was umpiring, didn't have the nerve to give him out. Next ball, he did walk, sending the crowd into paroxysms of excitement, only to return to the crease, 'leaving the multitude of spectators conscious of a "sell", for the ball had struck the ground before it went up'.[20] He was enjoying himself, but his fortunes changed when Boyle came into the attack. Sometimes described as a precursor of Bill O'Reilly, Boyle bowled fast for a slow bowler and had a distinct break from leg. He had come to Melbourne with his own personal barmy army of Bendigonians who cheered his every move. And when, as he had planned, he indeed got one between W.G.'s leg and his wicket, their joy was unconfined. The majority of the crowd would probably have preferred to see more, but even so, W.G.'s innings of 33 had come as a revelation, introducing a class of batting they had never encountered before. His timing and placing were particularly admired and called forth plaudits from the press.

The rest of the team did not fare so well. Apart from Grace, only Jupp (22) and Oscroft (12) made double figures as Allan and Cosstick gained total ascendancy. Allan bowled 54.1 overs, of which thirty-three were maidens, and took 6 for 44; Cosstick took 3 for 53 in sixty-one overs. The England total was 110, and they suffered the indignity of having to follow on.

The second innings started late on the Saturday afternoon, and Grace kept himself back until Monday. Heavy rain fell on Sunday night, and on returning to the ground Grace made a 'formal request to have the wicket rolled before commencing'.[21] There was no precedent for this and it was refused. The pitch played badly from the start, but the overnight pair of Greenwood and Gilbert held on for twenty overs, before Greenwood fended off a flyer to short-leg. This brought Grace to the wicket, with the score on 32 for 3. After a couple of overs he made a second, even more unorthodox, request for the roller, which was again refused. Shortly afterwards Gilbert was caught off a rising ball from Allan. Grace looked 'disgusted'. The score was 33 for 4. Soon it was 34 for 5, and all realistic hope of avoiding an innings defeat was gone. Fred joined him at this point, and the two brothers battled their way to a fifty-run partnership before Fred went for 28. Boult, whose umpiring left much to be desired, lost track of the number of balls bowled, and Oscroft was bowled for a duck off the *sixth* delivery of Conway's (four-ball) over. After that, only Lillywhite with 19 showed much resistance.

As so often, Grace appeared to be playing a different game. He was particularly harsh on Boyle, hitting him over the fence for a five. When the innings closed for 135, he was undefeated on 51. Victoria won by an innings and twenty-one runs. The crowd gave him a hero's reception, but the response to Victoria's first ever success against an English team was a mixture of elation and disappointment. The promoters had no such ambivalent feelings because 40,000 spectators had paid the very steep entrance fee of 2s. 6d. over the three days, and the takings reached £5,000, which remained a record up to the end of the century. Grace had proved his commercial value, and champagne flowed liberally in the pavilion at the end of the match.

But the English defeat – by such an overwhelming margin – sent shockwaves through the cricket-playing world. *The Times* was damning: 'It is said that [the tourists] were not in good form – they had only 10 days' practice after a six weeks' voyage – and that the self-denial necessary for getting into condition at Christmas in an hotel among hospitable people was too much for human nature, and was certainly not practised by some of the professionals.'[22] *Bell's Life* took a longer-term view of the Victorian victory: 'The effect . . . will be to make cricket between England and Australia now and henceforth really interesting . . . We may eventually see an Australian eleven . . . doing battle at Lord's.'[23]

Some of the Australian press reaction was rather less measured. One paper declared of the tourists, 'the stigma of their first defeat will rest on them for their professional lives, and can only be wiped out by a series of brilliant victories, crowned by a final triumph against the pick of the colonies'. Among the betting fraternity, who had lost heavily on the result, the match was seen in a more sinister light. 'They argue that the gentlemen of the grandest nation on the earth have sold themselves for lucre, and given away a match they could have won as easily as it has been lost . . . Mr Grace and his coadjutors have been wilfully and dishonourably dishonest'.[24] The suspicion that the side was 'a book-maker's team'[25] prepared to swindle the Australian punter had already taken root by the time the Englishmen batted a second time, and led to some harsh treatment of the English professionals. Jupp, for one, was 'hooted' when he was caught and bowled by Cosstick for a duck. As he had made the second highest score in the first innings, and also fielded brilliantly, this was unjust, and he felt it keenly.

The amateurs were not above reproach either. Though there was no suggestion that Grace himself did anything but try his impressive best to win the match, there were whispers that he had used the newly installed telegraph at the ground to warn friends in London to lay off their bets as the match was going to be lost,[26] while the *Sydney Mail* reported that one of the 'gentleman players of the English eleven' had advised a friend in the city not to back the team because 'the professionals were not working with them'. The reason for this was the 'marked distinction in the relative social positions of the members of the team'. The columnist continued: 'If Jupp and his brother professionals allowed private resentment to influence them in the match, their conduct is inexcusable; but I hope that the report has no foundation in fact. Such *contretemps*, however, might, and probably will, occur if the professionals continue to receive such scant courtesy.'[27]

Grace's response to the barrage of criticism was characteristic. The next match was at the mining town of Ballarat, known as the 'Golden City', some hundred or so miles to the north-west of Melbourne. In soaring temperatures ('about the hottest day in which I ever played cricket . . . about 100° in the shade')²⁸ he celebrated the New Year with an aggressive 126, which included two hits out of the ground for five. The local Twenty-two were strengthened by Cosstick and Allan, and it was a particular satisfaction to humble two of the main contributors to his team's defeat against Victoria. The Ballarat side also included the gifted slow left-arm bowler Tom Kendall, and Tom Wills, a legendary figure in Australian sport, not just for his work with the Aboriginal team in the 1860s but as a captain of Victoria and the inventor of Australian Rules Football.

The rest of the England team followed Grace's example. Fred matched W.G.'s century with one of his own, and Oscroft and Greenwood both scored fifties in a grand total of 470. This was the largest one-innings score ever made in Australia, and Grace's 126 just beat the 121 Richard Carpenter had made on the same ground in 1863–4 to set a new record for an Englishman in the southern hemisphere. Grace then took 7 for 71, alternating between medium pace and his slower style, and fielded as though his life depended on it. The *Ballarat Courier* thought him 'worth at least six good men in the field'. The performance should have silenced the critics, and most commentators allowed that the team were coming into something like their true form. But of course those who were convinced that the Melbourne match had been sold simply saw it as confirmation of their darkest suspicions.

Nor did success do anything to improve relations within the tour party. Although they acted in concert on the field – 'the most perfect subordination to authority prevails amongst the Englishmen. They act like a clock, wound up by their captain, whose orders and hints are scrupulously fulfilled, and never questioned'²⁹ – they remained strictly segregated off it. Once more they were billeted in different hotels, and events at the conclusion of the game only exacerbated the bad feeling.

The match ended on Saturday afternoon (petering out in a tame draw as the Twenty-two batted out time without difficulty). In his *Reminiscences*, Grace states that he stayed in Ballarat, and offers a dramatic description of the dust-storm that struck the following day: 'a hot wind swept over the city, scorching everything up and clouds of boiling dust whirled along the roads and streets. It was thoroughly unpleasant, as the whole town was in darkness while the storm raged.'³⁰ Grace did experience a dust storm that Sunday – 'one of the severest dust-storms ever experienced'³¹ – but in Melbourne, not in Ballarat. At the end of the match, according to the *Ballarat Courier*, Grace and the amateurs left the ground 'immediately they were dressed'. Then, heading for the nearby railway station, 'Mr and Mrs Grace left Ballarat for Melbourne on Saturday evening, accompanied by the remainder of the gentlemen players of the English team.'[32] As Agnes was missing the next, up-country, leg of the tour, Grace was understandably keen to escort her back to Melbourne where she would be staying. But not for the last time his conflicting duties as husband and captain produced friction with his hosts. His sudden departure was a public relations disaster. A champagne reception had been laid on to celebrate another financial success, but the star guest was missing. The professionals were perfectly happy to quaff the promoters' free drink, but the local committee was hurt by what they saw as Grace's snub.

While Grace was witnessing his dust-storm in Melbourne, the pros spent their Sunday driving out of Ballarat, sightseeing. A group of them were involved in the second accident of the tour, when a wheel came off their buggy. Humphrey and Greenwood were pitched out of the vehicle and thrown down an embankment, and Humphrey hurt his thigh sufficiently badly to miss the next two matches. The first of these was at Stawell, and Grace rejoined the team in Ballarat for their departure on Tuesday, 6 January. It was a journey memorable for its unpleasantness. There was trouble at the outset when the team assembled at 8.30 a.m. and saw what they would be travelling in – 'an old-fashioned Cobb's coach' with leather springs. As they were going across country most of the way it was obvious they were in for a dreadful experience. 'Several members of the team flatly refused to take their seats, and were only, after much coaxing, prevailed upon to do so,' Grace recalls.[33] It is conceivable that Grace's powers of persuasion were enhanced by the fact that he had a gun. It must have been an interesting scene: Ballarat with its broad streets and boardwalks lined with stores and saloons bore more than a passing resemblance to an outpost in the Wild West, and the resentful group being herded onto the coach might have been a gang of miscreants rounded up by the local sheriff. Eventually they set off, with, 'nine inside, four outside', the extra man being Sam Cosstick who was due to play against them once more when they reached their destination.

During the coach's tortuous journey through the bush, Grace, Fred and Gilbert reinforced the Wild West theme by blazing away at whatever wildlife came within range: 'Magpies, Parrots, Woodpeckers, Wagtails, + rabbits', according to Southerton, who was crammed inside with the other professionals. The first fifteen miles were on decent roads, but for the next sixty they suffered 'agonies' on the country tracks. 'The horses laboured along up to their hocks in white dust, with which we were literally cloaked, so that we looked for all the world like so many millers as we sat on the jolting and rickety vehicle.'[34]

The journey took twelve hours. Four miles out of Stawell, they were met by what seemed like the whole town's population. 'As we approached the crowd cheered wildly, and two brass bands struck up.' This was too much for one of the horses in the welcoming party. It overturned the wagonette it was drawing and kicked it 'to atoms', though no one was hurt. To cap an appalling day, the hotel was inadequate. 'No bath in the House, rooms very small,' Southerton scribbled disconsolately in his pocket-book. Most people would have taken it easy after such an ordeal, but the following morning, while the professionals went off to look wistfully at the best-paying gold mine in Victoria, Grace hired a buggy and drove off with Gilbert to a lagoon in the bush 'where we had a fine day's sport with our guns, but still failed to pot a kangaroo'.[35]

The match against the Stawell Twenty-two (strengthened by Conway, Cosstick, Cooper and Wills) started the next day, Thursday, and made a tragicomic contrast to the game at Ballarat. According to *Lillywhite's Companion*, '*the ground was simply unplayable*', having been a ploughed field only three months before.[36] Grace recalled in amazement that 'one slow ball actually stuck in the dust, and never reached the batsman'.[37] Conditions were so impossible he decided all-out attack was the only form of defence and 'did not block a single ball, but hit at everything'.[38] He scored 16 out of 43 and the 'ludicrous farce' was over in two days, Stawell winning by ten wickets. It was a wretched time, made worse by a plague of flies. Returning to the hotel after the match, Grace found the table in the breakfast room crawling with them and relieved some of his feelings with a mighty swat. His tally was nearly double the tourists' first-innings score – seventy-nine.[39]

Cricket still had to be provided on the third day, but Grace refused to demean himself further and headed back into the bush with his gun, leaving the six fit professionals – Greenwood, Oscroft, Jupp, Lillywhite, Southeron and McIntyre – to play twelve of the locals in a single-wicket match. The pros made it quite clear what they thought of this division of labour. In response to the Twelve's score of 29, they mustered precisely 2.

The next leg of the trip, to the seaside town of Warrnambool, was an even more horrific experience than the journey to Stawell. After the insufferable heat of the previous few days, the heavens opened and it poured. The rain 'fell pitilessly all the time, and we were soon drenched to the skin. The first thirty-one miles took five hours and a quarter, and though we changed horses now and then our progress was exasperatingly slow.'[40] The dirt tracks turned to mud, in which the wheels sank to the axles, and outside Hexham, the coach finally stopped. The horses were too exhausted to go any further with the whole team on board, so the party split up, Lillywhite, Jupp, Southerton, McIntyre and Humphrey staying behind to lighten the load.

It took the advance party nineteen hours to reach Warrnambool, and they arrived at half-past eleven at night wet through with their cricket bags and portmanteaus soaked. Even then, Grace's intolerably long day was not over. He had just retired to bed when a reporter knocked on the door wanting an interview. This was short and sharp and none of it was printable. The others arrived the following evening. '[T]he Gentlemen had been out all day shooting and fishing' and had forgotten to make any arrangements for the stragglers. After days of atrocious journeys, wild horses, worse wickets, the pros had reached breaking point, and this was the final straw, as Southerton made clear in his diary:

[T]here was no dinner prepared for us and they wanted to stick us, two in a room, [but] we had had enough of that, and the journey had not improved our temper, so we let them know it somewhat roundly. [I]n the end we got some tea; and a room each for 4 of us at another Hotel, so we are cut up in three pieces, this time, [–] infernal rot, not to be all together.

Whatever the professionals felt, Grace's determination to prevent their being 'all together' was so strong that he had already declined an invitation to a banquet on the eve of their match, and he also vetoed the professionals' presence at a ball on the evening of the last day. The local paper voiced the views of the bewildered welcoming committee:

The invitation sent was a general one, but . . . after all the arrangements had been made, [Mr Grace] distinctly refused to attend if the professionals were to be present. Cards of invitation were therefore sent to the 'gentlemen players' only. A ball in honour of the visit of the All-England cricketers, with more than half the number omitted, certainly sounds very queerly and forcibly illustrates the inconvenience of such a mixed team as Mr Grace has brought, who, it would appear, have no friendly understanding and cannot meet together in the same public room.[41]

Grace must have been sorely tried by constant attacks on him in the press, and he was also irked by the constant presence of Victoria's top players in the local teams. Cooper, Allan, Wills, Gaggin and Conway 'seemed prepared to regard themselves as representatives of any district in the Australian continent'.[42]

Although events off the field overshadowed the match, the professionals did at last put in an acceptable performance. Lillywhite and Southerton bowled throughout both the Twenty-two's innings, sharing forty wickets between them, and despite brilliant bowling by Allan, Jupp carried his bat for 58, 'one of the best innings he ever played' in Grace's view[43] and easily the highest score in the game. The tourists won by nine wickets on the second day. It was their first victory in Australia, and somewhat overdue.

To fill the rest of the afternoon, Grace teamed up with Fred, Bush and Gilbert to play a single-wicket match against Ten of Warrnambool. There wasn't enough time to finish it, and on the third day he called upon the six fit professionals to join five of the locals in a scratch game against another side of eighteen, and then set off once more in pursuit of kangaroos. At last he was in luck, and spent the day happily admiring the daring of the stockmen as they rode down their prey on bush ponies. His mood changed when he got back to the town in the evening and found out what had been going on at the cricket ground. The professionals were developing an eloquence of their own in these exhibition games. Having allowed the eighteen to amass the sizeable total of 172, the eleven were all out for 26, of which Greenwood scored 16, while the other five contributed no runs at all. As this third day's play had been largely for the benefit of the refreshment tent, the pros had obviously decided that they might as well patronize it. The ground was also swarming with 'card-sharpers and professional gamblers',[44] and with money changing hands and large amounts of liquor being consumed it was another bad day for the touring side's reputation.

The ball in the evening duly took place without the professionals. Fred records that it 'passed off really well'.[45] But the visit had not been a conspicuous success. The *Warrnambool Examiner* made no bones about the impression Grace and his fellow amateurs had made:

Those who have been among us have, with few exceptions, disgusted the community with their behaviour. We particularly allude to those of the team who have been called 'gentlemen'; but while making this allusion, we beg to state we do not refer to Mr Boult, who, so far as it was possible for him, redeemed the snobbishness of those who classed themselves as his equals. It is not a pleasant thing to have to speak in terms so strong of our visitors, but we do so because we are anxious to impress the community with the fact that those who conducted themselves so disgracefully here are no representatives of the gentlemen of England.[46]

The theme was taken up by other papers. One columnist pointed to the hypocrisy of

the gentlemen cricketers . . . trading on the professional cricketers of the team, and endeavoring to secure for their genteel selves as much of the three thousand five hundred pounds of colonial money as they can . . . They will not even lodge at the same hotel with them! Mr Grace and the other gentlemen cricketers take good care to secure the lion's share of the profits of the expedition; but they object to share the hospitality of the people of Warrnambool if the professional cricketers are permitted 'to come between the wind and their nobility' anywhere but on the cricket ground. The consequence of all this is what might be expected – insubordination in the ranks, a divided team, and humiliating defeats. We were not prepared to find such wretched specimens of snobbery as these amongst British gentlemen cricketers.

The writer finished by roundly condemning what he described as 'the vulgar pretentious species of gentility set up as the Grace standard'.[47]

Grace issued a denial, asserting that the arrangement by which the amateurs and players stayed at different hotels was 'by mutual consent, both parties ensuring to themselves greater freedom thereby'.[48] This was categorically denied, privately by Southerton ('rot'), and publicly by Lillywhite in a letter published towards the end of the tour.

*

They travelled back to Melbourne by sea. As luck would have it they ran into stormy weather, and Grace, for one, would happily have reverted to the Cobb's carriage. 'The steamer was abominably uncomfortable – the stench of the oil from the machinery pervading the whole vessel – while the pitching and tossing in the rough sea we encountered soon made us all feel ill. We were sixteen hours on the boat, and till then I had never spent so wretched a night on board ship.'[49] They had a couple of days in Melbourne before setting sail again, for Sydney. The same stormy weather was waiting for them around the coast, and they retired to their bunks clutching their basins once more. The beauties of Sydney Harbour revived their spirits, and they were given a royal welcome by a flotilla of smaller craft, while five or six thousand people were gathered to greet them on the dock. Although the Sydney papers had carried reports and comment on the tour to date, they were prepared to give Grace the benefit of the doubt, and this was an opportunity to make a fresh start.

That afternoon they went to look at the Albert ground where they would play the New South Wales Eighteen. Although destined soon to succumb to development, it was probably the best-appointed venue in Australia, with a big grandstand and a handsome pavilion. There was even a reminder of home in the shape of an avenue of trees that George Parr's team had planted in 1863–4. W.G. and Fred Grace also had the chance to exchange family news with their cousin, William Pocock, who was playing for the Eighteen. After the travails of the previous weeks, there seemed every prospect of the tour getting back on track.

As in Victoria, the encounter between the England team and the State side generated great excitement, and the same partisan passions over selection. One selector was forced to resign under the suspicion of bias, and the papers debated the respective merits of the players under consideration. One of these was the youthful Spofforth, back from his holiday in Tasmania. He went along to one or two of the practice sessions, but didn't participate. 'I never practise,' he told an interviewer several years later. 'I have always found that I require the stimulus and excitement of a match to put me on my mettle.'[50]

The chance to get the adrenalin pumping didn't really come his way on this occasion. When the big match started on Saturday, 24 January, Coates and Tindall ran through the England batting so easily that he wasn't required in the first innings. In the second, he took 2 for 16, and Grace noted him as 'a very fair bowler'. But the potential of Australia's greatest fast bowler was not uppermost in his mind as the match slipped away from him. He was twice caught at short third man off the slow left-arm spin of Coates, for 7 and 12, and on both occasions the crowd reacted as the Philadelphians had, with 'hats, caps, umbrellas, walking-sticks' flying into the air in triumph. William Pocock made the top score in the New South Wales second innings, and the tourists were beaten by eight wickets. But Grace still regarded the game as 'one of the pleasantest we played in Australia'.[51]

He did not, however, manage to keep his temper throughout the three days, and reports were soon circulating that 'Mr Grace grossly misconducted himself'.[52] The trouble arose on the second evening of the match when the promoters' agent argued for postponing the start on the third day until two o'clock to let the excitement culminate in the afternoon. To this Mr W. G. Grace objected, and he stated his intention to send his men into the field at the appointed time, 12 o'clock. The agent used some uncomplimentary language and reminded Mr Grace that the Eleven were paid to play, when the English captain seized him, and a scene was only prevented by the interference of some bystanders.[53]

Needless to say the game restarted at twelve o'clock.

As a result of Grace's obduracy, the game finished early, and the remaining time had to be filled with some form of exhibition game. A single-wicket match was arranged in which Grace led a combination of professionals and amateurs, though the others were hardly needed. Going in first, he scored 28 which, with two byes, made up the 30 required to win.

The next match should have been at Maitland, but it was cancelled due to flooding. Instead a fixture was arranged at Bathurst. While this saved them from another sea trip, the train journey over the Blue Mountains proved another hair-raising experience. '[A]t times our sensations were curious, as we were painfully conscious that the snapping of a coupling would send us careering down the precipitous slope to certain death'.[54] Grace was invited into the engine for the upward pull, but firmly declined to stay there for the even more terrifying descent.

Having survived this latest ordeal, the team carried off the match comfortably by eight wickets. It was played in a carnival atmosphere with a band in constant attendance. Someone bet Agnes a pair of gloves that her husband couldn't hit the ball out of the ground. He tried gallantly and cleared the scoring-box, but the ball dropped just inside the fence. The game was virtually free of incident, though Fred had to put the local umpire right when he confused the popping crease with the return crease. The no-ball awarded was subsequently struck from the score-book. On the Saturday evening there was a reception in the town hall, followed by a ball that lasted into the small hours. It appears that Grace made no objection to the players attending, and relations between the two factions seem to have been better in New South Wales. On the Sunday Grace spent a blissful morning massacring quails in his host's paddock.

After a relaxing interlude, the party returned to Sydney for a far more demanding match against a Combined Fifteen, drawn from both New South Wales and Victoria. This was really a dress rehearsal for the first Test match played three years later. Huge crowds again filled the Albert ground, and there were more scenes of unrestrained rejoicing when Grace was bowled by Cosstick for 9. At 104 for 7 the innings looked doomed, but McIntyre hit a face-saving 55 not out and hoisted the score to 170. Boult, who was umpiring, infuriated the crowd by giving Bush the benefit of not much doubt in a close call for a run-out. There was another controversial decision the following morning, which strongly suggested that Boult was little more than Grace's puppet: 'Cooper attempted a cut, but apparently missed the ball, which Bush took behind the wickets. W. G. Grace immediately appealed for the catch, and Boult gave Cooper out.'[55] Lillywhite was bowling superbly at the other end and took 9 for 39 as the Fifteen were dismissed for 98, just avoiding the follow-on. Grace survived a couple of early chances, but ended the day strongly on 56 not out, with his team 163 runs ahead.

Heavy storms overnight threatened to hold up the start of play on the third morning. But to everyone's surprise, play began an hour earlier than scheduled. This was on Grace's insistence, in order to improve his chances of winning the match (and, it was widely believed, substantial wagers laid on the outcome). The whole day was played with one eye on the clock and the English captain's aggressive drive to get a result created bad feeling both on and off the field. He continued hitting out until he was caught for 73, but inflamed the crowd by returning to the wicket later in the innings to give instructions to his batsmen. In the days before declarations were allowed the only way to end an innings was to give wickets away, and this is what Grace told his men to do. Although perfectly logical, this was seen as contrary to the spirit of the game, and the home side retaliated by bowling wide of the stumps and fielding sloppily. 'It was evident that a game at "cross purposes" was being played, one side trying to get out, and the other doing their best to frustrate such an intention,' reported the *Sydney Mail*.[56]

By these cat-and-mouse methods the innings was protracted until after lunch, and when it finally ended, on 236, the Fifteen were set an impossible 309 to win. Their only option was determined defence, and the English side had about three hours in which to winkle them out. On a sultry, sticky, bad-tempered afternoon, they did it – but not without more dubious umpiring by Boult. When he gave Cosstick out, hit wicket, from square leg, the crowd threatened to invade the pitch and shouted for the batsman to return to the crease. He did. By this time the next batsman, John Conway, had reached the wicket. 'The curious sight was witnessed of three batsmen being at the wickets at the same time,' Grace remembered.[57] The England captain led his team off in protest. They were met in front of the pavilion by embarrassed officials, who persuaded Cosstick to give up his stand for the greater good. To more booing, Grace led his men back out. The battle of attrition continued, and with the minutes ticking away, the England team finally took the last wicket and secured their victory by 218 runs. They may have won the match, but they lost something more important, if less tangible. The *Sydney Mail* commented:

It cannot be stated that the proceedings during the close of the match were characterised by that good feeling which the cricketing public hoped to witness from first to last; and those who have strenuously opposed any attempt to introduce the betting element into cricket had a specimen on Saturday of how a game may be marred when the players are pecuniarily interested in the result. It seemed to be generally understood that several of the English team had wagers on the match, and the tactics pursued by their captain towards the finish of the second innings of his men, with a view of obtaining sufficient time to get the combined team out and prevent a draw, resulted in a retaliation on the part of the majority of the Fifteen which was anything but creditable to them.[58]

Inevitably, Grace's own position came under the closest scrutiny. A local headmaster, whose measured and impartial column appeared in the *Sydney Mail* under the pen-name 'Square Leg', had this to say in the same edition:

I cannot see where Grace was at fault, if he were simply working for the honour of winning the game, but the accepted fact that he had wagers on the result of the play irritated some of our men, and rendered them obstinate in their desire to make the match a drawn one, and so spoil the speculations of those who cared more for what they had on the result than for cricket itself . . . It is stated, and I believe with some truth, that the leading bookmaker of Melbourne has an interest in the project which resulted in the visit of the English cricketers to Australia; and what is the result? The play of Grace and his team is looked upon with the utmost distrust, and even when they score an easy victory the public think they have all the more reason for saying that previous performances, where they were less fortunate, were not fair and above board.[59]

'Square Leg' returned to his assessment of Grace in his column the following week, referring to his 'unfortunate infirmity of temper' as the root cause of the unpleasantness that was marring the tour. Casting a last look at the New South Wales match, he remarked that 'the public are not likely to recover for some time from the feeling, akin to disgust, which the recent exhibition in the All-England match gave rise to.'[60] The *Australasian* was even more blunt in its condemnation of the English team, or rather the amateur component of it, especially the captain. On the eve of their departure, the paper's Sydney correspondent wrote: 'To-night we shall see the last of the English Eleven – at least such is the fervent hope of all those in this city who care to see the game played in a courteous and manly spirit.' At first the writer thought the Victorian press unduly severe on 'the brothers Grace and others'. 'I now beg to modify my views. In this colony, at least, we have an intense distaste for bumptious and overbearing captains.'[61]

Despite the hostile press, the tourists left Sydney with reluctance. They faced a three-day voyage back to Melbourne, and once more ran into dirty weather. On the third day the wind dropped and the frail passengers could once more totter on deck. Grace stumbled upon a great cache of oysters and persuaded the stewards to sell him a sack. Then, as though auditioning for a part in 'The Walrus and the Carpenter', he distributed his stockpile to all and sundry.

No sooner had the team disembarked at Melbourne than they were away up-country to play Twenty-two of Bendigo at Sandhurst, starting on 12 February. W.G. pointedly remarks of this team that it was 'unique in one respect – every man who played was an actual resident in the district'.[62] Conditions, though, were no better than for previous up-country matches. The wicket was poor and the heat appalling. On the second day it reached a scarcely endurable 140° in the sun.

This must have been a contributory factor in the next fracas Grace was involved in. He had promised to collect Agnes from town during the lunch interval on the second day, but as usual the proceedings were prolonged as toasts and speeches dragged on. Grace made his apologies and left. Mr Bruce, the chairman of the Bendigo Cricket Club, expressed his surprise at 'such a seeming act of discourtesy', which Grace heard about on his return to the ground. There are conflicting accounts of what happened next. The *Bendigo Advertiser* gives this version:

Mr Grace . . . asked him to publicly apologise for his remarks, but Mr Bruce declined to do so, whereupon Mr Grace threatened to wring an apology out of him, and he was desired by Mr Bruce to commence at once. Nothing further took place until the conclusion of the play, when in the dressing-room Mr Bruce went to Mr Grace and, in a frank manner, stated that if Mr Grace considered anything he had said required an apology he was perfectly willing to apologise. Instead of accepting this in the friendly spirit in which it appeared to be offered Mr Grace

1 Dr Henry Mills Grace,
father of three Test players and
cricketing empire-builder.

2 Martha Grace, cricket's First Lady,
who oversaw Grace's formative years.

3 A family team in all but name, and the nucleus of the first Gloucestershire county side,
West Gloucestershire CC v Knowle Park, Almondsbury, Gloucestershire, July 1866.
BACK ROW: Rev. H. W. Barber, Dr H. M. Grace, H. Grunning, Alfred Pocock MIDDLE:
W. G. Grace, Henry Grace, E. M. Grace, Alfred Grace FRONT: F. Baker, W. J. Pocock,
G. F. Grace, R. Brotherhood

4 E.M. and W.G.: companions in arms, but intense rivals.

5 Grace's first and happiest tour. R. A. Fitzgerald's all-amateur side for Canada and North America, 1872. BACK ROW: Alfred Lubbock, W.G., T. C. Patterson (promoter), C. J. Ottaway MIDDLE: Edgar Lubbock, R. A. Fitzgerald, Athur Appleby FRONT: Francis Pickering, Hon. George Harris, A. N. Hornby, W. M. Rose, C. K. Francis

6 Grace's first team to tour Australia, 1873–4. The mix of amateurs and professionals was disastrous and the party was dogged by scandal and controversy. BACK ROW: J. A. Bush, William Oscroft, Richard Humphrey, James Southerton, Martin McIntyre, F. H. Boult, Andrew Greenwood, Walter Gilbert FRONT: James Lillywhite, W.G., Harry Jupp, G.F.

7 The Game the Lawyers Couldn't Stop:
Grace's All England XI v 22 of South Australia, Adelaide, March 1874.

8 The United South squad, 1874: Grace's mercenaries, and the main source of his income
during the 1870s. BACK ROW: H. Phillips, R. Fillery, R. Humphrey, J. M. Cotterill, W. R.
Gilbert, John Lillywhite MIDDLE: J. Phillips, J. Southerton, E. Pooley, James Lillywhite,
W.G., F. Silcock, H. R. J. Charlwood FRONT: G.F., H. Jupp

Summary of W. G. Grace's cricket 1876

26 First-class matches

Runs.	Innings.	Not out.	Completed Innings		Average
2622 ..	46 ..	4 ..	42	..	62 — 18

13 Matches v Odds

| 1180 .. | 23 . | 2 .. | 21 | ... | 56 — 4 |

2 Other Matches v aside

| 106 .. | 3 .. | 1 .. | 2 | .. | 53 — |

41 All Matches

| 3908 .. | 72 .. | 7 .. | 65 | ... | 60 — 8 |

9 1876, Annus Mirabilis, in which Grace broke all records. Summary of his performances in his own hand (supremacy total but long division shaky).

10 Gloucestershire CC, County Champions, 1877. An all-conquering team built around the Three Graces and the Australian import Billy Midwinter. BACK ROW: W. Moberly, W. Fairbanks, G.F., F. G. Monkland, W. R. Gilbert, W. Midwinter FRONT: H. Kingscote, F. Townsend, R. F. Miles, W.G., E.M., C. K. Pullin (umpire)

11 'He killed professional fast bowling; for years they were almost afraid to bowl within his reach.'

12 'Nothing more childlike and bland than that slow, tossed-up bowling of Doctor Grace' – but he took more wickets than any other nineteenth-century bowler.

13 A formidable team for a Festival Match, Lord Londesborough's XI v the Australians at Scarborough, September 1888. A rare instance of the amateurs standing and the professionals sitting. BACK ROW: M. Sherwin (umpire), Lord Harris, C. I. Thornton, W.G. MIDDLE: G. Ulyett, W. Barnes, W. Gunn, J. Briggs, G. Lohmann FRONT: R. Peel, R. Abel, R. Pilling

14 'Never were there such people for family gatherings.' The Graces met regularly for cricket in the summer and other communal activities, on this occasion for a nutting party. The photograph was taken in the late 1880s, after the death of Martha Grace.

KEY TO THE NUTTING PARTY

1 W. G. Grace 2 Alfie Grace (nephew) 3 George Grace (nephew) 4 Mrs E. M. Grace 5 Mrs Page (niece) 6 Miss Bessie Grace (daughter) 7 E. M. Grace (brother) 8 Alfred. Pocock 9 W. G. Grace, jnr 10 Gerald Grace (nephew) 11 Mrs Bernard (sister) 12 Henry Grace (brother) 13 Mrs W. G. Grace 14 Dr Skelton (brother-in-law) 15 Miss Fanny Grace (sister) 16 Alfred Grace (brother) 17 Rev. J. W. Dann (brother-in-law) 18 H. E. Grace (son) 19 Mrs. Skelton (sister) 20 Mrs. II. Grace 21 Mrs. Dann (sister) 22 Charles B. Grace (son) 23 Mrs Alfred Grace

15 Country-house hospitality. Grace fraternizes with the old enemy: W. H. Laverton's XI v the Australians, Westbury, Wiltshire, May 1890. STARTING FIFTH FROM THE LEFT: E. J. K. Burn, H. F. Boyle, J. J. Lyons, W. L. Murdoch, W.G. J. J. Ferris is next to W.G. (with the gun) and C. T. B. Turner is wearing the bowler hat. J. A. Bush is standing third from the left.

16 Grace's second tour to Australia as captain of Lord Sheffield's team, 1892–3 (Botanical Garden, Adelaide). BACK: A. Shaw, A. E. Stoddart, M. Read, H. P. Philipson, O. G. Radcliffe FRONT: R. Abel, G. Lohman, G. McGregor, J. Briggs, R. Peel, W.G., W. Attewell, G. Bean, J. W. Sharpe.

turned round and said, 'You acted in a d— ungentlemanly way.' To which Mr Bruce responded, 'If you say so, you are a d— blackguard.' Mr Grace made a motion with his clenched fist to strike Mr Bruce, but several of the bystanders interfered, saying that he was wrong, and that he ought to have accepted Mr Bruce's apology.[63]

The *Castlemaine Representative* presented things in a different light:

When luncheon was pretty far advanced, Mr WG Grace saw that the toasts and speechifying were likely to be a diluted repetition of the previous day's utterances. He had an appointment to go into town to bring Mrs Grace down to see the play, and explaining to those nearest to him the reason for his leaving went out and fulfilled his promise. After the game was over, Mr Bruce, in anything but measured terms, 'tackled' Mr Grace for having left the table. Mr Grace again explained, and his explanation was not received in the courteous spirit in which it was tendered, the result being hotter and hotter words. Our reporter says that 'Mr Grace's manner was gentlemanly and quiet: that he was spoken to in a rude and rough manner.' Under such circumstances, it is hardly to be expected that he would preserve an equable demeanour. Whether everyone at the table heard Mr Grace's apology for leaving the festive board or not, he had surely a perfect right to do so if he chose, without question or cavil. The want of courtesy is in assuming that, because the cricketers do not pay completely gratuitous visits to the towns which ask for their presence, they are therefore *pro tem*, the actual servants, instead of the guests, of the people they play against.[64]

This is perhaps the best demonstration of a clear pattern that emerged during the tour. The papers in places Grace had yet to visit dismissed the accusations levelled against him as baseless smears, but the tune tended to change after they had had first-hand experience of him.

Whichever version is the more accurate, the incident could clearly have been avoided with a modicum of diplomacy on Grace's part. There was certainly no attempt at patching things up. Grace and the amateurs boycotted lunch on the third day, leaving it to Jupp and the professionals to swap toasts with the Bendigonians. But however graceless W.G. may have been off the field, he was pure Grace on it. He scored 53 and 72 not out and took 6 for 47 in the Bendigo second innings. *Lillywhite's Annual* was not far out in declaring, 'W. G. Grace won by seven wickets'.[65]

Accompanied by Agnes, Boult and Bush, Grace travelled to the next venue, Castlemaine, ahead of the rest of the team. There was a huge crowd waiting for them at the station – as many as had greeted the Duke of Edinburgh on his visit in 1867 – and 'Mrs Grace was the observed of all observers'.[66] The game itself was remarkable for the Alice-in-Wonderland quality of the umpiring. The local man refused to countenance a catch 'half-a-yard off the ground' and claimed he hadn't seen the bails come off when a batsman was bowled. His finest moment came when he turned down an appeal for a stumping because Bush had the tip of his nose over the stumps when he removed the bails.

The wicket was bad; according to *Lillywhite's Companion*, 'the worst ground possible – in fact really dangerous'.[67] Fred had good reason to say so. Having missed the previous match because of an attack of quinsy, he was now struck on the head first ball. W.G. retaliated by setting McIntyre loose on the locals, and the fast bowler 'played merrily about [their] ribs'.[68] 'The Castlemaniacs, however, stood up to the bowling like Britons and took the hard knocks with the greatest cheerfulness.'[69] No one was actually killed at the crease, but the tourists felt in mortal danger from another source. Every morning they were driven to the ground by sadistically reckless four-in-hand drivers, who gave the horses their heads on the steep hills and, Grace wrote, 'let them go galloping down at breakneck pace'.

They were glad to return to the spacious, and predominantly level, streets of Melbourne again for the return match against Victoria. The Victorians decided to lessen the odds, fielding fifteen rather than eighteen men. This should have increased interest in the game, but after the betting scandals that had dogged the tourists' important matches, the public's confidence was shaken and the attendances were poor. In the event the Eleven won comfortably by seven wickets. The match finished early, so once again an exhibition game was staged. This was an eleven-a-side match, and Grace showed what he could do against a normal field, running up an opening stand of 140 with Jupp and then going on to score 126. 'Nothing could have been grander from a cricketing point of view than the way in which he made his magnificent score . . . When Grace had been at the wicket 58 minutes, his score was 100. There is no other cricketer in the world who could accomplish that feat.'[70]

This was what the crowds had come to see, but although they enjoyed it, some of the Victorian players did not. Sam Cosstick, possibly still smarting from the incident in Sydney, lost his temper and, in the words of one of the local papers, 'deliberately shied three balls at Grace, the missile passing near enough to the upper part of the batsman's body to make him wince'.[71] A quarter of a century later Grace was prepared to be magnanimous about this, writing that it was 'an act which no one afterwards regretted more than the offender'.[72] It is possible he was less forgiving at the time.

With their record beginning to look healthier, and their captain in excellent form, the team sailed to Tasmania, reaching Launceston after another dreadful voyage lasting twenty-nine hours. A local journalist described his first sight of W.G. – 'like Peter, amongst the eleven, his towering form standing out boldly in the group'. A resounding cheer went up as the exhausted travellers staggered down the gang-plank.

The tourists found Tasmania a haven of hospitality and their stay was for once almost free of incident. Their reception 'won all our hearts', and the first game, against Twenty-two of Tasmania, was played in a good spirit, even though there was an argument when a stroke from Greenwood struck the dress of one of the ladies. The Tasmanian captain 'refused to allow more than was run for it, while Grace claimed the number allowed for a ball beyond the boundary. The umpires gave their decision in favour of the Englishmen'.[73] There were a great number of ladies at the ground – 'a bevy of fine girls', as the local paper put it. The tourists won the game comfortably and their mood was further improved when they discovered the road between Launceston and Hobart (a legacy from the convict days) 'was in magnificent condition'. As they did on other occasions, Grace and Agnes travelled separately, this time taking Bush and Gilbert with them.

The Twenty-two of Southern Tasmania gave the tourists 'a lively game', but the match was dominated by Fred's splendid innings of 154, which gave him the record his brother had held since Ballarat. The team won by eight wickets, but not before the Tasmanian batsmen had shown their quality. One hit six successive fours, while W. H. Walker drove W.G. 'out of the ground twice in one over'.[74] They rounded off their stay on the island with 'a couple of days' good shooting' on the way back to Launceston. Fred called the Tasmanian leg of the tour 'the most pleasant trip of all', adding, 'We were all exceedingly sorry to leave . . . and would much have liked to have stayed longer.'[75] In fact, he developed a strong enough liking for the place, or for one of its inhabitants, to return before the tour was over, and there were even rumours that he intended to stay.

The team returned to Melbourne for yet another match against Victoria – and more controversy. For the deciding game in the three-match 'series', Victoria reverted to Eighteen, and at last John Conway was entrusted with the captaincy. After the tourists' performances in Tasmania, public interest revived, and the match was far better supported than the previous one. Unfortunately, in addition to watching Grace score an excellent 64 out of a total of 166, the spectators witnessed yet another episode which revealed the other side of his cricketing mentality. Fred was fielding in front of the grandstand. A ball from Lillywhite was hit in his direction, and in full view of several hundred people it crossed the boundary and bounced back onto the outfield. The umpire, Budd, who was only standing in as a favour because Humphrey was indisposed, signalled four. Fred contested the decision, claiming that 'the ball had struck his foot and rebounded before it reached the chain fence'. 'This was so manifestly unfair that the people all round the ground protested, contending that the ball had gone to the chains, and should therefore count four.' Budd 'declined to alter his decision'. Grace, who was nowhere near the boundary, was nevertheless incensed that his brother's word should be doubted. He rounded on the hapless umpire, 'and spoke in such an insulting manner to Mr Budd . . . that he refused to remain in the field any longer.' No one was in any doubt that the incident 'occurred in consequence of the somewhat overbearing conduct of the English captain'.[76] So much for the sanctity of the umpire's decision that Grace had so forcefully upheld in the case of the Major run out at the beginning of the tour.

The game was going decidedly the tourists' way with the Victorian Eighteen on 53 for 10 when rain washed out the last day's play. The two not out batsmen were Conway and Midwinter, who were to feature prominently in the most famous of fracas four years hence.

To mark the end of the Victorian part of the tour, the promoters arranged a farewell dinner at the Criterion Hotel. This time it was the professionals' turn to make a point. They boycotted the evening. Mr Biddle, who took the chair on behalf of the promoters, regretted their absence but predictably talked up the success of the tour. Grace, replying, said he could not explain the professionals' absence, and added that 'Mr Biddle had done everything to make their visit a pleasant and happy one'. The rest of the amateurs also spoke. Fred, still sore after the Budd incident, made an outspoken attack on the Australian press. Those who wrote about cricket 'should know something about the game . . . there were no judges of cricket who wrote about it here, [and] those who did not know the game should not attempt to describe it. He thought the press, as a rule, . . . had been very hard on the eleven.' Conway, who replied as the Victorian captain, was trenchant in their defence: 'they were critical in the colonies, and the Englishmen should not object to the same standard of criticism as the colonial players'.[77]

To underline the colonial critical spirit, the *Argus* pulled no punches in its editorial, remarking: 'The Australian tour does not appear to have improved the tempers of the English cricketers.' After accepting that blame for the various controversies lay on both sides, the paper identified what it saw as the main problem: 'the distinction made between the gentlemen and the professional players was a piece of bad policy and worse taste on the part of whoever was responsible for it'.[78]

Just who was responsible was a matter for debate. The promoters claimed they had dealt directly with Grace himself, who, by implication, was answerable for the conditions under which the professionals toured. The professionals pointed the finger, publicly at least, at the promoters, as James Lillywhite made clear in a letter he wrote to the *Argus*:

The conditions were second-class passages out and home by the mail-boats through the Suez Canal, £170 per man, first-class hotel accommodation, and travelling and all other necessary expenses paid whilst they were in the colonies. Most of the professionals on being asked by Mr WG Grace objected to the second-class passage, upon which he telegraphed to Melbourne twice for first-class passages, but it was refused by the promoters. Eventually the players signed an agreement to come out and return second-class, which they repented after being three or four days at sea, it being bad accommodation and bad living. Upon arriving at Melbourne that distinction which has caused so much ill-feeling was immediately commenced – namely, the gentlemen sent to one hotel, the players to another, and so on through the whole chapter. Even when stopping at the same house, private apartments were reserved for the gentlemen in every instance except Stawell, and there it was because they couldn't get them. In Melbourne and Sydney the professionals have been perfectly satisfied with their hotels: in other instances they have not. In one place they were let out like a horse and trap, at 7s. 6d. per day, and in others have been neglected, and a long way from being satisfied. This is the fault of the promoters, in not arranging things properly for them ... I have requested them, for myself and brother professionals, to send us home first-class: it has not yet been positively refused ... Mr Biddle ... distinctly stated that it was for the good of cricket only, and not for money, that we were brought out, although they wouldn't object to its paying. Now if, after making some thousands, the men who have helped them to make it are doomed to a second-class passage, or in other words, seven weeks of misery, for the sake of a paltry £200, Mr Biddle must have stated what is not true. It has been stated that Mr WG Grace is the cause of this wretched second-class business, but I am very much deceived in the man if it is through him. Let the promoters send us home first-class, and the professionals will have at least one kindly recollection of them.

As for the reason why the professionals boycotted the farewell banquet, Lillywhite explained that one of the promoters had been overheard to say, 'second class was plenty good enough for us; at home we travelled third class and were glad to get a glass of beer; we could not appreciate champagne given us by these liberal-minded men'. And he concluded: 'I can assure you that the professionals will be very glad when they have fulfilled their agreement with these stuck-up persons, and they thank the public of Melbourne for the kind treatment they have received during their stay here. Jas. Lillywhite.'[79]

Enjoying the editorial prerogative of the last word, the *Argus* waxed satirical. It defended the press coverage of the tour two days later:

full justice has been done to GRACE's hits and to LILLYWHITE's twisters, but then the rude journals have dared to take exception to certain behaviour on the part of Mr. GRACE, of which they did not approve, and the promoters refuse to send Mr LILLYWHITE home first-class. We cannot decide the momentous question, Which of these two sensitive gentlemen has the greater cause for complaint? . . . What atonement can be offered to feelings which have been so cruelly lacerated?[80]

Thus, perhaps, was born the Whingeing Pom. The final stretch of the tour would reveal a much more established stereotype – Perfidious Albion.

THIRTEEN

THE last match of the tour was to be played in South Australia, but not, surprisingly, at Adelaide. After long negotiations with Biddle, the South Australian Cricket Association (SACA) had been pipped at the post by the Yorke's Peninsula Association for the right to stage South Australia's first match against an English touring team. The fee was enormous – £800 (Launceston, for example, paid £300 for their match) – but it secured a guarantee that the English team would only play one match in the state. Those in Adelaide who wanted to see Grace and his men would have to travel the hundred or so miles to Kadina to do so, and the Yorke's Peninsula Association were confident that their monopoly would ensure they made a profit.

The loss of the match was a bitter blow to SACA and a rancorous war of words developed between the two rival camps in the weeks leading up to the game. Throughout the period there were also persistent rumours that Adelaide would somehow get its fixture with the tourists despite the agreement with Biddle. The local paper on the peninsula, the *Wallaroo Times*, was tireless in denying them, pointing out that there would barely be time for the tourists to catch their boat home, let alone squeeze in another match after their engagement at Kadina. Anyway, they had Grace's word, and no flattering advances from Adelaide, declared the *Times*, would 'get the "Leviathan" to break faith with the men of the "Peninsula" '.[1]

Though the Adelaide press depicted the Yorke's Peninsula consortium as a bunch of vainglorious provincials who had bitten off more than they could chew, they took their responsibilities extremely seriously. The Wallaroo copper mine had generated great wealth, and if the three towns around it – Moonta, Wallaroo and Kadina – could only boast a population of just over 12,000 compared to Adelaide's 61,000,[2] they had a strong sense of civic pride, and no expense would be spared to stage the great event.

The game would be played on the Kadina racecourse, which was midway between Kadina and Wallaroo. The playing area was fenced at a cost of £140, and two grandstands were erected.[3] Partly out of necessity and partly as a placatory gesture, some of the leading Adelaide cricketers were invited to play, but when they declined the organizers agreed to recruit a coach from outside South Australia to lead the team's preparations. The man chosen was Tom Wills. Although Wills was past his best as a player, his experience with the Aboriginals and as captain of Victoria made him an ideal choice. His main responsibility was coaching, and he immediately instigated twice-weekly sessions for those hoping to play in the match. But he was also consulted about the ground and the wicket, and his opinion is particularly interesting in the light of the views subsequently expressed by Grace. The *Wallaroo Times* reported Wills as saying 'that no better place could have been chosen; the only thing wanted being . . . a good supply of water', and the paper added, 'There can be little doubt that . . . any suggestion of Mr Wills as to the improvement of the ground will be carefully carried out.'[4]

As the great day approached, the press carried notices of the game stressing that 'This will be the only match played by the Eleven in South Australia', alongside advertisements for consignments of 'Cricketing Shirts, Cricketing Trousers and Cricketing Caps . . . like those worn in Melbourne',[5] and the timetable of the 'Kadina and Wallaroo Railway and Pier Company' for the benefit of those travelling to the peninsula to watch the cricket.[6] The whole community was focused on this gala event, and nowhere on the entire tour was the arrival of the England team looked forward to with such keen anticipation.

But first they had to get there. This meant another sea trip round the coast to Adelaide, and they left Melbourne by steamer on Tuesday, 17 March. They were joined by Sam Morcom, a playing member of SACA who had been in Melbourne ostensibly to watch the tourists' match against Victoria, though the evidence suggests his real motive was to get in touch with Grace. He may have regretted his mission when yet another voyage turned into a nightmare, with storms prolonging the journey from the anticipated forty-eight hours to seventy-four. The whole team were horribly sea-sick, but the worst affected was Harry Jupp, who sought medicinal relief in the brandy bottle. This made matters considerably worse. He fell into 'a very excited state, seeing imaginary blue lights and beacons', and clearly suffered 'an attack of delirium tremens'. Southerton took him in hand, 'and had a rare time of it all night, for he kept waking about every five minutes, wanting the captain to come and examine him, then swearing at . . . some boys out of the porthole and who also kept dancing over his head'. He was also convinced there was a man 'climbing on the ceiling'. It appears that England's most famous medical student did not get involved, and when they arrived at Adelaide, Southerton remained in charge of the patient: 'Jupp was still very bad and [I] had to be with him all day.' A local doctor was called in, and Greenwood and Humphrey took over nursing duties during the night, but after a calm spell he began 'to rave and swear and he woke the whole house and was so evidently mad that Dr Herbert got an order to take him to the Hospital. We had great trouble to bind him with the assistance of two policemen and took him there in a cart . . . They took him in and put him in a padded room.'[7]

In addition to having his opening partner incarcerated in a padded cell, Grace had another problem. Fred had not sailed with the team when they left Melbourne. Instead, he went back to Tasmania, though whether for his health or for a matter of the heart remains unclear. Whatever the reason, he was going to miss the match at Kadina.

One thing the whole team was agreed on was that they were not going to set foot on another ship until they finally sailed home to England. They cancelled their steamer booking for Kadina, and opted instead for another bumpy ride in a Cobb's coach. They left Adelaide at five a.m. on Saturday, 21 March and spent the day rocking and jolting towards Yorke's Peninsula. Their driver for the last stage was one John Hill, the father-to-be of one of Australia's greatest cricketers, Clem Hill, who would find Grace still a formidable opponent over twenty years later.[8] When they eventually creaked into Kadina, they were met by a spectacular reception. A huge throng had gathered in the main square, a band played, and 'a fire balloon was sent up as an intimation to the Peninsula . . . that the great fact had been accomplished. The evening was beautifully fine . . . and the balloon rose to a height of some two thousand feet, and then sailed away to the northward and was soon out of sight.'[9]

This wild enthusiasm was dampened somewhat when it was discovered that neither Fred nor Jupp were with the party. Sam Morcom was, however, and despite having previously declined an invitation to play in the match, he now said he was available, and his offer was accepted at face value. Suspicious minds may have wondered at this late conversion of a member of SACA, and would certainly have been troubled by a brief paragraph buried in the paper reporting that 'Mr W. G. Grace telegraphed on Thursday from Lacepede Bay stating that he should be very happy to accept the invitation of the South Australian Cricketing Association to a banquet to be given in Adelaide on Friday evening, the 27th inst.' The editor passed over his own news story without comment, and devoted innumerable column inches to praising the preparations for the match, which, in addition to the building of the two grandstands, extended to the provision of 'plenty of urinals and latrines'. Most important of all, the paper claimed 'a first-class wicket has been obtained', and concluded that with 'such a ground and surroundings, if the Association does not have 3 great days, they will have cause to be disappointed'.[10]

To judge from his description of the facilities in *Reminiscences*, Grace might have been talking about a different venue:

When we reached Kadina, we went out in search of the cricket ground; and a search it really proved. We came to an open space, and then asked to be directed to the cricket ground. 'This is it,' some one said, and we whistled in astonishment . . . There was scarcely a blade of grass to be seen, while the whole area was covered with small stones. I fervently hope I shall never again have to play cricket on such a ground.[11]

The events of the next few days ensured he would certainly never be invited to play at Kadina again, and also suggested reasons why of all the indifferent grounds the team played on during the tour, the Yorke's Peninsula one was picked out for special disparagement.

After the fine weather on Saturday night, Sunday was a filthy day with violent winds and heavy rain. The weather had improved sufficiently for the game to start as scheduled on the Monday morning, though it remained cold with a persistent wind. Before play started, Grace ordered the ground to be swept and 'two large baskets of small stones' were collected.[12] There were only about 1,800 spectators to witness this interesting exercise, though 'accommodation was provided for 10,000'.[13] Ominously few had made the journey from Adelaide. And for all their conscientious practice under Wills's supervision, the locals were hopelessly out of depth against Southerton and McIntyre, who took 11 for 29 and 9 for 4 respectively. Twelve batsmen made ducks, including Wills, and no one outscored extras (eight) in a total of 42.

Jupp had made a miraculous recovery, proving that an English professional's constitution was equal to just about anything, and heroically reached Kadina in time to take part in the match. The tourists made 64 and Jupp's 10 was one of only two double-figure scores, the other being a lively 22 by Greenwood batting down the order. Grace himself got 5, and of the rest declared, 'Very naturally our men funked batting on a wicket like that'.[14] However, in his speech at the lunch interval he commended the association's efforts with the pitch, and said he 'admired the pluck of these gentlemen in bringing the Eleven to play in their neighbourhood'. He also predicted an upturn in the fortunes of the Twenty-two. They would, he hoped, 'do better as the game went on'.[15]

Grace may have offered encouraging words over lunch, but he gave them no help on the pitch. When the Twenty-two batted again the following day, he let Lillywhite and McIntyre bowl throughout the innings and the Yorke's Peninsula batting folded spectacularly. Only eight runs were scored off the bat, and from the fourth batsman down to extras (five), the card resembles nothing so much as a complicated binary sum: 0101000000010010000. The total of 13 left the Eleven victors by an innings and nine runs, and the match was over in a day and a half. Grace consented to play the Eleven's second innings. He went in four and proved that however bad the wicket, it was still possible to score runs on it. He made 54. Only Gilbert, with 23, joined him in double figures.

There was still one more day (Wednesday, 25 March) of the three-day engagement. The original agreement had been that in the event of the match ending in two days, a third day's exhibition game would be staged, the professionals being paid five pounds each and the amateurs appearing 'gratuitously'. But Grace saw the opportunity for a little extra profit, and on the extravagant pretext that his team had as yet bought 'no souvenirs', he insisted on payment of £110 – ten pounds a head – 'so that they could purchase something to carry home with them'.[16] After two ruinously disappointing days, the association had little choice but to take the gamble, and they reluctantly agreed to Grace's revised terms. Having extracted as much money from the situation as he deemed possible, Grace repaired once more to the cricket ground for a pointless day's exhibition cricket. What his hard-pressed hosts did not yet know was that, with Morcom by his side, he had been carrying on negotiations with SACA throughout his stay on the peninsula. But they did not have long to wait.

A farewell dinner had been arranged that evening at Kadina's main hotel. It was a short-lived affair. The opening salvos of the speechmaking had only just been exchanged when Grace stood up and made an unexpected announcement. With the minimum of preamble, and certainly no word of apology, he declared that as he and his team 'were expected in Adelaide next day and the coach was waiting at the door, he hoped they might be excused if they felt themselves compelled to depart'. The *Wallaroo Times* account continues: 'Mr Grace at once left the table, and was followed by the rest of the Eleven. This movement at once broke up the party and the room was soon left to the waiters.'[17]

When the men of the peninsula saw the *South Australian Register* in the morning, there, on the front page in the 'Amusements' column, was the stark announcement: 'All-England Eleven versus South Australian Cricketing Association. Cricket Match. The Oval. Thursday, Friday, & Saturday, March 26th, 27th, and 28th. Wickets Pitched Thursday, 2 o'clock. Admission to Ground, 2s 6d.' Beside it there was an urgent appeal for 'Twenty waiters and four female attendants for the Grand Stand on the Oval'.[18] This was no mere exhibition match, but a serious encounter like those in Melbourne and Sydney, and a fully fledged commercial operation into the bargain. (It had to be; in addition to an appearance fee – another £110 – Grace had also demanded half the gate money.)[19] The advertisements must have been placed with the paper the previous day. Even as he was taking more money off them to play the scratch game, Grace was double-crossing them with SACA. The Yorke's Peninsula Association were understandably outraged, and they sought immediate legal redress, applying for an injunction to prevent the game at the Oval from taking place. This application failed, as Grace knew it would. He had taken advice in Melbourne, and was confident that with the completion of the Kadina game, his contract with Biddle and the tour promoters was at an end. It wasn't his fault if they 'had foolishly agreed with the people of Kadina that no other match should be played in South Australia, forgetting that my agreement with them was for fourteen matches only'.[20]

Such contractual sophistry cut no ice on the peninsula. The association's losses came to around £700, but it was Grace's behaviour that they found most wounding. The *Wallaroo Times* of 28 March declared bluntly: 'The All-England Eleven, who seem to have a knack of getting into metaphorical hot water wherever they go, have left Yorke's Peninsula under circumstances highly dishonourable.' Even if there had been no breach of contract, there had clearly been 'some breach of faith between the Eleven and the Yorke's Peninsula Association'. What so incensed local opinion was the realization that Grace had been 'contemplating a mean evasion of the agreement under which he was morally, if not legally bound' before he even set foot in Kadina, and that his double-dealing had been the direct cause of the poor attendance. The Adelaide public 'were fully apprised many days ago that this breach of faith on the part of Mr Grace and his team' was intended from the start.

We scarcely know how to characterise the mean and sordid character of this business. For the sake of securing a few pounds in Adelaide, Mr Grace or his agents for him, have forfeited any claim that they had to the character of men of their word, or gentlemen; and they may be assured they will leave the colony with that stigma attached to them. This meanness is all the more inexcusable because, though Mr Grace without compunction received £110 for Wednesday's scratch match, he had admitted on previous occasions that at no place in the colonies had he been so liberally treated as on Yorke's Peninusula, where he received £800 and more, the highest sum anywhere else being but half that amount.[21]

He had done cricket no good, the paper said in its next issue, 'for instead of his brilliant and skilful play being remembered with profit and pleasure, his name will become a synonym for mean cunning and systematic fraud'.[22]

It was not just on the Yorke's Peninsula that Grace's actions provoked fury. Back in Melbourne, Biddle sent a telegram to Adelaide declaring that Grace 'has broken faith with the Promoters here' and had agreed to play the extra game 'entirely against their expressed wish'.[23] Needless to say, the situation was viewed rather differently in Adelaide. There was no sense there that anyone had connived in 'a sordid and even swindling transaction'. As the *South Australian Advertiser* put it, 'We do not see that there is ground for complaint against the Adelaide people in accepting or inviting the services of the Eleven for a match here. They have entered no contract, and they are bound by no conditions. If the Eleven feel at liberty to play, there is no reason why the Adelaide cricketers should not get up the farewell match.'[24] SACA had certainly pulled out all the stops, sending telegrams to the local clubs inviting the leading players to join the Twenty-two, taking out special supplements for the three main local newspapers, and preparing the ground and hiring the catering staff. Special excursion fares were negotiated with the railways, and, to ensure the maximum turn-out, a government half-holiday was granted on the Friday.[25]

Everything was ready for the start of the match on Thursday afternoon, but when the appointed hour came there was no sign of the tourists' coach. SACA officials spent an anxious lunchtime wondering whether Grace had had a change of heart. The answer was simpler, and contained a modicum of poetic justice. In the hurry to get away from Kadina, the coach had taken a wrong turning in the dark and become hopelessly lost. As Grace remembered it, they spent most of the night 'driving about in the bush, until at last, as we had taken seven hours to cover thirty-five miles, we thought it wiser to wait until daylight before proceeding on our journey'. This meant that they didn't reach Adelaide until after two p.m., and when they did finally arrive at the Oval, they were 'so stiff and tired that to play cricket decently was almost beyond us'.[26]

Even though they were late, Grace insisted on a net, and among those queuing to bowl at the tourists was a boy called George Giffen who would become one of Australia's outstanding players. The match had come as an unexpected birthday present – Giffen was fifteen on 27 March – and he was overjoyed at the chance to bowl at the Champion. 'Never in my life . . . did I try more earnestly to secure a wicket than I did when bowling at Grace's team in practice, but I had to be content then with getting the odd ball past the striker without once hitting the sticks, and pleased enough was I even with that measure of success.' As for the game itself, Giffen thought it would 'long live in the memory of those who witnessed it'. South Australia won the toss and batted first, but despite the exhausted state of the Englishmen, could do very little better than their despised neighbours at Kadina. Nor was the wicket notably superior. The home team lost eight wickets for ten runs, and Giffen was struck by 'the pitiable helplessness of most of our batsmen against the tricky bowling of Southerton, who, in the first innings captured 13 wickets for only 24'.[27] James Lillywhite took 8 for 38 and with a single bye the total reached 63.

There was no time for the Eleven to start their innings, and on the following day Grace held himself back so that the greatest number of spectators could see him bat. An estimated 5,000 were in the ground when he went in at number five. Giffen remembers the sense of anticipation as everyone expected 'to see the most wonderful batsman in the world make mincemeat of our bowlers'. But Grace was over-eager to oblige, and launched himself into a huge hit before he had got his eye in properly. He was well caught by a fielder 'standing on the edge of the boundary'.[28] No doubt hoping that the special circumstances would weigh with the umpire, he stood his ground, but the decision went against him. The Eleven made 108 and, with the cushion of a forty-four-run lead, set about dismissing a succession of inexperienced batsmen for what really was the last time on the tour. Perhaps to make up for his failure with the bat, Grace opened the bowling himself. He also invited Boult, who had hardly turned over his arm all tour, to share the new ball. If Grace intended making the South Australia Twenty-two look better than they were, the plan misfired. Boult returned the exemplary analysis of 7 for 14 in twenty-six overs. It was Grace himself who came in for what little punishment was going, his nine wickets costing fifty-nine runs.

On the Friday night, as planned the week before, a banquet, presided over by the governor, Sir Henry Ayers, was held at the town hall to honour the Eleven. Referring only in passing to the 'great many obstacles [that] were put in the way of our coming to play here', Grace gave generous praise to the organizers of the match who 'carried out every arrangement in the best possible manner'. His peroration, though flattering to his immediate audience, was hardly calculated to heal the wounds he had left in his wake at Kadina and further afield: 'We shall think of this visit as one of the pleasantest we have had. (Cheers). I am sure we have seen some of the best people here, if not the best that we have seen since leaving England. I won't say very much on that subject, but everyone here seems so thoroughly English. In some other places where we have been it is a little bit the reverse. (Cheers).'[29]

Although Grace was clearly determined to please his hosts in every way possible, the one thing he could not do was gratify the crowd's desire to see him make some runs. With only thirty-eight to win on the final day, Grace allowed the innings to run its course, and once again dropped down the order. But to no avail. He played a shooter hard into his wicket, and in his last innings he made his lowest score in Australia – 1. With Grace gone, interest in the proceedings evaporated. Only Greenwood (23) and Oscroft (20) made double figures, and the whole team must have been thoroughly relieved when the last wicket fell and the tour was finally over.

*

They caught a train that afternoon to rejoin the *Nubia* at Glenelg. Fred was waiting for them on board, having decided against an extended stay in Tasmania. Dozens of well-wishers from Adelaide came to see them off, and they left Australia with just as strong a demonstration of popularity as they had been met with at the outset.

It gave the appearance of a final seal of approval, and in Grace's summing up, the tour had 'on the whole, been conspicuously successful'.[30] Apart from his legalistic defence of his decision to play at Adelaide, the controversies surrounding his conduct were passed over in silence. The unsatisfactory aspects of the tour were addressed in Fred's summary for *Lillywhite's Companion*, but he echoed the professionals in attributing most of the friction to the promoters: 'It was most unfortunate for the team that they should have fallen into the hands of twelve speculators, all of whom were in business of some sort or another, and, I am sorry to say knew really nothing of cricket . . .' If this seems harsh on a man like Biddle who had long been associated with the Melbourne Cricket Club, Fred's strictures on the atmosphere in which the matches were played must have taken Australian readers aback. 'We were met,' he wrote, 'in a bad spirit, as if contending cricketers were great enemies.'[31]

In terms of results, the team produced a good overall record. They had played fifteen matches, winning ten and losing only three. For Grace as a cricketer it was another triumph. He had scored 711 runs at an average of 35.11, a considerable achievement given the rough wickets and packed fields. He also took seventy-two wickets and an astonishing forty-two catches, which was four more than Bush the wicket-keeper managed. Fred came a strong second in the batting, with 598 runs at 33.40 (the next highest average was Jupp's 16.13). Lillywhite and Southerton accounted for 170 and 145 wickets respectively. Both had an average of under six.[32] Away from the cricket Grace and Agnes had had a memorable honeymoon, enjoying a generous level of hospitality wherever they went. Grace had been able to indulge his other great loves: shooting and, on occasion, fishing. At one house where they stayed, he got up at dawn and amused himself by catching goldfish out of the pond and cooking them for his breakfast.[33]

However, Brownlee's over-enthusiastic description of the trip – 'as near as possible seven months of happiness and glory'[34] – falls wide of the mark. There were, undoubtedly, some extremely positive results of the tour. The very fact that an England team made the journey, after a ten-year gap, gave Australian cricket a much needed fillip. Only three years later a Combined Australian team was competing with an English XI on equal terms – and winning. Grace himself demonstrated a standard of batsmanship hitherto undreamt of, and his campaign to improve wickets also bore fruit. With the rapid advance in groundsmanship over the next few years Australian pitches became the best in the world and the bedrock for an ever-increasing improvement in all departments of the game.

But there were other legacies as well. It might not be thought that the Australians needed any lessons in competitiveness, but Grace's ruthless combative streak certainly made a lasting impression. Referring to some 'unpleasantness' in a club match in Sydney, 'Square Leg' lamented in the *Sydney Mail* 'that the example of the champion cricketer of the world, in starting disputes in the field, has not been without its ill-effect here'.[35] Grace's manner and behaviour both on and off the field would, in today's climate, have landed him in front of a disciplinary tribunal on charges of bringing the game into disrepute. He had gone to Australia pledging to 'maintain the honour of English cricket, and to uphold the high character of English cricketers'[36] and it cannot be said he did either. In fact he quickly exhausted almost limitless funds of personal goodwill towards him and his team. As an ambassador he had been an utter failure, and it has to be said that he sowed many of the seeds of mutual hostility and suspicion that intermittently soured Anglo-Australian relations in the years ahead. Not until Jardine led the Bodyline tour of 1932–3 was there a more unpopular and vilified English captain in Australia.

Much of the trouble arose from Grace's naturally overbearing personality. The Australians were sensitive to any assumptions of superiority, real or imagined, on the part of those coming out from England, and it was easy to cast the worst possible light on Grace's naturally abrupt manner. One of the most malicious attacks on him took the form of a fake letter supposedly written by Grace to an Australian friend on the eve of departure. In a style transparently different from Grace's own economical prose, it put a snide twist on all the most contentious aspects of the tour: 'The professionals were sulky with me for making them travel second-class . . . It is true I led them to believe up to the morning of sailing . . . that they would go in the saloon – but what else could I do? If I hadn't humbugged them they might have refused to go . . .' As to the occasions when he absented himself from various social functions, 'My reason was that I didn't want to fraternise with the tinkers, tailors, and snobs who are the great guns in your cricket world. To take their money was a fair thing in return for work done, but to hobnob with a lot of scum was a different thing. Fancy the chance of a greasy butcher in his travels walking up to me some day at Lord's with "How d'ye do, Mr Grace? I lunched with you in Australia."' With a sneer for the promoters whom he put 'in the hole nicely in the Adelaide match', and a confession that the tourists 'are at daggers drawn among ourselves', the letter ends with the gratuitous observation that Australia 'is a fine country, but wants steeping for 24 hours in the sea to rid it of the human vermin crawling over it'.[37]

This travesty appeared after Grace had left for England, but it returned to haunt him during his second tour when it was once again paraded before the Australian public. For all its ludicrous distortions, it does get near the bone in some respects, and was almost certainly inspired by Grace's speech at Adelaide with its gauche references to 'the best people' and everyone seeming 'so thoroughly English'. Nor was it unreasonable to detect snobbery as the root of the poor relations between Grace and his professionals. The decision to give them second-class passage may have been the promoters', but Grace reinforced their inferior standing at every turn once they reached Australia. It was a divided and unhappy touring party and the blame lay with him.

*

After their dreadful experiences round the coast of Australia, they had an uneventful return trip – 'the only untoward incident being a sand storm in the Suez Canal'. Once again they changed ships, and 'the latter half of the journey was made in the steamship *Kedive*, which stopped long enough at Alexandria to give us time to see the races, in which I saw dromedaries competing for the first and only time in my life.' They landed in England on 18 May to find 'that our doings in Australia had been followed by cricketers at home with the keenest possible interest, and that, for the first time, people in England had received the results of cricket matches played in Australia by means of the telegraph'.[38]

They also found that Disraeli was prime minister having led the Tories to power when Gladstone called a snap election. The papers were still full of Livingstone's life and last months in Africa before his death, which had been announced while they were away. Of more significance to Grace was the fact that a new cricket season had already started, and at some stage in the near future he was to become a father.

FOURTEEN

FOUR days after their return W.G. and Fred played for Thornbury against Clifton. The Clifton bowlers must have wished they'd stayed in Australia. Grace scored 259, Fred 123.

It took Grace a little while to hit his stride in first-class cricket, but when he did – with 179 for Gloucestershire against Sussex at Hove in June – he went on to enjoy a period of unprecedented success with both bat and ball. For the Gentlemen of the South against the Players of the North he made a century (104) and took eight wickets in the match. He then went into overdrive, scoring a century and taking ten wickets in the same match five times in the space of six games. There were only seven instances of this feat before 1874, and Grace himself accounted for four of them. According to Derek Lodge, it was 'certainly the best spell of all-round cricket seen to that time, and was arguably the best ever'.[1]

The run started with the Gentlemen–Players fixture at Prince's on 23, 24 and 25 July, a match that produced not only confirmation of Grace's undeniable superiority, but also further examples of the less acceptable side of his game. The Gentlemen batted first, and Grace made only 23 before being caught and bowled by Alfred Shaw. However, Fred hit 93 not out in a total of 222, and the two brothers then did the bulk of the bowling in the Players' first innings, W.G. taking 3 for 61 in 43.1 overs.

The Players gained a useful lead of twenty-one runs, and the match was in the balance when Fred joined his brother in the second innings. James Lillywhite was bowling and Fred, misjudging the length, hit a return catch back to him. All accounts agree that it was an easy catch – or would have been had W.G. not interposed his considerable frame between the bowler and the ball. Describing 'this curious incident', Sir Pelham Warner says that Grace 'palpably baulked the bowler'.[2] It was too much for Lillywhite. After all the tricks he had seen the Graces get up to in Australia, here they were practising them just as blatantly against English professionals in front of an English crowd. He was furious, as were the rest of the Players, who appealed vehemently to both umpires for obstruction. But Messrs Keeble and Luff, the two officials, declined to penalize Grace. With patrician understatement, Sir Pelham recorded that 'their decision was not received with equanimity', and the game continued in an atmosphere of smouldering hostility. Fred was bowled by Morley shortly afterwards, but Grace went on, indomitable and impervious, to 110, just over half the Gentlemen's second-innings total of 209. He then took 7 for 58 as the dispirited Players collapsed to 128 all out. One of Grace's victims was Richard Daft, the Players' captain, who was given out lbw for nought, a decision with which he was not happy. *Wisden* commented tartly that 'nearly every appeal by a Gentleman was decided affirmatively, and the Players' appeals were mainly met with NOT OUT'.[3]

On the match's major flashpoint, the obstruction of Lillywhite, Grace observed only that it was 'one of the remarkably few instances of a difference of opinion between my opponents and myself' – a comment in which Bernard Darwin detected 'some economy of historic accuracy'.[4] In fact Grace's long career was punctuated with differences of opinion between him and his opponents, arising from his overwhelming desire to win at virtually any cost. This excessive keenness had its roots in the orchard at Downend. All the Grace brothers played in the same way, and their highly competitive upbringing bred a single-minded ruthlessness that overrode considerations of propriety, and, far too often, fair play. Umpires could be conned or bullied, batsmen treated to a verbal barrage, and fielders belligerently challenged. No chink in an opponent's defence was too slight to be exploited, and the pressure was never relaxed for an instant. It was a boxer's mentality, and if in the heat of combat the odd blow went in below the belt, so be it.

The line between gamesmanship – the art of gaining advantage over an opponent within the strict letter of the law – and out and out cheating is a fine one. Whether Grace crossed it or not is a vexed question. Neville Cardus once asked an old Gloucestershire player, 'Did the old man ever cheat?' and received the answer, 'Cheat? No, sir, don't you ever believe it – he were too clever for that.'[5] That comment certainly suggests the spirit in which Grace played the game. While he would bridle at any suggestion of sharp practice, he had no truck with the emerging pieties associated with the phrase 'It's not cricket'. He never walked, never re-called a batsman even when he knew he should not have been given out, and appealed with authoritative conviction from any part of the field. And whatever the game threw up, however bizarre, he would try to turn to his advantage. On one occasion (Gloucestershire v. Surrey at Clifton in August 1878) a ball thrown in from the outfield lodged in his shirt. He simply kept on running, until finally 'collared by the fieldsmen'. Even then he refused to give back the ball, 'for by the strict letter of the law, had he handled [it] he could have been given out'.[6] But he was still prepared to claim the extra runs.

This was not how the majority of cricketers played the game, but there was nothing anyone could do to moderate Grace's behaviour, and he was generally accepted as a law unto himself. Most of his contemporaries recognized that 'any temporary friction in which he was ever involved was invariably due to his keenness'.[7] The incidents, when they occurred, arose on the spur of the moment. His action in 'baulking' Lillywhite was no more premeditated than his instinctive reaching for a low, hard catch off his own bowling. Though he could be exasperating, he was, in Lord Harris's words, 'so popular, and had the game so thoroughly at heart' that his excesses 'were readily forgiven him and indeed more often than not added to the fund of humorous stories about him'.[8] The rare occasions when he failed to get his way were seized on with universal delight. The most famous was when he stood up in the pavilion at the Oval and shouted 'Shan't have it; can't have it; won't have it' at a doubtful decision. Walter Read, who was fielding close by, secured anecdotal immortality by retorting, 'But you've got to have it.'[9]

Whether forgiven or not, there was no possibility of forgetting him. After the Prince's match he travelled up to Sheffield to score 167 and take 11 for 101 in Gloucestershire's victory over Yorkshire. The United South v. United North at Todmorden was the odd one out in this sequence of six all-round performances. He failed to score a century (by the comfortable margin of ninety-nine runs), but kept his hand in with another ten-wicket haul. Then he travelled back down south for what was a vintage Canterbury Week even by his standards. He scored 94 and 121 for Kent and Gloucestershire v. England and took 10 for 150, and then, for the MCC against Kent, he made 123 and took 11 for 129, including a hat-trick – the first time the feat had ever been performed by a centurian in a first-class match. On his return to Gloucestershire to play Yorkshire once more he scored 127 and took 10 for 121. That was the last of the season's eight first-class centuries, but his success as a bowler continued with fourteen wickets against Surrey at Cheltenham and a further seven against Sussex. And in his last first-class game of the season, the return between the United South and the United North, he took another ten wickets (for 125). This year, 1874, was the first in which he achieved the double of a thousand runs and a hundred wickets in genuinely first-class games (1,664 runs at 52 and 139 wickets at 12.64). The truly astonishing thing is that he actually did the double in his last eleven matches of the season, scoring 1,056 runs and taking 101 wickets.

Grace's all-round form lifted Gloucestershire to the top of most versions of the county table, though as Nottinghamshire still refused to play them after the previous year's row, they again avoided a showdown with their closest rivals. They nevertheless produced some outstanding results, beating Yorkshire twice and bowling Surrey out at Cheltenham for 27 and 73. The championship remained a matter of surprising indifference to Grace who makes no reference to Gloucestershire's supposed triumph, while, according to E.M., 'There ought never to have been [a championship], and the sooner it is done away with the better. It simply spoils the pleasure of cricket.'[10]

In addition to his first-class commitments, Grace continued his peripatetic life with the United South. His best performance was against Twenty-two of Leinster when he and Fred put on a stand of 272. W.G. made 153 – 'so far, the highest innings made against a twenty-two'[11] – and he now had the distinction of having scored centuries in England, Scotland, Ireland, Canada and Australia.

*

1874 marked a new phase in Grace's domestic life. On 6 July, Agnes gave birth to their first child, a boy whom they christened William Gilbert. It was a family tradition to give the eldest boy the father's names, but in this instance it was perhaps unfortunate. The difficulties of being the son of an eminent father were only pointed up by the burden of the world-famous initials.*

On their return from Australia, W.G. and Agnes had moved into The Chesnuts. Martha had something of an influx to cope with, as Walter Gilbert had decided to throw in his lot with Gloucestershire and accepted an invitation to pass his residential qualifying period at Downend. Fred had also returned to the family home after his brief stay in Aberdeen. He had attended classes regularly at the Medical School, but dropped out before sitting any of the first-year exams.

Grace was still registered as a medical student at Bristol, but at some stage it was decided that he should transfer to St Bartholomew's Hospital

---

* Sir Donald Bradman's son changed his name in an attempt to shake off the albatross of celebrity.

in London. Perhaps Agnes had some say in this. She was still a very young woman, and probably missed her family. Despite the wealth of medical experience to hand at Downend, she had insisted on returning home for her confinement, and she would almost certainly have welcomed a move back to the capital. They found accommodation initially in Earls Court, before moving further west to Acton, where they lived at 1 Leamington Park.

Bart's was one of the country's major teaching hospitals, and Grace was thrown in with students bent on reaching the top of their profession. He studied under Mr A. E. Cumberbatch, 'for many years the senior demonstrator of anatomy',[12] and took general surgery with Mr Howard. The discrepancy between his status as the country's most famous sportsman on the one hand and a very lowly medical student on the other must have struck his contemporaries forcefully, but Grace seems neither to have expected nor received any special treatment. Medicine was the one field in which he showed any deference to anyone, and his exaggerated respect for those who taught him is illustrated by a story in the *Memorial Biography*. Asked whether he had ever been nervous, he said,

Yes, once, when I was a medical student. My boss surgeon at Bart's, who hardly knew a bat from a ball, told me he would particularly like to see me play. So I said, 'On Thursday if I win the toss at the Oval, I shall go in first,' and he replied that he'd be there. Well, I won the toss and he had turned up to see me make runs. It was the first time since a boy I had played before a master, and having to do so absurdly bothered me. I felt altogether queer, and went in shaking like a leaf and was out for some five or six. He never came to watch me again and I was jolly glad.[13]

*

The match Grace was referring to was Gloucestershire's opening county match of 1875. The personal hex under which he was playing proved disastrous for his team, and they lost a low-scoring game by twenty-six runs.

The year was a wet one, and 'miserably cold the greater part . . . and wickets everywhere were sticky and very often unplayable'.[14] In these conditions Grace's batting resumed more human dimensions, and his average came down to 32.57. There were even suggestions that he had 'gone off'. But he still scored 1,498 first-class runs, which was more than anyone else, and completed the double again with a vast haul of wickets –

191 at 12.95. This was his most successful year with the ball, and a reminder that even if he had never scored a run, he would lay claim to greatness as a bowler alone.

In his own summary of the season he singles out Alfred Shaw for special note, saying he was 'simply irresistible'.[15] Alfred Lubbock thought Shaw caused Grace more trouble than anyone else and remembered how 'when W.G. had ten minutes at the net before a match began, he always selected Shaw to bowl to him', and that he used to 'bowl him out and beat him repeatedly'.[16] At Lord's in the match between Nottinghamshire and the MCC Shaw bowled through the home side's second innings, returning the extraordinary analysis of 41.2–36–7–7. Grace was the only batsman who had the technique to build an innings, and he scored 35 of the MCC's total of 98 before becoming one of Shaw's victims. He was just as effective with the ball, and his match figures of 9 for 86 helped the club win by fifty-two runs.

Rain saved the Gentlemen at the Oval, but the weather relented for the match against the Players at Lord's. After a failure in the first innings, Grace produced a marvellous display in the second. He opened with a first-year undergraduate, A. J. Webbe, who was making his debut in the fixture (as was Lord Harris), and between them they put on 203, which was a new record for the first wicket in Gentlemen–Players games. It was a remarkable achievement given the state of the wicket and the bowlers against them. Not only did they have Alfred Shaw to contend with, but his fellow Nottinghamshire bowler, Fred Morley, turned in a tremendous performance. Morley was decidedly quick, and unleashed a succession of leg-stump shooters. Edward Lyttelton was one of many connoisseurs fascinated by how Grace countered them: 'He brought his bat down with a curious dig, at such an angle that [the ball] not only went forcibly towards mid-on, but he positively placed it on each side of the field as he chose.' Webbe departed for a commendable 65 and Morley added five wickets to the six he had taken in the first innings, but Grace went on to 152 before being run out, after batting for just over three hours. According to Lyttelton, 'It was the most titanic display of batting that I have ever seen'.[17] With Hornby making fifty and the lower order taking advantage of the tiring attack, the Gentlemen ran up an unassailable total of 444, and the Players crashed to defeat by 262 runs. In addition to his magnificent century, Grace also took twelve wickets in the professionals' two innings.

He continued in this form in the third match at Prince's (where, as captain of the Gentlemen, he insisted on selecting the pitch), taking seven wickets against the Players as they were tumbled out for 70. Although the pitch he had chosen suited his bowling, Southerton and Shaw exploited it even more successfully. The Gentlemen were dismissed for 59, of which Grace made 20, and the Players extended their slender lead to 136 when they batted a second time, and with Southerton and Shaw again in complete control, won the match by forty-three runs.

There was a proliferation of the North v. South encounters this year with no fewer than seven played up and down the country. In the end, 'the public and the players themselves got tired of them'.[18] Grace played in all seven, and surprisingly failed to score a century in any of them, though he came close with 92 in the drawn match at Huddersfield.

Diplomatic relations were at last resumed between Gloucestershire and Nottinghamshire, and their two fixtures were restored. Nottinghamshire had the better of both: they won at Trent Bridge and were only denied a second victory by a century from Grace. This innings of 119 scored at Clifton on 18 August was his fiftieth century, and he was the first person to reach that milestone, by what Irving Rosenwater calls 'a truly vast margin'. Rosenwater has published some fascinating statistics associated with this particular achievement that underline W.G.'s absolute dominance in the 1860s and 1870s, and which go some way to establishing his position in the all-time league of great batsmen.

Grace was twenty-seven years and thirty-one days old when he made his fiftieth first-class century, the youngest until Wally Hammond in May 1930, who was fifty-two days younger, and it took him ten years and fifty-seven days from his first-class debut. In that time '*only 109 other centuries* were made in first-class cricket in England by all other players combined'. In other words, Grace scored '31.44% of all centuries scored in that period – a percentage quite unparalleled by any other player at any other time'. While Grace was reaching fifty centuries, Jupp managed ten, Daft six, Fred six and A. N. Hornby and Tom Humphrey four. 'In fact, in order to equal W.G.'s 50 centuries in the [same] period, it requires the combined centuries of the next 13 most successful century-scorers in England . . . evidence indeed of a vast superiority.'[19]

None of his contemporaries, of course, needed any convincing that Grace was in a class of his own, and to take the Champion's wicket was the highest ambition of any bowler in the first-class game. Two men who tested him to the utmost, J. C. Shaw and Ned Willsher, bowed out of the game in 1875. George Freeman, Emmett's partner for Yorkshire, had also faded from the scene to set up in business. Grace described the trio as 'three of the very best' he had ever faced.[20] After ten years in the game he had seen off his first generation of bowlers. Of those who would match their skills against him in the decades ahead, George Lohmann was a boy of ten, John Ferris was eight, Ernest Jones six, and Charles Kortright a doubtless scowling and petulant four-year-old.

Away from the great arenas, Grace had a triumphant season with the United South, for once achieving a better average against the odds than in his first-class innings. He scored 909 runs at 43, and took 186 wickets at a cost of only seven runs each. In September he made two huge totals – 152 against Eighteen of North Kent on the Bat and Ball ground at Gravesend, and 210 against Eighteen of Hastings and District at Hastings. This beat his record for an innings against the odds established in Ireland, but was destined to be capped dramatically in his next astonishing season.

*

Although Grace was now married with a child of his own (and another on the way), the ties with Downend remained strong, and he returned regularly to The Chesnuts. The Graces were a closely knit family, and they liked to keep in touch with one another. They had many similarities with the Browns as described by Thomas Hughes in *Tom Brown's Schooldays*: '[F]or clanship, they are as bad as Highlanders; it is amazing the belief they have in one another. With them there is nothing like the Browns, to the third and fourth generation . . . They can't be happy unless they are always meeting one another. Never were such people for family gatherings . . .'[21]

The Grace family now extended comfortably to the third generation. W.G.'s three elder brothers had long since married and settled down, though none of them outside the county boundaries. Henry had strengthened the Pocock connection, marrying his cousin Leanna Pocock and buying a practice at Kingswood on the outskirts of Bristol. E.M. had set up his standard in Thornbury, where he not only ruled the cricket club, but also exercised his natural authority as Coroner. Alfred had moved furthest from home, but only as far as Chipping Sodbury. Grace's three married sisters – Blanche, Annie and Alice – remained in Downend itself, while Fanny, who never married, stayed on at The Chesnuts. Like the Browns, the Graces were constantly visiting each other, but there were more formal gatherings of the extended family twice a year, for some mass activity like the nutting expedition recorded in a splendid group photograph (see Plate 14) or, characteristically, for a family cricket match.

For as long as she lived, Martha remained the head of the family. She had always been an important influence on Grace, and indeed on all her cricketing sons, and her interest in their performances never diminished. She kept voluminous scrapbooks of press cuttings recording their achievements, and invariably came to Gloucestershire's home matches at Clifton, sitting in her trap next to the pavilion. When playing away, Grace would send her regular telegrams to keep her informed: 'Self one hundred and forty not out. Fred one hundred and three; two hundred and ninety, four out' (from Dublin); 'Gloucester two hundred and eighty; Moberly one hundred not out. Ted eighty-nine. Notts. two out, seventeen' (Nottingham).[22]

A fleeting, and not very flattering, view of the Grace circle in the spring of 1876 is preserved in the diary of one of their neighbours, Nora Peache, who was the daughter of the Downend vicar, Revd Alfred Peache. (John Dann, Blanche's husband, was his curate before becoming a vicar himself when a second parish was created for the new church, Christ Church, in 1878.) Nora was a young woman with the usual accomplishments – and sentiments – of her age and class. She played the violin and piano, read poetry, and had more time on her hands than she knew what to do with. Although she was friendly with Fanny and Blanche, who were close to her in age, and paid social calls on Annie, she clearly had a low opinion of the Grace family as a whole. However, as her diary makes abundantly clear, there was one shining exception.

March 8th (Wednesday) [1876]

I went up with Fanny to Mrs Skelton's [Annie] & I played the violin. Fred was not there, & I did not care for it. In my estimation he is the nicest of the Graces, of course one could wish him in some things different, but Mrs Grace is so vulgar, she does say such things, & he does not go on like that. I went back with Fanny, & I played the violin with Mrs Grace . . . Perhaps it is conceited to put it, but I am sure Fred was watching me play, not that he might [not] watch anyone, but there are <u>different</u> ways of watching. I think he liked to hear me sing too, & I think it helped me. Then we played Whist, Fred & I (Fanny helping me) & Mrs Grace & Mr Pokcock [sic]. Fred took me into supper, & I feel sorry for him, I am sure he co'd be better if it was not for the rest. I should like to help him, & I believe I could . . . with God's help.

On saying Good Night, 'I gave his hand a little squeeze, & – he did too, I am sure, but it seems dreamy for F went out directly after, & I think it was well, for I am sure I must have blushed. Poor fellow I do feel sorry for him. I wonder if he does care for me a little bit . . . I should like to have his photo. I should like to see more of him without the other Graces . . .

Nora obviously cast Fred as a sensitive romantic surrounded by hearty vulgarians, and over the next few weeks developed a novelettish fantasy in which saving his soul and squeezing his hand assumed equal importance. Fred was indeed by far the most handsome of the Grace brothers, and as his unscheduled Tasmanian adventure suggests, he was not indifferent to female charms. However, reading between the breathless lines of Nora's diary, it appears he was anxious to keep her at a safe distance. Church was the traditional place for closely chaperoned Victorian young ladies to meet, or at least see, their admirers, and Nora looked forward to Sundays with particular keenness. Fred made sure he always had a chaperon of his own: 'Walter Gilbert and [Fred] sat in one of the middle pews. Once I looked up at him & he was looking at me, & it made me <u>blush</u> so, I got <u>so</u> red. Our eyes met two or three times after. Somehow I believe he does care for me a little.'[23]

Shortly after Easter, Grace was pressed into service as his brother's companion, though his appearance at Morning Service did not meet with Nora's approval. 'W.G. has come but I don't care for that.' Fred was all she did care for, and she spent the day on tenterhooks hoping that he would attend the evening service. He did, but he was late, and again he was not alone. 'I had prayed for him to come, & once when I looked to the side door I saw him there, but he did not come in for a minute or two & I was afraid perhaps he had gone away, but he soon came in with W.G.' Whether or not Grace was conscious of his role as gooseberry, his presence seems to have prevented the encounter Nora so desperately wanted. She disconsolately confided to her diary, 'We did not shake hands coming out; <u>when</u> shall we?'[24]

Nora continued to torment herself over Fred for the next few weeks. She and her family were spending the summer on the continent, and she was desperate to reach some sort of understanding before she left. Eventually, after many pages of scheming and soul-searching – '[27 April:] Shall I write a line & ask him to come to the summerhouse one night? . . . Perhaps it would not be right' – she steeled herself to call on The Chesnuts. Alas, the visit was abortive. '[6 May:] I did <u>see</u> him . . .

when we went to ask for Fanny, but I did not shake hands, he was playing cricket.'

For better or worse, that was what the Grace brothers did, and 1876 was to prove one of the most glorious in the family's cricketing annals.

FIFTEEN

EIGHTEEN seventy-six was Grace's *annus mirabilis*. He described it in *Reminiscences* as 'the most extraordinary batting year I had until 1895'.[1] But though the heights he scaled in that wonderful Indian summer were staggering, especially for a man in his forty-seventh year, 1876 saw him at his absolute peak.

As so often, he started slowly, making a string of low scores through May and the first half of June. But he carried his bowling success on from the previous season, taking ten wickets in both of his opening matches. (In the first of these, an England XI v. Cambridge University, Walter Gilbert scored 205 not out, the highest score by anyone apart from Grace all season.) His first century (104) came for Gloucestershire against Sussex at Brighton, but, as usual, it was the Gentlemen–Players matches that brought the best out of him.

The three games were played back to back over eleven days (29 June to 8 July), and during that period Grace bowled some 350 overs* and took twenty-seven wickets. In the first match at the Oval he took 5 for 103 in the Players' first innings (in seventy-eight overs). He then scored a duck, but again shouldered the bulk of the Gentlemen's bowling in the Players' second innings with 3 for 81 in another seventy-eight overs, and was leading the way to the 266 required for victory when dismissed by Ulyett for 90. The game petered out as a draw.

At Lord's he opened with his old partner from the Canada tour, C. J. Ottaway. They put on 126, at one point running a six and a seven in one over from Tom Emmett. Grace continued majestically to 169, and with a century from A. W. Ridley and a hard-hitting 68 not out from Fred, the Gentlemen reached their highest total of 449. This was far too much for the Players, and in harness with another Canada veteran, Appleby, Grace bowled them out for 219. He then took 6 for 41 when they followed on, and the Gentlemen won by an innings and ninety-eight runs. This was

---

* Although the five-ball over began to be experimented with this season, it was not universally adopted.

Fitzgerald's last year as MCC Secretary, and he no doubt had his attention drawn to Grace's bowling figures.

It was Grace's bowling that helped win the third match at Prince's. This looked likely to be a draw, but W.G. followed his five wickets in the Players' first innings with five more in the second, setting up an exciting run chase on the third afternoon. Grace set off in fine style, reaching 33 in quick time, but Lillywhite had his revenge for the obstruction incident of 1874, persuading Ned Willsher to give him out lbw. Tension mounted as wickets fell, but in the end Fred saw the Gentlemen home by five wickets with 30 not out.

After three consecutive matches of national interest, Grace next had to take a United South team up to Grimsby for a run-of-the-mill match against a local Twenty-two. With Agnes's second pregnancy coming to term, this was probably a chore he could have done without. His opponents did not seem particularly enthusiastic about it either, suggesting that the side he had recruited seemed rather under strength. Nevertheless, on Monday, 10 July he and Fred travelled north with Gilbert in tow to honour the fixture. Most of the rest of the team were late, so on winning the toss W.G. opened with Tom Humphrey, 'the old Surrey favourite', who was not noted for his batting but could prop an end up. When the others arrived just before lunch and saw Humphrey at the crease, they assumed the worst and rushed to the pavilion to put on their pads.

Grace's own pads, the yellowing pair once worn by Alfred Mynn, had been the focus of attention early in his innings. According to Mr Mortlock, the umpire, they were plumb in front of the wicket when he had scored only six runs. However, realizing that this really was an occasion where the crowd had come to see Grace bat and not some local non-entity bowl, he turned down the appeal. Quizzed about his decision that evening, he said, 'I did it all for the best, they really had such a bad team that I thought it inadvisable to give him out early in the game.'[2] At that stage neither Mortlock nor his companions could have guessed the full enormity of what he had done. Grace, after all, was only 136 not out.

While the townsfolk were mulling over the day's events, the three amateurs were running up their bar bill at the Yarborough Hotel, an unprepossessing but imposing pile next to the railway station. Quiet celebration was in order, as the overnight score was 217 for 2, and in addition to Grace's undefeated century, Fred had made a promising start with 29 not out. And there was still Gilbert to come. For a supposedly weak team, they were in a remarkably strong position.

Tuesday, 11 July was a red-letter day for Grace. He continued to plunder the Grimsby bowling at will. Appropriately, Fred was still with him when play was interrupted just before lunch by the arrival of a telegraph boy. Grace peeled off his gloves, tore open the envelope and showed the telegram to his brother, who was the first to congratulate him on the birth of his second son (Henry Edgar). Grace then called a halt to the proceedings and, in the words of Bob Lincoln who was one of the Twenty-two, 'invited us to adjourn and have champagne with him'. He proposed a toast to Agnes, adding, 'in a jocular way', the ominous afterthought: 'I should like to break a record, and celebrate it.'[3]

Play proceeded at a leisurely pace through the afternoon. Fred eventually holed out for 60, and Grace was joined by Gilbert. The score was 282 for 3. The first flicker of hope for the Grimsby men came when W.G. gave a chance on 180, but the wicket-keeper missed it. Grace put the lapse behind him and continued to treat every ball on its merits, occasionally despatching a delivery to the ropes, and even once or twice, to the delight of the crowd, lofting it out of the ground, but generally contenting himself with taking ones, twos and threes as he liked.

At 211 he passed his previous best against the odds. Was this the record he had had in mind? Apparently not. He carried on imperturbably past 250, though he did have a moment of fallibility at 260 when he was dropped at slip. He then equalled and passed his previous highest score in all cricket – 268 – but again showed no sign of relaxing his concentration. The 300 came in sight and was duly reached to applause that might have sounded a little perfunctory. Gilbert was also reaping a harvest of runs from the haplessly rotating bowlers. By the end of play he had reached 101, and Grace had made 313. The score was 537 for 4. Only one wicket had fallen all day.

On the Wednesday the crowds voted with their feet and stayed at home. They had seen enough. The Twenty-two trooped out to take up their positions once more, each finding the worn spot in the grass he had patrolled for the last two days, and perhaps wondering whether they were condemned to field for ever. Out came Grace again, as fresh and eager for the fray as on the first morning of the match. The torment continued.

Gilbert was dismissed after adding only twelve to his overnight score, and that led to a brief flurry of wickets, but Grace remained immovable, hitting runs at will as the score mounted inexorably towards 600. Lunch was taken. Play resumed. More wickets fell, but still the Champion went on, farming the bowling as best he could, though he lost Pooley in a run-out. The last man walked to the wicket. The score had reached astronomical heights, but Grace was still insatiable, his own tally well past the 350 mark. The telegraph showed only the grand total and the number of wickets, and when the last one fell – the chastened Mr Mortlock having absolutely no hesitation in raising his finger for an lbw appeal to see off the number eleven – it read 681. Grace strode off undefeated, and apparently unfatigued after nearly three full days at the crease. He went over to the scorebox where the scorer was struggling with his gargantuan task, and called up to ask how many he had made. '"399" was the answer. "Oh make it 400." Sam Haddelsey said, "Well you deserve it."' Bob Lincoln himself made the addition, and wrote afterwards: 'This is an absolute fact, and should once and for all settle the vexed question as to whether he ever scored 400 or not.'[4]

Even boosted to 400 it was still four short of the record score in all cricket, the 404 not out made by E. F. S. Tylecote in that house match at Clifton College back in 1868. Not that Grace minded; he had passed enough milestones already. His innings, made against fifteen different bowlers, comprised four sixes, twenty-seven fours, six threes, fifty-eight twos and 134 singles (including the bonus one), and was far and away the highest score ever made against twenty-two fielders.

Although Grace had used up most of the allotted time, there was still an hour or so in which to underline further the folly of criticizing a team he had taken the trouble to get together. The Grimsby team started batting at 4.30, and before a halt was finally called had lost eleven wickets for eighty-eight runs. Grace pounced on a couple of catches, and had the local vicar stumped by Pooley. Then, having paid off his men and collected his bags, he went home to see his new son, leaving the town in a state of shock. They may have felt they were the victims of some freakish conjunction of the planets portending wonders. The local newspaper that carried an account of the match also noted a sighting of 'Whales in the Humber', and reported 'one monster was seen swallowing a fine salmon'.[5]

Cricket's Leviathan moved on imperiously into the teeming waters of high summer, where he proceeded to gorge extravagantly without check. There were runs throughout the rest of July – a century for the South against the North at Trent Bridge, 69 and 50 in the return at the Oval, 19 and 57 for Gloucestershire against Yorkshire at Sheffield, followed by 60 and 26 against Nottinghamshire.

Then he was into August, and perhaps the single most remarkable month of his cricketing life. It started with a return to the Humber for a match at Hull between the United South and the United North. The night before there was a terrible storm, with high winds that blew down the tents on the cricket field. Richard Daft, the United North's captain, won the toss and fielded, thinking the rain-affected wicket would favour his bowlers. He was proved right, and his exceptionally strong attack – Alfred Shaw, Fred Morley and Allan Hill supported by Tye and Oscroft – duly routed the southerners. Between them Grace's team-mates managed twenty-eight runs with just one double-figure score, Pooley's 14. There were five extras. By rights the whole side should have been out for under fifty. The total in fact reached 159, of which Grace made 126.

Of all the matches where he seemed to be playing a different game from everyone else, this is perhaps the most notable. Jupp, Gilbert and Fred went for 1, 0 and 0 while Grace made 30, twice hitting Hill clean out of the ground. He had a sticky period after lunch against Morley, but warmed to his replacement, John Tye, whom he hit out of the ground and 'over two or three fields', the local paper added for good measure.[6] Almost immediately the ball had been fetched, he gave a sharp chance to Daft, who missed it, and he had another life shortly after that. Once Pooley's stubborn resistance was ended, wickets started falling rapidly, and Grace pressed on to his century and beyond. After a final boundary off Shaw, he 'tried to cut one late, and knocked down his wicket'.[7] He had batted for two and three-quarter hours, and hit nine fours (no sixes given even for hits out of the ground) and nineteen threes. It was an inspired innings, and Grace himself rated it as 'unquestionably one of the best I ever did, for the bowling . . . was extremely good'.[8]

Not content to rest on his laurels, he opened the bowling (with Southerton) and took the first wicket too, having one of the United North's openers caught by Pooley. This was a shy young man from Nottinghamshire who had made his debut for the Players at Lord's the previous month, and whom Grace would famously rank as second only to himself in years to come – Arthur Shrewsbury.

On the second day the pitch eased considerably. Ephraim Lockwood, Yorkshire's makeshift professional captain, made 108 not out (generously described as a 'really magnificent innings' by Grace),[9] and the northerners established a comfortable lead of just under a hundred. While not having much luck as a bowler, Grace's keenness in the field impressed the *Hull News* which remarked that 'the quantity of ground

[he] covered . . . was something marvellous'.[10] There was a dangerous period of forty-five minutes to negotiate before stumps, and Grace sent in Jupp and Fred, keeping himself back for the crowds on the third day, when he added eighty-two to his century in the first innings, and ensured an honourable draw for United South. As a one-man show it had been exceptional, and yet what followed would utterly eclipse it.

On Monday, 7 August Grace travelled down to Canterbury to continue his festival of high scoring. In the first match, Kent and Gloucestershire v. England he scored exactly 100 runs (9 and 91). He spent most of the first day of the MCC v. Kent game bowling at his old friend Lord Harris, who cut him 'again and again in his polished Eton way' while compiling 154.[11] Kent batted well into the second day, eventually making 473. Grace bowled seventy-seven overs and took 4 for 116. Then, despite the excellent wicket, both he and the rest of the MCC team failed. Dismissed for 144, they had to follow on, seemingly destined for a heavy defeat. Grace admitted that when he went in, he was more concerned with catching an early train back to London than with making a match of it. 'I played a rather freer game than usual. As I had to play at Bristol on the following Monday, and did not think we could save the match, I meant to get home as soon as possible. Consequently I opened my shoulders to the bowling . . .'[12]

The result was awesome. 'The first hundred was on the telegraph board after forty-five minutes' play, and when stumps were drawn the score stood at 217 for four wickets, of which my share was 133 (not out).'[13] The assault continued the next day when, in soaring temperatures, Grace extended his stand with P. C. Crutchley to 227 (Crutchley made 84). While this was a bonus for the crowd, it was an unexpected penance for the Kent team. Bill Yardley thought it 'about the hottest time I am ever likely to experience in this world'.[14] Grace was remorseless. Breaking off only to accept an invitation to quaff champagne and seltzer in a hospitable tent,[15] he passed 200, and 250. His own previous best score, 268, went next, followed quickly by William Ward's 278, which despite its doubtful provenance had been generally considered the first-class record for fifty-six years. After that, Grace pushed on through the psychological barrier of 300. He very nearly batted out the entire day, but in the end succumbed to Lord Harris who had been forced into service by the reluctance of his front-line bowlers to continue. One of those was Alfred Shaw, who had been drafted in to strengthen the Kent team and who now found himself under a towering drive with everyone on the field willing him not to drop it. He took it safely and, amid relieved congratulations, W.G. walked off with 344 to his name. He had batted six hours and twenty minutes without giving a chance, and hit fifty-one boundaries. 'Never,' according to *The Times*, 'was a more striking exhibition of endurance against exhaustion manifested.'[16]

Deprived by his own brilliance of a rare rest day, Grace made the halting cross-country journey to Bristol on the Sunday (13 August) and arrived 'rather tired' that evening. However, after a good night's rest he was perfectly fit for Gloucestershire's match against Nottinghamshire at Clifton College. The heatwave continued, but had no effect on Grace. He won the toss, batted, and scored 177 in three hours. Although the match is caught up in the tidal wave of his personal triumph, it was in fact a full family affair. 'The three Grace Brothers made 304 runs out of 419 from the bat, and, between us, had a fist in getting rid of seventeen of the twenty Notts wickets.'[17] E.M. was run out for 16 in the first innings of 400, but snapped up four catches at point. Fred scored 78 and then took five wickets as Nottinghamshire were bowled out for 265. In their second innings, W.G. took 8 for 69, and then sent in E.M. and Fred to knock off the thirty-three runs required for a ten-wicket victory.

The next match, against Yorkshire, was at Cheltenham, and there is no reason to doubt the story that the defeated Nottinghamshire eleven met the Yorkshire team at the station as they waited for their connection. When Emmett heard of Grace's second successive success, he laughed. 'Even the Big 'Un couldn't do it three times,' he said, adding, 'I'd shoot him first.'[18]

He may have felt less confident when Grace won the toss the following morning and remarked as he came out to the perfect batting wicket, '*You'll* have to get me out today. I shan't get myself out.' He was as good as his word, and by the end of the day had driven the Yorkshiremen to distraction – indeed, to the brink of mutiny. Ephraim Lockwood had the same problem as Lord Harris at Canterbury, but with rather less natural authority and rather more bolshie subordinates he had a thoroughly wretched time of it. When he called Allan Hill into the attack, the bowler refused point-blank. 'Make 'im bowl. Tha'rt captain,' jeered Emmett, and when Hill accused him of being frightened to bowl himself, he grabbed the ball and proceeded to unleash three of the widest wides ever witnessed in a first-class match.

None of this had any effect on Grace's concentration. At the end of the first day's play he had reached 216 and the Gloucestershire total was 353 for 4. Next morning the weather broke and it rained, but not long enough for the Yorkshire team, and at around one o'clock Grace chivvied them back out onto the field. The other batsman was G. O. Moberly, 73 not out overnight, and he helped Grace raise the total to 429 before departing with a well-made century to his credit. The partnership was worth 261. The lower order then collapsed, and Grace was in serious danger of being stranded. He was still a few runs short of 300 when the ninth wicket fell and the burly figure of Arthur Bush came out to join him. This was a greater responsibility than remembering the ring at the wedding, but he assured Grace he would stay in 'until you get your runs'. He made an excellent 32, and when Ulyett bowled him Grace had reached 318, which was to remain the highest score in a county match for the next twenty years. In three successive innings over a period of eight days (from 11 to 18 August) he had scored 839 runs at, as he liked to emphasize, an average of 419.5.

Success of such magnitude ran the danger of becoming farcical, and some of the lighter periodicals strove manfully to derive comic effects from Grace's stupefying achievements. One humorist imagined Grace taking on a Twenty-two of 'Wapshot' single-handedly. He wins the toss and bats, and as the runs mount up in staggering profusion, so the temperature rises inexorably, and bowlers and fielders fall out with sunstroke:

Score 106, and thermometer 97. W.G. now cut Jobson for 26 (the ball was sent clean over the village . . .), and afterwards collared Jollyboy's slows – 200 and the thermometer 100 . . . By mid-day the score stood at 724. W.G. had been at the wickets six hours (Play had commenced at six o'clock, as it was desired to have a good long day), and had never given a chance.

At one o'clock the score had risen to 965, and W.G. complained of being a little warm, but offered to play through luncheon time if the other side liked. It was thought better to adjourn, as the thermometer was 105 in the shade. . .

By the end of the day, the Wapshots are reduced to six men, and Grace has scored 2,001 'by as fine an exhibition of good all-round cricket as we would wish to see . . . and declared himself in readiness to go in the next day, but the Wapshots declined.'[19]

This would hardly have read as fantasy to the men of Grimsby, Kent and Yorkshire, and indeed it differs very little from a sketch in the *Saturday Review* of a typical Grace innings at Lord's during a heatwave:

Hour after hour passes, and there is the Champion in his old position. The field becomes demoralised, the bowlers are utterly exhausted, even the boys at the telegraph can hardly summon up strength to put up the numbers that are so perpetually increasing. At last some desperate appeal is made for leg before wicket, and an umpire, long since unconscious of what was going on around him, decides against the batsman. Immediately, eleven men prostrate themselves on the ground in a state of collapse, and the Champion marches indignantly to the Pavilion, inveighing against the stupidity of umpires, deploring his ill-luck in being given out just when he was so well set . . .

The article concludes that

Modern cricket . . . seems to have resolved itself into a match between Mr Grace on one side and the bowling strength of England on the other . . . At present, Mr Grace has clearly the mastery over his opponents. His powers, so far from showing signs of diminution, are showing signs of increase. No longer content with his hundreds and two hundreds, he has gone in this season for scores of three hundred and upwards, and there seems no reason why, if he can find anyone to stop in with him, and run his runs with him, he should not next season make five hundred off his own bat. How can a few bowlers of eminence hope to cope with such a man, who can go on all day, and every day in the week, and who, to all appearances, will be as good ten years hence as he is now?[20]

Not until Bradman would another batsman be written about in quite such awed tones.

Sussex were the next to face the music, and must have felt uneasy when W.G. set off strongly in the match at Clifton. He passed fifty and it would have taken a brave man to bet against his hitting a fourth successive century. In the event he fell on 78, and in the second innings made only 7. That match was drawn, and so was the next, against Surrey. Grace wound down with a humdrum 29, though he took 6 for 35 in the visitors' one completed innings. With Grace excelling even himself, Gloucestershire were far and away the best side in the country. They won five of their eight matches, and drew the remaining three, which was enough to secure them the championship.

August was the highest-scoring month of his entire career. 'I made 1,389 runs, a total which I may be forgiven for mentioning was greater than any other batsman made in the whole year in first-class cricket.'[21] He includes all his innings in that total, but most of the matches were first-class, and those yielded 1,278 runs. His 839 runs in three successive innings remains a record to this day, comfortably ahead of the next best 'treble', V. M. Merchant's 750 in 1943–4.

Though not overly concerned with records or averages, Grace liked to keep a record of his achievements, and usually totted up his runs for the season. His summary of 1876 recently came to light among his cricket books (see Plate 9). He played twenty-six first-class matches and scored 2,622 runs in forty-six innings, four of which were not out. (Engagingly, he makes a mistake with his average, giving it as 62.18 instead of 62.42.) In thirteen matches against the odds he scored 1,180, and, throwing in a couple of other non-first-class matches, he made a grand total of 3,908 runs throughout the season.

1876 was truly the year of Grace.

SIXTEEN

At the end of the 1876 season James Lillywhite led the fourth English cricket team to tour Australia. This was an epoch-making trip which saw the inaugural Test match played in Melbourne in March 1877 (though it was only recognized as such retrospectively). As with previous tours, it was a speculative venture, and Lillywhite had reverted to an exclusively professional squad. After the experiences of 1873–4, Grace would probably not have been welcome even had he been available.

Instead, the world's best cricketer settled down to a winter with his young family and his medical books. At the beginning of the year, almost certainly acting on advice from Henry, he had transferred from Bart's to the Westminster Hospital. The Westminster Medical School was much smaller than Bart's, with only about fifty-five students. This was probably the reason Grace moved. As George Cowell, the dean, emphasized: '[I]t is the boast of a small medical school, that there the opportunities of clinical study are very much greater than is possible in a large school where only a tithe of the students can obtain clerkships, and dresserships, and where in going round the wards, each student is but a unit of a large crowd.'[1]

The science of medicine had made some advances since Grace's father trained. The chloroform anaesthetic had been developed and was given universal credibility when the Queen availed herself of it during two of her confinements in the 1850s. But surgery remained a brutal affair. Richard Davy, the dresser at the Westminster, 'would often bring a set of carpenter's tools into the theatre' and 'an old frock-coat splashed with blood and pus was kept for operations and never cleaned'.[2] Before the paramount importance of hygiene was grasped, the surgeon himself was likely to be the most septic object in the operating theatre.

The standards of the London medical schools came under attack in the *Fortnightly* in 1879, and an article written in defence of the Westminster gives an indication of the conditions under which the students worked. One vaunted breakthrough was that 'Students whilst dissecting no longer were allowed to attend midwifery cases; among 102 midwifery cases attended by students in 1878 one death had occurred from collapse, and one from septicaemia after version . . . It was true, however, that once during the previous winter an offensive dead body had been brought up through a trap door in the "Clinical Theatre" for the operative surgery class.'[3]

The man Grace studied under was William Henry Allchin. Though only two years older than Grace, Allchin was a higher flyer. He became a Member of the Royal College of Surgeons at twenty-two, and his distinguished career was ultimately rewarded with a knighthood. He was an experienced tutor, having done a great deal of coaching to fund his own training, but 'it was . . . in the wards of the Hospital that Allchin was seen to the greatest advantage. He was an admirable clinical teacher, thorough and methodical in his examination of the patient, and never satisfied until he had regarded the case under consideration from all points of view.'[4] As Sub-Dean and then Dean of the Westminster School he had the reputation of being 'a firm disciplinarian', but Allchin was apparently no more successful than his predecessors in getting Grace to step up the tempo of his studies. In a letter of 16 February 1876 W.G. told a correspondent in passing, 'I go to Westminster Hospital twice or thrice a week',[5] which suggests he continued to take a fairly relaxed approach to the business.

*

Grace would have noted the result of the All England v. A Combined New South Wales and Victoria Eleven match, as the first Test was billed, and doubtless tugged his beard over a poor English performance which allowed the Australians to win by forty-five runs (they won the Centenary Test by exactly the same margin). He would also have been interested in the performance of Billy Midwinter, who took five wickets in England's first innings and chipped in with some useful runs.

Quite when Midwinter decided to try his luck as a cricketer in his native land is not known, but at some stage Grace must have agreed to give him a trial with Gloucestershire if he ever made the long trip back to the country of his birth. At the end of the Lillywhite tour, Midwinter packed his bags and followed the tourists back to England, arriving in London in May 1877. After a ruinously expensive taxi ride and a slap-up meal which further depleted his limited resources, he went straight to the Oval where Grace was playing for the Gentlemen of the South against the Players of the North. Grace signed him up for three United

South matches, and perhaps pressed a couple of sovereigns into his palm on account. If he proved his worth, he would play for Gloucestershire later in the season when the county championship campaign began in earnest.

Midwinter played in odds matches at Birmingham, Holbeck and Barrow-in-Furness, but must have felt impatient to show his colours in the first-class game. The travelling Elevens had really had their day. The first of them, the AEE, faded from the scene this season after thirty years on the provincial circuit, and although the United South 'continued to exist for three or four years longer, its fortunes declined rapidly'.[6] It only remained viable as long as it did because of Grace's continued involvement.

Grace had not started the season in the triumphant vein of the previous year – 1877 was wet, which helped the bowlers – and he didn't pass fifty until his fifth match, when he helped the South beat the North at Lord's towards the end of May. However, he was doing well with the ball, taking eleven wickets in the North–South match and then putting in another excellent all-round performance for the MCC against Derbyshire. He scored 35 out of 112 and 48 out of 123 and took fourteen wickets for 109.

He was back to his best batting form in the return between North and South at Prince's starting on 31 May. By the end of the first day he had scored 252 not out and the South had lost only two wickets for 385. The following morning the weather turned vile, with intermittent rain and a strong wind blowing over the ground. Grace was not exposed to the elements for very long, returning to the pavilion with only nine runs added to his overnight score. When the North batted, he showed his appreciation of the altered conditions with returns of 5 for 62 and 6 for 77. The South won by an innings and 152 runs.

Grace did a great deal of bowling in the three Gentlemen v. Players matches. In the first, at the Oval at the end of June, there was a great deal of bowling to be done, as the Players took advantage of a rare spell of warm, dry weather and on a perfect wicket made 405. The feature of this was the opening stand of 166 between Ephraim Lockwood and Arthur Shrewsbury, who was still only twenty-one. Lockwood fell three short of his century, but it was Shrewsbury's 78 that won the plaudits. *Wisden* called it 'the most perfectly played innings in the three Gentlemen v. Players matches of 1877'.[7] Grace bowled sixty-five overs, so had the opportunity to inspect this new batting talent at close quarters, and though he failed to dismiss him on this occasion, he took his wicket ten times over the course of the season. The Gentlemen made 427 thanks to Hornby's 144 and Alfred Lyttelton's 66. Grace failed with the bat, but still left his mark on a game destined for stalemate by taking five cheap wickets when the Players batted again.

The game at Lord's on 2, 3 and 4 July was altogether more exciting, and went down in the annals as 'The Glorious Match'. Grace had a relatively quiet game, which accounts for the evenness of the contest. The Players scored 192, which the Gentlemen exceeded by six runs, thanks largely to a magnificent innings of 92 by J. M. Cotterill. Cotterill was another cricketing medic, but unlike Grace he gave up the game to concentrate on his profession. He became an eminent surgeon and was eventually knighted, an honour steadfastly denied Grace. The wicket, which had been slow to start with, became more difficult, and the Players managed only 148 in their second innings. Grace showed his mastery of good bowling on a difficult surface, but when he went, caught and bowled Morley for 41, the rest of the batting collapsed. The Players looked to have the game in the bag when the ninth wicket fell and the Gentlemen were still forty-six short of their target. However, Fred, batting surprisingly low in the order, and W. S. Patterson dug in and gradually turned the situation round. When the winning run was hit the crowd stampeded onto the ground and chaired the two heroes back to the pavilion.

In the absence of a more socially acceptable candidate, Grace captained the amateurs in the third match, at Prince's. As E. F. S. Tylecote was also playing, the Gentlemen's team contained the only two batsmen who had reached 400. That, as it happened, was the Gentlemen's total in their first innings, though Grace and Tylecote made only thirty-three runs between them. Fred hit 134, and Walter Read made 72. The weather was appalling, with a fierce thunderstorm on the evening of the first day and an even more spectacular one on the second afternoon when loud claps of thunder accompanied by forked lightning and teeming rain drove the players from the ground. Despite two fighting innings of 53 and 118 from Ulyett, the Players succumbed by nine wickets.

This was the last Gentlemen–Players match at Prince's. Its location near Sloane Square had made it a prime target for development and the Prince brothers had been selling off lots for some time. 'First one corner, and then another piece . . . was cut off by the builders, and though two or three important matches were played there in the following year, Prince's Cricket Ground soon ceased to exist.'[8] Like the old ground at Hove, it had been a productive venue for W.G. He must have been sad to see it go.

As a prelude to the second half of the season, in which Gloucestershire played the majority of their matches, the county teamed up with Yorkshire to take on England at Lord's in the middle of July. The weather was still bad, and the first day's play was lost entirely. Grace had a good match, scoring 52 in the first innings. The second fell on 18 July, his twenty-ninth birthday, and he duly celebrated with a century which included one 'fine hit clean out of Lord's ground into Dark's garden for six runs'.[9] He was caught Barnes, bowled Lillywhite in both innings. The rest of the Gloucestershire contingent also did themselves justice, and Midwinter, drafted in for his first appearance at Lord's, took the wickets of I. D. Walker and Jupp. But with so much time lost, the match was left unfinished.

Gloucestershire continued their form of the previous summer, and Grace led them to seven victories in eight matches to retain the championship comfortably. Grace provided the driving force, ably seconded by Fred. Frank Townsend was a dependable batsman; Gilbert also scored runs, and gradually replaced E.M. as Grace's opening partner. When available, W. O. Moberly took Bush's place behind the stumps and could also score runs, while C. R. Filgate was a useful all-rounder. If there was a weakness it was the bowling. Grace wheeled away tirelessly, his nagging leg-stump line proving remarkably effective; Fred was always willing, if lacking in penetration; and Midwinter's medium pace could be made to seem fairly ordinary on a good wicket. They badly lacked the professional firepower of Nottinghamshire or Yorkshire. Given his limited resources, Grace came up with a tactical innovation. He had recruited the Oxford blue R. F. Miles, a slow left-hander who relied more on accuracy than dramatic turn; Grace instructed him 'to bowl wide on the off-side on purpose' to a packed offside field, and that, says Grace, 'is how off-theory came about'.[10]

Midwinter showed how useful he would be in the right conditions when Gloucestershire played an England side at the Oval at the end of July, taking 7 for 35 and 4 for 46. This was the first time for ten years that a single county had been deemed strong enough to take on a representative national team, and Gloucestershire justified the compliment by winning a low-scoring game by five wickets. Grace scored only 9 and 31, but gave Midwinter valuable support with 3 for 37 and 4 for 46. The two Gloucestershire giants bowled hundreds of overs in tandem in the years ahead.

After the England game, Gloucestershire travelled up to Sheffield to have the better of a draw against Yorkshire, and then beat Nottinghamshire at Trent Bridge on the way down south again (Grace took ten wickets in the match). The county programme was then suspended for Canterbury Week. There was no repetition of the previous year's astronomical scoring, though Grace hit a couple of fifties making his one guest appearance for Kent against an England eleven. He just missed a third half-century when he played for the MCC against the home team, and helped win the game with match figures of 9 for 83.

It was as a bowler again that he featured in the game against Nottinghamshire at Cheltenham. Gloucestershire scored 235, and then Grace started another marathon with the ball. In Nottinghamshire's first innings he bowled fifty-one overs and took 9 for 55 in a total of 111. Following on, the visitors did even worse, and things became comical. Grace set his usual crude leg trap with 'two fieldsmen at long leg', and batsman after batsman gullibly holed out to them. Richard Daft, the Nottinghamshire captain, became increasingly irate, but then delighted his team by falling into the trap himself. The two deep fielders were Gilbert and Fred and between them they took five catches. Grace ended with 8 for 34, the last seven wickets falling without a run being scored.

He took nine wickets in the match, as well as scoring 71, in the county's win over Yorkshire at Clifton, rounding off the season with eleven wickets against Sussex and eight against Surrey. In all he took eighty-one wickets for Gloucestershire at an average of 9.64, which more than compensated for his uncharacteristically few runs (327 at 32.70). Despite the relative falling-off in his batting, Grace still did the double quite comfortably in all first-class matches, with 1,474 runs at 39.83 and 179 wickets at 12.80.

Although it could not compare with 1876, it had been a marvellous season. It was also very nearly his last. In September Grace was involved in a shooting accident which threatened his life and came close to costing him the sight in one eye. He was combining some country house cricket with his other great love, partridge shooting, at Apethorpe in Northamptonshire. He had been invited by Lord Westmorland to avenge the defeat of his lordship's team by Lord Exeter's XI at Burghley the previous year. Grace left nothing to chance, bringing down a strong side that included Fred, Gilbert and Southerton, and scoring a century himself into the bargain. The next day, 6 September, he went out with the guns, but allowed enthusiasm to override caution. Slipping up 'a high hedge out of the line', he got ahead of the rest of the party, and when the birds went up over his head, he was caught in a sort of 'curtain fire'. He was hit, 'and not only hit, but hit in the eye'. A halt was called immediately, and Fred rushed up to assess the damage. The whole party stood round in silence 'watching G.F. winding bandages round W.G.'s head', and then followed in a funereal procession as he led his injured brother back to the house. Having cleaned up the wound, Fred was able to announce that W.G.'s sight would not be impaired.[11] He was lucky. Ranjitsinhji was caught in a similar incident many years later and spent the rest of his life with a glass eyeball.

It may have been this brush with serious injury (or worse) that prompted Grace to step back and review his life. At twenty-nine he was still a young man, but his widening girth and increasing weight meant that he was no longer the complete athlete he had been in his teens and early twenties. Even though he broke the amateur rules with profitable impunity, cricket could not guarantee long-term security for a man with a wife and growing family to support (Agnes was pregnant again).

Grace was offered a strong inducement to settle down to his chosen profession as a doctor from an unlikely source. The MCC agreed to give him a National Testimonial, with a view to buying him a practice from the proceeds. This was partly in recognition of his extraordinary achievements and the vital role he had played in reviving the club's fortunes, but it was also a response to the embarrassment caused by his blatant shamateurism. The hope may have been that with a busy practice to run, Grace would have to reduce his cricketing commitments, or even retire altogether; and if he did stay in the game, a regular income would at least end his reliance on appearance fees and grossly inflated 'expenses'.

The scheme was originated by two leading lights of Gloucestershire cricket, the Duke of Beaufort and Lord Fitzhardinge, who were also influential figures at Lord's. The Duke of Beaufort was president of the MCC in 1877, and Lord Fitzhardinge succeeded him in 1878, so between them they could keep a controlling hand on the project. They presumably consulted with Grace and outlined the thinking behind the club's unique and very generous gesture. As circulars were being sent out to every club in the country soliciting contributions, 'the recurrent rumour of [Grace's] imminent retirement' also started spreading.[12] Bernard Darwin, with whom Grace was intimate in later life, said that 'his decision had trembled in the balance',[13] though, of course, W.G. was canny enough to realize that the supposition that he was actually quitting cricket for good would probably have a positive effect on the final sum raised by the appeal.

However serious he really was about retiring, there was one factor above all others that kept him in the game. The Australians were due to send a touring team to England in 1878.

*

The first Australian tour, as it has always been referred to despite the Aboriginal precedent of 1868, was modelled on the English visits to Australia. The Australian players had seen how profitable touring could be, and under John Conway's management a group of them decided to try it for themselves, each putting fifty pounds into the kitty against expenses. James Lillywhite agreed to act as their agent and get them as many fixtures as he could, both first-class and against the odds. Following the English example, the team was only twelve strong, with six from New South Wales, five from Victoria and one from Tasmania. The captain was David Gregory, one of a cricketing family to rival the Graces, and the other players were Thomas Horan (who developed into an excellent cricket writer under the pen-name 'Felix'), Billy Murdoch, John Blackham ('the Prince of Wicket-keepers'), the brothers Charles and Alec Bannerman, T. W. Garrett, G. H. Bailey, and two bowlers who would rock English cricket to its foundations, Frederick Spofforth and Harry Boyle, backed up by 'the bowler of the century', Francis Allan. The last man was Billy Midwinter.

After a preliminary leg of the tour in New Zealand and a match against Eighteen of Victoria in Melbourne, the party set sail for England and arrived on 14 May. They probably regretted it immediately. If 1877 had been a bad year, 1878 was even worse, and they had a miserable time trying to acclimatize. With naive faith in the notion of an English summer, they had come equipped with fine silk shirts but no sweaters, and spent the early games shivering in the wintery temperatures. They got off to as bad a start as Grace's team in 1873–4, Lillywhite having done them no favours by arranging their first match at Trent Bridge. They proved unequal to Alfred Shaw and Fred Morley on a typical rain-affected wicket, and lost by an innings. This was only what was expected. Despite the result of the first Test in 1877 and one or two other warning signs from Grace's tour, no one in England took the Australians very seriously. Grace himself recalled '[we were] not very much alarmed about being defeated by them . . . [and] never for a moment thought of classing them with an English representative team'.[14]

That changed on 27 May in arguably the most momentous six hours in cricket history. Lillywhite had obviously decided to give the Australians a baptism of fire. The second match was against the MCC at Lord's, and on a damp, depressing morning the Australians must have looked around the famous ground with a sense of foreboding. The wicket was similar to the one at Trent Bridge and Shaw and Morley were on hand to put them through another rigorous examination. The MCC side also included the greatest bad-wicket batsman in the world, W.G. himself, though apart from Grace and Hornby, the batting was not particularly strong, and the notion that this was an English Test side in all but name is nonsense.

Play started at three minutes past twelve. The sun was now out, turning the wet wicket sticky. Allan bowled the first ball, and Grace hit it to leg for four. The few spectators clapped, and settled down to see the Champion put the colonials in their place. Allan ran in again, and again Grace hit a firm shot off his legs, only this time the ball went straight to Midwinter, who experienced no conflict of loyalty in sending his county captain marching crossly back to the pavilion. Boyle took a couple of wickets at the other end, but Hornby, who had opened with W.G., survived and scored a few runs. There was no sense of panic; not, that is, until Gregory replaced Allan with Spofforth. The crowd watched with interest as the tall, spare figure marked out his run and then came bounding up to the crease to deliver the ball with a terrifying leap and a very high action. His bowling had a naked hostility that intimidated all but the toughest batsmen, and very properly earned him the nickname 'the Demon'. His first spell at Lord's was truly demonic. He shattered Hornby's stumps and ran through the rest of the batting with a devastating display of guile and aggression. In 5.3 overs (just twenty-three deliveries) he took six wickets for four runs, his analysis reading: . . . 2 / . W . . / W . . . / 1 . . . / W W W . / . 1 W. Apart from Hornby (19), no one reached double figures in the MCC's total of 33.

Spofforth had the fast bowler's killer instinct, yet he was not exclusively a fast bowler. As a ten-year-old he had seen Tarrant bowl for Parr's team and spent his boyhood trying to generate speed above all else. But as he grew to maturity he started to experiment, and realized that accuracy was just as important as pace, and that pace itself would be more effective if it were varied. Two of his victims at Lord's were stumped, and throughout his career he liked to have his wicket-keeper standing up.* Spofforth's stock delivery was the break-back, the ball that came in sharply from the off to the right-hander, though he could move it away at will. (Later in life he claimed to have mastered swing bowling, but rejected it because it sometimes affected his length.) His high action meant he got lift on any wicket; on a track that gave him assistance he was nearly unplayable.

The MCC were by no means out of the match. Shaw and Morley had already proved their mastery over the Australian batsmen, and proceeded to demonstrate it again. They bowled unchanged, taking five wickets each as the Australians collapsed to 41 all out.

That left the game evenly poised, and the MCC needed only a moderately respectable score to be confident of winning. Grace and Hornby opened again, but this time Gregory opened with Spofforth. Grace took his position at the wicket. Spofforth stared at him icily from the end of his run-up. Even in his habitual nerveless state of total concentration, Grace may have heard the tiniest tick of premonition. The umpire's arm dropped like a railway signal and Spofforth burst into motion. Grace managed to get an edge on the first ball, but Murdoch missed the catch. There was no second chance. Spofforth castled him next ball. This was a fatal blow, and a mere fifty minutes later the last MCC wicket fell with the score on 19. Boyle had taken the majority of the wickets – 6 for 3 in a spell of 8.1 overs – but it was Spofforth who had seized the initiative, and he took three more wickets to finish with 4 for 16 (10 for 20 in the match).

Needing only twelve runs to win, the Australians lost Charles Bannerman to Shaw before Midwinter and Horan negotiated their way to an overwhelming and astonishing victory. The crowd which had swelled in the afternoon sunshine were thrilled by the unexpected drama they had witnessed, and mobbed the Australians as they left the field in a spirit of non-partisan enthusiasm. English cricket had found a worthy opponent, and a partner with whom to take the game on to greater heights. Henceforth a match between Australia and any representative English team would overshadow any of the 'great matches'. A new chapter had been opened; there was no possibility of Grace closing the book at this point.

* His first-choice wicket-keeper at this stage was Murdoch, who kept at Lord's. Spofforth had actually refused to play in the first Test match when told Murdoch wouldn't be wicket-keeper. He was quite as headstrong as Grace.

He gave the Australians due credit for their 'glorious victory' when he wrote about the match in his *Reminiscences*, and remarked that, subtracting the lunch interval and breaks between innings, the whole match had been completed in only 'four and a half hours of actual cricket'.* He also quoted the famous quatrain from *Punch* against himself:

> The Australians came down like a wolf on a fold,
> The Marylebone Club for a trifle were bowled,
> Our Grace before dinner was very soon done,
> And Grace after dinner did not get a run.[15]

*

The Australian invasion confirmed Grace's commitment to cricket at the top level, but his growing responsibilities meant his life was becoming a more complicated juggling act. By the time the new season opened, he and Agnes had moved back to the Bristol area, taking up residence with Henry at Kingswood, presumably so that Grace could complete the last crucial lap of his medical studies under his brother's personal supervision. Grace had been awarded a benefit match at Lord's the following July at which it was proposed to present the testimonial, so it was absolutely vital that he qualified in 1879. Once again, Agnes had returned to London for her confinement, and before the shattering events at Lord's had given birth to her third child, who was in due course baptized Agnes Bessie by W.G.'s brother-in-law, John Dann, though not until well through the cricket season.

With all his various domestic distractions, Grace's season had not started particularly well. He took ten wickets against the exceptionally strong Cambridge University team at Fenners, and scored 47 out of 93 for MCC against an England Eleven at Lord's, and when he played for the club against Derbyshire he bowled the visitors out for 36, taking 8 for 23. He hit something like his best form in the North–South match at Lord's, scoring 45 and 77 and taking nine wickets in the match, though this didn't prevent the North from winning.

The match he had been most keenly anticipating was the Gentlemen of England against the Australians in the middle of June. This was one of the few games staged at Prince's where the playing area was now

---

* Although this was the lowest-scoring first-class match on record, the MCC second innings of 19 bettered by three runs the club's all-out 16 against Surrey in 1872 (see pp. 106–7).

'ridiculously curtailed'[16] on account of the encroaching building sites. Workmen looking down from their scaffolding would have seen W.G. opening the batting with Gilbert and making a confident 25 out of the first-wicket partnership of 43 before being bowled by Boyle. The Gentlemen only made 139, but the limitations of the Australian batting were once more exposed, and they were all out for 75 and then 63, losing by an innings and one run. A. G. Steel, the brilliant Cambridge University slow leg-break bowler, did most of the damage, but Grace gave him excellent support, taking 4 for 25 in fifty-two overs and 2 for 27 in twenty-seven overs. His victims included Midwinter (twice) and Spofforth.

The match ended on Saturday, 18 June, and, honour satisfied, Grace could spend a relaxing Sunday with Agnes and their baby daughter before Gloucestershire's defence of the championship began against Surrey at the Oval on the Monday. Midwinter's inclusion in the Australian tour party had obviously threatened to deprive Grace of one of his leading players, but the two men had come to an understanding whereby Mid would play for the county when required, and Grace had notified him that he was wanted for the first match.

The events of Monday, 20 June have passed into the Grace mythology. The standard version is that W.G. arrived at the Oval and discovered that Midwinter had not turned up. Suspecting that his man might be found at Lord's, where the Australians were playing Middlesex, he got into a cab, drove to St John's Wood and barged into the Australian dressing room where Midwinter was indeed changed and padded up waiting to open the batting. Grace effectively kidnapped Midwinter and hurried him back across London to the Oval. Conway then set off in hot pursuit, catching up with them outside the Surrey ground, where a terrific altercation took place. However, according to Tom Horan, the sequence of events was slightly different. Once with the touring team, Midwinter had obviously had a change of heart and 'determined to return with them to the colonies, where he had been promised a benefit match in both Melbourne and Sydney'. But he did not fancy breaking the news to Grace in person, so Conway, taking Boyle with him for moral, and possibly muscular, support, 'went down to the Oval . . . to acquaint W.G. with Mid's decision'. That was when the altercation took place. Grace 'openly told Conway that the Australians were a lot of sneaks to try and entice Midwinter away. High words, of course, followed on both sides.'[17] The situation was made worse by the personality clash between Grace and

Conway, which had its origins in the 1873–4 tour. Both men were easily roused, and without restraining influences on both sides, they would almost certainly have come to blows.

Having delivered his message and traded insults, the Australian manager then returned to Lord's. It was at this point that W.G. hailed a cab, and summoning the trusty Bush as his second, he tore across London just behind Conway and arrived just as Midwinter was about to open with Bannerman. However, 'after about a quarter of an hour's pressing' from the Gloucestershire contingent, 'away walked Midwinter with his bag, and the Australians went in, of course, without him'.[18]

The idea that Grace bribed Midwinter (peddled enthusiastically in the *Sunday Times* as recently as 3 August 1997) is wide of the mark. In fact, according to Gloucestershire the reverse was true: the Australians bribed Midwinter. In the acrimonious correspondence that followed, E.M. wrote to the Australian captain, Gregory: 'With the knowledge of Midwinter's engagement staring you in the face you attempted to induce him to break his promise, desert his County, and play for you by offering him a much larger sum than we could afford to pay him.'[19] Midwinter certainly stood to gain far more than the eight pounds (plus expenses) a match Gloucestershire was offering him if he stayed with the Australians – the return on their initial stake of fifty pounds was something in the region of £700 to £750 per man. Grace may have bullied him, but he was in no position to bribe him. Horan admits that much of the blame lay with Midwinter, 'who did not seem to know his own mind for two minutes together', but is equally clear that 'Grace lost his temper and sadly forgot himself', adding that nothing could justify his 'passion and language, nor his conduct in coming to Lord's and almost forcibly leading away the captive Middy'.[20] Grace's account of this 'curious event' agrees in all important respects with Horan's, though unsurprisingly it tones down the drama, stating simply that Midwinter returned to the Oval with him 'after some persuasion'.[21]

Having lost his man from the sanctuary of the Australians' own changing room, Conway saw no point in trying to retrieve him from the enemy camp. Instead, he wrote a blistering letter of complaint to the Gloucestershire club. Whatever the arguments over Midwinter's vacillating loyalties, the Australians were not standing for Grace's behaviour. Grace wrote expressing regret for the misunderstanding, but that was not enough; the Australians threatened to cancel their fixture against the county at the end of the season. This forced the issue, and, a full month after the incident, W.G. made a final, rare, apology – but to David Gregory, not Conway:

The Cottage,
Kingswood Hill,
Bristol

July 21st

Dear Sir,

I am sorry that my former expression of regret to the Australian cricketers has not been considered satisfactory. Under the circumstances, and without going further into the matter, I wish to let bygones be bygones. I apologise again, and express my extreme regret to Mr Conway, Boyle and yourself, and through you to the Australian cricketers, that in the excitement of the moment I should have made use of unparliamentary language to Mr Conway. I can do no more but assure you that you will meet a hearty welcome and a good ground at Clifton.

Yours truly,
W. G. Grace[22]

Grace in fact derived little benefit from his piratical raid. Obviously unsettled by the storm that had broken over his head, Midwinter made only 4 and a duck, and bowled indifferently. Grace, on the other hand, was rather invigorated by the row. He scored 40 out of 111 and 31 out of 159, and bowled two long spells of forty-three and fifty-four overs taking 4 for 43 and 6 for 70. It was not enough, however, to prevent Gloucestershire losing their first match for two years, Surrey stealing home by sixteen runs.

Grace was again on comparatively good form when he returned to the Oval for the first Gentlemen–Players match. He batted through the amateurs' first innings for 40 out of a total of 76, and in the second, when the wicket had eased a little, he was again top scorer with 63. A. G. Steel, making his debut, took nine wickets in the match and the Gentlemen won by fifty-five runs. Lord's for once produced a better wicket than the Oval, but the story was the same. The Gentlemen had an exceptionally strong batting line-up which included four of the current Cambridge team – the brothers Alfred and Edward Lyttelton, A. P. Lucas and Steel – but Grace still dominated. He scored 90 before being caught by Shaw off Midwinter, now clearly resigned to being back in harness as an English professional, and set up a second comfortable win by 206 runs.

Towards the end of July Gloucestershire went up to Manchester for their first match against Lancashire. Neville Cardus's forerunner on the *Manchester Guardian* billed this as 'the "Derby" of the cricket year' (26 July), remarking that all that was wanted for 'a real cricket festival' was fine weather.[23] This was not forthcoming. The atmosphere on the first day was close and gloomy, and play was interrupted by heavy showers. In between the downpours Lancashire lost wickets regularly to end on 88 for 9. The weather relented for the second day, and, with the prospect of seeing the Champion at the crease, the crowds flocked to Old Trafford, as they had in the past to Broughton. The attendance was estimated at 10,000, and 'for once Manchester appeared to have forgotten that cotton was king, and gave itself up to the fascination of our national game with unrestrained enthusiasm'.[24] The last Lancashire wicket soon fell, and shortly afterwards Grace came out with Walter Gilbert to open the Gloucestershire batting. Gilbert didn't last long against the 'tremendous pace' of William McIntyre, but Grace held out for 32 before touching a lifter to slip. 'A tremendous shout announced the downfall of the big wicket.'[25] Only E.M., with 21, made much further resistance, and Gloucestershire were all out for 116.

Hornby and Barlow (mellifluously immortalized in Francis Thompson's poem; given the unhelpful title 'At Lord's', it is in fact a description of this match at Old Trafford) soon cleared the arrears in their different styles. Barlow was a dour professional stonewaller, while Hornby perfectly exemplified the amateur stylist. As an amateur he was the natural choice as Lancashire's captain, and because of his social credentials he took precedence over Grace when he played for the Gentlemen. This undoubtedly put a strain on their relations, though they were temperamentally very different. As his nickname, 'Monkey', suggests, Hornby was the physical opposite of the bear-like Grace.* The *Manchester Guardian* certainly thought 'The "opposition" of two such stars as Mr Hornby and Mr Grace was worth going miles to see.' If Grace had won the first round, Hornby came out the clear winner of the second, scoring a century during the course of which he took three successive fours off Grace, driving 'with extraordinary force'.[26] The huge Saturday crowd of over 13,000 saw Lancashire establish an invincible position.

They also witnessed another Grace incident. The ball was hit to the ring where a spectator stopped it and lobbed it to a Gloucestershire

---

* Once, when they were rooming together and Hornby got out of bed early, Grace asked where he was going. 'To have my cold bath, of course,' was the reply, to which Grace responded: 'Ooh . . . Monkey, you make me shudder.'

fielder. Patterson and Steel, the two Lancashire batsmen, were 'leisurely crossing' as the ball was thrown in and the wicket at Steel's end was broken. Grace immediately claimed the wicket, and Steel was given out. 'Directly this was seen, tremendous shouts of "no, no", "a four", were raised by the crowd. Mr Grace appealed to Storer [the umpire], who had given the batsman out "conditionally on its not being a boundary ball", and the point was hotly contested for some time.' E.M. broke the deadlock by going to the boundary to check what had happened, and as a result of his intervention Steel was re-called and play resumed. 'This was as it should be, of course, among gentlemen', the *Manchester Guardian* remarked pointedly.[27]

Lancashire were finally all out for 262, leaving time only for some exhibition batting. But Grace, still sulking from the run-out incident, declined to open, and only appeared at the crease when Gloucestershire crashed to 56 for 4. He was clearly in a vengeful mood. Steel went for eight boundaries, one a clean hit over the heads of the crowd, and a change of bowling only increased the scoring rate. 'Mr Grace did what he pleased with the bowling . . . His consummate command of the bat was never more conspicuous.'[28] By half-past six, when the game was abandoned, he had hit a belligerent 58 out of a total of 125 for 5.

After the draw with Lancashire, the team crossed the Pennines and were roundly beaten by Yorkshire, despite Grace's best efforts with bat and ball. He bowled 101 overs in the match, and scored 62 out of 201 and then 35 in Gloucestershire's miserable second-innings total of 73. He again shouldered the bulk of the bowling when they travelled down to Trent Bridge, getting through sixty-six overs in the Nottinghamshire first innings of 258. This gave the home side an advantage of nearly a hundred runs, so when Grace went in a second time the best he could hope for was a draw. This he achieved with his only century of the season. It took him five and a half hours to make 116, and if anything could have brought home to him the deficiencies of his own attack it would have been the bowling of Shaw and Morley, Oscroft and Barnes. Of the rest of the side, only E.M. coming in at six scored more than thirty runs. The game was saved, but with two draws and a defeat from their northern tour, any hope of retaining the championship was gone. They never won it again under Grace's captaincy (or indeed since).

Grace did little at Canterbury, and returned to Gloucestershire for the last round of county games and the salvaged fixture with the Australians. He once again bowled Nottinghamshire to defeat at Clifton, taking eleven wickets in the match, but when he took the side up to the Oval for the prestigious game against an England Eleven he was powerless to save them from a six-wicket defeat. They made just 118 in both innings.

For the first time there were two fixtures at Cheltenham, which laid the foundations of another well-loved week in the cricket calendar. James Lillywhite had a hand in this, and although his offer to pay for the right to manage the two matches was initially turned down, he was given the concession the following year for a flat fee of £120. Grace scored few runs, but ensured an innings victory over Sussex by taking thirteen wickets, *six* of which were caught and bowled, and in the drawn match against Yorkshire he sent down eighty-six overs in the first innings (6 for 77) and ten more in the second (2 for 10). He made 49 and 20 against Lancashire at Clifton, but again it was as a bowler that he shone, taking twelve wickets in Gloucestershire's eight-wicket win. And in the drawn match against Surrey, he redeemed his two failures with the bat by bowling eighty-eight overs for only eighty-six runs.

Gloucestershire's last match was against the Australians at Clifton starting on 5 September (the day after Bessie was baptized). After their glory day at Lord's the tourists had triumphed in the majority of their first-class matches (though Yorkshire and the exceptionally strong Cambridge University team had beaten them). They came to Bristol after a close win over the Players, but the match was more significant for the controversy surrounding it.

There had been growing resentment among the English professionals at the fact that although they were making money – considerable amounts of money – out of the tour, the Australians were granted amateur status with all its attendant privileges. They would have been prepared to go along with the fiction that they were playing their social superiors had the tourists been willing to share the proceeds of the proposed match a little more generously. The takings would obviously be large, and those selected to represent the Players demanded twenty pounds as an appearance fee. When the Australians stuck at ten, most of them withdrew, leaving Conway and Lillywhite little time in which to recruit replacements. This second eleven did remarkably well. Edward Barratt, the Surrey slow left-arm bowler, took all ten Australian wickets in the first innings, and the tourists only scraped home by eight runs.

The game at Clifton was far less dramatic. The crowds were even denied seeing how Midwinter fared at the hands of the team-mates he had deserted (he had an injured thumb and didn't play). It's doubtful whether he would have made much difference. The Gloucestershire batsmen were hopelessly out of their depth against Spofforth, who took 7 for 49 and 5 for 41. He did not number Grace among his victims, though he caught him off Boyle in the first innings (for 22), and when Australia batted he hit the top score of 44, during which he carted Grace's bowling all over the ground with studied disrespect. Grace bowled thirty-five overs, taking 1 for 90 as the Australians made 183. At fewer than three an over, it is by no means a bad performance, but he was taken to task for his 'great want of judgment in keeping himself on bowling long after he was fairly collared'.[29] He scored only five runs in the second innings, and that was the start of another dismal procession. The Australians bowled the county out for 85 and knocked off the seventeen-run deficit without losing a wicket to inflict Gloucestershire's first home defeat.

*

Eighteen seventy-eight is often taken as the start of the modern period in cricket. The Australians certainly shook English cricket with their surprise humiliation of the MCC. The bowling of Spofforth and Boyle was a revelation, while the fielding, and Blackham's wicket-keeping in particular, set an altogether new standard of excellence. But their visit also focused attention on the game's perennial problems of status and remuneration, and, as usual, Grace was the key figure.

The professionals' boycott of the Australian match was only a manifestation of their larger grievance against the shameless abuse of the system, and at last sufficient pressure built up for the MCC to issue a pronouncement on the subject. On 2 November the committee declared 'That no gentleman ought to make a profit by his services in the cricket field, and that for the future no cricketer who takes more than his expenses in any match shall be qualified to play for the Gentlemen against the Players at Lord's.'[30] This was only restating the existing position, but the committee also boldly asserted that the MCC had never broken its own guidelines. This brought forth a stinging rejoinder from *John Lillywhite's Companion*. The scandal of payment to amateurs should have been 'long since . . . nipped in the bud' declared the editorial, before going on to cite Grace as the worst offender and casting doubt on the probity, and indeed veracity, of the MCC to boot:

The Note issued by the MCC . . . should have been issued four or five seasons ago, but cricketers must be thankful that the leading club has, however late in the day, recognised an evil which has been injuring the best interests of the game for some years past. It is satisfactory to learn at last that 'no cricketer who takes more than his expenses in *any* match shall be qualified to play for the GENTLEMEN against the PLAYERS at LORD'S'; but it is somewhat surprising to read the assertion appended to the note that 'this rule has been invariably adhered to by the MARYLEBONE CLUB . . .', for ninety-nine out of every hundred cricketers know as well as we do that this statement is, to use a mild term, hardly consistent with [the] facts. One well-known cricketer in particular has not been an absentee from the GENTLEMEN'S eleven at LORD'S for many years past, and that he has made larger profits by playing cricket than any Professional ever made is an acknowledged fact. How the MARYLEBONE CLUB can reconcile their statement with this fact, even with any reasonable amount of word-twisting, we are unable to conceive.[31]

This would have made uncomfortable reading at Lord's when the *Companion* came out at the beginning of the following season, and the MCC hierarchy must have started counting the days until Grace could be given his testimonial and set up with a respectable source of income. Grace does seem to have made a small step to accommodate them. In September he played his last match for the United South against XX of Essex. He scored 4 and 10 and took twenty-six wickets. What he took in '£ s.d.' remains anybody's guess.

SEVENTEEN

THE winter of 1878–9 was the harshest and longest for years, lasting from October right through to May. It was so cold that lakes froze up for months, and a number of cricket matches were staged on the ice, including one by moonlight in Windsor Home Park. There was another at Grantchester in which 600 runs were made for the loss of fifteen wickets. '[O]ne batsman made 105 (not out)', W.G. noted in *Reminiscences*, adding, a touch wistfully, 'a record, I should think, for the game played in this manner'.[1] But for all his interest, Grace did not participate. Under Henry's watchful eye, he had no option but to devote himself to his text-books.

His medical studies did suffer one interruption in January. An Extraordinary General Meeting of the Gloucestershire Cricket Club was called to decide a virulent internecine conflict that had been festering since the previous November. Although the controversy outgrew its origins to throw the club into constitutional crisis, the root of the trouble was the old question of payment to amateurs.

After the county's match at the Oval in June 1878, E.M. had sent the Surrey authorities an invoice for expenses: 'Mr W. G. Grace, £15; Mr G. F. Grace, £11; Mr Gilbert, £8; Midwinter £10; the umpire, £6; scorer, £5; and Dr E. M. Grace £20'.[2] It is intriguing that the home club was expected to pay the visiting team's expenses, but beyond that, the figures clearly demonstrate that 'expenses' were nothing less than appearance fees graduated by status. Fred and Gilbert were living at the same address and so should have incurred the same travel expenses, and obviously the cost of W.G.'s journey could not have been nearly double that of Gilbert's. (The claim also confirms that Midwinter's reward for his defection scarcely constituted a bribe.) Surrey rejected the demand as 'exorbitant' and the Gloucester committee took a similar view when E.M. presented the accounts to them in November. They pruned twenty pounds off it and E.M. resubmitted it. Surrey duly paid, and the shortfall was made up out of Gloucestershire funds.

That was by no means the end of the story. The majority of the committee wanted to reassert control over the club's finances and curb E.M.'s freedom to agree, on his own authority, 'expenses' which noticeably benefited members of his own family and those for whom they took special responsibility. E.M. was incensed at the implied disparagement of his stewardship, repudiating the charges against him and claiming that he had 'secured vouchers for all items' in the controversial expenses claims. (He was also furious that some Surrey players were apparently saying on his authority that Gloucestershire players were each paid ten pounds a match, though his attempts to get their names from the Oval failed.) An attack on E.M. was, of course, seen as an attack on the whole Grace family, and the row developed into a bitter power struggle for the control of the club. The Extraordinary General Meeting was called to thrash the matter out, and in the process the club's dirty washing was paraded in public – even *The Times* covered it in embarrassing detail. The committee intended passing a motion depriving the Secretary of his club membership and thereby ending his right to vote. W.G., appealing over their heads to the wider membership, countered with an amendment guaranteeing the Secretary's position, saying 'they could not do better than follow the example of the Marylebone Club', whose Secretary was allowed to vote. He was seconded by his – and E.M.'s – brother-in-law, the Revd John Walter Dann, and the amendment was carried by twenty-three votes to seventeen. Although there were further resolutions requiring regular audits of the accounts and a closer control over the payment of expenses, the Grace faction had clearly won the day, and W.G. returned to his revision satisfied he had crushed a palace insurrection.[3]

It was, however, something of a Pyrrhic victory. The *Times* report offered a very rare insight into the inner workings of a county cricket club, and *John Lillywhite's Companion* seized on the embarrassing details to continue its campaign against 'the abuse of the term "Amateur"'. The *Companion* conceded that it was fair enough for gentlemen to claim their rail fare to a match,

But if hotel bills are to be included, and a gentlemen playing for his county is to be at liberty to drink Chateau Yquem with his dinner, and to smoke shilling cigars at the expense of the Club, and if the said Club is to be debited with £10, £15, or £20 for the privilege of retaining the services of such so-called amateurs, the MARYLEBONE NOTE is worse than useless . . . That a Professional's *wages* should be £5, and an Amateur's *expenses* £10, for playing in the same match, is simply absurd. It is high time that this unsavoury question was fairly met and disposed of for good and all.[4]

*

However hard a taskmaster Henry was, he had no realistic expectations that Grace would forgo all cricket until after his exams, though he did delay his start to the season until the start of June, when he played in Alfred Shaw's benefit match, North v. South at Lord's.

After the appalling winter, the summer of 1879 was to prove even colder and wetter than the two previous years (*Lillywhite's Companion* called it 'The Worst Season Ever Known')[5] and this game, like so many others, was ruined by the weather. The wicket was treacherous, so there was no chance of the sort of high-scoring game that beneficiaries preferred. Shaw's professionalism was pitched against his financial best interests, but he was unable to compromise his standards to benefit his pocket. In the South's second innings he took 8 for 21 in forty-three overs. For once Grace failed to produce something special, though in his first innings of 18 he hit Shaw for two massive sixes (possibly with the master bowler's connivance) to give the crowd something to cheer. The North won on the second day, and as a benefit match it had been a disaster.

Gloucestershire's fixture list had expanded to include Middlesex for the first time, and this meant their 'out' matches started slightly earlier than usual. They began at the Oval against Surrey, who were bowled out for 89 on what Grace described as 'a very dead wicket'.[6] Having taken five wickets, he proceeded to bat for the rest of the day, and had outscored the home side by stumps. Resuming on 93 in the morning he went on to complete an impressive century, his 123 being more than half the Gloucester total of 239. He took another four wickets when Surrey batted again, and the visitors won comfortably by ten wickets. The size of their expenses claim has not come to light.

Rain forced an abandonment of the match against their new opponents, Middlesex, at Lord's, but not before Grace had taken 6 for 16 as they collapsed to 41 all out. With twenty-four wickets in three matches, he might have expected to bowl for the Gentlemen when he returned to the Oval to meet the Players, but Hornby gave the ball to the Oxbridge pair Steel (slow) and A. H. Evans (fast), and they proved unplayable, dismissing the Players for 73 and 48. Grace scored a watchful 26 in the amateurs' only innings of 247, having a long duel with Shaw who sent down nineteen consecutive overs for only two runs before claiming his wicket. The match at Lord's was notable for Fred's

233

absence. After making their declaration of intent on eligibility for the Gentlemen's team, the MCC decided they had to be seen to be acting upon it, and Fred was sacrificed. W.G. of course remained untouchable. He even persuaded Hornby to give him a bowl, and took four wickets in the Players' first innings. But the rain had the final word.

Although no one could have deduced it from the weather, the season had now advanced into July, propelling Grace towards a different challenge. After spending a longer period as a medical student than it took him to score his first fifty centuries, he now had to pass his exams. He was entered for two qualifications, and following in E.M.'s footsteps he set off to Scotland to secure the first.

The Royal College of Physicians of Edinburgh was not a teaching institution, but its LRCP was highly regarded. Candidates were accepted from all over the country and there was no requirement to have studied at the University of Edinburgh Medical School – Grace certainly did not. Like all other applicants, however, he had to have attended a public hospital containing no fewer than eighty beds for at least twenty-four months and to have undertaken a medical course of no fewer than four years (hardly an issue in his case) before being examined in the following subjects: Anatomy, Physiology, Chemistry and Botany; Materia Medica & Pharmacy, Pathology and Analytical Anatomy; Practice of Medicine, Midwifery and Medical Jurisprudence. The examinations were partly oral and partly by written paper, with the final verdict being decided by a simple majority of the examining panel. If Grace was understandably anxious, it must have been an equally unnerving experience for those sitting across the table, quizzing the country's most famous sportsman on anatomical minutiae and midwifery, but both sides got through the ordeal, and on 16 July Grace added his name in the register of Licentiates, countersigned by Dr Charles Bell for the Examiners.

Grace's scope for celebration was limited as he had promised to be back in London the next day for Southerton's benefit match, the return between North and South at the Oval. On his way to the ground, Grace met Tom Emmett and told him he had at last got his diploma. This gave rise to one of the game's favourite bits of repartee. When Grace was batting, Emmett fell heavily on the slippery turf. W.G. asked him if he was hurt. 'No,' came the reply, 'but (turning to show the large grass stain on the seat of his pants) I have got my diploma!' This was the sort of joke Grace enjoyed enormously, and he must have been in excellent humour throughout the match, the second day of which was his thirty-first birthday. Not that he let his high spirits spoil his concentration. The North's bowling on the rain-affected wicket was severely testing, and he applied himself to score 21 out of 77 and then 41 out of 101. Though he couldn't prevent the North winning, he had at least produced a memorable demonstration of his skills.

The game ended early, but the two teams returned on the third day to play an exhibition match for the Saturday crowd. Grace scored only 2, and though he took five wickets, he would have been better employed getting in some last-minute revision. His second qualification was the MRCS (Member of the Royal College of Surgeons of England), for which he needed to demonstrate his competence in Clinical Medicine and Surgery. The timetable of these exams is obscure, but it seems clear that he would have sat any written papers by this stage. What is not in doubt is the date of his final meeting with the examiners. According to the records of the Royal College of Surgeons, confirmed by the *Lancet*, his viva voce was on Tuesday, 22 July.[7] This happened to be the second day of his own benefit match at Lord's. As this was also the day chosen for the presentation of his testimonial to launch his new career as a doctor, Grace could be said to have cut it rather fine, but that was entirely typical. After all, he had once left an important cricket match at the Oval to run in a hurdles race, so why shouldn't he clear the last hurdle of his medical qualifications during a fixture at Lord's?

In fact, the start of play was delayed until 1.30 p.m. (the first day was a wash-out), so he had plenty of time to meet his examiners in the morning before turning his attention to the cricket. The match was between the Under Thirties and the Over Thirties, and, according to *The Times*, it promised to be 'the most interesting of the season'. The paper went on: '[a] glance at the list of combatants will show that the amount of talent brought together . . . could not have been mended much by change'.[8] While this may have been the case from a cricketing point of view, 'the names of several prominent amateurs were conspicuously missing'.[9] Apart from Grace himself, E.M. and Frank Townsend, the Over Thirties team was all professional, which reflects something of Grace's standing with his exact contemporaries. The younger generation of amateurs was better represented in the Under Thirties side. Apart from Fred, Alfred Lyttelton, Frank Penn, Ivo Bligh and Vernon Royle turned out, and Lord Harris was only prevented from joining them by a family bereavement. At the start of the match Grace made an enormously generous gesture that would have endeared him to all the professionals: he insisted that the gate money should go to Alfred Shaw to compensate him for his ruined benefit earlier in the season.

When play finally got started the Under Thirties batted and found the going hard against an attack that included Emmett, W.G. and Shaw himself. They were briskly bowled out for 111, and then there was a lengthy interval for lunch and the presentation, which was made in front of the pavilion by Lord Fitzhardinge. The testimonial appeal had raised £1,458 (over £60,000 in today's terms), and in addition to a cheque, Grace also received two obelisks – one marble, the other bronze – and a clock. Lord Fitzhardinge said that the original intention had been to buy Grace's practice for him, but 'he had talked the matter over with the Duke of Beaufort and they thought Mr Grace was old enough and strong enough to choose a practice for himself'.[10] The Duke of Beaufort was abroad, but Lord Charles Russell deputized for him, and after Grace had uttered his few words of thanks, Russell delivered the speech of the day:

I agree with some friends that we have seen better bowling than we see now. You must not be surprised, then, to hear me say that I have seen better bowlers than Mr Grace, but I can say, with a clear conscience, that I have never seen anyone approach him as a batter, that I have never seen a better field. But he might be the good bowler that he is, the fine field, and the grand batter, without being a thorough cricketer; more than usual dexterity and agility of limb are required to play cricket – the game must be played with the head and heart, and in that respect Mr. Grace is very prominent . . . I have never heard the bell ring for cricketers to go into the field but he was first into it . . . I must hazard an opinion that HRH is grateful to Mr Grace for having afforded him an opportunity of showing his respect for the one great game of the people [the Prince of Wales had sent a cheque for five pounds]; requiring in those who·play it the national essentials of patience, fortitude and pluck, and fostering the respect for law and love of fair play which are characteristics of the Englishman. And now, sir, in conclusion, let me have the pleasure of addressing you as Dr. W.G.; you have entered upon a liberal profession, you have adopted the healing art. My best wish for your future is, that your right hand may never forget its cunning, and in time to come you may be as successful in alleviating pain and promoting health as most assuredly in time past you have been in promoting and satisfying to the full the enjoyment of all those who take delight in the grand game of cricket.[11]

When play resumed, W.G. opened for the Over Thirties with E.M., but, as *The Times* reported, 'the start was to some extent ominous, as the hero of the day lost his wicket from the third ball, delivered by Morley'.[12] It is ironic that after so many glorious feats in other benefit matches, he should have got a duck in his own, but perhaps for once the occasion got the better of him.

E.M. and Frank Townsend upheld family and county honour with 40 and 43 respectively, steering the Over Thirties to 138. On the last day Grace finally came into his own, bowling forty-six overs and taking 6 for 33 as the Under Thirties were dismissed for 80, setting their seniors a target of fifty-four runs. A large crowd had gathered for the closing stages of the match, and they cheered Grace loudly when he came out to open with E.M. It may have been W.G.'s match, but the old competitive streak was still there, and E.M. had no hesitation in upstaging his younger brother. He blazed away at his aggressive best, hitting four fours in an over from Barlow, and easily outscoring W.G. in their stand of thirty-five. Grace eventually went, caught Royle, bowled Bates, for 7, but E.M. continued to hog the limelight and saw the Over Thirties home by seven wickets.

Grace barely had time to bank his cheque and lodge his obelisks and clock in safe hands before setting off on Gloucestershire's northern tour. This was not a success. Lancashire beat them by an innings at Old Trafford, dismissing the whole team for 52 in their first innings, and an equally disastrous effort in their second innings cost them a close match against Yorkshire at Sheffield. Rain made the game something of a lottery, and they must have been bitterly disappointed to be bowled out for 63, just seven runs short of their target, after making a potentially match-winning 253 when they batted first. The weather continued to hound them as they travelled down to Trent Bridge. The first day's play was completely washed out and the wicket remained too sodden to produce a result. Grace scored a watchful 102 in a little over four hours out of 197 in the only innings there was time for.

After scoring a couple of fifties at Canterbury, he returned to the championship campaign for the rest of August, but although he did well enough personally, the rest of the team underperformed. Grace hit 85 in an opening stand of 161 with Gilbert against Middlesex, but the visitors exposed the Gloucestershire bowling in posting a total of 476, and it needed another fine innings, of 81, from him to save the game. There were further drawn matches against Yorkshire, Lancashire and Surrey and a six-wicket defeat by Nottinghamshire, the first county game Gloucestershire had lost at home. Grace was top scorer in both innings with 27 and 33, and took 6 for 37, but got little support. Against Lancashire he scored 75 not out in a total of 123 and also took 7 for 37.

But his best bowling of the season came against Surrey at Cirencester: 8 for 81 and 7 for 35 (six clean-bowled). There was one other county match, in the second week of August against Somerset at Clifton. Although no longer regarded as a first-class match, it was considered so at the time, and the 113 Grace scored counted towards his hundred centuries. But the visitors were out of their depths, and as Grace conceded, it was 'an easy walk-over for us'.[13]

At the end of the season, Grace made his first appearance at the Scarborough Festival, which had come into being three years earlier thanks to the enthusiasm of C. I. Thornton. Thornton was the greatest hitter of the age (possibly of any age), and his approach to the game set the tone for one of the most successful weeks in the cricketing calendar. Grace became a familiar figure at the Scarborough ground over the years, and though he could never quite match Thornton's legendary hits, he regularly despatched the ball into the surrounding streets. On this occasion, playing for Gentlemen of the South against Gentlemen of the North, he made 45 in his first innings and added to the 1,000 overs he had already bowled with another long spell in which he took 3 for 93. But his season ended on a low note: bowled A. G. Steel, 1.

Grace played less cricket than usual in 1879 – eighteen first-class matches compared to the twenty-four in the two previous seasons (and only two minor games). The appalling weather and the difficult wickets that resulted were further factors in his failure to reach 1,000 runs, thus missing the double for the first time since 1874. Nevertheless, he could still be satisfied with 880 runs at 35.20 and 105 wickets at 13.46.

However, he had more important concerns than his averages at the end of the season. He had to establish himself in his new practice. There had never been much doubt that he would put up his brass plate in Bristol, but rather than opting for remunerative work in a middle-class neighbourhood, he chose the relatively run-down area of the Stapleton Road. He clearly felt he would be more comfortable among the working class, and he soon followed in the family tradition by taking up appointments as the local Public Vaccinator and as Medical Officer to the Barton Regis Union, which involved tending patients in the workhouse.

By the end of the year he had moved the family into Thrissle Lodge, 61 Stapleton Road, and started applying himself to his new duties. It was still widely assumed that he would gradually drop out of cricket. *Lillywhite's Companion* remarked: 'It is now generally understood that we shall see but little of him in the future, except, perhaps in County and Gentlemen v Players matches . . ."[14] If that was his intention to begin with, it did not last very long. In the two decades ahead he would play more cricket than ever before.

EIGHTEEN

O VER the winter, while Grace was listening to wheezing chests in the workhouse and practising his midwifery skills along the Stapleton Road, British troops were massacred by the Zulus at Isandlhwana, and a tiny contingent facing overwhelming odds fought their way into the history books at Rorke's Drift.

Lord Harris found himself in the thick of his own Rorke's Drift on the Sydney Cricket Ground. He had taken a team of amateurs, strengthened by Emmett and Ulyett, out to Australia, and after losing the only Test at Melbourne, moved on to play New South Wales. Unfortunately Harris recruited a Victorian umpire, George Coulthard, whose impartiality was doubted; when he gave Murdoch run out in the New South Wales second innings, the crowd invaded the pitch. In trying to defend Coulthard, Lord Harris was struck with a whip or a stick, though how seriously was disputed subsequently – as was the allegation that one of the English professionals made an unhelpful reference to 'sons of convicts' while trying to defend his captain with a stump. Hornby effected a citizen's arrest on the 'larrikin' who assaulted Harris and had his shirt half torn from his back for his pains. The mêlée lasted a considerable time, because Lord Harris refused to leave the field, and play had to be abandoned for the day.

Although he accepted the apologies with which he was showered, Harris also wrote a highly inflammatory account of events for the English press, questioning Australian sportsmanship and concluding ominously: 'We never expect to see such scenes of disorder again; we can never forget this one.' This may have relieved his injured feelings, but rather than closing the matter, it triggered a new wave of accusations on both sides and put future relations between the two cricketing communities in serious jeopardy. Walter Hadow, one of Harris's companions in Canada, weighed in, accusing the 1878 tourists of abusing the privilege of their amateur status by their rapacious pursuit of gate money, and declared, 'it is sincerely to be hoped that we have now seen and heard the last of

Australian cricket and cricketers; at any rate until they have learned the true spirit in which the game should be played'. His letter appeared in the *Daily Telegraph* on 1 April, and must have been taken as a bad April Fool's joke when it was reprinted in Australia. It called forth lively ripostes with sarcastic references to the remuneration received by English amateurs touring Australia, and a reminder that his lordship's well-attested tantrum in which he threw his bat across the pavilion on losing his wicket hardly argued much for his own sportsmanship.

None of this augured well for the proposed Australian visit to England in the summer of 1880, but there were also domestic complications arising from the rivalry between Victoria and the New South Wales Cricket Association over control of the tour. A compromise was eventually reached, but the delay had a knock-on effect, and James Lillywhite, who was again acting as agent, only received confirmation in February that the Australians were coming, by which time the first-class fixtures had been agreed.

The team finally chosen for what many regarded as a fools' errand was managed by George Alexander. Harry Boyle was the captain, and his players were Alec Bannerman, John Blackham, George Bonnor, Thomas Groube, Arthur Jarvis, Percy McDonnell, William Moule, Billy Murdoch, George Palmer, James Slight and the Demon, Spofforth. Eight were from Victoria, four from New South Wales and one from South Australia. As before, each man put up fifty pounds against a division of the profits at the end of the tour (except for Bannerman, who played as a professional). The speculative aspect of the tour assumed greater importance for some than for others. Murdoch, for instance, had just been declared bankrupt. He had qualified as a solicitor in 1877, but had branched out into a disastrous shipping investment which left him with nothing more than the clothes on his back and £24 19s 5d in his bank account.

Murdoch's cricketing fortunes received an unexpected fillip when a bloodless coup during the voyage demoted Boyle and installed him as the team's new captain. This apparently caused no ill feeling between the two men, and Boyle may well have seen it as a blessing in disguise when it was discovered that the team had little cricket to look forward to when they arrived in London in May. They were reduced to advertising for fixtures in the press, offering to donate the proceeds to the Cricketers' Fund, but the only response was a deluge of abusive letters. It was quite clear that they were not welcome, and Boyle for one suspected a concerted plot to cold-shoulder them. In one of the regular despatches he sent back home, he wrote:

The feeling here is very bitter; but it is only nursed up by Lord Harris, Hornby, Hadow, and some more of that kidney . . . We could not be treated worse if we were a set of blacklogs [sic] . . . We have been assured that if the Marylebone club had met us, then all the counties and the gentlemen too would have played, but Harris, Hornby and Penn being on the committee of the club, spoiled all show for us.[1]

The tourists had to resign themselves to playing the series of odds games Lillywhite had fixed up for them in the provinces.

Not everyone was against them however, and in their first match they found two English amateurs prepared to break ranks. The Eighteen of St Luke's Cricket Club, Southampton, included Fred Grace and Walter Gilbert. With the United South on its last legs now that W.G. had stopped playing for the team, the two young mercenaries made no secret of their general availability. The Australians proved a very acceptable source of income, and they followed them up and down the country making guest appearances for local teams, rather as Conway, Cosstick and Cooper had dogged the England team's footsteps in 1873–4. In this instance, though, the ringers were warmly welcomed. The Southampton match was of interest only in indicating the pattern of the rest of the tour. Murdoch played a captain's innings of 97, and Fred was the only man on the St Luke's team who could handle Spofforth and Boyle. He played two excellent innings of 45 not out and 46 – very nearly half the runs scored by the entire St Luke's team.

In addition to providing some worthwhile opposition, Fred was also useful to the Australians in opening a direct channel of communication to his brother. Grace was not of the '"H" party', as Boyle dubbed Harris's clique. Although he played the game hard and fought his corner as determinedly as anyone, he was always prepared to bury the hatchet after the smoke of battle had rolled away. If the Australians were worth playing – and Fred could confirm that they were – then he wanted to meet them, and had no hesitation in breaking the unofficial Lord's embargo and offering them a match with Gloucestershire.

And Grace went further. There was no point in having an Australian team in England unless a fully representative team could be put up against them. With three Test matches already played and Australia holding the advantage 2–1, it would be folly to lose momentum. After all, if the Australians were snubbed badly enough they simply might not come again, and Grace could see how disastrous that would be. So, not for the first nor the last time, he intervened, throwing his full weight into rehabilitating the tourists. He made representations to the MCC and came close to securing a match for the Australians in July. In his own account, he says 'the MCC granted the use of the ground, but it was found impossible'[2] – presumably because there were not enough amateurs prepared to turn out. The Australians must have been bemused. Two years before they had been boycotted by the professionals; now the amateurs wouldn't meet them. And all they wanted to do was play cricket. Grace, however, was a powerful ally and he wasn't beaten yet.

His own season had started late and slowly. Although his bowling remained impressive, he was badly out of form with the bat. He took ten wickets against Surrey at the Oval in his first match (10 and 11 June), but made only 9 and 27 (though the latter was nearly half the team's total of 62). He made 69 in a drawn game against Middlesex, but then had his worst ever Gentlemen v. Players match at the Oval at the start of July, making 6 and 3 and failing to take a wicket. The Players, who had had the advantage of batting before the pitch deteriorated, seized the opportunity to win their first match on the Surrey ground since 1865.

To some extent Grace resumed normal service at Lord's, top-scoring with 49 in the Gentlemen's first innings of 226. This was described in *Lillywhite's Companion* as 'probably the most patient innings he has ever played. His defence to Morley's shooters on a half-dried wicket was magnificent.'[3] The Players crashed to 95 all out, but made an excellent recovery when they followed on, and, exploiting some very slack fielding and Hornby's uncertain captaincy, scored 248 to set a target of 118. The wicket was still difficult and Shaw began by bowling fourteen consecutive maidens. But after a gritty start from Grace, Frank Penn scored 48 to shepherd the Gentlemen home by five wickets. (For the second year running, Fred was not selected, but after consorting with the Australians he can't have been surprised.)

After another game between the Over Thirties and Under Thirties, in which Grace scored 51 and 49, and the county's northern tour, which was ruined by rain, it was time to meet the tourists at Clifton. Gloucestershire was only the third first-class county to play them thus far, the other two being Derbyshire and Yorkshire – who showed their independence from Lord's by meeting them twice. The Australians had beaten both counties comfortably (the second Yorkshire match was a draw), and only the weather had foiled them in their minor fixtures. They were a strong team whose talents were hardly stretched as they traipsed triumphantly around the north and the Midlands (with a trip over to Dublin to play two more one-sided matches). The Gloucestershire match, which started on August Bank Holiday Monday, offered them the prospect of a large crowd and the sort of cricket they had come to play.

The game excited a great deal of local interest, and there was apparently considerable betting on the outcome. With their unbeaten record, the Australians were favourites, but Grace had his own ideas about that. When the visitors batted he put in a spell of forty-five overs and took 6 for 44 as they struggled to 110 all out. There was a short delay for rain, but at 4.25 p.m. the Australians took the field, and W.G. emerged from the pavilion. He opened with E.M. rather than Gilbert on this occasion, but the story was the same as in his benefit match at Lord's the previous year: he failed and E.M. shone. W.G. fell to a fine diving catch by Boyle at mid-on off the bowling of Palmer, leaving E.M. to show how few terrors the Australian bowling held for him. He was stubborn in defence, but always ready to swing Spofforth around to leg when he saw the chance. The total moved on smartly past fifty, with the loss of Midwinter (unambivalently in the Gloucester camp this year) and Frank Townsend, and when Fred joined his brother at the wicket, the scoring rate improved further. Spofforth was taken off, E.M. reached his half-century, and sailed on with irrepressible gusto. The scores drew level – to a warm round of applause – but next ball E.M. played on to Palmer. He was so angry he knocked all three stumps out of the ground before striding off disgustedly to the pavilion. If anyone had dared to tell him, his 65 was the highest single innings yet made against the tourists. Having got the breakthrough, Murdoch brought Spofforth back into the attack and was immediately rewarded with the wicket of Cranston. Fred followed shortly afterwards, for 25, and it was left to Moberly and Gilbert to play out time until stumps at 6.30. Gloucestershire were ten runs ahead, but with only four wickets left must have felt they had let their hold on the game slip.

The pitch was easier on the second day and the weather 'splendid'. After a close call in the first over he faced from Spofforth, Gilbert gradually played himself in and then started to make a score. He hit Spofforth for several boundaries through the offside, and, for the second time in the innings, the Demon was tamed. The innings closed on 191 with Gilbert 48 not out, and the Australians trailed by eighty-one runs.

They found the wicket more to their liking in the second innings, and cleared the arrears without difficulty before accelerating to post a respectable total, thanks mainly to a cultured 79 by McDonnell and some terrific late-order hitting by Bonnor. George Bonnor was six and a half feet tall with a physique to match, and his approach to batting was entirely consistent with his appearance. One blow off Midwinter carried over 140 yards, but when he tried to serve Grace the same way the ball fell just inside the boundary where there was a fielder on patrol. Bonnor had clubbed 35, and with useful contributions from the tail the Australians made 246. Grace finished with 5 for 90, boosting his haul to eleven wickets in the match. The Australian innings closed at twenty past six which saved Gloucestershire from having to bat that night. They needed 166 to win, and had the whole of the third day in which to get them. Weather permitting, the match looked perfectly balanced.

The final day started with a row, something the Australians were coming to accept as a fact of life when they played against Grace. The wicket had been rolled at the end of play the previous evening, but W.G. decided it needed rolling again. Murdoch protested, but though he might be denied at the MCG, at Clifton Grace's word was law, and out came the roller once more. To the Australians' delight it didn't do him much good, as he fell lbw to Spofforth for 3. E.M., though, carried on from where he had left off in the first innings, and Midwinter also played well as they put on thirty-three for the second wicket. But after Midwinter left, E.M. found no one else to stay with him. He continued to play Spofforth with confidence, getting him away to leg and occasionally driving him. One last straight drive to the pavilion took his score to 41, but he was then deceived in the flight and gave the Demon a return catch. With his departure, the county's hopes of registering a famous victory ended and Spofforth wrapped up a comfortable win by sixty-eight runs when he had the number eleven caught by Murdoch at silly point just before two o'clock.

Despite the run-in over the roller, W.G. remained a staunch supporter of the tourists in their quest for further first-class fixtures, and even a fully representative encounter. As they travelled up to Leeds to continue their undemanding progress around the northern circuit, Grace went down to Canterbury to argue their case with the one man who could give them what they wanted, Lord Harris. Grace and the Australians had an ally in Charles Alcock. He was all in favour of an England–Australia match, and from where he sat, in the Surrey Secretary's office, the Oval seemed the ideal place to stage it. In *Background of Cricket*, Sir Home Gordon gives Alcock the credit for persuading Lord Harris to relax his antipathy towards the tourists and consent to captain an England team against them, but Grace also added his weight – though bowling his old friend when within sight of a century was arguably not the best way of starting his mission when he arrived at Canterbury. Grace may have had to lend a sympathetic ear while Harris recounted the horrors of Sydney once more, but almost certainly passed on conciliatory messages from Murdoch, and gave his personal opinion that the Australians were decent sorts and worthy opponents. He also made further converts among the two teams in the match in which he played. Three of the England Eleven that played at the Oval were drawn from either the Gentlemen of England or the Gentlemen of Kent.

Once 'the potentate of cricket'[4] was finally won over, the success of the venture was more or less assured, but there was very little time, and Alcock, who undertook to make all the arrangements, had much to do. His first task was to fix a date, and at such a late stage of the season that meant targeting an already existing fixture. Lillywhite, with his Sussex connections, had arranged for the Australians to play the county at Brighton on 6, 7 and 8 September, and that was the game Alcock chose. With Harris's blessing and the Australians' eager compliance, he negotiated a postponement of the county match and secured the three days for the Test. Harris insisted that Sussex were compensated with a donation of £100.

Alcock then had to find a team. As Fitzgerald had found on the eve of the Canadian tour, players tended to be heavily committed at that stage in the season, assuming they hadn't already departed for the grouse moors. Alcock's month of shuttle diplomacy even included a recruiting drive up to Scotland. But his efforts were successful, though some of those who agreed to play grumbled at the inconvenience. Home Gordon recorded that 'years after, A. G. Steel recalled to me what a rotten journey he and Alfred Lyttelton had from Scotland, where they were having some splendid shooting, in order to take part in the game'. At least they were willing to play. Others weren't. 'The two professionals who had witnessed the scene at Sydney flatly refused to take part in the match for England.'[5] A. N. Hornby also declined.

While Alcock was working frantically behind the scenes to ensure the success of the first Test match on English soil, Grace's season continued with Gloucestershire. He led the county to a five-wicket win over

Middlesex at Clifton, and they held Nottinghamshire to a draw at Cheltenham. Cheltenham also saw an unlikely victory over Surrey. So unlikely was a result on the last day that at lunchtime Fred bet L. A. Shuter, brother of the Surrey captain John Shuter, that the game would not be completed by stumps. As Surrey still had a full innings to play, a draw looked certain, but Shuter accepted the bet at odds of 100/1 ('i.e. £5 to 1s.'). Grace seems to have taken the bet as a personal challenge, and proceeded 'to make things hum', and after lunch he bowled Surrey out for 117, taking 7 for 65 in thirty-seven overs. This still left Gloucestershire fifty-two runs to get in forty-five minutes. E.M. hurried off the field to put his pads on, but Grace decided to open with Gilbert. E.M. was furious, and as they went out sneered, 'There go the slowest pair of batsmen in England.' The runs were knocked off with twenty minutes to spare, and Grace scored thirty-one of them, before returning to the pavilion to enjoy both brothers' embarrassment. It apparently took Fred some time to pay up. When he did, Shuter declined to cash his cheque, preferring to preserve the evidence in his scrapbook.[6]

Grace continued in cracking form in the two remaining Clifton matches. He scored 89 and 57, and took six wickets to help beat Yorkshire, and then made 106 to set up a seven-wicket win over Lancashire. He then went off to Kingsclere, in Hampshire, for a short shooting holiday, leaving the rest of the country to indulge in excited speculation over the composition of the England team for the Oval Test match.

All three Graces were chosen. W.G. and Fred were obvious choices, but E.M. had also earned his place, having proved capable of taking on, and even dominating, the Australian attack. The full team, in batting order, was W. G. Grace, E. M. Grace, A. P. Lucas, Barnes, Lord Harris, F. Penn, A. G. Steel, Hon. A. Lyttelton, G. F. Grace, Shaw and Morley.

The Australians' preparations for the match were spoilt by an incident quite as unpleasant as the one in Sydney in February. In their game against Eighteen of Scarborough and District they found themselves in serious trouble against a local fast bowler called Frank who was clearly throwing. Murdoch waited until the end of the first innings before asking Charlwood, who was captaining the Eighteen, not to bowl Frank in the second innings. This was ignored, and when Alec Bannerman was struck a painful blow on the leg, Murdoch went onto the field to remonstrate. Charlwood was adamant, Frank unrepentant, and the umpire indifferent. 'During this time frequent cries were heard from the spectators of "another Lord Harris affair" and "go on", etc.' Murdoch was anxious to avoid a row at all costs, and so reluctantly allowed the game to continue, and had to watch the rogue bowler hitting his men 'so frequently and with such force, that it caused them to limp about the ground in the most painful manner. This seemed to give the spectators no end of amusement, judging from the laughter that burst out after each knock.'[7] Among those hit was Spofforth, who got a stinging blow on his glove. He carried on batting, but when he returned to the pavilion it was discovered that he had broken the bottom joint of the third finger of his right hand. In trying to safeguard his team from any bad publicity on the eve of the Test match, Murdoch had inadvertently sacrificed his most potent weapon.

With this startling exhibition of British fair play still fresh in their minds, the Australians arrived at the Oval with a large portion of humble pie to consume. They were still on shaky ground as far as relations with their hosts were concerned, and must have been relieved when they finally saw Murdoch and Lord Harris shake hands and formally make peace. The peer of the realm told the bankrupt solicitor, 'You find the timber and we will find the workmen to build a bridge which will endure for ever, on which to struggle.'[8] Having delivered these worthy sentiments, Lord Harris won the toss, and at shortly after 11.30 a.m. Murdoch led his men onto the field to loud cheers. There was even more noise when W.G. and E.M. followed them out to open for England. Alcock's confidence in the enterprise was fully justified. The weather was favourable, and 48,000 spectators paid for admission over the three days. With guests and Surrey members, the total attendance was estimated at around 65,000.

The Australians' opening attack of Boyle and Palmer held no terrors for the two brothers, and once E.M. had clubbed his first boundary to square leg, they proceeded to dominate the bowling, hitting up sixty in less than an hour. E.M. had a life when he gave a sharp return chance to Alec Bannerman who had come on as first change with his innocuous round-arm medium pace – a sure indication of how desperately the tourists missed Spofforth – and celebrated his reprieve with two cracking drives for four on either side of the wicket. W.G. was playing with equal freedom and scoring at an ever faster rate, placing the ball with his usual certainty and cutting anything slightly wide with great force.

E.M. finally made one drive too many and was well caught by Alexander at mid-off for 36. The score was 91, of which Grace had scored 48. A. P. Lucas, the quintessential amateur stylist (Uppingham, Cambridge and Surrey), came out to join W.G. and congratulated him on his fifty which followed five minutes later. Once the 100 was passed, Lucas launched into a cultured attack on both Palmer and Bannerman. Although Murdoch shuffled his depleted bowling resources, there was no stemming the flow of runs, and at lunch the score was 167 for 1, with Grace on 82, well on the way to his maiden Test hundred in his maiden Test match.

This he achieved ten minutes after the resumption of play during an accelerated onslaught on the Australian bowling which also saw the hundred partnership up (the first in Test cricket). When Lucas gave Bannerman his second wicket (playing on), he had scored 55. The score stood at 211. The classical amateur was replaced by the representative professional. William Barnes had had an excellent season for Nottinghamshire, and received warm appreciation for his efforts from the Oval crowd (the old animosity between Nottinghamshire and Surrey having transmuted into a fierce but mutually appreciative rivalry). The scoring rate slowed somewhat – Barnes was a sound bat in the professional mould – but there was no loss of momentum as the score rose to 250. The stand was worth fifty-eight when Barnes unluckily played the ball hard onto his wicket off another second-string bowler, the team's manager George Alexander, drafted in as a makeshift substitute for Spofforth. 269 for 3. Grace saluted the arrival of Lord Harris with a drive and a cut for four, which brought up his hundred and fifty and took the score to 281.

No sooner had the applause for Grace died down than Palmer bowled him off-stump, and the cheering started up again. 'He retired amid the most deafening round of cheers that had probably ever greeted him.'[9] His 152 had taken three hours and fifty-five minutes, and he had hit twelve fours, ten threes and fourteen twos. He had given one chance – an 'exceedingly hard' one out on the boundary in front of the pavilion when he was on 134 – but otherwise had played an unblemished innings. He rated it highly himself – 'one of the best I ever played'[10] – and it gave the Oval crowd, with whom he had always been a favourite, enormous pleasure.

It also provided England with the foundation for an impressive total. Frank Penn joined his Kent captain and helped to add forty-one, and then A. G. Steel came in to keep up the momentum. Lord Harris made his fifty and was then caught by Bonnor at slip off Alexander with the score on 404. Alfred Lyttelton, the third member of the team who had played at Canterbury, made his entrance. Six runs later, Steel hit Moule to Boyle at mid-on at the same total and this brought Fred to the wicket. 410 for 7 was hardly a crisis, but he must have been terribly anxious to make a contribution to the England effort. It was not to be. Moule, the most occasional of occasional bowlers, found the edge of his bat, and Bannerman snapped him up at slip. There was no time for another batsman to come out; the umpires lifted the bails, and Fred had to drag himself back to the pavilion with the exhausted Australians in his wake.

There was another huge crowd for the second day (Tuesday). Play started at 11.05 a.m., and by 11.20 the England innings was over. Alfred Lyttelton was left stranded on 11 not out as Shaw was bowled for a duck by Moule and Morley ran himself out for 2. An interesting feature of the Australian bowling was that Boyle and Palmer between them took only one wicket, while Bannerman, Alexander and Moule shared eight.

Murdoch and Bannerman opened the Australian innings, and surprisingly, in view of his reputation as a stubborn stone-waller, it was Bannerman who made the running. He hit his first two balls for four, and when Murdoch was caught for a duck off Steel, the score was 28. The combination of Steel's leg-breaks and Morley's pace worked well, and wickets fell steadily. At 84 for 5, Bonnor decided to try to hit his way out of trouble. Alfred Shaw had come into the attack by now, and the Australian giant wound himself up for a massive hit that would become legendary.

As with so many legends, there is conflicting evidence as to the details. Some say the ball was lofted towards the pavilion, others state it was aimed at the gasometer at the Vauxhall end.* What is not in dispute is that it was a towering hit, that the batsmen had completed two runs as it hung, hawk-like, high in the sky, and that the man waiting underneath it on the boundary was Fred Grace, who caught it perfectly cleanly. It was a truly magnificent catch which momentarily stunned the crowd before they burst into a storm of cheering and applause which was heard as far away as Vauxhall station. It was not only a superb catch, but a potentially match-winning one. An hour, or even half an hour, of Bonnor in full flow could have revitalized the Australian innings, and as the events of the last day proved, an extra forty or fifty runs could have made all the difference.

---

* At the lunch interval that followed shortly, Frederick Gale measured the distance the ball had travelled with a chain. It had carried a minimum of 115 yards, which, given the position of the wickets in relation to the boundary, proves that the catch was taken in front of the gasometer. Home Gordon, writing many years later, had no doubts: 'an excited boy's memory of such a feat is likely to be accurate: it is certainly as vivid as though it had happened a month ago'. (*Background of Cricket*, p. 50.)

Although Boyle batted sensibly for 36 not out, the Australian innings came to a close at three o'clock when W.G., with the first ball of his second over, had Moule caught by Morley for 6. Their total was 149, giving England a lead of 271. Hardly anyone on the ground thought they would have to bat again, and many imagined that the match would be over that evening.

When the Australians slumped to 14 for 3 in their second innings that seemed even more likely. Timetables were consulted and those who lived out of town began to pack up and leave. But those who hesitated, thinking they would stay for just one more wicket, found they were missing their trains as Murdoch and McDonnell dug in and began to build a stand. After his failure in the first innings, Murdoch had dropped down to three, sending in Boyle to partner Bannerman. It didn't offer him much respite as the first wicket fell with only eight runs on the board, but he started more confidently, and with McDonnell showing good form the score rose to fifty. and Harris replaced Morley and Shaw with Barnes and Grace. Barnes gave way to Steel, but Murdoch hit him for two fours in his second over. McDonnell hit two fours off consecutive balls to bring the Australians to within three of the hundred, but then fell to an importunate appeal for lbw from Grace. He had made 43, with nine fours, and had done something to revive the tourists' hopes of at least taking the game into the last day. But with only four more runs added, James Slight made the mistake of trying to slog Grace for a boundary to get off the mark, and Lord Harris took the catch at long-off – 101 for 5, and the match seemed all over bar some fairly desultory shouting.

Murdoch was still there and playing well, but Blackham looked out of touch and was simply concerned with survival. The return of Shaw to the attack surprisingly seemed to ease the pressure. Murdoch cut him for four, and Blackham also got him away to the boundary twice. However, after scoring nineteen runs he popped up a simple catch to point off Morley. E.M. tossed it up disdainfully. 143 for 6. He remained in his place close to the bat for Bonnor, even when three powerful cuts flashed past him. Murdoch also hit some boundaries as the two saw out the rest of the overs. At stumps the score was 170 for 6, of which Murdoch had made seventy-nine 'in irreproachable style'.[11]

In a moment of foolhardy bravura, Murdoch had bet Grace a sovereign he would beat his first-innings score. Grace was always prepared to accept a wager, provided, as he no doubt emphasized to Fred, it was a sensible one. He must have offered Murdoch hearty congratulations on his splendid knock, while commiserating with him on the near certainty that he would run out of partners before he could get close to his target.

With eighty-one still needed to make England bat again, the result of the match looked a foregone conclusion and there was a much smaller crowd on the third day. They were privileged to see one of the greatest and most dramatic day's Test cricket. The likelihood of Murdoch being left stranded increased when Steel hurried one through Bonnor's defence after only eleven had been added to the overnight score, and his chances of reaching even a well-deserved century looked slim when, just six runs later, Palmer went, skying an easy return catch to the same bowler. Only Alexander and Moule remained to give him support, and neither could claim to be much of a batsman. However, from this point the character not only of the innings but of the match began to change. The Australian captain and manager put on a magnificent display of determination and defiance. Murdoch continued to bat superbly while Alexander concentrated on defence. Eventually he came out of his shell with a four off Steel, and shortly afterwards, at ten to twelve, the 200 came up. Alexander's continued assault on Steel forced Harris to turn to Grace. Murdoch was close to his hundred, but tight bowling kept him penned in the nineties for several overs. Mental anguish was compounded by physical agony when, on 99, he was hit by a ball from Morley and was unable to resume for several minutes. From the length of time he was incapacitated and the absolute silence of contemporary accounts as to the nature of the blow, it seems reasonable to conclude that he was struck in the box – if, indeed, he was wearing one. The two qualified doctors on the field could probably do little more than assure him he would live once the vision-clouding pain subsided. Eventually he stepped gingerly back to the crease to resume his innings. Just before 12.30 he scored the single that brought him to three figures, and the small crowd cheered vociferously.

Alexander celebrated by cutting Grace for three and hitting Morley to the legside boundary for four. But that was his last scoring shot. Morley had his revenge, having him caught at slip by Shaw. He had made 33, more than two thirds of the fifty-two runs added for the ninth wicket. Considering how little match practice he had had, it was a heroic performance. But at 239 for 9 Australia still needed thirty-two more runs to make England bat again.

William Henry Moule had done little to earn selection for the tour, and nothing since arriving in England to suggest he was worth a place in the Test team. His team-mates almost certainly regarded his three cheap wickets in England's innings as an unexpected bonus, and would not have expected great things from him with the bat. He started badly, playing and missing but somehow managing to keep out the straight ones. Murdoch hit Grace for four while he still had the chance. The 250 came up and Steel relieved Grace. Moule provokingly snicked him for four. Murdoch hit Morley for three. Australia were now within ten of making England bat again. The crowd watched intently. Shaw replaced Morley at the gasworks end and tightened the screw. Only two runs came from five overs. Then, after Murdoch had taken a single off Steel, Moule broke the tension by driving him to the off for four. One run was needed to avert an innings defeat, and when Murdoch called for a single the crowd again reacted clamorously. It had hardly seemed possible, and yet they had done it.

Nor had they finished. Elated with their success, both men started to play more freely. Murdoch drove Shaw for four, and Moule took seven off an over. Morley came back on and the two Nottinghamshire professionals checked the run rate for a while, conceding only five runs in ten overs. But still no wicket. At 297 for 9 Harris tried a double bowling change, bringing back Grace with Lucas at the other end. It didn't work. In W.G.'s second over Moule cut him for two and three, and Murdoch hit him for four. The 300 came up, and with lunch fast approaching Murdoch was tantalizingly close to claiming Grace's sovereign.

Harris took Grace off and brought on Frank Penn. Murdoch cut Lucas for three, which brought his score level with Grace's 152. But there the matter had to rest as, after a maiden, the lunch bell rang. The score was 324 for 9, Moule had made 32 not out, and Australia had a scarcely credible lead of fifty-three runs. But Murdoch was still not in possession of W.G.'s sovereign. It must have been a long luncheon interval for him.

The players returned to the middle at ten to three. Moule drove Steel for two, and then Murdoch faced Barnes and at last scored the single that took him past W.G. It was not a moment too soon, as Barnes produced a very fast delivery in the same over which bowled Moule all ends up. Australia were all out for 327 with Murdoch 153 not out. In his *History of a Hundred Centuries* Grace wrote fulsomely in praise of his rival's performance:

Mr W. L. Murdoch's superlatively fine innings of 153 *not out* will always stand in the history of cricket as one of the most heroic performances that has ever been achieved by a batsman in a thoroughly first-class match. Especially it was a triumph for him to have not only exceeded my own fine score of 152 by one run, but also to have achieved the distinction of being *not out*, and I take this opportunity of congratulating him most heartily and sincerely in print, as I did at the time verbally, on having enrolled his name for ever on the scroll of cricket fame by his gallant achievement.[12]

Despite his bankruptcy, W.G.'s sovereign (about forty pounds in today's money) was far too precious a trophy to be frittered away in day-to-day expenditure. Murdoch wore it on his watch-chain for the rest of his life.

England needed fifty-seven to win, a seemingly innocuous task on a very placid wicket. After their success in the first innings, W.G. and E.M. stood down as openers and Harris sent in Lyttelton and Fred. It was a misguided act of kindness, given that Fred was on a pair and had also developed a slight cold. Lyttelton took two off Boyle's first over, but when G.F. faced Palmer he was clean-bowled second ball. His personal disappointment paled into insignificance when Lucas was caught behind off the same bowler, and shortly afterwards Lyttelton gave Palmer his third wicket. At 22 for 3, there were the makings of a crisis. Palmer and Boyle were bowling superbly, and the tension was palpable. Frank Penn and Barnes steadied things for a while, inching the score past thirty, but one run later the Nottinghamshire man skied the ball uncharacteristically over Boyle's head and was caught by Moule. E.M. came purposefully to the wicket, clearly bent on putting an end to the nonsense, but was soon on his way back to the pavilion, bowled second ball by Boyle for nought.

Enter W.G., probably reflecting that if he had opened there wouldn't have been a crisis in the first place. There certainly was one now. With half their batting gone England still required twenty-six runs to win. The Australians were keyed up to their hostile best, and memories of 1878 must have risen uncomfortably in the minds of those still waiting to bat. Another couple of wickets and the unthinkable would become a very real possibility.

Penn decided that attack was the best policy and quickly hit two fours and a two off Palmer. He then caused palpitations in the England dressing room by giving a chance to Bonnor at slip, but it didn't stick. Penn marked his reprieve with a two and another boundary, which brought victory within reach. Appropriately, Grace, who had been playing cautious second-fiddle, unleashed a superb cut for four off Palmer to bring the scores level, and later in the same over he pushed the ball away for the single that won the match. England were home by five wickets, but it had been a damned close thing. The crowd cheered and the Australians clapped their vanquishers back to the pavilion, where Spofforth looked on with pursed lips, flexing his damaged hand.

The three Graces, making their only appearance together in a Test match, could look back on a stalwart family effort. W.G.'s century had obviously been crucial, but E.M.'s first innings had helped him lay the foundations, and although he had collected a pair, Fred could console himself with the thought that his catch to dismiss Bonnor was the single most dramatic incident in a gloriously memorable match.

NINETEEN

ALTHOUGH the Test match marked the end of the first-class season for the Grace brothers, there were still some minor games during the rest of September. Despite his cold, Fred went from the Oval to play for United South at Stroud. The weather was bad and the sensible course would have been to pull out, but that was not the Grace way, and despite being soaked twice by showers, which made his cold worse, Fred threw himself into the game, scoring 44 in what proved to be his last ever innings. He then went home to Downend to recuperate for a couple of days before his next engagement. He had promised to play in a benefit match at Winchester on Wednesday, 15 September, and although he hadn't shrugged off his cold, he set off for Basingstoke on the Tuesday and put up at the Red Lion Hotel.

On Wednesday Fred's cold was worse, and the weather inclement. A friend, Dr Charles Frere Webb, who was the town's medical officer, managed to persuade him to give up the day's cricket and return to his bed at the hotel. When Webb visited him on Thursday he was no better, but there seemed to be no complications. Fred should simply stay put until he recovered.

The following day, Friday, there was more cause for alarm. Webb found that Fred's right lung was affected, and wrote to Henry at Kingswood and Martha and Walter Gilbert at Downend. Gilbert immediately set off for Basingstoke where he remained constantly at the patient's bedside. There were still no serious symptoms, but Henry took the train over on Saturday, returning to Bristol that evening. W.G. was obviously informed, but with good medical attention at hand and Walter in attendance he saw no reason to go and see his brother himself.

Gilbert sent a telegram on Sunday morning confirming that there was no cause for alarm. Fred 'was going on very well'. On Monday Henry again went over to Basingstoke, 'and found him worse, but no immediate danger was apprehended'. On Tuesday morning Gilbert sent another telegram saying the patient had 'spent a good night, and was much better'.[1] The outlook changed dramatically the following night, and at about four a.m. on Wednesday, 22 September Fred's condition became alarming. Henry was away from home at Bradford-on-Avon, and on receipt of Gilbert's telegram W.G. sprang into action, arranging to meet his elder brother at Bradford en route for Basingstoke. Meanwhile Blanche and her husband the Revd Dann had set off from Downend, but they were too late. Fred died at 1.15. The cause of death was given as 'congestion of the lungs'. W.G. and Henry received the news on the platform at Bradford station.

The news must have stunned them both. Fred was a superbly fit, athletic young man of twenty-nine who only a fortnight before had been haring over the vast spaces of the Oval, revelling in every moment of his first Test match. And now he was dead, snatched away as suddenly as their father had been nine years before. As the train rattled drearily through the Wiltshire and Hampshire countryside, Henry must have wondered if any more could have been done to save him, while W.G. can only have reflected bitterly on his decision not to make the journey before it was too late.

Fred's death 'cast a deep gloom over the close of the season'[2] and sent a wave of genuine dismay through the cricket world. *The Times* wrote, 'his manly and straightforward conduct and genial manners won him not only popularity, but the esteem of hosts of friends',[3] and such sentiments were echoed in the many obituaries that appeared. The last match of the Australians' tour, against the Players at Crystal Palace, started on 27 September, the day of Fred's funeral, and 'each cricketer wore a bow or band of black crape'.[4] An estimated three thousand people turned out to follow the coffin on its short journey from The Chesnuts to the church, including the Gloucestershire team and representatives of a large number of clubs from Cheltenham, Oxford, Bath, Chepstow and the Bristol area. The church obviously could not hold such a multitude and the crush in the churchyard was so great the family had difficulty positioning themselves at the graveside. The Revd Dann gave a brief address, but broke down in the middle of it, and as the crowd dispersed the family trailed home to reflect on a life halted on the threshold of a future full of promise. After the failure of his year at Aberdeen, Fred had persisted with his medical studies and intended to qualify the following summer. And after his various romantic entanglements, he had finally found a girl he wanted to marry, a Miss Robinson who, as though guided by some unwritten family law of inclusivity, eventually became E.M.'s second wife.

Of all his brothers, Grace had been closest to Fred, and he continued to miss him for years to come. His admiration for him shines through the encomium he wrote in *Reminiscences*:

I need scarcely enlarge on the brilliance of his career. He was one of the finest all-round cricketers I have ever seen, and a first-rate sportsman in every sense. As a batsman he was an invaluable run-getter; as a bowler he always rendered his side timely assistance; while as a fieldsman he was unsurpassed. He loved the game, and threw himself heart and soul into his play, whether it was batting, bowling, or fielding.[5]

Like E.M., Fred was destined always to be in W.G.'s shadow, but although they competed fiercely on the rare occasions when they found themselves on opposing sides, there seems to have been little of the overt rivalry that existed between the two elder brothers. Like E.M., Fred has been underrated by posterity because he missed having a Test career, but his first-class statistics place him in the top rank of contemporary cricketers. He scored 6,906 runs at 25.02, which compares extremely well with Richard Daft's career average of 25.42 (throughout the 1870s Daft was regarded as second only to W.G. himself). E.M.'s first-class average was 18.66 (though it would have been higher had he retired earlier). Fred's bowling is less impressive, though 329 wickets at 20.06 is not bad for a batting all-rounder. Tom Emmett's wickets came at 13.56, Arthur Appleby's at 15.67, W.G.'s at 18.14, while E.M. matched him almost to the decimal point on 20.37. There can be little doubt that he would have remained a regular in the England side throughout the 1880s; his might have been the first, but certainly not the last, great Test career to start with a pair.

*

The 1881 census shows Grace and his family still at 61 Stapleton Road at the beginning of the year, though they would soon move round the corner to the more spacious Thrissle House at 57 Stapleton Road. The household consisted of W.G. and Agnes, William Gilbert junior (6), Henry Edgar (4) and Agnes Elizabeth (Bessie, 2). They had also had visitors, John and Carline Nicholls, relatives of Agnes, and were continuing in the tradition of accommodating younger members of the family with medical aspirations. Stewart B. Day (20), one of Agnes's brothers, is listed as a medical student. There were also two servants: Elizabeth Pullin (22), who may well have been a niece or even daughter of C. K. Pullin, the Gloucestershire umpire; and Susannah H. Fowler (35), who came from Munsley in Herefordshire.

Harriet, as she was known, is an interesting figure. There is no record of when she joined the family (though the fact that Grace listed her by her first name may indicate that she had not been with them very long; in the 1891 census her accustomed second Christian name is used), but she stayed with them for many years, and her loyalty was eventually rewarded by the gift of one of W.G.'s easy chairs* which, with his increased girth, he had outgrown. Harriet was the unmarried mother of two children, a boy and a girl. Her daughter, Emily, was brought up by her sister back in Herefordshire; the boy's story is more shadowy, but he was reputedly brought up 'a gentleman' and remained sufficiently in touch with his mother to attend her funeral. It is, of course, possible that she concealed the existence of her children from her employers, but if, as seems likely, Grace and Agnes knew her circumstances, it speaks highly of their tolerance during a period of punitive Victorian respectability. It may even have been the case that they contributed towards the upbringing of Harriet's son.[6]

On 1 April 1881 the Gloucestershire committee met, as usual, at the Grand Hotel in Bristol. W.G. proposed that Pullin should be given a benefit for his service to the club, but another member of the committee attempted to veto it with a reference to 'the state of our Funds at the present time'. A compromise was reached, postponing the decision. Then, as now, the most pressing question for any county committee was 'the state of our Funds', and the same meeting agreed to advertise the refreshment franchise for matches at Clifton in the local press, 'But with the proviso that they shall not sell anything after 7 o clock'. James Lillywhite was to be offered the week at Cheltenham for a set fee, 'as last year'. His request for a refund of ten pounds in the event of rain was turned down. '[H]e should give the £140 wet or dry, success or no success.'[7]

Beyond a proposal to pay J. Painter £2 10s if he played in the Colts match at Bedminster, there was no discussion of the cricketing prospects for the new season. This may well have been because the members of the committee knew the futility of trespassing on W.G.'s personal domain. He, and he alone, was responsible for selecting the side and, by extension, for any forward planning. But beyond the annual Colts match there was none, and in years to come the club would pay a heavy price for its reliance on Grace's form and his personal judgement.

---

* Now in the Gloucestershire C.C. museum at the County Ground, Bristol.

He did not have a good season in 1881. As a result of his growing professional commitments he played even fewer matches than the previous year, and, apart from one or two outstanding performances, fell markedly below his usual standards. He scored only 792 runs – 'the low-water mark of my batting career'[8] – and his bowling was less effective. He bowled only 500 overs and took forty-five wickets at just under twenty each. It's possible that in the aftermath of Fred's death the game lost some of its savour. Gloucestershire too missed the young all-rounder, who had played in every single county match since 1870 (even W.G. had missed some when he toured Canada), and their performances mirrored their captain's relative decline. Having come a good second to Nottinghamshire in 1880, they slid down the championship table in 1881, losing as many matches as they won. This was to be the pattern for the 1880s. They could no longer rely on W.G. to win them matches singlehandedly, and with Fred gone and E.M. in his forties, the family powerhouse was no longer what it had been in the 1870s.

As the championship expanded, success could only be sustained by a well-balanced side into which new blood was judiciously introduced. At Old Trafford, Lancashire showed what was needed, building up an exceptionally strong team which blended the amateur talent of Hornby and A. G. Steel with the professional skills of Barlow, Briggs and the remarkable (if dubiously generated) pace of Crossland. Grace acknowledged Lancashire's success, and admitted that, even if the leading professionals were playing under residential qualifications, 'other counties would have been only too glad to have them on similar conditions, and . . . it was owing to the committee and the excellent judgement of Mr Hornby that they had been originally selected and their powers developed'.[9] Gloucestershire's attempts at following their example were to be halting at best.

However, they made a deceptively good start, winning their first two matches in London. They beat Surrey by eight wickets, W.G. seeing them home with an unbeaten fifty and taking five wickets in the game. Against Middlesex he was in even better all-round form, scoring 64 out of 160 and taking 7 for 30 as the home team collapsed to 77 all out. They scored 195 in their second innings, the improvement in the wicket reflected in W.G.'s bowling figures of 1 for 54 in only eleven overs, but Gloucestershire reached the 114-run target with six wickets in hand.

Grace also made an influential contribution to an exciting Gentlemen

v. Players match at the Oval. While the amateurs were nearly at full strength, the Players were weakened by the absence of the Nottinghamshire professionals. This was not a boycott on their part. As an indication of the shift in the balance of power since the 1860s, they were not invited to play because they were in dispute with their committee over pay and conditions. (William Gunn, who was on the Lord's staff, did play though, batting down the order and scoring a few runs.) Tom Emmett captained the Players, and Hornby, as usual, was given the job for the Gentlemen. Facing a total of 197, he opened with W.G. and scored 20. A. P. Lucas made 25, but then Barlow and Hill tore the heart out of the middle order. Only Grace stood between the Gentlemen and defeat. He scored exactly 100, a performance described as 'the finest innings seen in London during the season'.[10] Grace was also instrumental in reining back the Players in their second innings. He bowled Midwinter for 35 and later dismissed Ulyett, whose brilliant 80 followed a forceful 57 in the first innings. W.G. bowled thirty-two overs and took 7 for 61. With only 144 to win, Hornby decided to alter the batting order. The Gentlemen promptly lost five wickets in three quarters of an hour and ended the day on 41 for 5. This time Grace was not able to dig them out of trouble. He was bowled by Bates for 9.

The third day was a cliff-hanger, reminiscent of the Glorious Match of 1877 when Fred and W. S. Patterson only just steered the Gentlemen to victory. The heroes on this occasion were C. T. Studd, making his debut, and E. F. S. Tylecote, who scored 25 not out and 22 not out respectively. The Gentlemen sneaked home by two wickets, 'a much narrower margin in point of fact than it appears on paper'.[11]

The return match at Lord's was played on a bad wicket. There had been a dry spell, and the ground was rough. (The notion of interfering with the natural course of events by watering the square was still some years off.) It was a low-scoring game, with the pace of A. H. Evans proving too much for the professionals. He took five wickets and Grace and Steel took the other five between them. (For the second time in succession Grace accounted for Midwinter, who had been given the privilege of captaining the Players.) The Gentlemen found batting no easier, though the openers Grace and Hornby together made fifty of the eventual total of 131, W.G.'s 29 being the top score. Evans proved less effective in the second innings, and Grace only bowled three overs. Steel and C. T. Studd did most of the work and took eight of the Players' wickets as they struggled to 112 all out. The Gentlemen lost Grace and

Hornby early, both bowled by Barlow, and lost three further wickets getting the seventy-seven runs required.

Grace and Hornby were opposing captains when Gloucestershire travelled up to Old Trafford later in July. The gulf that was opening between the County of the Graces and the top sides in the country was emphasized when the visitors were bowled out for 42 (of which Grace scored 14), and were thrashed by an innings. A victory over Yorkshire restored some pride, but they were forced to follow on at Trent Bridge after trailing the Nottinghamshire first innings of 240 by eighty-five runs. Grace had scored 51 in the first innings of 155, and held himself back in the second innings. When he did get to the crease he continued in good form, and led a tremendous fight-back to save the match. When he was finally trapped lbw by Attewell he had made 182, a record for the ground, and with 83 from Moberly and 54 from Gilbert, Gloucestershire reached safety with a total of 483.

This, though, proved a flash in the pan. The two sides met again immediately, at Clifton, and Nottinghamshire bowled their hosts out for 63 and 116 and beat them by ten wickets. The second Clifton match, Pullin's delayed benefit, against Middlesex was washed out, but Grace did his best for the beneficiary with an 80 in Gloucestershire's only innings. Both Yorkshire and Lancashire had by far the better of drawn games, but the season ended as it had begun with a comfortable win over Surrey at Clifton.

This was a successful game for Grace. He took 3 for 7 and 5 for 58, and in the Gloucestershire innings he delightedly stole a march on E.M., scoring 34 to his brother's 10, 'a proportion he gleefully talked about at luncheon'.[12] He also made a barnstorming 80 against Somerset at Bath, though his professional commitments prevented him going up to Scarborough to continue putting bowlers to the sword. Despite his relatively disappointing season with the bat, he was still second only to Hornby in the national averages, but he fell below both Midwinter and Gilbert in the county bowling averages.

At their parting at the end of the season, Grace may have looked somewhat askance at the giant Gloucester pro. Midwinter was returning Down Under for the winter to take part in the series between Australia and the team Alfred Shaw, Arthur Shrewsbury and James Lillywhite had got up together. There were four Tests, and Mid played in all of them – for England.

TWENTY

THE Australians beat Alfred Shaw's team 2–0 in the four-match series, and came to England at the start of the 1882 season full of confidence and assured of a warmer welcome than two years before. They also came prepared to repay old debts: Gloucestershire were rewarded for being prepared to meet them in 1880 with two fixtures, while Yorkshire, who had played them twice, were now given no fewer than five matches. These were valuable favours. The Australians were the biggest draw in English cricket and, barring rain, any match in which they played was guaranteed to generate healthy revenues. The deal they offered Gloucestershire, and presumably the other counties, was a fifty-fifty share of 'the gross receipts at the Gate'.[1] Billy Murdoch was again the Australian captain, the manager was Charles Beal, and the other members of the party were: Alec Bannerman, John Blackham, George Bonnor, Harry Boyle, Tom Garrett, George Giffen, Tom Horan, Sammy Jones, Percy McDonnell, Hugh Massie, George Palmer, and Frederick Robert Spofforth.

The trip to England provided the usual mixed bag of entertainments. Murdoch brought the house down as Bones in a Christy Minstrel show, while his appearance as a monk won plaudits at the fancy dress ball. Spofforth went as Mephistopheles, and 'needless to say he looked the character almost to the life'. The Demon further combated the tedium of the voyage by managing to get himself challenged to a duel by a Frenchman, though a diplomatic intervention, presumably by Murdoch, prevented this unscheduled diversion from taking place. Murdoch may have saved Spofforth from needlessly risking life and limb in defence of his honour, but there was nothing he could do to prevent Bonnor picking up a nasty injury when the ship lurched in a storm and the giant was flung violently against the bulwarks. Onlookers were convinced he was seriously hurt, but he survived with nothing worse than a few bruises. More worrying in the longer term was the illness that kept McDonnell confined to his bunk, and which affected his form throughout the tour.[2]

Eventually the long ordeal was over, and the ship docked at Plymouth. Bonnor had bet a number of passengers that he could throw a cricket ball 115 yards with his first attempt on dry land. With a hundred sovereigns resting on the outcome, he wound back his arm and unleashed a massive throw measured at 119 yards 'and some odd inches'.[3] It was a titanic exhibition of skill and confidence, and it set the tone for the whole tour.

On arrival in London the tourists checked in at their old haunt, the Tavistock Hotel in Covent Garden. After a few days' practice out of the city at Mitcham, where they were looked after by James Southerton who ran a pub near the ground, they caught the train to Oxford for their first match, against the university. Hugh Massie hit a sensational double century in under three hours, scoring 206 out of the 265 runs notched up while he was at the crease.* In the next match, against Sussex at Brighton, Murdoch went one better, compiling a massive 286 not out in a phenomenal total of 643 to ensure a crushing victory by an innings and 355 runs. Seldom has a touring side got off to such a flying start.

Grace's start to the season had been anything but flying. He went down with an attack of mumps, which severely limited his opportunity to practise and took the edge off his usually tireless physical energy. He was still working hard to establish himself as a GP, and his responsibilities were increased with the birth of his fourth (and last) child, Charles Butler Grace, on 26 March 1882. He was obviously feeling the financial pressure of providing for his family because the Gloucestershire committee meeting of 24 March 'Resolved that Dr W. G. Grace was not satisfied at his allowance for expenses out of pocket last year. He shall be allowed the sum of £6.1 od towards paying his Assistant in addition to the £20 already paid.' (In future years he was paid thirty-six pounds, which was occasionally topped up with further allowances.) However, with the Australians once more carrying all before them, he was eager to rejoin the fray, and was happy to accept C. I. Thornton's invitation to meet them at Twickenham, turning out for the Orleans Club. This was the first of Grace's eight matches against the tourists, and they were just as interested in his form as he was in theirs. Horan noted that he had lost a little weight as a result of his illness, but he had lost none of his appetite for battle, and drew first blood in this initial encounter.

He opened with E.M., though there was no repeat of their great Oval

* This remained the best first innings in England by an Australian until Bradman's 236 at Worcester in May 1930.

partnership of 1880, E.M. departing early for a duck. W.G. made 34 before being bowled by Palmer, and then A. P. Lucas went on to score an unbeaten 87 to help build a useful total of 271. Overnight rain changed the character of the wicket, and the following day Grace and Steel dismissed the tourists for 75, W.G. taking 5 for 26. He was less effective as the wicket improved during the visitors' second innings. He bowled thirty-eight overs at a cost of sixty-six runs, but took only one wicket (that of Bonnor, who had just struck a huge six out of the ground). The Australians relied heavily on Murdoch to save the game. Batting with great assurance, he remained undefeated on 107 when time ran out with the visitors' score on 240 for 9 (the game was limited to two days to allow the tourists to watch the Derby on 24 May).

Quite as worrying, from the Australian point of view, as their poor batting was the fact that Spofforth failed to take a single wicket in the match. He started the tour in indifferent form with only eight wickets at an average of thirty-nine in the first five games. In his only Test appearance over the winter he had taken just one wicket for 128. There seemed to be grounds for cautious English optimism. Fortunately for the Australians, they were by no means wholly dependent on the Demon. In addition to the experienced Boyle and Palmer, they had the newcomer George Giffen. Giffen had developed rapidly since bowling at Grace's team in the nets at Adelaide in 1874, and was now embarked on a career that would produce all-round performances to rival those of W.G. himself.

He gave notice of his outstanding talent in Grace's next match against the tourists at the Oval. Faced with an Australian total of 334, the Gentlemen made heavy weather of their reply. Only Grace showed much confidence and, having survived a caught and bowled chance off Spofforth, he was scoring freely when Giffen came on to bowl to him for the first time. It was a big moment for the South Australian: 'I tried for his wicket as though my life depended on the result. Success rewarded my efforts, for I bowled out his middle stump.' He was overjoyed. 'Was it not excusable, too, seeing that at the first time of asking I had clean bowled the batting wonder of the age when he was well set?' Grace had made 61, and returned to the pavilion to watch Giffen run through the rest of the side. As the Australian progressed to his final figures of 8 for 49, he received great encouragement from Bob Thoms, England's leading umpire. '"Beautiful ball, my boy; beautiful ball!" he would say at one moment. Again it would be, "Splendid, splendid! Stick to it – great future!" and then when I bowled some one, "Beautiful ball, my boy; would have beaten any one."[4] When the Gentlemen followed on, Grace was again top scorer, though this time he made only 32 before being bowled by Palmer. In an atmosphere heavy with foreboding, the stunned crowd saw the Gentlemen fail – by one run – to make the Australians bat a second time. As Horan reminded his readers in the *Australasian*, 'this disastrous defeat' was the mirror image of that inflicted by the Gentlemen on Gregory's team in 1878.

Any thought that Grace might have shaken off the Demon's jinx was rudely dispelled in the next match at Chichester. This was the first of two encounters between the tourists and the United Eleven, whose bland title, shorn of all regional affiliation, indicated its status as the absolute rump of the great peripatetic Elevens of the 1860s and 1870s. The United South had died with G.F., but both Grace and Gilbert had seen some benefit in keeping up the tradition, in however attenuated a form. Grace gave the enterprise credibility, and of course captained the side in the field; Gilbert undertook the secretarial and management duties. When, as in this instance, contractual problems arose, Gilbert was the one who carried the can.

Despite the picturesque setting of Priory Park, with the pavilion 'formed of a portion of the old ruined Priory itself',[5] the Chichester match was an undistinguished affair. Between them Grace and Gilbert had raised a poor side. E.M. and James Cranston joined them from the ranks of the Gloucestershire amateurs, and they were supported by a largely colourless group of professionals. Midwinter was down to play, but is recorded 'absent' in both innings, and the bulk of the bowling was done by W.G., E.M. and Gilbert. This was hardly the attack to warrant inserting the opposition, but, deceived by the apparent softness of the wicket, that is what Grace did. The Australians rubbed their eyes and then went enthusiastically to work. Every batsman who completed his innings scored more than twenty-five runs and Horan hit 112 in a total of 501. W.G. toiled away for fifty-three overs and took 3 for 118. Things were no better when the United Eleven batted. Had it not been for an excellent 90 by Maurice Read of Surrey (not to be confused with the Surrey amateur W. W. Read), the game would have been even more farcically one-sided. W.G. and E.M. both failed twice, and ominously Spofforth twice claimed Grace's wicket (for 4 and 11). The Australians won by an innings and 263 runs.

To add to the embarrassment, one of the professionals, Charlie

Howard of Sussex, who had been called up as a late replacement, took Gilbert to court over his fee. Typically, Grace had offered him the minimum five pounds which, considering he made 0 and 5 and took no wickets, was perhaps no more than he deserved. Howard, however, claimed ten pounds, and when the Chichester magistrates heard he had been paid six pounds to appear for his county against the 1880 tourists, they ruled that he should be paid the same in this case.[6]

Before meeting the Australians again, Grace played in the two Gentlemen v. Players matches. His performances did nothing to dispel worries over his form. He scored 21 and 1 and took two wickets in the Oval game, which the Players won; and at Lord's, after being dismissed for 4, he spent a long first day watching A. P. Lucas and C. T. Studd scoring centuries, followed by A. G. Steel, who made 76. The Gentlemen won by eight wickets, but Grace only managed seven runs in his second innings.

It had looked at some stage as though the Australians might go through a second tour without appearing at Lord's. The MCC had rejected the usual deal splitting the gate and offered a flat fee of £210 instead, which was not accepted. An accommodation was eventually reached, and the tourists played two consecutive matches at Head-quarters at the beginning of July. They beat Middlesex comfortably, and then faced an extremely strong MCC & Ground team on 10, 11 and 12 July. Most of the first two days were lost to rain, and when the MCC batted the pitch was so wet the bowlers could hardly get a footing. Nevertheless it was an impressive display. W.G. scored 46, Hornby and Lucas 45 each, and then C. T. Studd, who was having a wonderful season, scored his second century against the visitors in a total of 302. In what remained of the third afternoon the Australians started badly, but Horan and Bonnor put up some resistance, while Spofforth, going in at number eleven, batted well in the difficult conditions before Grace bowled him to bring the innings to a close on 138. The match was abandoned as a draw, but the signs were good for the Test to be played at the Oval at the end of August.

Although, as W.G. noted, the Australians dominated the season to such an extent 'that the ordinary inter-county matches suffered eclipse',[7] there was still a county programme to be played. Gloucestershire had started badly with a defeat by Middlesex at Lord's and were lucky to escape with a draw against Surrey at the Oval. Now they had an easy game at Gloucester against Somerset, admitted to the first-class ranks at last after years of indeterminate status. But they were really no stronger. Gloucestershire scored 348, and Grace made up for his failure with the bat by taking 8 for 31 to speed the visitors on their way to a massive defeat.

It was Gloucestershire's turn to be outplayed when they went up to Trent Bridge. 1882 was another damp summer, and on a rain-affected wicket the Nottinghamshire bowlers were devastating. Grace was caught by Shrewsbury off Shaw for 4, and the whole team was brushed aside for 49. He did better in the second innings, making 37 out of 108, but it was not sufficient to avert an innings defeat. He made another useful score in a small total at Old Trafford, hitting 31 out of 88, but although he also bowled well, taking seven wickets in the match, Lancashire's first-innings lead of eighty-four runs was a sufficient cushion and their victory was never in doubt.

The northern tour finished with the match against Yorkshire at Sheffield. Grace was bowled for a duck by the lugubrious left-hander Ted Peate, but Gloucestershire still managed a first-innings lead of eight runs. Yorkshire scored 146 in their second innings, Grace taking three wickets as he had in the first. He then led the pursuit of the 138 needed with 56, but as so often lacked support. The visitors were all out for 109.

They returned home for the first of their two matches against Australia at Clifton. This was another one-sided affair, which once more showed up Gloucestershire's weaknesses. Although Midwinter's medium pace had been supplemented by the left-arm seamers of William Woof, the attack lacked penetration. W.G. shared the burden with his two professionals, sending down fifty-seven overs, but his three wickets cost 146 as the tourists reached 450. Horan scored 141, and only two members of the team failed to make double figures, while the last four batsmen each scored over thirty. Grace and E.M. made something of a start, but both went for under twenty. Midwinter and Moberly scored 25 and 29 respectively, but the county's soft amateur underbelly was no match for the Australian bowling, even though Spofforth was not playing. Grace took advantage of the Demon's absence in the second innings and scored an excellent 77, but it was a one-man show, and Gloucestershire slumped to inevitable defeat by an innings and 159 runs.

They then had a sequence of four home county matches. Grace continued in good form against Lancashire at Clifton, but his 86 and 25 plus five wickets in the match were not quite enough to prevent Gloucestershire losing by thirteen runs. They were soundly beaten by

Middlesex at Cheltenham, but beat Yorkshire by an innings in the second match of the week. In the washed-out game against Nottinghamshire at Clifton Grace scored 38 and 55.

Gloucestershire then played the Australians again on the eve of the Oval match. The tourists had suffered two shock defeats since their first visit to Clifton at the beginning of August. A strong Players Eleven had beaten them by an innings and thirty-four runs, thanks largely to Maurice Read, who scored a century, and William Barnes, who made 87; and then Cambridge University Past and Present had snatched victory by twenty runs (though Horan attributed their success to atrocious umpiring). Powerful though they were, they were not invincible, and the rigours of the tour were beginning to take their toll. Horan reported: 'Giffen has given way in the knees. Palmer is very much prostrated, and Garrett is fast becoming stale and done up.'[8] Even Murdoch had to withdraw from the Gloucestershire match, coming down with cold shivers the night before.

On yet another rain-affected pitch, Grace took 8 for 93 in the Australians' first innings of 190. One of his victims was Bonnor, promoted up the order in a bold attempt to save the innings from stagnation. He rapidly reached 29 and then sent up a towering hit which most spectators thought would clear the boundary. But Midwinter was underneath it, and brought off 'one of the best catches ever seen', according to Horan. Bonnor returned to the pavilion grumbling that the catch was no credit to him as there was 'no glove in England large enough to fit his right hand'.[9]

The match was important to Grace for the last opportunity it offered to face the Australian bowling before the Oval. The one innings he had was not promising: he was clean-bowled by Spofforth for 4. The bad weather prevented a result, but after Gloucestershire had been dismissed for 131, there was time for Grace to take four more wickets as Australia batted again. More significantly, Massie made an undefeated 55.

*

The public interest in the Test match was, if anything, even greater than in 1880. There were none of the last-minute uncertainties that had surrounded the first Oval match, and the England selectors – Lord Harris, F. Burbidge, I. D. and V. E. Walker – had the opportunity to sit down and pick the best eleven cricketers in the country. They chose A. N. Hornby as captain, along with the amateurs Alfred Lyttelton (wicket-keeper), W.G., A. P. Lucas, C. T. Studd, A. G. Steel; and the professionals Barlow, Ulyett, Barnes, Peate and Maurice Read. There was no genuine fast bowler in the team – Fred Morley was injured, and although Crossland of Lancashire was decidedly quick, his action was decidedly questionable, and Lord Harris was a stickler on this point. But even without pace, the bowling was sufficiently varied, and the batting, on paper at least, looked very strong. Studd had already scored two centuries against the Australians, Read one century and a 90. Barnes had made 87 for the Players, and was a useful change bowler. Ulyett had been less successful in the various Yorkshire matches, but had topped the English batting in Australia the winter before with an aggregate of 1,424. Only six Englishmen would make 1,000 runs in the 1882 season, and five of them were in the England side. Grace fell twenty-five runs short, but no one would have dreamt for a moment of leaving him out. Hornby had, if anything, an embarrassment of batting, which perhaps accounted for some of the dubious decisions he made during the match.

The Australian eleven more or less chose itself. Palmer was unfit. Although rested for the previous four matches, his groin strain had not recovered sufficiently for him to play and so, for the second Oval Test running, Australia were deprived of one of their leading bowlers – 'our most notable bowler', according to Horan.[10] He sat out the game with Percy McDonnell, who lost the last place in the side to Sammy Jones.

The team returned to London from Clifton late on the Saturday night, and spent a quiet Sunday at the Tavistock. As they left their hotel at eleven o'clock on Monday morning a large crowd gathered to see them off. It was a gloomy day, but despite the threatening clouds at least 10,000 people were packed into the Oval to see the Australians bat after Murdoch had won the toss. At noon, Hornby led out his team to great cheers, followed by the Australian opening pair, Bannerman and Massie. They faced the two Yorkshiremen, Peate and Ulyett. Peate was steadiness personified, keeping a miserly line and length with a natural movement away from the right-hander. Ulyett was quicker, varying his pace according to conditions, and, though less dependable than Peate, was always a potential match-winner. He took the first wicket, knocking back Massie's leg-stump with a full toss when just six runs were on the board – a typical Ulyett dismissal. Murdoch joined Bannerman, and together they took the score past twenty after about an hour's play. Then, on 13, he edged a ball from Peate into his stumps. Peate at this stage had bowled nineteen overs, fifteen of which were maidens, and taken 1 for 7. Ulyett gave way to Barlow's bustling medium pace, and the Lancashire all-rounder immediately bowled Bonnor for 1. 22 for 3.

Grace had been watching proceedings intently from point, and now he made his first intervention in the match, brilliantly catching Bannerman low down and left-handed off Peate. He took a second catch later, a skier from Blackham, and throughout the innings was an intimidating presence just at the edge of the batsman's peripheral vision. In an exemplary English fielding performance he was outstanding, as Horan generously acknowledged: 'W.G. at point was a host in himself, and by his dextrous movements, his judgement, and his unceasing brilliance in that important position, gained round after round of hearty applause. I do not think I have ever seen a better point than W.G. was on this occasion.'[11] With their anchorman gone, the rest of the Australian batsmen succumbed to Peate and Barlow in a dispirited procession. Blackham made 17 and Garrett 10, but those were the only double-figure scores after Murdoch's, and the innings closed at quarter past three when Jones was caught off Barlow by Barnes at third man. The total was a miserable 63. Barlow had taken 5 for 10 in thirty-one overs, and Peate finished with 4 for 31 in thirty-eight.

The ground had continued to fill during the day and spectators were still pushing through the turnstiles at five o'clock to take the figure of those who paid for entry to 19,601. Horan gives a vivid description of the scene from the playing area:

On the sloping embankment close to the chains people were standing 20 deep all round, and further back on the terraces the throng was equally dense, while on the spacious covered stand, close to the pavilion, and on the two equally spacious uncovered stands placed at intervals around the ground, not a vacant seat could be had for love or money. The roofs of the dingy brick houses surrounding the Oval, too, bore their quota of eager spectators, and every window overlooking the . . . ground was also thronged.

To Australian eyes, the most striking feature of this vast crowd was the complete absence of colour: '[E]very article of clothing was sombre and funereal . . . in strict unison with the gloomy weather which prevailed throughout the day.'[12]

However, the crowd were enjoying themselves, and after England's clinical dismemberment of the Australian batting they gave a somewhat triumphalist cheer when Grace and Barlow came out to open the batting. They were confronted, inevitably, by Spofforth, who was partnered on this occasion by Garrett. Tall, slightly gaunt, like the Demon, Garrett was a fast-medium bowler capable of moving the ball either way, especially on a helpful wicket. He might have been Australia's second string, but he was a more than useful foil for Spofforth.

The England pair negotiated the opening overs carefully, and the score edged into double figures. Then, with thirteen runs on the board, Grace was yorked by Spofforth, for 4. Five runs later the Demon had Barlow snapped up by Bannerman at forward point for 11. 18 for 2. Hornby had sent in Ulyett at three, and with A. P. Lucas watching aghast at the other end, Happy Jack proceeded to hit out in his most carefree vein. The Australians were not impressed: 'He scarcely made a good stroke, and had his stumps grazed a half-a-dozen times.'[13] It may not have been pretty, but it was effective, as long as it lasted. When he eventually took one risk too many and was stumped by Blackham off Spofforth, he had made 26 and the score stood at 57.

Ulyett's aggression was largely vindicated as the more correct amateur bats of the middle order floundered against the Demon and Boyle, who had replaced Garrett. Lucas, Lyttleton and Studd made eleven between them, and although the Australian total was reached, there seemed little hope of a significant lead. Maurice Read played sensibly, and with support from Steel took the score to 96. Steel then played on to Garrett, having made 14, and Read was joined by his captain, unaccountably coming in at number ten. There was relieved cheering as the hundred was reached, but one run later Spofforth produced a vicious break-back to bowl Hornby for 2. Peate, the one man in the side of whom nothing was expected with the bat, made his way out to the wicket, and Spofforth quickly sent him back with no addition to the score. Read was left undefeated on 19, and the England total of 101 gave them a lead of thirty-eight.

The second day was no more propitious than the first. It was unseasonally cold, and overnight rain had left the pitch soaking. Piles of sawdust marked the end of the bowlers' run-ups and each crease was also covered to give them a chance of a foothold. When it started drying out, the wicket would become a vicious sticky, but for an hour or so conditions favoured the batsmen, if they were brave enough to seize their chance. Hugh Massie was, and, possibly inspired by Ulyett's long-handled spree the previous day, hit out with calculated aggression. Hornby opened with Ulyett and Barlow, but he was soon forced to change them as Massie's assault continued. It was a stunning performance, which rapidly saw the deficit wiped off with all ten wickets standing. He was dropped once after scoring thirty-eight runs – a hard chance to Lucas at long-off – but he didn't allow that to deflect him. While Bannerman bided his time at the other end, the score passed fifty, and Massie had reached his own half-century when he eventually missed Steel's quicker ball and had his leg-stump knocked out of the ground. He had made 55 at exactly a run a minute and given his team an invaluable start.

As on Monday, there was a huge crowd, and their applause for Massie's magnificent innings was levened with relief. The wicket was now becoming more and more difficult, but even though wickets fell in rapid succession, they sensed that Massie had caught the tide and swung the match Australia's way. The English players felt it too, and responded with renewed aggression. Once Bannerman went, caught by Studd off Barnes, Murdoch stood as the Australians' great hope – as he had two years before. The circumstances were different, but the pressure was just as great. W.G., encroaching ever closer at point, picked up two catches off Peate. Bonnor had failed, bowled by Ulyett for 2, and runs were painfully hard to get. At 99 for 6, Sammy Jones came and helped his captain raise the score to 110.

Then came the flashpoint, and arguably the turning-point of the match, though the incident has tended to be lost in the dramatic avalanche it set off. Murdoch turned Steel away fine on the leg side. There was no fielder, and the batsmen crossed for an easy single while Lyttelton left his post at the stumps to retrieve the ball, which ended up in Grace's hands. Jones, having made his ground, and assuming the ball was dead, left his crease to pat down a divot on the pitch. Grace whipped off the bails and appealed. The umpire Thoms gave Jones out.

Those seem to be the facts, though different accounts vary as to the details. Horan says Peate took Lyttelton's place at the wicket but missed the wicket-keeper's return, which went through to Grace who was backing up from his position at point. Grace then 'held it for two or three seconds', which was enough for Jones to assume he regarded it as dead.[14] Evidence that Grace was more actively complicit in Jones's misapprehension comes in one of two letters that Hugh Massie's son, R. J. A. Massie, wrote to English friends in 1956, giving his father's version of the incident. According to Massie, once the ball had come to rest in Grace's hands, 'Jones nodded to Grace', establishing, as he thought, a tacit understanding that he was now safe to leave the crease. The Massie account continues: 'to the amazement of the Australians, the umpire gave Jones out.'[15]

Thoms really had little option, though there are conflicting reports as to his reaction. According to Horan, he was reluctant to give the decision, saying, 'If you claim it, sir, it is out.'[16] In other versions Thoms denied casting any doubt over the probity of the appeal. Horan admitted, 'In strict cricket no doubt Jones was out,' but added, 'I do not think it redounds much to any man's credit to endeavour to win a match by resorting to what might not inaptly be termed sharp practice.'[17] It is difficult to dissent from this view, especially if the detail the Massie letter gave about Jones's nod to Grace is true. The account contains some inaccuracies – Jones is credited with the original scoring shot, the batsmen crossing for two runs rather than a single, and there is no mention of Peate coming up to the wicket and missing Lyttelton's throw-in – but on the central issue, Grace's effectual duplicity, it has the ring of truth. Massie's son wrote, 'I have no reason to doubt what my father told me – he was not given to romancing.'[18]

Murdoch's anger was plain for all to see, but Spofforth was equally indignant. During England's first innings he had had the opportunity to run Hornby out while backing up at the bowler's end, and had told him: 'I could stump you now – you're out of your ground.' Hornby said, 'Yes . . . but surely that's not your game, is it?' To which the Demon replied, 'Well, no.'[19] Having let off Hornby, who was after all attempting to gain some marginal advantage, Spofforth was all the more outraged by Grace's blatant bad sportsmanship. He now came in and tried to relieve his feelings by slogging at Peate. He was bowled for a duck and retired to the pavilion still boiling.

Just how furious Spofforth was is revealed in the other letter Massie's son wrote in 1956:* 'when the Australians were all out and the English team left the field, he went into the Englishmen's dressing-room and told Grace he was a bloody cheat and abused him in the best Australian vernacular for a full five minutes. As he flung out of the door his parting shot was, "This will lose you the match."'[20]

The last three wickets fell quickly, Murdoch also being run out, though in his case by a brilliant throw from the boundary by Studd. The total stood at 122, leaving England the seemingly straightforward task of scoring eighty-five runs to win the match. After Spofforth's tirade, Hornby decided the captain's place was at the head of his troops, so

* R. J. A. Massie was reminded of the match when he was sent a copy of John Masefield's poem, 'Eighty-five to Win', published in *The Times*, 29 August 1956. In his first letter he volunteered his father's account of the Jones incident, providing further details in the second.

he opened with W.G. The Demon, grimly focused on the task ahead, told his team-mates, 'This can be done,' and paced out his run at the Vauxhall end, waiting to give the England batsmen the benefit of his baleful glare. Bonnor, the only man on the field who could look down on Grace, came up to him and gave him another ear-bashing, seconded by Garrett.[21] Grace no doubt gave as good as he got, and far from unsettling him, the set-to only increased his determination to get the runs needed.

The innings got off to a good start, with Hornby taking the lead. Fifteen runs came up quite quickly. But then Spofforth struck, bowling the England captain for 9. Barlow, his dour opening partner for Lancashire, replaced him, under instruction to play his natural defensive game. An hour or so of stubborn resistance to blunt the attack and the game would have been England's. Spofforth knew that as well as anyone, and he produced another beauty to bowl him first ball. The next man was Ulyett. Refusing to recognize the situation as a crisis, he went for his shots as he had in the first innings, and with Grace scoring with more freedom too – he hit seven off one over, on-driving Spofforth twice – the total reached fifty. With only thirty-five to get and eight wickets in hand, the game, in Horan's quaint phrase, 'looked a guinea to a gooseberry on England'.[22]

But although the rest of the team might have lost heart, Spofforth was still in furious overdrive. Murdoch had switched him to the Pavilion end, and in the thickening light, visibility was appalling. Ulyett seemed intent on finishing the game as quickly as possible, but a wild slash gave Blackham the chance to take a spectacular catch behind. 51 for 3. The crowd shifted uneasily in their seats, but took comfort from the continuing presence of W.G., who had become only the second batsman in the match to reach the thirty mark. A. P. Lucas joined him.

Boyle was now bowling from the Vauxhall end, varying his trajectory and trying to tempt Grace into the drive. With only two more runs added, he succeeded. Grace went for a ball that dipped just short of half-volley length and at mid-off Alec Bannerman gratefully received the catch. Grace had made 32. It was a splendid innings, hovering on the brink of greatness. If the early afternoon had shown him at his belligerently competitive worst, the last hour had seen him at his incomparably competitive best. He had stood in the eye of the storm, his temperament and technique alike proof against everything the Australians could hurl at him. It should have been enough, but even as he plodded back to the pavilion he may have doubted whether it would be. With his massive presence removed, England were about to reap the whirlwind he had sown.

Grace's departure was a huge psychological boost to the Australians, and a corresponding blow to English morale, but the game was still there to be won, and the next passage of play was vital. After a flurry of runs which took him rapidly to double figures, Lyttelton clearly decided consolidation was the priority. Both he and Lucas had been commended for their defence as undergraduates, and now the Cambridge pair began to play a waiting game. As John Masefield put it in his poem, 'Eighty-five to Win': 'Twelve deadly overs followed without score, / Then came a run, then deadly maidens more'.[23] The one run was a snick by Lyttelton off Boyle, which brought him down to Spofforth's end. The great bowler was operating with the intense purpose of an avenging figure in a Greek drama, and he now produced another crippling stroke of retribution, dismissing Lyttelton with a ripping off-cutter to break the deadlock. 66 for 5; last man, 12.

Lyttelton had made a useful contribution, but he had also surrendered the initiative, and this made the job of those still to bat all the more difficult. All the same, only nineteen runs were needed and there were still five wickets standing. However, it was at this point that Hornby started to lose his nerve. Rather than sending in Studd, he held him back like a timid card-player hoarding an ace. Steel came out instead. He survived the remaining two balls of Spofforth's over, and then the tension was relieved slightly as Lucas cut Boyle away for four. The crowd which had been suffering in silence at last had something to cheer as the score crawled to seventy.

But that still left the new batsman at Spofforth's end, and in the rapidly deteriorating light he was completely defeated by the Demon's slower ball, hitting up an easy return catch. 70 for 6. Still Hornby kept back Studd, and sent in Maurice Read. These stays of execution were not doing anything for Studd's state of mind. The young Middlesex batsman was feeling the cold and wrapped himself in a blanket to stop his shivering. He gazed out wretchedly as Read survived his first ball from Spofforth, but the second bowled him middle stump. 70 for 7. Yet again Hornby ordered Studd to wait and Barnes set off on the long walk to the middle.

The atmosphere in the English changing room must have been dreadful. Draped in his blanket, Studd looked anything but the saviour of his side, while Peate was apparently in such a state that some members of the team decided the champagne waiting for England's anticipated victory could be put to better use as a medicinal 'tonic'.[24] Hornby was trapped in a captain's living nightmare, while Grace, as he always did when agitated, resorted to vigorous beard tugging.

Barnes had one ball of Spofforth's over to negotiate, and got it away for two. Three joyfully sprinted byes followed. 75 for 7, and only ten to win. Lucas faced Spofforth and survived the first three balls of the over. But the fourth brought his long resistance to an end as he edged the ball into his stumps. He had made five. 75 for 8. At last it was Studd's turn. Throwing off his blanket and trying to shake some life into his arms and legs, he wound his way through the pavilion, oblivious to dry-throated croaks of encouragement from the Surrey members, and out into the murky light.

The Australians were gathered round their captain. The match would be decided one way or the other in the next few minutes, and Murdoch required one last, Herculean effort from them. Studd reached the wicket but was denied the strike. The over had been called, and now Barnes faced Boyle. Boyle took his time, bending to dust the ball in the sawdust pile to gain maximum purchase on the seam, before turning and starting his run from the Vauxhall end. Seconds later his front foot pounded into the footmarks and the ball flew from his grasp. It hung momentarily in the heavy evening air. Barnes pushed forward, but not quite far enough. At the most critical moment of his cricketing life, Boyle had produced the perfect delivery. It turned and lifted, striking the glove to loop up to Murdoch at point. 75 for 9.

Studd looked on in disbelief. After that interminable delay, he was still left on tenterhooks, his fate in someone else's hands. He waited anxiously for the man who would share the stage with him at the climax of the drama played out under the impassive gasometers. It was an audacious pairing for the denouement: Studd, 'Cambridge Studd, the bright bat debonair', classically coached amateur and future Christian missionary; and Ted Peate, the Yorkshireman, professional cricketer to the soles of his boots. Droopily moustached, left-handed, short-sighted, tall without any vestige of athleticism, he had the slightly comic demeanour entirely consistent with his pedigree as one of Arthur Trelor's troupe of Clown Cricketers. Although the sight of him blinking his way towards the wicket was not calculated to inspire confidence, he had been known to score runs, albeit by unorthodox methods. He had made 48 in the Under Thirty v. Over Thirty match, and in the last of Yorkshire's fixtures against the Australians had slogged a useful twenty. Now, in worsening light and fortified with several measures of 'tonic', he had a captive audience of twenty thousand. There was no knowing how he would react.

Three balls remained in Boyle's over. Peate mowed the first one with the spin into the outfield. Studd charged down the wicket and for a moment was at the striker's end. Prudence might have suggested staying there, but runs were inexpressibly precious and he turned for the second, only to hear Peate proposing a suicidal third as they crossed. It was a close enough call as it was. Garrett fielded the ball and many years later remembered 'old Luke Greenwood, who was umpiring, [throwing] himself on his stomach to see' as Peate just made his ground.[25] Eight more runs needed. More importantly, two more balls in the over for Peate to negotiate. 'Boyle launched another, subtly not the same.' The subtlety was wasted on Peate, who wound himself up for another dreadful heave and missed. In Masefield's poem, those who had them 'Bit their umbrella handles in suspense'. And if the oft-cited but never identified heart-attack victim really did succumb to his angina in the final stages of the match, then it must surely have been Peate who did for him. One delivery of the over remained.

> Boyle took the ball; he turned; he ran; he bowled,
> All England's watching heart was stricken cold.
> Peate's whirling bat met nothing in its sweep.
> The ball put all his wickets in a heap;
> All out, with Studd untried; our star had set,
> All England out, with seven runs to get.*

At ten to six on the second day, Australia had brought off an implausible victory. After a collective gasp of disbelief, the crowd broke into a torrent of cheering. Though England had lost, they knew they had witnessed a historic occurrence, and a sense of non-partisan elation swept across the ground. The two batsmen set off for the pavilion, Peate with a rueful grimace, Studd tight-lipped, as the spectators mobbed the victors, hoisting Boyle and Spofforth aloft and bearing them to the pavilion fence, an uncomfortable homage they undoubtedly deserved. Spofforth had

---

* Though Masefield's poem is extremely accurate, he in fact describes five balls in the last over, not four.

taken 7 for 44 in twenty-eight overs, the last eleven of which had yielded four wickets for only two runs. 'Irresistible as an avalanche' is how George Giffen summed it up. His fourteen wickets in a Test against England remained a record until Bob Massie's match at Lord's ninety years later. Boyle had been equally brilliant, each of his three wickets proving a crucial turning point. He took 3 for 19 in twenty overs, of which eleven were maidens.

The excitement at the conclusion of the match was unparalleled. Charlie Beal rushed down the pavilion steps to congratulate his players and sent the man at the gate flying. Beal's mother was equally excited and flung her arms around George Giffen and planted 'a mother's kiss' upon his brow.[26] The crowd called for the heroes by name and each had to step forward and acknowledge the cheers. The Australian dressing room was thronged, not just with their supporters, but with the English players, who mixed a loving cup of 'champagne, seltzer, and lemons' for their vanquishers. Hornby went up to Murdoch and said, 'Well, old fellow, it would have been the proudest moment of my life to have won, but I cannot help congratulating you sincerely on the splendid uphill game you played and your well-merited success.'[27] The Australians were mobbed again as they left the ground; women waved handkerchiefs at them all along the Kennington Road, and as word spread through the capital, 'the passers-by looked at us as if we had done something to make us famous for all time'.[28] Which, of course, they had.

*

The aftermath for the defeated team was altogether more sombre. Although the *Sporting Times*'s spoof obituary – 'In Affectionate Remembrance of ENGLISH CRICKET, which died at the Oval on 29th August, 1882. Deeply lamented by a large circle of Sorrowing Friends and Acquaintances R.I.P.' – is rightly remembered for its throwaway last line, 'The body will be cremated, and the Ashes taken to Australia', its facetiousness was hardly in tune with the mood of the country. The first defeat of a fully representative English side was a severe shock and national pride was badly dented when it was realized that Australia could now claim 'the cricketing supremacy of the world'.[29] The inquest was long and severe. ' "The Decadence of English Cricket" was the theme of leader-writers in a hundred papers', *Lillywhite's Companion* noted,[30] and many accused the English batsmen of funk. The team selection was questioned, and Hornby's worth as captain disparaged.

Spofforth sided with those who accused the English batsmen of timidity. Lyttelton, he thought, had played 'fatally correctly'[31] and should have tried to get after Boyle. But Peate, of course, was condemned for his impetuosity. He is reputed to have justified himself with the laconic retort, 'Ah couldn't troost Mester Stood', expanded, according to an account of a dressing-down Lord Harris gave him immediately after the match, to 'Ah warn't afeerd for mesen; Ah were afeerd for Mester Stood; Ah knew Ah could play old Spoff!'[32] It was obviously ridiculous to hold Peate personally responsible for the defeat. Grace summed it up with his usual blunt simplicity: 'I left six men to get thirty odd runs and they could not get them.'[33] While this is undoubtedly true, it leaves out his wider role in the match. It is impossible to know what would have happened had he not broken Jones's wicket. Jones might have batted on with Murdoch and taken the game out of England's reach; he might have been bowled next ball. What is certain is that by running him out in what the Australians thought an unsporting manner, Grace roused Spofforth to produce one of the greatest bowling efforts of all time to drive his team to their extraordinary victory. In other words, Grace was, to a very large extent, personally responsible for the birth of the Ashes.

Two days after the Test match Grace took the field against the Australians again, this time at the head of his United XI at Tunbridge Wells. The Australians were emotionally and physically drained, and found it impossible to raise their game. They were bowled out for 49 in their second innings by Grace and an unknown slow left-armer, J. T. Parnham, who took 7 for 25 (12 for 126 in the match) and must have wondered what all the fuss was about. The game was cut short by rain and abandoned as a draw.

This was the last of Grace's encounters with the tourists, and they must have felt that they had got the better of him. Spofforth had clearly kept the upper hand, dismissing him on five occasions, on four of which he failed. Grace had made his highest score (77) when Spofforth was not playing, and the other time he passed fifty Spofforth had missed a caught and bowled chance. However, the Australians had not had it all their own way. Grace made 340 runs against them in twelve innings at an average of 28.3, and put in some splendid bowling performances, including his 8 for 93 at Clifton, to accumulate thirty-two wickets at 18.59. But it had been a disappointing season for him. For the first time since 1867 he failed to score a first-class century, and in missing his thousand runs he also recorded his lowest average in his first-class career to date – 26.35. Even his haul of 101 wickets was poor in comparison to the 182 he had taken the previous year, and it was a reflection of his relatively poor form that he found himself on the winning side in only four matches out of twenty-two.

The last of these was a rousing victory over Surrey at Clifton, which demonstrated just how important Grace's performances were to his county. He scored 88 out of 193 and 51 out of 132 for 4, and took 7 for 44 and 2 for 90. But it was far too late to revive Gloucestershire's fortunes. They had been out of contention from early in the summer, and the championship was shared by Lancashire and Nottinghamshire, whose success was grounded in their pool of professionals. Lancashire had eight professionals listed in *Lillywhite's Companion*, Nottinghamshire a staggering twenty-seven. Gloucestershire had just two, Midwinter and Woof – fewer than any other first-class county. As the new decade went on, Gloucestershire's continued failure to live up to the glories of the 1870s became a matter of growing concern, especially as suspicions grew that, paradoxically, the blame lay largely with the man on whom the club depended for its very survival.

TWENTY-ONE

IN 1883 the MCC introduced amendments to the laws on two subjects close to Grace's heart: umpires and the use of the roller. Henceforth the batting side had the option of having the pitch rolled on the morning of the second and third days rather than simply between innings. As the veteran of several contretemps on this issue, W.G. was delighted:

Before this new rule came into operation the side winning the toss secured an altogether unfair advantage over their opponents, who, in many cases, lost the chance of having the wicket rolled in the morning through getting a few minutes' play overnight. If rain had fallen in the night, or a heavy dew had damped the ground, the batting side often found the wicket detrimental to their chances. The new rule swept away this grievance.[1]

The insistence on neutral umpires for county matches was generally welcomed, but it also threw up fresh difficulties. At the end of the season E.M. wrote to Lord's 'complaining that our nomination C. K. Pullin stood in seven County matches only in 1883 instead of Twelve, the number of Matches played by Gloucestershire'.[2] Although they had grasped the nettles of qualification and now neutral umpiring, the authorities still put off giving the county championship the thorough shake-up it required. The tradition by which the side losing the fewest matches claimed the title was exposed as ludicrous when Nottinghamshire were declared champions having won a mere four matches with only one defeat, while Yorkshire won nine but lost two. But nothing was done to change the system.

Gloucestershire's interest in this issue was purely academic. They would have come last anyway. Grace organized a Colts match as usual in April, but despite this laudable enthusiasm for bringing on young cricketers, there remained no policy for increasing the county's immediate competitiveness. This was further reduced by Midwinter's decision to pursue the next stage of his chequered career in Australia. As a result, an even greater burden fell on Grace and Woof, and Gloucestershire were left with one of the most innocuous attacks in county cricket.

It was no surprise therefore that they won only three of their matches – and two of those were against Somerset, who were so weak they were excluded from most versions of the championship. Despite the team's disappointing form, Grace threw himself into the game with his usual gusto and produced a few outstanding personal performances. He scored 89 and 35 and took twelve wickets in the Middlesex match at Lord's in May, but still saw Gloucestershire lose the game. He took six wickets against Surrey at the Oval and made 34 and 51, with five wickets in the match against Yorkshire at Bradford, but only found consistent form in August. He scored 40 and 43 and took ten wickets against Somerset at Clifton, and then did even better when Gloucestershire travelled down to Taunton for the return – eleven wickets, and 75 and 58. He then scored 85 against Middlesex at Clifton, though his one wicket cost 154 runs as the visitors ran up a huge total of 537. It was not until the last county match of the season, against Lancashire, that he scored his first and only century, 112. He was ably supported by the left-hander James Cranston, with whom he put on 126 for the fourth wicket. Cranston went on to score 127 out of a total of 324 which set up victory by six wickets. It was a poor consolation prize for a wretched season. Cranston, for one, decided that he had had enough and departed for Warwickshire (though he returned to play for Gloucestershire at the end of the decade).

In addition to county games Grace played his normal quota of other first-class matches. He scored exactly half the South's total of 128 against the North at Lord's and bowled seventy-four overs in the match (6 for 96), but was 'absent hurt' nursing an injured finger in the South's second innings, when the rest of the team made exactly the same number of runs as they had in the first – 64. He made a fifty for the MCC against Nottinghamshire, enjoying the increasingly rare experience of being on the winning side, and had his best match in the first half of the season when he took his own team down to Sheffield Park in Sussex to play Lord Sheffield's XI.

The third Earl of Sheffield was a shy, idiosyncratic man who loved the game and became its greatest patron in the last years of the Victorian period. After serving in the diplomatic service, and then as an MP for East Sussex for several years, he succeeded to his title in 1876 at the age of forty-four and immediately set about creating a first-class cricket field in the grounds of Sheffield Park. The result was a perfect setting with a splendid pavilion set among rhododendron bushes, a bandstand and, on match days, tiered seating for the public, who were allowed in free of charge. As a longstanding member of the MCC and president of Sussex, he was well connected in the cricket world and over the years played host to many of the leading players of the day, most notably a succession of Australian touring sides. He also developed an important relationship with Grace. This was Grace's first match at Sheffield Park, and he rewarded the cricket-mad peer with two quality innings of 81 and 51. His lordship was further recompensed for his lavish hospitality when his team triumphed by six wickets.

For the first time since 1867 Grace missed the Gentlemen v. Players match at the Oval, owing to unspecified 'medical duties'. His presence would almost certainly have spoiled the closest match in the history of the fixture. It ended in a tie. The return at Lord's took place on 9, 10 and 11 July, and the first day was notable for a spectacular display of batting by the amateurs. Grace started it with a brutal assault on a young Yorkshire player called G. P. 'Shoey' Harrison who was making his debut at Lord's after some impressive performances in county cricket. He was new to Grace, and on being told by A. P. Lucas that he was 'pretty fast', W.G. said, 'Well, let me have a look at him,' and took strike. Lucas recalled what happened next: 'I never in all my life saw any one ever crumple up a bowler as he did poor Harrison. I never received a single ball from him so long as my great colleague was in. He simply laid in wait for him, punished and snicked him, and I have always believed that small score of 26 . . . broke Harrison's heart so far as bowling was concerned.'[3]

Although he was generally very kind to young cricketers, there were occasions when Grace took a sadistic delight in reminding them of their place in the scheme of things. Harrison, however, recovered pretty well from being 'crumpled'. Grace departed, bowled Peate, for 26, and the young Yorkshireman took the next three wickets, albeit at some cost; but to clean-bowl Lucas, C. T. Studd and Lord Harris was not a bad performance. Nevertheless, the score continued to mount. Lucas made 72, Steel 64, A. W. Ridley 51 and E. F. S. Tylecote a century in a total of 441. Despite some good individual scores, the Players were never in the match, and lost by seven wickets.

Grace played one of the two matches at Canterbury Week, and had another reminder of what it was like to be on the winning side when the MCC beat their hosts. He also finished his season in Kent, playing for a South XI v. a North XI at Tunbridge Wells. He made 41 in his second innings, dismissed by the tearaway Lancashire fast bowler Jack Cross-land.

As in 1882 he just missed the double, though this time he fell short in the bowling department, taking ninety-four wickets at 22.09. It had been a much warmer summer and the wickets were firmer, so batting was generally easier. Nine men reached 1,000 runs, the largest number ever to do so, and Grace was third with 1,352 behind Walter Read and Ulyett, who were separated by a single run (1,573, 1,572). Read (47.22) and Studd (41.4) also kept him third in the averages on 34.66. (E.M. recorded a very respectable 638 runs at 24.14.) Grace took thirty-five catches and also claimed a stumping in Yorkshire's first innings at Bradford, during which he also bowled fifty-four overs. Only the laws of physics prevented him from keeping to his own bowling.

There was a poignant tailpiece to the season. At the autumn committee meeting held on 26 October it was 'Resolved that we cannot accede to Mrs Lillywhite's request, of returning her some of the money paid for the Cheltenham week'. James Lillywhite had died the previous November. He had obviously been left out of pocket on the week, and his widow had hoped to recoup some of that loss. But the terms of the agreement were clear. Gloucestershire were not a wealthy club, and charity began at home.

*

With Henry Grace in the chair, the first committee meeting of 1884 took place on 29 February and unanimously passed the motion 'That the Secretary be presented with a Bonus of £25. 0. 0. for the admirable manner in which he has conducted the affairs of the Club during the past Year.' The meeting then passed on to matters of wider importance. The previous year's resolution on neutral umpires had been a step in the right direction, but had failed to grasp the nettle of throwing. As the Australians had found at Scarborough on the eve of the 1880 Test match, umpires simply refused to no-ball bowlers with unfair actions. As a result, bowlers had a licence to do much as they pleased, and throwing was becoming an epidemic.

One of the worst offenders was Crossland, whose action was so bad that Lord Harris would not countenance his selection for England. However, he was protected by his county captain, A. N. Hornby, to the disgust of many in the game. In a symposium in *Lillywhite's Companion* for 1884, the Hon. R. H. Lyttelton publicly appealed to Hornby to force Crossland out of county cricket, but he stuck by his man and continued to bowl him for Lancashire. This produced considerable ill feeling around the county circuit, and Ted Peate brought matters to a head in the Roses match at Old Trafford. George Wootton was umpiring and had, as usual, allowed Crossland to bowl without interference. Peate warned Wootton that he was going to throw a delivery and challenged him to call a no-ball. When Wootton failed to respond, Peate rounded on him: 'There, that shows what you umpires are all worth!'[4]

Grace does not seem to have been particularly exercised by the problem, though he came in for his fair – or unfair – share of throwing. Sometimes bowlers let fly at him out of frustration, like Sam Costick in the exhibition match at Melbourne in 1874; sometimes there was a more calculated plan to dismiss him by foul means. Once, in a United South game against Batley, he was well set against the local Eighteen. Then 'a bowler whom I had never seen before was commissioned to have a try at me. The very first ball was a deliberate throw, and it hit my wickets, and I had to go out.'[5] Having taken the vital wicket, the unknown thrower was taken off. Such incidents caused Grace's hackles to rise, but he faced the likes of Crossland without complaint. Indeed, on one occasion at Clifton when the Lancashire bowler was giving him a very hard time and attracting hostile comments from the home crowd in consequence, Grace stopped play, walked to the boundary and told the barrackers to be quiet before returning to his ordeal at the crease. And after his legendary encounter in 1896 with the Australian Ernest Jones, whose action was also doubtful, he showed off his trophies, 'six or seven black puddings around his heart', saying 'I don't mind how fast they send them down to me. They can chuck them if they like; the faster they are the better.'[6]

But Lord Harris did care, and had sent a circular to all the counties appealing for the practice to be stamped out once and for all. The difficulty was that umpires were ex-pros, and as such were hardly likely to challenge a bowler sanctioned by someone like Hornby. Class solidarity also made them reluctant to jeopardize a fellow professional's career by calling him. On the practical side, only the umpire at the bowler's end was allowed to call for throwing. It was this point that the Gloucestershire committee addressed in their submission to Lord's. They suggested 'That as an Umpire cannot keep his eyes on the crease and the bowler's arm at the same time, Both Umpires shall have the power to No Ball an unfair delivery.' While they were about it, they added a further suggestion: 'That the Marylebone Cricket Club shall provide every County Umpire with a properly authenticated Gauge to decide the width of any Bats, when requested to do so.'[7] This almost certainly came from Grace, who developed a slightly comic fixation with the subject.

On 21 April the MCC amended the laws of cricket, insisting that umpires must be 'absolutely satisfied' with a bowler's delivery before passing it as fair. However, as the remaining decade and a half of the century would show, this was not enough on its own. Until the real powers in first-class cricket, the captains, gave their active support to the rules, the problem would remain. The MCC also climbed onto the Test bandwagon at last, agreeing to stage a match against the 1884 Australians at Lord's in July. In the aftermath of Ivo Bligh's triumphant tour of 1882–3 when he reclaimed the Ashes and came home with the actual urn (and an Australian wife), a proper three-match series was arranged, with the other two Tests at Old Trafford, and, of course, the Oval.

The fourth Australian tourists did not achieve the glory of the 1882 team, though they did for once experience an English summer at its best. The core of the side remained the same. Murdoch was again captain, and the great bowling trio of Spofforth, Boyle and Palmer remained intact. A fourth, of whom great things were expected, was the leg-spinner William Cooper, but he suffered a bad injury to his bowling hand on the boat and was never much of a force as a result. The voyage's toll of misfortune also included George Giffen's loss of *two* diamond rings as a result of throwing some orange peel over the side of the boat.[8] The British public were bemused to find Billy Midwinter once more in the tourists' ranks. He had played in the fourth (unofficial) Test against Bligh's team and decided, on balance, that he was an Australian after all.

Grace entered the lists at the earliest opportunity. This was at Sheffield Park, in what was to become the traditional curtain-raiser, Lord Sheffield's XI v. The Australians. Giffen records that 'His lordship met us with a smiling face, [and] an open hand; . . . we repaid his hospitality by defeating his team with an innings to spare.'[9] (Horan noted that the hospitality was such that the two-day match cost Lord Sheffield £1,300.)[10] Grace made 1 and 30, but salvaged something from the game by taking 6 for 72. He had another six-wicket haul playing for the MCC against Lancashire at Lord's, but he went into his next encounter with the tourists for MCC & Ground without a decent score to his name. Any fears that his batting might be in terminal decline were dispersed when he made a fine 101. This was William Cooper's first match, and he had wretchedly bad luck. He opened the bowling, and to begin with W.G.

was 'sadly troubled' by the amount of turn the leg-spinner was getting. He survived a close call for a stumping which left the Australians 'very much dissatisfied',[11] and then decided that attack was the best means of defence. He gave Cooper the Harrison treatment, virtually hitting him out of contention for a place in the Test side, and indeed out of first-class cricket altogether. Cooper took only seven wickets throughout the tour, and retired from the game when he got back to Australia. Grace's blistering start set the tone for the rest of the MCC & Ground innings, and both Steel and Barnes also scored centuries in a total of 481 – the highest score ever made against the Australians in England, and the first time there had been three centuries in a first-class innings. MCC then bowled out the touring team for 184 and 182, Grace taking 3 for 18 and 4 for 61, to clinch a psychologically important victory by an innings and 115 runs.

Before the end of May the tourists were back at Lord's to meet the Gentlemen of England. This had always been something of a litmus test, and the English camp took heart from a six-wicket win for the amateurs (though once again Spofforth had a hand injury and hardly bowled). Grace spent some useful time at the crease, scoring 21 and 20. He returned to Lord's for his next two games. He took five wickets in the South's win over the North, but failed twice with the bat in a low-scoring game. He was in better form for Gloucestershire against Middlesex, missing a century by six runs, but that was overshadowed when he strained a muscle in his leg and was unable to take the field for Middlesex's second innings. Gloucestershire conceded 345 runs and, despite leading by seventy-three on first innings, lost the match by 122 runs.

They lost their next two fixtures as well, against Surrey and Sussex. Grace doggedly turned out for both games, though he was severely handicapped by his injury which, he admitted, 'ought to have laid me up, but I never stopped playing for a day, although very lame'.[12] At the end of June he scored another century against the Australians in the second Gentlemen of England match at the Oval. It was 'a very remarkable performance', considering his leg was still bad, and his domination of the innings was reminiscent of earlier days.[13] The next highest score after his 107 was Lord Harris's 35, and no one else passed thirty. The Gentlemen secured a modest first-innings lead, and at 104 for 3 chasing 188 to win looked well set. However, Spofforth, recovered from his injury, was riled when a slip catch was disallowed, and moved onto that plane of supercharged hostility where few could live with him. Setting an intimidating slip cordon, he tore in from the Pavilion end and demolished the rest of the batting, taking 7 for 68. The last five wickets fell for twenty-three, and Australia won by forty-six runs.

The two Gentlemen v. Players games at the beginning of July gave a last opportunity to prepare for the first Test. Ulyett's magnificent 134 helped the Players win the game at the Oval; W.G., batting down the order, was top scorer for the Gentlemen in both innings with 35 not out and 66. Ulyett and Grace continued in excellent form at Lord's, the Yorkshireman scoring 94 and 64, the Champion 21 and 89. His second-wicket partnership of 137 with A. G. Steel swung a closely fought match, and the Gentlemen won by six wickets.

The game ended on 9 July, and those chosen for England went straight up to Old Trafford where the first Test was due to start the following day. Selection was left to the authorities of the ground hosting the fixture, so it was no surprise that Hornby was captain, though the temptation to include Crossland was wisely resisted. Test cricket at Old Trafford got off to a predictable start. Rain washed out the first day completely, though the two captains had gone ahead with the toss, and Hornby had elected to bat. He almost certainly regretted his decision when he opened with Grace the following day against Spofforth and Boyle. Whether or not he was haunted by memories of the Oval two years before, he was clearly out of sorts and was stumped off Boyle for a duck. When Grace and Ulyett followed him with no more than thirteen runs on the board there must have been a depressing sense of *déjà vu* in the England dressing room. Only a superb 43 from Arthur Shrewsbury prevented a total disaster, but 95 all out was a dismal score.

Although none of the Australians could match Shrewsbury's mastery of the conditions, neither could Peate, Ulyett and Barlow emulate Spofforth and Boyle's metronomic destructiveness. Wickets fell but runs also came, with all but four of the team making double figures. The top scorer was none other than Midwinter, who proved that he always gave good value whichever country he happened to be playing for. He finally went for 37 when Grace took a sharp catch off Ulyett. Australia were all out for 182, which gave them a commanding lead of eighty-seven runs.

As usual, England's survival depended largely on Grace, and he rose to the occasion. Although concentrating on defence, he 'hit heavily when an opportunity offered', and produced one 'prodigious drive, nearly square, off Spofforth, into the pavilion enclosure', which was the shot of the match.[14] Hornby again showed his lack of mettle as a Test captain, tinkering with the batting order for no very good reason. He sent Lucas in to open with Grace, and dropped himself down to number nine, where he made four runs before being stumped for the second time in the match. However, the rest of the team built on the foundation Grace's 31 had given them, reaching 180 for 9 to make the game safe.

England could consider themselves lucky to have escaped defeat, and inevitably criticism was levelled at their performance. There would be changes for the second Test in a fortnight. The most obvious of these was the replacement of Hornby with Lord Harris, who had found some form himself – 85 in the second Gentlemen v. Players match – and who clearly felt competent to resume the captaincy. There was a perceptible amateur bias in some of the other selections. The Hon. Alfred Lyttelton took Pilling's place behind the stumps, Walter Read of Surrey came in for his first home Test, and Stanley Christopherson, the Kent fast bowler, made his debut on the strength of a good performance for the Gentlemen.

While the Australians had an encouraging innings win over Middlesex, Grace went down to Gloucester and scored 47 and 20 (out of 79) against Nottinghamshire. He also took 5 for 54, though this was not enough to save the match. Though his enthusiasm for any sort of cricket never flagged, Test cricket now provided the most stimulating challenge, and he must have been impatient to get back to the England dressing room on 21 July.

The public anticipation was also great, and 35,501 paid at the turnstiles over the three days. They saw a good Test which, if hardly a classic, produced some excellent individual performances. Australia batted first, and England gained the early initiative through Peate, who removed McDonnell, Bannerman, Murdoch and Midwinter cheaply. Giffen stood firm and received useful support from Bonnor until Grace snapped up the giant off Christopherson. Blackham was run out for a duck, but then 'Tup' Scott, coming in at eight, produced a fighting innings of 75 to complement Giffen's 63. Scott's innings ended when he was caught by his own captain. Grace had left the field with a hand injury and, in the absence of a twelfth man, Murdoch had come on as a substitute. Like all the Australians, he had a very safe pair of hands.

Grace returned to dismiss Spofforth for a duck and the innings ended on 229. The Demon would dearly have liked to retaliate in kind, but Lord's proved a less productive venue for him than the Oval. As it was, Palmer and Giffen posed enough problems. Grace was caught by Bonnor off Palmer for 14, and Lucas, Shrewsbury and Ulyett all went relatively cheaply. When Spofforth came back to account for Lord Harris, England were teetering on the brink of another collapse at 135 for 5. As the England captain returned to the pavilion he told the incoming batsman, 'For Heaven's sake, Barlow, stop this rot!'[15] The Lancastrian stonewaller followed his instructions to the letter, and his ninety-eight-run stand with A. G. Steel turned the match. When he finally succumbed to the occasional bowling of Bonnor, he had scored an invaluable 38 and Steel was well on the way to a century. With good support from the lower order, Steel went on to 148, and England were finally all out for 379.

The Australian second innings belonged to Ulyett. Bowling with Steel, he whipped out the top order before stumps on the second day. The wicket was cut up at one end, and finding the conditions helpful, 'the famous Yorkshireman bowled his very best, breaking back several inches at great pace'.[16] In the middle of this triumphant spell he pulled off what Pelham Warner described as 'one of the historic catches of cricket'.[17] As with other historic catches, the victim was Bonnor. However, this was not a towering blow plummeting out of the sky, but a drive of immense power hit straight back at the bowler. Ulyett had barely released the ball when it came back at him like a stone from a catapult. He injudiciously threw up his hand, and it stuck. It was one of Happy Jack's days, and the following morning he continued irresistibly to finish with 7 for 36. England emerged winners by the surprisingly comfortable margin of an innings and five runs.

At some stage in July, Martha fell ill, but her condition was not thought serious enough to prevent Grace and E.M. from going up to Old Trafford for Gloucestershire's match against Lancashire starting on the 24th. They found the Manchester skies dark with portent, and heavy storms broke over the ground on the first day. W.G. managed a characteristic 53 out of 119, though Lancashire were in a relatively strong position overnight at 104 for 6. The second day – Friday, 25 July – was as gloomy as the first, but the news received by telegraph from Downend was 'of a reassuring character'.[18] Despite a break for a thunderstorm after only one over, Gloucestershire quickly took the last four wickets, and E.M. and Walter Gilbert went out to open their second innings. E.M. hit the first ball for four and the sun came out. Shortly after lunch E.M. was brilliantly caught off Barlow, and W.G. took his place. He scored a single and survived a confident appeal for lbw when play was brought to an abrupt halt by the news that Martha had died.

Hornby immediately suggested that the match should be abandoned, and the crowd filed quietly out of the ground in the brilliant sunshine, leaving E.M., W.G. and Gilbert to pack their cricket bags prior to the long train journey home to Downend. For the second time in five years Grace had been absent from a family death-bed, though it may have been some slight consolation that he had been where his mother was most proud of him when the news came through – at the wicket, batting for the county his father had done so much to create.

Martha died a week after her seventy-second birthday, and her death broke another link with the past, as well as leaving a vacuum at the heart of the family. From her first meeting with William Clarke, she had impressed generations of cricketers with her knowledgeable interest in the game, and visiting cricketers would attend her carriage drawn up beside the pavilion at Clifton to pay their respects. She had forthright views – harbouring a lifelong aversion to left-handers and despising fielders who jerked the ball in under-arm – and her influence on Grace's career was inestimable. The First Lady of cricket, she was, until the recent addition of Rachel Heyhoe-Flint, the only woman included in *Wisden*'s Births and Deaths of Cricketers, where she remains to this day flanked in the game's roll of honour by her husband and her most famous son.

Grace missed the county's away matches against Yorkshire and Nottinghamshire, and the first game he played after the funeral was at Clifton against the Australians. He saluted Martha's memory in the most fitting way possible, scoring 116 not out in Gloucestershire's total of 301. It was his highest score of the season, and his third century against the Australians.

The match, which petered out as a draw, was played in a perfectly friendly and indeed respectful spirit, but there was, inevitably, an incident involving W.G. Watching Percy McDonnell score 62, he had managed to persuade himself that his bat was suspiciously broad. At the end of play he called for a gauge to test its legality. Giffen remembered the tourists' astonishment: 'If we had bats which had been specially made in Australia, there might have been some reason for his action, but we all had blades bearing the names of the best known and most reputable English makers. I know Percy Mac's was found to be a trifle too wide, but no more so than a bat often becomes after severe usage, for the faces of many blades have a tendency to spread.' The Australians retaliated by calling for Grace's bats to be subjected to the same test. Much to their delight, 'the very first one would not pass muster'.[19]

The tourists returned to the Oval for the last Test with mixed feelings. Although the site of their greatest triumph, their previous match against the Players had been disrupted by a pitch invasion. They had only eleven to make with nine wickets standing at the lunch interval on the third day, and though Murdoch was perfectly happy to play on, the ground authorities insisted on breaking for lunch for the benefit of the caterers. The crowd smelt a rat, but jumped to the conclusion that the blame lay with the Australians, intent on screwing every last penny of gate money from the fixture. They charged onto the square, pulled up the stumps and then converged on the pavilion. The mood was sufficiently good-humoured for some of the players to be cheered. One was Ted Peate, but when Alcock approached him to appeal for calm, he declined, saying, 'Ah didn't cum here t'quell riot; Ah cum t' play cricket.'[20] With the help of police reinforcements the situation was eventually defused and the match finished, but it left the Australians wondering about the reception they might receive during the Test.

They need not have worried. The August sun beat down, the wicket was perfect, and they gave the Ovalites a banquet of batting, to which the crowd responded with warm appreciation. In fact they were positively surfeited with runs, and in an era of farcically low-scoring matches, this was a farcically high-scoring one. After Alec Bannerman had been dismissed by Peate for 4, the next three Australian batsmen scored centuries, Murdoch making the first double century in Test match cricket (211). McDonnell's broad bat brought him 103 and Scott made 102. Scott's stand with Murdoch of 207 was a Test record for any wicket.

As the law allowing declarations was still five years off, the Australians had no option but to keep on batting, while the English bowlers wheeled away futilely hour after hour. As a veteran of Grace's triple century at Canterbury in 1876, Harris had some experience of flagging bowlers and immovable batsmen. At some stage on the second day he decided to introduce an element of Canterbury Week into the game, and after everyone else on the team had bowled, he invited Alfred Lyttelton to discard his pads and try his luck. Grace insisted on taking his place, so the crowd were treated to the spectacle of the Champion crouching bulkily behind the stumps while Lyttelton went on to bowl under-arm lobs. The air of farce was heightened when Midwinter swung wildly at a ball going down the leg-side. It lodged in the wicket-keeping gloves and Lyttelton appealed. Grace was not convinced there had been any contact with the bat, but 'I had no time to prevent the umpire giving his decision, so Midwinter had to go'.[21] Whether acting under orders, or simply mesmerized at finding such playground stuff served up in a Test match, the Australian tail rapidly self-destructed, and Lyttelton ended the innings with the astonishing figures of 4 for 19. Australia finished with the equally astonishing total of 551.

After nearly two full days in the field, England started their innings at 5.10 p.m. Grace had a new opening partner, the left-hander William Scotton, who might be described as the stonewallers' stonewaller. In Grace's view, the Nottinghamshire professional had 'perhaps the most impregnable defence I ever saw'[22] and for stagnation at the crease was rivalled only by Barlow. He was perfectly suited to the situation, though not an ideal partner for W.G., for whom deliberately slow scoring was anathema. His impatience on this occasion led to a run-out, and he returned fuming to the pavilion for 19.

Wickets continued to fall regularly through the innings, though Scotton remained immovable. At three o'clock on the last afternoon, he was still there – on 53 – but England had slumped to 181 for 8 and were not entirely out of danger. At this point Scotton was joined by Walter Read. The Surrey amateur was enjoying a wonderful season, and can't have been pleased to find himself occupying the number ten position that seemed to hold such a bizarre fascination for England captains. Read immediately began to work off his frustration. He hit Spofforth into the crowd at square leg, and also lofted Giffen over the ropes. After an hour and three quarters he caught up Scotton on 84. Eight minutes later he reached his century, off only thirty-six scoring strokes (no sixes). Scotton was still on 84. It must have been as great a shock for the Australians as it was for the batsmen when he was finally caught by Scott off Giffen, exactly twenty-four hours after he went in. He had scored 90 in five hours and forty minutes at the crease, and made thirty-seven of the 151 he and Read put on for the ninth wicket. But for all the tedium involved, he had shepherded England to safety.

The innings ended shortly afterwards on 346 when Read was bowled by Boyle for 117, made in two and a half hours. It was probably the most exciting century in a Test at the Oval until Jessop eclipsed it eighteen years later to the day (13 August). Shrewsbury was sufficiently inspired to hit a rapid 37 in England's hour-long second innings, but Grace was happy to take his ease on the balcony.

England had won the series and retained the Ashes, though the notional prize for which the two teams fought had not yet achieved the significance it assumed for later generations. The Australians had been unlucky, robbed of probable victory by the rain at Manchester and paradoxically sabotaged by their own prolific run-scoring at the Oval. Unlike today, the last Test did not signal the end of the tour, and there was another month before the Australians sailed home.

Grace, too, had more cricket to play, and he returned to Bristol for what proved to be the high point of the championship for Gloucestershire, the return against Lancashire at Clifton. He scored 31 and 43, and took five wickets in the match, which culminated in an exciting finish with the visitors losing by seven runs. As in 1882, two matches had been arranged with the Australians, but the second, at Cheltenham, was a dismally one-sided affair after the well-balanced match at Clifton. The tourists plundered the county bowling to the tune of 402, winning easily by an innings and 136 runs. Cooper, making one of his rare appearances, had a tantalizing glimpse of what might have been, getting Grace caught for a duck and taking two more quick wickets, while in the second innings Spofforth dismissed W.G. for 2, precipitating a Gloucestershire collapse to 83 all out.

The county ended the season surprisingly well, making 388 against Middlesex at Cheltenham and 484 against Surrey at Clifton, of which W.G. scored 66 before being bowled by the diminutive Bobby Abel. Both games were drawn, but showed that there was ability in the Gloucestershire batting line-up if only it could be applied. Overall, though, it had been 'a disastrous season'.[23] They had even contrived to lose to a Philadelphian touring team by the embarrassingly huge margin of 168 runs. When asked about the reasons for Gloucestershire's lack of success, Grace blamed bad luck, bad form, and the fact that at times '[we] have played some very poor men in our elevens, owing to inability to get our best men to play'.[24] Grace gives no hint that there might be some underlying structural problems, or that the haphazard selection policy needed review. As Edward Lyttelton said, 'No one ever had a more unanalytical brain.'[25]

Grace played once more against the Australians, for the South of England at the Oval on 11 and 12 September. Although the North had beaten the tourists twice, the South were completely outplayed. Spofforth had yet another field-day on his favourite English ground. He took 12 for 77 in the match, including an impressive hat-trick of Grace, J. R. Painter and Maurice Read, and Australia won by an innings and five runs. Grace produced two typically defiant innings in the losing cause, scoring 24 out of 56 and 26 out of 102.

The long season finally wound down with an end-of-term beano, Smokers v. Non-Smokers, played for the benefit of the Cricketers' Fund at Lord's on 15 and 16 September. The main concern was to divide the Australians equally, and the qualifications of the abstainers were not too closely inspected. Bonnor hit a whirlwind century for the Non-smokers, which included some clattering blows off Spofforth, and was then seen perambulating round the boundary puffing on a cigar. His 124 out of the 156 made while he was at the crease was the highlight of the match, though Peate in one spell for the Smokers took 6 for 10 in thirteen overs. Grace showed the benefit of clean lungs – or, as he believed, one clean lung – bowling thirty-four tight overs and taking 5 for 29.

Although he still enjoyed his cricket, his thoughts were turning once again to reducing the amount he played. With his thirty-sixth birthday behind him, he was no longer a young man. He was picking up injuries more often now, and with his increasing bulk he was, if hardly a liability, certainly not the nimblest player about the field. His responsibilities to his family and his medical practice remained onerous, and the person to whom his success meant the most was now gone. Perhaps, at last, it was time to start a staged withdrawal from the game.

That was certainly the tenor of an article published in the *Pall Mall Gazette* in October. The piece purported to be an interview conducted by H. H. Spielmann during the Smokers match, but it was largely based on a questionnaire Grace answered in his own hand a few days later, now kept in the library at Lord's. To the question, 'Do you play as well as ever you did?' he replied, 'My defence is as good, but I cannot punish the bowling as I used to and as you get older, you cannot field well. You lose your activity.' Asked whether he had any intention of discontinuing, he wrote, 'Yes, I shall only play for the county next season as my professional duties will keep me at home. I really mean this. I shall only take about 3 weeks holiday next year.' And he admitted that playing cricket did interfere with his practice 'a great deal, as patients do not like an assistant, never mind how good he is . . . I have a good practice which increases every winter when I am at home, and decreases when I am away from home. This is the reason I shall not play much away from home next season.' Among a number of other enquiries which might have been modelled on Lewis Carroll's 'You Are Old, Father William', he deflected a question on the Australians with studied diplomacy. 'How do they compare with English Cricketers? What do you think of them as players + as business-men?' 'They compare favourably with English cricketers. There is no reason why they should not. I know nothing of them as business men.'

The whole cricketing world would soon have the chance to weigh them up as businessmen as they sailed back to Australia and straight into a storm of opprobrium over their refusal to play in home Tests against Shrewsbury's English tourists unless they were given a share of the gate money. But by then Grace was back on his rounds, apparently confident that he would never be exposed to the acrimonious cut and thrust of international cricket again.

TWENTY-TWO

MEMBERS of the Gloucestershire committee who subscribed to the *Pall Mall Gazette* would have read the Grace interview with interest, but also with a large pinch of salt. They would believe in his semi-retirement when they saw it. In the meantime, as long as he was involved in the club, he would remain in charge. In addition to running the side, he was also the club's representative at the annual Lord's meeting at which fixtures for the following season were agreed, and his mandate had been renewed at the October committee meeting. The same meeting had also set up a sub-committee to look into the possibility of acquiring a home ground in Bristol. W.G. was on that, along with Frank Townsend, Arthur Bush, H. W. Below and R. J. G. Matthews. All the signs were that he had no intention of fading from the scene.

And so it proved. In 1885 he played twenty-five first-class matches (only one fewer than the year before), of which fourteen were outside the county boundaries. Furthermore, he returned to something like his form of the 1870s, comfortably achieving the double and ending up with his best figures since 1877. They hadn't seen the last of him by a long chalk. Grace makes no reference in *Reminiscences* to any intention to reduce his cricketing commitments, and so gives no insight into his change of heart. But a clue can perhaps be found in his remark that 'Warm, dry weather kept the wickets hard and fast throughout the season, and large scores were frequent.'[1] After the wet summers of recent years, he simply couldn't resist batting with the sun on his back once again.

He started undramatically in the match between Lord Sheffield's XI and Alfred Shaw's team which had just completed a successful campaign in Australia, and then went up to Lord's to play for the South against the North. This was a benefit match for the family of Fred Morley, who had died in September. Although Grace only scored 28, his 5 for 25 and 4 for 48 helped the South to an emphatic win. In his next game, MCC v. the Champion County, Nottinghamshire, he produced an outstanding all-round performance. In addition to scoring 63 out of 199, he bowled right through both innings, taking 7 for 40 and then 9 for 20 as Nottingham-shire were skittled out for 40. He took this form into Gloucestershire's first game against Surrey at the Oval, scoring 55 with six wickets in the match, which they won by two wickets. He had another five-wicket haul at Hove, though Sussex put 401 on the board and won by an innings. Two fifties and another six wickets were the main cause of Middlesex's defeat at Lord's, and Grace went into the first Gentlemen v. Players match at the Oval on something of a roll.

In the absence of Lord Harris and Hornby, W.G. was the only contender for the captaincy. He did not have a particularly strong team, while the majority of those picked for the Players either were or would become Test players. Trailing badly after the first innings, Grace (76) and Walter Read (159) just managed to force a draw. In the return at Lord's Grace failed twice and Peate and Barnes bowled the Players to their first win at Headquarters since 1874.

Grace scored fifties in his next two matches, South v. North at Old Trafford and Gloucestershire v. Yorkshire at Gloucester, but still reached the mid-point of the season without passing three figures. He put that right when the county played Yorkshire at Bradford. Over 1,000 runs were scored in the three days, but Grace was the only centurian, his 132 forming, as he put it, 'a fair proportion of the 287 we made in our first innings'.[2] The game ended in a draw, with honours even, but at Old Trafford the visitors were beaten by an innings, despite Grace's individual contribution of 50 and 39. Apart from an equally one-sided victory over Somerset, they also lost at home to Nottinghamshire, Lancashire again, and Sussex before Grace stopped the rot with his second century, against Surrey at Cheltenham. The next match, against Middlesex at Clifton, was notable not only for another stunning all-round performance, but as the occasion for one of his best-loved jokes.

Gloucestershire batted first and Grace was in all day, scoring 163 not out. He was then up all night attending a difficult confinement. He reappeared at the ground the following morning looking ominously fresh, and when asked about his professional vigil replied roguishly, 'It was fairly successful. The child died and the mother died, *but I saved the father*.' Resuming his innings, he continued in ebullient mood, playing the Middlesex bowling with even more 'masterly freedom'[3] than on the first day to reach his first double century for nine years – 221 not out (which represented 63.5 per cent of the Gloucestershire total of 348). He then shed his pads and took 11 for 120 in Middlesex's two innings. It was the second time he had scored a double century and taken ten wickets in a match, a feat which remained uniquely his until George Giffen emulated him (twice) in the next ten years. It was a Herculean display for a man of thirty-seven, and seemed to dispel any lingering doubts as to whether he could successfully balance the demands of cricket and his practice.

Gloucestershire's fuller fixture list meant that Grace could no longer get down to Canterbury Week in August for the match between Kent and the MCC, but the Scarborough Festival in September was a more than adequate substitute. After Gloucestershire's ritual obliteration of Somerset to end the county season, Grace decamped to the seaside for a fortnight's holiday cricket. He started in cavalier fashion, scoring 68 for the Gentlemen of England against I Zingari and eclipsing the great 'Buns' Thornton by hitting twenty-six of the thirty runs they put on together. Then in the third encounter between the Gentlemen and Players he again revived memories of his 1870s heyday. He was confronted by the combined bowling might of Nottinghamshire and Yorkshire, but on a treacherous pitch and through frequent interruptions for rain he scored 174 out of 247, rated by those who saw it as 'one of the finest performances ever credited to a batsman'.[4] The next highest score was 21. As he pointed out, with a rare note of quite justified self-congratulation, 'at the conclusion of this match I had played consecutive innings of 104, 19 *not out*, 221 *not out*, 68, and 174, making a total of 586, and giving the remarkable average of a trifle over 195'.[5] Emmett and Ulyett combined forces to bring this sequence of high scores to an abrupt end when he played for MCC against Yorkshire (c. Ulyett b. Emmett 4), but in his last match of the season, playing for an England XI against Alfred Shaw's XI at Harrogate, he signed off with a scintillating 51 out of 53 runs made while he was at the wicket.

It had been a triumphant year. He had achieved the double in style, with 1,688 runs at 43.28 and 117 wickets at 18.79, scored four centuries, won several matches single-handedly, and led Gloucestershire out of the doldrums. There was no further mention of retirement.

*

1886 was a year of extremes. Grace continued in the same excellent form as the previous season and achieved what would prove to be his last double. He lost and then immediately reclaimed the record for the highest individual Test score by an Englishman and England had their most successful home series against the Australians, though once again W.G.

was passed over for the captaincy. Far more painfully, the family was touched by an unsavoury scandal which it took all the Grace influence to hush up.

Walter Gilbert had been experiencing financial difficulties for some time. The few United XI matches were no substitute for the lucrative fixture list of the United South, and although he was paid his thinly disguised appearance fee by Gloucestershire, this was proving inadequate. In 1885 he had asked for more and Grace had obviously told him he would get it, though this had to be ratified by the committee. The matter had come up at the meeting of 3 July. Grace was absent, playing in the Gentlemen–Players match at the Oval, and those present had resolved 'that the Committee cannot accede to Mr WR Gilbert's request to be paid an additional sum per match, and in regard to a promise as stated to have been made to him, this Committee as a Committee had nothing to do with it.'[6]

By the start of the new season, Gilbert's plight was even worse, and he decided to break ranks and turn professional. His motive is not as obvious as it might seem. He knew exactly what professionals were paid. The same committee meeting that turned down his request for more money 'Resolved that Woof be paid the sum of £6 for each match', with a rider that any professional playing in a winning side should be paid an extra pound. With the way Gloucestershire were performing, no one was going to get rich on win bonuses, and it is difficult to see how Gilbert was going to make any more money from the county by turning pro. Yet in terms of the readjustment of his social status, it was such a drastic step that he can't have taken the decision lightly. One possibility is that he threatened to make the change hoping that family pride would force Grace to push harder for the increased fee. When his bluff was called, he went ahead out of pique. As subsequent events showed, he was reaching the end of his tether.

He was, perhaps surprisingly, promised a little additional income on the announcement of his decision. At their January meeting, the committee resolved 'that if Mr WR Gilbert plays in all the Gloucestershire matches in 1886 the sum of £25 extra be given to him as a Donation at the end of the season. But this is conditional on Mr WR Gilbert treating this as a strictly private communication'[7] – an indication that he was being offered preferential treatment. But Gilbert's needs were more pressing, and he signed up as a professional for the East Gloucestershire Club, Cheltenham. His first match as a hired hand for Gloucestershire was the opening game against Surrey at the Oval at the end of April, and by coincidence another amateur who turned professional, E. J. Diver, was also making his first appearance shorn of his 'Mr' on the scorecard. (Diver was also deprived of his initials, but in deference, presumably, to Gilbert's connections with W.G., *The Times* gave him the anomalous status of 'W.R.Gilbert' in its match report.)

The switch from amateur to professional was almost unprecedented, but the cricketing fraternity was sympathetic. 'Pavilion Gossip' in the 29 April 1886 issue of Charles Alcock's magazine *Cricket* handled the matter with delicacy:

Circumstances have caused, as was the case with Daft, the two cricketers named to join the professional ranks, and the public will thoroughly appreciate the motives which have prompted them to take a step which involves, as everyone will readily understand, no small amount of moral courage. The relations between amateurs and professionals, though well defined and strictly kept, are of such a pleasant character that the change is not after all such a hard one, and as both are excellent players their prospects ought to be of the best.

Gilbert's prospects, along with a summary of his achievements and role in the Gloucestershire side, were discussed further in the magazine's 'Weekly Portrait' in May. And yet, for all the high hopes that his relaunched career would be long and successful, he never played for Gloucestershire again, vanishing suddenly and as completely as if he had never existed.

His downfall came at the end of the first week in June. He was playing for East Gloucestershire at home against Stroud. On the first day – Friday, 4 June – Stroud batted, and Gilbert bowled well. On the Saturday he turned up at the ground at about noon, greeted those members of the team who had already changed and were knocking up in front of the pavilion, and walked straight into a trap the club officials had reluctantly laid for him. The changing room was empty; trousers, coats and waistcoats were left hanging invitingly on their hooks, and in one of them there was a marked half sovereign. There was also a detective standing by. Gilbert changed, and then, after listening for the footsteps that would have saved him and hearing none, started rifling through his team-mates' pockets. The game was up. When confronted by the detective, he produced the marked coin and subsequently pleaded guilty to two charges of theft, though clearly money had been going missing for some while before. He was sentenced to twenty-eight days' hard labour.

The family's reaction was swift. Grace's match against the Australians at Lord's had finished a day early, and there is strong circumstantial evidence that he went over to Cheltenham to start the damage-limitation exercise in person that afternoon. The process whereby Gilbert 'disappeared' began immediately. Press reports of the match credited his wickets to 'Smith', while in the East Gloucestershire innings it was stated that 'Mr E.L.Even did not bat'. Gilbert had been due to play in the next Gloucestershire match against Sussex at Hove starting on the following Monday (7 June). Obviously he would not be making the trip to the south coast. The man who replaced him, C. H. Margrett, was a Cheltenham cricketer, which adds to the probability that Grace was in the spa town that Saturday. Recruiting players at very short notice in circumstances of extreme embarrassment is best done face to face. Having stood in for Gilbert at Hove, Margrett never played another game for the county.

While Gilbert was breaking rocks with a shackle round his leg, his fate was decided. Like other Victorian black sheep he would be sent to the colonies, in his case Canada. There could be no arguing with a tribunal consisting of W.G., E.M. and Henry Grace, and he was packed off at the earliest opportunity to begin a new life, which happily proved to be successful and above reproach. He settled in Calgary, found work as a government official, married and started a family, and continued to play cricket to a high standard.

But that was in the future. The immediate concern was to hush up the scandal and expunge, so far as it was possible, the disgraced name from the records. W.G. obviously contacted Alcock; despite the high profile that *Cricket* had given Gilbert early in the season, there was no further reference to him in its pages. *Lillywhite's Annual* noted his loss without comment; *Wisden* also mentioned him, adding darkly, '. . . about whose subsequent disappearance from cricket there is no need to speak'.[8]

It was a squalid business, which illustrated the pressures imposed by the two-tier class system of English cricket on those without the means to sustain their amateur status, or the exceptional talent 'to run with the amateurs and hunt with the professionals'.* Although he was obviously furious with his cousin – their interview that Saturday afternoon in Cheltenham must have been a terrible occasion – Grace would have grieved for him as well. They had been close companions on the cricket

---

* Gilbert's first-class career figures were 5,290 runs at 19.16 and 295 wickets at 17.93.

trail that had taken them to the extremities of the British Isles as well as round the world to Australia. Gilbert was also a link with Fred, having been his companion at Downend and his faithful nurse during the last days of his life. Despite his capacity for wrath, W.G. was a forgiving man, and in all probability at the final parting offered his hand and uttered some brusque benediction from the depths of his beard, before turning on his heel and walking massively away.

*

If the Gilbert affair overshadowed the start of Grace's season, the violent passions aroused by the 1884 tourists' insistence on a share of the gate in the home Tests of 1884–5 had cast, in Horan's view, 'a universal gloom' over Australian cricket.[9] (Spofforth alone had dissociated himself from this mercenary move.) Murdoch, who was badly bruised by the controversy, was not available to lead the 1886 tourists, and his place as captain was taken by H. J. H. Scott. Scott was a fine cricketer and a decent man, but his team was rent by internal bickering and further weakened by injuries.

England also had an inexperienced captain. Once again Grace's obvious claims were overlooked, and A. G. Steel, ten years his junior, was given the job. Steel had been an outstanding schoolboy cricketer at Marlborough and a triumphant captain of the exceptionally strong Cambridge team in the late 1870s. That was still the preferred pedigree. Grace's behaviour in Australia may have counted against him, and his abrasive competitiveness was always likely to spark an incident – as it had with fatal consequences in the 1882 Test. As long as there was a credible alternative, the authorities were clearly determined to play safe. Whatever his private feelings, Grace seems never to have uttered a word of reproach for what came close to a public rebuff, and continued to serve his country to the best of his ample ability. In the event, Steel's record as captain left no cause for complaint. With the younger professional stars like George Lohmann, Johnny Briggs and Arthur Shrewsbury coming to the fore, he had a very strong team, and England wrapped up the series in July winning the first two Tests by four wickets and an innings and 106 runs. Grace had failed in his three innings (8, 4, 18) and had seen Arthur Shrewsbury beat his record for the highest Test innings by an Englishman when he made 164 at Lord's.

He arrived at the Oval in August needing a good performance. His opening partner for the third time in the series was Scotton, and the two of them made heavy weather of it to begin with. The wicket was slow and

304

gave the bowlers plenty of encouragement. Only nineteen runs were scored in the first hour, and the whole of the first session was a dour struggle. Grace was dropped twice, on 6 and 23, but towards lunch began to regain his touch, and by two o'clock, when the score was 56, he had made forty runs to Scotton's sixteen. Conditions improved a little after the interval, and Grace soon reached his fifty after batting for two hours and twelve minutes. He then accelerated dramatically, reaching his century just forty-two minutes later when the England total stood at 129. He had survived two more chances, one in the deep off Spofforth on 60, the other off Giffen at slip on 93, but pressed on remorselessly, leaving Scotton utterly becalmed. For a period of sixty-seven minutes he failed to score a single run, and at 134 Grace established a lead of exactly a hundred over his partner. Perhaps distracted by the statistical enormity of the situation, Scotton was then bowled by Garrett. The opening partnership of 170 was the highest first-wicket stand by either country and a record for any England wicket.

Shrewsbury came in at three, but although he had more of an open mind about scoring runs than his Nottinghamshire colleague, W.G. continued to dominate proceedings, playing the Australian bowling with something like his former majesty. Shrewsbury was still at the wicket to congratulate him when he reclaimed his Test record, but he was obviously tiring, and gave a fifth chance on 169. Almost immediately afterwards, at 5.30, he was finally caught by Blackham off Spofforth having scored 130 in the two hours and thirty-eight minutes after lunch. His 170 out of 216 constituted 78 per cent of the runs made while he was at the crease, the highest proportion for any century in an Ashes Test.[10] He hit twenty-two fours, including one huge drive off Spofforth into the crowd. He certainly rode his luck, but nevertheless it was, as he put himself, 'a pretty good performance'[11] and the basis for England's most comfortable win of the series. They continued to pile on the runs the following day, Walter Read scoring 94 and Johnny Briggs hitting 50 down the order to bring the total to 434. It then rained, and on a lively wicket the demoralized Australians were bowled out by George Lohmann and Briggs for 68 and 149, losing the match by an innings and 217 runs.

Grace met the Australians twelve times in all during 1886, and his 170 was the third century he scored against them. The first was for the Gentlemen of England at the Oval in June when he took advantage of Spofforth's absence with yet another hand injury to reach 148. Spofforth was still out of the game when the tourists came down to Clifton at the beginning of August, when Grace scored 110. He also took 7 for 67, making sure the county had the better of the draw.

Although Grace was fallible, as the five chances at the Oval showed, and Spofforth was convinced he had the measure of him, he was still the batsman the Australians feared and respected most. When discussion in the visitors' changing room came round to the respective merits of Murdoch and W.G., Alec Bannerman said simply that Grace had forgotten more about batting than Murdoch ever knew.[12] George Giffen had a similarly elevated view of him: 'As I stood there watching him bat, I would think to myself, "What a difference to the Australian Elevens it would make, if there were no WG to go in first and kill our bowling!"'[13] Giffen had plenty of opportunities to form his opinion. Grace played nineteen innings against the tourists and made 812 runs at an average of 42.

Grace scored one other century in 1886, against Oxford University for the MCC on 21 and 22 June. The match was an extraordinary personal triumph, and was vividly recalled by those privileged to play in it. One of those was George Scott, a freshman who was given a place in the MCC team. When it was announced that Grace was coming, much thought was given to the problem of getting him out. The nation's élite came up with an innovative game-plan. They would get him drunk. Though commendably original, this strategy was flawed. As Scott admitted, 'due consideration' was not given to the fact 'that a bottle or even two bottles of champagne could have no more effect on his mighty frame than a liqueur glass of Kummel on a bunker on a golf course'. Nevertheless, J. H. Brain, a member of the Oxford XI who had already played a few matches for Gloucestershire, arranged a dinner party for the first night of the fixture, and persuaded Grace to attend. By the time they gathered in the evening, the undergraduates had already had an instructive session with the Champion, watching him make an untroubled and undefeated fifty in the afternoon. Scott was impressed:

I was only one of many undergraduates who had never before seen W.G. batting, and when he advanced towards the wicket I personally wondered if he were really so wonderful as he was said to be. His physique was splendid. He looked huge, and his large, dark beard gave him . . . a dominating appearance . . .

When facing the bowling his methods appeared to be simple. He gave a considerable uplift to his bat in a bee line from the bowler's arm to his wicket. The bowling obviously gave him no trouble, and it was delightful to see how, when playing back, he put such power into his defensive strokes that, if the fielders failed to stop the ball, it generally went to the boundary. The Parks wicket was . . . a lively one, and I was personally more impressed by the way he treated the bumping balls than anything else in his play. When a ball got up high on his off-stump or outside it, instead of leaving it alone he appeared to tap it down to the ground, generally to the boundary, as if he could place each delivery as he liked. I had never seen anything like it.

There was no reason to doubt that he would continue in the same vein the following day. All hope rested on the subversive power of alcohol. Grace almost certainly realized he was being set up, but played along, jovial as Bluebeard on a bridal night. The champagne flowed and W.G. consumed encouragingly large amounts of it. The results were eagerly awaited the following morning.

As usual, Grace made his way to the nets before resuming his innings. Possibly to turn the screw of expectation a little tighter, he allowed a ball to bowl him. 'This,' says Scott, 'was really encouraging, and the fiction spread like wildfire, "WG was tight last night and can't see the ball this morning" . . . The whole of cricketing Oxford smiled with joyful satisfaction.' There were smiles aplenty during the rest of the day, but they all originated in the dark undergrowth of Grace's beard. The little pantomime was over, and when play began it soon became obvious 'that no Oxford bowler was going to get past WG's bat'. He moved effortlessly to his century before the umpire took pity on the students and gave him out lbw. His 104 contained fifteen fours and one six. The next highest score was 36 and the MCC were all out for 260, which gave them a lead of 118. This was quite enough for Grace, who proceeded to bowl the university out for 90, taking all ten wickets for 49 runs in 36.2 overs. He thus joined E.M. in one of cricket's most exclusive clubs. Only V. E. Walker (England v. Surrey, 1859) and E.M in 1862 had previously scored a century and taken ten wickets in an innings in the same match.

Scott gave his impressions of Grace's bowling:

With a rather low action he seemed more to put the ball towards the wicket than to bowl in the conventional manner. I thought that his bowling looked easy for a quick-footed batsman, but he did what he liked with the batsmen that day, and this was probably where the snare lay. [Being on the same side, Scott didn't have to face him.] WG was said at that time to be the best change bowler in England. I imagine that, given a fast wicket, he required a full-sized ground even more than most slow bowlers. And although he might be hit hard and even frequently, his knowledge of the game and complete control of length enabled him to detect any weak spot in the batsman's armour.

Four of his ten victims were caught – J. H. Brain brilliantly by T. R. Hine-Haycock sprinting round the boundary, which prompted Grace to exclaim, 'I haven't had a man who could dot it like that for me since poor old G.F.' But no fleeting pang of memory could take the gloss off a perfect day, and Scott records that he 'looked supremely happy . . . when MCC won by an innings and 28 runs'.[14]

Upsetting the best-laid plans of undergraduates was one thing, raising the standards of Gloucestershire County Cricket Club was quite another. They won only three county matches in 1886 and 'sank again to the bottom of the table'.[15] One of the victories was against Derbyshire, who shared Somerset's anomalous position of having first-class status without being reckoned strong enough to be included in the championship. The committee had decided not to renew the Somerset fixture, invariably an easy win, so the county's record was even worse than it might have been.

Although Grace led, as usual, from the front and produced some excellent individual efforts, critics might point to his comparatively poor showing for the county. Although he achieved the highest national aggregate, only 560 of his 1,846 runs came in county matches, and his Gloucestershire average of 28 was significantly lower than his overall average of 35.50. The bowling spoils were more evenly divided. He took half of his 122 wickets for the county. In all he played thirty-three first-class matches in the season, by far the highest number in his career to date. In addition to the twelve games against the Australians, there were the two Gentlemen v. Players encounters. The amateurs' bowling was weak in both games, and in the first at Lord's Grace shouldered the bulk of the work, sending down 63.3 overs and taking 5 for 79. The Players were exceptionally strong, and two England stars in the making, Bobby Abel and George Lohmann, made their debuts, Lohmann taking seven wickets in the match to help his side to a comfortable five-wicket victory. Grace captained the Gentlemen at the Oval, a match which saw the return of E.M. to the fixture after a lengthy gap. This was the last time the two brothers appeared together in the great fixture, and of course they opened the Gentlemen's innings. They got off to a good start with a stand of sixty-seven in an hour and a quarter. When E.M. was out for 21, W.G. went on to make 65, 'a really meritorious effort'[16] against the bowling of Peate, Lohmann, Ulyett, Barnes and Flowers. It was the highest score in a total of 183. Then Shrewsbury showed up the discrepancy between the two sides with 127, as once again W.G. toiled away (supported in part by E.M.) to take 4 for 55. He completed his captain's duties by batting out the remainder of the match. When play was abandoned at the bizarrely early time of two p.m., the Gentlemen had scored 111 for 4, with Grace 50 not out.

Once his duties with Gloucestershire were over, he headed for Scarborough where the first match, the Gentlemen of England v. I Zingari, produced one of the great performances of the festival. Going in when the Gentlemen's score was 133 for 5 in the second innings, 'Buns' Thornton hit 107 not out in seventy minutes off only twenty-nine scoring strokes. This included seven shots out of the ground for six, including the legendary one into Trafalgar Square. The principal victim was the England captain, A. G. Steel, who must have thought it was his lucky day when he got Grace out early for 28. This may have also been the occasion of the joke played on W.G. to remind him of the spirit of festival cricket. P.J. de Paravicini recounted how Grace

had been given out, caught at the wicket by Farrands, and did not think he was out. With much pains we wrote a letter to Lord L[ondesborough] – we were all dining with him – purporting to come from Farrands. We arranged that the letter should be delivered at a suitable moment. [It] read something like this: 'My lord, I really must complain of Mr Grace. He said he was not out, which, I consider, reflects on my standing as an umpire, etc.' Of course, W.G. indignantly explained that he had said nothing except the merest commonplace, but we all looked very serious, as if we had discovered some great crime, until someone laughed and gave the show away.[17]

A priceless moment.

After that chastening experience, Grace scored 92 for his Lordship's XI against the Australians, and then shadowed the visitors as they made their last farewells around the country. He scored 31 and 38 for the South of England at Hove, 74 for an England XI at Lord's and took 3 for 47, also for an England XI, at Birmingham. All four matches were drawn, and as Grace remarked, the tourists' programme was 'too long for all practical purposes [and] towards the end of their thirty-nine matches public interest in their doings somewhat dwindled away'.[18]

It was an anti-climactic end to an absorbing summer, but already interest was focused on the ninth English team to tour Australia. Led again by Shrewsbury, this was an exceptionally strong professional side of which much was expected. Regularly alternating tours kept up the competitive momentum, and the public and players of both countries were now thoroughly enthralled by Test cricket. Grace was no exception.

This new dimension of the game had given him a fresh lease of life, and the next time the Australians came to try their fortunes on English soil, he would at last come into his own as England's captain.

TWENTY-THREE

EIGHTEEN eighty-seven was a fallow year as far as Test cricket was concerned, but the public had other things to get excited about. It was the Queen's Golden Jubilee and a tide of unprecedented enthusiasm engulfed the nation. Though there were clouds on the horizon – the problem of Home Rule for Ireland, and the threat of civil unrest from a disaffected underclass cut off from the rest of society's limitless prosperity – the summer was glorious, and such troubles were forgotten as everyone basked in what became known as the 'Queen's Weather'. With Lord Salisbury as her prime minister in place of the detestable Mr Gladstone, the Queen herself was in unwonted good spirits, and she appeared before her adoring subjects 'smiling, good and gracious beyond words'[1] to complete the rehabilitation of the monarchy after the long years of reclusive mourning for Prince Albert.

That other venerable and sometimes vulnerable institution, the Marylebone Cricket Club, was also celebrating a triumphant landmark – its centenary. After the doldrums of the 1860s, the club was firmly established as cricket's ultimate authority, and in July it at last addressed its responsibilities for the domestic game by countenancing the formation of a County Cricket Council. Unlike the Cricket Parliament proposed twenty years earlier, the council was designed to augment the MCC's role rather than challenge it (though it was short-lived, expiring in some procedural confusion in 1890). The membership had grown steadily and now stood at over 3,000, and the ground's facilities continued to improve. Indeed, the club had just extended its domain with the purchase of the Nursery end from the Clergy Orphan corporation for £18,500 – a measure of its wealth and confidence.

A week before the Queen's big day (21 June) it held a centenary match between the Club & Ground and an England XI, starting on 13 June. Grace, as the universally acknowledged monarch of the game, was of course the first man invited to play for the MCC, though, perhaps surprisingly, he was denied the honour of captaining them on this special occasion. That went to Hornby. The crowds that thronged to St John's Wood on the first day of the match had every hope of seeing a fittingly imperious innings from the Champion. He had started the season in fine form, scoring 81 not out for MCC against Sussex and then an excellent century (113 out of 197) for Gloucestershire against Middlesex, also at Lord's. But there was to be no repeat performance. George Lohmann bowled him for 5, and then with Briggs rattled through the rest of the MCC team, who were all out for 175.

However, those who had come to see great batting were not disappointed. In one of the highlights of an exceptional summer, the England openers A. E. Stoddart and Arthur Shrewsbury put on 266 for the first wicket. It was magnificent stuff, with both men reaching 150, and England went on to amass a mammoth total of 514. W.G. gamely sent down thirty-six fruitless overs for sixty-five runs. Batting a second time, Grace was determined to leave some mark on the game and he missed his fifty by only five runs. The two professionals, Barnes and Flowers, made 53 and 43, but the rest of the team did no better than they had in the first innings, and the game ended rather tamely in an England victory by an innings and 117 runs.

At the end of the match there was a dinner for the great and the good. This was held in the tennis court, 'while employees on the ground, about ninety in number, were entertained in the members' dining room'. 'A perfect repast was provided by Mr Reeder, and the band of the S Division of Police discoursed an excellent selection of music.'[2] Inevitably there were toasts and speeches, given and replied to by the full panoply of the English establishment. After the Lords, Sirs, Honorables and Reverends, W.G. stood up to speak on behalf of the medical profession, replying to the toast 'The Great Army of Cricketers'.

The assembled regiments of that great army dispersed in genial disarray at a late hour, thoroughly satisfied with their evening and all it celebrated. A week later cricket was suspended so that cricketers could join the rest of the country in saluting Victoria's fifty years on the throne and, by extension, the sustained success of British industry, enterprise, political stability and the British Empire. A service of thanksgiving was held in a Westminster Abbey packed with nobility, while outside the crowds waved their Union Jacks and cheered themselves hoarse. Every town and village had its Jubilee procession; bands and bunting were the order of the day; and at night the Queen was treated to 'a torch light procession of the fire brigade' on the terrace at Windsor Castle.[3]

No one embodied the national mood of triumphant self-confidence better than Grace. He was back at Lord's at the end of June to score a century for the MCC against Cambridge University, which included one hit 'clean into the upper part of the pavilion'.[4] He then went down to Gloucester for a heroic effort against Yorkshire. He made 92 in the county's first innings of 369, and then had to watch as Ulyett and Louis Hall put on 173 for Yorkshire's first wicket. As a desperate last resort he gave the ball to E.M. who then wreaked havoc with his under-arm lobs. He took seven wickets and Yorkshire were surprised to find themselves conceding a first-innings lead of sixty-nine runs. Possibly inspired by E.M.'s success, Grace then proceeded to bat for the rest of the match. On the hottest day of that very hot summer he occupied the crease for five and a half hours, adding 143 for the ninth wicket with Arthur Newnham and finishing on 183 not out. As he may have found occasion to remark to Tom Emmett, it was quite like old times, though now that the Hon. M. B. Hawke had replaced Ephraim Lockwood as Yorkshire captain there was no hint of mutiny from the long-suffering bowlers. In the return at Dewsbury three weeks later, Grace made 97 and 20 to bring his aggregate against them to 392 runs in four innings.

His triumphal progress through the summer was halted by the Players, who fielded a team of virtual Test strength. Captained by Shrewsbury, who scored a century in the first match at Lord's, they won both games by an innings. The Gentlemen were so short of bowling that Appleby was drafted in after an absence of nine years. Grace took 5 for 116 in the first match and was top scorer in three of the Gentlemen's four innings – making 24, 49, 15 and 35 – but the days when he could take on the might of England's professionals single-handed were over.

He took 6 for 45 and scored 73 for the MCC against Lancashire at Lord's on 18 and 19 July only to find himself on the losing side once more, and then followed the Lancastrians up to Manchester for Gloucestershire's match at Old Trafford. The game would contribute another dramatic incident to Grace lore, but provided much of incidental interest on the way. Gloucestershire batted first and W.G. opened with E.M. According to the *Manchester Guardian*, 'The brothers Grace gave a grand display of batting, that of the elder being on this occasion unmistakably the better of the two. He showed the greatest skill in defence, combined with heavy hitting, and some of his strokes on the leg were wonderfully good.' W.G., 'after making some magnificent off-drives', drilled a square cut at Hornby at point who took an excellent catch. Grace made 41, E.M. went on to 84, and the whole team was bowled out for 248.[5]

Resuming on 44 for 1 in the morning, Lancashire soon took control of the match. Hornby was dropped on 51 and was 93 not out at lunch when the score was 186 for 3. Gloucestershire had a success immediately after the interval when Grace bowled his opposite number three short of his century, but thereafter their 'worn-out bowling was hit to all parts of the field'.[6] Although Grace kept plugging away – he bowled 64.1 overs and took 6 for 138 – the score continued to rise, eventually passing 400. It was when Lancashire's last pair were together making a bit of tail-end hay that the accident for which the game is remembered occurred. Pilling slogged the ball high towards the pavilion and A. C. Croome, in the best traditions of Fred Grace, hared round the boundary to try to reach it. Having already spilled a catch off Grace over the boundary he was especially keen not to make another mistake, but in launching himself at the ball he fell, and in falling impaled his throat on the spikes of the railings surrounding the enclosure.

The generally accepted version of what happened next originates with Croome himself. Grace rushed over to him and held the wound tight to stop the bleeding for nearly half an hour – 'something near a miracle'[7] – while a needle and thread were sought. This, in Croome's view, 'saved my life'.[8] However, he wrote his account of Grace's heroics nearly thirty years after the event as part of his contribution to the *Memorial Biography*. As with Spofforth's confident assertion that he was bowling to Grace in the nets at Melbourne when the evidence places him in Tasmania, it's possible that the passage of time and the desire to accord due homage to the great man led to a certain licence on Croome's part. Certainly the facts as reported in the Manchester newspapers are less dramatic. The *Manchester Guardian* said simply 'the injury was not a serious one' and that play resumed after 'a brief delay',[9] while the *Manchester Courier* gives a fuller picture. The spike entered Croome's neck

for an inch or so, just below the chin. Mr Croome at once extricated himself, and called out for Dr W. G. Grace, who, with his elder brother, immediately ran to him and partly carried him into the pavilion. These medical gentlemen, assisted by Dr Royle, paid the greatest attention to the injured player, and the wound was stitched up with the utmost promptitude. Fortunately the injury was not a dangerous one, as the rail just missed all the vital parts, and we understand that no serious results are anticipated.[10]

Croome obviously took no further part in the match, and in what seems to have been something of an accepted procedure, the Lancashire captain himself came out to substitute for him during the remainder of the home team's innings. They were eventually all out for 444 when Frank Townsend caught Pilling off Grace at twenty past six. The game ended prematurely on the third day when, faced with a deficit of 196, Gloucestershire threw in the towel and collapsed to 98 all out, of which Grace made 23.

The county's condition seemed more critical than poor Croome's. They had simply lost the ability to win matches. At their April meeting the committee had agreed on the urgent need to recruit 'a First Class resident Professional Bowler with the least possible delay'.[11] Grace had duly scouted around and came up with a fast left-armer, Frederick George Roberts, to partner the indefatigable Woof. Roberts made his first appearance at the end of July in the Yorkshire match that followed the Lancashire game, and it was a sensational debut. He took fourteen wickets, but even with Grace's first-innings 97 Gloucestershire still lost. Indeed, with the exception of a six-wicket win over Sussex at Clifton at the start of August, they lost seven games on the trot. Grace did his best to stem the flood, but his best was not sufficient. Following on against Nottinghamshire at Clifton, he carried his bat for 113 on a lively wicket, but the next highest score was 30, and beyond that no one made more than twelve runs as Gloucestershire stumbled to yet another innings defeat. They were arguably unlucky to lose their next game to Middlesex. Grace was once more in the van, with 63 and 31, backed up by some tight if unpenetrative bowling, but the visitors just scraped home by one wicket.

The county did manage to get things right in their last game of the season. This was their first fixture against Kent, at Clifton on 25, 26 and 27 August, and it proved another extraordinary triumph for Grace. Gloucestershire batted first, and the old firm put on 127 for the first wicket. E.M. scored 70, W.G. went on to 101. Most of the second day was lost to rain, and with Kent scoring 317, another defeat or a draw were the only two possibilities when Grace went out to bat again. In fact there were only two and a quarter hours left for play, so once disaster had been averted the game looked set to lose all interest. But Grace stayed in and kept scoring runs. The possibility of a second century began to take shape, though with only fifteen minutes left he was still eighteen short. At this point Lord Harris intervened: '[H]e put on an underhand bowler, so that I might, as he said, get out or complete the hundred before "Time" was called."[12] Even so, it was a close-run thing. With two balls of the match remaining Grace had reached 99 and must have felt a rare twinge of anxiety. However, whether by accident or design, the next ball dipped towards his leg-stump and he smote it away for a boundary. That was the second time he had scored two centuries in a match, though, as he ruefully remarked, on neither occasion did his side win the match. In the nineteen years since he first performed the feat for South of the Thames v. North of the Thames at Canterbury in 1868, no other batsman had done it once.

Grace finished his season in the bracing air of Scarborough, and although the cricket was played in the light-hearted country-house manner, there was a serious matter at stake. He was just fifty-seven short of 2,000 runs, and obviously decided to put it beyond doubt at the first opportunity, in the game between the Gentlemen of England and I Zingari. The IZ team included Prince Christian Victor, one of the Queen's grandsons, making his only appearance – and indeed the only appearance of a member of the royal family – in first-class cricket. His Royal Highness kept wicket, which was the best place to be as Grace and C. I. Thornton opened the innings for the Gentlemen. Seventy-four runs were on the board after thirty-five minutes, and they continued in murderous vein to put on 173. Grace passed the 2,000 mark, and Thornton said that he hadn't often seen Grace hit so hard. Even so, it was Thornton who took the lead, hitting three sixes and seventeen fours as he raced to his century. Grace made 73, and Stoddart followed in the same aggressive fashion to help boost the Gentlemen's score to 300 in only two and a half hours. When I Zingari batted W.G. kept wicket and no doubt made suitably encouraging noises as Prince Christian scored a cultured 35.

Grace's record against Yorkshire was dented somewhat when in the second game he scored only 17 and 21 not out against them for the MCC, but he played a leading part in the football that followed the cricket, nearly scoring a goal as he brushed aside both Emmett and Hawke. And when, ten minutes from the end of the game (with the MCC two goals up), they switched from soccer to rugby, W.G. rumbled over for what can only have been a largely unopposed try.

Then, after one last match between North and South in which Grace scored 8 and his only duck of the season, it was all over for another year. And what a year it had been. His 2,062 runs was by far the highest national aggregate, and although Shrewsbury was way ahead of him in the averages (1,653 at 78.15), he took second place with a more than respectable 54.26 – his best performance since 1876. In addition, he fell only three wickets short of completing another double. At thirty-nine he could still perform as he had in his heyday. Like the Queen herself, he endured, a part of the national landscape apparently impervious to time.

His uniquely high profile was not lost on publishers, and in 1887 the first of many books about him appeared – Methven Brownlee's biography, written with privileged access to the great man himself. Brownlee was a Scot who had moved to Bristol and befriended Grace. Over many evenings in the study at Thrissle House he had elicited a fund of personal stories, from which he built up an engaging portrait of his subject. Grace scribbled a prefatory note, reproduced in facsimile immediately after the title page, in which he said the project had 'my entire approval', and stated that 'the cricket doings have been checked by myself, and that the personal incidents are entirely new to the public'. Until the Bristol publisher J. W. Arrowsmith persuaded Grace to produce his own memoir, *Cricket*, four years later, Brownlee's biography was the most authoritative account of W.G.'s life and career, and remains a valuable source to this day.

*

After a dismal winter which saw mounted police riding down protesters in Trafalgar Square and continued threats from the Fenians, the summer of 1888 was one of the most miserable on record. The Australians must have wondered what they had done to deserve such a succession of awful English seasons. There were some notable absentees from the sixth team to brave the home country's inhospitable weather. Murdoch was again unavailable and the captaincy was taken by P. S. McDonnell. Giffen, too, had stayed at home, and the great bowling triumvirate of Boyle, Palmer and Spofforth had been dissolved by retirement.* Having lost one devastating combination of bowlers, Australia simply produced another – J. J. Ferris and C. T. B. Turner. Turner was known as The Terror, and had such strength in the first two fingers of his right hand that he could place an orange between them and reduce it to pulp, a party trick to make any batsman wince.[13] He had made an impressive Test debut in 1886–7 with twenty-nine wickets in his first four matches, and in 1887–8 he became the first (and only) bowler to take 100 wickets in an

---

* Spofforth had married an English girl at the end of the 1886 tour and settled in Derbyshire, though he could still burst in upon unsuspecting batsmen in club or festival matches.

Australian season.[14] His partner in intimidation was John James Ferris, a lively left-armer of phenomenal accuracy. Between them they were to take a quite astonishing 534 wickets on the tour.

They introduced themselves in no uncertain terms in the first match of the tour, against C. I. Thornton's XI at Norbury Park. Turner had Grace lbw for 10, and in the second innings he was stumped by Blackham off Ferris for 4. The Australians romped home by six wickets. Things were different when they next met the Champion, playing for the Gentlemen of England at Lord's at the end of May. Grace had taken advantage of the season's only dry spell to revive his previous year's form, and against Sussex at Hove had scored 215. Now he took a long hard look at the Australian bowling and made it emphatically clear that he could cope with it. He opened with the Surrey captain, John Shuter, and together they put on 158 in a partnership 'which from the aspect of sheer delight has never been surpassed'. The two men matched each other run for run until Shuter was bowled by Ferris for 71. Grace went on to his hundred in an innings placed among his best by those who saw it. 'On no other occasion were Turner and Ferris so ruthlessly handled.'[15] He was eventually caught by Bannerman off Ferris for 165 early on the second morning. In the established tradition, the match was limited to two days to let the tourists see the Derby, and so ended inevitably in a draw, but it had given Grace the chance to seize the psychological high ground.

However, the weather then turned hostile, and wickets started favouring the bowlers. After 95 against Oxford at the start of June, Grace's scoring fell away, and in his next two encounters with the Australians he failed. The first of these was for an England XI at Edgbaston, and such was his popularity that when he appeared at the pavilion gate the crowd mobbed him and carried him round the ground. Perhaps unsettled by this unorthodox start to a day's cricket, he was run out for 18, but gave his fans something to cheer about when the Australians batted. In fifty-two overs, half of which were maidens, he took 6 for 74. In the England XI's second innings he was yet again dismissed by Ferris, for 4, and the two Australian strike bowlers swept through the rest of the batting to set up a ten-wicket victory for the tourists. The story was the same in the next match, MCC v. Australians at Lord's, though the margin of victory was narrower. This time it was Turner who accounted for Grace cheaply – for 4 and 0.

As usual, the Gentlemen v. Players matches preceded the Test series. The first, at Lord's, was extraordinary. Grace was the only man to reach double figures twice (10 and 21); when the Players, set 78 to win, reached 71 for 6 in their second innings, it looked as if the match was over. But Sammy Woods, an Australian fast bowler whose brilliance at cricket did not rub off on his academic studies at Cambridge, came back into the attack, and the last four wickets fell for one run to give the Gentlemen a sensational victory. Woods' fellow destroyer was C. A. 'Round the Corner' Smith, in later years Sir Aubrey Smith, one of the earliest English film stars in Hollywood. The second match at the Oval was spoilt by rain. The Players had by far the easier conditions for batting, and bowled the Gentlemen out for 76 and 61 to win a very one-sided affair by an innings.

Whatever the Australians thought of the appalling weather, they had no cause for complaint when they came to Lord's for the first Test, starting on 16 July. Steel, who had retained the England captaincy, must have cursed the rain that presented them with another wet wicket for their bowlers to exploit. The visitors batted first, and scraped to 116. Turner and Ferris then went into action and dismissed the entire England team for 53. Grace made 10, which was the only double-figure score until the tail-ender Johnny Briggs introduced some Lancashire brawn into the proceedings. Lohmann and Peel found the conditions just as helpful, but Turner and Ferris came up trumps again, scoring 32 of Australia's meagre total of 60. One hundred and twenty-four to win on that ruined strip was an impossible task, though no one apparently explained this to Grace. 'He began as freely as if it were Saturday afternoon cricket'[16] and raced to 24 out of the first 34 on the board. He then gave a catch to Bannerman off Ferris, and the match was as good as over. In rapidly deteriorating light, Turner and Ferris took five wickets each, combining to remove the last English batsman – Sherwin, caught Ferris, bowled Turner, 0 – to win the game by sixty-one runs. England made 62 in their second innings, and between them the two sides had produced the lowest aggregate for any completed Ashes Test: 291.[17]

That was the end of Steel's England career. The most brilliant schoolboy and university cricketer of his dazzling generation, and a natural choice for his country, he was not a stayer. Over recent seasons his bowling skills had deserted him, and his confidence in his batting was such that he put himself at eight in the England batting order. Now, two months short of his thirtieth birthday, he decided it was time to quit and concentrate on his career as a barrister. There was, at last, no alternative, and Grace, whose fortieth birthday had fallen on the unused third day of the first Test, was appointed England captain for the second Test. This, unusually, was to be staged at the Oval, while Old Trafford hosted the third. Grace would be starting his captaincy on what was virtually a home ground for him.

He did nothing spectacular in the intervening month, though he would have been buoyed by the three consecutive victories Gloucestershire recorded in August. They beat Nottinghamshire at Trent Bridge for the first time in many years, defeated Sussex by seven wickets at Clifton, and, sweetest of all, overwhelmed Australia by 257 runs on the eve of the Test match. Grace took five wickets in the game and scored 51 in his second innings.

Grace modestly makes no mention of his elevation to the captaincy in *Reminiscences*, but it is impossible to believe it did not give him, and the nation at large, immense satisfaction. His first duty was the toss, which he lost; but it was a very good one to lose. The science of reading a wet wicket was not an exact one. Cricket captains were rather like their maritime equivalents trying to gauge the tide in unfamiliar waters. At Lord's, McDonnell's decision to bat had been vindicated; Australia got their first innings in before the wicket started to do its worst. On this occasion the pitch improved, but only to the benefit of England. McDonnell must have wondered what would have happened had he unleashed Turner and Ferris on the first day. As it was, his own side's fallibility was clinically exposed by the England attack. Lohmann, Peel, Briggs and Barnes took wickets regularly, and between them dismissed Australia for 80.

Grace went out to open with John Shuter, the Surrey captain, making his first (and only) Test appearance. The two had batted wonderfully together at Lord's in May, but hopes that they would repeat their performance were dashed when Grace was dismissed by Turner for 1. When George Ulyett followed him for a duck and the scoreboard read 6 for 2 the outlook was bad. However, by the time the next batsman was out, more than half the arrears had been knocked off, and as the wicket continued to ease, the two professionals in the middle order, Bobby Abel and William Barnes, gradually turned the match in England's favour. Abel made 70, Barnes 62, and, after useful contributions from Sugg and Peel, Lohmann hit an outrageous 62 not out which contained just one single. England made 317 and were left with the relatively simple task of bowling out Australia again cheaply to square the series. Peel and Barnes took the nine wickets that fell to the bowlers, and only McDonnell with a captain's innings of 32 showed much resistance as his side collapsed to 100 all out. In his first match in charge Grace had led England to victory by an innings and 137 runs, despite having the least successful Test match of his career as a batsman.

It is difficult to say whether failure or success made him the more dangerous. When he was on a roll there was simply no stopping him. Yet his response to failure could be just as awesome. Any Test player is likely to regard a county match as something of a holiday after an encounter with Australia, but Peel and Ulyett, travelling down to Clifton for Yorkshire's match against Gloucestershire, were in for an unpleasant surprise. At Cheltenham in 1876 Grace had scored 300 runs against Yorkshire in a single innings. This year at Clifton it took him two innings. It was, he thought, his 'champion match', 'for it was the third time in which I had managed to make a century in each innings, and there was no mistake about the century being reached on each occasion, for in the first innings I made 148, and in the second 153'.[18] Emmett had retired, so the only survivor of the 1876 team was George Ulyett, who had the satisfaction of first catching Grace and then having him caught to end his second innings. He also had the welcome relief of a long rest in the pavilion as Louis Hall carried his bat for 120, guiding Yorkshire to a total of 461, supported handsomely all the way down the batting order. Grace, by contrast, got virtually no help from anyone. Brain made 47 in Gloucestershire's first innings, but there was only one other double-figure score, and the highest score in the second innings after Grace's 153 was 37. Yorkshire, needing only seventy-six runs to win, ran out of time, and as Grace conceded, 'we were pretty lucky not to lose this match'.[19]

Gloucestershire did better against the Australians at Cheltenham. Grace continued in top form and was eight short of a third consecutive century when he was bowled by Turner. The tourists' brittle batting was exposed yet again as they were bowled out for 118. They did only marginally better when they followed on, and Gloucestershire would almost certainly have won had time allowed.

Rain returned to ruin the remaining two home matches. Grace scored 19 and a duck in a defeat by Middlesex at Clifton. Then, for the only time in his first-class career, he scored a second consecutive duck – the closest he came to a pair – in Gloucestershire's catastrophic performance against Surrey. They were all out for 39, the lowest score in their history to that point. Fortunately the game was consigned to oblivion by the weather.

Unsurprisingly, rain had also been falling in Manchester, but Grace nevertheless opted to bat when he won the toss at the start of the third and decisive Test at Old Trafford. Abel and Ulyett were both bowled by Turner for ducks, but Grace survived the early onslaught, and with Walter Read even started to dominate. It's a measure of his confidence that he was out hitting a lofted drive to the long-on boundary where Bonnor took a splendid catch. Grace's 38 was not only the best score in the innings, but the highest in the entire match. England struggled to 172, and then dismissed Australia for 81 and 70 to win by an innings and twenty-one runs, clinch the series and retain the Ashes. The game was over just before lunch on the second day, the shortest ever completed Test match. The Manchester crowds were delighted, and milled around the pavilion calling enthusiastically for W.G. and Peel who had led the victory charge with 7 for 31 and 4 for 37. Grace had helped Peel to three of his four second-innings wickets with three catches, including 'a magnificent left-handed one' to account for Edwards. News of the result, though not the details, had proceeded him to Londesborough Lodge where he joined others gathered for the Scarborough Festival late that night. His fellow guests were obviously keen to find out how Australia had been dismissed. 'I cot 'em out,' Grace summarized succinctly en route to the table to salvage something from the remains of dinner.[20]

Something of the country-house flavour of the Scarborough week is suggested by the team photograph of Lord Londesborough's XI to play the Australians, posed indoors amid the lavish furnishings of High Victorian decor. As a concession to the end-of-term holiday atmosphere, the professionals are seated while the nabobs of the game stand behind them (see Plate 13). It was close to a full England Test side, and it proved too strong for the tourists, who were bowled out for 96 and 57. Grace scored 35 out of 145 in the second innings and also added three more to his tally of catches.

This wasn't the last the Australians saw of him. The cricket circus moved down to Hastings, though the public's interest was diverted by the lurid press coverage of the Whitechapel murders that had started on August Bank Holiday and would continue, with mounting gruesomeness, into October, leaving the nation with one of its most enduring criminal mysteries. Grace scored 44 in the South's win over the North, and signed off with a fine 53 for the South of England against the tourists, though he once again found himself on the losing side.

*

It had been another wonderful season for Grace. He had played thirty-three first-class matches and his aggregate of 1,886 was far and away the highest, though his average of 32.51 was second to Walter Read's. Bobby Abel was the only other batsman to score 1,000 runs. Grace also took something near his usual tally of wickets, though given the helpful pitches ninety-two at 18.18 indicated a decline in his powers (the astonishing George Lohmann took 142 wickets at under nine apiece in only fourteen county matches). In fact, Grace would never again be the bowling force he had been for over twenty years, and 1888 was the last year in which he came close to doing the double.

Although he had had a quiet Test series, no one could cavil at his debut as England's captain with two wins by an innings in two matches, and his success with the bat in other games against the tourists proved that he could still dominate the best bowling in the world whatever the conditions. Gloucestershire's fortunes improved as well. Although Surrey were unchallenged champions with twelve wins, followed at a distance by Kent and Yorkshire, Gloucestershire came fourth with five wins to their credit.

This was a marked improvement on recent years, and came against a background of exciting developments in the club's progress towards a proper headquarters at Bristol. The quest for a ground had been a long and painstaking one involving many sorties to inspect various green-field sites in and around the city. One possibility, first mooted in April 1886, had been some land at Eastville which the club could have leased from Sir Greville Smyth 'for fourteen years at the rent of one Hundred and Twenty Pounds per Annum'. Although renewing the Smyth connection after two generations might have appealed to E.M. and W.G., there were complications involving the re-routing of a public footpath and the negotiations over the lease proved protracted. An agreement had been reached early in the year, but before the proposal was put to the AGM in March a more attractive alternative came up. This was some farmland at Ashley Down, and having decided that they preferred it, the committee threw themselves into a flurry of activity. In February 1888 it was decided to set up 'The Gloucestershire County Ground Company Limited' to purchase, prepare and run the County Headquarters on twenty-six acres at Ashley Down. It would cost 'not less than £2000' to get the site ready for first-class cricket, and that was on top of the £6,500 purchase price for the land. In an early example of an internal market, the club would then pay the new company £300 p.a. to use its facilities, while taking the gate money from home matches. At the following meeting on 2 March, it was proposed 'that Dr W. G. Grace be the first member of the GCCC Committee nominated as a director of the GC Co Ltd to represent the Club on the board'. The proposal was passed, and for good measure committee members signed their approval in the minutes book.[21]

In addition to his new director's topper, Grace still wore his old hat as the club's representative at Lord's. These duties were increased with the formation of the County Cricket Council, and Grace attended the meeting held at Lord's on 5 December. The council was purely an advisory body with no powers of its own, and its members were a heterogeneous mix of first-class, soon-to-be first-class and non-first-class counties. Then, as now, the wide diversity of interests among counties of different size and status militated against any common acceptance of a wider vision of the game, and the council ran the danger of becoming a mere talking shop.

With Lord Harris in the chair, they debated a possible revision of the lbw law to counter the pad play prevalent among the new generation of professional batsmen. Nothing was resolved and delegates were encouraged to raise the matter with their own committees. Grace made no contribution, confident perhaps that with his hold over umpires he needed no alterations to the law. He did, however, speak when the discussion moved on to hours of play in county matches. 'He thought every county match should begin on the first day at twelve o'clock, and on the second and third days at eleven, though he was afraid Gloucestershire were very slack in that matter at home.'[22] It was a long way to go to make one common-sense suggestion coupled with the engaging confession that his own club couldn't put it into practice. Judging by the full report in *Wisden*, it must have been a staggeringly boring occasion, but Grace was now a middle-aged committee man, well versed in the art of letting verbiage wash over him while keeping a monitoring ear cocked for anything that threatened his interests. It was a far cry from the days when with his buccaneering brilliance he had shaken up the game from top to bottom and single-handedly set it on the course it would follow into and through the next century.

TWENTY-FOUR

BY the end of the 1880s the pattern of Grace's life in Bristol was thoroughly established. At the close of the cricket season he would return home to Stapleton Road, pay off his locum, and resume his medical duties. He wobbled out on his rounds on an ancient bicycle, and attended the sick in the workhouse. For recreation he went shooting or followed the beagles. And then, as soon as it was feasible, cricket would begin again in the garden. As in so many things, Grace adhered rigidly to routines laid down by his father. Constant practice was the foundation stone of success. The net at Thrissle House not only provided exercise for him, but also gave his boys, and indeed Bessie as she grew up, the opportunity for the same solid grounding in the game he had had as a child. If anything, practice started even earlier in the year than at Downend. On 17 *January* 1884, Grace had dashed off a note to a hopeful young Lansdown cricketer: 'I hear . . . that you are a fast bowler, if you can get down here on Saturday next at 3 o'clock I shall be pleased to see you bowle [*sic*]. I have a good wicket here.'[1]

His two elder sons, W.G. junior (Bertie) and Edgar, were now day-boys at Clifton College. The school was three and a half miles from Stapleton Road, and in the family tradition of Uncle Pocock, they walked there and back – twice a day for a time, until they were allowed to stay at school for lunch. Both were better scholars than their father had been, but of course neither could begin to compete with him as a cricketer. As the eldest son and bearer of his father's world-famous initials, W.G. junior carried a huge burden of expectation which it was obvious he could not hope to live up to. A contemporary remembered him in his teens: 'I used to watch him at Clifton College matches and at College sports, but to me this tall, bespectacled young man always seemed to be out of his element. Quiet, reserved and unemotional, he was entirely different from other members of the Grace family.'[2] Like other sons who follow in their famous fathers' footsteps, Bertie was cursed with a yardstick by which he could only be judged a failure. (Richard Hutton once returned to the pavilion after a low score for Yorkshire to be greeted with the words, 'Tha'll nivver be as good as thi' faither.')[3]

It is hardly surprising that Bertie was 'reserved', living so close to the epicentre of such a powerful and volatile personality. Grace was a loving father, but along with his well-attested kindness and ebullient sense of humour went an explosive temper on a very short fuse, and it is impossible to imagine that his sons did not from time to time experience the rough edge of his tongue or feel the weight of his hand. Grace desperately wanted them to do well, and gave them every encouragement to follow in his distinguished footsteps in all forms of sport, though sometimes his enthusiasm went to embarrassing extremes. Both W.G. junior and Edgar had inherited some of his athletic talent, and Grace went to watch them whenever he could. He was no passive spectator. On one (wet) sports day when Edgar was running in the quarter mile, he completely forgot himself. As Edgar came into the home straight pressing for a place, Grace abandoned his umbrella and the pile of clothes he was meant to be minding and broke into a sprint, running neck and neck with his son down the last hundred yards chivvying him into greater efforts all the way to the line.[4]

Whatever his sons may have felt about such breaches of parental etiquette, their peers were thrilled by W.G.'s association with the school. The *Bristol Mercury* reported 'the glee with which they welcome to their annual supper one who is to English boys the greatest hero of all living men'.[5] And in addition to appearing as guest of honour on formal occasions, Grace was also prepared to turn up at the nets and offer some coaching. He had great empathy with boys and would join in any game without a thought for his dignity. In winter, if someone had the temerity to shy a snowball at his inviting bulk as he was out on his rounds, he would respond in kind, though undoubtedly with far greater force and accuracy. Ted Spry, the son of the groundsman at the new County Headquarters, told a typical story of Grace's spontaneous, if rather rough, sense of fun. Ted was exploring the half-finished pavilion one day when he met the huge bearded form of the Ground Company's first director. Grace invited him into one of the changing rooms where the plumbers were still working on the showers. Pointing to a hole in the ceiling he told the boy to look up, saying mysteriously, 'You'll see the monkey.' As soon as his victim was in place, he pulled the shower lever and soaked him.[6]

The less playful side of Grace's character could be activated just as readily. From his earliest maturity he had reacted furiously to being crossed and this tendency increased with advancing years. The county ground at Ashley Down gave him a new sphere of influence, and he became jealously concerned with every aspect of its development, walking up to inspect progress almost every day. This rapidly led to open conflict with the foreman on the site, a large man vociferously confident that he could direct his men quite adequately without constant interference. Grace also had rows with Ted's father, John Spry, an equally strong-minded individual who similarly disliked being told how to do his job. On one occasion when Grace went to the ground and found something he didn't like, he sacked Spry on the spot. Spry retorted that he couldn't without the agreement of the whole board and refused to go. Grace stormed off, and when he cooled down let the matter drop.

A much more serious outburst of temper occurred in May 1889. It had been raining, and one look at his precious ground decided Grace to put up a notice forbidding practice. On his return later he was enraged to find that his instructions were being ignored by some Colts who were playing in the nets. The extraordinary letter he wrote on 26 May shows how seriously he over-reacted. It was written on club notepaper from his own address to the president, J. W. Arrowsmith:

Dear Arrowsmith,
    Many thanks for saying you would see White's father about the assault if I wished it. As I did not see him last evening when I saw the son, perhaps it would be as well, if not troubling you too much. The lad I know bears me no ill will, but I fancy, he was kept in bed to make it look worse, you will find this out, if you call. I told the boy's father and mother that I was sorry I had struck the boy, but that 9 out of every 10 persons would have done the same, under the provocation. I could do no more than apologize etc, which I did, and of course would pay the lad for loss of time, etc. but I shall certainly not stand Black Mail being levied on me, which I fancy the father has been put up to, by some of his friends. The father I think you could reason with, and would after some persuasion forego proceedings which would save a lot of trouble and annoyance if it could be managed. You must not let him know that I know you are going to see him as it might make matters worse, but if you call as President of the Club he belongs to, you might see the son as well as the father and let me know the result. Please drop me a line to Lord's Cricket Ground, St John's Wood Rd, as I shall then know how to act.
    Thanking you in Anticipation for the trouble you are taking.
    Believe me, yours truly
    W. G. Grace[7]

327

With the cloud of a potential scandal hanging over him Grace went off to London for the MCC's annual meeting. There were several proposals to take his mind off the assault, and, after much debate, three changes to the rules were introduced: the over was set (for the time) at five balls; restrictions on how often a bowler could change ends during an innings were lifted; and, most radical of all, the principle of declarations was at last accepted, though an innings could only be declared closed on the third day of a first-class match. Grace welcomed the last innovation as a means of reducing the number of drawn games, 'which are nearly always unsatisfactory, and often exasperating'.[8] It also ended the farce of batting sides trying to throw away their wickets while bowlers bowled deliberately wide to try to keep them in, which, as he knew from his experiences in Australia, could cause unpleasantness. At some stage he must have heard from Arrowsmith that he had mollified the White family and the 'trouble and annoyance' of a court case had been averted. More surprisingly, the matter was kept out of the papers.

Grace left London with a light heart, bound for Essex. Charles Green, his old companion-in-arms against Freeman and Emmett in 1870, and now president of Essex, had persuaded him to join an MCC team for a match on the county ground at Leyton (31 May, 1 and 2 June). Leyton had only been a county venue for three years, and Green was quite candid in hoping that Grace's presence would help to put it more on the map. In return, he invited W.G. to stay at his country house, where he proved a generous and accommodating host. As Master of the Essex Hunt, he called out the hounds and lent Grace a favourite horse. A good time was had by all, and Grace was the life and soul of the party, getting on particularly well with the younger members of the household. He also scored 71 in the match, which was watched by a sizeable crowd. Less happily, at the conclusion of the game he shot off, despite being billed as the guest of honour at a smoking concert that evening. The aftermath was even more unexpected. According to Home Gordon, 'After WG had left, he wrote his host a warm letter of thanks, adding that he would like to receive twenty guineas of the advertisement he had afforded the new ground.'[9]* Green sent the cheque, but made no secret of the fact that the demand was out of order. Of course Grace could have argued that given the increased takings at the gate and the extensive press coverage he was cheap at the price, but it was some time before the two were on speaking terms again.

* In calling the ground 'new', Home Gordon has misled subsequent writers into thinking the date was 1886; according to Neville Weston, Grace's first appearance at Leyton was in 1889.

The match against Essex was Grace's second appearance for the MCC. In the first, a low-scoring affair against Sussex at Lord's, he took 8 for 37 in the first innings (and ten in the match), but although this was a promising start, he only managed to take five wickets in an innings once more during the rest of the season. Gloucestershire's first championship match was also at Lord's, against Middlesex. They 'made a shocking display'[10] in their first innings, bowled out for 79. Things improved in the second innings when Grace scored 101, though as so often his own outstanding efforts were not enough to stave off defeat.

They went on to the Oval, where they met George Lohmann in devastating form. Grace made nearly half the runs (94 out of 206), and then, after Surrey made the first declaration in history, hit thirty-four of the fifty-one runs scored while he was at the wicket before Gloucester-shire collapsed abjectly to 92 all out. At Hove he scored 70 against Sussex, and declared himself for the first time, though the game was still drawn. The county won their first match against Yorkshire at Gloucester at the end of June, but their first championship encounter at the new ground at Bristol produced a disappointing innings defeat at the hands of Lancashire.

Grace was also on the losing side in both Gentlemen v. Players matches. The whirligig of time was now bringing in its revenges. With the increase in representative matches, the majority of those selected for the Players had Test experience. Shrewsbury, Gunn and Abel, supported by all-rounders like Barnes and Ulyett, made for a formidable batting line-up, while as for bowling – always the professionals' strong suit – there was no comparison. Since 1885, when each side won one match with one draw, the Players had won six games, often by an innings, to the Gentlemen's single victory (by five runs) in 1888. Although Grace had a successful match at the Oval, scoring 49 and 67, and got some good support from his batsmen, there was no stopping the professionals. They were set 177 to win, and Gunn and Quaife knocked off 156 of them for the first wicket. Gunn went on to 98 not out to see his side home by nine wickets. The Players went one better at Lord's, though they were greatly helped by overnight rain after the first day's play. On a difficult wicket Lohmann and Briggs bowled the Gentlemen out for 148 and 137, while Barnes, Peel, Attewell and Flowers looked on, redundant.

Gloucestershire's northern tour saw them reverse their results against the two Roses rivals. They beat Lancashire in a low-scoring match at Liverpool by three wickets, but lost to Yorkshire by five wickets, despite

Grace's 52 in the second innings. At Trent Bridge they met a Nottinghamshire side which seemed destined for the championship (though Surrey challenged them hard in the closing stages) and lost by an innings.

Back at Bristol they recorded their first win at Ashley Down against Sussex, and Grace came close to registering his first century on the new ground. Ted Spry's new square had not yet settled down, and the wicket was 'so treacherous' that there was no other score over forty and only three batsmen made more than eighteen. 'Yet Grace played grandly, with a vestige of a mishit, never showing a sign of difficulty and tackling all the bowling with ease'[11] to reach 84, which was more than the visitors managed in either innings (79 – Grace 5 for 32 – and 82). He then had a poor spell, during which Gloucestershire drew with Kent and Surrey and lost for the second time to Nottinghamshire, but regained his touch in the return against Middlesex at Cheltenham. Grace scored his second century of the season against them, carrying his bat for 127 not out. Middlesex were forced to follow on, but rallied in their second innings, finally setting an unlikely target of 137 in just over an hour. This proved quite long enough for the home team to cook up a crisis, and when the umpires called an end to the proceedings they had reached the unhappy no man's land of 48 for 5. The county's topsy-turvy season ended at Clifton, which had not been entirely replaced by Ashley Down, with a nine-wicket defeat by Kent.

This game ended on 28 August. The next day Grace was at Scarborough, where he celebrated his release from the frustrations of captaining Gloucestershire with a carefree 58 which helped the Gentlemen of England beat I Zingari. He then made his third and best century of the season, for the South against the North. After being dismissed for 197, the South had to follow on, and Grace opened with Bobby Abel on a wicket described as 'decidedly tricky'.[12] They were together for three and three-quarter hours, and had scored 226 when Abel 'unluckily played a ball on, having made 105 in admirable style'.[13] He must indeed have batted well to have kept within twenty runs of Grace, and doubtless the Yorkshire crowd derived additional pleasure from the contrast between the largest and the smallest cricketers on the first-class circuit. Grace batted for a further forty-five minutes and was finally out for 154 to signal the end of the match.

Both sides then climbed onto a train for the south coast, and played the match again at Hastings. In two innings the South only just scored more runs than Grace had on his own at Scarborough, and lost heavily. But Grace finished his season on a winning side, leading the Gentlemen to a thrilling victory over the Players by one wicket. He had a quiet game himself, bowled by Lohmann for 12 in his first innings and caught one-handed by the six-foot-three William Gunn stretching 'to the extremity of his reach' on the boundary for 6 in the second.[14] The man who knocked off the winning runs with two consecutive boundaries was a popular Hastings cricketer, E. J. McCormick, who was praised in a short speech by the mayor, Mr Alderman Stubbles. It was a suitably parochial note on which to end a season wholly focused on domestic cricket.

Grace had had a pretty satisfactory year for a man of forty-one. He again scored more first-class runs than anyone else – 1,396 – though at 32.46 could claim only fifth place in the averages. His bowling, however, 'showed the effects of increasing years and weight',[15] and his brilliant start against Sussex proved a false dawn. In fact the match provided him with nearly a quarter of the forty-four wickets he took all year. Gloucestershire fell away slightly, winning two fewer matches than the previous year, but maintained their position in the middle of the championship table. Despite teething problems, the new ground had successfully opened its gates to the public. The club seemed stable and its prospects looked bright. There were few signs of the turmoil it would experience through the last decade of the century.

*

In so far as it makes any sense to put a date to cricket eras, 1890 may be said to mark the beginning of the Golden Age. Two luminaries of that incomparable period, Archie MacLaren and F. S. Jackson, made their respective debuts for Lancashire and Yorkshire, signalling a new amateur revival which would once more redress the balance of power with the Players and, with the genius of Ranjitsinhji and the technical brilliance of C. B. Fry waiting in the wings, take the art of batsmanship to new heights.

The game had already started on the course which would extend the Test-playing community far beyond the two pioneers, England and Australia. In 1888–9 the first English team had travelled to South Africa. They played two Tests, though England won so overwhelmingly they were hardly worth the name. Cricket was unfortunately doomed to fail in North America, despite the continuing enthusiasm of the Philadelphians and the Canadians, who sent teams to England in the 1880s; but it was, however, destined for glory on the other side of the world, in the Indian subcontinent. The Parsees had already toured England, in 1886 and 1888, with a measure of success, and in the autumn of 1889 G. F. Vernon took a team of English amateurs to India and Ceylon.

It was a time of expansive optimism, and cricket was perfectly in tune with the wider assumptions and aspirations of the nation. Despite the consolidation of German power under Bismarck, there seemed few direct challenges to Pax Britannica with its promise of ever-increasing influence and prosperity, and the game was seen to have its appointed part to play in the global scheme of things. Grace wrote: 'I believe that the interchanging of visits by cricketing teams has helped to deepen British interest in our colonies and to bind us in closer harmony with other nations . . . and I am disposed to think that the good fellowship born on the cricket-field has done more than is recognised to knit together the various sections of the British Empire and to advance the cause of civilisation.'[16] Grace's own role was also widely acknowledged. The *Australasian*, demonstrating a closeness of identity between the colonies and the mother country, wrote:

We are a race of explorers, colonists, and sailors. An adventurous strain is in our blood. We somehow hold one-fourth of the planet in fee. We possess, we do not know how or why, a curious faculty for the leadership of half civilised races. And amongst qualities which have made the British Empire possible, and which makes English history intelligible, are exactly those which are admired in W.G. – vigour of limb, joy in physical effort, endurance, hardihood, combativeness. No nation but one rich in physical energy and rejoicing in strenuous physical effort, could take the place in the world the British nation fills. And these are exactly the qualities of which W. G. Grace is the symbol.[17]

The end of the Age of Grace did not, of course, mean the end of Grace. The Old Man, as he was now known, as cricket's counterpart to the Grand Old Man of British politics, had no more intention than Gladstone of letting the accumulating years interfere with his life's work.

*

1890 was not a conspicuously successful season (he mustered only twenty-five runs in three innings in the Gentlemen v. Players matches), but Grace comfortably cleared 1,000 runs, albeit at the disappointing average of 28.38, and his bowling showed an improvement on the previous year with sixty-one wickets at 19.37. The Australians were over once again, and that presented him with his main challenge.

The opening match of the tour provided an emphatic reminder of their dangerous potential. They bowled out Lord Sheffield's XI for a scarcely credible 27, of which Grace scored 20 before being bowled by Turner. In the second innings he fell to Ferris for 9.

He met them again a week later in a similar country-house setting in rural Wiltshire. The teams were invited down to Leighton Park, Westbury, by W. H. Laverton (see Plate 15) who gave his name to the XI that Grace captained – a combination of Gloucestershire amateurs reinforced by the pick of England's professionals: Maurice Read, Ulyett, Peel, Briggs, Lohmann and Mold. The first innings produced a shoot-out between Turner and Ferris and Briggs and Lohmann, which the Englishmen won (Australia 67, Laverton's XI 141), but in the second innings the wicket became easier and Grace scored a lively 64 which included one hit out of the ground onto the roof of the farm. It broke a tile, and a glass one was put in its place as a memorial. He was given good support by O. G. Radcliffe, who was unlucky to miss his hundred by two runs, and the resulting total was well beyond the Australian batting strength.

Australian cricket was not going through a good period. In Ferris and Turner they had the best bowling combination in the world, but their batting was weak. Murdoch had come out of retirement, but though still capable of prodigious scores on hard pitches he lacked the necessary skills to make runs consistently on all types of English wicket. Murdoch was often described as the Australian W.G., but the man with the best claim to that title was George Giffen, and he had declined to make the trip. They sorely missed Alec Bannerman's dogged resistance and Bonnor's unbridled aggression, though John Barrett and Harry Trott adopted their respective roles with some success. Blackham remained behind the stumps, quietly consolidating one of the most astonishing careers in cricket history.

As usual they came up against Grace with great regularity. He captained a variety of sides against them on no fewer than ten occasions, and showed an overall record of six wins and three defeats. However, he never regained the heights of 1886 or 1888 and had to be content with 35 for the MCC, 49 and 35 for the South of England, and 43 for Gloucestershire on the eve of the first Test.

The series went very much as might have been expected, and though the Australians fought with characteristic tenacity, England had greater all-round strength. At Lord's J. J. Lyons played a similar whirlwind innings to the one with which Massie had swung the Oval test in 1882. Opening for the tourists, he hit the same score, 55, but in even less time, reaching his half century in a record thirty-six minutes. It was a measure of the Australians' weakness that his opening partner was Charlie Turner, though his 24 was a better effort than those of any of the batsmen who followed him. Australia made 132, and Turner continued to serve his team well by dismissing Grace for a duck, caught and bowled. This, surprisingly, was his only wicket in England's reply. Equally surprising was Lyons' five-wicket haul, but despite his success the home side reached 173, thanks largely to George Ulyett's 74.

The Australians' second innings was in marked contrast to their first. Murdoch shuffled his batting order, dropping Lyons down to four and promoting Barrett to open with Turner. Barrett dropped anchor, withstanding the full range of England's bowling – Lohmann, Peel, Attewell, Barnes, Ulyett, and even Grace himself – to become the first man to carry his bat through a completed Test innings, for 67 not out. He received little support, apart from a second useful contribution of 33 from Lyons, but the Australian total of 176 was the highest of the match, and gave their bowlers something to bowl at. With 136 required on a wearing pitch, England faced a considerable challenge. That they rose to it was due almost entirely to Grace who led the way with an assured and aggressive 75 not out. Shrewsbury failed, but Gunn stayed with him for a second-wicket partnership that realized seventy-four runs, effectively sealing the match, and Grace saw his team home by seven wickets.

This was the start of a run of excellent form, for both W.G. and, by extension, Gloucestershire. He scored 94 at Old Trafford, and when Lancashire were bowled out for 60 a rare win looked on the cards, but the home team recovered to save the game. There was a similar reversal of fortunes in the match against Yorkshire, though with a happier outcome. After being dismissed for 72, Gloucestershire came good in the second innings. Grace scored 98, 'hitting at times with all the freedom of youth',[18] and put on 188 with James Cranston in two hours and twenty minutes. Gloucestershire made 341 and bowled Yorkshire out for 120 to win the match comfortably. They then completed a highly successful northern tour with a narrow win over Nottinghamshire, in which Grace took 5 for 37 in the second innings. There was a third consecutive victory, by an innings, over Sussex at Bristol, and Grace scored his third ninety in as many weeks in the return against Lancashire at Clifton, though the wicket was too good to allow a result.

The weather then changed, and the Oval Test was played on a bowlers' wicket. Peel and Ulyett missed the match, as Lord Hawke put Yorkshire before England and insisted they play for the county. Fred Martin, the Kent left-arm fast bowler, was drafted in and made a startling debut. He took 12 for 102 in the match, which remained the record for a first appearance until Bob Massie's sixteen wickets at Lord's in 1972. Backed up by Lohmann (3 for 34), Martin bundled the Australians out for 92 in their first innings. But the conditions were just as helpful for the Australian bowlers, and Grace as usual was first in the firing line. It was Ferris's turn to dismiss him for a duck, and apart from Gunn (32), the English batsmen seemed out of their depth as they struggled to establish a lead of eight runs. The Australian second innings followed the pattern of the first. Martin again took six wickets (for fifty-two runs) and Lohmann once more claimed three (for thirty-two runs). Australia made 102, which left England ninety-five runs to win. Eighty-five had proved too much for them on the same ground eight years before, and few people would have predicted the outcome with any confidence.

History might have been repeated – as well as made – had Harry Trott taken the chance Grace offered to him at point off the first ball he received. It was a catastrophic lapse. Relieved at having avoided what would have been the only pair of his first-class career, Grace struggled to 16 before succumbing to Ferris once more. The value of his opening stand of twenty-four with Shrewsbury was immediately emphasized when four quick wickets followed, and the situation became ominously reminiscent of 1882. For Maurice Read, who until his recall at Lord's had not played a home Test since the fateful day of Spofforth's triumph, the ghosts must have been particularly insistent, but he was determined to lay them. He scored 35, and built a partnership of fifty-one with James Cranston, who must have owed his surprise selection to W.G.'s personal influence. But even this did not guarantee victory. Once the breakthrough had been achieved, Turner and Ferris harried the English tail mercilessly, and it was left to numbers nine and ten to secure the winning runs, with Fred Martin watching nervously in the pavilion devoutly hoping that the mantle of Ted Peate was not about to fall on him.

England therefore won the series, and Grace maintained his one hundred per cent record as a Test captain. Australia's opportunity to dent that record in the third Test at the end of August was lost to the Manchester weather. The match was abandoned without a ball being bowled.

The tourists still had a couple of encounters with W.G. before they sailed home. He scored 7 and 36 when they defeated Gloucestershire in the second match at Cheltenham. Once again he fell victim to Turner and Ferris, caught by Percie Charlton on both occasions. Grace got his revenge when he scored 84 in the last game of the season at Hastings. '[H]is punishment of Charlton was something to remember.'[19]

Grace's season had one or two other highlights. He made 70 and took five wickets when Gloucestershire completed a gratifying double over Nottinghamshire at Clifton, and he scored 57 in the next match at Cheltenham when the county beat Middlesex. Their record of five wins was an improvement over the previous season, and they could also point to Cranston's elevation to Test status as a positive sign. However, the bowling was still weak. The damp wickets had enabled Grace to return to something like his old form with the ball, but there remained a notable lack of penetration when it was dry. As the standard of pitches generally was improving every year, it was a problem that could only become more pressing.

However, Grace had a plan. Although unable – or, more likely, unwilling – to strengthen his attack from the pool of English professional bowlers, he was not averse to recruiting assistance from further afield. (Apart from the embarrassments of 1878, the experiment with Mid-winter had proved a success.) One advantage of playing against the Australians so frequently was that he got to know them well. He had first-hand experience of just how good a bowler Ferris was and at some stage, fairly early in the season, the question of his playing for Gloucestershire was mooted. The committee members were delighted, and at their meeting at the end of June resolved 'to arrange for a necessary qualification to be provided without delay so that, if an arrangement is ultimately concluded, Time should be running in favour of the engagement'.[20] An arrangement was duly concluded, and Ferris was given the keys to his new home, though the fiction that he had actually settled in Gloucestershire was not widely believed. A. G. Steel commented in the following year's *Wisden*, 'We are told that Ferris has taken a house or cottage of some sort near Bristol in order to secure some so-called qualification for Gloucestershire, though from all accounts he himself is at present in Australia.'[21] This observation of the letter of the law while its spirit was so clearly breached produced a fine piece of hypocrisy the following spring. Billy Murdoch had also decided to try county cricket, throwing in his lot with Sussex, but when his new county wrote asking permission to play him in their fixtures with Gloucester-shire, E.M. was instructed to reply 'That the Committee very much [crossed out] regret that they feel bound to uphold the Rule of Residential Qualification for County Players. Therefore they cannot consent to anyone playing who is not properly qualified.'[22]

At the end of the 1890 season, the Cricket Council made a heroic effort to impose order on the domestic game. There was now a great diversity of county clubs, ranging from the 'octarchy' of indisputably first-class counties – Nottinghamshire, Kent, Sussex, Yorkshire, Surrey, Middlesex, Lancashire and Gloucestershire – through those whose status was less certain but whose ambitions were clear, like Somerset and Derbyshire, down to counties destined to remain minor, such as Devon and Cheshire. Those pressing to join the élite argued for a system of promotion and demotion, and a special meeting of the council, which Grace attended, proposed a league of three divisions with end-of-season play-offs for the bottom club in one division and the winner of the division below. This would have given English cricket a more competitive culture, while casting beyond the closed circle of first-class counties to bring in more of the country's cricketing talent. But as Lord MacLaurin discovered when he tried to introduce a similar proposal just over a hundred years later, the national good seldom outweighs parochial self-interest.

There was another meeting of the council at Lord's in December to make a final decision on the scheme. No such decision was reached. As Grace wearily records, 'there was a hopeless conflict of opinion, and eventually a resolution suspending the Council *sine die* was carried by the casting vote of the chairman (Mr M. J. Ellison)'.[23] Though it was doubtful whether Ellison was acting within his rights, there was no attempt to revive the council, and the MCC resumed full responsibility for all aspects of the game. As a sop to those clamouring for admission to the county championship, Somerset were allowed to participate for the first time in 1891, but the wider questions the council had tried to address were shelved.

*

Over the previous twelve months or so Grace had spent much time closeted with Methven Brownlee, working on the first of the four books which have his name on the title page. As that name had for so long been synonymous with the game, the book was to be called, simply, *Cricket*. It was part autobiography, part potted history, part season-by-season résumé of first-class cricket since Grace first made his appearance in the 1860s, rounded off with portraits of those with whom he had played, chapters of practical advice on batting, bowling and fielding, and an appendix of Records and Curiosities. It was a huge undertaking, falling just short of 500 pages. Grace was a reluctant author – 'writing is not a recreation I care for', he stated bluntly in the preface to *Reminiscences,* the next project for which he was forced into the role – and it taxed his patience sorely. It also put a huge strain on his friendship with Arrowsmith, who had commissioned the work.

Like Charles Green, Arrowsmith discovered just how completely Grace could compartmentalize business and personal relations. For a man as much given to having his own way as Grace, conceding the last word to his publisher was always likely to produce friction, and Arrowsmith's previous good offices counted for nothing once differences of opinion emerged. From being 'very pleased you are going to publish the book' in December 1889, Grace became increasingly critical of Arrowsmith's handling of the project. By August 1891 the usual peremptory note had entered the correspondence: 'You seem to have commenced this book, without my knowing exactly what you intend to do. I must see the binding & covers before giving my consent, as it must be done nicely or not at all.' He was also suspicious of Arrowsmith's apparent intention to sell advertising for the back pages, and demanded to know what his cut would be.

Things got worse as Arrowsmith tried to mollify his author while defending his own interests. Grace was as hard in business matters as he was on the cricket field: 'I do not say you are or you are not within your rights, in doing what you propose, but I never for one instant dreamt of you doing anything I did not approve of. If you are still going to print the book as you like and not as I like then I have done with you.' This put Arrowsmith in the unenviable position of having to choose between friendship and financial self-interest. He pressed on, obviously hoping that Grace would acquiesce in a *fait accompli,* and even, extraordinarily, that he would show some flexibility over his own remuneration. Grace wrote on 10 September 1891, 'Now the murder is out, you have agreed to supply the book at 6d per copy, and cannot possibly do it properly for this sum. It is not my fault but yours, and how you can suggest that I should forego my royalty I cannot understand. As I told you before, it is absurd to publish it as you propose and will bring ridicule on you and me, and I will certainly not give you my consent.' In the end he was forced to give way, but with very bad grace. On 1 October he sent a final letter on the subject: 'I have put your letter in the fire, and hope our private friendship will be the same as before, although on business matters we do not agree.'[24]

After all the furore, the volume Arrowsmith produced was a handsome one, both in its cheap version and the de luxe edition (of which there were 652 signed and numbered copies). Very few people read *Cricket* now. *'W.G.' Cricketing Reminiscences and Personal Recollections*, which came out in 1899 (and was reprinted as recently as 1980), covers the same ground and takes the story further. It is also much better written. *Cricket*, by comparison, is unduly earnest. There are moments of unconscious comedy, as when Grace lists 'a few points which every beginner should carry in his mind', solemnly numbered I to XI ('IX. Do not go into the field with a cigarette or a pipe in your mouth').[25]* But for all its shortcomings, it does contain valuable details on the early years, and it certainly met the contemporary demand for big books crammed with the minutiae of a life and career.

It is also a masterpiece of modesty. Grace was genuinely reluctant to talk about his achievements. 'Other cricketers will tell you of their own doing, but he never,' C. C. Clarke wrote in the *Memorial Biography*.[26] This, potentially, was rather a problem, given that Grace's astonishing career was the main theme of the book, but though he does, inevitably, write about his great innings and prodigious bowling feats, it is with an absolute lack of self-glory. He is also habitually generous about the efforts of others, picking out in any given season the best performances and heaping praise on everybody he mentions. He even manages to find something positive to say about the likes of Barlow and Scotton, whose approach to batting was the antithesis of his.

Unfortunately, from a publicity point of view, Grace had his worst season on record in 1891, scoring only 771 runs at an average of 19.71. His highest score was 72 not out against Middlesex at Cheltenham in August. He managed only one other fifty in what was usually a productive month. July had been even worse, with a string of single-figure scores. This run of failures was in part attributable to a troublesome knee injury which should have kept him out of the game. But as always, enthusiasm and a keen sense of responsibility for the county team kept him at his post.

His poor county form continued into the Gentlemen v. Players matches. The amateurs gained a welcome victory at the Oval, and W.G. would have

---

* This may have been prompted by the sighting of an elderly member of I Zingari smoking a pipe in the outfield at Eastbourne. (R. L. Arrowsmith and B. J. W. Hill, *The History of I Zingari*, p. 42.)

been delighted to see Ferris take 7 for 28 in the Players' second innings, but managed only eight runs himself. In the drawn match at Lord's he scored ten. In the third game at Hastings he made a more typical contribution – 21 out of an all-out total of 68 in the first innings – but the Players emphasized their overwhelming superiority by making 390 (Gunn 169) to win by an innings and 128. Grace's best match as a batsman was the North v. South game, also at Hastings, when he made 54 and 36. His best bowling was in Gloucestershire's match against Surrey. Rain produced a responsive Oval wicket, and Grace and Lohmann both took eleven wickets – for 105 and 93 respectively. Grace's victims included Maurice Read, Lohmann himself, Abel and Walter Read, and as he also made 20 and 37 (out of 144 and 113), it was an excellent all-round performance. Gloucestershire still managed to lose the match, however.

The county's poor showing and his painful knee may account for the growing asperity in his correspondence with Arrowsmith, but he had something else on his mind as well: preparations for his second tour of Australia. In the spring he had been engaged in negotiations with Lord Sheffield who had offered to underwrite a tour and whose enthusiasm – and bank-book – extended to having Grace as his captain. To many it seemed a lunatic proposal. W.G. was clearly past his best, and a gruelling Australian trip was not a sensible undertaking for a man of forty-three. His subsequent poor form in the domestic season – and his knee trouble – seemed to confirm his friends' worst fears. He would break down on the hard Australian pitches or, worse, prove inadequate as a cricketer. He was putting his unchallenged reputation as the world's greatest cricketer needlessly at risk. Grace remained unmoved and, with a parcel of the de luxe edition of *Cricket* to disperse as complimentary copies, set sail in October to write another chapter in the extraordinary story of his cricketing life.

TWENTY-FIVE

G RACE left England with more than his cricket bag and a parcel of books, of course. Whatever toll the years had taken on him as a cricketer, Grace had lost none of his formidable power when it came to agreeing a contract. Just as his first tour in 1873–4 had been an all-expenses-paid honeymoon, so his second was to be the holiday of a lifetime for Agnes and their two youngest children, Bessie (13) and Charles (9). As for his fee, it had simply doubled to £3,000 – roughly £140,000 in today's terms. Grace had warned Lord Sheffield that he wouldn't be able to afford his services, but his lordship was determined to go ahead, whatever the cost. (There are suggestions that he was egged on by friends in diplomatic circles worried by the stirrings of antipodean republicanism, and hopeful that a successful cricket tour would help shore up the colonial status quo. If that was the case, insufficient attention seems to have been given to W.G.'s ambassadorial qualifications.)[1]

Alfred Shaw, who had for some time been Lord Sheffield's right-hand man in cricketing matters, was appalled at Grace's 'princely fee'.[2] Arthur Shrewsbury, who was drafted in as an adviser on the strength of his experience of Australian tours, acknowledged the commercial sense in taking Grace – 'his presence would at the very least make a difference of £1500 or £2000 in the takings'[3] – but the detailed budget he drew up was knocked sideways by the deal Grace struck. 'I didn't know that Lord Sheffield had to pay for Grace's wife and family expenses . . . I thought he had repudiated that before leaving England. If he hadn't taken Grace out, Lord Sheffield would have been £3000 better off at the end of the tour, and also had a better team.' For good measure he added, 'I told you what wine would be drunk by the Amateurs. Grace himself would drink enough to swim a ship.'[4] Shrewsbury clearly felt that his lordship's generosity to his 'amateur' captain meant that he could not afford to give the professionals a fair deal. They were offered a mere 10 per cent of Grace's fee – £300 plus expenses, 'exclusive of wine and cigars' – and he, along with William Gunn, was having none of it. Alfred Shaw did, however, agree to act as manager.

Grace's selection difficulties were compounded when it emerged that another tour – to South Africa – had been arranged for the winter. Walter Read, who would certainly have been on Grace's list, was captain, though the only other players of international stature in his side would not have been candidates for Lord Sheffield's party. J. J. Ferris and Billy Murdoch were happy to represent their adoptive country, but neither would have followed in Billy Midwinter's footsteps and actually played against Australia.* In the end Grace and Shaw found eight professionals who were prepared to accept Lord Sheffield's terms: Bobby Abel, George Lohmann, John Sharpe and Maurice Read (Surrey); William Attewell (Nottinghamshire), Bobby Peel (Yorkshire), Johnny Briggs (Lancashire) and George Bean (Sussex). In addition to Grace there were four amateurs: Gregor MacGregor, the brilliant Cambridge blue, now established as England's first-choice wicket-keeper; A. E. Stoddart and Hylton Philipson, who had captained Oxford and was now MacGregor's understudy (Middlesex); and Octavius Goldney Radcliffe, who sometimes opened with Grace for Gloucestershire and was a serviceable off-break bowler. It was not a bad team – some even considered it the most powerful team ever to leave England – though Bean, Philipson and Radcliffe had never played in a Test match, and the two untried amateurs were hardly serious contenders at that level.

The tour inevitably created huge public interest both in England and in Australia. One Sydney journalist wrote: 'Cricketers for a certainty, and the public in all probability, will go to see Grace; while University men will be interested in Gregor MacGregor, captain of Cambridge . . . [while] upon society folk the presence of Lord Sheffield will exercise a strong fascination, and as the team is intrinsically a very powerful one it may be said to unite all the elements requisite to make its visit successful'.[5] Australia's volatile economy was entering a downward phase in its cycle of boom and bust, but the public appetite for international stars was undiminished. Sarah Bernhardt had toured Australia in June 1891, reaping appearance fees to make even Grace rub his eyes – in Melbourne tickets changed hands on the black market at hugely inflated prices – and the Englishmen could certainly look forward to being fulsomely lionized and lavishly entertained.

---

* Midwinter's strange life had come to a sad end when he died in a Melbourne asylum in December 1890 following the death of his wife and two children. He was thirty-nine.

The party left England on the P&O's premier steamship, the *Arcadia*, on 2 October. Henry Morton Stanley, the discoverer of Livingstone, joined the ship in the Mediterranean, bound for a lecture tour (he complained that it was oppressively crowded, and made no mention in his letters of his distinguished fellow passengers). The tedium of the voyage was varied by the usual deck games and evening entertainments. Johnny Briggs took the lead in a Christy Minstrel act in which Grace, with face blacked and beard powdered, had a mainly looming part.[6] The team played two matches: against Eighteen of Malta, when they wore Lord Sheffield's colours – purple, crimson and gold – for the first time; and at Colombo where they played another match against the odds.

This produced one cricketing curiosity, a reverse of the 'Windy day, umpire' story of popular myth. It was excessively hot, and although provided with pith helmets and even cabbage leaves as protection, all the players found the conditions trying. Grace, with his vast bulk, was particularly affected. After he had notched up fourteen runs, a ball shot and cut back in at him, and in attempting to keep it away from his stumps he apparently dislodged a bail, though neither bowler nor wicket-keeper could quite tell how. The umpire was in the same predicament, and declared that he had to give it not out. 'That's all right,' said Grace, 'but I'm going anyway,' and retired to the shade, leaving Stoddart to sweat it out for 70. Grace obviously made the sensible choice as the next day Stoddart's 'arms from elbow to wrist were one huge blister, and his face was a study in red'.[7]

They reached Albany in Western Australia on 6 November and three days later arrived in Adelaide. They were given a typical Australian welcome, though Grace was chagrined to find that Lord Sheffield, while generous to a fault with his cheque-book, was parsimonious in the matter of personal appearances. Almost the whole responsibility for public relations devolved onto him, and he wearily got down to preparing some serviceable speeches, delivering the first at a mayoral reception in the town hall the day after they docked. As they drove through the city they saw the billboards adorned with huge posters announcing simply 'W. G. Grace'.[8]

Harry Boyle, who had urged the importance of a tour to Lord Sheffield when manager of the 1890 Australian team, travelled over from Melbourne, and telegrams of welcome were received from the wider cricket community. Lord Sheffield responded by making a generous donation of £150 to supply a trophy for which the three cricketing states,

New South Wales, Victoria and South Australia, would compete: the Sheffield Shield. There was one administrative hiccup when the team's original liaison man suddenly went missing. At very short notice, Major Wardill was seconded from the Melbourne Cricket Club to fill his place.

Though they were still lodged in different hotels, the distinction between the amateurs and professionals which had caused such problems in 1873–4 was not, it seemed, going to be an issue, at least within the team itself. In the magnificent group photograph taken in Adelaide's Botanical Gardens, it is impossible to tell the players from the gentlemen as they strike superbly relaxed poses in their light suits and boaters (see Plate 16). Only Grace seems a man apart, with his heavy three-piece suit, his vast beard (now the only one in the party, apart from Shaw's, which was trimmed to modest proportions) and Derby hat, staring in a completely different direction from the majority of the team. (Lord Sheffield is characteristically absent.)

Again in contrast to the previous tour, things started auspiciously when they took to the field for their first match, against South Australia, on 20 November. There had been some rain and Grace had no hesitation in fielding when he won the toss. He then dropped one of the openers, who were in fact both tail-enders sent in to play and miss until the wicket eased. They succeeded remarkably well, staying together until the interval and scoring forty-one runs. The makeshift openers continued their stand after lunch, but when they were separated with the score on 63, the English attack, led by Lohmann and Attewell, ran through the rest of the team at a cost of only a hundred more runs. George Giffen, the captain, was the danger man. He had started the year with a double century and twelve wickets against Victoria at Melbourne in January, and in his previous match the week the tourists arrived he had produced another all-round performance to rival any of W.G.'s, scoring 271 (out of 562) and taking 9 for 96 and 7 for 70. Grace made no mistake when, after a stay of over two hours for 27, his opposite number gave him a chance off Peel.

England were faced with a short but dangerous period before close of play, and Grace followed Giffen by holding back his regular openers. Bean and Briggs survived until stumps, and resumed the following morning. A huge crowd turned up to see Grace, and when Giffen bowled Bean for 15, his appearance was met by clamorous cheering, which was echoed by the South Australian team grouped together to greet him at the wicket. Grace got off the mark with a two, and then opened his shoulders and sent the ball sailing to the boundary. The crowd's roar dwindled to a collective gasp when J. C. Reedman, sprinting 'fully twenty-five yards', stuck up a hand and plucked it out of the air. This was an exact replica of Grace's dismissal on the same ground eighteen years earlier when George Giffen had been looking on from the boundary. Now he was the bowler. In 1874 Grace had stood his ground. On this occasion he responded more sportingly, telling Giffen 'that it was one of the most extraordinary catches he had ever seen', though he did add, 'with one of his characteristic chuckles, "I think, though, it was a bit of a fluke."'[9]

It was virtually the last piece of luck the South Australians had in the match. Stoddart joined Johnny Briggs, who, like any tail-ender given a rare opportunity to build an innings, was keen to make the best of it. They put on 140 together, Briggs missing his century by nine runs. The Surrey professionals Abel and Maurice Read piled on more runs, and the last England wicket fell at close of play with the score on 323. Giffen, who shared Grace's propensity for doing the lion's share of the bowling, took 7 for 152 in forty-one overs. Faced with a deficit of 160, the home side proved unequal to the task. Attewell added six wickets to the five he had already taken and the tourists won by an innings and sixty-two runs at 3.30 on the third day. This allowed time for an exhibition game in which Grace scored a brisk 48. It had been a thoroughly satisfactory three days, with virtually every member of the team contributing to a convincing victory, and Grace must have travelled on to Melbourne in high spirits.

A huge crowd greeted them at Spencer Street station, and they were then driven round the city in coaches decked with Lord Sheffield's colours. The self-effacing earl had once again ticked the No Publicity box, electing to travel round the coast by boat. Grace was left with the role of public spokesman for the tourists, and at the town hall was light-heartedly installed as Melbourne's 'Cricket Mayor'. In all, he had to make three speeches on the first day, and remarked that had he known he would have been asked to make so many he would have stayed at home.

When at last the cricketers got to the cricket ground for their first practice, Grace noticed some changes. A well from which the players used to refresh themselves had gone, as had the vine growing along the pavilion wall. He himself was, of course, the object of close scrutiny. The unforgettable figure had filled out considerably over the intervening years, but if he had lost some of his agility, he was still obviously fit and just as energetic as before. Tom Horan wrote eulogistically:

345

For 27 years he has trod the cricket field, and . . . as he walked from the MCC pavilion to the practice nets, he looked what he is, the king of cricketers, and the personification of robust health and manly strength and vigour. With his flannels on, his giant-like proportions were seen to the fullest advantage, and an old cricketer who saw him here 18 years ago remarked; 'Why he is just the same as ever, except that his chest has slipped down a little.' He smote the bowling to all parts of the field, and played on under the powerful rays of a real Australian summer as if he thoroughly enjoyed himself. Indeed, with his flowing beard, dark features, and loose gait, he seemed more like an Australian than an Englishman, and would easily pass for a sun-tanned squatter, fresh from the grassy downs of Queensland.[10]

When it came to the match against Victoria, John Blackham, who would also lead the Australians in the Test series, won the toss and elected to bat. The Englishmen made a better start than they had at Adelaide, and at lunch the Victorians' score was 35 for 4. Lord Sheffield arrived in the afternoon; the band played 'A Fine Old English Gentleman' and the crowd broke into repeated cheers as Major Wardill escorted him round the ground. A press report recorded that he wore 'an alpine hat with the colours of his Eleven as a band, dark blue shooting coat and roomy nankeen trousers. A newspaper parcel was in one coat pocket, and a warm-tinted kerchief in the other.'[11] Though gratified by his enthusiastic reception, the reclusive peer found the public attention too much, and he retired to his hotel complaining of the heat.

In his absence the team increased their stranglehold on the match. Attewell and Sharpe had bowled the home team out for 73, and Grace and Abel got the English reply off to an excellent start. Grace, inevitably, took the lead, playing with the aggression that marked his approach throughout the tour. He survived an early chance – to third man – but thereafter laid into the undistinguished Victorian attack, racing to his fifty while Abel proceeded at his own pace at the other end. When he fell to Worrall for 29 the score stood at 91. George Lohmann joined his captain for another excellent partnership which took the total to 161. However, when he went for 39, the tourists suffered something of a collapse. Stoddart made 10 and Bean got a duck. But Grace continued in full flow – indeed, he was so well set that he refused to go off for the tea interval, and such was his authority that the home team were forced to carry on bowling at him. Just before stumps he brought up his century with his tenth boundary, and returned to the pavilion to rapturous applause.

Fourteen thousand people thronged to the ground on the second day to see Grace continue his innings. The Victorian bowling and fielding improved, and Grace made only thirty-eight runs in the morning session, going on to 140 while the score increased to 258 for 7. At lunch Lord Sheffield at last took a turn in the speech-making, saying that the welcome he had extended to visiting Australian teams in England had already been more than repaid, and thanking the Melbourne Cricket Club for their generosity in giving his team free use of the ground. Afterwards Grace strode out to continue his innings to the strains of 'See the Conquering Hero Comes', and with only the tail left he decided to increase the tempo somewhat. He hit a five over long-on, and had added nineteen to his score by the time the last wicket fell. His 159 not out was more than half the total of 284. Horan led the chorus of appreciation in the press:

Timing, placing, and finished execution in cutting formed special features of his innings . . . His cuts, whether square or late, were all along the grass, with one or two exceptions; his leg play was marked by characteristic judgement and skill; and that he can hit pretty nearly as hard and clean as ever was made amply manifest by his fiver off Worrall. Considering his great weight and his 43 years, it cannot be expected that he would be as quick on his feet as of old. By reason of this he merely sends back to the bowler many balls that I have seen him in his younger days drive like a shot to the outfield . . . [Nonetheless] it was in every sense worthy of his best days.[12]

The result of the match was a foregone conclusion. Attewell took his tally of wickets to twenty with 5 for 41, assisted this time by Lohmann, who returned exactly the same figures. He bowled the last Victorian at 5.20 to give Lord Sheffield's XI victory by an innings and 107 runs.

The team moved on to Sydney, where the separation of the amateurs and professionals inspired the same criticism that Grace had become familiar with on his first tour. The new republican strain in Australian politics that had troubled Lord Sheffield's friends back in England found expression in the pages of the radical Sydney paper the *Bulletin*, and a team sponsored by an earl and captained by a richly rewarded 'amateur' whose professionals were clearly discriminated against offered easy pickings. Though the paper was hardly flattering about Lord Sheffield, describing him as 'a fat, stumpy man . . . Hair long and straggly, lips and face roughly shaven, and a little fringe of a beard left under the chin, eyes small and cute; thick-necked, heavy-jowled . . . his Lordship is just the sort of man that would make a fine landlord for a bush pub',[13] they had nothing against him personally: 'Lord Sheffield is merely a non-aggressive representative of deplorable social and political systems . . . regarded as a simple-minded old fellow who runs a wholesome show for its own glory, and with an amiable desire to amuse more people than himself, Sheffield is not so displeasing to the democratic eye.'[14] Grace, who could never be called 'a non-aggressive representative' of anything, was the main target. As the embodiment of the corrupt system of amateur privilege, he was simply made to order: 'W. G. Grace said . . . that he was not nearly done with cricket yet. We smile. £3000 and exs. for a pleasure trip.'[15] As the embodiment of the hard school of competitive cricket, he filled the bill as well – 'he plays the game like a professional card-expert; the veteran is master of every form of "bluff", and appeals on the slightest pretext'.[16] Unfortunately, as the tour progressed Grace gave those prejudiced against him all the ammunition they needed.

At this stage, however, things were still going well. Grace even seems to have managed to keep out of the controversy over the umpires which held up the start of play on the first morning of the match with New South Wales. Harry Moses, the NSW captain, refused to accept the tourists' nominee, the Victorian D. F. Cotter, but with the restraining presence of Alfred Shaw by his side Grace agreed to let the point go, and Shaw took Cotter's place.

The game, once it started, was much more evenly balanced than the two previous ones, largely because Charles Turner was playing. The wicket was always going to help the bowlers, and on winning the toss W.G. decided to defer his encounter with the Terror and put the opposition in. Briggs and Lohmann promptly bowled them out for 74. Things were going to be no easier for the England team, especially as a heavy shower had injected even more life into the pitch, and Grace tried to hit his way out of trouble, clubbing both Turner and his fellow opening bowler, Sydney Callaway, for boundaries. Callaway dropped him off Turner, but when Grace gave Turner a chance off Calloway, he took it, despite being knocked over by the wicket-keeper. Grace stood his ground until given out by the umpire. Though suffering a bruised face as a result of the collision, Turner then lived up to his nickname and took 6 for 45 as the Englishmen struggled to 94 all out. Their twenty-run lead was made to look insignificant as Turner, Donnan and Moses all passed thirty, but on the third morning, when a substantial total beckoned, Attewell once more came up trumps, rattling through the lower order to finish with 6 for 49.

A total of 153 was a sufficiently difficult target to guarantee the 12,000 spectators an exciting day's cricket. Grace and Abel put on thirty-six for the first wicket, before Turner lured the English captain into giving him a return catch. He made 19. Abel battled on, but when he went for 31 Turner forced a breach in the middle order, removing Stoddart for 28, then Read, Briggs and Bean for ten between them. At 88 for 6 the tourists were in trouble, but Lohmann and Peel came to the rescue with 34 not out and 26 not out respectively, and Grace's team got home by four wickets.

Beating the three state sides was enormously encouraging, but there would be no more first-class cricket before the first Test in the New Year. Instead, there was a string of up-country games against the odds. Grace found himself in familiar territory, and rapidly reverted to his old cantankerousness. At Parramatta, where they were due to play Eighteen of Cumberland District, he got embroiled in an argument about the number of players each side should have. He insisted on taking the field with twelve men. The local captain eventually agreed, provided he could field twenty, which neatly cancelled any advantage to the visitors. More serious was a dispute about the toss. Both captains claimed to have won it. An unseemly incident was only avoided when the Cumberland captain gave way, but even this did not satisfy Grace who marched off muttering that 'he would have an apology or he would break things, by thunder'. The local paper commented, '[he] may be a very good cricketer, but he has some decidedly funny ways'.[17] The game demonstrated how pointless it was matching first-class, indeed Test-class, players against provincial cricketers. Grace used only two bowlers in the Cumberland first innings. Sharpe took 7 for 22 and Briggs 12 for 38 to dismiss the locals for 67. As he did in most of the odds matches, Grace held himself back, but was forced to bat all the same. To round off a thoroughly bad day he was bowled for a duck. Cumberland District did better in their second innings, clearing the deficit of forty-six and setting the tourists just under a hundred to win. There was not enough time to force a result, and Grace showed his continuing disgruntlement by refusing to bat a second time.

The next match, against XXII of Camden, followed the same pattern, with Lohmann taking 12 for 17 and Peel 9 for 36 in the first innings, and Briggs 13 for 29 and Grace himself 6 for 32 in the second to secure victory by an innings and forty-three runs. At Bowral they played against a team of twenty-four and won by sixty-seven runs (Grace 46). *Wisden* records that 'the home players were a poor lot', though their number included one Richard Whatman whose sister, Emily, married George Bradman and produced a son who ensured his home town a rather higher profile in the years to come. The last in the round of rural fixtures in New South Wales was Goulburn, where once again the tourists had an easy win – by an innings and sixteen runs.

The team returned to Victoria for the Christmas period and had a more demanding match against a XVI of the Melbourne Cricket Club which included three of the Australian Test team – captain John Blackham, Hugh Trumble and William Bruce. The game was a draw, but Lohmann took 6 for 44 and Bean played himself into contention with a top score of 57.

The rest of the batsmen spent profitable time at the crease after the holiday when they ran up 424 against XX of Ballarat. Grace clearly enjoyed his return to the ground which had seen his maiden Australian century eighteen years before: surviving four chances, he scored 62. Stoddart, with whom he opened, made 45, Maurice Read made 40, and then George Lohmann, coming in at eight, hit a spirited 106. Grace gave himself a bowl for old times' sake and collected seven wickets, while Sharpe and Briggs were the most successful of the front-line bowlers. The tourists won by an innings and 134. Even the gate receipts were good – £225, of which only 15 per cent went to the local club, and the *Ballarat Courier* reported the Englishmen 'very well satisfied'.[18] (Lord Sheffield had generously offered to divide any profits among the professionals at the end of the tour.)

They returned to Melbourne brimming with confidence and firm favourites to win the first Test, starting on Friday, 1 January 1892. There were behind-the-scenes ructions when John Cresswell, Secretary of SACA, threatened to withdraw Giffen and Jack Lyons unless Adelaide was given the third Test. Lord Sheffield had little option but to agree, but he was deeply offended and refused to have anything further to do with Cresswell.

But for now all eyes were focused on Melbourne. Although the recession was biting hard – one prominent businessman shot himself in despair during the course of the match – 20,000 people packed the ground on the first day. The series nearly got off on the wrong foot when Grace took exception to the ancient penny Blackham produced for the toss. It was so worn that it was difficult to distinguish one side from the other. Grace's suspicions were roused, and having lost the toss he insisted on testing the coin a few times to make sure that it wasn't 'loaded'.

Blackham watched patiently, well versed by now in the Old Man's foibles. Grace declared himself satisfied; the Australian captain retrieved his penny and said he would bat.

He sent out Bannerman and Lyons, the blocker and the hitter, to open. Grace caught Lyons off Peel for 19 when the score was 32. Four runs later Peel claimed the key wicket of Giffen, lbw for 2. Bruce and Bannerman steadied the ship with a patient partnership of 87, but then Sharpe bowled Bruce for 57 and followed that by dismissing both Donnan (9) and the limpet-like Bannerman (45) on 136. Australia suffered another blow when Moses tore a muscle and could only continue with a runner. At close of play they had reached 191 for 7.

A violent dust-storm blew up early on the second day, but when it died down another huge crowd made their way to the ground through streets strewn with broken tiles and glass. They were encouraged by a ninth-wicket stand of forty-one between Callaway and Turner which helped to push the total up to 240. Sharpe had been England's most successful bowler with 6 for 84 in fifty-one overs (for this series the over was six balls). Grace opened with Abel and immediately benefited from a tactical ploy on Blackham's part which failed to come off. Convinced that Grace was more susceptible to slow bowling than fast, he gave the ball to Harry Trott (leg-spin) and George Giffen (off-breaks). Neither troubled the batsmen, who got off to an assured start. Abel hit two fours off an over from Trott, and took a further eight off one of Giffen's. When Turner did bowl, Grace thumped him to the legside boundary.

It was rousing stuff. It certainly roused the crowd, especially the vocal minority of barrackers. George Giffen gives a rather anodyne explanation of this 'distinguishing characteristic of Australian crowds': 'Throughout the match . . . a running fire of audible comment is maintained by a number of spectators, and some very amusing advice is tendered to the players.' Grace, though, was not amused, and decided to retaliate. When McLeod came on and just shaved his leg-stump he resorted to his old trick of pretending he was out. With a wag of his beard, he took three strides towards the pavilion. A huge shout of triumph went up and 'twenty thousand pairs of hands' burst into applause. Then the ponderous figure wheeled back to the crease ready to face the next ball, and the crowd fell silent, 'crestfallen' that 'a rise has been got out of them'.[19]

McLeod had the last laugh. He bowled Abel for 32 and then with the first ball of his next over got through Grace's defence. He had made 50 exactly, and played 'fine, masterful cricket'. Stoddart staved off the hat-trick, but two balls later fell to a slip catch by Giffen. McLeod had reduced England from 84 for no wicket to 85 for 3 in five deliveries. George Bean, making his Test debut, rose to the occasion and produced a colourful half century. His dismissal, however, provoked another row. Bean hit the ball into the outfield where Bruce claimed the catch. When the players came in from the field, Grace challenged Bruce, asserting that the ball had bounced. Those with sufficiently long memories would be able to recall Grace's outrage when Fred's word was doubted under similar circumstances on the same ground in 1873-4. Maurice Read made 36 and late in the day Johnny Briggs scored 41 to take the England total to 248 for 7 at stumps. Briggs failed to add to his total in the morning, and the England innings petered out with the addition of only sixteen runs, giving them a slender lead of twenty-four.

Bannerman and Lyons cleared the deficit, the combination of aggression and defence working better than it had in the first innings. Lyons struck out boldly, and when Abel caught him with a brilliant one-handed catch off Briggs he had scored fifty-one of the sixty-six runs on the board. Attewell then bowled Giffen for a single and the game swung England's way. But Bannerman remained, and he proceeded to inflict on the English the sort of grim stonewalling Scotton had produced in the 1886 series. In the hundred minutes of the afternoon period Bannerman scored just seven runs, but however tedious ('intolerably slow to look at' was *Wisden's* judgement)[20] it was tactically justified. Unlike English Tests, this was a five-day match, and the longer a team occupied the crease the more likely they were to win. Though ringed by close fielders, nothing disturbed the opener's adamantine concentration, and when Sharpe finally induced an error to have him caught by Grace at point, he had batted 230 minutes for his 41 and a total of 435 minutes for 86 runs in his two innings. Australia ended the day on 152 for 5.

On the fourth morning Moses and Trott added thirty before they were separated by a run-out. Blackham, who was running for Moses, was sure he had made his ground and was angry when the decision went against him, but it wasn't long before he was back at the crease in his own right. He made 0, but by that time Trott (23) and McLeod (31) had given the total more respectability. Australia's 236 left England 213 to win. The match was perfectly poised.

Grace opened with Stoddart, dropping Abel down to five to give the middle order more solidity. He seems to have been confident of victory –

Giffen quoted him as saying he expected to score the runs for the loss 'at most' of six wickets[21] – and when, despite Blackham's reversion to the more orthodox attack of Turner and McLeod, the fifty came up with the two England openers still together, it looked as though he would be proved right. But the game changed dramatically when the score was on 60: first Grace fell to a good catch by Bannerman off Turner for 25, and then Stoddart was bowled playing across the line to Callaway. The score soon became 71 for 3, then 75 for 4 as both Read and Bean failed, and Abel was left with the task of rebuilding the innings. He and Peel added eighteen, but then England suffered another collapse. Three wickets fell for five runs in the nineties, and at close of play the score was 104 for 7 with Abel 16 not out and MacGregor on 3.

No Test had ever gone into a fifth day before, and it was obvious that without a minor miracle the long battle would be won by Australia. Abel continued to bat well, but eventually fell to Turner for 28. MacGregor made 16 and Attewell a brave 24, but the innings ended when he was caught by Donnan off Turner. England had made 158, leaving the Australians worthy winners by fifty-four runs. The crowds surged happily onto the field to bear their heroes back to the pavilion. There was much to celebrate. Australia had defeated arguably the most representative English XI ever seen Down Under (Grace had regularly claimed that title for it), and had broken an appalling run of results in which England had won eleven out of the last twelve Test matches. And it wasn't simply the fact of their success, but the manner in which it had been achieved that offered hope that Australia had turned an important corner. George Giffen commented, 'The batting of our men was the soundest all round we had ever exhibited. It had taken twenty years for the English batsmen to teach us that, on good wickets, matches were to be won by sound, rather than risky, batting. This match was the first great one in which Australian batsman after Australian batsman put these precepts into practice.'[22]

It was a lesson the English team seemed to forget just as their opponents learned it. The tourists batted for just eight hours and twenty minutes in the match, compared to Australia's thirteen hours for only fifty-four more runs. Grace made no apology for their attacking approach. Lord Sheffield had promised that his team would play attractive cricket, and his captain supported him: 'It is the game I have tried to play all my life: it is the game every lover of cricket desires to see played, and it will be a bad day for our national game when it is given up, and a slow defensive game takes its place. Matches are played to be won, not lost, and slow defensive play is against that, and in my opinion opposed to everything that is conducive to the welfare of the game.'[23]

Brave sentiments, but Grace would have given much for the professional discipline of Gunn or Shrewsbury, and there is no doubt the result hurt him badly. He lost his unbeaten record as England's captain and conceded a dangerous advantage in the three-match rubber. He did, of course, congratulate the Australians 'on their well-won victory', though the *Australasian* reported 'he seemed surprised at the failure of his own batsmen after his departure in the second innings. The light, he added, was bad, but that was hardly sufficient to account for so feeble a display on a wicket which was still good.'[24] Away from the public gaze he was less magnanimous and, according to the *Bulletin*, 'grossly insulted a newspaper man who asked him in a civil way' for a comment.[25]

One slight consolation for the tourists was the amount of money taken at the gate. The total attendance of 63,652 over the five days was an Australian record and, given the generosity of the Melbourne Cricket Club in granting free use of the ground, some £2,000 went into the kitty to offset Lord Sheffield's expenditure.

The second Test was due to begin in Sydney on 29 January, but again the tourists' schedule included no first-class cricket in the interim. The next round of country matches was particularly frustrating for Grace, whose last three innings before the Test were 0, 1 and 0. Most of the games degenerated into meaningless battles of attrition as the local sides set out doggedly to achieve an honourable draw. The cumulative effect of such pointless cricket became apparent when Twenty Combined Juniors came dangerously close to inflicting a humiliating defeat on the tourists. Everyone must have been relieved to get back to Sydney and the serious matter of retrieving the series.

By the end of the second day, they had made more progress towards this objective than they might have dared to hope, having bowled out Australia for 145 and then built up a seemingly impregnable lead of 162 runs. This happy position had not been achieved without friction, and as usual Grace had been at the centre of it. The first problem had been Moses' leg. This had not completely recovered from the injury he sustained in the first Test, and Grace was well within his rights in warning Blackham that if it went again he would refuse a runner or substitute fielder. Blackham accepted the risk, and when Moses pulled up limping after a quick single, Grace stuck to his guns. Though this was perfectly justified, it was not popular with the crowd, who started barracking. Grace's standing with them fell even more when he was involved in the dismissal of Walter Giffen, George's younger brother, who was making his debut. He hit the ball back to Lohmann who, in an attempt to catch it on the half-volley, scooped it to Grace at point. Grace threw it triumphantly in the air, and the unsighted umpire at the bowler's end was persuaded that the catch was clean. As the *Australasian* put it, Grace 'assisted in the deception by tossing up the ball',[26] which was particularly rich in view of his protests over Bruce's catch to dismiss Bean in the first Test.

The chances were that Lohmann would have accounted for Giffen anyway. He was in the middle of one of the great bowling spells in Ashes history, and he finished the innings with 8 for 58. There were thirty minutes for England to bat at the end of the day, and once again spectators witnessed Grace trying, successfully, to influence an umpire's decision when he waved his glove vigorously in response to a confident lbw appeal. As Moses, refused a substitute, was limping gamely from end to end to take up his enforced position at slip, the crowd had plenty to fuel their ire. Grace, as usual, refused to let the barracking distract him, and he remained undefeated on 23 at the close. Abel was not out 15, the score was 38 for no wicket, and England had got off to an excellent start.

On the second morning – Saturday, 30 January – Moses was told he was in danger of inflicting permanent damage to his leg if he continued to field, and Grace reluctantly agreed to allow a substitute, though he was quick to ban Syd Gregory, one of Australia's best fielders. In the end Garrett took his place. Grace went early, bowled by Turner, having added three to his overnight score. Though most of the English batsmen got a start, only one went on to make a big total. The day belonged to Bobby Abel. Under a bright sun in front of a crowd of 24,000, he played patiently and with consummate skill, accumulating runs steadily as his colleagues departed at regular intervals at the other end. When the last man, Sharpe, joined him he had notched up ninety-five runs. Throughout his career Abel had a reputation for making heavy weather of the nervous nineties, and he now spent an agonizing twenty minutes before reaching his century, courtesy two overthrows. He had been at the crease for four and three-quarter hours and it was his first Test hundred. Partly out of relief and partly in response to the situation, he then began to open up, hitting thirty-two runs in forty minutes before Sharpe was finally caught by Bannerman off George Giffen for a valuable 26. Abel was left on 132 not out and became the first Englishman to carry his bat through a Test match innings. It was a splendid performance, and recognized as such by Lord Sheffield, who gave him a cheque for fifty pounds. It also put England in a very strong position, especially as there was just time to take the first Australian wicket before stumps, Trott falling to Lohmann for a single. The English team could enjoy their Sunday off, confident that the match was all but won.

There were some, however, who had no wish to allow the English, least of all Grace himself, a peaceful rest day. A local Sunday paper, laughably called *Truth*, chose this moment to revive the fake letter Grace was supposed to have written at the end of his previous tour. Printed under the headline 'Dr. Grace Extraordinary Behaviour. He Abuses and Insults Australians', it was prefaced by a poison-pen portrait of 'the famous professional English cricketer, who calls himself an amateur, while making fortunes at the game'. The line of attack was similar to the *Bulletin*'s, though developed with rather less finesse:

[I]n spite of . . . the uniformly kind and generous treatment, which has attended him here, he don't seem able to behave himself as an 'English gentleman' is supposed to know how to do. His behaviour on the cricket field, not to mention his demeanour in private, has been caddish, snobbish, or anything else you like, except gentlemanly . . . [He] has deeply outraged Australian sportsmen's sense of honour, by making the most cruel and uncalled for reflections against the credibility of the word of Bruce, one of Australia's best-known and most popular cricketers. But what can be expected from a man who takes £3000 as his share of the spoils of a cricketing tour, and then claims to be regarded as an amateur? He was here among us once before – nearly twenty years ago – and what he thought of us he placed on record in the following letter, written to a friend of his in Melbourne, just as he was leaving our shores . . .[27]

Whether he saw this piece of journalistic malice on the Sunday or not, Grace soon heard about it and sent the more reputable *Sydney Morning Herald* his 'positive and most emphatic denial of being the author or writer of the letter referred to'. But by the time his rebuttal appeared – it was dated 3 February, the last day of the Test – the damage had been done, and the popular prejudice against him further inflamed. The third day of the match, which had seemed to promise so much, was a wretched one for him. He was constantly barracked and, far worse, things went disastrously wrong out on the field.

Play started with Bannerman and Lyons making their way to the middle just as though they were opening the innings. And indeed, the bonus wicket of Trott soon seemed a thing of the distant past as Lyons tore into the English attack. The South Australian had recently produced a ferocious display of hitting in a state match against New South Wales, striking the ball so hard that the fielders were seen withdrawing their hands from the line of fire. His whirlwind 145 gave him the confidence to back himself to score 200 runs over the two innings of the Test match. At odds of 20/1 he put down two fifty-pound notes, looking to make a small fortune. He fell short, but only by twenty-five runs, and a side-bet that he would outscore Abel in his second innings covered his initial wager. (Ironically Abel missed him in the slips – twice – when he was on 49.) His 134 scored in three hours helped Australia to a vital lead, and all the time Bannerman was grittily keeping his end up. He scored just sixty-seven runs during the whole of the third day, and laboured on well into the fourth. *Wisden* recorded that 'out of 204 balls bowled at him by Attewell he only scored from five'.[28] He even drew Grace out of retirement as a bowler, but although he was troubled by the slow, hanging deliveries on his leg-stump, he refused to be deflected from the path he had set himself. By the time Grace eventually caught him off Briggs he had scored an invaluable 91. Giffen left a vivid portrait of Bannerman during this marathon of stubbornness:

[T]he field crowded around him as he stone-walled. There was W.G. at point, almost on the point of his bat; Lohmann a couple of yards away at slip; Peel at silly point; Stoddart only a dozen yards away at mid-off; and Briggs at silly mid-on . . . A barracker once called out, 'Look out, Alec, or W.G. will have his hand in your pocket.' But Alec stone-walled on, imperturbably blocking the straight ones, sardonically smiling at the off-theory, and judiciously tapping a rare loose one to leg. Suddenly he swished at an off ball, and cut it past W.G.'s ear to the boundary, and then what a yell rent the air! [He was eventually caught by W.G. off Briggs] who had simply tossed the balls down slowly, with as much twizzle as possible on them, in the hope that he might lead Alec into an indiscretion. But the Englishmen had to wait seven and a half hours for that indiscretion! Truly patience is a virtue.[29]

It was not one Grace was noted for, and suffering the taunts of the crowd for hour after hour while watching Bannerman slowly strangling the life out of England's hopes can't have improved his temper. When Briggs brought the Australian innings to a surprisingly swift end with a hat-trick, Grace returned to the pavilion to encounter yet another request for a substitute fielder. McLeod had received news in the morning that his elder brother had died. As he couldn't leave for the funeral before five in the afternoon, he decided to stay at the ground and have his innings. Now he had gone, Bannerman wanted someone to field for him. Grace obviously couldn't refuse, but he asked whether the player chosen was a better fielder than McLeod. Bannerman admitted that he was. 'Then get someone else,' said Grace, and stumped off to put on his pads.

Australia's total of 391 had left England needing 230 to win the match, and they had an awkward fifty minutes to negotiate before stumps. There had been a break for drizzle earlier, and with the cloud cover persisting Grace was worried that conditions would deteriorate on the following day. Instead of holding himself back, he decided to open, reportedly saying, 'If there's any trouble out there, who's more likely to deal with it than me?'[30] His tactics also involved a spirited attempt to get as many runs on the board as possible that evening. The plan misfired horribly. First Abel spooned a catch off George Giffen to his brother Walter, then Bean drove Turner to Lyons at mid-on, and finally Grace himself edged Turner to Blackham. The score was 11 for 3. To end what was almost certainly the worst day of W.G.'s cricketing career, it then began to rain.

England regretted the loss of those three wickets all the more bitterly the following day when the wicket proved less bad than anticipated. As Abel said many years later, 'the Sydney wicket is the easiest I have ever played on'[31] – this from a man whose home ground was the Oval – and Maurice Read and Stoddart certainly seemed untroubled as they took the score past fifty. With ten or even nine wickets in hand, England might well have made their target, especially as the Australian bowling was weakened by the absence of McLeod. However, although Stoddart played brilliantly for his 69, Giffen and Turner worked steadily through the wickets and the match ended in Australian triumph mid-way through the afternoon session when the last English wicket fell with the score on 157. Australia thus won the rubber, and, in George Giffen's quaint phrase, 'regained possession of our own treasured emblems'.[32] *Wisden* justly pronounced it 'one of the finest performances in the whole history of Australian cricket, a performance, indeed, fully comparable to the seven runs victory at the Oval in 1882, or the great, but unsuccessful, fight on the same ground in 1880'.[33] The crowds milling round the pavilion were understandably ecstatic, flinging their hats into the air and calling for the players, while 'the ladies who crowded the reserve smashed their parasols on the seats and battered umbrellas were kicked about the lawn'.[34] Grace probably felt like kicking a few umbrellas about himself.

He had had a dreadful three days, culminating in the loss of a Test match he ought to have won, and with it the Ashes.

The defeat was obviously a terrible blow to the whole team, and not for the first time there was criticism of Grace's captaincy. Lohmann, who had done so much on the first day to ensure victory, clearly felt Grace had squandered a magnificent opportunity, and was reported shouting at him within earshot of a number of Australians: 'Not for a thousand a week would I join another team captained by you!'[35] There was to be no repeat of the breakdown in relations that had marred Grace's first tour – Alfred Shaw's presence as manager ensured that – but tensions began to surface, and Tom Horan wrote with his usual authority that Grace 'was not popular with his team, especially [after] the second test match'.[36] One topic likely to have come up repeatedly among the pros was the question of money. Even though they had been drawing record crowds and taking impressive receipts on the gate, it was by no means certain that the tour would show a profit to divide between them after Lord Sheffield had covered all his expenses, and undoubtedly the largest item on his budget was Grace's disproportionate fee.

The mood in the party was reflected in the next few matches. These were against the odds, and the tourists did not distinguish themselves. The nadir was reached when they allowed Twenty-Two Juniors of Sydney to run up a total of 318, which included two scores of 71, and were then forced to follow on after being bowled out for 162. Grace no doubt had words with his players, although his own form had hardly been inspiring – one fifty and one other score over thirty – and on their return to first-class cricket they pulled themselves together, chalking up a resounding victory in the return against New South Wales. Grace led the way scoring forty-five out of the first fifty-two runs on the board. Abel made 48 and Read and Lohmann both made centuries in a total of 414 – an impressive effort, given that the New South Wales attack was led by Turner and Callaway. The tourists also did well with the ball. Grace had the satisfaction of dislodging Alec Bannerman for 29, and apart from Turner, who was run out for 66, and Syd Gregory, who made a promising 46, the home team did not give them much trouble.

But trouble there was. As so often it involved Grace and an umpire. The umpire in question was E. J. Briscoe who, it is clear, had become irritated by the Englishmen's readiness to appeal. When they went up for a catch behind off Charlton's first ball from Lohmann late in the innings, he gave the batsman not out. That Grace said something was not disputed. What Grace said he said was, 'I wish you would pay attention to the game; we all heard the catch.' What Briscoe said he said was, 'You will give no one out. It is unpardonable. You must be blind. We might as well go home tomorrow.'[37] Whatever he said, Briscoe went home that very afternoon, though again there are two versions as to when and under what circumstances. Australian accounts suggest that the umpire left the field immediately. Grace tells a different story. According to an article he published in the *Cricket Field* on his return to England, Briscoe officiated throughout the remainder of the NSW first innings. It was only 'when New South Wales, who had to follow on, were going in for their second innings, we heard for the first time that Mr Briscoe had decided not to umpire any longer. I need not say that all of the team were surprised, for not one word had been said at the time of the incident to lead us to believe that Mr Briscoe had such a thought in his head.' Grace blamed ill-wishers in the pavilion who 'kept harping unnecessarily upon the point, and caused Mr Briscoe to act in a way that he would not have acted if he had been left to his own judgment'.[38] Finding a replacement caused some delay, but eventually Charles Bannerman, Alec's brother, agreed to take Briscoe's place, and the following day the tourists won comfortably by seven wickets, despite Syd Gregory's brilliant knock of 93 not out which earned him a place in the last Test.

The Briscoe affair rumbled on. The unhappy umpire lodged an official complaint with the New South Wales Cricket Association, who wrote to Grace for a response to the allegation that he had used offensive language. Grace penned his reply from Launceston during the tourists' two-week stay in Tasmania. After rehearsing the minutiae of the decision which caused the controversy, he stated categorically, 'I did not insult Mr Briscoe, nor did I think him a cheat', before going on to grind his own axe: 'The umpiring question will have to be gone into thoroughly, and some new plan adopted or cricket will not be worth playing as there is not the slightest bit of pleasure in playing under the present system of umpiring in Australia.' The NSWCA wrote again – did he or did he not make the insulting remark umpire Briscoe had complained of? Grace replied:

I did tell Mr Briscoe that his decision was unpardonable, and that he must pay more attention, as everyone except himself knew Mr Charlton was caught at the wicket. Any other remarks were not addressed to the umpire, but to me by Attewell, and I agreed with him. I did not insult Mr Briscoe, nor do I think him a cheat, but, I am sorry to say, he is not a good umpire. Lohmann denies that Mr Briscoe told him he got in his way. He [Lohmann] says Mr Briscoe said he did not know Charlton hit the ball. I must decline to go any further into this matter.[39]

And there the 'unfortunate disagreement', as *Wisden* described it, was allowed to rest. After all, what power had the NSWCA to make Grace apologize? Neither he nor his team would be returning to Sydney.

Apart from having to deal with aggravating correspondence, Grace enjoyed his return to the 'most English' of the colonies. As in 1873–4, he found it a peaceful haven after the hostility he faced on the mainland, and remembered with gratitude 'a delightful time of hunting, fishing and shooting'.[40] There was also some cricket. Two matches had been arranged for the tourists. At Hobart they played an Eighteen of Southern Tasmania which included the veteran left-armer Tom Kendall, who put in a marvellous performance. He took 7 for 79, including all the top-order batsmen, but a fine 84 not out by Stoddart ensured a big enough total for the tourists to take the match by an innings. Against Northern Tasmania at Launceston they rattled up exactly 400, with Stoddart again in good form and Read just missing a century by five. Although with a total like that only two results were possible, the third day's play was nearly aborted when Grace arrived at the ground to find that the wicket had been rolled and watered. The Tasmanian first innings was still in progress, and although the MCC had recently changed the rules governing the use of the roller, apparently the match was played under the old dispensation, which, in Grace's view, had been violated. It was some time before he could be persuaded to allow play to continue. When it did, the Northern Tasmanians were soon forced to follow on, but they batted well enough in their second innings to save the match.

The cricket had not been demanding, and the English party had a restful fortnight's holiday in congenial surroundings. Lord Sheffield liked the island so much he decided to stay on, taking rooms in a hotel in Hobart while his team sailed back to Melbourne for the return against Victoria on 17, 18 and 19 March. (He did, however, get involved when it looked as though the Victorians were not going to be able to raise a full side, telegraphing that he would cancel the fixture if a strong team were not put into the field. Trumble and McLeod found that they could, after all, get time off from their bank.) His lordship did not miss a particularly enthralling game, though a nine-wicket victory was a welcome result. Grace returned to form with a top score of 44, and Lohmann, Peel and

Attewell were all among the wickets, while Briggs took 5 for 33 in Victoria's second innings. The team travelled on to Adelaide for their final engagement of the tour in good heart.

When they arrived, Grace immediately showed that even on his last appearance in Australia there would be no relaxation of his jealous protectiveness of what he saw as his own team's interests. There was another row over the umpires. Grace wanted Phillips, and when he was told he couldn't have him, he interdicted Flynn, who was highly respected, out of pique. Two far less experienced men were drafted in, with predictable results. When Grace inspected the ground, he found fault with the fact that the wicket had been covered before the match started. He also wanted the boundaries squared off at the ends to lessen the carry for a straight hit. This was refused, but when he insisted that instead of Blackham tossing the coin, he should do it, on the flimsy grounds that he had lost on the previous two occasions, the Australian captain decided it was easier to give in than delay the start of the match with yet another argument. He lost, and Grace announced he would bat. It was a sunny day and the wicket seemed to have suffered no adverse effects from its twenty-four hours under the tarpaulin. Conditions for batting were perfect.

Indeed, everything went England's way. Grace played an innings of consummate skill and looked certain to make a century when he was surprisingly yorked by McLeod for 58. Stoddart did reach three figures – with three cracking boundaries in an over from Giffen – and went on to a magnificent 134. Maurice Read made a fifty, Bobby Peel 83, and substantial lower-order contributions from Briggs, Attewell and Mac-Gregor guaranteed an intimidating total. England batted on all through the second day, though by this time the weather had deteriorated. There were interruptions for rain, and the last passage of play continued in persistent drizzle, much to the dismay of the Australian bowlers.

England began the third day on 490 for 9, with MacGregor 29 not out and Attewell 36, but the start was postponed because the umpires deemed the pitch unfit. Although delay would actually help England, as the wicket could only get more difficult as it dried out, the decision was not well received. The *Australasian* reported: 'Grace and several members of his team were much annoyed and disagreeable insinuations were freely made . . . It was apparent that the Englishmen considered the Australians responsible in some way for the decision of the umpires, though Blackham had refused to hold any communication with them, and left them the entire responsibility.' As the paper pointed out, the poor quality of the umpires was solely due to Grace's rejection of Flynn. 'In this the members of his own team admitted that he was entirely wrong.' Having threatened to abandon the match (and with it his chance to retrieve something from the series), Grace 'finally insisted on the umpires examining the pitch every quarter of an hour'.[41] Even so, they refused to be bullied into letting play start until they were satisfied with the conditions.

When they did give the go-ahead, the question was whether England could score the ten runs necessary to bring up the 500. In the event, MacGregor was narrowly run out going for a second to reach the landmark, and they had to settle for 499. This was still their highest Test total, and given the rain-affected wicket, more than enough to ensure an easy victory. Briggs (6 for 49) and Lohmann (3 for 46) destroyed the Australian first innings, and they followed on having cleared only a fifth of the huge deficit. The wicket gradually improved and batting became less difficult, but the Australians were still attempting the impossible. Only rain could have saved them, and it was not forthcoming. Briggs took 6 for 87 to bring his match total to twelve, and Attewell managed 3 for 69 as Australia's resistance ended on the fourth day with their score on 169. England had won by an innings and 230 runs.

Grace was delighted to have won, but he must also have been aware that he had lost something as well – the affection and respect of a large section of the Australian public. While he was on the field he was constantly barracked, while a chorus, made up mainly of boys, greeted his every move with rounds of mock applause. Tom Horan observed in his Felix column, 'Grace seems to have fallen under the ban of the crowd which in November last on the same oval were ready to bow down and worship him as a sort of cricket god.'[42] Amid the hostile cacophony of the popular press, Horan remained the steady voice of reason and fairness. He offered his final judgement of Grace more in sorrow than in anger. He had greeted the great man with just as much enthusiasm and warmth of feeling as the majority of his compatriots, but at the end of the tour he had to admit his feelings had changed:

Grace is . . . a bad loser, and when he lost two of the test matches in succession he lost his temper too, and kept on losing it right to the finish. Blackham stated that Grace behaved like a thorough sportsman during the second combined match, and the great wicketkeeper's remarks served to successfully combat adverse comment passed upon Grace in connection with that contest. But since that match Grace seems to have developed a condition of captiousness, fussiness, and nastiness strongly to be deprecated. His objection to Flynn was nothing short of a gratuitous insult to a first-class umpire, and I regret to be obliged to say this, for I have always endeavoured in my comments to show that Grace was not as bad as he was painted . . . [but] the great cricketer has only himself to blame for any strictures passed upon his conduct by those who were inclined to view him in the best light.[43]

And so, after its brilliantly promising start, Grace's second tour followed the same sad trajectory as his first. At forty-three he had behaved just as he had at twenty-five, and rather than learning from his mistakes, he simply repeated them, seemingly confident there was nothing to regret and nothing to apologize for. As he sailed away from Adelaide with his family and the rest of his team on the SS *Valetta*, Australians with a love of English poetry might have found themselves murmuring Robert Browning's words:

> [L]et him never come back to us!
> There would be doubt, hesitation and pain,
> Forced praise on our part – the glimmer of twilight,
> Never glad confident morning again!

17 W.G. not only scored more runs than anybody else, he travelled more miles than any other cricketer and probably consulted Bradshaw as often as Wisden.

18 A highly marketable figure.
19 A wholesome role-model in the year of Oscar Wilde's disgrace, 1895.

20A W.G. senior

20B W.G. junior

20C E.M.: the Coroner

20D Arthur Shrewsbury

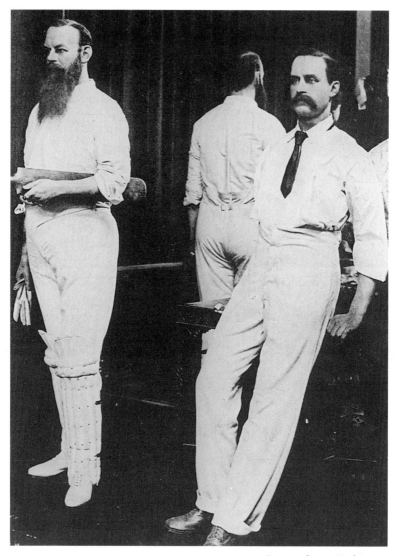

21 Immortality at Madame Tussaud's with another victorious England captain, A. E. Stoddart.

22 Keepsake from a memorable occasion. W.G. had medallions struck for those who played in his Jubilee Gentleman v Players match, July 1898.

26 Rare action photographs of W.G. playing in a minor match at Witney, Oxfordshire,
September 1903.

27 Billy Murdoch, C. B. Fry, W.G. and L. O. S. Poidevin at the Crystal Palace, 1902.

28 W. G. Grace throwing himself into the spirt of Ranji's extravagant summer at
Shillinglee Park, May 1908.

29 Eminent Victorian.

30 The removal of a national symbol from the Long Room at Lord's, September 1939, signifying the inevitability of war.

TWENTY-SIX

THERE is little likelihood that Grace was familiar with 'The Lost Leader'. Reading was an activity he distrusted, and as his library of predominantly pristine volumes testified, he kept it to an absolute minimum. He once said to a younger player who was given to sitting quietly in the dressing room reading Greek tragedies, 'How can you make runs when you are always reading? I am never caught that way.'[1] Even if he had known Browning's poem, he would have failed to see how it applied to him.

From what little he wrote about it, it seems he regarded the Australian tour as a success, but not one he cared to dwell on. In contrast to the lively chapter devoted to his first Australian expedition, the 1891–2 tour is given just two pages in *Reminiscences*. He comments on Australia's improved communications – 'Railway extensions enabled us to dispense with the tedious coach drives through the bush and the uncomfortable coasting voyages which had been the bugbears of our tour in the seventies'[2] – but fails to say much about the cricket. More revealing is the article he wrote for the *Cricket Field* on his return. There, in addition to exhuming the Briscoe affair, he does go into detail in an attempt to explain the loss of the first two Tests. Dismissing as 'sheer nonsense' the excuse that the tourists were troubled by the 'dazzling light', he attributes the defeats in part to losing the toss, but much more to basic cricketing errors:

In the first match our batting failed in the second innings. One or two had bad luck, but, after the first wicket fell for 60 runs, most of the eleven failed on a fair wicket when they ought to have made the necessary 213 to win. We did not get them, and we had only ourselves to blame. The second match was lost by missing catches . . . Had three-fourths of the catches offered been accepted, there would not have been more than twenty runs left for us to make in our second innings, and the match would have been over before the rain came.

As to the criticisms of his tactics at the end of the fourth day, he remained unrepentant: 'There was an hour left for play on an indifferent wicket, with little hope of a better one next day, and I acted as I would certainly act again under similar circumstances.' This is a fair and sensible analysis. Grace certainly hated losing, and all too often his behaviour reflected his frustration, but he never tried to shirk the responsibility. And once the initial disappointment had passed, he was generous in defeat:

A great fuss was made over the loss of the two test matches, and opinions were gravely expressed by some to the effect that the tour was a failure on account of it. Perhaps they will be surprised when I say that it was the best thing that could have happened for the game in Australia, and that it served the purpose Lord Sheffield had in view, viz, the revival of the game there. He did not go out to show how immensely superior English form was to Australian, but to give an impetus to the game, which according to all accounts, was very badly wanted . . . Had we won all three of the test matches, or even two of them, I believe the rising generation and the enthusiasts would have lost heart and the game out there received a blow that would have taken years to recover from. Instead of that, interest was quickened considerably, and before we left there was nothing talked about but making sure of a thoroughly representative team to come to England in 1893.[3]

The fact that his lordship was left out of pocket – to the tune of some £2,700 – was a disappointment, but as Grace remarked, 'Lord Sheffield had no desire for pecuniary benefit'.[4] Assuming this to be true – and Lord Sheffield was a very wealthy man – the real losers were the professionals, who were to have shared any profits there might have been.

Quite apart from his own 'pecuniary benefit', which went a good way towards ensuring him financial independence for the rest of his life, the tour could certainly be judged a conspicuous success for Grace as a player. He had topped the batting averages for both first-class and odds matches, and came a close second in aggregate to Stoddart who played one more match. He scored 921 runs in all, 448 at 44.80 in first-class matches, and 164 in the Tests. As *Wisden* commented: 'When we remember that he was in his forty-fourth year, and that his position as the finest batsman in the world had been established at a time when all the other members of the team were children, this feat must be pronounced nothing less than astonishing.'[5]

His captaincy and rows with or about umpires aside, he came home with his reputation greatly enhanced, and returning to the English press must have been like slipping into a warm bath after a regime of very cold showers. 'We begin to wonder what manner of man is this,' enthused one correspondent who attached himself to the party even before the boat docked at Plymouth. Grace politely declined to be interviewed, guessing perhaps that nothing he said could embellish the glowing coverage he would receive: 'He looked the picture of health, his bronzed features plainly showing the pleasure he felt at finding himself at home again. He was accompanied by Mrs Grace, whose kindness and tact throughout the tour have made her, if that is possible, even more popular among the members of the team than the Champion himself.'[6]

*

Ten days after they had taken leave of each other at Plymouth, the whole team reassembled at Trent Bridge on 16 May to play a benefit match for Alfred Shaw against the Rest of England. They were bowled out for 89 (Grace 2) which set heads nodding, but recovered in the second innings. Grace made 63 and the match, which was shortened by rain, was drawn.

The 1892 season was not a great one for Grace, though there was a marked improvement on the previous year, and 'it was thought that his Colonial experiences had increased his aggressiveness in comparison with the unusually tame cricket he had shown in 1891'.[7] Once again he was troubled by his bad knee, which had made a welcome recovery on the long voyage to Australia and gave him few problems once there, yet he soldiered on, often playing when he clearly should not have done.

One reason for this was the disastrous form shown by the county side. After a handsome win over Kent in their first match at Bristol, they failed to win another game, and with six defeats plummeted down the championship table. This was particularly disappointing in view of the high hopes invested in John Ferris. The great Australian bowler had had a stunning tour of South Africa during the winter. In the only Test match he took thirteen wickets, and over the whole tour he took 235 wickets at the astonishing average of 5.9. But 'for some inexplicable reason' he was a failure in the championship. Grace commented sadly, '[H]is collapse seemed to discourage the other bowlers, and the team, weak in this department, spent many a long day in the field.'[8]

Despite the depressing results, W.G.'s sheer keenness for the game remained as sharp as ever. The match against Nottinghamshire at Cheltenham, in which Richard Daft made a comeback (as an amateur), provided a characteristic vignette. Rain fell during the interval on the second day, and although Daft appeared after lunch ready to resume, there was no sign of the professionals. Grace marched over to their tent and threatened to report them to Lord's if they didn't get out onto the field. Barnes replied they would turn out when the rain stopped. Grace retorted that it was not raining. Barnes then enquired why he was standing under an umbrella.[9]

There were four Gentlemen v. Players matches, and Grace missed two of them. His knee forced him out of the Oval game, and he didn't go up to Scarborough. He captained the side at Lord's, and on losing the toss was given a painful reminder of the class he had missed in Australia. Shrewsbury scored 98 and Gunn 103 (though Grace should have had him stumped on 4). The Players made 454. Grace and Stoddart scored eighty-eight runs together, but then rain intervened, transforming the perfect batting wicket into a much more helpful surface for the bowlers, and the Gentlemen were bowled out twice without making the Players bat again.

It was the professionals who had to follow on in the match at Hastings in September. Grace added a 54 to his 41 at Lord's, but the Gentlemen made only a modest 211. Terrific fast bowling by Sammy Woods (8 for 46) reduced the Players to 109 all out and seemed to give the amateurs a chance of a rare win. However, they found the Players in more determined mood in their second innings. Abel scored a 'faultless' century and Lohmann, Peel and Attewell all made fifties. Grace pulled up limping after only three overs, leaving Woods and Stoddart to do the bulk of the bowling. In contrast to his triumph in the first innings, Woods took 3 for 201 in sixty-five overs. In the end the Gentlemen were hard pushed to make a draw of it. In his last innings of the season, Grace scored 5 (c. Abel b. Attewell).

He had played in a total of twenty-one matches and made 1,055 runs at 31.02, but it was another of the rare years in which Grace failed to add to his tally of centuries, although he came as close as possible in the county match against Sussex at Gloucester. Though unaware of his score, he became becalmed for a while before skying a caught and bowled chance to George Bean. When he discovered he had made 99 he rounded on E.M. for not alerting him to the situation: 'I could have scored off any of those balls.' 'And if I had told you,' E.M. replied, 'you would have been the first to complain.'[10] The bulk of his runs came in the county championship (802 at 36.45), so Gloucestershire's ills could not be laid at his door as a player. It was, however, inevitable that the county's repeated failures should generate a groundswell of discontent in the committee.

W.G. was absent from the meeting in October, at which he was voted the usual thirty-six pounds to pay for his locum. As a reflection of the club's far from healthy financial situation, it was resolved not to supply free lunch interval drinks at home matches, and that it was still 'premature' to offer Woof a benefit. If there was discussion about the state of the club and the way W.G. was running the side, it was not recorded. The topic certainly did arise at the next meeting in December, at which Grace was present, but E.M. at his most economic simply wrote in the minutes book:

Re selection of Players

E. Lawrence spoke
A. Robinson "
J. W. Arrowsmith "
H. Grace "
E. G. Clarke "
W. G. Grace "

But no resolution was put to the meeting.

Those laconic dittos conceal a heated debate. The issue was simple: the committee was not satisfied with Grace's selection policy. He seemed unduly biased in favour of public school and university cricketers, while less privileged but no less promising candidates were ignored. To counter the captain's prejudices, they wanted a selection committee. Grace would have nothing to do with it. The committee had little option but to back down, assuring him that they 'did not wish to take any action distasteful or antagonistic to him', and that they continued to have the same confidence in his captaincy as they had always had. They may have thought that that would be the end of the matter. It wasn't. Grace brooded over it during Christmas, and when the committee next met, on 26 January 1893, they faced a crisis. He had resigned, both from the committee and as captain. Having dropped this bomb-shell, Grace left them to stew. As he must have suspected, they could see only one course of action, abject surrender, and the minutes record an agreement to request him 'in the interest of the County XI & of Cricket generally to reconsider his determination and withdraw his resignation'.

He did not withdraw his resignation, but he did carry on as captain, leading the county in fourteen of their sixteen matches in 1893. At some stage someone, possibly E.M., pointed out the anomaly and persuaded Grace to write a letter to formalize the situation. However, there was another twist to the story. Perhaps in writing to withdraw his resignation he was reminded of how angry he had been when he had offered it in the first place, and he became angry all over again. Or perhaps some new grievance arose. Either way, no sooner had he written to rescind his first resignation than he resigned a second time. That is the only explanation for the extraordinary minutes of the committee meeting of Tuesday, 5 September of 1893. The first item is 'W. G. Grace's letter withdrawing resignation read', and yet, further on, E.M. recorded 'That this Committee receives with much regret the letter from Dr W. G. Grace of August 20th resigning the Captaincy of the Club and while declining to accept the same, decide to adjourn the meeting to a date at which it would be convenient for Dr Grace to attend.' Obviously emboldened by the suspicion that Grace was crying wolf, they went on to resolve 'That in the meantime all endeavours be made to ascertain whether if it was the general wish of the Committee Dr Grace would be prepared to concur in the appointment of a Selection Committee as a means of preventing in future the recurrence of such observations as are referred to in the Doctor's letter.' The gentle hint that offensive 'observations' would cease if he gave way was wasted on Grace. At the next committee meeting, on 31 October, they had another letter to consider. Its content and tone can't have come as a surprise:

After due consideration as it is the wish of the Committee I will withdraw my letter of resignation. I do this simply for the sake of our County Cricket.

With regard to the Selection Committee I will have nothing to do with it, I do not think it will help us to win matches, or that it would work at all satisfactorily. What is more, most if not all of the playing members of the Club are of my opinion.

To what extent Grace really was in tune with his players was debatable. After it had 'come to the knowledge of the Committee that certain of the Professionals had made complaints', four of them were called to the October meeting to say what was troubling them. Murch, Board and Roberts aired grievances, though as usual E.M.'s note-taking was minimalist. They are recorded simply as being 'not quite satisfied'. A fourth, Painter, was 'quite satisfied'. He was obviously more astute than his colleagues (though he probably had more to complain of; Grace underbowled him scandalously). 'After consultation' the three malcontents 'were told by the Chairman that no Guarantee could be given them that they should play in all matches next Year'. As the chairman, H. W.

Beloe, had been on the point of resigning himself, only withdrawing his resignation at the same meeting, it is fair to conclude that the club was not a happy one in 1893.

*

Serious though Gloucestershire's internal problems were, they paled into insignificance compared with those of the eighth Australian touring party which had arrived in May hoping to build on the triumphs of 1891–2. Although captained by the experienced Blackham, the tour turned into an utter shambles, with players of different state sides forming factions and continuing virulent domestic rivalries. Once, when the team had travelled by train to Brighton, the porters found their carriage spattered with blood.[11] Private quarrels erupted into public rows, drunkenness was rampant, and a thoroughly unpleasant trip was rounded off with threats of violence accompanying allegations that the profits were being inequitably shared out. This acrimonious spirit affected relations with their hosts. In the view of Victor Cohen, the unhappy manager, the tourists' behaviour was 'so bad ... that the next team will not be welcomed at all. Another team should not visit England for years to come.'[12] They certainly didn't endear themselves to the English authorities by taking a leaf out of Grace's book and complaining bitterly about umpires. But their demand to be allowed to choose one of the officials selected for each Test was granted, albeit reluctantly.

As in previous years, the Australians saw a great deal of W.G. He led Lord Sheffield's XI to victory over them in May, scoring 63 and 18, but when they came down to Bristol a week later they inflicted an utter humiliation on the county side. The Australians made 503, of which Giffen scored 180, and then to confirm his position as the world's best all-rounder he took seven wickets for eleven runs as Gloucestershire were brushed aside for 41. (Grace, who had dropped himself down the order, was stranded on 4 not out.) Rain caused the match to be abandoned as a draw, but the Australians had given notice that however much at odds they were among themselves, they were still a force to be reckoned with.

Certainly their batting strength was greater than that of any previous Australian side. In the match against the MCC immediately after the game at Bristol, Lyons put on a magnificent display of controlled aggression, scoring a century in an hour and going on to a barnstorming 149 in ninety minutes to save the game. This was one of the occasions when Grace's captaincy came in for criticism, *Wisden* finding it strange that the score reached 215 before J. T. Hearne was put on at the Pavilion end after his success in the first innings. When he was given a chance he took six wickets. Throughout the season, the Australians were capable of amassing big scores. Against an admittedly weak Combined Universities side, they set a new record for a first-class innings with a mammoth total of 843.

Ironically, given their superiority in the bowling department throughout the 1880s, they now found their attack wanting. Ferris's decision to play for Gloucestershire deprived Turner of his accustomed partner, and although he could still be a most dangerous bowler, he was no longer the Terror of old. He also missed several matches through illness. Giffen and his fellow off-spinner Hugh Trumble were lethal on any wicket that helped them, but 1893 was predominantly dry and proved to be a batsman's summer. (Though it could be cold: Arthur Coningham, the left-arm fast bowler who had stepped into Ferris's boots, lit a fire in the outfield at Lord's.)[13]

After the long drought caused by Grace's demoralization of an earlier generation of fast bowlers, England had entered a period of plenty in the pace department. Though Lohmann was just beginning his desperate battle with tuberculosis and had left England for the healthier climate of South Africa on Christmas Eve 1892, Surrey alone could supply two replacements of Test potential and undeniable speed in Bill Lockwood and Tom Richardson. As Giffen remarked wryly, 'We missed a fast bowler badly . . . but their fast bowlers did not always miss us.' Richardson was 'positively dangerous . . . on a broken pitch'.[14]

Grace met the tourists three more times before the Test series got under way, and showed excellent form on each occasion. After scoring 128 – his first century in England since 1890 – for the MCC against Kent in the second week of June, he made 75 and 45 in the club's return against the Australians, which resulted in a convincing win by seven wickets. In the next match at the Oval he helped the South of England inflict another defeat on them, this time by an innings. His 66 saw him pass the almost unimaginable milestone of 40,000 runs in first-class cricket. His next innings, against Nottinghamshire at Bristol, produced his only duck of the season, but he was quickly back into his stride with an aggressive 49 for Arthur Shrewsbury's XI against the Australians at Trent Bridge. Shrewsbury's team made 416 and won by an innings and 159 runs. With scores of 57, 68 and 32 in the two Gentlemen v. Players games, Grace could look forward to the first Test at Lord's in July with some confidence.

In the event he didn't play, having split a finger in Gloucestershire's match against Lancashire at Bristol. It was the first time he had to miss a home Test. Stoddart took over the captaincy, and England had the better of a match curtailed by rain on the third day. F. S. Jackson and Bill Lockwood both made brilliant debuts. Jackson's 91 was made with the ease and fluency which became the hallmark of the Golden Age, while Shrewsbury produced a superbly professional century on a difficult wicket, becoming the first man to reach 1,000 Test runs. In Australia's only innings Lockwood bowled forty-five overs and took 6 for 101. A second-wicket stand of 152 between Shrewsbury (81) and Gunn (77) allowed Stoddart the luxury of the first declaration in Test cricket, but the weather prevented any possibility of a result.

Grace rejoined the team for the Oval match in August, and wasted no time in reasserting his right to a Test place despite having just celebrated his forty-fifth birthday. On winning the toss he opened with Stoddart and they put on 151 together, Grace making 68, Stoddart 83. Although the Australians got both men out on the same score, there was to be no relief as, with the exception of Gunn (16), each of the top seven England batsmen passed fifty. The centrepiece of the innings was Jackson's 103. Coming in late on the first day, he took advantage of a tiring attack to reach 49 at the close. The England score was 378 for 5. The following morning Jackson continued to pile on the runs, though when he found himself on 98 with the number eleven, Arthur Mold, as his partner, he decided that desperate measures were called for and became the first player in England to bring up his century with a hit over the ropes. In fact, the ball struck the roof of one of the stands and bounced over it, but he still only got four. It had been a sensible risk to take. Mold ran him out straight afterwards.

England's 483 gave the Australians no chance of winning the match, and Lockwood and Briggs soon drastically reduced the likelihood of their saving it by bowling them out for 91. Lockwood took 4 for 37 and Briggs 5 for 35. Their share of the wickets was exactly the same in the second innings, but their analyses were rather different. The Australians dug deep and produced a rearguard action to compare with their great fightback on the same ground in 1880. Bannerman must have stirred painful memories when he settled down to bat out the last day, and during the course of his innings he joined Shrewsbury with 1,000 Test runs. Much to England's relief, he didn't go far past that great landmark, falling to a catch by Walter Read off Lockwood for 55. Almost all the other batsmen offered stout resistance, Harry Trott leading the way with 92, and even when all hope was gone they went down with guns blazing. Lyons ended his innings of 31 with five consecutive fours – the last two, towering drives into the pavilion – before Grace gratefully clasped a catch off Lockwood. Briggs finally ended resistance when he bowled Turner for a duck with the Australian score standing at 349. England were winners by an innings and forty-three runs, but they had been made to work for it.

One up with one to play, Grace went to Old Trafford the following week knowing that a draw would be enough to regain the Ashes, though he doubtless had every confidence that his side would win, even though he was missing two key players from the Oval. For the second time Lord Hawke, who had made disparaging remarks about the value of representative matches against Australia, withheld his Yorkshire players, so Grace was without Jackson and Peel. Lockwood was also out with a strained side. His place was more than adequately filled by Tom Richardson, who took ten wickets on debut, but their Surrey colleague, William 'Band-box' Brockwell, was no substitute for Jackson.

In fact the England batting looked decidedly shaky. After Richardson and the ever-dependable Briggs had bowled Australia out for 204, only Grace and Gunn made more than twenty. After losing Stoddart to a run-out for a duck, Grace laid the foundation of the innings with a solid 40, and the following day Gunn gave the Australians a taste of their own stonewalling taking nearly three hours to reach his half century. Thereafter, with wickets falling regularly, he accelerated, and once again the hapless Mold had to shoulder the responsibility of surviving while his senior partner reached three figures. Gunn just made it, his 102 the first Test century made at Old Trafford, and England had a useful lead of thirty-nine runs. When Australia batted again, Bannerman, playing his last Test innings, was once more the anchorman with 60, but the rest of the side was vulnerable against Richardson, and when Blackham joined Turner on 200 for 9 England's chances looked good. However, the last wicket proved elusive, and Turner in particular was batting very well when he dislocated a finger. Yet again at Old Trafford Grace's medical skills were called upon, though his reward was to see Turner go on to 27 and support his captain in a vital stand of thirty-six. When the two were at last separated, England faced a target of just under 200 at more than a run a minute. Although Grace and Stoddart began with a stand of seventy-eight runs in even time, three quick wickets by Trumble sounded the alarm, and W.G. called off the chase. Shrewsbury batted sedately to close of play, thus securing England's fifth consecutive home series win.

Grace had won back the Ashes at the first opportunity, and although he had been overshadowed by younger men, he had still made valuable contributions with the bat, ending with the very acceptable average of 51 for his three Test innings. Indeed, as the Australians set sail for America for the final leg of their ill-fated tour (they were well beaten by Philadelphia), Grace could look back on a thoroughly successful season. He made 1,609 runs in all at an average of 35.75, added another century to his collection, and with his 40,000 runs set a landmark that no other batsman would approach until well into the next century. The one cloud was Gloucestershire's dire record. They had lost eleven matches and dropped to last place in the championship table. He could only hope things would get better in 1894.

*

In fact, they got worse. The county lost thirteen matches, and *Lillywhite's Annual* commented gloomily: 'Of Gloucestershire's cricket little can be written that has not been written of late years. The brothers Grace are not getting younger, and although W.G.'s batting showed little if any falling off, as an all-round cricketer he did not stand out so prominently . . . In batting as well as in bowling the figures were decidedly poor . . . Nor did the bowlers as a rule get the support they might have expected from the field.' There was, however, 'one hopeful sign' – 'the introduction of Mr G. L. Jessop, a fine hitter, a fair bowler, and a smart field. He bids fair to be of great use.'[15]

This cautious prediction turned out to be an understatement. The club had attracted a future star to its ranks. In fact, it gained two young cricketers both of whom would prove exceptional. The previous year Frank Townsend had retired after long and loyal service. The committee voted him 'the gift of one hundred Guineas as a slight acknowledgement of those services' and unanimously elected him a life member of the club.[16] In the same season his sixteen-year-old son, Charles, made his debut, though still a schoolboy. While Frank had been a doughty county player with no aspirations to anything better, Charles Townsend was something of a prodigy. He bowled leg-breaks with such excessive turn that even the most experienced batsmen found him baffling. In only his second match, against Somerset, he took a unique hat-trick – all three victims were stumped (by W. H. Brain) – and although his (left-handed) batting would take longer to develop, he was the most exciting young prospect since A. G. Steel.

Grace could point to both Townsend and Jessop as vindications of his very personal selection policy. Townsend came from within the wider family circle of the club (Grace was his godfather), but Jessop was a rank outsider. He was called up at short notice to the trial match between a Universities and Public Schools XI and the Rest of the County towards the end of the 1893 season, and immediately caught Grace's attention by running out W.G. junior. He also scored 53 and took 4 for 39 to ensure a more serious trial in 1894. His debut match was at Old Trafford and Gloucestershire were in their usual dire straits when he went in on a hat-trick to face Mold. He hit his first ball for four, followed by two more, and went on to make the top score of 29 in a total of 99. W.G., sitting in the pavilion (b. Briggs 0), was delighted: 'Well, we've found something this time.'[17]

Grace, very naturally, had high hopes of his own son making up a triumvirate of talented young amateurs. After three years in the Clifton XI, he had fulfilled one of his father's ambitions by getting a place at Cambridge. However, despite making 88 in the Freshmen's match, he showed no sign of breaking into the exclusive ranks of the XI. Grace decided to intervene. If Cambridge wouldn't give his son a proper trial, then he would. In a transparent attempt to influence selection, Grace picked him for his MCC team to play at Fenners at the end of May. The two W.G.s opened the innings together, but Grace's dream of watching his son batting his way to a blue was shattered when he edged one to the university keeper, Druce (yet another W.G.), for a duck. No doubt wishing the ground would open up in front of him, W.G. junior trailed back to the pavilion to spend a wretched four hours watching his father compile a punitive 139. Not one to admit defeat readily, Grace summoned Bertie to London for the return at Lord's a month later. There was still time – just – for a really splendid performance to get him into the side for the Varsity match. Perhaps the pressure of opening had been too much for him at Fenners. Grace put him in at five and opened with Lord Hawke. He was soon out, for 23, and strode back to the pavilion to sit on the balcony with his son, pointing out the various things to watch with each of the bowlers.

Also sitting with his pads on waiting to bat was another man who had found it hard to win acceptance at Cambridge, though Kumar Shri Ranjitsinhji's problem had been the colour of his skin and his unorthodox batting style rather than any question of his ability. After being overlooked in 1892, he had won his blue in 1893, but financial difficulties had compelled him to leave the university. Though Grace

376

would have been interested in seeing this gifted young cricketer bat, his attention was focused on his son. The third wicket fell at last, and with one last word of parental advice buzzing in his ears, W.G. junior set off on the long walk to the middle.

Only to return, a few beard-tugging minutes later, caught W. G. Druce again, again for a duck. If he couldn't ensure that Bertie scored any runs, Grace could certainly give him every opportunity to take some wickets. In a lengthy spell he dismissed six of the Cambridge side, including Druce, caught and bowled. That was something, but Grace had a little more for the Varsity men to consider. The MCC's second innings was an experience none of them would ever forget. Grace himself sent them running to every corner of Lord's as he ruthlessly dismembered their bowling. Not content with a mere century, he carried on tirelessly, apparently bent on a double or even triple hundred. He put on 200 with Ranjitsinhji, who scored a scintillating 94, and then at last had the satisfaction of batting with Bertie, who took full advantage of the exhausted attack to help himself to a fifty and a proud mention in *The History of a Hundred Centuries*: 'my boy, W.G. jun., 54'.[18]

Grace himself made 196, which was his highest ever score at Lord's, and the highest first-class innings of the season. But even after both father and son were back in the pavilion, the slaughter continued. Grace finally called a halt with the score on 595 for 7. Later he regretted not going on to 600. As it was, that was the highest total ever made at Lord's, and the game's final aggregate of 1,332 was also a record for Headquarters. The last stage in the demolition of the Light Blues was executed with ruthless efficiency, Grace himself taking 4 for 33, and, as he put it with rare relish in his account of the game, the university 'were terribly beaten by 374 runs'.[19] A drubbing of that magnitude was hardly the best preparation for the Varsity match, and it is not surprising that when they met Oxford a week later they lost by eight wickets. The following year W.G. junior gained his blue.

Grace continued in fine form, scoring 71 in the Gentlemen's first innings against the Players at the Oval. But this was emphatically Bobby Abel's match. He was leading the Players for the first time and played a true captain's innings, carrying his bat for 168 in a total of 363. The amateurs had a torrid time late on the second day. The light was very bad and Mold worked up a lively pace. Mold had taken over from Crossland as Lancashire's fast bowler, and like his predecessor had a distinctly dubious action. One contemporary remembered Grace saying Mold 'hurt him more than any bowler he ever knew . . . And why? Because he threw.'[20] Grace coped with him better than anybody else on this occasion, but fell to Briggs for 20. The overnight score was 31 for 6, and the match ended early on the third morning, the Players winning by an innings and twenty-seven runs.

The roles were neatly reversed in the return at Lord's on 9 and 10 July. Grace won the toss and on a wicket always likely to get worse decided to force the pace from the outset. He made 56, and with support from Stoddart and Jackson got the hundred on the board in seventy minutes. Batting became increasingly difficult, but with that start the Gentlemen were always ahead of the game. When the Players had to bat they found Sammy Woods and Jackson a difficult proposition in bad light on a lifting pitch, and lost four wickets for forty-nine runs before rain stopped play. Woods and Jackson continued the destruction the following morning, and also bowled all the way through the Players' second innings when they followed on. Woods took six wickets, Jackson twelve, and the Gentlemen won by an innings and thirty-nine runs.

That was the high-water mark of Grace's season. Indeed, from the second week of July he was never on a winning side, and, under the handicap of yet another injury, this time a leg strain, his own form fell away. He did, however, make a typically defiant 49 out of 113 against Lancashire at Bristol and a similarly dogged 41 out of 108 against Yorkshire at Headingley in a match Gloucestershire should have won, given that they reduced the home team to 19 for 9 in their second innings. But they let them off the hook, and then failed narrowly to meet the small target they were set. Grace ploughed on with 61 against Nottinghamshire at Trent Bridge and 52 at Edgbaston against Warwickshire (now, with Leicestershire, Derbyshire and Essex, numbered among the first-class counties, though not yet included in the championship).

However, after these respectable if hardly outstanding performances, his season took a further dive in the home matches in August. He started with a public relations disaster in the August Bank Holiday game against Sussex. There had been some rain overnight, and when a further heavy shower fell, play was abandoned for the day. Gilbert Jessop takes up the story:

In order to provide some entertainment for the holiday crowd, W.G. arranged to play Sussex at Soccer on the practice ground, but on emerging from the Pavilion with his valiant band of warriors attired in hastily improvised accoutrement, he quickly found, from the attitude of the crowd, that such form of amusement was hardly at that moment to their taste. If it was fit enough to play football, it was fit enough for cricket, was their ultimatum, and they voiced their sentiments in no uncertain fashion. They came to see cricket, and if that was not provided, then – return their money.[21]

The gathering in front of the pavilion was fairly good-natured, if determined, until Charles Fry, Sussex's new and brilliant recruit from Oxford, responded provocatively to one particular sally. This enraged the crowd, and as the players tried to leave the ground they were mobbed and heckled. A splinter group set off to vent their wrath on Ted Spry's precious square, though the canny groundsman, sensing trouble, had roped off another strip as a decoy, and the match wicket was left unscathed. Despite the loss of a day's play, Sussex won comfortably by an innings, Grace making 33 and 9 (out of 77).

That was not the only example of the family's imperious ways. In the Somerset match at Bristol earlier in the season, E.M. had batted bravely under the handicap of an infected thumb. Sammy Woods remembered 'matter oozing from under the nail', and made things worse by rapping him on the gloves a couple of times. Even E.M. couldn't help showing he was hurt, and 'someone in the crowd called out "Why don't you hold an inquest on him?" for E.M. was coroner for West Gloucester'. With a curt word to T. H. Hewett, the Somerset captain, E.M. charged into the crowd and chased the offender out of the ground and some way down the road outside, before returning to resume his innings.[22]

This was in fact E.M.'s last season. He obviously decided if he could no longer collar an obstreperous spectator, it was time to call it a day. In his fifty-third year he had been easily the most senior cricketer in first-class cricket, apart from Richard Daft who had been forced out of retirement by the needs of his county. There may have been times during some of Gloucestershire's more spineless performances when his younger brother thought about following suit. But Grace was not one to quit when things got tough, and there was another reason to carry on playing. He was tantalizingly close to yet another astonishing landmark; his 196 at Lord's had been his ninety-seventh century.

At the end of the county's programme he took a break for some partridge shooting with his old friend William Yardley, who may have taken this opportunity to sound out Grace about a new publishing venture, *The History of a Hundred Centuries*, which Yardley was willing to compile and edit. The idea had a certain appeal, but as Grace would have pointed out, he had to score them first. He still had three more matches to play, but in a damp September can't have held out much hope of his getting any nearer the target that year.

He must have wished he had stuck to shooting when he scored 2 for the South against the North in his first game at Hastings, but he had better luck in the Gentlemen–Players match. Gunn, who was captaining the Players, won the toss and made the rash decision to bat on 'a muddy, sticky wicket'.[23] Grace was unusually short of bowling, but was well served by Ferris and Stoddart, who got the professionals out for 85, taking five wickets apiece. The wicket was still difficult when the Gentlemen batted, but Grace, after surviving a ball from Mold that cannoned off his pad onto the stumps without dislodging the bails, proceeded to bat with all his old authority and notched up his ninety-eighth century. The next highest score after his 131 was 40. It wasn't quite enough to win the game. The Players fought back to reach 268 for 8 and set a target of 107 against the clock. For no very obvious reason, Grace held himself, Stoddart and Billy Murdoch back, and the rest of the rather undistinguished batsmen fell thirty runs short, the game ending in a draw with honours even.

Grace played one more game well into September for Gentlemen of the South against the Players of the South at Lord's. He took four wickets, but scored only 6 and 7, a performance that gave no hint of what was to come the following year.

TWENTY-SEVEN

T HE winter of 1894–5 provided the most exciting Test series since Anglo-Australian battles began. There were five matches, and each produced a result. A. E. Stoddart was the England captain, and his team astonished the cricketing world by winning the first Test at Sydney, after following on. Thanks to Stoddart's magnificent 173 (which just beat Grace's record), they also won the second at Melbourne, despite making only 75 in their first innings. But Australia took the third and fourth matches, and so everything rested on the fifth which began on 1 March 1895, back at Melbourne. The Australians rashly left out Turner. (On the same day Oscar Wilde even more rashly applied for a warrant against the Marquess of Queensberry on the grounds of libel.) Grace records that 'news was telegraphed every few minutes, [and] was awaited with extraordinary interest'. Even Queen Victoria was reported to be following events closely. Heroic bowling by Peel and Richardson, with centuries from MacLaren and J. T. Brown of Yorkshire, were the leading contributions to a splendid team effort which saw England win 'a brilliant victory' by six wickets and so take the series and retain the Ashes. 'The jubilation in English cricket circles was unbounded', wrote Grace.[1]

It was the perfect prelude to a domestic season in which public interest in the game reached new heights. Britain was in a febrile state: South African gold produced a huge speculative boom; the country was whipped into moralistic hysteria by the trials of Oscar Wilde; and the Liberal government, led by Lord Rosebery (against whom there were rumours in connection with Wilde and the wider homosexual 'conspiracy'), was in deep trouble. Who better to restore confidence in the robust certainties on which Victorian society was founded than the greatest exponent of 'the manly game', W.G. himself? Stoddart's team had barely recovered from their heroes' reception when Grace swung the spotlight firmly onto the centre-stage, which he was going to occupy for most of the summer.

His first match, beginning on 9 May, was at Lord's for the MCC & Ground against Sussex, now captained by Billy Murdoch. He also renewed his acquaintance with the man whose mercurial rise to sporting fame would rival even his own. After leaving Cambridge, Ranjitsinhji had dropped out of sight, but now claimed to be qualified to play for Sussex. This was his first match for the county. Hornby was captaining the MCC and when he won the toss he sent Grace out to open the innings. Ranji caught him at slip for 13. When Sussex batted, no one was comfortable against J. T. Hearne and Martin (both Test bowlers), except Ranji. He went in at five and carried his bat through the remainder of the innings for 77 not out. It was a sparkling performance, but a mere vignette compared to what was to come. MCC went in again, with a useful lead of seventy-four runs. When he had scored 14, Grace again edged a catch to Ranji at slip. This time he dropped it – not the least of his contributions to this extraordinary match. As he had always done, Grace put the mistake behind him and carried on, scoring with ever-increasing ease, powering the ball to the boundary and placing it between the fielders to take sedately ambled singles, until he reached three figures for the ninety-ninth time in his career. No sooner had he received the congratulations of the fielders than Ranji intervened again. Although not considered much of a bowler, Murdoch gave him the ball, and now, to everyone's amusement, he dismissed the Old Man. Grace returned to the pavilion, tired but happy with his 103. MCC made 330 (Ranji taking 6 for 109), setting Sussex the fanciful target of 405 to win.

After several years in the country, Ranji was now *au fait* with English conventions. He knew that amateur batsmen always played to win, went for their strokes and never said die, so when Hearne and Martin nipped out the first four Sussex batsmen cheaply he was not disconcerted in the least. He simply did what his role demanded, and played his natural game. Ranji's batting was recognizable as a continuation of what had gone before, but only just. It was based on a perfect eye and impeccable timing, grounded in a sure defence, constructed during interminable net sessions at Cambridge, but with a flamboyant emphasis on attack that was almost shocking. In a way he combined the irrepressible aggression of E.M. and the technical correctness of W.G., but beyond that his style was wholly his own creation. Although physically slight, he had the wristy strength of a tennis player (initially his preferred game) and could place his cuts with astonishing accuracy and power; his loose shoulders might have been envied by any golfer, giving his driving a ferocity that left fielders motionless as the ball skimmed past them or soared effortlessly over their heads to the boundary.

But there was an extra dimension to his play – footwork. Grace decreed that sound batting was based around the stable pivot of a firm back leg. 'Shift your left foot in hitting as much as you like, but be cautious of moving your right', he told his readers in the *Boy's Own Paper*.[2] This was certainly appropriate for Grace, especially as he put on weight, and was undoubtedly sound advice for the vast majority of English batsmen, men or boys. But Ranji refused to be chained to the crease. This surrendered too much initiative to the bowler. He utterly rejected the notion of a 'good length ball', dancing down the wicket to meet slow bowling on the half-volley. And when the harassed bowler dropped short in self-defence, Ranji would dart back and flick him away behind the stumps. It was perhaps his range of options on the legside that most alarmed his contemporaries. Grace had developed the firm push through mid-wicket and wide mid-on, and cracked anything short away through square-leg. But Ranji invented something new – the leg glance. Anything remotely near his leg-stump was exasperatingly deflected away to fine leg. After all the refinement bowling had undergone in response to Grace's initial batting revolution, here was a new batsman to whom it was impossible to bowl.

Surprisingly, he had never scored a first-class century. Now he did, and he continued to lacerate the MCC bowling until he reached 150, at which point Grace took a turn himself. The first ball looped up, high and easy, and any thoughts Ranji may have entertained of treating it with respect evaporated. But in deciding which of the many beckoning spaces to hit it to, he missed it altogether and was bowled. This completed a symmetry which gave both men enormous satisfaction and provided the material for much good-natured banter. Grace always recognized talent in others, and he knew what he had witnessed as not mere talent, but genius. He and Ranji would have got on anyway, but the bedrock of their friendship was a deep mutual respect for each other's astonishing abilities.

With Ranji's departure the game should have been over, but his example lit a flame in the Sussex lower order, and with the number ten scoring 47 and number eleven 64 not out, they came within twenty runs of winning the match. In the four innings 1,227 runs had been scored, with centuries by the two greatest batsmen of the period. The match was a perfect showpiece for the most dazzling decade in English cricket.

Ranji's performance was of course recognized for what it was by all who saw it. 'Anything finer than his hitting has never been seen at Lord's' was one representative assessment.[3] But by getting his ninety-ninth century, Grace stole most of the headlines, and the public flocked to Lord's for his next match, MCC v. Yorkshire, to see if it would bring the hundredth – though even at the time there were querulous letters in the press questioning whether it really would be his hundredth genuinely first-class century (see Appendix, page 497). But the crowds were disappointed. Grace scored 18 and 25, and the club went down to a heavy defeat by nine wickets.

Attention shifted to Bristol, where Gloucestershire opened their championship campaign against Somerset. Although dry, May was very cold that year, and the exposed acres of Ashley Down were hardly welcoming. Grace spent most of the first day in the field as Somerset batted through to stumps, scoring 303. It looked as though they would make a great deal more, as Gerald Fowler and Lionel Palairet (another golden boy of the Golden Age) put on 200 for the first wicket, but Grace gave himself a long spell of forty-five overs and took 5 for 87. The Gloucestershire innings started late that afternoon. Sammy Woods was convinced he had the Old Man 'plumb Leg Before when he'd made only three or four',[4] but must have known he was wasting his breath appealing. After that Grace played with great authority to reach 38 by close of play.

The following day, 17 May, was even colder than the first. A biting wind blew across the ground, and at one point there was even a flurry of snow. But that didn't trouble Grace. He had an infallible antidote: scoring runs – at the brisk rate of fifty an hour. The other not out batsman overnight was Charles Townsend. He stayed with his godfather, batting as well as he had ever done, and was privileged to still be at the wicket when the stupendous milestone appeared in view. It was then that Grace faltered. Townsend said: 'This was the one and only time I ever saw him flustered, namely when the last runs were needed for his hundredth hundred. Poor Sam Woods could hardly bowl the ball and the Doctor was nearly as bad.'[5] By this time the crowd had been swelled by late-comers who thronged to the ground as the news spread around Bristol. An atmosphere of intense anticipation grew until at last Grace latched onto an innocuous full toss lobbed down by Woods and drove it triumphantly for four to end the agony. The crowd erupted, the fielders applauded, Woods ran down the wicket to be the first to congratulate him, and E.M. sitting in the pavilion said he would have given anything to be out there for the historic moment. All three brothers were in fact present, Alfred and Henry along with E.M.; also Uncle Pocock, who had reason to be proudest of them all. Grace's reception at lunch was predictably warm, and when Beloe proposed his health, he replied with characteristic brevity: 'I sincerely thank you. I hope you will excuse me from saying more, as I have a long afternoon before me.'[6]

That put paid to any notion that he might be prepared to rest on his laurels. Somerset returned to the field knowing they had an uphill climb. Grace continued in absolutely top form, impregnable in defence, lethal in attack, and the runs kept coming at a terrific rate (the Somerset wicket-keeper would say afterwards that Grace only let five balls through to him in the entire innings). It soon became clear that his next target was 200, and the only question was whether he would get there before Townsend made his century. He did, and with the Gloucestershire total on 340, play stopped once more as the cheers and applause rang round the ground. E.M. sent out a magnum of champagne, and everyone drank the Old Man's health again.

Then battle recommenced. The first casualty was Townsend, given out lbw five short of his maiden century. Perhaps the umpire had been emboldened by the champagne, or piqued because he hadn't been offered any. It was a brave decision under the circumstances. Reflecting on the stand with his godson, Grace wrote, 'I suppose I ought to feel very much older than I do when I come to consider the number of times that his father and I have been associated in similar long partnerships for Gloucestershire.'[7] Continuing to show the appetite for runs that had set him apart as a young man, Grace pressed on, but apart from Painter (34), he got precious little support from the Gloucestershire lower order. He was eventually ninth out, caught off Woods for 288 out of 463 in five and a half hours. It was a superlative effort, reminiscent of his heyday twenty years earlier. In fact, it was his highest score since his 318 against Yorkshire in 1876. And just as his fiftieth century had offered a yardstick by which to judge his dominance in the opening phase of his career, so his hundredth century confirmed his continuing superiority. The next bats-man in the league of centurians was Arthur Shrewsbury with forty-one.[8]

The match ended the next day, Saturday, with Gloucestershire comfortable winners by nine wickets, and Grace shot off to catch the train to London, bound for the victory banquet in Stoddart's honour at Hampstead Cricket Club. He was late, arriving at about 8.45 p.m., after the meal had started, but as he made his way into the room the dinner guests to a man rose to cheer him, a standing ovation that lasted a good few minutes. It was typical, Stoddart may have reflected wryly, that the champion should upstage him even at the celebration for an Ashes triumph in which he had played no part at all.

England's two cricket captains travelled up to Cambridge together on the Monday to play for A. J. Webbe's XI at Fenners. Once again, the university experienced Grace in full flow as he and Stoddart put on a hundred in under an hour. But he let them off lightly in comparison with the previous season, giving a catch when he had made 52. W.G. junior was still not in the team, but Grace had a quiet word with the new captain, W. G. Druce, and extracted a promise that he should be given a try.

After the undergraduates had been put in their place – W.G. took six wickets in their two innings – it was down to Gravesend to rejoin the county team for their match against Kent. Kent had been the other main victims of his phenomenal run in August in 1876, though of course none of the side that turned up at the Bat and Ball ground on 23 May had been playing nineteen years before. (Lord Harris had retired in 1890.) They were probably rather excited to be meeting the Old Man so soon after his record, but can have had no presentiment of history repeating itself – especially after they ran up the huge total of 470 in their first innings, of which Alec Hearne made 155.

Grace bowled forty-three overs and took 2 for 115, but showed no signs of fatigue when he batted on the second day. His extraordinary form continued, and apart from a couple of chances, he sailed effortlessly to his century, and then, by close of play, to his second double hundred in eight days. But Gloucestershire were still 115 behind with only three wickets standing, not a promising situation. Indeed, as Grace rather archly wrote afterwards, 'On the morning of the last day the papers said that Kent had every chance of winning the match and no chance of losing. Of course we have all been taught from youth upwards that anything in the paper must be true.'[9] Resuming on 210, his first objective was to make Kent's task as difficult as possible, and he gave his lower-order batsmen strict instructions to put safety first. Under his watchful eye, they carried out his orders to the letter. He too was cautious, adding only forty-seven runs to his personal total in the two and a quarter hours of the morning session. The last three wickets managed to reduce the Kent lead to twenty-seven before Grace himself was last man out, caught in the deep off the only lofted shot in his innings. He had batted seven and three-quarter hours, made 257 out of 443, and saved the game. He was ready for his lunch.

There doesn't seem to be a rational explanation for what happened in the afternoon. The match was dead. All Kent had to do was amuse themselves for a while at the expense of the Gloucestershire bowling, and then they could all go home. Grace can't have seen it any differently. The first two innings had produced over 900 runs, and although the wicket was wearing and showed a few cracks, a fourth day seemed to be required to produce a result. Perhaps that's why he relented for once and threw the ball to the underbowled but uncomplaining Painter. Painter didn't need to be asked twice, and promptly bowled Kent out for 76. This left Gloucestershire with 104 to win in an hour and a quarter. It was more than enough time. After losing his opening partner, Grace was joined by Painter, who was a hard-hitting batsman in his own right (not that he needed to do much more than give his captain the strike). Grace was in the form of his life, placing the ball at will and cracking anything short or overpitched to the boundary. He reached his fifty in forty-seven minutes, and the score at six o'clock was 73. He then 'repeatedly opened his shoulders',[10] and by 6.15, barely an hour after the innings started, the runs were hit off. Grace had made 73, with eleven fours, two threes and five twos. He had been on the field for every ball of the match, and in recognition of a feat extraordinary even by his standards, the Kent crowd cheered him to the echo. For Grace, though, it was all in a day's work, and Hubert Preston, the future editor of *Wisden*, remembered him '[trotting] from the dressing tent in his tweed tail suit and hard felt hat, carrying his heavy cricket bag to a four-wheeler cab which took him to the station', accompanied by a mob of irrepressible schoolboys.[11] The news travelled fast, and there was a similarly enthusiastic reception committee waiting for him when he got back to Temple Meads in Bristol that evening.

By a coincidence likely to lift the spirits of every right-thinking paterfamilias up and down the country, the following morning's papers also carried reports of the last day of the second and final Oscar Wilde trial. While W.G. was vigorously promoting the robust virtues of healthy physical exercise, Mr Justice Wills was telling the disgraced playwright that he had 'been the centre of a circle of extensive corruption of the most hideous kind among young men', and expressing his regret that the severest sentence he could pass was two years' hard labour.[12]

As Wilde was led away to be broken on the treadmill, Grace set himself to scale yet another cricketing peak: 1,000 runs in May. By the end of the Kent match he had scored 829 runs. He had two more games – potentially four innings – in which to score the remaining 171; not too much to ask of a man averaging 118. The first match was a revival of the old fixture, England v. Surrey, which was played for the benefit of Walter Read. The omens were good. Grace had scored his first first-class century (224) in the same match twenty-nine years earlier, and a huge crowd gathered at the Oval to see him do something similar. Instead they had to settle for a magnificent 163 by Albert Ward, one of Stoddart's heroes. Grace was bowled by Richardson for 18. He was further frustrated when the Leicestershire professional A. D. Pougher tore through the Surrey batting, taking 9 for 34 as they collapsed to 85 all out. They did better when they followed on, but not well enough to make England bat again, so Grace was now left with only the first two days – 30 and 31 May – of the Gloucestershire–Middlesex match in which to score 153 runs.

Although it was a tall order, there was a lot of confidence that he would do it, and yet another large crowd turned up at Lord's to see him try. The first hurdle was the toss, one of the most crucial of his career. He didn't want to spend a day in the field watching Stoddart scoring his runs. He was in luck. Having called correctly, he started his innings cautiously but was soon batting 'beautifully', according to *The Times*: 'There was all the old power in the drive and the cut, while few balls to leg escaped unpunished.'[13] He negotiated the morning session without alarms and went in to lunch on 58. He took a little time after the interval to get back into his stride, and was particularly troubled by the slow leg-breaks of R. A. Nepean, once or twice popping the ball up perilously close to fielders. He also narrowly avoided being run out. But after that he settled down and went imperiously on to his century, which he reached with a single off a deferential long-hop. It had taken him three hours, and his proportion of the total runs scored was down to an uncharacteristic 50 per cent.

Though gaining three figures normally reduces the pressure on a batsman, on this occasion it merely increased it. He still had fifty-three to make, and without showing any sign of nerves or allowing himself to get bogged down, he worked on methodically until he reached 149, when another gentle long-hop saw him home. The 7,000-strong crowd, which had watched his steady progress anxiously, broke into loud and sustained cheering, and the Champion's name rang out around the ground. He was given another tumultuous ovation when he was finally bowled for 169 and made his way back to the pavilion where the members stood to acknowledge his unprecedented achievement.

The Times seemed rather vague as to just how unprecedented it was: 'It must be something of a record even for Dr. Grace to make over a thousand runs in the first month of the season.'[14] Grace himself had no doubt about its value as the pinnacle of his batting career: 'The feat had never been achieved before, and it was naturally a matter of supreme satisfaction to me that I should, in my forty-seventh year, be enabled to surpass all the achievements of my youth.'[15]

What makes Grace's feat even more astonishing is that he didn't make a run until 9 May. His 1,016 in fact took him just twenty-two days. The strict record of a thousand runs *in May* (rather than *before June*) is shared only with his great Gloucestershire successor Wally Hammond, who also needed only twenty-two days in 1927, and Charlie Hallows, who took twenty-seven days in 1928 (getting there on 31 May with the last run of an innings of 232). (Only five other batsmen have scored 1,000 runs in the season before June (in April and May): Tom Hayward, Don Bradman (twice), Bill Edrich, Glenn Turner and Graeme Hick.)

A tidal wave of excited rejoicing washed over the country. As a hastily produced penny pamphlet, 'The Hero of Cricket', emphasized, 'his performances have been followed with pleasure and satisfaction by all classes of the community, from the heir to the throne down to the humblest urchin in the street'.[16] Indeed, one of the first letters Grace received came from Marlborough House, dated 1 June:

The Prince of Wales has watched with much interest the fine scores which you continue to make in the great matches this year. He now learns that you have beat all former records by scoring 1000 runs during the first month of the Cricket season as well as completing more than 100 centuries in first class matches.

His Royal Highness cannot allow an event of such deep interest to all lovers of our great national game to pass unnoticed by him, and he has desired me to offer you his hearty congratulations upon this magnificent performance . . .[17]

The entire nation succumbed to Grace mania and there was a universal clamour for some form of public recognition. In an adroit marketing move, the *Daily Telegraph* leapt onto the bandwagon, announcing its National Shilling Testimonial and inviting what it hoped would be an increased readership to send in their donations. (A list of fresh subscribers was published every morning.) This was sniffed at in some quarters. A. G. Steel remarked that with 'the flood of shillings pouring in, accompanied by such varied correspondence, one could not but feel a little alarm for the dignity of our great game'.[18] Not wishing to be sidelined, the MCC set up their own testimonial fund for those who might find the *Telegraph*'s distasteful, while a committee was formed in Bristol to drum up local donations. In its editorial of 17 June, *The Times* gave its Olympian approval to these fund-raising efforts, but also aired another widely canvassed proposal: 'Many would have been glad to see his name in the Birthday list, since Lord's is at least as national as the Lyceum and since a PRIME MINISTER [Lord Rosebery] who twice wins the Derby might be supposed to have a fellow-feeling for the man who has made the other national sport illustrious.' Rosebery, however, was too embroiled in the disintegration of his government to make this populist gesture, and within a week had given way to Lord Salisbury. The new prime minister, whose luxuriant beard was the only serious rival to W.G.'s in late Victorian England, was less in tune with the nation's obsession with sport, and contented himself with making a personal contribution to the testimonial: 'I beg to enclose a centenary of shillings to use the current phrase. I have not touched a cricket ball for more than fifty years, so I am afraid that I can only claim a *locus standi* as owner of a village cricket ground.'[19]

Grace didn't mind where the shillings came from as long as they kept coming. He certainly stuck to his side of the bargain by keeping the runs flowing. In his next match after the epoch-making game against Middlesex, he just missed another century by nine runs at Hove, and on the day the MCC announced his testimonial he repaid them by scoring 125 for the club against Kent at Lord's. Given the difficult state of the wicket, this was a superlative display. *Lillywhite's Annual* commented, 'Never throughout his career had the champion been seen to better advantage.'[20]

He was back at Headquarters a fortnight later, playing for The Gentlemen of England against I Zingari in their Jubilee match. Although they had never invited him to join, England's most exclusive cricket club was more than happy to have him at their fiftieth birthday celebrations. He obliged with yet another century (101 not out in the second innings to secure a ten-wicket victory), but derived infinitely more pleasure from W.G. junior's 79, which was the highest score in the Gentlemen's first innings of 411. This was a very fair achievement, as I Zingari fielded a strong team, including Jackson, Stoddart (who was elected for the occasion) and A. G. Steel, whose flight was still sufficient to beat W.G. all ends up in his first knock. Bertie's performance in this match cemented his place in the Cambridge XI. When Grace turned out for the MCC against the university at Lord's, his son was at last on the opposite side, and 'shaped extremely well'.[21] They lost, but W.G. senior let them off lightly with 47. Then, on the eve of the Varsity match, he softened up the Oxford attack with a pugnacious 72.

Nothing short of a summons to the Palace would have kept Grace away from Lord's on 4 July. Risking the mockery of his friends – Stoddart for one made a great joke out of affecting not to recognize him – he decked himself out in the full regalia of frock coat and silk top hat and attended the social pinnacle of the English cricket calendar, not as 'the hero of a hundred centuries', but as just another proud and pitifully nervous parent. When Druce won the toss for Cambridge and elected to bat he must have been even more nervous, while the pressure on the younger Grace as he walked out in front of a full house to open the innings doesn't bear thinking about. But he gave W.G. no cause to be ashamed, scoring a solid 40 before falling to C. B. Fry. It was by some way the highest score until a lower-order flourish from the Light Blues' number eight.

Grace's wonderful day was further improved when he bumped into C. E. Green. Generously forgetting the mercenary aftermath to Grace's Leyton visit, Green was once again open-handed in his hospitality, inviting Grace and Agnes to his box for the afternoon session. At the end of the Cambridge innings, Green and his party went down to join the fashionable throng in front of the pavilion. Grace stayed put, out of the public eye. He did not, however, remain alone. When Green returned he could hardly get through the door. 'The explanation for this was that dear old W.G., in the fullness of his heart and the intensity of his happiness, had himself invited most of the members of both the Oxford and Cambridge teams into my box to celebrate the occasion!'[22] Basking at last in the success of his boy, surrounded by the hero-worshipping sons of the country's élite and dispensing large amounts of someone else's champagne to all and sundry, it was probably the most enjoyable moment of Grace's extraordinary summer.

The Varsity match ended, in a satisfactory win for Cambridge, on Saturday, 6 July and W.G. was back at Lord's on Monday, 8 July in his more accustomed role, as a participant in the other great fixture, Gentlemen v. Players. It was a terrific match, and with a wicket cracking up after the drought and a bowler of genuine pace in Tom Richardson (making his debut), it was reminiscent of the previous period that Green and Grace had no doubt talked nostalgically about the week before. Following the Players' first innings total of 231, Grace and Stoddart put on 151 for the first wicket, but when Grace lost his partner for 71 he got virtually no support from anyone else. A combination of Richardson's frightening speed and Peel's mercilessly accurate spin produced a regular procession, but Grace played on sublimely, eventually falling to Peel for 118. As with so many of his triumphs this year, Grace had to look back to 1876 for the last time he scored a century against the Players at Lord's, and of all his great performances of 1895 this was reckoned his finest. Pelham Warner records, 'he gave a masterly exhibition to the younger generation of how to play fast bowling on a fiery wicket, his defence against Mold and Richardson being magnificent'.[23] Despite their slender lead, the Gentlemen lost the initiative when the Players batted again, though it was the bowlers Peel (93 not out), Attewell (71) and Richardson (43) who were responsible for their eventual target of 336. Grace and Stoddart failed to repeat their performance of the first innings, but when Fry rallied the middle order with 60, it looked as though an improbable victory might just be achieved. In the end the might of the professional bowling told, and they went down by thirty-two runs, but the game had proved another high point in this season of peaks.

Another soon followed, though this one meant that Grace entered his forty-eighth year deprived of a record he had held for nineteen years. Two days before Grace's forty-seventh birthday, A. C. MacLaren completed an innings of 424 against Somerset at Taunton, eclipsing Grace's 344 at Canterbury in 1876. There's no evidence that W.G. begrudged him his success, and he was generous in recognition of his talents in *Reminiscences.**

With Grace in the form of his life, there was every probability that he would create a new record by becoming the first batsman to score 3,000 runs in a season, but after the prolonged dry spell the weather changed, and with it the wickets. To suggest that the second half of his season was an anti-climax would be wrong – he continued to produce marvellous things right to the end – but the drama certainly eased as he fell back into the familiar round of county matches.

*

* In stark contrast, when Bill Ponsford made 429 for Victoria against Tasmania in 1923, MacLaren made strenuous attempts to have the match demoted to second-class status. (Kynaston, *Archie's Last Stand*, p. 115.)

1895 was the first year of the expanded championship. With the counties admitted to first-class status in 1894, there were now fourteen teams in the competition, and public interest increased to a pitch of 'feverish excitement'.[24] The competition had not been completely overhauled. Counties were still allowed to determine the number of matches they played, and Gloucestershire played the same eighteen fixtures they had played the year before, the only difference being that the Warwickshire matches now counted in the championship table. Surrey, the eventual champions, played twenty-six matches.

With victories already secured against Somerset, Kent and Middlesex, Gloucestershire went on to beat Nottinghamshire (twice), Warwickshire, Sussex and Yorkshire. Jessop played his first full season with the county, and remembered it as a wonderful time. 'From the position of "wooden spoonist" [Gloucestershire] rose to the honourable position of fourth in the list, and became once again a team whose drawing capacity as regards "gate" was unsurpassed by any other County.'[25] Jessop himself was a major factor in this recovery, but the undoubted star was Charlie Townsend, who took 124 wickets of which ninety-three came in August alone.

After his personal triumph against the Players at Lord's Grace had a quiet July. He missed the return at the Oval (which saw the welcome reappearance of Lohmann after his two-year convalescence in South Africa) and passed the rest of the month without another fifty. He had a particularly miserable match at Bradford when Peel dismissed him twice for 0 and 3. He scored 70 in the county's defeat of Warwickshire at Gloucester at the beginning of August, and then led the side to an unlikely win over Sussex at Bristol.

Rain washed out the first day, and allowed only forty minutes' play on the second, during which Sussex scored 30 for 2. The third day was sunny, but there seemed no chance of a result. Nevertheless, when Sussex were bowled out for 99, Grace changed the batting order and gave instructions to attack. This was a perfect situation for Jessop who hit a rapid 53 out of a total of 159 reached by 3.45. Although Gloucestershire had a lead of sixty runs, there was only an hour and a half to dismiss a batting line-up that included Fry, Ranji, Murdoch and George Bean. There could be no complaints about Grace's captaincy on this occasion. Chivvying his men to race to their positions after each over, he kept the Sussex batsmen under intense pressure as Townsend ran through them, taking 7 for 28 (12 for 87 in the match). They were all out for exactly 60 thirteen minutes from stumps. The scores were tied, but there would, Grace established with the umpires, be just time for one over. Most of the Sussex team had changed, and Ranji had already left, but Murdoch led them out once more, with Grace as substitute. He sent in Ferris and Jessop to get the one run required. Jessop was deputed to face. 'The first ball from Tate came at a perfect length, and nipping back missed the bails by a hair's-breadth. I managed to connect with the next, but not with sufficient force as to become remunerative, and then with the third came a short push towards point, and by the time the Old Man's fingers closed over the ball Johnny [Ferris] had reached sanctuary.'[26] It was a famous victory which spoke volumes for both Grace's leadership and his lifelong commitment to attacking cricket.

W.G.'s forcefulness was seen to less advantage in the Kent match. There had been more rain, and getting to the county ground before the umpires, he decided unilaterally that play should be abandoned for the day. 'On the strength of Grace's word the gates were closed, and the telegraph clerks, the members of the press, and the attendants departed.'[27] Later the sun came out and it was agreed to start play at four o'clock. The Kent professionals, however, had taken their chance to escape and were nowhere to be seen.

There was a happier outcome at Cheltenham a week later. On a difficult wicket Grace scored his eighth century of the season, 119 out of 257. Nobody else reached forty, and Nottinghamshire (without Gunn and Shrewsbury) were bowled out for 66 and 99, Townsend taking 13 for 111. The second Cheltenham match provided another victory, over Yorkshire, and saw Townsend reach his hundred wickets. He took a further twelve against Surrey at Clifton, but Gloucestershire's winning run was over. In the second innings Richardson and Lohmann reduced the home side to 37 for 7, and they were lucky to get away with a draw. They then went down to Taunton for their last match which, despite another twelve wickets from Townsend, Somerset won by fifty-seven runs. Grace ended his own season, as usual, at Hastings, and scored his ninth century (104) to help the South beat the North, but his final game was a disappointment, particularly for the festival crowds. Tom Richardson got him for 0 and 8 as A. E. Stoddart's XI crushed the Rest of England by 218 runs, a reminder perhaps that for all the semi-miraculous performances of a man fast approaching fifty, the future belonged to men half his age.

One of those, Archie MacLaren, just pipped him for pride of place at the head of the averages, but Grace's aggregate of 2,346 at exactly 51 was universally accepted as the batting display of the summer. In the desperate hunt for untried superlatives, *Lillywhite's Annual* (1895) came up with the formulation: 'Of W.G.'s batting in 1895 the highest praise which can be given him is that he excelled himself.'[28] Grace's own reaction to events is described by the compilers of the *Memorial Biography*: 'Amid all the bewildering plethora of runs the veteran had amassed, his own head was quite unturned by all the praises so deservedly lavished upon him. He took success as imperturbably as failure, but he enjoyed it fervently in his quiet way.'[29]

However much he might have preferred to savour his triumph without fuss, public enthusiasm made this impossible; 'Until the end of the summer I went through a period of lionising, which, though gratifying, was distinctly embarrassing.'[30] Hard on the heels of his 288 against Somerset, Arrowsmith and Brownlee set to work arranging a banquet in his honour. This took place on 24 June at the Victoria Rooms, Clifton, and some four hundred guests attended. The Duke of Beaufort returned from Ireland especially to preside over the evening. He had news of two recent additions to the testimonial fund: 'The Prince of Wales had written through his private secretary a kindly letter enclosing a cheque for five guineas towards the testimonial, as "he could not be left out in the cold when there was a subscription going," and the Duke of York had sent three guineas.'[31] When the Duke proposed the toast to the centurian of centuries, Grace's reply was typically brief, 'brief, perhaps, because the Speaker – though showing no signs of it – was struggling to keep his emotions under control'.[32] There were more speeches to follow. The Bishop of Hereford allowed himself a few flights of fancy. If Grace had been

born an ancient Greek . . . the Iliad would have been something different. They would have heard not only of Ajax and Diomed, but they would have been adding a third name – that of a hero who would have had the pleasure of killing a great number of people and of being sung in immortal verse! If he had been born in the Middle Ages, Dr Grace would have been a Crusader, of course, and would have been lying with his legs crossed in one of those niches in Bristol Cathedral.[33]

It was a minor wonder he did not end the night in a similar attitude anyway. According to Sammy Woods, 'He drank something of everything, before and during dinner, and afterwards he sent for the whisky . . . [But] you couldn't make the Old Man drunk. His nut was too large.' Nor, apparently, could you tire him out. 'About midnight, some of us thought we might start for home; but the Old Man said to me: "Shock'ead, get two others, and we'll play rubbers of whist till two in the morning." So we did.'[34]

Proving his stamina was as gargantuan as his appetite for living life to the punishing full, Grace was out the following night as well – as the guest of the Bristol Century Club, which had been formed simply to honour his hundred hundreds. There was also a dinner at the Sports Club in London on 19 July. Grace complained that he had been brought along under false pretences as he had been promised 'there would be no "speechifying"', and, of course, there was.

The whole country was gripped with enthusiasm for the great cricketing warrior. Brownlee's biography was reprinted and sales topped 21,000 copies; *The History of a Hundred Centuries* came out (carrying several pages of lucrative advertisements for Brooke's Soap, Dark's Bats and Bird's Custard Powder), and Grace astutely dedicated the volume 'To Colonel John Thomas North, a Thorough all-Round Sportsman, and The First Subscriber to my National Testimonial Fund'. (North was also a millionaire, known as 'The Nitrate King' on account of the fortune he had made from his investments in Chile.) The public needed little prompting to dip into their pockets, and when the three funds were finally closed they had raised a staggering £9,073 8s 3d (around half a million at present values) of which the MCC appeal raised over £2,000, the local Gloucestershire fund nearly £1,500, and the *Telegraph* Shilling Testimonial £5,281 9s 1d. In the letter accompanying the *Telegraph*'s cheque, the paper's proprietor, Sir Edward Lawson (afterwards Lord Burnham), wrote:

Such a magnificent demonstration, sir, is due in the first place to a warm appreciation felt throughout the land and the Empire for your own high and worthy qualities as an English cricketer. It comprises, however, above and beyond this – as cannot possibly be doubted – a very notable and emphatic expression of the general love for those out-of-door sports and pursuits, which – free from any element of cruelty, greed or coarseness – most and best develop our British traits of manliness, good temper, fair play, and the healthy training of mind and body.[35]

Not everybody was happy to worship at the Grace shrine. Max Beerbohm struck a satirical blow against the hearties' triumphalism with a cartoon in which a huge Grace with bulging biceps stands in the foreground with a minuscule cricket bat in one hand and a large cheque in the other, while behind him the funeral cortège of one of his neglected patients sets off to the cemetery. Oscar Wilde would not have been allowed to see this in his bare cell, but even the prison walls could not keep the national obsession entirely at bay. The condemned guardsman in Wilde's poem 'The Ballad of Reading Gaol' walked among the Trial Men with 'a cricket cap [up]on his head'.

TWENTY-EIGHT

O N 15 November 1895 Henry Grace died of apoplexy at the age of sixty-two. It was a cruel blight on a magnificent year. Since 1871 Henry had been head of the family, and though overshadowed by W.G. and E.M., he had played a vital role in the Grace story. Had it not been for his enthusiasm as a schoolboy, Dr Grace might never have been drawn back to the game to which he devoted the rest of his life. Whatever their differences in the early years, Henry had always adopted a protective role towards his infinitely more talented younger brother – most notably on the South Wales tour of 1864. Without him W.G. would not have had the chance to make his brilliant century at Brighton. Henry also helped him greatly over the course of his protracted medical training, and W.G. had a high opinion of him as a doctor. He had played an important part in Gloucestershire's affairs, and although always of the Grace camp, he was a voice for moderation on the committee. When Alfred Pocock lost his wife, Henry offered him the sanctuary of his home at Kingswood, and the two must have spent many companionable evenings reliving the glories of the Mangotsfield and West Gloucestershire clubs and everything that had sprung from those humble beginnings. Although written when he was still very much alive, Brownlee's words will serve as an eloquent epitaph: 'In him the father had an exemplary son, the mother, in her widowhood and sorrow, the best of his thought and care, and the younger members of the family a brother ever ready with time and means to lend a helping hand.'[1]

Henry was sadly missed at a 'pleasant function' at the Clifton Club on 4 February 1896 when Grace was presented with the proceeds of the Gloucestershire testimonial. It was a relatively low-key affair compared with the celebratory banquets of the previous year, but the Duke of Beaufort presided, and among the seventy guests were Brownlee, Arrowsmith and W.G.'s two surviving brothers, Alfred and E.M. In addition to a cheque, Grace was also given 'a gold chronometer watch, while Agnes was presented with an inscribed silver kettle'. Giving thanks,

Grace 'declared that but for his wife's help he never would have done as well as he had even in cricket'.[2]

W.G. and Agnes would not have had far to go home after the evening. The lease on Thrissle House had run out the previous year, and their next-door neighbour, who had acquired the freehold on the property, warned Grace that he had no intention of renewing it. Net sessions in January had obviously been too much for him. The Graces were now living, in some opulence, at 15, Victoria Square, Clifton, though it wasn't long before they moved again, to Ashley Grange, where W.G. would be only a short walk from the county ground.

*

1896 saw the publication of the first serious attempt to get to grips with the welter of statistics spawned by Grace's career. Arthur Waring's 'W.G.' or The Champion's Career owed much to the number-crunching tradition of Jeremy Bentham: 'Up to the end of 1895, his thirty-ninth cricket year, [Grace] has contested 991 matches, occupying 2,396 days, equivalent to *six years two hundred and six days* . . . He has played 1,614 innings, and scored off his own bat 59,910 runs. Had each of these been run out . . . taking the actual distance of each run at twenty-two yards, he would have covered a distance of 748 miles, 1,540 yards, or within a mile of the distance between London and Thurso.' As for his bowling, if each of the 114,221 balls he had bowled had been allowed to pass unimpeded and carried for fifty yards, 'a simple calculation' could show 'that he has exerted sufficient energy in their delivery to have caused the ball to travel 3,244 miles, 1,610 yards, a distance equal to over one-eighth of the equatorial circumference of the earth'.[3] No doubt Grace had his leg pulled over that one, but he could deflect the chaff by pointing to a rather more sensible finding of Waring's – that in that huge number of deliveries, he had bowled only twenty-two wides and a solitary no-ball. There were very few bowlers who could match that.

Although there could be no expectation that 1896 could possibly rival 1895, it was nonetheless an eventful season, with some spectacular incidents. Considerable controversy surrounds one of them, the single most famous delivery W.G. ever faced. This was the ball the Australian fast bowler Ernest Jones (Jonah) bowled through his beard. No one doubts that it happened, but just as those who saw Lord Byron's body after his death at Missolonghi could not agree whether his club foot was his left or right one, so those who claim to have seen the Jones delivery disagree as to where it took place. F. S. Jackson and C. B. Fry, both of whom were playing for Lord Sheffield's XI, were sure it occurred when Jones bowled his first furious over on English soil in the touring Australians' opening game at Sheffield Park in May. Fry's account is as follows:

In that match W.G. went in first with Arthur Shrewsbury. I was playing too, and I vouch to you that it is true that in the first over a ball from Ernest Jones did go through W.G.'s beard, and that W.G. did rumble out a falsetto, 'What – what – what!' and that Harry Trott [the Australian captain] did say, 'Steady, Jonah,' and that Ernest Jones did say, 'Sorry, doctor, she slipped.' . . . W.G. topped the twenties, and his huge chest was black and blue. F. S. Jackson made a score and had one of his ribs broken. Ranjitsinhji made 80 [actually 79], and flicked Jonah's faster rising ball off his nose. The wicket must have had a sandstone subsoil so viciously did the ball fly. But about that first over. W.G. played it, partly, as I say, with his beard. When Arthur Shrewsbury got to that end, having watched the first two balls, he deliberately tipped the next into the hands of second slip, and before the catch was held had folded his bat under his right armpit and marched off. Then the 6 feet 3 inches of William Gunn walked delicately to the wicket. His first ball from Jones whizzed past where his head had just been. William withdrew from the line of the next ball and deliberately tipped it into the slips, and he too had pouched his bat and was stepping off to the pavilion before the catch was surely caught.[4]

This is lively stuff, but Fry was writing from memory, without the details of the match in front of him. Grace in fact opened with Jackson, and neither Shrewsbury nor Gunn got a duck as Fry suggested (and as he did himself; they scored 1 and 5 respectively). Furthermore, Grace did more than 'top the twenties' – he made 49. It would appear therefore that Jackson should be the best witness, given that he was actually at the crease rather than watching from the pavilion. In the 1944 *Wisden* he confirmed that the setting was definitely Sheffield Park, but denies that the incident took place in the first over, though that contained quite enough drama to be going on with. Grace was 'hit under the arm' (Jackson), and, according to *The Sportsman*, he received 'three nasty blows', the second of which caused a brief stoppage, in Jones's opening salvo. Jackson puts the 'beard ball' later in the innings: 'I can see W.G. now. He threw his head back, which caused his beard to stick out.' Jackson, in fact, claimed responsibility for the story, 'as when I returned to the pavilion, I said "Did you see that ball go through W.G.'s beard?"'[5]

But two of the compilers of the *Memorial Biography* (1919) were equally certain that it happened at Lord's in the first Test in June. Lord Harris wrote: 'I saw the incident. W.G. was not quite quick enough. The ball grazed his beard, touched the top of the handle of his bat, ricocheted far over the wicket keeper's head and went to the screen for four.' Harris went on: 'I did not notice his being at all upset, and I was told that the remark he made to Jones as he ran up the wicket was: "Whatever are ye at?"' Home Gordon, while siding with Harris as to the venue, disagreed on Grace's response. According to him, Grace was 'conspicuously ruffled'; 'The veteran looked volumes, [and] was so seriously discomfited that he took some time to recover his composure and then only after having made some observations to the wicket-keeper, while the twelve thousand spectators positively hummed, so general were their audible comments.'[6] Grace himself always referred to Jones as 'the fellow who bowled through my beard', though without specifying the exact occasion. The one thing that was not in dispute was that in the hard-drinking ex-miner, the Australians had unearthed a bowler of genuine pace and undoubted aggression to match the likes of Richardson, Lockwood and Mold – though, as with Mold, there were aspersions cast on Jonah's action. In George Giffen's opinion he was, for a few overs, 'absolutely the fastest of bowlers', though he admitted he had neither the steadiness nor staying power of Tom Richardson.[7]

The other thing that became clear, given the two Nottinghamshire professionals' reactions, was that the man expected to tame this new terror was the forty-eight-year-old Grace. In the Sheffield Park match, under the admiring eye of the Prince of Wales, he coped admirably, following his first-innings 49 with 26 in the second. Jackson also performed well, scoring an unbeaten 95 which ensured him a Test place, and Ranji again emphasized his brilliance, following his 79 with 42 in the second innings to save the game for Lord Sheffield's XI.

Grace's form remained encouraging without threatening a repeat of the previous year's marvels – until he went to Hove at the end of May. Then he gorged on the weak Sussex bowling, hitting 243 out of Gloucestershire's total of 463. When Sussex lost three wickets, including Ranjitsinhji, for ten runs, victory looked likely, but the home team rallied in their second innings, which contained three centuries. One of these was, inevitably, scored by Ranji (114).

His omission from the England side for the first Test at Lord's caused a considerable stir, as no one doubted that he was worth a Test place. The MCC's decision not to include him has been widely attributed to the same racial prejudice that initially kept him out of the Cambridge XI, and there is no doubt that the club had its racist elements. Home Gordon, one of Ranji's champions, was threatened with expulsion by a senior member if he 'had the disgusting degeneracy to praise a dirty black'.[8] However, Lord Harris, the previous year's president and the man most responsible for the decision to exclude Ranji, would not have thought of him as 'a dirty black'. During his time as Governor of Bombay (1890–5) he had courted unpopularity by overriding the established racial barriers and arranging matches between the Parsees and Europeans. Nor does a charge of institutional racism against the MCC seem particularly convincing in the light of the warm reception given at Lord's to the Aborigines in 1868 and the two Parsee sides that toured in the 1880s.

But the fact remains that the batsman who had reached 1,000 runs by the middle of June and who was electrifying crowds up and down the country with his brilliant performances was not picked for the Test team. The reasons given at the time were vague and unsatisfactory. *The Times* gave the official version without comment: 'Some cricketers were, on principle, against the inclusion of Ranjitsinhji in the English side. The Marylebone Club committee thoroughly weighed the matter, and, while recognizing the wonderful ability of that cricketer, thought it scarcely right to play him for England against Australia. And Mr Perkins [the Secretary], on behalf of the M.C.C., sent a letter to K. S. Ranjitsinhji explaining the reason why the M.C.C. did not choose him.'[9] Behind the scenes, it was said that Lord Harris had developed scruples against playing 'birds of passage'[10] in the England team, though given the precedent set by Murdoch and Ferris, not to mention Midwinter, that hardly held water.

Simon Wilde, Ranji's most recent biographer, has no hesitation in laying the blame on Harris, but suggests he himself was acting under pressure from the government. In 1892, an Indian standing as a Home-Rule Liberal had won a seat in the House of Commons despite strenuous opposition from Lord Salisbury. Now the Conservatives, with Salisbury prime minister once more, were again hostile to anything that might increase or in any way seem to validate Indian involvement in British domestic affairs, and that included picking an Indian prince (as he was widely believed to be) for the national cricket team. Having served as an under-secretary in Salisbury's previous administrations, Harris was clearly in tune with his party's sensitivities, and it was his understanding of the 'international implications', Wilde argues, that motivated him to persuade the rest of the MCC committee not to pick Ranji.

They were not won over easily. The decision was delayed, and Ranji was instructed to 'hold himself in readiness' right up to the last minute.[11] This had the effect of heightening the public's interest in the match, which was already intense. The Australians had made an excellent start to their tour, but had suffered an appalling set-back ten days before the Test when they were caught on a wet Lord's wicket by the MCC & Ground. The whole team was dismissed by Jack Hearne and A. D. Pougher for 18, their lowest ever total. How would they fare with a full England attack? And how, in turn, would the English batsmen cope with the raw pace of Ernest Jones?

By the end of the first day's play, the Lord's crowd had an answer to both questions. On a fast but otherwise blameless pitch, the Australians had been demolished again. Richardson produced a classic spell of accurate, hostile fast bowling and, well supported by the rehabilitated Lohmann, had the whole side back in the pavilion before lunch for 53. At stumps England were 233 runs ahead with two wickets standing, and the match seemed as good as won.

Despite his difficulties in the opening over, Grace had held the line against Jones. When he lost Stoddart at 38, he was joined by Bobby Abel, who was thought to be suspect against the fastest bowling. However, his resolve stiffened no doubt by Grace's authoritative presence at the other end, the Surrey professional played a courageous innings and helped his captain put on a hundred for the second wicket. Grace went, mishitting Giffen, for 66, during the course of which he passed 1,000 runs in Test cricket. Abel carried on the good work and got as close as he ever would to a century in a home Test, falling short, as so often, in the nervous nineties. His 94 was England's highest score, and Jackson was the third main contributor with 44. Jones had been tamed to the extent that he took only one wicket in his twenty-six overs.

The England innings ended early on the second morning with only six more runs added, but Australia still faced a deficit of 239. When Richardson took two more quick wickets at the start of their second innings, the English team must have started making plans for a day off. But Harry Trott played a captain's innings and, with support from Syd Gregory, took the attack to England. In sixty-five minutes before lunch ninety runs were added, and the score at the interval was 152 for 3. In the afternoon both men went on to centuries, though Trott was missed on 98 and then nearly ran himself out on 99. He made 143, and Gregory was brilliantly caught by Lohmann at slip off Jack Hearne for 103. They were out within five minutes of each other, and their partnership of 221 was a new record for any wicket in Test matches. It left Australia fifty runs ahead with five wickets in hand.

Thanks to Richardson and Jack Hearne, those five wickets produced only another sixty runs. Richardson took 5 for 134 in forty-seven overs to finish with match figures of 11 for 173. This left England only 111 to win, but they got off to a bad start. To his obvious disgust Grace fell to Trumble, caught off bat and pad by Clem Hill, for 7, and Abel succumbed to Jones for 4. Overnight rain made things more difficult, and J. T. Brown considered his 36 against Jones bowling flat out in poor light at least as good an innings as his century in Melbourne in March 1895. Stoddart, coming in at five, saw England home by six wickets with a nicely judged 30 not out.

Grace had a productive three weeks between the first and second Tests. He scored 51 and 102 against Lancashire at Bristol (a match Gloucestershire still contrived to lose), and 186 against Somerset at Taunton. He made a heroic 53 not out in the Gentlemen's second innings against the Players at the Oval, batting through the innings as Richardson swept imperiously aside the rest of the amateur batsmen, until R. P. Lewis, the Oxford wicket-keeper, came in at number eleven to scamper the winning run. The amateurs coped better with Richardson at Lord's, where Ranji hit an aggressive 47 for the benefit of any MCC committee members who happened to be watching. Grace took 5 for 97 and scored 54 in his second innings to lead the Gentlemen to another victory. There was only one disappointment: in the Varsity match W.G. junior bagged a pair. It was an altogether less happy occasion than the previous year as the Cambridge captain's decision to instruct E. B. Shine to bowl no-balls to prevent Oxford having to follow on was widely regarded as an unsporting blemish on the fixture, and the Light Blues were roundly booed by the crowd. To make matters worse, the ploy backfired, and Oxford made an unprecedented 330 in the fourth innings to win by six wickets.

The main talking point in the build-up to the Old Trafford Test was again the selection of Ranji. The Lancashire authorities took a different line from the MCC and invited him to play. Ranji diplomatically asked them to check whether his presence would be acceptable to the Australians, and Trott decently said they would be delighted. It was to be a historic debut, but Ranji spent his first day in Test cricket in the field as the Australians reached 366 for 8. Despite another magnificent effort by Richardson, Iredale, Giffen and Trott took control and wickets were few and far between. Grace gave himself a rare spell, but to no avail. Then, remembering Alfred Lyttelton's success with the ball in 1884, he called upon Brown to relieve Lilley behind the stumps to see if the current England wicket-keeper could repeat the trick. He conceded fourteen runs off his first over and continued to bowl net-fodder for four more overs, at the end of which he induced Trott to snick a long-hop to Brown. Any thoughts he may have had of emulating Lyttelton's four-wicket spell were quickly dashed. W.G. told him to get back behind the stumps, saying, rather ungraciously, 'You must have been bowling with your wrong arm.'[12]

With the breakthrough achieved, Richardson did the rest, finishing with 7 for 168 in sixty-eight overs. But by the time he bowled the last man, Jones, the following morning, the Australians had scored 412. When England batted, Trott followed Grace by serving up a surprise. He reverted to the ploy Blackham had tried in the 1891–2 series and opened the bowling himself. This time it worked. He had Grace stumped for 2 in his first over, and as a bonus he accounted for Stoddart in the same way twenty runs later. Ranji was barely off the mark at this stage, but with the dependable Bobby Abel as his partner, he soon settled down and started playing with his usual fluency. After a stand of seventy, Abel departed for 26 and Ranji soon followed, caught suspiciously low at point, for an excellent 62. The impressive middle order of Jackson, Brown and MacLaren produced only forty runs, and it was left to Lilley to salvage some respectability with the top score of 65 not out. But England were nearly two hundred adrift when they followed on.

This time Jones did make the first inroads, having Grace caught by Trott for 11, and so, with fifty-five minutes left to play, Ranji went out to bat a second time with England facing a dangerous situation. This rapidly developed into a crisis as Stoddart was bowled by McKibbin, and then Giffen accounted for Abel and Jackson. At close of play the score was 109 for 4, with Ranji not out 41.

On the third morning England's prospects looked bleak. But Ranji was getting the hang of things, and having scored a hundred runs on his first day as a Test batsman, he proceeded to score another hundred – before lunch. He started cautiously against a barrage of short deliveries from Jones (one of which struck him a glancing blow, splitting the lobe of his ear), but then, having played himself in and taken the edge off Australia's most lethal weapon, he began to open up, treating the rest of the bowlers with imperious impartiality. He simply hit them all over Old Trafford. He reached his century at 12.45, and when Trott brought Jones back, Ranji showed a complete mastery of him, dismissing the short stuff to leg and mercilessly driving anything overpitched. When the innings ended an hour later with the total on 305, Ranji was still there, undefeated, with 154 to his name. In two hours and ten minutes of the morning session he had scored 113, which is still the most any batsman has made before lunch in an Ashes match, and he became only the second England player – Grace was the first – to score a century on his Test debut. He had also given his team an outside chance of stealing the game.

The pitch was still good, but the pressure was immense; 125 was not a big target, but Australia had to win, and England, back from the dead, had nothing to lose and everything to play for. Richardson was the key, and once more this remarkable bowler gave England his magnificent all. A wicket at 20, a wicket at 26, a wicket at 28. Suddenly the crowd began to sense that they might be about to witness a historic victory. The tension proved too much for Trott, who chose to drive round outside the ground in a hansom cab rather than watch. In the event, thanks to a top score of 33 from Syd Gregory, Australia made it by three wickets, but the crowd had certainly had their money's worth, having seen one of the greatest England batting feats complemented by one of the greatest spells of fast bowling. When Richardson walked off at the end of the match he had bowled flat out for three hours and taken 6 for 76. This gave him match figures of 13 for 244 and brought his tally in the first two Tests to twenty-four wickets at 17.37 apiece. It would have seemed inconceivable that anything short of injury could have kept him out of the third and deciding Test at the Oval three weeks later. Yet he very nearly didn't play.

*

This was because of a threatened strike on the part of the professionals. The third Test, at the Oval, was due to start on 10 August. Those picked were notified in advance and offered the usual terms: ten pounds each. The fee for representative matches (Gentlemen v. Players, Tests) had remained the same for twenty-five years and had been a source of discontent for some time. The English professionals had long bemoaned the fact that though treated as amateurs, the Australians always made a handsome profit out of their tours. An individual's share of the gate receipts could reach as much as £500. There had been problems over this as far back as

1878 when the top professionals boycotted the Australia–Players match after their demand for twenty pounds a head was turned down. Now, the five professionals selected for the third Test – Lohmann, Richardson, Tom Hayward, Abel and William Gunn – decided to hold out for the same sum. On 3 August they wrote to the Surrey committee: 'We . . . do hereby take the liberty to ask for increased terms viz. twenty pounds. The importance of such a fixture entitles us to make this demand.'[13]

This was not well received. Both the tone and the timing grated, and the fact that four of the five rebels were Surrey players was a further affront to the Oval authorities. They told their own players that the fee remained ten pounds plus expenses, or they would 'be out of the match', while Gunn was separately informed that his 'terms were not accepted'.[14] So far the matter had been kept private. Now the players went public. One of them, almost certainly Lohmann, gave an interview to the *Daily Mail* which was published on the Saturday before the match:

We want £20 apiece and expenses. The Australians will probably take away £1,700 or £1,800 and the Surrey Club will probably benefit to the same extent or more. We professional cricketers in England do not get anything like adequate payment for our services. The enormous crowds which now follow the game benefit the clubs and, in fact, everybody but those who have done at least their fair share towards bringing the game towards its present state – the professional players.[15]

This may not have made comfortable reading for the Oval authorities, but it was an unexceptionable statement of the case. Lohmann really caused waves when he extended his fire to include the amateurs who 'will be paid more than us professionals'.[16] This revived the controversy over amateur payments that had flared up at the end of the 1870s. The MCC Note of 1878 had been an acknowledgement that there was a case to answer, but despite the dropping of Fred Grace from the Gentlemen's side, few people believed the abuse of the system had ended.

However, Lohmann's decision to rake it up on the eve of the decisive Test match caused a huge stir, and gave the papers a field-day. Harry Trott injudiciously allowed himself to be dragged into the controversy, and was quoted as saying, 'I am astonished and deeply sorry to hear that Lohmann is the leading spirit of the movement, especially after the handsome treatment he has received at the hands of the Surrey Club and the English public generally.' As one of the papers remarked, 'The charm of this criticism would be more apparent were Trott to tell an excited public the exact terms upon which he, personally, undertook the trip to this country. If I mistake not, the burden of the complaint made by Lohmann and his brethren is that the terms are not equal all round. Given fine weather, the Australians will benefit to an extent undreamt of by the English professionals. Of course, the Australians are amateurs . . .'[17]

The row inevitably focused the spotlight on Grace once more, and he was furious. He was still seething three years later when he came to write *Reminiscences*. It was, he said, 'an unseemly controversy, in the course of which many irritating statements of an absolutely false character were made with regard to prominent amateur cricketers'.[18] There was, of course, no more prominent amateur cricketer than Grace himself and the Sunday papers weighed in enthusiastically. 'Orbit' of the *Weekly Sun* wrote on 9 August, 'My sympathies are entirely with the pros., and whether they get what they are asking for or not, they are entitled to our respect for having raised another protest gainst the shoddy amateurism which waxes fat on "expenses".' Grace acted swiftly, giving the Surrey authorities an ultimatum of his own. He would withdraw from the match unless they published an immediate denial.

This appeared on the morning of the match:

The Committee of the Surrey County Cricket Club have observed paragraphs in the Press respecting amounts alleged to be paid, or promised to, Dr. W. G. Grace for playing in the match England v. Australia. The Committee desire to give the statements contained in the paragraphs the most unqualified contradiction. During many years, on the occasions of Dr. W. G. Grace playing at the Oval, at the request of the Surrey County Committee, in the matches Gentlemen v. Players and England v. Australia, Dr. Grace has received the sum of £10 a match to cover his expenses in coming to and remaining in London during the three days. Beyond this amount Dr. Grace has not received, directly or indirectly, one farthing for playing in a match at the Oval.

Signed on behalf of the Committee, C. W. Alcock, August 10, 1896.

This was no more convincing than the MCC's assertion in 1878 that it had never broken its own guidelines, which *John Lillywhite's Companion* had dismissed as tantamount to a lie. Sydney Pardon, the editor of *Wisden*, was far less abrasive. In his Notes for the 1897 edition, he attempted to smooth over the embarrassment with a line from the Bard: 'Mr W. G. Grace's position has for years, as everyone knows, been an anomalous one, but "nice customs curtsey to great kings" and the work he has done in popularising cricket outweighs a hundredfold every other consideration.'[19] As the phrase is uttered by the all-conquering Henry V after the battle of Agincourt, the quotation was particularly apt. Grace's power remained unchallengeable.

Suitably mollified, Grace was now prepared to play, but Stoddart, another unnamed but easily identified shamateur, cried off, claiming indisposition. As for the five disaffected professionals, Abel, Richardson and Hayward climbed down as soon as the committee got tough, and were reinstated in the side. Gunn stayed firm, and Lohmann prevaricated in solidarity until warned that he would not be picked again for Surrey, let alone for England, until the issue was resolved. Having tried to use the press to further the professionals' cause, he was now forced to put his name to an open letter of apology that was circulated to the papers. The establishment had closed ranks, called the professionals' bluff, and cruelly exposed their lack of bargaining power. The mutiny, such as it was, was over.

This was hardly the ideal build-up to such an important match, and there was plenty of time for feelings to fester on the first day as rain prevented a start before the late afternoon. As the crowd waited for play to begin, a reporter from the *Star* went eavesdropping: 'The talk round the ropes amongst the spectators is all about the great strike and its probable consequences. The voice of the people in this instance is unmistakably in favour of the professionals.'[20]

Perfectly indifferent to the things that might be said about him in the cheaper seating, Grace went out to open with Jackson on a sopping pitch, and the two gave England a firm foundation with a stand that produced fifty-four runs. Grace was caught by Trott off Giffen for 24. England were 69 for 1 overnight, and the following morning developed this to 114 for 3 with Jackson making 45 and Abel 26. (Ranji came down to earth with 8.) After that Hugh Trumble wrapped up the rest of the innings with his medium-paced off-breaks, and England were all out for 145.

There may have been a punitive aspect to Grace's judgement that the conditions were unsuitable for Richardson's pace, but his decision to give the bulk of the bowling to Peel and Jack Hearne was fully justified. After an opening stand of seventy-five runs between Jack Darling and Iredale – ended by a spectacular throw from Ranji to run out the latter who was going for a fifth run – the two slower bowlers proved a winning combination. Hearne took 6 for 41 while Peel kept up the pressure, conceding only thirty runs in twenty overs. Australia were bowled out for 119, giving England a lead of twenty-six.

As the pitch dried out it became even more difficult. Jackson was bowled by Trumble for 2, and Grace followed for 9. Ranji made 11, Abel, who was happier dealing with Trumble's jagging turn than with Jones's uncomplicated pace, 21, and MacLaren 6. England were 60 for 5 overnight, only eighty-six runs ahead. Tom Hayward and Major E. G. Wynyard, who had taken Stoddart's place at short notice, were the two not out batsmen. Wynyard, playing in his first Test, had survived the twenty minutes up to the close and felt he had seldom batted better. The following morning he arrived at the ground looking forward to building an innings. He was to be disappointed. Grace went out to inspect the pitch, and returned to give clear but drastic orders to his remaining batsmen: 'Sorry, you must all be out in half an hour. We must have them in by twelve-thirty at latest.'[21] They were all out for 84, only Hayward (13) and Richardson (10 not out) making double figures.

This left Australia 111 to win, and all day to get them. Grace opened with Richardson, who bowled a maiden, but when Hearne bowled Darling for a duck he took off his fast bowler and called up Peel. The result was devastating. Australia collapsed to 14 for 7, and only some defiant hitting from the number eleven McKibbin (16) got them to their final total of 44 – their lowest in a Test in England up to that time. In twelve overs Peel took 6 for 23 (passing a hundred Test wickets in the process), and Hearne added four wickets to the six he had taken in the first to end with match figures of 10 for 60. England won by the deceptively large margin of sixty-six runs, and so took the rubber and retained the Ashes yet again.

For all the unpleasantness that had preceded it, the match was a triumph for Grace. His own batting was undoubtedly a factor, and whatever the divisions within his team, he marshalled them into a winning unit. But most importantly, he had read the pitch correctly and had had the nerve to back his judgement. Wynyard, for one, was deeply impressed, and he regarded Grace as 'incomparably the best captain he had ever known'.[22]

W.G.'s record in county cricket was less impressive. Although he had another excellent season as a batsman, and his best for some time as a bowler, Gloucestershire were unable to build on their recovery in 1895. Winning only five matches and losing ten, they slipped down the table once more. Although Townsend took only twenty-three fewer wickets than the previous year, he started slowly; 'In the early part of the season he was quite unsuccessful, and though he improved considerably later on, still he was only a shadow of his former self'.[23] Jessop was absent for the first half of the season, having gone up to Cambridge where he joined W.G. junior in the XI, but his return to the county did not signal any upturn in their fortunes. The true cause of their poor season was probably the old one – Grace's idiosyncratic selection policy. Twenty-eight names are listed in the batting averages – more than any other county – and most of those were amateurs who came in for the odd game here and there. It was impossible to build a serious challenge for a place in the top half of the championship table with a team of part-timers.

Bertie also reclaimed his county place at the end of the university term, and Grace had the pleasure of seeing him atone for the pair at Lord's with his highest first-class score of 62 against Nottinghamshire at Trent Bridge. However, when he took him out to open the batting against Sussex at Bristol a fortnight later (3 August), there was a grim repeat of the nightmare of 1894. This time it was even worse: W.G. junior made 1; W.G. senior made exactly 300 more.* Exploiting the weak Sussex bowling for the second time in the season, he made 193 on the first day and was finally ninth out, with the total on 548, after eight and a half chanceless hours at the crease. History does not relate how Bertie spent the time. Perhaps he buried his head in a book.

This was the high point of Grace's county season. There were also the inevitable bad days. Against Surrey at the Oval in May he damaged his hand stopping a stinging cut at point, and had to leave the field. The injury rankled, and he claimed that the ball was too hard. He took up the matter with the Surrey captain, K. J. Key, who told him he was talking nonsense and that match balls at the Oval were kept at least two years to season them properly. Grace wouldn't have it, and demanded that the ball be cut open. To prevent the argument developing into a full-scale row, Key consented. The ball was disembowelled; Grace unravelled the cork and twine and then gleefully produced a twist of newspaper bearing a tell-tale date from earlier in the year. Being proved right restored his humour, and more than compensated for the original injury. 'That night from the bottom of the long flight of stairs at Fenchurch Street Station, he shouted to a friend at the top how he had scored off "the Surreyites", and he went on talking of this for many a day afterwards.'[24] The 'Surreyites' may have lost the skirmish of the ball, but they won the battle of the match by ten wickets.

Gloucestershire's nadir came against the Australians at Cheltenham,

* This was the third and last of W.G.'s triple centuries. At that time only Walter Read, Murdoch and MacLaren had passed the three hundred mark in first-class cricket.

shortly after the third Test. On a wet wicket they scored 133, of which Grace made 26, and had the tourists 138 for 8. They then dropped a string of catches and the last two wickets added sixty-six runs. Grace and Rice put three runs on the board before stumps on the second day, but the following morning the pitch was lethal and Trumble and McKibbin proved 'practically unplayable'.[25] In less than an hour the whole team was out for only fourteen more runs. Grace scored 9 out of the total of 17, and there were six ducks.

The Australians' last sight of the Old Man was a fortnight later at Hastings in their match against the South of England. Conditions were more favourable for batting, at least to begin with, and Grace signed off with a festival fifty, 'hitting McKibbin, Trumble and Giffen with great severity'.[26] The next highest score after his 53 was Jack Hearne's 29. In the Australians' second innings Hearne outdid his performance at the Oval, taking 6 for 8 in seventeen overs. His foil on this occasion was George Lohmann, who followed up his four wickets in the first innings with 4 for 45 to help dismiss the Australians for 63.* Grace declined to bat a second time, letting others knock off the forty-five runs required for victory so that he could shake hands with Trott as he came off the field and clap the Australians back into the enclosure at the end of their long tour. Although they lost the Test series, Grace rated them highly. Their record of nineteen wins out of thirty-four matches with six defeats was better than that of any side since 1884. More importantly, he noted that 'the tour was singularly free from hitches and unpleasantness of any kind'.[27] Whether he would still be there to oppose them the next time they returned they could only guess. Most must have suspected that he would be.

His figures for the season certainly showed no obvious waning of his powers. His 301 was the highest innings in first-class cricket, and for the second year running (and for the fifth time in his career) he scored over 2,000 runs, a distinction shared only by Ranji and Abel. Ranji's aggregate of 2,780 narrowly beat the 2,739 Grace scored in 1871, a record that had stood for twenty-five years. (Ranji also equalled Grace's record of ten centuries in a season.) Abel registered 2,218, but W.G.'s 2,135 was some way ahead of the rest of the field, and he was fifth in the overall averages with 42.70. He also took fifty-two wickets at 24.01. These figures would have been outstanding for someone half his age. For a man of forty-eight they were astonishing.

* This was Lohmann's penultimate first-class match in England. He had decided to return to South Africa, where he finally succumbed to tuberculosis in December 1901, aged thirty-six.

TWENTY-NINE

Eighteen ninety-seven was the year of Queen Victoria's Diamond
Jubilee. On 21 June she presided over a banquet for Europe's royalty
at Buckingham Palace (the Archduke Franz Ferdinand, heir to the
Austrian throne, sat on her right). The next day there was a six-mile
procession through streets lined with cheering crowds. With the Prince of
Wales on one side of her carriage and her grandson, the Kaiser, on the
other, the Queen was escorted by 50,000 troops from all over the Empire,
stopping first at the Mansion House and then proceeding to a
thanksgiving service on the steps of St Paul's.

Grace started his season in celebratory mood, hitting 55 off the
previous year's champions, Yorkshire, at Bristol and producing a string
of entertaining vignettes throughout the rest of May and June. Though
popular with the crowds, this uncharacteristically cavalier approach was
frowned upon by purists. *Wisden* commented, 'For several weeks the
great batsman laboured under the impression that it was imperative upon
him to make runs at a quick pace. The result was that . . . he frequently
lost his wicket at a time when he might have been considered well set, and
so long did he continue to play in a manner quite foreign to his normal
methods as to create a feeling of dismay.'[1]

Whether Grace was trying to keep up with the astounding Ranji, who
had come back from a convalescent tour of Europe to score a dazzling
260 for Sussex against the MCC at Lord's, or was simply carried away by
the carnival mood sweeping the country, common sense eventually
prevailed, and after Jubilee Day he began to play more circumspectly. In
the first Gentlemen–Players match at the Oval he scored 41, though his
handling of the amateurs' bowling drew criticism. On the second day the
Players ran up a huge score as he kept himself and Charles Townsend on
for seventy-five overs. They took seven wickets between them, but at a
cost of 234 runs, and the Gentlemen were hard pressed to avoid an
innings defeat. A similar miscalculation in the return at Lord's resulted in
another big deficit on first innings, and the Gentlemen ended up being set

the almost impossible task of scoring 352 to win the game. Grace batted 'in his finest form' for 66, but when Richardson tore out the middle order, including Ranji and Jackson, the match seemed lost. This was not how Jessop, making his first appearance in the fixture, saw things. On the fall of the sixth wicket he joined F. G. J. Ford, a tall, languid left-hander with a reputation for 'gentle violence'.[2] Jessop's violence was anything but gentle, and of the eighty-eight runs the two added for the seventh wicket, he scored 67 in thirty-five minutes. However, although Ford continued to take the fight to the professionals, he got little support from the tail and ended on 79 not out, with the Gentlemen falling short of their target by seventy-eight runs.

Jessop's emergence as far more than just a tail-end slogger proved a huge bonus to Gloucestershire, as Grace readily acknowledged: 'His hitting was simply terrific, and the nerve which he threw into his play stimulated every other member of the team'[3] – not least, Grace himself. Both men scored centuries at Bristol in their next match after Lord's. This was against the third Philadelphian tourists who had persuaded the authorities to grant them first-class status. Though their batting was certainly not first-class, J. B. King was one of the greatest of all fast bowlers. With a hint of disapproval Grace records that King had developed 'the baseball trick of making the ball curve in the air after leaving his hand',[4] but on this occasion both he and Jessop mastered the swing, scoring 113 and 101 respectively, and Gloucestershire won by an innings.

Grace then had a well-earned rest to celebrate his forty-ninth birthday on the Sunday before focusing his attention on the championship for the second half of the season. Although lacking the depth and consistency required for a serious bid for the title, Gloucestershire regained their confidence and on their day could compete with any team in the country. They came very close to beating Warwickshire at Edgbaston, thanks almost entirely to Jessop's 126 in ninety-five minutes, during which W.G. was frequently seen standing up in the verandah of the pavilion, clapping his hands and shouting 'Well hit, Gilbert!'

It was W.G.'s turn in the next match against Nottinghamshire at Trent Bridge. He also produced an innings of 126, though at a rather more sedate pace, and Gloucestershire won by three wickets. When they travelled further north to Manchester they lost to the eventual champions Lancashire by ten wickets, but not before Jessop had hit 49 in the second innings. The runs came in twenty-five minutes against Mold, Johnny

Briggs and the fast-bowling find of the season, Bill Cuttell. If the Old Trafford crowd enjoyed that, they would have been even more delighted with his performance against Yorkshire at Harrogate the next day (29 July). Gloucestershire were 72 for 3 when Jessop came in twenty minutes before lunch. He returned to the pavilion with 43 not out. In eight overs after the interval he hit a further fifty-eight runs to reach 101 in only forty minutes. This was the fastest century ever scored in a first-class match to date, and it was made against an attack which included Jackson, George Hirst, J. T. Brown (whom Jessop rated the quickest Yorkshire bowler he ever faced) and Frank Milligan, who was also genuinely quick. In eight consecutive balls from Milligan and Hirst, Jessop belted thirty-three runs (6, 4, 4, 1; 4, 6, 4, 4). In all he hit four sixes, which in those days were only given when the ball went out of the ground. Jessop admitted he had a soft spot for Harrogate: 'it was so small'. Grace could barely contain himself, going up to Lord Hawke at the earliest opportunity and crowing, 'He gave you some, didn't he?' Hawke conceded that batting like that 'baffles description', though doubtless the Yorkshire bowlers made some attempts to do it justice.[5] Jessop got a duck in his second innings, but bounced back to take nine wickets and win the game for Gloucestershire by 140 runs.

In just fifteen days Jessop had given the cricket world another wonder to marvel at, and the prospect of seeing him with Ranji in the same match brought huge crowds to the county ground at Bristol on August Bank Holiday Monday for the game against Sussex. They saw a fine match, but the only centuries came from the two veterans of the previous age, Grace and Murdoch. Grace's 116 was a rather laboured affair, but after fifties against Middlesex and Kent, he produced his best innings of the season at Cheltenham against Nottinghamshire. He was in for four hours for his 131, and 'scarcely made a bad hit'.[6] He also had a successful match with the ball, taking 2 for 22 and 6 for 36 as Gloucestershire won by an innings.

Surrey had their revenge for the defeat at the Oval when they came to Clifton towards the end of August. Richardson, who was on fine form, bowled Grace for a duck and the whole team was out for 53. At a reception for the players of both teams that evening the host took the Surrey fast bowler aside and congratulated him on his performance, but insisted that 'the Old Man must not get a pair'. The following morning Richardson, 'the most good-natured of men',[7] obliged with an easy one, but Grace was almost immediately dismissed by Hayward, for 3, and

Gloucestershire collapsed again, losing by an innings and 134 runs. Richardson took 12 for 54 in the match.

Grace was on the losing side in his last two games of the season, North v. South and a final Gentlemen v. Players match at Hastings. For the South he made 36 and 30, and was twice bowled by Cuttell. For the Gentlemen he scored 46 in the first innings when only he and Frank Mitchell played Richardson with any confidence, though he became one of his six victims in the end. In the second innings the great fast bowler was simply irresistible. He bowled Grace for a duck and dismissed the rest of the team for 67, taking 7 for 43. During the course of this clinically destructive spell he accomplished 'the great feat of securing 1,000 wickets in four seasons'.[8]

Grace had reason to be proud of his achievements over the same period of time, and though 1897 had proved nothing like as successful as the two glorious years before it, he had still made 1,532 runs at 39.28 and taken fifty-six wickets at 22.17. There were, however, indications that his extraordinary run at the very top of the game might be coming to an end. The fact that in five out of his last six innings he had been clean-bowled by the fast men was a hint that even his wonderful eye was losing some of its sharpness. His huge bulk was also slowing him down. As he approached his fiftieth birthday his weight was nudging ever closer to the twenty-stone mark.

But for the public at large his position remained unassailable. His praises were sung and his deeds retold in the spate of books published to satisfy the explosion of interest in the game. Several prominent players had produced volumes cast in the same mould as Grace's own *Cricket* – a potted history of the game followed by a more personal account of the recent past. In 1893 Richard Daft had published his *Kings of Cricket* (one chapter sub-heading read: 'Dr. W. G. Grace: his Mastery of the Game'); Walter Read had followed with *Annals of Cricket* in 1896 ('My esteemed friend, Mr. W. G. Grace . . . his marvellous exhibitions of superb cricket'); and now Ranji, with some help from C. B. Fry, presented his *Jubilee Book of Cricket*, 'Dedicated, by her Gracious Permission, to Her Majesty the Queen Empress'. This distilled all the hard thinking the great batsman had given to the game as he had struggled from indefatigable apprenticeship to acknowledged mastery, and inevitably W.G.'s role was recognized as central:

[T]here is one great landmark that separated the old batting from the new – the appearance of Dr W. G. Grace in the cricket world . . . He revolutionised batting. He turned it from an accomplishment into a science. All I know of old-time batting is, of course, gathered from books and older players, but the impression left on my mind is this: Before W.G. batsmen were of two kinds – a batsman played a forward game or he played a back game. Each player, too, seems to have made a speciality of some particular stroke . . . What W.G. did was to unite in his mighty self all the good points of all the good players, and to make utility the criterion of style. He founded the modern theory of batting by making forward- and back-play of equal importance, relying neither on the one nor on the other, but on both . . . I hold him to be, not only the finest player born or unborn, but the maker of modern batting. He turned the old one-stringed instrument into a many-chorded lyre . . . Those who nowadays try to follow in his footsteps may or may not get within measurable distance of him, but it was he who pioneered and made the road. Where a great man has led many can go afterwards, but the honour is his who found and cut the path. The theory of modern batting is in all essentials the result of W.G.'s thinking and working on the game.[9]

Fine praise indeed from one who had certainly got within measurable distance of Grace, even relieving him of his record for the highest aggregate in a season, and who had produced new variations on the many-chorded lyre that left his contemporaries gasping in astonishment.

*

Grace's own Jubilee in 1898 caused almost as much national fervour as the Queen's the year before. After the unexpected, but very thorough, defeat of Stoddart's team in Australia over the winter, English cricket needed a fillip, and a celebration of the Champion's continuing prowess fitted the bill. In his honour the MCC decreed that the Gentlemen–Players fixture at Lord's should start on his actual birthday (18 July), and that was clearly going to be the game of the season. Grace began his preparations early, commandeering the pre-season Colts match for an extended net, in which he scored 146 not out in just under five and a half hours.

He started his first-class campaign in fine style with 65 at Lord's for the MCC in their innings victory over Sussex at the beginning of May. A week later he made 18 and 17 (out of 69) in the club's defeat by Yorkshire, and was back in London at the end of the month for Gloucestershire's game against Surrey at the Oval. Once more Richard-son had the measure of him, bowling him for 18 in the first innings. Grace made 51 in his second innings, before Richardson claimed his wicket again. This was a strenuous match for W.G. as he had bowled fifty-one overs in the Surrey second innings of 500 for 4 (he took three of the four wickets for ninety-four runs). Such an endurance test inevitably put great strain on Grace's fifty-year-old body, and he was not to get through the season without a recurrence of his knee problem. But nothing could take the edge off his keenness, and he soldiered on, uncomplaining.

The county drew against Sussex at Hove, but won their first game at the beginning of June, beating Middlesex by eight wickets at Lord's. Grace followed his 39 not out in that match with 73 against Kent at Gravesend, and then made the relatively modest contribution of 63 to Gloucestershire's phenomenal total of 634 at Bristol against Nottinghamshire (Walter Troup, C. O. H. Sewell and Charlie Townsend all scored centuries in what remained the county's highest score until 1928, when they made 653 for 6 against Glamorgan – also at Bristol). Pleasing though such a huge score must have been, it is arguable that Grace should have declared as his bowlers had barely the time to bowl out Nottinghamshire once.

Grace then went back to London for the Gentlemen v. Players match at the Oval. As a dress rehearsal for his big day a month later it was slightly disappointing. Although the amateurs held their own against Jack Hearne and Lockwood on the first day, with Townsend and Murdoch both making fifties, the Players' greater strength told over the remainder of the game. William Storer and Lockwood racked up ninety-six runs for the last wicket to establish a lead of fifty-one, and when the Gentlemen batted a second time only Grace had an answer to Lockwood. He stayed in for two hours for a determined 50, but the rest of the side mustered only another 105 between them and the Players won by eight wickets.

Low scores in the drawn game against Lancashire at Gloucester and in the MCC's surprise defeat by Oxford University followed, but the game against Essex at Leyton on the eve of the Jubilee match provided something altogether more dramatic. The two protagonists were, inevitably, W.G. himself and the Essex amateur fast bowler Charles Kortright.[10] Kortright was one of those characters it is more fun to read about than to confront, especially at a distance of twenty-two yards. Moody and aggressive, he was generally reckoned to be *the* fastest bowler of his time, perhaps, as some have claimed, of all time. In contrast to the mild-mannered Richardson, he had a notoriously mean streak and took considerable pleasure from hurting batsmen. As one insurance company liked to remind readers of *Wisden*, 'More accidents are met with at Cricket than at any other pastime', and this was certainly true when Kortright was playing.

Two stories illustrate his lethal nature. Once, playing an army team, he noted that one of the batsmen cocked his left toe as he prepared to face. Kortright told him that he only allowed one man to do that to him, and that was W.G. The cocked toe remained cocked, but not for long. Kortright quite deliberately broke it with a yorker. On another occasion when he was playing golf, the four behind teed off too soon and one of their balls landed close to Kortright. Kortright drove it straight back. In his determination to have things his own way and his general irascibility he was quite the equal of Grace, so when the two were brought together in the highly charged atmosphere of a very competitive match, a clash was almost inevitable.

This was the first time Gloucestershire had played Essex, and there was at least one person in Leyton to whom Grace was not as familiar as the sovereign or the recently deceased Mr Gladstone. The policeman on the gate refused to let Grace into the pavilion because he couldn't produce the right pass. Once Grace's identity had been established to the satisfaction of the law, he was at liberty to meet his opposite number, Hugh Owen, and proceed to the toss. Grace called wrongly and Essex batted. Just in case there was anyone else on the ground who didn't know who he was, he then bowled Essex out for 128 before lunch, keeping up a nagging line on the leg-stump and taking 7 for 44 in 16.1 overs.

Although there was no denying this was a splendid performance, bad feeling was created over the dismissal of Percy Perrin, who was given out caught and bowled when he hit the ball back low to Grace. Grace lunged heavily forward and then turned in triumph to the umpire exclaiming, 'Not bad for an old 'un.' To everyone who saw it, it was apparent that he had taken the ball on the half-volley, but the umpire was unsighted and with Grace waving the ball in his face put his finger up. Grace increased the bad feeling when on telegraphing the score to Bristol he received the reply 'How cruel of you to bowl the rabbits out', and couldn't resist pinning it up inside the pavilion. Kortright reckoned he knew something about rabbits, and when Gloucestershire batted he soon had five back in the hutch. But he couldn't shift Grace, who scored 126. It was a classic contest, still vividly remembered by Kortright half a century later when he was interviewed by John Arlott. 'The Old Man made me look as simple as dirt. He wasn't attempting to hit the ball with his bat outside the off-stump, but he was punching it – punching it – with his thick felt gloves through the slips and I was bowling fairly fast then. He was punching me with his hands down the slips to third man and everyone was very much surprised at that.' With the obvious risk of injury, let alone the chance of being caught, it seems an unlikely approach, and it is quite possible that from the privileged vantage of old age, Kortright was over-dramatizing; the *Memorial Biography* states simply that Grace was 'severely knocked on the hand several times'.[11] Kortright's suggestion that Grace made him 'look as simple as dirt', and by implication took a large proportion of his runs off him, is certainly not borne out by his figures. He took 5 for 41.

Charles Townsend (51) was the only batsman to give Grace support, and the Gloucestershire innings closed first thing on the second morning with the score on 231. The wicket was still good and Essex knocked off the arrears and ran up a total of 250. This might have been more but for a second controversial dismissal. A. P. Lucas, veteran of the 1882 Test who turned out occasionally for Essex, was adjudged caught behind, but made it quite clear the ball had brushed his shirt not his bat. As he walked back to the pavilion, the crowd shouted 'Cheats never prosper'.

The presence of Lucas might have reminded Grace how dangerous fast bowlers could be when provoked, and if it didn't, Kortright's opening salvo certainly did. In his first over he clean-bowled Board and Troup, and when he got Grace down his end he gave him a very torrid time. But although unsettled, Grace couldn't be intimidated. Nor, it seemed, could he be got out. He gave such a clear return catch to Walter Mead that none of the Essex team appealed – until they saw Grace calmly taking up his position again. Mead then did appeal, and the umpire, George Burton, put up his finger and said 'Out!', only to reverse his decision when Grace roared down the wicket, 'What, George?' If Kortright was angry before – and he was – this drove him to a pitch of homicidal fury, and he sprinted in with redoubled venom. Gone was the off-stump line of the first innings; now he aimed straight at his man – and got him, repeatedly. One blow in the stomach doubled Grace up, and the bruise was spectacular. Jessop called it 'quite the most extraordinary extravasation of blood that I have ever witnessed. The seam of the ball was quite clear, and you could almost see the maker's name impinged on the flesh. The horrid thud of the impact could be distinctly heard in the pavilion. An unpleasant noise – especially for those who had to come after him.'[12] Grace's discomfort pleased sections of the crowd, and gave rise to some jeering laughter. It was an unedifying spectacle, and Kortright was roundly ticked off by the following year's *Wisden*: 'Balls dropped little more than half way down the wicket at his tremendous speed bring cricket within the category of dangerous pastimes.' Precisely. This was war.

In all his time in first-class cricket Grace probably never experienced anything quite as hostile as that last spell on the second day at Leyton, but, just ten days short of his fiftieth birthday, he still had the strength of character and skill to survive. He gave one very sharp chance off a full-blooded cut, but the slip didn't even get a hand to it. When he overheard Kortright remonstrating with the fielder as they came off the field, he muttered, 'Cheats never prosper'. He was more voluble back in the pavilion, expressing his opinion of Kortright's assault 'vigorously and adjectivally'.

Gloucestershire had scored eighty-one of the 148 runs they needed to win for the loss of three wickets. The opening overs on the third morning would in all probability prove decisive. Grace resumed on 36. Kortright resumed in the same mood of unbridled hostility. The duel continued. For a while Grace seemed to be getting the upper hand, alternating rock-like defence with controlled aggression, and he had eased the total up to 96 and his own score to 49 when Kortright summoned every ounce of energy for one last effort. The first ball hit the pad plumb in front of the stumps. Kortright appealed, and then, from his position half-way down the wicket, watched in disbelief as Grace seemed to hypnotize the umpire into keeping his hand by his side. He snatched up the ball, strode back to his mark and sprinted in again. This time Grace got an edge to the keeper. Another clamorous appeal; another magnetic stare; another shamefaced shake of the head. The next ball was probably the fastest delivery ever bowled up to that time. It sent the middle stump flying towards the slips and knocked the leg-stump crooked. Grace surveyed the wreckage with a thunderous face and set off for the pavilion. Kortright raised a quizzical eyebrow and uttered his immortal line: 'Surely you're not going, Doc? There's still one stump standing.'

Grace claimed he had never been so insulted in his life, which wasn't true, but he had certainly never been put down so emphatically. Kortright had won the personal battle. It now remained to be seen whether he could win the game. When he got Townsend soon after to reduce Gloucestershire to 129 for 5, it looked as though he would. Whatever the rights and wrongs of the preceding two days, the match had now developed a competitive dimension that lifted it out of the run-of-the-mill championship encounter. Jessop, who replaced Townsend, later recalled, 'Excepting a Varsity or a Test, I'm sure I can never have more devoutly wished to win a match than this one.'[13]

And it was very much down to him. He soon lost Champain (132 for 6), but Wrathall stayed with him until, with only three required, it looked as though the visitors were safe. However, Mead made the breakthrough, and although Brown scored a single, that only took him down to the other end. Kortright shattered his stumps first ball. Edward Wright, the number ten, wasn't so lucky. He got his foot in the way of his first ball, and could barely hobble back to the pavilion using his bat as a crutch. Fred Roberts was the last man, and Grace collared him before he went out. On no account was he to move his bat or run away. Roberts pleaded wife and family. Grace countered with the assurance he would never play for the county again if he got out, sweetened with the promise of an extra pound if they won.

With much to think about Roberts walked out to face the firing squad. He might just as well have been blindfolded for all he knew of the rest of the over. Having missed the stumps by a fraction with his first two deliveries, Kortright finally found the edge of Roberts's motionless bat with his third. The ball flew away through the slips, and Jessop hared down the wicket, intending to win the match then and there. However, in his shocked elation at finding himself still alive, Roberts took too long over his first run, and as the return came in Jessop had to tell him to stay where he was. This left him on strike to Walter Mead.

Mead's medium pace was no threat to life or limb, but he was a canny bowler, and more than a match for Roberts's rudimentary defensive skills. Jessop looked on in anguished impotence as the number eleven survived an appeal for lbw and a catch behind, narrowly missed being bowled and played a ball onto his stumps without disturbing the bails. It was with positive relief that Jessop faced Kortright again, and after playing two balls he ended the agony with a lofted drive to the pavilion.

Although Grace was delighted to have won, the victory was achieved at some cost. Relations between the two teams were soured, and once again Grace's friendship with C. E. Green went into cold storage. In his contribution to the *Memorial Biography*, Green wrote of Grace's 'excessive keenness' which led to what he considered 'rather sharp practices', but went on to say that 'eventually after mutual explanations and most handsome admissions on his part, we became greater and warmer friends than ever.'[14] There seemed no likelihood of his ever patching things up with Kortright, who was so incensed that he threatened to pull out of the Gentlemen's side for the match at Lord's. In the end he was persuaded to go, but it took yet another remarkable finale to break the ice between the two men.

There were still two county matches before the great day, and Grace played in both of them, despite a bruised heel possibly picked up in his battle with Kortright. Against Warwickshire at Edgbaston Gloucestershire ran up another huge total of 504, and although he only contributed 24 runs, Grace bowled over fifty overs and took 6 for 73 in the match. The game at Bristol against Somerset was an almost exact replica. Gloucestershire made 505, and again, though he only made 20, Grace was successful with the ball, taking 7 for 85 and 5 for 53 to secure the second innings victory in a week. It was perfect preparation for 18 July. All that was needed was correspondingly perfect weather.

*

The weather was fine, and 17,500 spectators pressed through the turnstiles to witness, and indeed participate in, W.G.'s Jubilee match. When Grace arrived at the ground with Agnes and Bessie he was virtually mobbed, and in the welter of greetings and congratulations there was no time for his customary knock-up.

The two teams, however, were hard at work in the nets, closely scrutinized by the milling crowd. The announcement of the sides had been eagerly awaited and their publication caused the usual stir. The Players were inexplicably given two wicket-keepers (Storer and Lilley) and denied their leading fast bowler, though perhaps, given the number of times Richardson had clean-bowled Grace over the last year and a half, his absence should be seen as an additional birthday present. Ranji was pursuing his political interests at home in India, but the next biggest draw, Jessop, was passed over for Sammy Woods. Palairet was another absentee, Captain (as he now was) Wynyard getting the last batting place. Johnny Dixon of Nottinghamshire was fortunate to be chosen, but his inclusion probably indicates one of the selectors' criteria: he, like six of his team-mates (seven including Grace), was captain of his county.

Though the two teams contained sufficient material for extensive bar-room analysis, there was no doubting that they largely comprised the cream of English cricket. In addition to Woods, Wynyard and Dixon, the Gentlemen had Stoddart, Jackson, MacLaren, Mason, Townsend, Gregor MacGregor and Kortright, while the Players could boast an equally formidable line-up: Shrewsbury (captain), Abel, Gunn, Storer,

Tunnicliffe, Brockwell, Alec Hearne, Lilley, Lockwood, Haigh and Jack Hearne. The young Wilfred Rhodes was twelfth man. Grace had a commemorative medallion struck for the occasion which he presented to all those playing with their names inscribed on the obverse (see Plate 22). The two sides were captured in a famous, if flickeringly brief, piece of film, walking two by two in Chaplinesque style towards the camera. Grace, looking like a jovial gorilla in his bulging blazer, leads the way, and just manages to doff his cap in salutation as he passes out of shot. It was, as David Kynaston said, 'the gesture of a man who would have been a media superstar in any age'.[15]

He certainly got a superstar's reception when, having lost the toss, he led his team out, just after twelve o'clock. For a man who had been given rapturous receptions on three different continents, this must still have been an exceptional moment. Here, at the heart of the game with which his name was inextricably linked the world over, he was given a hero's welcome. The capacity crowd rose to their feet and thunderous applause punctuated with yells of praise and birthday greetings poured from every side of Lord's in an unbroken torrent of sound. Grace raised his hand in a casual salute, and then, almost before the noise had died away, another huge cheer went up for the Players' opening pair, Shrewsbury and Abel.

Without consulting Kortright, with whom he was still not on speaking terms, Grace set a field and the Demon of Leyton raced in to get the match under way. His speed drew gasps from the spectators as he put both batsmen through a rigorous test of technique and character. This was clearly not Bobby Abel's idea of a birthday party, and he departed with no visible sign of regret after a humiliating fifty minutes when Kortright found his exposed leg-stump. He had made 7. Kortright also had a hand in the dismissal of Shrewsbury, taking a smart catch at slip off a rather wide leg-break from Townsend. After an hour, the score was 29 for 2. Grace, who had limped off the field to attend to his heel which was troubling him, now grasped the nettle and asked Kortright whether he wanted a rest. Kortright said he would carry on, but gradually, as the heat took its toll and Gunn and Storer played themselves in, he lost his edge and the runs started to come. Grace eventually took him off, and, to renewed cheering, had a spell himself. He and Sammy Woods bowled in tandem until lunch, when the score stood at 85 for 2.

If the morning had belonged to the Gentlemen, the Players claimed the afternoon. Storer went on to 59, and Gunn played one of the great innings in the history of the fixture. His 139 was the highest score for the

Players at Lord's to that date. Brockwell made 47 and Alec Hearne and Lilley also made useful contributions. Play ended half an hour earlier than advertised when the ninth wicket fell at 328. The probable explanation was that the MCC was holding a banquet for W.G. in the pavilion that evening, but with no public address system beyond a man with a megaphone, the crowd – and the groundstaff – were caught unawares, and the square was soon lost to sight as the spectators, who had been cramped for hours in the hot sun, stretched their legs and inspected the wicket.

The second day was less propitious than the first, with rain falling over London in the morning. However, another large crowd gathered and play started shortly after 11.30 a.m. The Players' last wicket soon fell, and the Gentlemen faced a total of 335. Another great cheer greeted Grace as he came out to open the innings with Stoddart on a wicket made lively by the morning showers. The crowd watched anxiously as Grace made an uncertain start against Jack Hearne's medium pace. Lockwood's greater speed posed equally difficult problems at the other end. Neither batsman looked comfortable against the steeply rearing ball, and when Grace sparred at one, Lilley first juggled with, then dropped, what appeared to be a chance – though the Champion was back to his Leyton tricks and made a great display of rubbing his side to indicate he hadn't hit it. After another let-off when Hearne seemed to misjudge a tame caught and bowled, he changed tactics and started to give the crowd something to cheer with a few thumping drives and a huge pull that cleared the ring. Haigh, the Yorkshire fast bowler, replaced Hearne, and though the fifty came up, batting was still difficult. Lockwood eventually got Stoddart, caught at slip for 21 with the score on 56.

Jackson joined Grace, who shortly afterwards received a stinging blow on the hand from Haigh which made him drop his bat in pain. His bruised heel troubled him almost from the start and he had been in obvious difficulties running between the wickets for some time. But the old war-horse carried on, as he always had done, combative and uncomplaining. With the score on 79 he gave another chance off Lockwood and Lilley made no mistake this time. He had been in for an hour and a half and, though never at ease, had put up a dogged fight for his 43. Although Townsend, who came in next, made only 2, Jackson (48) and MacLaren (50) both batted beautifully, Mason and Dixon made useful thirties, and all the tail-enders reached double figures in a highly creditable total of 303. Lockwood took 4 for 82, Hearne 5 for 87.

Fifty minutes remained for play at the conclusion of the Gentlemen's innings. The light was bad, the wicket had deteriorated and Kortright, loosened up by a vigorous little innings of 17, was fresh. Who would be an opening batsman? Abel demonstrated even less enthusiasm for the role than he had the day before, and soon lost his leg-stump for a second time to Kortright. Shrewsbury didn't seem to have much more stomach for the fight, and followed him for 11, bowled Woods. At 21 for 2 the Players faced a crisis. Gunn was held back – he had been off the field all day nursing an injury picked up during his long innings on Monday – and it was left to Storer and Tunnicliffe to weather the storm for the last twenty-five minutes of the day. Another wicket would almost certainly have swung the match the Gentlemen's way, but though journalists were debating whether Kortright would face charges of murder or manslaughter in the likely event of his killing someone, he could not get the breakthrough and the Players lived to fight another day, closing on 42 for 2.

In the meantime, Grace had another dinner to eat and another speech to make. Along with the entire Gentlemen's team and 150 guests drawn from the great and the good of the cricket world, he was entertained at the Sports Club in St James's Square. Sir Richard Webster, the Attorney-General, presided over the evening and declared that

1848 would be celebrated not by the French revolution or by the abdication of Louis Philippe, but for the fact of the birth of W .G. Grace . . . He would be remembered . . . because he had elevated sport, because he had played cricket as a sportsman's game, and had played from beginning to end courageously, honourably and straightforwardly, and not simply to make a great many runs, but to make his side play the game as they ought to play it. They honoured him because he was a large-hearted Englishmen.[16]

Grace pulled himself wearily to his feet and engagingly reminded his audience that his prowess on the field of play was not matched by his skill as a public speaker: 'I wish I had Stoddart's happy knack of saying the right words in the right place. If I cannot say the right words, I feel them. You all know my speeches are few and short. When I am pleased they may be all right. When I am not they may be all wrong.'[17] But of course on such an occasion he could do no wrong, and his halting pleasantries delighted his audience. Of the match in hand he said:

I am very proud to be captain of the lot we have got here tonight. I have played on a good many wickets, and I know when they are a little bad, and I can tell you to get over 300 runs on the wicket we have played on today was better than we expected. My old friend Stoddart and myself, when we got 50, thought we had done pretty well. The 300 wasn't made by one man, but by everybody on the side. I must say if we had won the toss the game would have been nearly over tonight.[18]

As it was, the match was perfectly balanced. Grace had not gone out to field the previous evening as the blow on his hand from Haigh was still troubling him. It was no better in the morning, so Stoddart led out the Gentlemen while W.G. remained in the pavilion. It was a fine day, but a cold wind blew across the ground. That helped complete the drying-out process, and the wicket was much easier than the day before. Storer and Tunnicliffe soon showed that they were in command, running quick singles and punishing anything loose. They had put on 106 together when Mason induced Tunnicliffe to drive uppishly into the covers, where he was caught by the substitute fielder, Rhodes. Gunn came in and got off the mark with a crashing square-cut off Kortright, and the runs kept coming at a good rate until Storer was tempted by Townsend and gave Rhodes his second catch of the morning. He had made 73 to add to his 59 in the first innings, and thoroughly justified his place in the side. Gunn also passed fifty for the second time in the match, and with some useful runs down the order the Players reached 263. The innings ended at 3.45, which left the Gentlemen just two and a half hours to get 296 – an unlikely proposition on a third-day pitch against a strong attack.

However, when Stoddart and MacLaren came out to open for the Gentlemen (Grace was still not fit enough to bat), it was clear that the amateurs were going to give it their best shot. Stoddart lashed out at Lockwood, hitting a powerful four past point's right hand, but was then caught at slip fencing at a rising ball. Jackson, coming in at three, was also prepared to chance his arm and hit Hearne for several offside boundaries. Hearne retaliated by removing MacLaren with a ball that rebounded in awful slow motion off his pads onto the stumps. At 41 for 2 Sammy Woods came in and smacked nine runs off his first four balls, but whereas Jessop might have gone on to set the afternoon alight, Woods then succumbed to Hearne. The score moved rapidly from 55 for 3 to 56 for 6 as both Wynyard and Mason made ducks and Jackson was bowled by Hearne, who was breaking the ball down the Lord's slope prodigiously.

Jackson's departure for 33 ended any last hope of a romantic victory.

The Gentlemen would be hard pressed now to save the match. Townsend and Dixon knuckled down to the task. It took Dixon twenty-five minutes to get off the mark, but after some patient play Townsend began to get restless. He hit Hearne for a couple of fours, but then gave him his fifth wicket of the innings when he was well caught by Tunnicliffe at slip. And now, at 77 for 7 with just under an hour to play, Grace made his dramatic entrance.

Another huge shout went up and then cheering broke out round the ground as he made his way slowly to the wicket. There had been rumours that he wouldn't bat, but it was his party and he wasn't going to sit it out in the pavilion. It did, however, look as though he was going to run out of partners. He lost Dixon, bowled Haigh, with the score still on 77, and Gregor MacGregor, having scored only a single, then became Hearne's sixth victim – 80 for 9. All eyes turned to the pavilion where the tall figure of Charles Kortright strode purposefully through the massed ranks of MCC members. For possibly only the second time in three days, Grace approached to talk to him. As Kortright remembered years later, it was a brief encounter. Grace said, 'Korty, don't be nervous, play your usual game,' to which he replied, 'All right, Doc, I'll do my best.' The two men then separated to display their British phlegm in their individual ways.

It was nerve-racking stuff. Kortright was nearly bowled first ball, and looked very shaky, though his determination not to get out was clear. Grace, too, caused some anxious moments, especially when he mishit a lofted drive and Bobby Abel, running back, just failed to get his hands to the ball. But, as the minutes agonizingly ticked away, the alarms became fewer and the runs mounted up. When Lockwood came back on, Grace cut him for four, and Kortright brought up the hundred with a classical drive off Hearne. The crowd were enthralled, applauding every run, shouting out encouragement and greeting every passing over with relief. Shrewsbury turned to Alec Hearne's round-arm leg-breaks, but without result, and then, just before 6.30, he called up Storer to try to tempt Kortright with some out-and-out rubbish. The number eleven solemnly patted back an over of slow long-hops, and then, as the crowd broke into wild cheering, turned on his heel and made for the pavilion.

But the match was not, in fact, over. The captains had agreed earlier to play through to seven if a result looked possible, though in another failure of communication nobody had bothered to tell the spectators. Or, indeed, Kortright. He returned to the crease and the crowd settled down once more. With the Gentlemen's score standing at 130 for 9, the agony continued. Shrewsbury shuffled his pack trying to break the batsmen's concentration with a succession of bowling changes while ensuring that he got in as many overs as possible. This didn't necessarily help his bowlers, and Kortright in particular hit some crashing boundaries, each bringing fresh torrents of sound from the stands and the cheaper seating. At a quarter to seven Grace lumbered down the wicket and shook hands with his erstwhile antagonist and now companion-in-arms. It was a typically big-hearted gesture which was clamorously received by the crowd.

The great stand continued, though with the removal of the personal tension between them both Kortright and Grace showed signs of fallibility. But they survived until at four minutes to seven Shrewsbury tried one last throw of the dice and brought Lockwood on at the Pavilion end, behind which the declining sun was shining brightly. Kortright, on 46, was the man on strike. He blocked the first two balls, but then, with his fifty beckoning, drove at the third, Lockwood's notorious slower ball, got a leading edge and watched horrified as Haigh ran back from cover to take the catch and finally win the match. The two heroes of the seventy-eight-run last-wicket stand buffeted their way through the jubilant throng arm in arm, and later, with the crowd baying for them, appeared together again on the balcony. The Players had thoroughly deserved their victory, but for all the great performances from Gunn, Storer, Lockwood, Hearne and the others, the undoubted star of the show was W.G.

*

After three such physically, emotionally and gastronomically demanding days, most men – of any age, let alone fifty – would have wanted a day off. Grace was emphatically not most men. He was unique, and to prove it he travelled up to Trent Bridge the following morning for Gloucestershire's match against Nottinghamshire. Despite his troublesome heel – which made him 'very lame'[19] – and the continuing discomfort from his damaged hand, he batted all day, scoring, appropriately enough, his fiftieth century for the county. He was 143 not out at stumps and carried on the next day to reach 168 out of 307. The match ended as it had started, with Grace at the wicket shepherding his side to a draw with 38 not out.

He failed at Old Trafford, and the team was bowled out for 44. Although they made a spirited recovery in the second innings, the match was beyond saving, but Lancashire were the last side to beat them. At

Bristol, Grace was looking set for another century as he played out the last afternoon against Sussex, but when he reached 93 he surprised everyone by declaring. It was, he explained, the only score between 0 and 100 he had never made.

After an equally tame draw with Middlesex, in which Grace made 55, Gloucestershire had a triumphant finish to the season, winning their last four matches. Grace failed against Kent, falling twice to Fred Martin, and went quietly in the return against Essex at Clifton, which the county won uncontroversially by an innings and forty-two runs. But at Taunton he produced a scintillating 109 to set up another innings victory over Somerset. When a friend later hinted that it was a small ground, he bridled: '[L]et me tell you it takes as much trouble to hit to the ropes at Taunton as at the Oval.'[20] Against Surrey in the last championship game, the card had a familiar ring to it: Grace was bowled by Richardson for 27. But the county still won comfortably by five wickets.

Gloucestershire's record of nine wins and three defeats lifted them above Surrey (eleven wins, four defeats) and Essex (ten wins, six defeats) to take third place in the final championship table, below Yorkshire and Middlesex. It was their highest position since they were (dubious) runners-up to Lancashire in 1881. They were playing with much more confidence now, and were far less dependent on Grace to win their matches for them. This was fortunate in view of the drama that was about to unfold.

Grace ended his own season by the seaside as usual. He made 58 and 0 for the Rest of England against A. E. Stoddart's XI, and 40 and 8 for the Rest of England v. Surrey and Sussex. Tom Richardson claimed his wicket on three occasions out of four, clean-bowling him twice in his last match. But though some things appeared to stay the same, everything in Grace's life was about to change, radically and irrevocably.

THIRTY

ALTHOUGH 1899 is generally taken as the cut-off point for the life Grace had been leading since setting up his practice in 1879, most of the important changes to that settled existence either happened or started happening the year before. 1898 was the year of decisions.

They were not, however, premeditated. In December 1896 Grace wrote to a Dr A. C. Greenwood from his new home at Ashley Grange, offering him a job as his assistant. In addition to providing a rare instance of Grace giving an inch over money – 'I did not mean to give more than £90 but still if we suit each other, I will give you £100' – the letter shows that he had every intention of remaining as he was for the foreseeable future: 'I would rather you did not accept my offer unless there is a chance of your staying with me for a year or two or more. I do not want to keep changing my Locum Tenens.' The two men obviously did suit each other, and Dr Greenwood started work as Grace's assistant in January 1897. His son recalled his father telling him 'how he once watched "W.G." do a circumcision on a young lad of about 19. No anaesthetic of any kind was given. The young lad did not make a sound, but my father never forgot the look of agony on his face.'[1]

Grace was so pre-eminent as a cricketer that his contemporaries found it hard to take his medical activities seriously. E. V. Lucas wrote, 'Between September and May one thought of him as hibernating in a cave',[2] and Max Beerbohm's cartoon of 1895 pandered to the popular prejudice that W.G. put cricket (and the money he made from it) before his patients. He was certainly not above using his privileged position as a doctor to further his cricketing purposes. When Walter Troup, who was still an officer in the Indian Police when he started his long career with Gloucestershire, was threatened with a re-call, Grace displayed acute diagnostic precision to avert disaster. His doctor's note read: 'I have to-day examined Mr W. Troup. He is in a very low state of health. I strongly recommend out-door exercise and cricket for preference.'[3]

Although a large body of humorous anecdotes grew up around Grace's medical career ('Is Dr Grace in?' 'Of course. He's been in since lunchtime on Tuesday,' etc.), the evidence suggests that in fact he was as conscientious a GP as he was a cricketer. 'From early morn till late in the evening you will find W.G. toiling at his profession, trudging through rain, sunshine and storm as cheerful as if he were playing cricket,' his biographer Brownlee recorded,[4] and those he served held him in high regard. His bedside manner may have been gruff, but he was undoubtedly kind; his huge presence must of itself have been reassuring, and his naturally optimistic personality can only have worked as a tonic. His expertise was probably no greater than might have been expected, though he apparently had one talent of particular value in the crowded slums of Stapleton Road. He was 'tremendously good at smelling the air when there was smallpox around' and distinguishing it from the far less dangerous chicken pox.[5] The oral tradition also suggests that he often omitted to send bills to his poorest patients.

Like his father before him, Grace had first-hand experience of industrial accidents. In February 1886, for instance, there was an explosion at the Easton Colliery. Eight men died, and eight more were so seriously injured that they could never work again. Grace was called to the horrific scene at eight a.m. to do what he could.[6] Far from hibernating in a cave, W.G. spent the best part of twenty winters building up a deserved reputation as a competent, trusted and well-loved doctor in the Bristol area.

But early in 1898, wide-ranging reforms to the administration of the Poor Law resulted in a radical restructuring of the provision of care in the Bristol area, including the Barton Regis Union, whose No.2 District W.G. served as Medical Officer.[7] Grace found himself under a new authority, and took exception to the terms he was offered. He was just as determined in defence of his own interests as a doctor as he was as a cricketer, and, along with a number of other union doctors, he resigned. In compensation, he was paid an annuity for the rest of his life.[8]

This effectively brought his medical career to an end. He could have soldiered on in private practice, but the summer was to throw up an opportunity that might have been, and indeed probably was, tailor-made for him. The Directors of the Board of Crystal Palace Company decided to establish a first-class cricket club, to be known as London County, at the Crystal Palace site in Sydenham. The suburbs were fast becoming the natural home of the lower middle classes, and the population was expanding rapidly. As *The Times* commented, 'If the London clerk is often slack in his employer's service, he is pretty sure to be a master of the last information about batting averages and about the chances of the county championship.'[9] It was on this growing army of enthusiasts that the board rested its hopes. And who better to draw them through the gates than W.G.?

Approaches were made to him during the 1898 season, and given Grace's hard-nosed business sense, negotiations were doubtless protracted. In addition to reaching an agreement on terms, there were two further problems: Crystal Palace already had a cricket club, and so had Grace. As far as Grace was concerned, he didn't see the difficulty. He had always shared his time between Gloucestershire and his other cricketing commitments – Gentlemen v. Players, North v. South, MCC fixtures – and he had been organizing teams of first-class standard since the days of the United South. He saw no reason why he should not do the same for London County while continuing to play for and captain Gloucestershire. The question of divided loyalties simply did not arise.

The first problem, the prior existence of a cricket club at Crystal Palace, he left to be resolved by the board. As Ian Maxwell Campbell, one of the younger members of the existing club, recalled fifty years later, 'There was considerable and outspoken opposition on the part of members of our old and well-established Crystal Palace Cricket Club to this unexpected intrusion and to their being taken over lock, stock and barrel by the new concern. We have become accustomed in recent years to possessive aggressions, both internal and international, but in those days they were uncommon and deeply resented.'[10] It is doubtful that Grace lost much sleep over that; since the days of the amalgamation of the Mangotsfield Cricket Club and the West Gloucestershire Cricket Club, 'possessive aggressions' had run in the family. He probably felt impatient at the compromise whereby the two clubs led separate and independent lives for the first season before Crystal Palace CC finally bowed out in 1900.

Grace's appointment as secretary and manager of the new club was announced in *The Times* on 11 October 1898. The paper noted that 'Dr W. G. Grace . . . will reside on the spot, in order to be able to devote his whole time and attention to the new club.' This provoked an instant response, published the following day: 'A telegram has been received from Dr W. G. Grace stating that . . . the appointment will not involve his retiring from the Gloucestershire eleven.' The paragraph ended, 'Dr Grace's contract with Crystal Palace was signed last Thursday' (i.e. 6

October). His salary was to be £600 per annum, plus a shilling out of every guinea collected in subscriptions or taken at the gate. Despite his disclaimer, the announcement can only have caused the Gloucestershire Committee deep unease, but there was nothing they could do. Grace, as ever, was a law unto himself.

Before this state of affairs led to its inevitable acrimonious denouement, there was a busy winter settling in at St Andrew's in Laurie Park Road, which was conveniently close to Grace's new operational headquarters. With Bertie launched on his career in teaching – after Cambridge he taught first at Uppingham and then at the Royal Naval College, Osborne on the Isle of Wight – and Edgar starting his naval training, only Bessie and Charles remained under the parental roof. Bessie, like any other young lady, would stay at home until she married. Charles was to attend the Crystal Palace Engineering School, and as part of the deal with the directorate his fees would be found for him. It must have been a wonderful place to study. The school was only a couple of hundred yards away from Paxton's monumental feat of engineering which, after looming like an iceberg over Hyde Park when it housed the Great Exhibition in 1851, had been miraculously resurrected at the top of Sydenham Hill, giving dramatic focus to the acres of formal gardens that stretched down to the cricket ground.

Another major project that finally got under way in 1898 was the preparation of a second volume of Grace's cricketing memoirs. Since the publication of *Cricket* in 1891, his forays into print had been limited to *The History of a Hundred Centuries* and occasional articles for the cricketing periodicals. Now, despite the drudgery involved, he had been persuaded, with the usual financial inducements, to submit himself once more to the toils of authorship. Ranji's *Jubilee Book* had done very well, and with the glories of 1895 and all the other triumphs of the decade still fresh in the memory, Grace's name retained more than enough lustre to guarantee a commercial success. The book had initially been planned to coincide with his own Jubilee in 1898, but as Arrowsmith had found, Grace's busy lifestyle and the vagaries of his thought processes did not sit well with publishing deadlines, and his new publisher, James Bowden, eventually despaired and called in professional help. The man given the job of eliciting Grace's recollections and getting them down on paper in a coherent manner was the journalist and religious affairs writer Arthur Porritt, who left an engaging, if slightly exasperated, account of the process:

It is not a breach of faith now to say that I wrote the book. Grace was choke full of cricketing history, experience and reminiscence, but he was a singularly inarticulate man, and had he been left to write his own cricketing biography it would never have seen the light . . . Grace accepted me as his collaborator with the utmost heartiness, and, although the task of getting the material from him was almost heartbreaking, I enjoyed the work immensely. My plan was to spend three half-days a week with W. G. in his own study – he was living at Sydenham then – and by every conceivable artifice that an experienced interviewer could bring into operation, lure him into a flow of reminiscence. Many days I drew a blank and came away with scarcely sufficient material for a paragraph. On other days I managed to enveigle him into a reminiscent vein, and he would send me off with data enough for one or two chapters.

W. G.'s mind functioned oddly. He never stuck to any train of recollection, but would jump from an event in the sixties to something that happened in, say, the last Test Match. Often I left his house in absolute despair. Once, at least, I asked leave to abandon the enterprise; but I was urged to persist. I remember very distinctly one age-long afternoon when I was trying to get out of W. G. something of the psychology of a batsman making a big score in a great match. All that he wanted to say in recording some dazzling batting feat of his own was, 'Then I went in and made 284.' 'Yes,' I would reply, 'but that is not good enough. People want to know what W. G. Grace felt like when he was doing it; what thoughts he had and what the whole mental experience of a big innings means to a batsman.' 'I did not feel anything; I had too much to do to watch the bowling and see how the fieldsmen were moved about to think anything.'[11]

In point of fact this is a brilliant description of the state of Zen-like concentration required for sporting achievement at the highest level. However, Porritt eventually badgered Grace into the far less illuminating statement that 'some days a batsman's eye is *in* and other days it is not. When his eye is *in*, the cricket ball seems the size of a football and he can't miss it. When his eye isn't *in* then he isn't in long, because he's soon bowled out.'[12] It is this stunning *aperçu* that Porritt pads out to a page and a half in *Reminiscences*. But for all his amenability, Grace had lost none of his sharp sense of what readers expected from him, and he vetted every page of the manuscript. Porritt recalled his taking exception to the word 'inimical'. '[T]hat word can't go in. Why, if that went into the book I should have the fellows at Lord's coming to me in the pavilion and saying, "Look here, W. G., where did you get that word from?"'[13]

Pressure on Porritt, and Grace for that matter, was suddenly increased when they were told without prior consultation that Bowden had sold serial rights to a daily newspaper. Porritt was 'horror-struck. I gravely doubted my capacity to keep up the regular supply of "copy".'[14] This extra complication may explain some of the imbalances in the book – the short shrift given to the second Australian tour, for example – but in the end Porritt triumphed over all his difficulties and produced a far more readable volume than *Cricket*. However, before Grace's public life was revealed to his readers, his private life was blighted by calamity.

Bessie Grace was a strong, healthy and attractive girl of twenty when the family moved to Sydenham. She had inherited the family love of cricket, and was always seen at the county ground at home matches when Grace was playing, 'busily engaged in keeping a complete record of the score'. Her devotion to her father was seen in other ways: 'one rather cold day during the summer of 1898 [she] was observed to insist on his wearing a muffler, which she had thoughtfully brought with her'.[15] She was apparently quite a good cricketer in her own right. In June 1895 Grace wrote about her in one of the many questionnaires to which he was periodically subjected. In reply to the prompt *A little gossip about Miss Grace's appearance in the field*, he scrawled: 'a real good bat for a girl very hard & splendid fielder – fair underhand bowler – highest score 63 not out 4 years ago for Ladies of Clifton v Ladies of Glamorgan'. He went on to add, 'she is just 17 & has given up cricket as I consider it is only a game for school girls & should be given up when grown up'.[16] Like any other Victorian young lady, Bessie was to put away childish things and become a companion and help to her mother until it was time for her to fulfil her own matrimonial destiny. The young Pelham Warner, who met her when entertained by W.G. in Bristol, remembered her as 'a very nice-looking girl with grey-green eyes'.[17] All accounts suggest she was a delightful, vivacious girl for whom life held nothing but promise.

Just before Christmas she fell ill. It was a terrible irony that no sooner had he given up his medical practice, Grace found himself with a patient in his own household. Bessie was put to bed, and after his own examination Grace sought a second opinion. But he hardly needed confirmation. She had contracted one of the most terrifying scourges of the day: enteric, or typhoid, fever.

Although largely confined to the cramped and insanitary slums, typhoid fever was no respecter of class boundaries and could strike anywhere. It was a water- or food-borne bacterial infection that could be transferred from a carrier who had simply prepared a meal without washing. Those who came down with it could expect considerable discomfort and possible death:

[T]yphoid brought sustained fever, headache, malaise, and gastrointestinal problems (constipation or diarrhoea) to its victims . . . The body temperature slowly rose – to 104 or 105 degrees – and could remain high for two weeks; with only cold baths to relieve the fever, it often did not disappear for four weeks or more. Victims developed a characteristic rash on the abdomen and chest, which lasted for a few days . . . Sick for over a month, the patient weakened and became susceptible to complications. Although many mild cases occurred, typhoid fever carried a case fatality rate of about 10 per cent.[18]

As for a cure, there was none.

After twenty years' experience in Bristol, Grace would have known the grim statistics, and how little could be done beyond alleviating the patient's worst torments. With memories of his father's death at Christmas an inevitable cloud over the festive season, it must always have been a slightly difficult time of the year for him. Now he had to endure it with the knowledge that Bessie was in mortal danger.

She put up a brave fight, drawing on all the resources of her young life as she lay in her bed day after day, half-hearing the muted sounds of the household going about its business beyond her bedroom door. But despite the family's best efforts, she grew weaker and weaker as the fever refused to relax its hold. The end came on 6 February 1899. The death certificate gives a graphic indication of the slowness of the process: 'Enteric fever 46 days Exhaustion'. Bessie's 'Occupation' reads simply, 'Daughter of William Gilbert Grace M. R. C. S. Eng'. But his hard-won qualification had not given W.G. the power to save her.

Bessie's death has been variously misdated and mislocated. Some biographers, thinking she died in Bristol, confidently cite that as a reason for Grace's readiness to move to London. But whatever the inaccuracies surrounding his bereavement, no one doubts it was a terrible blow, and throughout the seismic events of 1899 it should be remembered that Grace was still in the state of shock we dignify as mourning.

*

The Victorian antidote to grief was work, and Grace threw himself into his fresh commitments with all his customary vigour. There was a new ground to oversee and a new groundstaff to break in, and all the administration to deal with. One of the several publications devoted to a schoolboy readership, *The Captain*, carried an account of a day with Grace in his new role. The editor found Grace 'up to his neck in documents':

[T]he doctor's desk is littered with notepaper and envelopes; . . . the morning, afternoon, evening, and late-night postmen fill the doctor's letter-box with a never-ending supply of cricketing correspondence. But he loves not pen or ink, and so he arose and shook himself like a St. Bernard dog, put on a square felt hat and a black overcoat, and led me away in the direction of the Crystal Palace grounds, talking gruffly, but good-temperedly, and with no little enthusiasm, about the new venture of which he is the head, the middle, and the tail.[19]

Grace let them into the ground with his own key, and conducted a tour of inspection. Just as he had at Bristol, he showed an interest in every aspect of the playing area, and in order to attract the attention of the groundstaff he carried a whistle, blowing loud blasts whenever he wanted something done. The trees around the edge of the ground were a constant source of worry. Some threw early shadows across the pitch towards the end of play (the editor of *The Captain* reported that Grace 'promptly gave orders that the ends of those branches were to be ruthlessly executed'), and a row of limes behind the bowler's arm made sighting the ball difficult. Similarly distracting foliage had been removed at Lord's, but the Crystal Palace authorities preferred to keep their ground picturesque in keeping with the rest of the site. The lime trees remained inviolate.

A new pavilion was being built to replace the existing structure at an estimated cost of £3,000. It was clear that no expense was being spared in an effort to establish a club that could stand comparison with the best. London County was indeed modelled on the MCC – a private club staging first-class matches for the public, while providing first-class facilities for its members. These included the services of a professional ground bowler or two, and Grace had brought H. W. Murch, the old Gloucestershire pro, with him to be head of the groundstaff. The annual subscription was three guineas (two guineas for schoolboys and under-graduates) and included a season ticket to the Crystal Palace. Members also had access to the Palace itself: 'a suite of courts, abutting on the North Nave, was set aside for a club room . . . with a ladies drawing room and loggia overlooking the grounds'.[20] Grace had arranged a full fixture list for the club's first season, which included games against Oxford University, the MCC and some of the newly promoted county sides like Worcestershire. But London County's first match was a modest two-day affair against Wiltshire at Swindon on 5 and 6 May.

The first day of the match happened to be the day of the memorial service for the Duke of Beaufort, a long-standing patron of Gloucester-

438

shire cricket and a man to whom Grace had owed much over the years. His death removed an influence that might conceivably have helped moderate attitudes over the bitter weeks ahead. At this stage, though, Grace's ties with the Gloucestershire Club were still intact. He remained, and intended to remain, captain, and he had no hesitation in inviting county players to help him in his new venture. As the *Devizes and Wiltshire Gazette* of 11 May 1899 reported, 'The London team was entirely composed of amateurs, and besides Dr. W. G. Grace, included Messrs. C. L. Townsend, W. S. A. Brown, and W. Troup of Gloucestershire.'

The game, played in cold but bright conditions, followed a predictable course. Grace took a prominent role in all departments. When Wiltshire batted, he opened the bowling and took 6 for 60 in thirty-four overs. He also opened the batting, and looked well set for fifty at least before discovering that the local umpire had sufficient character to give him out lbw. His 42 was still the top score. He left Townsend to take the wickets in Wiltshire's second innings, and only made 13 when he batted again, but the ninety runs required came easily enough and London County won their first match by six wickets.

It was a satisfactory start, but the new club had a great deal to do to establish its credentials. It was in many ways an anomaly. Unlike all the counties competing for the championship, which had grown gradually from local club cricket until they reached first-class status, London County had sprung up overnight. It hadn't even built on the existing Crystal Palace Cricket Club, but simply supplanted it. With little grounding in its locality, it could be seen as something of an impostor, staking a claim within Kent's territorial boundaries. Though modelled on the MCC, it had no past, no tradition, nothing beyond Grace's massive presence to give it any standing. In view of that, Lord's decreed that its matches should not, initially at least, be given first-class status. This meant that when Crystal Palace played host to the Australians, Grace called his team The South of England. Apart from a Gloucestershire contingent of Townsend, Jessop and wicket-keeper Jack Board, it was a home counties side: J. R. Mason from Kent, Fry and Ranji from Sussex, and a quartet of professionals from the Oval: Brockwell, Abel, Lockwood and Tom Hayward.

The tenth Australian tourists, captained by Joe Darling, arrived at the end of April, and on Saturday, 6 May London County held a banquet in their honour at the palace. Grace, just back from Swindon, welcomed the visitors saying he was 'sure they were a rare good lot of cricketers', and wishing them well.[21] Just how good some of them were would rapidly become clear. Among the new faces there was a shy teetotaller called Victor Trumper.

Trumper didn't play in the South of England fixture, but Monty Noble did. Noble had already won his first Test cap, against Stoddart's side in 1897–8, but this was his first trip to England and his first experience of Grace. One of the old hands, Hugh Trumble, had a word with him before he went out to bat: '[T]ake care "W. G." doesn't talk you out.' Trumble explained that the great man 'had a reputation for getting young players bustled if he could only get them to talk while at the wicket'. Noble found the advice timely:

Sure enough, after the first over, 'W. G.' came up and said: 'Good day, young fellow. ' 'Good day,' I replied and walked away. At the end of the next over he again tried, but I ignored him. For several overs this went on without my taking any notice of him. I had a very uncomfortable feeling about my apparent rudeness, and wondered just what he was thinking of me. After a while, however, I convinced myself that I was well enough set not to be talked out of the game, so, next time he approached me, I replied, and from then on we conversed freely.

Looking back on the incident twenty-five years later, Noble thought that rather than attempting to put him off, Grace's 'object was really to encourage me', and that Trumble had been pulling his leg.[22] It seems more likely that Grace was testing him, trying to gauge the mettle of a new opponent whom he would be meeting in far more demanding circumstances in the first Test at Trent Bridge three weeks later.

He certainly came away with a strong impression of Noble's ability, as he scored 105 not out. Syd Gregory made 124, and the Australians reached 375 in their only completed innings. The game also offered a reminder of the problems posed by Ernest Jones. Despite being called for throwing in the second Test of the 1897–8 series, Jonah remained the spearhead of the Australian attack and had lost none of his pace. Grace dropped down the order to seven, leaving to Fry and Abel the job of facing Jones at his fiercest (and in effect to compete for the other opening batsman's slot in the England team – Abel failed twice, Fry secured his first Test cap with 81). W.G. still fell to the fast bowler in both his innings. He was bowled for 5 in the first, but on the third day he and Ranji, who had recently returned from a trip to India to pursue his claim to the throne of Nawanagar, put on seventy-eight runs for the sixth wicket.

Grace, 'while scoring much more slowly than Ranjitsinhji, made some fine cuts, while his twos and threes out of reach of cover-point and extra mid-off showed the champion in his best style'.[23] By the time Jones bowled him for 47, the match was effectively saved.

The occasion had been a great success and *The Times* of 11 May was very positive: 'Under Dr Grace's instruction the ground men at the Palace have secured a playing field which is equal to either Lord's or the Oval'; a crowd of 8,000 attended on the first day, and 10,000 on the second; and the paper wrote that all those responsible, especially Dr Grace, should 'be congratulated on the *debut* of the London County Club'.[24]

Having got his new club off to a satisfactory start, Grace then travelled the short distance to Blackheath on Thursday, 11 May to captain his old club against Kent. On the surface everything was fine; Grace scored 16 and 31 and Gloucestershire won comfortably. But his refusal to take the side up to Yorkshire prompted the committee to resolve to seek clarification as to his intentions, though just as Grace had kept them in the dark over his contract with London County, so they kept their cards close to their chest for the time being. (It seems that there was no warning from E.M., from whom Grace might have expected a word on the matter.)

Grace led the side at the Oval, and may have strengthened a belief that he was no longer indispensable by registering a duck in a total of 404 when everybody else made double figures, and Wrathall and Board put on over 100 for the last wicket. (Grace did take 5 for 86 in Surrey's first innings.) His main contribution to the Whit Bank Holiday victory over Sussex was winning the toss and inserting the home side on a wet wicket under a hot sun. Sussex were dismissed for 97. When Ranji looked like hitting them out of trouble W.G. came on and promptly had him caught, for 30. Grace tried the hitting game himself in Gloucestershire's reply, scoring all but one of the first twelve runs on the board before holing out. He only managed a 6 in his second innings, but that hardly took the gloss off a four-wicket victory.

As with so many happier landmarks in his long career, Grace's last match for Gloucestershire was destined to take place at Lord's. He was apparently still unaware of the impending crisis when he arrived at St John's Wood on Thursday, 25 May, and the game in hand gave him quite enough to think about. The wet weather that had made the Hove wicket so difficult made the Lord's pitch equally helpful to bowlers, and in Jack Hearne Middlesex had just the man to exploit the conditions fully. Grace again decided to hit out and scored 11 before being brilliantly caught one-handed on the legside boundary. No one else made double figures and Gloucestershire were dismissed for 52. The Middlesex batsmen fared only a little better, but in the context of the match a lead of forty-four runs was significant.

Grace then went out to play his final innings for Gloucestershire. It was not a glorious century, nor even a stylish fifty. In a way it was more fitting that it should have been a determined, workmanlike 33 carved out in a losing cause against good bowling on a damp wicket, typical of the hundreds of innings he had played day in day out up and down the country since the club's foundation. It was easily the visitors' best effort, and although periodically beaten, *The Times* noted 'his strokes on the leg side were very good'.[25] His proportion of the Gloucestershire total was pretty good too: the rest of the team scored eighty runs. The innings closed at the end of play and Middlesex were left to gather seventy runs the following morning.

This proved a formality, but Gloucestershire's defeat was completely overshadowed by the bombshell awaiting Grace in his post bag. In amongst the welter of correspondence brought by one of the hard-worked Sydenham postmen was a letter from the committee requiring Grace to tell them 'exactly' which matches he was proposing to play. Grace found this offensive. Indeed, the more he thought about it the more furious it made him, until twenty-four hours later he reached boiling point:

May 28th, 1899

To the Committee of the Gloucestershire County Club.

Gentlemen, in answer to yours of the 26th, re resolution passed on the 16th and kept back from me for reasons best known to yourselves, I beg to state that I had intended to play in nearly all our matches, but in consequence of the resolution passed and other actions of some of the Committee, I send in my resignation as captain, and must ask the Committee to choose the teams for future games, as I shall not get them up.

I have always tried my very best to promote the interests of the Gloucestershire County Club, and it is with deep regret that I resign the captaincy. I have the greatest affection for the county of my birth, but for the Committee, as a body, the greatest contempt.

I am, Yours truly, W. G. Grace.[26]

Grace wrote at the height of his anger, but attempts to get him to retract the last wounding thrust were doomed to failure. Walter Troup, the man who succeeded him as captain, and J. A. Bush, his best man and one of his longest-standing friends, did their utmost to make him retract. Troup records that they sat up with him one night 'drinking until the early hours, waiting until the time was ripe before carefully tackling him on the sore point. He saw through the ruse only too clearly, and said laughingly: "No good, my boys, you can go back and tell the committee to *underline* it a hundred times."'[27] In the absence of an apology, a reconciliation was impossible, and minutes of the next committee meeting recorded that while they were 'conscious of the great services rendered by Dr Grace to the Gloucestershire Cricket Club as well as to cricket generally, and [felt] deep regret at his severance from them in spite of the efforts which have been made by them to avoid it', there was 'no course open to them but to accept his resignation'.[28]

And so Grace's connection with the club that went back thirty years and more was broken. He had helped to found it, captained it and proved its backbone through the heights of the 1870s, the dark days of the 1880s and early 1890s, and back to the sunlit uplands again in recent seasons. Apart from forced absences due to his American tour or injury, he had never missed a match and had never given less than everything to the cause. In all, he played 359 matches for the county, scored 22,808 runs at an average of 40.51, and made fifty-one centuries. His bowling was barely less impressive: 1,339 wickets at 18.48. Grace was saddened by the break, and according to Troup he offered to come back and play under him, an idea Troup rejected as 'too ridiculous for words'. But he was not given to brooding, and with the first Test coming up there were other demands on his attention.

Another of the developments that occurred in 1898 that had an impact on him in 1899 was the setting up of a board of control to oversee international matches. The initiative came from Lord Hawke, who argued that it was unfair to limit Test cricket to London and Manchester. It was agreed to follow the Australian precedent of having five matches in the series, and Trent Bridge and Headingley were the two new Test venues. And in the wake of the nonsense over Ranji in 1896, it was also decided to regularize the selection process. Ironically, after fighting the principle so long on his home turf, Grace now found himself on a selection committee at last. Officially, he was joined by Lord Hawke and H. W. Bainbridge, the captain of Warwickshire; unofficially, C. B. Fry and F. S. Jackson were invited to the meeting at the Sports Club to help choose the side for Trent Bridge. This did not make the process more efficient. Fry later wrote: 'Any one of us could have selected the right England team; or right enough. What happened with such a band of experts was that each came along expecting someone else to have the necessary clear-cut ideas. The discussions were interminable . . . Strictly speaking, the whole problem was whom to leave out.'[29]

It seems clear that Grace did not dominate the proceedings. Perhaps he was beginning to harbour doubts about his own place in the side; or he may have felt an inhibiting deference to Lord Hawke, the committee's chairman. Whatever the internal dynamics of the committee, decisions were eventually reached, and one of those left out was Arthur Shrewsbury. Fry makes it clear 'that he would most certainly have been selected to play in that match but for the fact that the team could not carry both W.G. and him, since both of them could field at point and nowhere else.'[30] Shrewsbury was understandably hurt by the decision, and watched the first Test on his home ground from underneath George Parr's tree.

Apart from their difficulties with the position of point, the selectors had had a more serious problem with their fast bowler. For one reason or another none of the leading contenders – Richardson, Lockwood, Mold or Kortright – were available, and it was decided to play George Hirst, who in those days was a genuine medium pacer. Lord Hawke's involvement meant an end to his reluctance to release his own players, and in addition to Hirst, Jackson and, for the first time, Wilfred Rhodes were chosen. The rest of the team comprised Grace himself, C. B. Fry, William Gunn, Ranjitsinhji, Tom Hayward, J. T. Tyldesley, William Storer (wicket-keeper) and Jack Hearne. There was great depth in batting and, apart from the lack of out-and-out pace, an impressive variety in the bowling.

That Rhodes should make his debut in the twilight of Grace's long international career now seems another example of the felicitous continuity that runs through so much of cricket history, but of course no one in the Trent Bridge ground on 1 June 1899 could have guessed that the twenty-one-year-old would eventually become the only man to play Test cricket at a greater age than the Champion. Grace was now fifty years and 317 days old, and although the crowd of over 14,000 gave him his usual acclaim as he led out the team, nothing could disguise the fact that he was at least twenty years older than anybody else on the field. He was still worth his place in the side as a batsman – on the eve of the Test he had scored 175 for London County against Worcestershire, a first-class match in all but name – but in other departments he was past it. Although his hands were as safe as ever, his elephantine bulk meant he was helpless if the ball did not come straight to him, and as other members of the team had to do his running for him, sections of the Nottingham crowd began to give him the bird. It was a poor return for the man who had scored the first first-class century ever made at Trent Bridge, but the glory of those all-conquering days of his prime was now a folk memory. Nearly thirty years on, the truth was that he was a liability in the field.

Thinking, perhaps, that an early involvement in the game would quell any nerves, Grace gave Rhodes precedence over the more experienced bowlers and opened with him in partnership with Jack Hearne. Hearne removed Iredale cheaply, but then Joe Darling and Monty Noble added seventy-one runs for the second wicket. Grace put himself on, but the Australians were content to treat him with respect. His twenty overs contained eight maidens and cost only thirty-one runs, but he remained wicketless. Indeed, the Australian policy of safety first drew criticism – there was 'never anything very attractive in the Australian batting' according to *The Times*.[31]

It was the original pair that broke up the stand. Hearne, who kept one end tight all day, got Darling for 47, and Rhodes bowled Noble for 41 to claim his first Test wicket. But the middle order continued in the same steady vein, with Syd Gregory making 48 and the brilliant left-hander Clem Hill 52, before being run out. Victor Trumper walked to the crease for his first Test innings with the score on 166 for 4. He had already shown enough evidence of his exceptional talent to be considered a major threat by the English team, but Hearne dismissed him with a terrific break-back, a ball that 'might have bowled any man in the world' in the opinion of one of the Nottinghamshire professionals who was watching.[32] One of the most glorious of all Test careers began with a duck. After that wickets fell regularly and the innings ended early on the second day at 252. Rhodes and Hearne shared the bowling honours with four wickets apiece.

Fry, who opened the batting with Grace, remembered the wicket as 'perfect' – hard, fast and true. But these qualities were potentially very helpful to Jones, and the Australians had high hopes of an early breakthrough. Grace took strike and the crowd watched in awed silence as Jonah tore in. *Cricket* described his first ball as 'sensational', adding 'if

Grace had not been to some extent prepared by previous experience . . . there might have been a bad accident; as it was he ducked in time.'[33] The drama was heightened by a cry of 'No-ball!' The crowd assumed Jones had been called for throwing, but it was made clear he had merely overstepped the mark ('getting right outside the return crease').[34] There could be no doubting Jones's intention, and the rest of the over was equally intimidatory. Grace survived, but was clearly ill at ease. When Fry got down to the danger end, Jones was called again. 'He hit Fry's middle stump and the ball went to the boundary, but Fry made no attempt to play the ball. Titchmarsh, the umpire, ostentatiously pointed to the crease to show the reason of his decision. Dr Grace and Mr Fry played beautiful cricket while they were together.'[35]

After that explosive start, things settled down. Grace was never really comfortable, but fought on indomitably, while Fry gave intimations of his future brilliance. Runs came faster than at any time during the Australian innings, but even so, Fry felt inhibited by Grace's lack of mobility. 'We lost innumerable singles on the off-side, and I never dared to call W.G. for a second run to the long-field.'[36] Nevertheless, the score had reached 75 in seventy minutes when Grace relaxed his guard against Noble and was caught behind for 28. '[I]t was not one of his finest efforts, but as far as could be seen at the time it had paved the way for a fine score by England.'[37] However, Jones proved too much for the rest of the team, and after Fry was bowled for 50 only Ranji with 42 and Tyldesley with 22 gave the Australians much cause for concern. Jones took 5 for 88 as England conceded a first-innings lead of fifty-nine.

Australia built a solid second innings. Noble opened in place of Iredale and made 45, putting on nearly a hundred with Clem Hill for the second wicket. Hill was just getting into his stride when, to the crowd's voluble dismay, Grace failed to bend quickly enough to a sharp chance at point. He went on to score 80, and though Grace caught him brilliantly in the end, ('a great one-hand catch low down at point')[38] he had done enough to ensure an imposing lead. The innings closed on the third day with the score at 230 for 8.

This left England 290 to win in under four hours. They started disastrously. Bill Howell had played a supporting role in the first innings. Now he made a dramatic mark on the match, bowling Grace for 1 with a break-back similar to the delivery Hearne had found for Trumper, and then dismissing Jackson for a duck. Jones bounced back with the wickets of Fry and Gunn, and 19 for 4 on the scoreboard revived 'memories of

England's dismal failure of 1882'.[39] Grace was condemned to a long afternoon with his beard.

England's saviour was Ranjitsinhji. He batted with more restraint than he had at Old Trafford in 1896, but still played in his own incomparable style. Darling tried to restrict his favourite legside strokes with two short legs, 'but he merely reverted to a series of conjured drives to all corners of the field off Jones, Noble and Trumble'.[40] Gradually and bewilderingly the prospect of Australian victory receded. The English card suggests one of the more exaggerated flights of fantasy from boys' fiction: 1, 9, 0, 3, 93 not out, 28, 10, 3. Hayward and Tyldesley gave Ranji support as he batted through to the end, sacrificing the chance of a well-deserved century in the interests of the team. The evening newspaper placards proclaiming 'Ranji Saves England' were more than adequate compensation.

Grace, understandably, had a lot of time for Ranji and gave a glowing account of him in Porritt's labour of love: 'Without a doubt "Ranji" is one of the most interesting figures in the cricket-field. His popularity has two sources – his extraordinary skill as a batsman and his nationality. How a man of his slender physique and apparently delicate constitution has so completely mastered the art of batting as to score with astounding rapidity and ease off all manner of bowling upon every variety of wicket is simply wonderful . . .'[41]

'W. G.' Cricketing Reminiscences and Personal Recollections was already making its lucrative way into the public domain via serialization in not just one but several newspapers, but there was much more to talk about than the Old Man's reflections on seasons past. The rift with Gloucestershire was a matter for wide discussion, though Cricket, always the soul of discretion, announced it in three lines tucked away at the bottom of a column. But the major debating point was now Grace's future as England captain. The barracking at Trent Bridge had drawn attention to his fallibility in the field, and although he had kept the Australian attack at bay in the first innings, he had been powerless to halt what was beginning to look like a helpless rout in the second. Could he go on?

In his own mind, the answer was no. On the train back to London he told Jackson, 'It's all over, Jacker. I shan't play again.'[42] He did not make this decision public, and on the evidence of his next innings against the Australians, in the MCC match at Lord's immediately after the Test, he still looked worth his place in the side. He survived a couple of chances, but then batted 'with absolute imperturbability' against Jones bowling at his fastest, and scored 50. When the Australians batted, he claimed the wickets of Hill and Trumper. He also looked every inch the part when the two teams were presented to the Prince of Wales and the Duke of York on the second day. 'Grace, quite at his ease, much amused the Prince with some remarks about the game', and even refused a cigar from the royal cigar-case.[43]

The game, which the Australians won by eight wickets, ended on 7 June. The following day a lifelong enthusiast wrote to Grace from Gravesend. He had witnessed many of Grace's performances, including his 257 and 73 not out at the Bat and Ball ground in 1895, and expressed his dismay at events in the first Test – 'to think a Cricket crowd should be so unmindful of the Splendid Service rendered to Cricket by yourself. How different to the match at Leyton last year [–] in the covered stand where I was, a laugh was raised when Mr Kortright struck you in the chest with a fast ball[;] a cry of Order! Order! from all soon silenced that.' He then went on to voice a very representative view of the two topics of the hour – the severance from Gloucestershire and Grace's Test future:

I trust that notwithstanding the ungrateful conduct of the Gloucester Committee you will still delight thousands with your play – & that the 'test' match (as it is now the fashion to call them) at Lord's will be graced by your presence at the wicket. Thousands including myself[,] members of my family & friends, have determined to see at least one full day's play – & would not so have determined had it not been thought you would play. We don't care for Shrewsbury; or the Notts 'scientific' mode of playing & making draws, but we do care for 'W.G.', & sentiment or no sentiment, he ought to play.[44]

The fact that Grace kept the letter showed that it touched him, but his mind was made up when he joined the other selectors at the Sports Club that Sunday. Fry was late and Jackson was unable to come, but Grace immediately told Lord Hawke and Bainbridge that he was standing down. They were appalled and tried to dissuade him, arguing that as long as his batting justified his place in the team, he should stay. At their urging, he agreed to reconsider, provided the whole committee was unanimous. Then Fry turned up:

The moment I entered the door W. G. said, 'Here's Charles. Now, Charles, before you sit down, we want you to answer this question, yes or no. Do you think that Archie MacLaren ought to play in the next Test Match?' . . . I answered without hesitation, 'Yes, I do.'

'That settles it,' said W. G.; and I sat down at the table. Then, and not till then, did I discover that the question W. G. had asked me meant, 'Shall I, W. G. Grace, resign from the England eleven?' This had never occurred to me. I had thought it was merely a question of Archie coming in instead of one of the other batsmen, perhaps myself. I explained this and tried to hedge, but the others had made up their minds that I was to be confronted with a sudden casting-vote. So there it was.[45]

Within a fortnight of resigning the captaincy of his county, Grace had lost the England captaincy, and a Test career that went back nearly twenty years was over. Apart from one match missed through injury, he had played in every domestic Test since the first at the Oval in 1880, and had captained the side since the second Test in the 1888 series. He had played in twenty-two Tests, taking part in a record nine different series. Of the thirteen in which he was captain, England won eight, lost three and drew three, and lost only one series.* As a player he scored 1,098 runs at 32.29 with two centuries, and took nine wickets at 26.22. He also claimed thirty-nine catches. It was a proud record, especially since he played his first Test at the age of thirty-two. As B. J. Wakley, the magisterial chronicler of centuries scored in Anglo-Australian Tests, emphasizes, 'Had Test Matches been played when he was in his prime, his record against Australia would have been even more outstanding than it is.'[46] Fry was horrified at what he had done, but Grace was at pains to put his mind at rest, insisting that he 'felt he ought to retire, not because he could not bat or bowl to the value of his place',[47] but because of his fielding. As he told a number of friends, 'The ground was getting too far away.'

It was obviously an emotionally charged meeting, and the committee made some odd decisions. In deference to the man they had just reluctantly deposed, they included his two young Gloucestershire protégés. Jessop was brought in as the solution to the fast-bowling problem, and, on the strength of his 78 for the MCC against the Australians, Townsend was chosen to bat at four in place of William Gunn, which must have caused some muttering in the changing room at Trent Bridge. The team was further weakened by the replacement of Jack Hearne with Walter Mead – 'sheer madness'[48] according to many even though Mead was currently heading the bowling averages with sixty-nine

* Grace's record as captain compares favourably with Mike Brearley – played 18, won 11, lost 4, drew 3. Their percentage of wins is almost identical: Brearley 61.11, Grace 61.54 (Gerry Cotter, *The Ashes Captains*, p. 312).

wickets at 11.44. Far more serious in its long-term effects was the promotion of MacLaren to the captaincy before F. S. Jackson, who was the senior amateur in the team. Fry suggested this was something of an oversight, though as Lord Hawke, his county captain, was there that seems hard to credit. According to his biographer, 'Hawke's silence at the moment of decision is perhaps best described as inexplicable', even 'an act . . . of betrayal'.[49]

As for the most dramatic outcome of the selection meeting, the response seems to have been muted. *The Times* saw nothing particularly newsworthy in the ending of Grace's career, noting simply that 'five changes have been made from the side that played at Nottingham. Dr Grace, Gunn, Hirst, Storer, and Jack Hearne are succeeded by Mr MacLaren, Mr Jessop, Mr Townsend, Lilley, and Mead. This radical change from the first team is not wholly surprising on the form of some of the men in the opening test match.'[50] *The Sportsman* merely commented, 'After the moderate show made by "W.G." at Nottingham the omission of his name from the list will create little surprise, and we are sure that he was in no way wanting in recognising the facts.' As a reminder of the facts, the batting averages followed. Grace was eighty-third, on 18.92.[51]

*

Grace turned up at Lord's for the second Test in an unaccustomed role as one of 25,000 spectators, and must have shared the crowd's horror as Jones demolished the England top order. From 66 for 6, England fought back through Jackson (73) and Jessop, who in his first Test hit 51 out of 95 in an hour, a performance *The Times* characterized as 'a quiet game'.[52] But 206 all out was a sorry first-innings total.

There was more to appreciate, from an objective standpoint, when Australia batted. Clem Hill scored a century, but had the misfortune to choose the day Trumper announced his genius at the game's highest level. The two men made exactly the same score, 135, but there was only one name on everybody's lips. Lilley, from his privileged vantage point behind the stumps, pronounced Trumper 'undoubtedly the greatest Australian batsman I have ever seen',[53] and *The Times* said 'He played like a master on a great occasion.'[54] H. S. Altham, writing twenty-five years later, had no hesitation in elevating him to the game's pantheon: 'Before he had batted for half an hour it was obvious that a new star of unsurpassed brilliance and charm had joined the cluster of the Southern Cross'.[55] Grace was equally impressed, and later in the tour appeared in the Australian dressing room demanding a bat with Trumper's autograph on it. He then handed over one of his own, saying, 'From today's champion to the champion of tomorrow.'[56]

With a lead of over 200 Australia were virtually assured of victory, and despite a belated captain's innings of 88 by MacLaren, England lost the match by ten wickets. That was the only result in the five-match series. Although England led Australia on first innings in the remaining three games, their bowling was never quite penetrative enough. And so the Australians won two consecutive series for the first time, bringing down the curtain on the dominance England had maintained almost unbroken since the 1880s. Grace's retirement certainly marked the end of an era.

*

Grace met the Australians on three further occasions during the season. In July they returned to Sydenham to meet a London County side thinly disguised as W. G. Grace's XI. This was described as 'a very slack game',[57] though the home team ran up an impressive total of 431, bearing out Grace's contention that Crystal Palace was the 'best wicket in England'.[58] He made 25 before succumbing once more to Noble, but bowled Trumper in the Australians' first innings and injected some interest into the dying stages of the drawn match by taking 3 for 29 late on the third day. He failed twice for the MCC at Lord's at the end of the month, and Jones got him for 7 and 29 when the tourists beat a South of England side at Hastings in September.

Although a match against the Australians was always an occasion, Grace's greatest challenge after he had made his bow on the international stage was the Gentleman–Players fixture. After the wet weather in the early stages, the summer of 1899 became one of the best on record, and a vintage year for batting. Bobby Abel had already stamped his name on the season by carrying his bat for 357 against Somerset at the Oval at the end of May. His home ground proved a fertile source of runs once more when he scored a chanceless 195 for the Players in early July. As his occupation of the crease continued hour after hour, Grace used nine different bowlers, though the bulk of the work was left to Townsend, who sent down 64.4 overs and took 2 for 180. Grace managed 2 for 82 in thirty-six overs, and another long-suffering bowler was B. J. T. Bosanquet, then a very ordinary medium pacer, who may have had time to reflect, over the course of a day and a half in the field, on the need for some new initiative to counter the domination of technically sophisticated batsmen on perfect wickets. To emphasize the impotence of the amateurs' attack, the Players' last pair put on 135 to boost the total to

451

647. Grace scored 28 and 60 as the Gentlemen struggled gamely to avert the inevitable. They reached 300 twice, but still lost by an innings and thirty-six runs.

The return at Lord's on 10, 11 and 12 July was Grace's swansong at Headquarters, and it proved a fine match on which to go out. As he had done at the Oval, he dropped himself down the order and came in towards the end of the first day which had seen English amateur batting at its best. Fry led the way with a century, but MacLaren, Ranji, Townsend, Major Poore and Jackson all made runs against an attack that included Lockwood, Hirst, Rhodes and J. T. Brown. Grace, determined to be at the crease for the start of the second day, batted watchfully, taking an hour and forty minutes to score thirty-three runs. The next morning he set a different tempo, striking forty-five in barely an hour. It had been thirty-one years since he made his first century for the Gentlemen at Lord's, and everyone on the ground was hoping he would pass three figures again. Unfortunately Mason got carried away and called him for a quick single that was clearly beyond him, and he was run out twenty-two runs short of his target. The two had added 120 for the seventh wicket, and for all the disappointment of missing a century, Grace could be well pleased with his 78 against the best bowling in England on the eve of his fifty-first birthday. The Gentlemen made 480.

One bowler who had certainly given some thought to the problem of getting batsmen out on perfect pitches was Surrey's Digby Jephson. A stockbroker, journalist and poet, Jephson had the self-confidence to ride out the storm of mockery and single-handedly revived the ancient art of under-arm lob bowling. This was his finest hour, and he proceeded to make complete fools of the professionals whose antics, according to the *Manchester Guardian*, were 'truly ludicrous'.[59] Grace enjoyed the show hugely, no doubt reminded of E.M. at his most provocative, and when MacLaren ran thirty yards round the boundary to dismiss Hirst with a brilliant catch, he must also have thought of Fred. To the delight of the crowd W.G. lumbered over to the rail to shake MacLaren's hand, saying 'Well caught, Archie!' Jephson finished with figures of 18.4–7–21–6 and the Players were all out for 196. Rain on the third morning ended any hope they had of saving the game, and on the more helpful surface Grace let his more orthodox bowlers do the damage. The professionals made 225, and Grace had the satisfaction of leading off a victorious team at the conclusion of his last Gentlemen–Players match at Lord's.

For the rest of the season, with the exception of the three Australian matches and a final appearance for the Rest of England v. Home Counties at Hastings in September, Grace played minor cricket for London County. Needless to say, he made no distinction in terms of his approach; a game of cricket was a game of cricket, and as many unfortunate club bowlers discovered, he was incapable of lowering his standards or lessening his appetite for runs. In addition to his 515 first-class runs at 23.40, he scored 1,092 runs in his other matches at an average of 84.

Although one of personal poignancy for Grace, it had been a memorable summer in which the game he had done so much to promote was seen to its best advantage. Ranji – who else? – became the first man to score 3,000 runs in a season, but Abel and Fry were not far behind him, in technical mastery if not in stylistic wizardry, and lesser stars from the ranks of both amateurs and professionals delighted crowds with levels of skill that would have been unthinkable thirty-five years before. Major Poore, in one of his rare extended breaks from army commitments, scored 1,399 runs for Hampshire in just two months at an average of 116.58, and put on 411 in four hours and twenty minutes with his fellow officer Wynyard at Taunton.[60] A schoolboy, A. E. J. Collins, compiled the highest individual score of all time, 628 not out in a house match at Clifton – a testimony to the virtues of sound defence and tireless application that Grace, by his example, had inculcated into successive generations of cricketers. But the older tradition of unbridled aggression had hardly been killed off by the new emphasis on technique. Jessop was as electrifying as E.M. had ever been, and in August Albert Trott (the younger brother of Harry) out-howitzered even C. I. Thornton, becoming the only man in history to hit a ball over the pavilion at Lord's. In recognition of his unquantifiable but quite undeniable part in the game's glorious transformation, the MCC made Grace a life member.

THIRTY-ONE

IN 1900 London County's matches against first-class opposition were granted first-class status, but their application to join the county championship was turned down. There were limits even to Grace's power to get what he wanted.

In fact, the way things turned out probably suited him better. The MCC required the club to play a minimum of nine first-class games (six home, three away), which put far less strain on Grace than having to arrange a full championship fixture list. In the end he settled for about thirteen matches a season. Neighbours Surrey were happy to play home and away, as were the relative newcomers Warwickshire, Derbyshire and Leicestershire. MCC offered two Club & Ground matches, and Grace worked on his old Cambridge connections to secure visits to and from the university. He also offered the touring team of the season a friendly, if competitive, welcome. But with one or two exceptions, the more established counties were conspicuous by their absence. The club's host county, Kent, never played them.

There is no doubt that London County merited its first-class status. Grace's presence guaranteed high standards on the field, and the ground and facilities could bear comparison with any in the country. But the feeling that the club was in some ways an interloper with no *raison d'être* beyond the commercial imperative was never shaken off. As Clifford Bax put it, 'A Schoolboy could not care a common marble whether Grace's friends or their opponents were victorious',[1] and without that lifeblood of popular support the club remained a curiosity, the creation and personal dominion of one man, W.G.

It was entirely appropriate that Grace ended his career at a palace, albeit a glorified glasshouse, and like any monarch he had his court and inner circle of favourite courtiers. In 1900 Billy Murdoch came to London County after relinquishing the Sussex captaincy to Ranji the previous season. He still wore Grace's sovereign on his watch-chain as a memento of his great innings in the 1880 Test, and the friendship

454

between the two old war-horses set the tone for the club. Percy Gale, a nondescript cricketer but clearly a clubbable man, was another accepted into the fellowship. '[T]he inner group of the London County Club was like a happy family. Grace himself was known as Father, W. L. Murdoch as Muvver, "Livey" Walker as the Babe and I as Granny – why I was given that nickname I do not remember, unless it was because I was slow in the field.'[2] Grace and Murdoch had been horsing around together for years. Sammy Woods recalled one occasion when they were playing in a match at Cambridge. As usual Woods and his room-mate Gregor MacGregor invited the visiting amateurs to dine at their palatial digs. 'What times we had! Generally a dance and cards after dinner.' It is clear that the dancing was all-male, and merely an excuse for a bit of a scrum. 'I remember W.G. and Billy Murdoch bumping A. J. L. Hill and myself into the fireplace . . . just like a couple of boys.'[3] The combined weight of the two great cricketers must have been awesome, and Hill was lucky to escape serious injury. (Woods once tossed MacGregor through a window on the eve of the Varsity match; he too survived unscathed.)

Unscripted comedy was never far away when Father and Muvver were together. On one occasion they both leapt heavily into a cab and the floor fell out under their combined weight. It is very doubtful whether the cabby received any compensation; it was hard enough getting a fare out of Grace. As a boy, Clifford Bax once saw W.G. and Murdoch arriving at a cricket ground:

[A] ramshackle four-wheeler drew up at the main gate. A huge man with twinkling eyes and a great black bushy beard got out of the cab, lugging after him a capacious cricket bag. He wore a 'square bowler' hat, and looked like a prosperous farmer. 'There he is,' said Uncle Harold in an awed voice, 'Look, look – it's W.G.' Another large man emerged, the springs of the cab audibly sighing with relief. 'That's Murdoch . . . the Australian crack,' and [we] heard the square-faced Australian calling out 'Hi, Gilbert, hi!' But Grace, not answering to Hi or to any loud cry, strode majestically towards the pavilion, as though no cabby in his senses would expect payment from one who had been Emperor of the Cricket World for thirty years. We watched Mr Murdoch fumbling in his waistcoat pocket for a shilling and two coppers.[4]

Bax also told the story of the two of them on a cricketing jaunt to Wiltshire. There was a river near where they were staying, and in the spirit of their first great wager Grace bet Murdoch he could catch more fish than the Australian could score runs. To make sure he won, Grace got up at four in the morning and landed a round hundred. Murdoch scored 103.

The atmosphere of larky good humour pervaded the field of play, though never to the detriment of the game. Cricket at Crystal Palace was fun, but deeply serious at the same time. Grace himself was the focal point, and though he kept everyone up to the mark, he was tolerant of the shortcomings of the lesser players who surrounded him, and even acknowledged the joke against himself when he lapsed from his own high standards. On one occasion when a number of chances had been missed off his bowling, he dropped one himself and remarked with elephantine wit, 'Missing catches seems catching.'[5]

Arthur Conan Doyle was another drawn into Grace's London County circle, playing both with and against W.G. on several occasions. Once, when playing for the MCC at Crystal Palace, he claimed the great man's wicket and celebrated his triumph in verse:

> Before me he stands like a vision,
> Bearded and burly and brown,
> A smile of good-humoured derision
> As he waits for the first to come down.
>
> With the beard of a Goth or a Vandal,
> His bat hanging ready and free,
> His great hairy hands on the handle,
> And his menacing eyes upon me.

After dealing contemptuously with the first two deliveries, Grace took a heave at the third, but didn't quite middle it. The ball went straight up – 'Up, up, to a speck in the blue' – and after hanging above the wicket for an unconscionably long time, plummeted into the gloves of Bill Storer:

> Out – beyond question or wrangle!
> Homeward he lurched to his lunch!
> His bat was tucked up at an angle,
> His great shoulders curved to a hunch.[6]

'Out – beyond question or wrangle!' is particularly fine, though what Conan Doyle omitted to mention is that Grace had scored 110 before he was brought into the attack. W.G. got his revenge in the same fixture the following year, but that only inspired a rueful reflection in prose: 'There was nothing more childlike and bland than that slow, tossed-up bowling of Doctor Grace, and nothing more subtle and dangerous. He was always on the wicket or about it, never sent down a really loose ball, worked continually a few inches from the leg, and had a perfect command of length.' After Conan Doyle had hit him for two successive fours, Grace held one back a little, 'which gave the delusion that it was coming right up to the bat, but as a matter of fact it pitched well short of my reach, broke sharply across and Lilley, the wicket-keeper, had my bails off in a twinkling. One feels rather cheap when one walks from the middle of the pitch to the pavilion, longing to kick oneself for one's own foolishness all the way.'[7] But Conan Doyle was in good company. Grace took thirteen wickets in the match.

The two famous doctors might just as easily find themselves on the same side. On another occasion they were batting together at Lord's against the fast bowler Bill Bradley (Kent and England):

His first delivery I hardly saw, and it landed with a terrific thud upon my thigh. A little occasional pain is one of the chances of cricket, and one takes it as cheerfully as one can, but on this occasion it suddenly became sharp to an unbearable degree. I clapped my hand to the spot, and found to my amazement I was on fire. The ball had landed straight on a small tin vesta box in my trousers pocket, had splintered the box, and set the matches ablaze . . . W.G. was greatly amused. 'Couldn't get you out – had to set you on fire!' he cried in the high voice which seemed so queer from so big a body.[8]

However, for all his joviality, Grace remained an uncompromising autocrat and would react furiously to any unlicensed levity or challenge to his dignity. Once, when it was necessary to use a pitch a second time, the visiting team's groundsman, who was also a player, remarked, 'Surely we ain't going to play on this wicket?' 'Why not?' said Grace in a tone that should have warned against further impertinence. 'Why, it's an old pitch. I s'pose it's some old dodge of yours,' came the insulting response. Grace was incensed. 'Unless that man apologizes,' he told the opposing captain, 'there'll be no match to-day.' The apology was duly forthcoming; Grace won the toss, and batted on till nearly five o'clock, 'just to show 'em there's nothin' much the matter with the wicket'. When another visitor had the temerity to question an lbw decision off Grace's bowling, he was given his marching orders in no uncertain terms. 'Pavilion, you,' Grace thundered, pointing his way. He went.[9]

Such instances, though, were rare. The vast majority of cricketers were delighted at the facilities at the Palace, and felt honoured to play against the Champion in his declining years. This applied to touring teams as well as club cricketers, and for a time Grace took over Lord Sheffield's role, playing host not only to the Australians, but the South Africans and the West Indians.

Led by Aucher Warner, the elder brother of P. F. Warner (now captain of Middlesex), the West Indians made their first visit to England in 1900, and played their first game at Crystal Palace. Warner's heterogeneous band of 'white colonists and coloured players'[10] were not deemed first-class, but Grace nevertheless put out a strong team against them, including (apart from himself) four past or future Test players – Billy Murdoch, J. R. Mason, the Kent captain, Bill Storer of Derbyshire and a promising young professional, Len Braund. Not all the team were so experienced. James Gilman was twenty and this was his first match for London County. With memories of his own early days as a boy among men, Grace was invariably kind to young players unless they were sloppy, cocky or unpunctual. Gilman, who lived to an advanced age, gave his memories of the occasion in *Wisden* in 1977. Grace asked if he was nervous, and on being told 'I'm terrified, Sir', replied, 'I'm taking you in with me to open the innings.'[11]

The West Indian attack relied heavily on the two black professionals 'Float' Woods and W. J. Burton. Burton was the more accurate, with a particularly effective yorker, but Woods was faster, generating surprising pace off a short run. Of the two he had the most difficulty acclimatizing to English conditions and conventions. He hated having to wear boots, and when Jessop went on the rampage at Bristol (scoring 157 in an hour) later in the tour, he felt his only chance was to bowl barefoot. Warner, of course, rejected his request out of hand. The West Indians had come to England not so much to compete as to learn, and playing the game properly was just as important as playing it well.

The London County match was their first masterclass, and Grace was in the right form to teach them a few lessons. He repeatedly turned good-length balls away to leg, and whenever the ball was wide of the off-stump he cut it with astonishing power to the boundary. Anything slightly overpitched was punished with a thunderous drive, and any attempt to intimidate him with the rising ball was futile. He either used his great height to play it down off his chest, or sent it humming like a shell into the middle distance over square leg. It was a hot day – the whole country was sweltering in a heatwave – but that didn't bother Grace, and though the back of his shirt darkened and beads of sweat glistened in his beard, he carried on relentlessly. There was no let-up at the other end either; Gilman was a strong player, eager to capitalize on his good fortune. The runs kept coming, and both batsmen had reached their fifties by the time the umpires called a halt for lunch.

Luncheon was a feast. Gilman remembered it as 'sumptuous', and couldn't help noticing that his partner 'was very keen on the catering'. Grace had 'a real whack of the roast, followed by a big lump of cheese', washed down with whisky and seltzer.[12] It was not perhaps surprising that Grace was marginally less alert in the afternoon session, and he departed for a well-earned post-prandial rest, bowled by a Burton yorker for 71. The next day's *Times* complimented him on having 'played beautiful cricket for his runs'.[13]

Mason carried on from where the Champion had left off, hitting a century in two hours. The West Indians were kept in the field all day, and the score at the close was 432 for 8. The last two wickets added another hundred runs the following morning, and the match was put even further beyond the tourists' reach when a thunderstorm transformed the wicket. With Grace wheeling away at one end for most of the innings and Mason getting sharp movement with his seamers at the other, the West Indians did well to reach 237, but they collapsed when they followed on. Grace took 5 for 52 and they were all out for 103, leaving London County winners by an innings and 198 runs. Grace never minded how completely he trounced the opposition. It might have seemed an inauspicious start, but Billy Murdoch gave a speech in which he recalled the early Australian tours, and said 'He was sure that the West Indians would as years went on develop their talent as Australia had done.'[14] Grace no doubt clapped his massive hands and raised a glass. But neither he, nor anyone else present, could have guessed how prophetic Murdoch's words would prove.

Grace had a glimpse of future West Indian glories when he met the tourists again, playing for the MCC. L. S. Constantine (the father of Learie Constantine) very nearly didn't make the trip. Classed as an amateur, he hadn't sufficient funds to pay his own way, and it needed an impromptu public subscription to get him on the boat, which had already left harbour.[15] At Lord's 'Cons', as he was known, fully justified the faith of his supporters. He made 24 not out in the first innings; in the second he and Burton put on 162 in sixty-five minutes for the eighth wicket. Grace had him stumped, but not before he had scored the first West Indies century in England (113).

Before the West Indies game, London County had played their first first-class matches, home and away, against Surrey. After one defeat and one draw, they travelled to Worcester to register their first first-class win. Grace was unable to repeat his magnificent batting of the previous year, but made 30 and 20 as well as taking 9 for 155 in the match. His bowling was treated with less respect at Oxford, where the university ran up a total of 539. R. E. 'Tip' Foster, fresh from emulating Grace by scoring two centuries in a match, made it three in succession by hitting 169. In one sensational over he hit W.G. for four consecutive sixes. At the end of the over Grace came up to him. 'Not very respectful to an old man, was it, Tip?' he said, adding generously, 'But it was worth seeing.'[16] Despite the onslaught, W.G. kept pegging away, bowling thirty-four overs (now six balls) and taking 2 for 130. At some point in the Oxford innings he picked up an injury which was sufficiently serious to prevent him batting. Without him London County were bowled out for 116 and 93. He was fit to play against Cambridge University at Fenners, and made 86 and 62. Undaunted by his savaging at the hands of the Dark Blues, he gave himself forty overs and took 5 for 99. He remained in good form against Derbyshire, scoring 87 and 44 in the club's first win on home territory.

Grace's biggest match of the season was the Gentlemen–Players game at the Oval in July. There was a reminder of times past when he cavilled at the umpiring arrangements. The Surrey authorities had always chosen two of their professionals to stand, but this year Grace demanded a change, so two substitutes had to be sent over from Lord's. Abel, captaining the Players, scored half their runs, carrying his bat for 153. Grace also played a captain's innings when the Gentlemen replied, though with a more modest contribution of 58. Bradley and A. O. Jones took eight wickets between them when the Players batted again, and the Gentlemen were set 351 to win. Thanks mainly to a century on his debut by C. J. Burnup, they made a spirited attempt but were denied by another debutant, John Gunn, who took six wickets, including that of Grace for 3, to add to the five he had taken in the first innings. The Players won by thirty-seven runs.

For the first time in thirty-five years Grace was not chosen for the return at Lord's, and he missed a remarkable match. Set 502 to win in the fourth innings, the Players made the runs for the loss of eight wickets. Grace's omission from the Gentlemen's team may have been the spur he needed, or he may have been galvanized by the death of Richard Daft (aged 64), which fell on his fifty-second birthday. Whatever the explanation, he proceeded to put together an impressive run of scores: 82 and 48 against Warwickshire at Edgbaston, 72 and 110 against Worcestershire, 76 in the return against Warwickshire, then, after two failures, the 110 against the MCC which ended in Conan Doyle's moment of metrical glee. Both Bertie and Charles played in these last two home games, and the Warwickshire match proved quite a family success story. W.G. junior for once matched his father's score exactly, while C.B. took 3 for 62 in Warwickshire's first innings with his slows.

As usual, Grace went down to Hastings in September. He made 36 in his first innings for the Rest of England against Surrey and Sussex, but in his second he was bowled by Tom Richardson for 1. He left his best until last. In his final game of the season, at Lord's, he made a rousing 126 for the South against the North to emphasize that he was by no means a spent force. In fact, in eighteen first-class matches in 1900 he made 1,277 runs at 42.57 and took thirty-two wickets at 30.28. In minor matches he comfortably did the double.

*

In 1901 the world changed. The Victorians did not regard 1 January 1900 as the beginning of the twentieth century, but held on pedantically until 1 January 1901. Twenty-one days later Queen Victoria died, and the whole nation was plunged into a state of shock in which genuine grief was mixed with a deeper sense of loss. She had reigned over her subjects – glorious, if not particularly happy – for so long that very few could remember a time when she had not been monarch. For the vast majority she had always been there, a comforting absolute throughout a period of great and sometimes alarming change. And now she was gone. As the Prince of Wales (at last) acceded to the throne as Edward VII, Grace also took a step up in the national hierarchy to become unquestionably the most eminent living figure from the Victorian period.

Not that the thought would have crossed his mind. As always there was the cricket season to prepare for, and Grace got on busily with his piles of correspondence. One innovation that was sanctioned by Lord's was that London County's drawn matches should be decided on first innings – provided the opposing captain agreed. As was generally the case when Grace wanted something, they did, and in consequence the club claimed an extra four victories to add to the four they secured in completed games. Perhaps the most surprising fixture, given that

Kitchener was still trying to stamp out the bush-fires of guerrilla resistance in the Transvaal, was against a South African touring team. With a leavening of Test players, the visitors proved strong enough to win by sixty-one runs. Grace played them again at Lord's when the MCC beat them by a similar margin.

The highlights of Grace's season for London County were the games against MCC & Ground and Worcestershire. Against the MCC at Lord's he took 11 for 110 (proving Conan Doyle's nemesis in the second innings), and in the return at Crystal Palace he made 132 in just under four hours, despite a heavily bandaged hand. This was one of the matches London County claimed on first innings – indeed, there was only time for one innings a side; London County made 633, MCC 501. At Worcester he scored 30 and 20 and took 9 for 157, and in the return at Crystal Palace helped secure a second win with scores of 72 and 110 not out.

In 1901 Grace also played in two Gentlemen–Players matches. The first at the Oval turned out to be another personal triumph for Bobby Abel. Grace had a poor team, with very few recognized bowlers. In the end he gave nine of the side a bowl. They all came alike to Abel, who methodically helped himself to 247. As he had the previous year, Grace top-scored for the Gentlemen with 57, but the imbalance in the captains' respective scores accurately reflected the gap between the two sides, and the Players won by ten wickets. Grace scored another fifty in the match at Hastings, but his captaincy raised questions. Having used nine bowlers at the Oval, he went to the other extreme and refused to change the bowling at all, leaving Mason and the South African J. H. Sinclair on throughout the Players' first innings of 238. When the Gentlemen batted again, he changed the order then watched from the pavilion as Rhodes and Hirst wreaked havoc. When he eventually went in he was left stranded without a run as the whole team was bowled out for 59. Only rain deprived the Players of certain victory.

Grace just scraped his thousand runs (1,007 at 32.48), but had a healthy total of fifty-one wickets at 21.78. The national averages were dominated by the Sussex trio of Fry, Ranji and George Brann, who took the first three places. Fry had an extraordinary season, making 3,247 runs at 78.67. He scored thirteen centuries, including six in succession, a record subsequently matched only by Bradman and Mike Proctor. Bobby Abel claimed the highest aggregate with 3,309.

Over the winter of 1901–2 MacLaren took a depleted England side to

Australia. He lost the series but found a bowler of genius in S. F. Barnes. Hard on the returning party's heels came the eleventh Australian team, and they played their opening match at Crystal Palace. The match was ruined by the weather, but Grace showed something of his old wiles with the ball, taking 2 for 25 in the first innings and removing the Australian captain, Joe Darling, when he was well set in the second. A fellow Australian, L. O. S. Poidevin, was looking on. Poidevin had missed selection for the tour through injury, but came to England anyway to pursue his medical studies, subsidizing his stay by writing match reports for the Australian press, and Grace welcomed him warmly to the ranks of London County. He gave his readers back home a picture of the Old Man in action:

Taking about three or four steps to cover the two yards 'run' to the bowling crease, and delivering between round and overarm, he bowls a slow ball on the leg stump, or a little outside, that does nothing but 'tantalise' the batsman. With four men on either side of the wicket peculiarly well placed, and one about fifteen to twenty yards behind himself, he sets out to get you caught or stumped or bowled (hit on mostly), or anything else that his wily nature may suggest. At first I was quite at a loss to see the use of the man stationed behind himself, but, curiously enough, that is where W. G. snared the Australian captain [see Plate 23 for Grace's field].[17]

Grace met the tourists a second time when he captained the MCC against them at Lord's shortly before the first Test, and he clearly fancied his chances of 'tantalizing' a few more victims. *Cricket* had remarked a couple of years earlier, 'About six times out of ten he is fatal to any batsman who meets him for the first time',[18] and so it proved with the new generation of Australians. He took 5 for 29, and narrowly missed a hat-trick. In addition he made 29 and 23, but had some bad moments when Trumper made his declaration look ludicrously generous. In the end the MCC escaped with a draw.

The summer of 1902 was miserably wet, but after the batsmen's jamboree of the previous three years, this was a welcome relief to the bowlers. In the opening Test at Edgbaston Rhodes and Hirst got their retaliation in early, dismissing Australia for their lowest score ever – 36. It was typical of MacLaren's luck as captain that the Australians were saved by rain, and went on to win an epic series 2–1.

Grace could only tug his beard in sympathy as he pursued his humbler path through the London County fixture list. Although the experiment of claiming a win on first innings was discontinued, the club still won five of its first-class matches, and Grace maintained the form of his previous year, though scores of under ten regularly punctuated his better efforts. Billy Murdoch was also staying the course well, and the two had a number of good stands together. They opened the batting for the MCC at Lord's and comfortably beat their combined age of 101, putting on 120 before they were parted. Had they been able to run with any speed, this would have been doubled. As it was, Grace saved his legs with a huge hit out of the ground off Hallows. Ian Maxwell Campbell, who played regularly for London County, saw several of their partnerships: 'To see Billy and W. G. in batting together was a feast for the eyes and the spirit, the former an exponent of the more graceful and elegant, the latter more dominating and majestic; in his hands the bat looked a mere toy; he used it like a toy, too, and rarely allowed a ball within reach to pass it – wonderful mastery and a wonderful eye.'[19]

In July, a week before his fifty-fourth birthday, Grace captained the Gentlemen at the Oval and had the opportunity to see the great Sydney Barnes for himself. He gave a couple of chances, but made 82, driving with all his old power. The rest of the batting fell away, and the Players had much the better of the draw. W.G. followed that with 131 against the MCC at Crystal Palace, and scored his second century of the season (129) against Warwickshire in August. By then the whole country was buzzing with England's dramatic one-wicket victory in the final Ashes Test, set up by Jessop's record-breaking century in eighty-five minutes. There was no disguising the fact that Grace was now playing in the backwaters of the game.

He was still a popular attraction at Hastings, however, and his 70 for the Rest of England which secured victory over Kent and Sussex was greeted with a great show of appreciation. In his final encounter with the Australians, for the South of England, he dropped down the order and was 17 not out on declaration. He ended the season at Lord's where he made 29 for the Rest of England against Yorkshire. This was the last season in which Grace made 1,000 runs – 1,187 at 37.09. He also took forty-six wickets at 23.34.

*

On the evening of 19 May 1903 Arthur Shrewsbury shot himself in the chest with a five-chambered revolver, and then put the gun to his head, 'death from the latter bullet proving almost instantaneous', as *The Times* told its readers the following morning. Shrewsbury had always been something of a hypochondriac, and a recent illness had increased his tendency to depression. From the mid-1880s to the early 1890s he had been England's best professional batsman, and Grace once gave him a higher accolade. Asked who was the best bat after him, he answered, famously, 'Give me Arthur.'

When the news broke, Grace was playing for London County against the MCC at Lord's, the setting for Shrewsbury's 164 in the second Test of 1886. There was no Father Time with his scythe in those days, but thoughts of mortality must have played beneath the surface of Grace's mind as he looked out over the largely empty stands of the great arena. Already the makings of a pretty good team had been culled from among those with whom he had played: G.F., Daft, Ulyett, Morley, Peate, Lohmann, Midwinter, Briggs. And now, to strengthen the batting, Shrewsbury.

But time's healing properties were also in evidence this year. Despite the acrimony surrounding his departure from the club, Grace's ties with individual Gloucestershire players had never been broken, and with goodwill on both sides a rapprochement was achieved, and consolidated with two fixtures, home and away. The first took place at Crystal Palace in the first week in June, and although his old team came in a spirit of peace, Grace still had some points to make. Summoning all his powers he produced easily his best all-round performance of the season, taking 6 for 102 and scoring a magnificent 150 to lay the foundation for a deeply gratifying win by seven wickets. London County also won at Gloucester, though the crowds that turned out hoping to see something special from the returning Champion were disappointed. W.G. made only 8 and 21. In a final gesture of reconciliation, Gloucestershire made Grace a life member of the club.

Although no longer considered for Lord's, Grace was still invited to lead the Gentlemen against the Players at the Oval. He scored only 15 and 19, but, after the vagaries of his captaincy the previous year, he effected a stunning turn-around in the professionals' second innings, summoning G. H. Simpson-Hayward into the attack when the game hung in the balance. Simpson-Hayward had followed Jephson in adopting the under-arm lob, and once more the unorthdox proved the Players' undoing. In three overs and one ball he took the last four wickets for five runs, to give the Gentlemen victory by fifty-four runs.

The match at Hastings was marred by rain, as so many other games had been during a cold, wet summer. Only one innings a side was possible, and at one stage on the first day the players were driven from the field by the wintery conditions. George Hirst turned up the heat with a free-hitting century, and Grace kept himself warm with a spell of twelve overs, taking 2 for 52. When the Gentlemen batted, only MacLaren had an answer to the Players' bowling on a difficult wicket. Grace, going in at eight, was not out 22 when a halt was finally called.

His final average for the season was 22 (from a total of only 593 first-class runs), and apart from his century against Gloucestershire and 43 and 81 in the first match against Surrey, he only once passed thirty, when he scored 31 for the MCC against Kent at Lord's.

If the writing was on the wall for Grace as a player, there were equally strong indications that London County itself was in terminal decline. Although Grace could still muster some good players – both Murdoch and Poidevin scored centuries in the club's total of 597 against Lancashire at Old Trafford, and the Dutch left-arm fast bowler C. J. Posthuma gave a much needed edge to the attack – the side was beginning to have a hand-to-mouth feel about it. Their first-class record of four wins, four defeats and three draws was respectable, but not enough people were interested. As the club's self-appointed Gibbon, A. D. Taylor, wrote in his article in *Cricket*, 'The London County CC – Its Rise and Fall', 'matches at the Crystal Palace did not secure any large amount of public patronage'. Taylor thought part of the problem was that 'the Sydenham resort' offered so many other attractions, and too many intending cricket spectators succumbed to 'the temptations of the palace of glass'.[20] Whatever the reasons, the future looked bleak.

For one last year things continued unchanged, and at the start of the 1904 season the club had a welcome injection of talent. Another South African tour had been arranged and a number of the team readily accepted the invitation to acclimatize to English conditions by playing in London County's early matches. These included the fast bowler J. J. Kotze and the brilliant all-rounder J. H. Sinclair. Not surprisingly the club started well, with three wins out of the first four matches. Grace also began well, scoring 52 in the opening game against Surrey and 34 against the MCC at Lord's. A string of low scores followed, but he regained form at the end of May with 45 against Cambridge University at Fenners. Then on 30 May he travelled to St John's Wood for his final first-class appearance at Lord's. It was, suitably, a match of some importance, MCC v. South Africa. Kotze bowled at great pace, but W.G. played him with 'genuine ease'[21] before falling to a brilliant catch behind for 27.

He followed that with a splendid match against Leicestershire at Crystal Palace. He scored 73 and 54, and once again found himself in competition with Billy Murdoch, who pipped him in both innings with 74 and 57. Another run of low scores, including 0 and 1 against the South Africans, might have suggested that Grace's season had passed its high point. But, as always, he was capable of springing a surprise, and on 18 July, his fifty-sixth birthday, he went in to bat against the MCC on the Crystal Palace ground and scored his last first-class century, 166. He occupied the crease for five and a quarter hours, hit fourteen fours, and despite some faulty shots gave no chance against an attack that included A. E. Relf, Walter Mead, Alec Hearne and Arthur Fielder (who the following year took all ten wickets in the Gentlemen's first innings at Lord's).

For the first time in thirty-nine seasons Grace didn't play in any of the Gentlemen–Players matches, though astonishingly his record number of appearances in the great fixture was not in fact complete. He did meet the Players of the South in his last game of the season, but it was something of an anti-climax: he made 2 and 6 not out. His only match of note after his birthday triumph was an excellent all-round game against Derbyshire at Chesterfield. Overlooked by the famous crooked spire, he scored 37 and produced his last significant bowling performance in first-class cricket – 6 for 73 and 3 for 82. Over the season as a whole, he played fifteen first-class games, scored 637 runs at 25.48 and took twenty-one wickets at 32.71.

Despite the early successes, the situation with London County deteriorated further. The wet summers of 1902 and 1903 had been particularly unkind to the new venture, and the financial burdens of running a first-class side were great. Even without the luxury of contracted professionals, amateurs' expenses had to be met. Grace had already asked Lord's to reduce the number of away matches the club had to play, but this was refused. Now it was apparent that first-class status would have to be relinquished. The club applied to join the Minor Counties, but that too was turned down. From 1905, therefore, London County would simply become another club, no different in status from the original Crystal Palace Club it had so brusquely replaced. For there to be continued first-class cricket at the palace, Grace would have to sail under a flag of convenience, The Gentlemen of England.

*

Before the start of the 1905 season Grace suffered another personal tragedy. After an operation for appendicitis, Bertie died on 2 March. He was thirty, virtually the same age as his uncle Fred in 1880. What scant evidence there is suggests that father and son were not particularly close. With an excellent Cambridge degree, Bertie could have taught anywhere he pleased, but he chose to pursue his career first at Oundle and then at Osborne, well away from the family home. There was no breakdown in relations – in 1901 Grace readily travelled north to score 141 for W. G. Grace Junior's XI against the Oundle first team – but a certain coolness is suggested by the inscription in Grace's copy of *The Walkers of Southgate*. It reads simply: 'Father from Bertie Xmas 1900'. But for all their differences in temperament and Grace's understandable, if ill-concealed, disappointment that cricketing ability was less easily passed on than a pair of initials, Bertie's death was a second terrible bereavement so soon after the loss of Bessie.

Grace came away from burying his eldest son to preside over the first-class debut of his natural cricketing heir. Though London County had lost their first-class status, Grace still kept a number of the old fixtures. As usual the first game was against Surrey, starting on Easter Monday, 24 April at the Oval. In the absence of a suitable amateur, Tom Hayward was given the captaincy of the home team, and, in the absence of Bobby Abel who had retired at the end of the previous season, the partner he took in to open the innings with him was a young man called Jack Hobbs.

The first of the four great batting partnerships which formed the framework of Hobbs's career began under the watchful eye of W.G. at point. The bowlers were the brilliant sports photographer George Beldam, who as a medium pacer swung the new ball prodigiously, and Walter Brearley, who would claim a place in the England team by the end of the season, so Hobbs faced a considerably stiffer test than anything he had met in club and ground matches. Hayward's advice on the way to the wicket had been to get the first single as soon as possible, and he showed the way in the first over. Not long afterwards Hobbs registered the first of his many thousands of runs at the Oval. Once off the mark he played the bowling quite comfortably, but edged an outswinger to slip on 18. This proved to be equal top score as Brearley and Beldam ran through the Surrey batting for 86.

Grace's Gentlemen of England fared little better against the pace of N. A. Knox. Grace was bowled for 12, and only Charles Townsend showed much resistance as the team was bowled out for 115. This left an hour for play, and so for the second time on his first day in first-class cricket, Hobbs went out to open the batting. With growing confidence he stroked forty-four runs before the close, and carried on the following morning with persuasive fluency. Grace normally reckoned he could get a newcomer out, and came on for a short spell, but Hobbs proved equal to his blandishments. He did, though, have a taste of the Old Man's canniness when his plans for a quick single were halted by the peremptory request to hit the ball back to save Grace the trouble of retrieving it. Afterwards Alcock congratulated him on the way he had stood up to W.G., who, he said, 'was very artful at getting out youngsters'.[22] Hobbs just missed a century on debut, mis-hooking Brearley to square leg when he had made 88, but it had been a highly impressive start. The game, which was interrupted by rain, held little else of interest. Surrey reached a far more respectable total of 282, and by the end the Gentlemen were in trouble at 164 for 7, of which Grace had scored 32.

The next match was against the Australians at Crystal Palace. After the surprise win of Pelham Warner's side in 1903–4 – during which Grace's vanquisher at Oxford, Tip Foster, had scored 287 in his first Test innings and Bosanquet had proved the devastating potential of the googly – the tourists were eager to seize an opportunity to get into shape to reclaim the Ashes. They used the Crystal Palace match as an extended net session, scoring 270 and then killing the game by running up a massive 526 in their second innings. Grace made 5 in his one innings and bowled a mere three overs.

He had a better match against Oxford University at the Parks, though he still found disrespectful undergraduates prepared to hit him into the surrounding greenery. In twenty-eight overs he conceded 121 runs, claiming four wickets in the process. In his second innings he made 71, his highest first-class score of the season, but with the loss of London County's status his opportunities were restricted to just nine matches. He played against both universities in June, managed a top score of 26 against Oxford at Crystal Palace, but then played no first-class cricket until the end of August when he met the Australians again at Bournemouth playing for an England XI. By then Jackson, who had at last been given the captaincy in preference to MacLaren, had led England to a 2–0 win in the Test series to retain the Ashes. Grace fell twice for 2 and 22 to Warwick Armstrong, a future Australian captain who would make a habit of crushing England sides. It was a close match with an extremely tense finish. Grace had scored his 22 when wickets were going down quickly, and he shored up the innings sufficiently for the Australians to be set 159 to win. Overnight rain made the pitch treacherous, and the game see-sawed throughout the last day. When the scores were level Australia still had three wickets in hand, but two further successes by the England XI made a tie a real possibility. In the end, the last pair scampered a leg-bye.

Grace stayed in Bournemouth for a match between Gentlemen of the South and Players of the South and scored 43 and 4. He then moved round the coast to Hastings for a virtual re-run of the Bournemouth fixtures. This was his last appearance at the festival, and it was a dismal anti-climax. In the first game, which was spoilt by the weather, he didn't bat at all, and in his final appearance against the Australians he scored 2 batting at number nine before being bowled by Monty Noble. The game was spoilt by bad weather, and according to *Wisden* 'the play at the finish was a travesty of cricket' as Armstrong was fed full tosses in a vain attempt to help him to the double of 2,000 runs and 100 wickets that Grace had first achieved in 1876.[23]

Twenty-nine years on, W.G.'s first-class figures were 250 runs at 19.23 and seven wickets at 54.71. Grace was now fifty-seven and a grandfather (Edgar having married and started a family), and this might have been the moment to quit. But his job remained open, albeit on a yearly contract, and for all his demonstrable loss of form at the highest level, he still relished the game. The next season would, however, be his last hurrah.

*

Grace started the 1906 season by leading the rump of London County, thinly disguised as the Gentlemen of England, to defeat against Surrey in April. In June, the side became W. G. Grace's XI for their match against Cambridge at Fenners. They won, and Grace had a good match, displaying 'really fine form and decisive mastery'[24] of the university bowling in scoring 64 and then 44 not out. Immediately afterwards, they played host to the second West Indian touring side. Although now granted first-class status, the tourists did no better than in 1900 and were heavily beaten by 247 runs. Grace was not the scourge he had been six years before, making only 23 and 3, but in the visitors' first innings he again demonstrated his fatal innocuousness with the ball, taking 4 for 71. Constantine showed his class with 89 out of a total of 156. Grace took another four wickets in the second innings, including Constantine caught and bowled for a duck, but came in for some terrific punishment from

A. E. Harrigin, who hit him for three sixes off an over. The next match, on 18 and 19 June, saw the end of first-class cricket at Crystal Palace, W. G. Grace's XI suffering a comprehensive defeat at the hands of Cambridge University. It was a personal disappointment for Grace too. Although he bowled nine tidy overs, taking 1 for 27, he was dismissed for 0 and 1.

There was, however, one more first-class engagement in his diary. After an absence of two years he was once again invited to captain the Gentlemen against the Players at the Oval on 16, 17 and 18 July. Whether or not the Oval authorities had been moved by the coincidence of the fixture falling on his birthday, Grace certainly accepted this unlooked-for present with enthusiasm. After two quiet days, he made his fifty-eighth birthday almost as memorable as his fiftieth. He took a wicket with his first ball when he had J. H. King caught for 88. It was his last in first-class cricket, and typically it was an important one as it ended a stand of 182. And when he batted, with the Gentlemen in serious danger of losing, he made 74. (He helped himself to George Beldam's bat which he had apparently been coveting, with the proviso that if he scored a century he would return it signed. At the end of the season he did send it back, autographed with his score.) He played 'with much of his old power, placing the fast bowling with the old certainty and showing the same consummate ease at the wicket'. As *Wisden* commented, 'Though he tired towards the end of his innings, his play while he was getting his first fifty runs was good enough to give the younger people among the crowd an idea of what his batting was like in his prime.'[25] When Grace was finally caught by Albert Trott off Tom Jayes he had saved the game, and he made his slow way back to the pavilion to the last great ovation of his staggering career. It had been forty-one years since he first played for the Gentlemen, and he was as happy as the crowd that his last appearance should have been a triumph. When he got back to the changing room he flung his bat on the table and said, 'There, I shan't play any more.'

In all he had played in eighty-five Gentlemen v. Players matches. The first had been at the Oval in July 1865 just a few days before his seventeenth birthday. The Players won, as they were accustomed to, but such was Grace's influence on the fixture over the next three and a half decades that Pelham Warner labelled the second part of his history of the fixture 'The Domination of Dr W. G. Grace'. In total Grace made 6,008 runs in 151 innings at an average of 42.60, sharing out the bulk of his runs almost equally between Lord's (2,417) and the Oval (2,563) at an almost identical average, 41.67 and 41.34 respectively. He scored fifteen centuries, with a highest score of 217. In addition he took 271 wickets at 18.72 with ninety-seven catches. It is an astonishing record, quite unmatched in his own day and rivalled subsequently only by Hobbs, whose career figures for the Players were: 4,052 runs in seventy-nine innings at 54.75, sixteen centuries, highest score 266 not out, and twenty catches.

*

Of course, Grace had no intention of giving up cricket when he flung down Beldam's bat. But it meant he acknowledged that he had reached the end of the road as far as big matches were concerned. Even so, in May 1907 he continued the tradition of taking a W. G. Grace XI to the Oval in May, managing 16 and 3 in an eight-wicket drubbing by the professionals. Also in May he came into contact with the South Africans again. They had at last been offered a Test series, but, though there was no first-class match against London County, Grace invited some of the players down to the palace to practise and play in a warm-up club game against Beckenham. Among those who accepted was A. E. Vogler, one of the South African quartet of googly bowlers. This gave W.G. the chance to 'take stock' of the new bowling, and he concluded that when bowled well, the googly 'is the most troublesome of all deliveries'. He devoted some space in *W.G.'s Little Book* to the problems of playing it, which, he admitted, were considerable. His solution was simply to 'watch the ball from the pitch' as he clearly saw no possibility of reading it from the hand.[26] In the three Tests Vogler, Schwarze, Faulkner and White took all but nine of the forty-nine English wickets that fell, and only C. B. Fry showed anything approaching confidence against them, though England still managed to win the one Test completed. In the minor cricket that now filled his season, Grace still found many takers for his own gentle leg-breaks, and he scored three centuries.

At the beginning of the 1908 season he took a Gentlemen of England side to the Oval for what really was his last ever first-class match. It was played on 20, 21 and 22 April and he made a dogged 15 in the first innings and a more aggressive 25 in the second. He was bowled both times by a Barnes amateur, Sydney Busher, who was making his first-class debut. This year also marked the end of London County. Grace scored his last century, 111 not out (Grace says 110 in his own summary for the year), against Whitgift Wanderers on 26 June, and he also took a hat-trick in a seven-wicket haul which helped the club win the match comfortably.

In August he made his final appearances at Lord's, playing in two consecutive matches. In the first, for London County on 17 and 18 August, he scored a single in his only innings and took no wickets, but in his final game at Headquarters, playing for MCC & Ground against Dorset on 19 and 20 August, he revived a few memories with an innings of 33 and three wickets. He was in good form and looked set for a thousand runs in the season, but as he told Ashley-Cooper, 'I injured my foot . . . on August 19 and played only twice afterwards'.[27]

London County struggled on and played their last match in September, thrashing a hapless XV of Penge. By then a new managing director had been appointed, and his main priority was not cricket. The brave experiment had failed, and a decision was made to discontinue the club and turn the playing area over to tennis 'as a more paying proposition'. As Ian Maxwell Campbell recalled, 'It was a melancholy and shattering reversion of policy . . . [t]he offer of loyal diehards to revive the former self-supporting club was incontinently rejected', which caused as much bad feeling as the sidelining of the original club had in the first place.[28] Grace took the news as badly as anyone. When it was broken to him, he stormed up to the committee room and challenged the board to a single-wicket match.[29] It was a splendid, but futile, gesture. In fact, they had already delayed too long. The savings made by the closure of the cricket club and the termination of Grace's contract were not enough to avert disaster, and in 1909 the company went into receivership.

It would be easy to dismiss the London County as merely a comfortable sinecure for Grace in the twilight of his career, but he certainly didn't see it like that. No one could have worked harder to make it a success. He was incapable of doing things by halves and spent endless hours on the ground harrying the groundstaff with his whistle, and equal amounts of time in his study working his way through piles of paperwork. On the field, Grace led from the front as always, doing his utmost to make the club as competitive as possible. In the five first-class years he played sixty-three matches in which he scored 3,485 runs at 34.14 and took 135 wickets at 27.40. The results were respectable rather than outstanding, and the strength of the team varied depending on who was available, but on their day London County could certainly hold their own in the best cricket company. To have entertained three Australian teams and two each from the West Indies and South Africa in the club's

473

short lifetime was no mean achievement. In addition, London County provided a warm welcome to many individual overseas players, as well as bringing on a number of promising English cricketers. Grace was particularly proud of this: 'There has been no club like the London County CC for giving invaluable first-class match experience to many cricketers who could not otherwise get it and who would one day be all the better for it when they came to play in County Cricket.'[30] London County was a high-risk venture, and the eventual outcome always likely. That Grace raised the club to the heights it reached and kept it there as long as he did is one of the less recognized accomplishments of his life in cricket.

*

Just as circumstances were conspiring to deprive Grace of his personal fiefdom, a convenient death led to Ranjitsinhji's installation as the Jam Sahib of Nawanagar. To celebrate, and possibly to avoid the attentions of a court poisoner, he returned to England, installed himself at Shillinglee Park in Sussex and proceeded to live like the prince he now was. With Archie MacLaren, who was a great deal less grand off the cricket field than on it, as his personal secretary, he embarked on a Wodehousian summer of country-house cricket and creditors' summonses. Grace was among those who enjoyed his hospitality, taking a team of twelve down to play the Jam of Nawanagar's XII in May. W.G. threw himself into the spirit of Ranji's piratical extravaganza, posing in a turban in Shillinglee's extensive grounds (see Plate 28) and taking six wickets in the home team's first innings, though he failed with the bat and gratified his host by losing the match.

In October, on the eve of the Jam's return to his bewildered people, Grace headed a distinguished guest list at 'a complimentary and farewell dinner' in Cambridge. After sitting through countless speeches, including Ranji's and Conan Doyle's on the relationship between India and Britain, W.G. responded to the toast 'Famous Cricketers and County Cricket' – something about which he was qualified to speak.[31]

THIRTY-TWO

NEEDLESS to say, even as he dropped out of first-class cricket Grace remained the most famous of famous cricketers, the personification of the game itself for old and young alike. There were periodic revivals of the call for Grace to be knighted, though nothing came of them. However, it has very recently come to light that he was seriously considered for a peerage. In 1911 his name was included on a list drawn up by Prime Minister Herbert Asquith when, with George V's tacit approval, he planned to use the Honours List to swamp the Conservative majority in the House of Lords, which was threatening to block his Parliament Act (just as the Lords had blocked the Reform Bill in 1831). Also on the list were C. B. Fry, Ranjitsinhji and H. G. Wells (himself the son of a first-class cricketer).[1] Though many would have been delighted to see Grace elevated from Lord's to the House of Lords, it would have been ironic for him to have done so as a Liberal peer. Arthur Porritt recorded that after umpires who gave him out, he most 'detested Radicals in politics'.[2] In the end the Conservatives climbed down, Asquith's list was put away, and the tantalizing prospect of W.G. making his maiden speech – a Canadian variation? – to a packed upper chamber was consigned to the realm of fantasy.

In truth, no honour could have enhanced his stature, a point made with typical élan by Neville Cardus: 'the very idea of "Sir W. G. Grace" is comical . . . He was an institution. As well might we think of Sir Albert Memorial, Sir National Debt, Sir Harvest Moon – or Sir Cricket!'[3] He had already been elevated to the national pantheon by Madame Tussaud's (see Plate 21), though sadly his waxwork has not survived; his image appeared on pub signs; he remained a gift to cartoonists; and he was a favourite subject with the makers of figurines, busts, plates and other commemorative crockery. While the makers of bats had long been keen to associate the 'Beard' with their products, Grace was almost certainly the first sportsman to feature in an advertising campaign for a product with no obvious sporting connection when Colman's printed a handsome poster in which he emerged from a pavilion under the legend 'Colman's Mustard' wearing a shirt proclaiming 'Like Grace' and about to step over the words 'Heads the Field' (see Plate 18). He was recognized everywhere, even when it wasn't him. It was the proudest boast of C. B. Fry's heavily bearded housemaster that he had once been mistaken for W.G. by a porter on Nottingham station.[4] In 1908, Grace was due to unveil a granite obelisk to the Hambledon Club on Broad Halfpenny Down during a match between an All England XI and the local side, and a large crowd turned up. For some reason, Grace didn't. However, the crowd were not disappointed:

A train arrived and a burly bearded figure emerged. 'Dr Grace,' cried an enthusiastic porter who ushered him into the only vehicle. On the way the local photographer managed several snap-shots but found it singularly difficult to elicit anything about cricket from the smiling traveller. On arrival at the ground, the cricketers of course at once recognized that this was W.G.'s double, Mr Henry Warren of West Byfleet . . . The double was subsequently introduced to Dr Grace, who was amused by his description of his reception at Hambledon and gave him his signed photo.[5]

On another occasion, when he missed his train having promised to perform against an army team at Sandhurst, a more deliberate deception was practised. As some top brass had been assured that Grace would definitely play, Captain Wynyard decided to impersonate him from arrival at the station all the way to the wicket, 'beard, voice, batting style and all'.[6]

Whenever he appeared in public he was treated as a celebrity. E.M.'s son, Edgar Mervyn Grace, recalled being taken to a football match at Crystal Palace by his uncle in 1909. W.G. was hailed at every turn as they made their way through the crowd, and obviously enjoyed it, returning jovial greetings to one and all.[7] But he was not always so genial. In 1911 he captained an MCC side at St Dunstan's College in Catford. The school won by six runs, and the *College Chronicle* wrote up the match with understandable enthusiasm, reporting that 'Doctor Grace complimented us on our brilliant fielding and bowling'. But Ken Phillips, who was a pupil at the time, though too young for the 1st XI, remembered the great man rather differently: 'He was absolutely terrifying, not just because of his bulk and his frightening beard, but also because of his shockingly bad temper. Even the umpires were scared when he was at the crease – they used to look to him before making up their mind. If Grace didn't agree

476

with a decision, he simply overruled [them]. Also he wasn't above making loud uncomplimentary remarks about any of our players he took a dislike to.'[8]

But of course, for the vast majority of sports-mad schoolboys he remained a hero. Clement Attlee, looking back over a long life in the early 1960s, told an audience at a Cricket Society function that for him and his schoolfellows cricket had been a religion, and W.G. stood second only to the Deity.[9] Grace's status was not wasted on those with an eye to the market, and in November 1903 *The Times* noted the launch of 'a greatly improved form of table cricket'. Naturally Grace had been involved in its development ('additions and rules by Dr. Grace'), and just as naturally he was there at *Wisden*'s showrooms to put on an exhibition match with its inventor, Mr A. Weintrand.[10] The *Wisden* premises were also the setting for an auction of bats for the benefit of the Cricketers' Benevolent Fund in 1907. The prices give an interesting confirmation of Grace's standing. As reported in the following year's Almanack, the bidding for W.G.'s bat 'rose from £25 to £30. Then a wire brought 30 guineas, a telephone message £40, and a little before ten £50 was realized.' The next highest price was £42 for Trumper's bat. Ranji's fetched thirteen guineas, but after that there were no more double-figure scores, even though the names of those whose bats were on sale included Jessop, Shrewsbury, Abel, Fry, MacLaren, Murdoch, Joe Darling, Tom Hayward and Clem Hill. The great Fuller Pilch's willow weighed in at £5 10s, and C. I. Thornton's weapon went for a song at £1 17s 6d. Making the most of an opportunity, the article concluded with a couple of lines in large bold type: 'Dr. Grace's bat was a Wisden's Crawford Exceller'.[11]

Grace, too, was happy to take advantage of an undiminished asset, and in 1909 produced the last of the four volumes that bear his name as author: *W.G.'s Little Book*. As its title indicates, this was a more modest volume than either *Cricket* or *Reminiscences* and was designed to 'appeal by its price to a wider public than Mr Grace's former popular books'.[12] It was issued in paperback at one shilling. The cover features a photograph of Grace still sporting his MCC cap, though his beard is nearly white, strikingly framed in red to stand out on railway bookstalls. The text, intended to be both 'useful and entertaining', includes chapters on Batting, Bowling and Fielding, an overview of Past and Present, and some trenchant observations on contemporary standards in cricket journalism. By way of anecdote and observation it takes the story of Grace's cricketing life through to the demise of London County, and concludes with a brief chapter on Australian cricket and a summary of all the Anglo-Australian Tests since 1877. In one of the copies in his own library he wrote, 'W. G. Grace's own Little Book', adding 'with Corrections', and inside he tucked a postcard from F. S. Ashley-Cooper who had provided some of the emendations. Ashley-Cooper was the country's leading cricket statistician, and as Grace represented the greatest challenge (then as now), he devoted much time and effort to updating Waring and establishing W.G.'s full first-class career figures, eventually publishing the results in 1916 (see Appendix, pages 495–6). Grace gave him every encouragement, responding to queries and volunteering information on his performances through the remaining years of his life, and proving particularly helpful when Ashley-Cooper undertook his biography of E.M.

Other scraps of Grace's correspondence survive, showing that he remained the oracle for anyone interested in cricket, however ill-informed. A Harry Smith wrote out of the blue asking for the definition of a yorker. 'A Yorker must hit the ground first, if not it is a full pitch', Grace scrawled back. F. B. Wilson of Trinity College got a more considered response to what was obviously a gratifying question: 'My dear Wilson, One of my greatest innings was for the Gentlemen v Players at Lord's June 29 & 30 in 1868. I went in first wicket down with the total at 10 and scored 134 not out out of a total of 201. BB Cooper 28 was the only double figure beside my own. The ground was hard and bumpy and the bowlers were Willsher, Grundy, Wootton and James Lillywhite.'[13]

Although cricket never lost its savour, it was not the only sport Grace was interested in. His responsibilities at Crystal Palace had extended to managing the bowls club, which led him to take up the game himself. At the turn of the century Scotland was the senior bowling nation, and Grace applied for membership of the Scottish Bowling Association. He then invited the Scots to send down a team to the Palace. This was a huge success, and a return visit cemented the relationship and soon led to regular internationals. The first England–Scotland bowls match took place at Crystal Palace in July 1903. Grace captained the England team to a close victory, giving the game south of the border a great boost. Wales and Ireland also became involved, and in 1906 the *News of the World* put up a challenge trophy for the four national teams. Grace captained England for six years, and played his last game in Edinburgh in 1908.

The more leisurely pace of bowls, coupled with its lack of a hypothetical dimension, gave Grace's intense competitiveness less scope for gamesmanship than cricket, but he could still become voluble in his pursuit of victory. In the climactic moments of a close match at Wandsworth Common, he urged one of his team, an expatriate Highlander and Scottish international, 'Play to my foot, man, play to my foot.' Back came the crushing reply: 'Play to your fut, mon, play to your fut, why your fut is all over the green.' Unused to anyone answering him back, 'Grace remained quiet for several minutes'.[14]

It was through his Scottish connections that Grace was introduced to curling, and he struck an imposing presence on the ice. 'His figure, erect, broad and towering, had something kingly, and for all that he was built on such massive lines, his well-knit trunk and limbs possessed the spring of a step-dancer.'[15] However, his massive build undermined his kingly dignity when he went out to play on the frozen pond at the Palace in January 1905. As the *Daily Telegraph* reported, without a hint of levity, he went through the ice and got soaked.[16]

Another late passion that also involved threats to his dignity was golf. He made his first ferocious assaults on the new discipline while still playing cricket. Every year on the Sunday of the Hastings Festival he could be found 'removing huge divots on the fascinating course of Rye'. His early accomplice was Billy Murdoch, and Jessop recorded an epic of incompetence spiced with all their usual rivalry in which the two slashed and hacked their way round from bunker to rough, cheating whenever they thought they were unobserved. The match was reaching its climax after 'some surprising golf', and Grace 'led off with a low screamer which caught the top' of a notorious bunker. Murdoch was delighted but made an equally maladroit drive, and had taken seven shots to gain the green in front of the clubhouse before Grace started the steep ascent to his ball. 'It looked a "cinch" for the Old Man as he slowly and strenuously climbed the face of the bunker, and probably would have been if the weight of his oncoming tread had not caused his ball . . . to roll down towards him.' Grace took 'an almighty swipe at it', missed, and fell back down the slope. The match was halved, Murdoch winning the last hole in twelve to Grace's thirteen.[17]

After his retirement from cricket, Grace applied himself more seriously to the game, and got his handicap down to eight. He was an accurate, though not particularly powerful, driver, and deadly on the green, but Bernard Darwin, a regular companion on the links, recalled his difficulty with the bits in between: 'When he had his driver in his hand, one perceived that here was a ball-hitting genius who had come to golf a little too late; with an iron he seemed a very ordinary mortal.' He had a favourite iron, 'of niblick ancestry', which he called his 'cleaver'. This he used 'in all possible situations, but it was not, in my recollection, very effective'.*[18] Grace's shortcomings took nothing from his enjoyment of the game. Sir George (later Lord) Riddell, chairman of the *News of the World*, remembered him as 'one of the most enthusiastic golfers I have ever met – never tired and never bored. No weather deterred him. I have played with him in rain, snow, hail and thunderstorms. When he started for a day's golf, nothing kept him in the club-house. In the early days of motoring we made a trip to Huntercombe. On the road we had a breakdown which detained us for several hours. W.G. wasted no time. He spent all morning in an adjoining field, practising approach shots.'[19]

Grace also played regularly with Prince Albert of Schleswig-Holstein, a grandson of Queen Victoria, who would travel overnight from mainland Europe arriving in time for a round before lunch. On one occasion the party went on from the golf course to the skating rink at Prince's where Grace gave a demonstration of curling. They then dined and saw their royal companion off at Victoria. Grace was surprised to find his activities written up in the press the following day, especially as the reporter had paired him with the wrong prince. The story, filling three quarters of a column on a prominent page, gave 'full details of how the great W.G. had been playing golf with little Prince Albert [eldest son of the Prince of Wales]', and then went on to curling 'where the little chap ran beside the burly form of W.G. clapping his hands in delight, and had afterwards been taken to Buckingham Palace by the Old Man, who, after dining there, caught the last train back to the Crystal Palace'.[20] Grace was never remotely as intimate with the palace as this flattering fabrication suggests, though in 1911 he met and was photographed with the then Prince of Wales, the future Edward VIII, when he played for Prince Albert of Schleswig-Holstein's XI against Charterhouse at Cumberland Lodge. The Prince looked in at the match after the Garter ceremony at Windsor.

In addition to his punishing recreational programme in and around the metropolis, Grace remained devoted to field sports. He never missed an opportunity to fish, and received many invitations to shoot. He wrote to

* It was perhaps more versatile than Darwin gives it credit for. Grace was once stranded on a station which had two lines to Crystal Palace. He had come up on one line but the next train was on the other. He asked at the booking office whether his ticket was valid. On being told no, he stuck the 'cleaver' through the ticket-office window and elicited a more acceptable answer. (*Memorial Biography*, p. 337)

his friend Richard Bell in December 1907 telling him of a successful expedition to Norfolk: 'We killed over 1000 head in two days, principally pheasants, but the weather spoilt the fun. We shot through the wet all the first day.'[21] (Even Grace's iron constitution could not withstand that and he was laid up in bed for a week with bronchitis.) Grace was also an ardent follower of the Worcester Park Beagles. In fact he was rather too ardent for some, as he used to jog around blowing his whistle excitedly whenever he spotted a hare. Attempts to ban the whistle were singularly unsuccessful. In the summer he arranged matches between the Worcester Park Beaglers and London County, and such were his loyalties that he once batted for both sides in the same game.

Everything Grace undertook was marked by total concentration, and his range of activities showed an unquenchable zest for life and a truly flabbergasting stamina. After cataloguing the pursuits of a typical day with him, George Beldam remarked, 'it would have been too much for many a younger man'.[22] It is a mistake to think of the period after 1900 as Grace's 'declining years'. He probably packed more physical exercise into the last fifteen years of his life than most people get into an entire lifetime.

*

In the second half of 1909, the address at the top of Grace's letters changed from 'St Andrews', Laurie Park Road, Sydenham to 'Fairmount', Mottingham, a secluded property in over an acre of land. Grace took it for seven years at a rent of £110 per annum, and signed the lease on 13 July 1909. Situated between Bexley and Bromley, Mottingham was a little further out of town than Sydenham, but there was a station near by at Eltham, and as Grace emphasized to a friend, he was hardly less accessible than before – 'it will only take you about 20 or 25 minutes to get to Eltham, and 18 minutes to walk up, or a cab is only 1/-'.[23]

Grace thoroughly enjoyed his new domain. There was a large vegetable garden, to which he devoted much time (his asparagus bed was particularly splendid); he also kept chickens, '13 fowls' being listed under 'Garden Effects' when his assets were assessed for estate duty.[24] Though there was no cricket net (Grace laid out a clock-golf course instead), W.G. had no intention of giving up the game, and in 1910 both he and Charles joined Eltham Cricket Club. Grace wrote proudly to Ashley-Cooper at the end of the 1910 season, 'I played in 17 matches . . . and had 15 completed innings scoring 418 runs. Average 27.13. My highest score was 71. I only bowled in a few matches but took over 20 wickets.'[25]

481

Before the following season got properly under way, Grace had news of the deaths of two men to whom he had been exceptionally close. Billy Murdoch had returned to Australia and was watching the Test between Australia and South Africa at Melbourne in February 1911 when he suffered a stroke from which he did not recover. Grace had lost touch with him for a while, and was delighted when Murdoch sent him a postcard a couple of years before, hinting that he might be coming back to England. Their friendship grew from their initial rivalry and developed into a boon companionship in the London County days. Murdoch was the perfect foil, sharing Grace's puerile sense of fun and having the stature – and stamina – to behave as his equal. Like his great compatriot, Spofforth, Murdoch felt equally at home in England as in Australia, and left instructions that he was to be buried in Kensal Green Cemetery. His body was duly embalmed and shipped back for interment.

Three months later Grace suffered an even greater loss. E.M. died at the age of sixty-nine on Saturday, 20 May 1911 (by chance, the day Ted Alletson hit his extraordinary 189 in ninety minutes at Hove, of which the last eighty-nine runs came in just fifteen minutes – a rampage E.M. would have enjoyed). E.M.'s services to cricket, especially the Gloucestershire Club, were immeasurable. He had only resigned as Secretary in 1909, and in recognition of his thirty-nine years in the post a testimonial was raised and a presentation dinner held at the Grand Hotel in Bristol. He continued to play for Thornbury, even though he required a runner when batting, until 1910, when he collapsed from exhaustion at Weston and was carried off the field insensible. There was no discernible mellowing in his last years and the stories of his obduracy are legion. But for all his ferocious reputation, the Coroner was a revered and popular figure and his funeral was the occasion for a public demonstration of deep affection.

In his speech of thanks at the Grand Hotel E.M. had projected a rather anodyne picture of his time as Secretary, declaring 'there has never been a mis-word; everything has gone pleasantly and well'.[26] His personal views on W.G.'s break with the club remained private, but it is legitimate to suppose that he had sympathized more with the club's position than with his brother's, and the move to Sydenham clearly worked against family intimacy. In July 1901 W.G. wrote to Spofforth ('My dear Spof') who had hoped to meet him at a match at Hampstead. Grace said he wouldn't be playing, adding, 'You will be sorry to hear old E.M.'s second wife died this morning, telegram just arrived, she has been ill some time, but we did not know it was so serious until last week, they kept it to themselves and told no one, so it has given us rather a shock.'[27] (E.M. married again the following year, and for a fourth time in 1907.) E.M.'s son, Edgar, remembered that when W.G. made his last appearance on the county ground at Bristol for Ted Spry's benefit match in 1908 there was some friction between the two of them. Grace disappointed the crowds by failing to make a score, and disgusted his brother by going off to play bowls rather than stay and talk to him.[28]

E.M. was without doubt one of the great cricketers of the Victorian period, and, as the 1912 *Wisden* obituary put it, 'But for the accident that his own brother proved greater than himself, [he] would have lived in cricket history as perhaps the most remarkable player the game has produced.'[29] Praising him for his brilliant eye which, coupled with his unorthodox approach to batting, made him a terror to bowlers from Lord's down to the village green, *The Times* recalled his 65 and 41 for Gloucestershire against the 1880 Australians: 'It has always been said that these two innings astonished Mr Spofforth, who never dreamed that anybody could be found who could pull his best length balls so daringly.'[30] E.M.'s influence on W.G. is obvious, and their rivalry during Grace's early years almost certainly made him an even more focused and determined cricketer than he would otherwise have been. For all their run-ins – and run-outs – there was a huge mutual respect between them, and Grace felt the loss deeply. For some time after the funeral he wore a black armband when he played bowls.

Other friends and companions had been gathered in over the recent years. Alfred Shaw, the man who claimed his wicket forty-nine times, had died in 1909, and Tom Emmett, who shared second place in that particular roll of honour with thirty-six dismissals, a couple of years before. Charles Alcock had also died in 1907. Grace remarked to a friend, 'It shows how old I am getting that there is hardly anyone left now to call me Gilbert.'[31] He was beginning to show his age too, as the photographs record. The beard becomes whiter, the clothes begin to hang a little looser, and that sense of vast physical power begins to ebb away. Grace makes no compromise with the camera, gazing unsmilingly into the lens or far into the distance as though the present were losing its interest for him (see Plate 29).

But he continued to play cricket. His figures for 1911, sent as usual to Ashley-Cooper, were: 'Batting No of innings 16 Runs 352 Highest score 79 average 22 Bowling Matches bowled in 8 wickets taken 30'.[32] He also kept busy with his other various commitments. In March 1913 he sent Jessop a three-line postcard, pulling out of an engagement: 'Very sorry I cannot come on Monday next, but I find I have to attend a meeting on that day. Yours in haste'.[33]

In 1913 Grace played his last game for the MCC, scoring 18 against Old Charlton at Charlton on 26 June. His records in first-class cricket were under continual pressure, and this year he had to make room on the plinth he had occupied alone since 1895 when Tom Hayward joined him as the second batsman to score a hundred centuries. As the 1914 *Wisden* pointed out, 'The change that has come over modern cricket in the way of an extended programme of first-class fixtures is brought home to us by the fact that Hayward made his hundredth century in his twenty-first season',[34] whereas it took Grace thirty years to reach the landmark. In addition, the wickets Grace played on in his early years (when Tom Hayward's uncle, after whom he was named, was still playing) were so inferior to those in the 1890s that a comparison of the two feats is almost meaningless. The next man to a hundred centuries was Hayward's opening partner, Jack Hobbs, who also went on, amid frenzied public excitement, first to equal and then to beat W.G.'s record of 126 first-class centuries in 1925 – on one of Grace's favourite grounds, Taunton.

Grace's keen eye for talent had already picked out Hobbs, and the Old Man would have been cheered by the news of his record opening stand of 323 with Wilfred Rhodes in the Melbourne Test of February 1912 (England's triumphant team was led by a London County old boy, J. W. H. T. Douglas). Apart from the ill-fated Triangular Tournament of 1912, there was no further Test cricket between England and Australia before the war, so when Grace died the Ashes were where they belonged – in England. There was a series against South Africa over the winter of 1913–14, which England won comfortably by four Tests to nil. On 22, 23 and 24 June 1914 a match was arranged between those who had toured and a Rest of England Eleven to celebrate the centenary of cricket at St John's Wood. Grace made his way to Lord's to watch, and was cheered whenever the large crowd caught sight of him. He was also honoured at the dinner held after the second day's play in the Hotel Cecil, presided over by Lord Hawke. Grace received an ovation 'worthy of a prince', and C. E. Green was rapturously hear-heared when he said, 'Dr Grace is, as you all know, the greatest cricketer that ever lived or ever will live.'[35]

The greatest cricketer that ever lived took the train home and returned to the humdrum world of club cricket. He missed the third day of the match at Lord's because he was playing himself. He had been persuaded to get up a team to play the Army Ordnance Corps at Woolwich on 24 and 25 June. This was the last time a W. G. Grace's XI took the field, and W.G. led his side to victory by nine wickets, scoring an undefeated 12 in his only innings. On 11 July he had a long day in the field for Eltham as Blackheath scored 305. He went in last and saved the game with 3 not out. On 25 July, a week after his sixty-sixth birthday, he played for Eltham against Grove Park (away). This is often cited, wrongly, as his last match, but it was the last in which he batted. In a fitting finale he scored 69 not out in a total of 155 for 6 declared. The *Eltham and District Times* reported: '"WG" batted admirably, going in with the score at 31 [for 4], and carrying his bat for an excellent 69. He got his runs all round the wicket, being especially strong on the off side. His chief hits included one five, six four's, and seven two's. The "Doctor" found a valuable partner in D.E. Henshall, who helped to put on 71 runs in 80 minutes.'[36] The next highest score was 30 not out. Grove Park made 99 for 8 in reply, and Charles Grace took 4 for 48. Apart from the fact that Eltham couldn't quite force a win, it was a thoroughly satisfactory game.

*

Five days after Grace's last innings, Albert Trott, worn down by poverty and a sense of failure, committed suicide at the age of forty-one. But the time for mourning individual tragedies was running out. As England basked in a heatwave, developments on the continent were becoming more ominous by the day. On Friday, 31 July *The Times*' headlines warned of 'Russian Military Concentration' and 'German Mobilization Imminent'. Europe was on the brink of the abyss. Germany declared war on Russia the following day, and the momentum towards conflict in the west was too great to halt.

On the Bank Holiday Monday (3 August) most people preferred to trust the weather than heed the headlines, and thousands crowded into the Oval to see Hobbs make the highest score of his career to date, a majestic 226 with, as he admitted, 'never a thought of war'. But the war was coming nevertheless. The Germans invaded France and were poised to violate Belgium's neutrality, which Britain was pledged to defend. The following day, the *Sportsman* still clung to the hope that Britain might stay out, but offered the scant consolation if she couldn't that during the Crimean conflict 'race meetings were held as usual'.[37]

That night Lionel Tennyson, grandson of the poet, dashing amateur batsman and army officer, went to bed in his London flat and dreamt he was batting at Leyton. He brought up his century with a six to loud applause. However, though he 'acknowledged it in the orthodox fashion . . . [it] refused to stop.' The scene grew dim, and he awoke to the fact that someone was banging on the door. It was the night porter summoning him to the telephone. He was being recalled to his regiment in Colchester. The time was two a.m., and Britain had been at war with Germany for an hour and three quarters.[38] Within a month Tennyson would take part in the retreat from Mons and the battle of the Marne. The future captain of England had dreamed the last dream of cricket's Golden Age.

Although the war had an immediate impact on the cricket season – others beside Tennyson were recalled to the colours, leaving proleptic gaps in the white-flannelled ranks – the government told the counties to carry on with their fixtures. The Oval was briefly requisitioned by the army, leaving Hobbs with the unenviable choice of cancelling his benefit match or playing it at Lord's (he opted for Lord's but the game was a failure). Club cricket also continued, and on 8 August Grace played his last match. It took place at Eltham against Northbrook, and ended in a draw. Grace neither batted nor bowled, but by then cricket was becoming an irrelevance.

The day before, the first units of the British Expeditionary Force had crossed to France. Their role was to try to put a brake on the German flanking movement to the north-west of Paris. They were involved in heavy fighting from the onset, and as they fell back from Mons the casualty figures rose shockingly. On 26 August, alongside the cricket reports and news of probable runners in the St Leger, the *Sportsman* noted 2,000 British casualties. Grace reached for his pen, and the following appeared in the next day's edition:

CRICKETERS AND THE WAR
DR W. G. GRACE'S VIEW. TO THE EDITOR OF 'THE SPORTSMAN'

Sir, – There are many cricketers who are already doing their duty, but there are many more who do not seem to realise that in all probability they will have to serve either at home or abroad before the war is brought to a conclusion. The fighting on the Continent is very severe, and will probably be prolonged. I think the time has arrived when the county cricket season should be closed, for it is not fitting at a time like the present that able-bodied men should play day after day and pleasure-seekers look on. There are so many who are young and able, and

486

yet are hanging back. I should like to see all first-class cricketers of suitable age, etc, set a good example, and come to the help of their country without delay in its hour of need.

Yours, etc.,
W. G. Grace[39]

This elicited a spate of letters from the representatives of other sports, not all of them expressed so moderately: 'Are Rugger men . . . going to follow the perfidious example of their chicken-hearted brethren among cricket amateurs? Can this be possible? [signed] "Britain Uber Alles".'[40]

Although Grace's appeal is often assumed to have brought the cricket season to an abrupt halt, one more round of county matches was in fact played. With the Oval temporarily released by the military authorities, Surrey, who were heading the championship, played Gloucestershire. Some of the Gloucestershire team had already joined up, and the visitors took the field with only ten men. Those who came to watch saw Hobbs and Hayward opening together for the last time, and took away one final memory to tide them through the darkness of the next four years.

With two sons of his own, Grace had not written his letter to the *Sportsman* lightly. Edgar had been in the Royal Navy since leaving school, and had attained the rank of commander some years earlier. When his ship, HMS *New Zealand*, docked at Melbourne before the war, he had visited the Melbourne Cricket Club where he was warmly welcomed. By 1915 he had been promoted to captain, and his ship, HMS *Grafton*, was involved in covering the Gallipoli evacuation in December, remaining off the Anzac beach until the end.[41] He finished the war a vice-admiral (attaining his final rank of full admiral in the 1930s). After his training at Crystal Palace, Charles joined the Kent Fortress Engineers, making regular trips home to Fairmount on his motorbike. He too had attained the rank of captain within the first year of the war.

Grace was kept occupied during the winter of 1914 responding to the various queries Ashley-Cooper put to him as he wrote his biography of E.M. It is clear from this correspondence that Grace took the minutiae of cricket records very seriously. He had in his own library all fourteen volumes of *Scores and Biographies*, and these show signs of regular use. Grace was quick to spot mistakes: 'The wicket you say E. M. was credited with was T. P. Sainsbury not T. B. as in Scores & Biogs', he wrote to Ashley-Cooper three days before Christmas. In the same letter he offered help with 'Scores and Analyses of the West Gloucestershire and

Knole Park matches, I have them all I think. Anyhow I have the West Gloucestershire score books. Let me know what you want and any other Biogs mistakes I may be able to put right . . .' In another letter (20 December) he admitted defeat on some early games, suggesting, 'Perhaps our old friend John Lloyd might help you, he was Capt of the South Wales team', and supplied his address.[42]

He must have enjoyed this excuse to immerse himself in the past. The present was too awful to contemplate. For Grace, who had spent so much of his life surrounded by young men, the slaughter on the Western Front was intolerable. Bernard Darwin remembered how badly it affected him: '[N]obody took it more to heart. In addition to a father's anxieties, he had to bear the loss of so very many young friends – not only the boys he knew but their fathers who had once been boys to him. He could not endure the thought of them being, as he said over and over again, "mowed down".'[43] A. E. Stoddart registered a personal protest against the general appalling-ness by committing suicide on 3 April 1915 at the age of fifty-two. He had had a nervous breakdown the year before which forced his resignation as Secretary of Queen's Club. *The Times* reported that he was 'in financial difficulties and lost all his money through the war'.[44] Shortly afterwards the cricket world suffered another loss when Victor Trumper died of Bright's Disease on 28 June, aged only thirty-seven. Even in England the death of the master batsman momentarily pushed the war from the newspaper placards.

A week earlier, on Whit Monday, 23 June, Grace made what was to prove his last public appearance at a cricket match. Archie MacLaren was stationed at Catford, the home of the great Kent stalwart Alec Hearne. Together they agreed to get up a cricket match for the benefit of the Belgian refugees. Hearne wrote to Grace inviting him to play, and received the answer that he would. Posters advertising the fact went up all over the town, and a large crowd gathered. However, on the day Grace felt unwell. Captain Percy Burke, a Kent amateur who was playing in the match, wrote: 'I can see him now coming through the gate and walking across the ground. No bag and in ordinary clothes. He must have seen our faces and he at once compromised by offering to stay all day and go round the ground with a collecting box.' This went down well with the spectators. 'I could hear every now and again great bursts of laughter from the crowd where W.G. had scored a repartee.' MacLaren's team batted first, and Hobbs scored 126. Burke was playing for Alec Hearne's team and also scored a century. At the end of the match Grace presented him with a bat. Of infinitely more value was the conversation that accompanied the presentation:

'A very fine innings indeed – How is it you are not playing for Kent County?'

'I could probably have done so if I had turned professional which I would not do and Kent are very well served now by Amateurs.'

'Ah yes,' the Old Man replied, 'they are, and I can understand, but thank you for the innings.'[45]

He continued to enjoy the company of cricketers, and always welcomed their visits to Fairmount. A famous photograph shows him flanked by MacLaren and Ranjitsinhji, both in uniform. MacLaren had sounded a far more bloodthirsty call to arms than Grace, calling the Kaiser a 'crowned madman' and 'that hog in armour' in *World of Cricket*.[46] Ranji, inspired by the same hyper-patriotism that had fuelled his Test career, had raised his own troops in India, though his ambition to lead them personally into battle was frustrated by the army authorities.

In the autumn of 1915 the war took a new and malevolent turn for the worse. In response to the British blockade, the Germans resolved to hit back at the British mainland. In comparison with the Blitz, the Zeppelin raids may seem innocuous, but as the first civilians ever to be subjected to aerial bombardment, Londoners regarded them with terror and outrage. In the novel he wrote with Violet Hunt, *Zeppelin Nights*, Ford Madox Ford spoke of a population 'driven almost to death by the horror set free [by] the Night Hag of Germany'.[47] Conan Doyle referred more bluntly to 'the Zeppelin murderers'.[48] The first trial runs took place in September, and proved how defenceless London was. The damage inflicted was slight, but German propaganda promised greater numbers of Zeppelins and a rain of fire from the sky. The threat put everyone on edge.

On 9 October Grace suffered a stroke while working in his garden. It was a relatively mild attack, leaving him the use of his limbs and only slightly affecting his speech. He was put to bed at home, and as the letter Agnes wrote to Ashley-Cooper three days later indicates, he had suffered no mental impairment and was fully expecting to recover very soon:

The doctor is ill & may not do anything in the way of going through your proofs for a week at least from now – he was taken ill on Saturday but read the first lot of proofs through & told me of a lot of mistakes but they are not marked, & I am sure that I could not remember all, he would be very sorry for it to be published with such a number of errors If you must have the proofs back before he can revise them, I must send them to you, but I am not allowed to bother him in any way.[49]

The following night, 13 October, the Germans launched their great raid. One of their targets was the Woolwich Arsenal, only a few miles north of Mottingham, but bombs were also dropped as far south as Croydon, and the sound of explosions could be heard all over south-east London. Grace reacted badly. H. D. G. 'Shrimp' Leveson-Gower, who visited him twice, tried to josh him out of his depression, asking how he could be bothered by Zeppelins having seen off generations of fast bowlers; 'I could see those beggars,' W.G. replied, 'I can't see these.' He was never likely to have made a model patient, but it seems that he was driven to new levels of restlessness by the raids. In attempting to get out of bed, he fell heavily, which inflicted a further shock on his system. Although there were hopeful bulletins about his condition in *The Times*, the mighty frame was now at the end of its tether, and on Saturday, 23 October he died of a heart attack.*

The news travelled fast, and even among the remorseless bulletins of annihilation from France and Gallipoli it struck a special chord of sorrow in the nation, and, indeed, the world. The distinguished journalist A. G. Gardiner ('Alpha of the Plough') was spending the weekend in the country. By six o'clock his hunger for a paper drove him to walk two miles to the nearest station.

As I stood on the platform . . . devouring the latest war news under the dim oil lamp, a voice behind me said, in a broad rural accent, 'Bill, I say, W.G. is dead.' At the word I turned hastily to another column and found the news that had stirred him. And even in the midst of world-shaking events it stirred me too. For a brief moment I forgot the war and was back in tht cheerful world where we used to be happy, where we greeted the rising sun with light hearts and saw it setting without fear. In that cheerful world I can hardly recall a time when a big man with a black beard was not my King.[50]

Similar sentiments were voiced in hundreds of obituary notices. Sir Arthur Conan Doyle wrote in *The Times*:

The world will be the poorer to many of us for the passing of the greatest of cricketers. To those who knew him he was more than a great cricketer. He had many of the characteristics of a great man. There was a masterful personality and a large direct simplicity and frankness which, combined with his huge frame, swarthy features, bushy beard, and somewhat lumbering carriage, made an

---

* It seems clear that the Zeppelin raids were a contributory cause, but the claim that the Germans made propaganda out of Grace's death has not been substantiated by a trawl through the German papers held at Colindale.

impression which could never be forgotten . . . Few men have done more for the generation in which he lived, and his influence was none the less because it was a spontaneous and utterly unconscious one.[51]

Telegrams flooded in from around the world, and a message of condolence from King George V was passed on to the family via the MCC.

The funeral took place in bitterly cold weather on 26 October at Elmer's End Cemetery, Beckenham, and despite the war there was a large attendance. Both Lord Harris and Lord Hawke were there, along with Ranjitsinhji, despite the recent loss of his eye in a shooting incident. Other notable cricketers included MacLaren, Pelham Warner, Gregor MacGregor, Leveson-Gower, Grace's fellow selector of 1899, H. W. Bainbridge, J. R. Mason, Alec Hearne and the great Kent hitter C. I. Thornton; C. E. Green, J. A. Bush and Frank Townsend from the early days of the Gloucestershire Club; C. L. Townsend and S. A. P. Kitcat from the later years; and P. J. de Paravicini and E. H. D. Sewell, who had played with Grace for London County. Edgar could not return from active service in the Dardanelles, but Charles was present to escort his mother. The coffin was enormous and weighed well over twenty stone. It required eight pallbearers. Sentiment rather than sense had determined that Bobby Abel should be one, and there was an appalling moment when he stumbled on the steps of the cemetery chapel.[52]

Grace was buried in the same plot as Bessie and Bertie. The simple tiered gravestone, surmounted by a plain cross, enshrines Grace as a family man. He had followed the path his father had mapped out for him, pursuing his profession and achieving, by the end of his career, a position of modest middle-class affluence. Of course he was greatly helped by the windfall of his 1895 testimonial, much of which was invested (his portfolio included shares in the Bukit-Rajah Rubber Co., the Waiki Gold Mining Co. and the Royal Hotel Edinburgh Co.); he also had seven life insurance policies worth £2,651. His entire estate, including 'Household Furniture, Plate, Linen, Personal Effects and Garden Sundries', was valued at £7,278 – £6,590 when outstanding debts had been deducted. Once estate duty of £264 had been paid, this left £6,326, well over £200,000 at today's values. It was not a fortune, but it guaranteed Agnes financial security for the remaining fourteen years of her life.[53]

*

Although it went to the nation's heart, Grace's death was inevitably

491

overshadowed by the war, in particular by the outrage felt at the shooting of Nurse Edith Cavell as a spy a fortnight earlier. Formal recognition of his great achievements had to wait until after the Armistice. In 1919 the MCC published the *Memorial Biography*, a unique tribute to W.G.'s qualities as both man and cricketer, made up of personal memoirs by many who had played with him. Edited by Sir Home Gordon, Lord Harris and Lord Hawke, the volume paints a warm human portrait and offers undeniable testimony to the affection in which Grace was held by the whole cricketing community. Feeling that something more substantial was required, the MCC commissioned the Grace Gates for the main entrance to Lord's in 1923. A great debate ensued as to the wording underneath Grace's name, and among the submissions were English verse, Latin tags and even homages in Greek. In the end, F. S. Jackson came up with the classic English understatement: The Great Cricketer.

When cricket resumed after the war Rhodes and Hobbs continued to rival Grace, as the most complete all-rounder and the world's finest batsman respectively. In 1925 Hobbs overhauled W.G.'s record of 126 first-class centuries, and the following year Rhodes was recalled to the England side at the age of forty-eight for the fifth Test at the Oval. Hobbs scored 100 and Rhodes took 4 for 44 to help win the match, and with it the Ashes. By that time the young Wally Hammond had embarked on a career that would beg comparison with his great Gloucestershire forebear. Hard on his heels came George Headley and the Don himself, who would rewrite the record books as they had been rewritten only once before. By the end of the inter-war period, Compton and Hutton were bidding fair to join the pantheon of great batsmen.

No one, however, could challenge Grace's position in the game, or his place in the English consciousness. His potency as a national symbol was illustrated when his bust was removed for safe-keeping from the Long Room at Lord's in September 1939 (see Plate 30); one member turned to his neighbour and said simply, 'That means war.' The following year, a Spitfire pilot was forced to bale out after a dog-fight over south London, caught sight of the Oval, and later confided to a radio audience that he had had 'a momentary vision of a man with a beard'.[54] It seems fair to conclude that the image of a man with a beard, his bat poised imperiously awaiting the next ball, will endure for as long as cricket is played.

William Gilbert Grace: A Statistical Survey

Compiled by BILL FRINDALL

His First-Class Career: The Traditional Figures

BATTING

Season	M	I	NO	HS	Runs	Avge	100	50
1865	5	8	1	48	189	27.00	–	–
1866	8	13	2	224*	581	52.81	2	1
1867	4	6	1	75	154	30.80	–	1
1868	8	13	2	134*	625	56.81	3	2
1869	15	24	1	180	1,320	57.39	6	3
1870	21	38	5	215	1,808	54.78	5	9
1871	25	39	4	268	2,739	78.25	10	9
1872	22	32	3	170*	1,561	53.82	6	7
1873	24	38	8	192*	2,139	71.30	7	9
1874	21	32	–	179	1,664	52.00	8	2
1875	26	48	2	152	1,498	32.56	3	5
1876	26	46	4	344	2,622	62.42	7	10
1877	24	40	3	261	1,474	39.83	2	9
1878	24	42	2	116	1,151	28.77	1	5
1879	19	29	3	123	993	38.19	3	5
1880	16	27	3	152	951	39.62	2	5
1881	15	25	1	182	917	38.20	2	5
1882	22	37	–	88	975	26.35	–	8
1883	22	41	2	112	1,352	34.66	1	9
1884	26	45	5	116*	1,361	34.02	3	6
1885	25	42	3	221*	1,688	43.28	4	10
1886	33	55	3	170	1,846	35.50	4	9
1887	24	46	8	183*	2,062	54.26	6	8
1888	33	59	1	215	1,886	32.51	4	7
1889	24	45	2	154	1,396	32.46	3	7
1890	30	55	3	109*	1,476	28.38	1	9
1891	24	40	1	72*	771	19.76	–	5
1891–2	8	11	1	159*	448	44.80	1	2
1892	21	37	3	99	1,055	31.02	–	8
1893	28	50	5	128	1,609	35.75	1	11
1894	27	45	1	196	1,293	29.38	3	5
1895	29	48	2	288	2,346	51.00	9	5
1896	30	54	4	301	2,135	42.70	4	11
1897	25	41	2	131	1,532	39.28	4	7
1898	26	41	5	168	1,513	42.02	3	8
1899	13	23	1	78	515	23.40	–	3
1900	18	31	1	126	1,277	42.56	3	8
1901	19	32	1	132	1,007	32.48	1	7
1902	22	35	3	131	1,187	37.09	2	7
1903	16	27	1	150	593	22.80	1	1
1904	15	26	1	166	637	25.48	1	3
1905	8	13	–	71	250	19.23	–	1
1906	5	10	1	74	241	26.77	–	2
1907	1	2	–	16	19	9.50	–	–
1908	1	2	–	25	40	20.00	–	–
Totals	878	1,493	105	344	54,896	39.55	126	254

BOWLING

Season	Balls	Runs	Wkts	Avge	5wI	10wM
1865	630	268	20	13.40	1	1
1866	1,215	434	31	14.00	3	–
1867	799	292	39	7.48	5	2
1868	⎧ 1,384	686	48	14.29	5	3
	⎩ –	–	1	–	–	–
1869	3,138	1,255	73	17.19	7	1
1870	1,817	782	50	15.64	4	–
1871	3,060	1,346	79	17.03	5	2
1872	⎧ 1,835	736	62	11.87	9	3
	⎩ –	–	6	–	–	–
1873	⎧ 2,727	1,307	101	12.94	10	3
	⎩ –	–	5	–	–	–
1874	4,101	1,780	140	12.71	17	9
1875	6,757	2,468	191	12.92	22	8
1876	6,321	2,458	129	19.05	11	2
1877	7,170	2,291	179	12.79	17	7
1878	6,680	2,204	152	14.50	12	6
1879	4,420	1,491	113	13.19	14	1
1880	4,062	1,480	84	17.61	9	3
1881	2,434	1,026	57	18.00	3	–
1882	3,404	1,754	101	17.36	8	2
1883	4,417	2,077	94	22.09	9	4
1884	4,150	1,762	82	21.48	5	–
1885	5,738	2,199	117	18.79	8	2
1886	6,102	2,439	122	19.99	10	1
1887	5,094	2,078	97	21.42	7	1
1888	4,390	1,691	93	18.18	6	–
1889	2,313	1,014	44	23.04	2	1
1890	3,048	1,183	61	19.39	3	–
1891	2,364	973	58	16.77	5	1
1891–92	385	134	5	26.80	–	–
1892	2,128	958	31	30.90	2	–
1893	1,705	854	22	38.81	–	–
1894	1,507	732	29	25.24	1	–
1895	900	527	16	32.93	1	–
1896	2,768	1,249	52	24.01	3	1
1897	2,971	1,242	56	22.17	4	–
1898	2,378	917	36	25.47	3	1
1899	1,220	482	20	24.10	1	–
1900	1,759	969	32	30.28	3	–
1901	2,815	1,111	51	21.78	5	1
1902	2,917	1,074	46	23.34	4	–
1903	798	479	10	47.90	1	–
1904	1,308	687	21	32.71	1	–
1905	510	383	7	54.71	–	–
1906	506	268	13	20.61	–	–
1907	–	–	–	–	–	–
1908	12	5	–	–	–	–
Totals	⎧ 126,157	51,545	2,864	17.99	246	66
	⎩ –	–	12	–	–	–

The Disputed Matches

Any chronicler of first-class careers involving matches played in the nineteenth century has entered a minefield. Apart from assessing which matches should qualify for first-class status, he has to decide which figures to take as correct when even contemporary publications could not agree, and original scoresheets have been lost.

Not until 19 May 1947, more than thirty years after W. G. Grace's death, was the term 'first-class match' officially defined by the Imperial Cricket Conference meeting at Lord's. The six countries represented agreed that 'a match of three or more days' duration between two sides of eleven players officially adjudged first-class, shall be regarded as a first-class fixture. Matches in which either team has more than eleven players or which are scheduled for less than three days shall not be regarded as first-class. The governing body in each country shall decide the status of teams.' The ICC's ruling gave the MCC the authority to decide the status of all matches in Britain for the first time, but it did not have retrospective effect. Although the MCC had controlled the status of the counties since 1895, classification of matches outside the County Championship had rested largely with the Cricket Reporting Agency, who compiled the first-class averages for the leading publications of the day and only occasionally consulted the MCC. Prior to 1895 the status of matches was even more of a lottery.

The season-by-season career figures which precede these notes are those compiled by F. S. Ashley-Cooper and published in *John Wisden's Cricketers' Almanack for 1916* to supplement Grace's obituary. Ashley-Cooper was the leading statistician of his era and these figures remained unquestioned until 1951, when the first edition of Roy Webber's *Playfair Book of Cricket Records* was published. Webber had made a detailed study of Grace's figures and had revised the accepted figures, jettisoning matches he did not regard as first-class and correcting a number of errors to published scores. He detailed his revisions in the February 1961 issue of *Playfair Cricket Monthly*.

In 1973 the Association of Cricket Statisticians (ACS) was formed, one of its primary aims being to agree a list of first-class matches. The first stage was completed in 1976 when its list of British Isles matches (1864 to 1946) was published. This list, to which all subsequent ACS publications have adhered, has superseded Webber's. The various differences were fully documented by Philip Bailey in an article entitled 'W. G. Grace Revisited' published in 1987 in the ACS journal *Cricket Statistician* (No. 58).

Which career figures should we accept? I make no apology for confessing that my own views are ambivalent. Whilst I fully sympathize with blinkered mathematicians who, quite rightly, condemn Victorian chroniclers for including minor matches to enable Grace to reach certain milestones, I also respect the view of the Doctor's contemporaries who considered any match in which he played to be elevated to first-class status by the great man's very presence. Acceptance of the ACS version would inevitably turn history on its head as two of his hundreds (nos. 37 and 63 in the list which follows) would disappear, reducing his tally to 124; the historic scenes which followed the equalling and breaking of the record 126 by Jack Hobbs at Taunton in 1925 would be rendered meaningless. I prefer to compromise, and whilst I have kept to the traditional figures, incorporating corrections to scores without discarding matches of dubious status in the records I compile for *Wisden, Playfair Cricket Annual* and my *Wisden Book of Cricket Records*, in the latter I have noted the revised version. For the record, here are Grace's career totals as they now appear in *Wisden*, etc., and in ACS publications:

Batting	M	I	NO	HS	Runs	Avge	100
Wisden	878	1,493	105	344	54,896	39.55	126
ACS	869	1,478	104	344	54,211	39.45	124

Bowling	Runs	Wkts	Avge	5wI	10wM
Wisden	51,545	2,876	17.92	246	66
ACS	50,980	2,809	18.14	240	64

Highlights of His First-Class Career

1869 First batsman to score a hundred before lunch on the first day of an 'important match': 116* for MCC v. Kent at Canterbury. Repeated the feat six times, including twice in successive innings, and achieved it three times on other days.

1871 First batsman to score ten first-class hundreds in a season.
First batsman to score 2,000 runs.

1876 His score of 126 out of 159 for United South v. United North at Hull remains the highest proportion of a first-class total (79.2%) by an Englishman and was the world record until 1943–4.

His 344 for MCC v. Kent at Canterbury was the first triple century, remained the highest first-class score until 1895, and is still the record for MCC anywhere. It contained the first instance of fifty fours (51). Ten days later he made 318* v. Yorkshire at Cheltenham – still Gloucestershire's highest score.

1895 Achieved the first instance of 1,000 runs in May alone (aged forty-six years and ten months). First batsman to score 100 first-class hundreds. His record of 126 centuries (including ten doubles and three triples) stood until 1925. Scored a hundred in each innings of a match three times and on five occasions scored hundreds in three successive innings.

1896 Carried his bat through a completed innings for the seventeenth time (world record equalled by C. J. B. Wood for Leicestershire).

1902 Exceeded 1,000 runs in a season for the twenty-eighth time (a record equalled by F. E. Woolley), including 2,000 on five occasions.

BOWLING

1865 Took 13 for 84 in his first first-class match, Gentlemen of the South v. Players of the South at the Oval – bowling unchanged throughout both innings with I. D. Walker.

1885 Took fifteen wickets in a match for the fifth time; his 17 for 89 for Gloucestershire v. Nottinghamshire at Cheltenham in 1877 included a spell of seven wickets in seventeen balls.

1886 Took 100 wickets in a season for the tenth time.

ALL-ROUND

1874 First to achieve the 'double' of 1,000 runs and 100 wickets in a first-class season. He repeated this feat in each of the next four seasons, but not until 1882 was it emulated.

1876 Achieved the first instance of 2,000 runs and 100 wickets in a season.

1886 Scored 104 and took all 10 for 49 for MCC & Ground v. Oxford University at Oxford. Achieved the match 'double' of 100 runs and ten wickets on fifteen occasions (six more than any other cricketer), including the only three instances in Gentlemen v. Players matches, a fixture in which he made the record total of eighty-five appearances.

Achieved the 'double' for the eighth time.

FIELDING

Held 887 catches in 878 matches, a total exceeded only by F. E. Woolley (1,018 in 978).

His First-Class Hundreds

No.	Score	Match	Venue	Season
1	224*	England XI v. Surrey	The Oval	1866
2	173*	Gentlemen of South v. Players of South	The Oval	1866
3	134*	Gentlemen v. Players	Lord's	1868
4	⎧30	South of Thames v. North of Thames	Canterbury	1868
5	⎩ 102*			
6	117	MCC & Ground v. Oxford University	Oxford	1869
7	138*	MCC & Ground v. Surrey	The Oval	1869
8	121	MCC & Ground v. Nottinghamshire	Lord's	1869
9	180	Gentlemen of South v. Players of South	The Oval	1869
10	122	South v. North	Sheffield	1869
11	127	MCC v. Kent	Canterbury	1869
12	117*	MCC & Ground v. Nottinghamshire	Lord's	1870
13	215	Gentlemen v. Players	The Oval	1870
14	109	Gentlemen v. Players	Lord's	1870
15	143	Gloucestershire v. Surrey	The Oval	1870
16	172	Gloucestershire v. MCC & Ground	Lord's	1870
17	181	MCC & Ground v. Surrey	Lord's	1871
18	118	Gentlemen of South v. Gentlemen of North	West Brompton	1871
19	178	South v. North	Lord's	1871
20	162	Gentlemen of England v. Cambridge University	Cambridge	1871
21	189*	Single v. Married	Lord's	1871
22	146	MCC & Ground v. Surrey	The Oval	1871
23	268	South v. North	The Oval	1871
24	117	MCC v. Kent	Canterbury	1871
25	217	Gentlemen v. Players	Brighton	1871
26	116	Gloucestershire v. Nottinghamshire	Nottingham	1871
27	101	MCC & Ground v. Yorkshire	Lord's	1872
28	112	Gentlemen v. Players	Lord's	1872
29	117	Gentlemen v. Players	The Oval	1872
30	170*	England XI v. Nottinghamshire & Yorkshire	Lord's	1872
31	114	South v. North	The Oval	1872
32	150	Gloucestershire v. Yorkshire	Sheffield	1872
33	145	Gentlemen of South v. Players of North	Prince's	1873
34	134	Gentlemen of South v. Players of South	The Oval	1873
35	163	Gentlemen v. Players	Lord's	1873
36	158	Gentlemen v. Players	The Oval	1873
37	152	Anglo-American XI v. XV of MCC	Lord's	1873
38	192*	South v. North	The Oval	1873
39	160*	Gloucestershire v. Surrey	Clifton	1873
40	179	Gloucestershire v. Sussex	Brighton	1874
41	150	Gentlemen of South v. Players of South	The Oval	1874
42	104	Gentlemen of South v. Players of North	Prince's	1874
43	110	Gentlemen v. Players	Prince's	1874
44	167	Gloucestershire v. Yorkshire	Sheffield	1874
45	121	Kent & Gloucestershire v. England XI	Canterbury	1874
46	123	MCC v. Kent	Canterbury	1874
47	127	Gloucestershire v. Yorkshire	Clifton	1874
48	152	Gentlemen v. Players	Lord's	1875
49	111	Gloucestershire v. Yorkshire	Sheffield	1875

No.	Score	Match	Venue	Season
50	119	Gloucestershire v. Nottinghamshire	Clifton	1875
51	104	Gloucestershire v. Sussex	Brighton	1876
52	169	Gentlemen v. Players	Lord's	1876
53	114*	South v. North	Nottingham	1876
54	126	United South v. United North	Hull	1876
55	344	MCC v. Kent	Canterbury	1876
56	177	Gloucestershire v. Nottinghamshire	Clifton	1876
57	318*	Gloucestershire v. Yorkshire	Cheltenham	1876
58	261	South v. North	Prince's	1877
59	110	Gloucestershire & Yorkshire v. England XI	Lord's	1877
60	116	Gloucestershire v. Nottinghamshire	Nottingham	1878
61	123	Gloucestershire v. Surrey	The Oval	1879
62	102	Gloucestershire v. Nottinghamshire	Nottingham	1879
63	113	Gloucestershire v. Somerset	Clifton	1879
64	106	Gloucestershire v. Lancs	Clifton	1880
65	**152**	**England v. Australia**	**The Oval**	1880
66	100	Gentlemen v. Players	The Oval	1881
67	182	Gloucestershire v. Nottinghamshire	Nottingham	1881
68	112	Gloucestershire v. Lancashire	Clifton	1883
69	101	MCC & Ground v. Australians	Lord's	1884
70	107	Gentlemen of England v. Australians	The Oval	1884
71	116*	Gloucestershire v. Australians	Clifton	1884
72	132	Gloucestershire v. Yorkshire	Bradford	1885
73	104	Gloucestershire v. Surrey	Cheltenham	1885
74	221*	Gloucestershire v. Middlesex	Clifton	1885
75	174	Gentlemen v. Players	Scarborough	1885
76	148	Gentlemen of England v. Australians	The Oval	1886
77	104	MCC & Ground v. Oxford University	Oxford	1886
78	110	Gloucestershire v. Australians	Clifton	1886
79	**170**	**England v. Australia**	**The Oval**	1886
80	113	Gloucestershire v. Middlesex	Lord's	1887
81	116*	MCC & Ground v. Cambridge University	Lord's	1887
82	183*	Gloucestershire v. Yorkshire	Gloucester	1887
83	113*	Gloucestershire v. Nottinghamshire	Clifton	1887
84	101	Gloucestershire v. Kent	Clifton	1887
85	103*			
86	215	Gloucestershire v. Sussex	Brighton	1888
87	165	Gentlemen of England v. Australians	Lord's	1888
88	148	Gloucestershire v. Yorkshire	Clifton	1888
89	153			
90	101	Gloucestershire v. Middlesex	Lord's	1889
91	127*	Gloucestershire v. Middlesex	Cheltenham	1889
92	154	South v. North	Scarborough	1889
93	109*	Gloucestershire v. Kent	Maidstone	1890
94	159*	England XI v. Victoria	Melbourne	1891–92
95	128	MCC & Ground v. Kent	Lord's	1893
96	139	MCC & Ground v. Cambridge University	Cambridge	1894
97	196	MCC & Ground v. Cambridge University	Lord's	1894
98	131	Gentlemen v. Players	Hastings	1894
99	103	MCC & Ground v. Sussex	Lord's	1895
100	288	Gloucestershire v. Somerset	Bristol	1895
101	257	Gloucestershire v. Kent	Gravesend	1895

No.	Score	Match	Venue	Season
102	169	Gloucestershire v. Middlesex	Lord's	1895
103	125	MCC & Ground v. Kent	Lord's	1895
104	101*	Gentlemen of England v. I Zingari	Lord's	1895
105	118	Gentlemen v. Players	Lord's	1895
106	119	Gloucestershire v. Nottinghamshire	Cheltenham	1895
107	104	South v. North	Hastings	1895
108	243*	Gloucestershire v. Sussex	Brighton	1896
109	102*	Gloucestershire v. Lancashire	Bristol	1896
110	186	Gloucestershire v. Somerset	Taunton	1896
111	301	Gloucestershire v. Sussex	Bristol	1896
112	113	Gloucestershire v. Philadelphians	Bristol	1897
113	126	Gloucestershire v. Nottinghamshire	Nottingham	1897
114	116	Gloucestershire v. Sussex	Bristol	1897
115	131	Gloucestershire v. Nottinghamshire	Cheltenham	1897
116	126	Gloucestershire v. Essex	Leyton	1898
117	168	Gloucestershire v. Nottinghamshire	Nottingham	1898
118	109	Gloucestershire v. Somerset	Taunton	1898
119	110*	London County v. Worcestershire	Crystal Palace	1900
120	110	London County v. MCC & Ground	Crystal Palace	1900
121	126	South v. North	Lord's	1900
122	132	London County v. MCC & Ground	Crystal Palace	1901
123	131	London County v. MCC & Ground	Crystal Palace	1902
124	129	London County v. Warwickshire	Crystal Palace	1902
125	150	London County v. Gloucestershire	Crystal Palace	1903
126	166	London County v. MCC & Ground	Crystal Palace	1904

He scored his first hundred at the age of eighteen years and twelve days and completed his 126th on the day after his fifty-sixth birthday.

DISTRIBUTION OF HUNDREDS
His hundreds were scored for the following teams:

Anglo-American XI	1
England (Test matches)	2
England XI	3
Gentlemen (v. Players)	15
Gentlemen of England	5
Gentlemen of South	7
Gloucestershire	51
Gloucestershire & Yorkshire	1
Kent & Gloucestershire	1
London County	7
MCC	4
MCC & Ground	15
Single (v. Married)	1
South	10
South of Thames	2
United South	1
Total	**126**

	Total			100th Hundred	
	Hundreds	Inns	Inns/100	Season	Inns
J. B. Hobbs	197	1,315	6.67	1923	821
E. H. Hendren	170	1,300	7.64	1928–9	740
W. R. Hammond	167	1,005	6.01	1935	679
C. P. Mead	153	1,340	8.75	1927	892
G. Boycott	151	1,014	6.71	1977	645
H. Sutcliffe	149	1,088	7.30	1932	700
F. E. Woolley	145	1,532	10.56	1929	1,031
L. Hutton	129	814	6.31	1951	619
G. A. Gooch	128	988	7.71	1992–3	820
W. G. Grace	**126**	**1,493**	**11.84**	**1895**	**1,113**
D. C. S. Compton	123	839	6.82	1952	552
T. W. Graveney	122	1,223	10.02	1964	940
D. G. Bradman	117	338	2.88	1947–8	295
I. V. A. Richards	114	796	6.98	1988–9	658
Zaheer Abbas	108	768	7.11	1982–3	658
A. Sandham	107	1,000	9.34	1935	871
M. C. Cowdrey	107	1,130	10.56	1973	1,035
T. W. Hayward	104	1,138	10.94	1913	1,076
J. H. Edrich	103	979	9.50	1977	945
G. M. Turner	103	792	7.68	1982	779
G. E. Tyldesley	102	961	9.42	1934	919
L. E. G. Ames	102	951	9.32	1950	915
D. L. Amiss	102	1,139	11.16	1986	1,081

50,000 Runs in a Career

	Career	I	NO	HS	Runs	Avge	100
J. B. Hobbs	1905–34	1,315	106	316*	61,237	50.65	197
F. E. Woolley	1906–38	1,532	85	305*	58,969	40.75	145
E. H. Hendren	1907–38	1,300	166	301*	57,611	50.80	170
C. P. Mead	1905–36	1,340	185	280*	55,061	47.67	153
W. G. Grace	**1865–1908**	**1,493**	**105**	**344**	**54,896**	**39.55**	**126**
W. R. Hammond	1920–51	1,005	104	336*	50,551	56.10	167
H. Sutcliffe	1919–45	1,088	123	313	50,138	51.95	149

2,800 Wickets in a Career

	Career	Runs	Wkts	Avge	100w
W. Rhodes	1898–1930	69,993	4,187	16.71	23
A. P. Freeman	1914–36	69,577	3,776	18.42	17
C. W. L. Parker	1903–35	63,817	3,278	19.46	16
J. T. Hearne	1888–1923	54,352	3,061	17.75	15
T. W. J. Goddard	1922–52	59,116	2,979	19.84	16
W. G. Grace	**1865–1908**	**51,545**	**2,876**	**17.92**	**10**
A. S. Kennedy	1907–36	61,034	2,874	21.23	15
D. Shackleton	1948–69	53,303	2,857	18.65	20
G. A. R. Lock	1946–70/71	54,709	2,844	19.23	14
F. J. Titmus	1949–82	63,313	2,830	22.37	16

MATCH-BY-MATCH SUMMARY

				Batting							Bowling					
				1st Innings			2nd Innings				1st Innings			2nd Innings		
Season	Ref	Test	Venue	No	R	HO	No	R	HO	Ct	Balls	R	W	Balls	R	W
1880	1		The Oval	2	152	b	7	9	*	1	5	2	1	112	66	2
1882	2		The Oval	2	4	b	1	32	c	4	–			–		
1884	3	1	Manchester	1	8	c	1	31	b	2	44	2	1	–		
	4	2	Lord's	1	14	c	–			2	28	13	1	–		
	5	3	The Oval	1	19	ro	–			1	96	23	1	–		
1886	6	1	Manchester	2	8	c	2	4	c	2	36	21	1	4	1	0
	7	2	Lord's	1	18	c	–			2	–			–		
	8	3	The Oval	1	170	c	–			4	–			–		
1888	9	1	Lord's	1	10	c	1	24	c	3	–			–		
	10	2+	The Oval	1	1	c	–			1	–			–		
	11	3+	Manchester	1	38	c	–			4	–			–		
1890	12	1+	Lord's	1	0	c	1	75	*	1	–			70	12	2
	13	2+	The Oval	2	0	c	2	16	c	–	–			–		
1891–92	14	1+	Melbourne	1	50	b	1	25	c	2	–			–		
	15	2+	Sydney	2	26	b	2	5	c	5	–			96	34	0
	16	3+	Adelaide	1	58	b	–			2	–			–		
1893	17	2+	The Oval	1	68	c	–			1	–			–		
	18	3+	Manchester	2	40	b	2	45	c	1	–			–		
1896	19	1+	Lord's	1	66	c	1	7	c	–	–			30	14	0
	20	2+	Manchester	2	2	st	2	11	c	–	35	11	0	–		
	21	3+	The Oval	1	24	c	1	9	b	–	–			–		
1899	22	1+	Nottingham	1	28	c	1	1	b	1	100	31	0	10	6	0

All his appearances were against Australia. * not out; + captain

HIGHLIGHTS OF HIS TEST MATCH CAREER

Ref

1 With E.M. and G.F. he provided the first instance of three brothers playing in the same Test.
Scored England's first Test match century on his debut and, until G. P. Thorpe emulated his feat in 1993, was the only Englishman to score a hundred against Australia in England in his first Test.
With A. P. Lucas shared in Test cricket's first hundred partnership – 120 for the second wicket.

5 Only player to hold a catch off his first ball as a wicket-keeper in Test cricket when he deputized for A. Lyttelton, who was bowling.

8 Made 170 out of 216 in 270 minutes to reclaim the record England score he had lost to A. Shrewsbury in the previous match.
Shared a partnership of 170 with W. H. Scotton which remained the Test match first-wicket record until 1899.

19 Completed 1,000 runs in his twenty-ninth innings.

22 Ended his England career at the age of fifty years and 320 days and remains the oldest Test captain.

SERIES-BY-SERIES SUMMARY

Series	M	I	NO	HS	R	Avge	100	50	Ct	Balls	R	W	Avge	Best
1880	1	2	1	152	161	161.00	1	–	1	117	68	3	22.66	2–66
1882	1	2	–	32	36	18.00	–	–	4	–				
1884	3	4	–	31	72	18.00	–	–	5	168	38	3	12.66	1–2
1886	3	4	–	170	200	50.00	1	–	8	40	22	1	22.00	1–21
1888	3	4	–	38	73	18.25	–	–	8	–				
1890	2	4	1	75*	91	30.33	–	1	1	70	12	2	6.00	2–12
1891–92	3	5	–	58	164	32.80	–	2	9	96	34	0	–	
1893	2	3	–	68	153	51.00	–	1	2	–				
1896	3	6	–	66	119	19.83	–	1	–	65	25	0	–	
1899	1	2	–	28	29	14.50	–	–	1	110	37	0	–	
Totals	**22**	**36**	**2**	**170**	**1,098**	**32.29**	**2**	**5**	**39**	**666**	**236**	**9**	**26.22**	**2–12**

SUMMARY BY VENUES

Venue	M	I	NO	HS	R	Avge	100	50	Ct	Balls	R	W	Avge	Best
The Oval	8	12	1	170	504	45.81	2	1	12	213	91	4	22.75	2–66
Manchester	5	9	0	45	187	20.77	–	–	9	119	35	2	17.50	1–2
Lord's	5	8	1	75*	214	30.57	–	2	8	128	39	3	13.00	2–12
Nottingham	1	2	0	28	29	14.50	–	–	1	110	37	0	–	–
In England	**19**	**31**	**2**	**170**	**934**	**32.20**	**2**	**3**	**30**	**570**	**202**	**9**	**22.44**	**2–12**
Melbourne	1	2	0	50	75	37.50	–	1	2	–				
Sydney	1	2	0	26	31	15.50	–	–	5	96	34	0	–	–
Adelaide	1	1	0	58	58	58.00	–	1	2	–				
In Australia	**3**	**5**	**0**	**58**	**164**	**32.80**	**–**	**2**	**9**	**96**	**34**	**0**	**–**	**–**
Totals	**22**	**36**	**2**	**170**	**1,098**	**32.29**	**2**	**5**	**39**	**666**	**236**	**9**	**26.22**	**2–12**

BIBLIOGRAPHY

Reference works

CRICKET: W. G. Grace

Ashley-Cooper, F. S., *W. G. Grace, Cricketer: A Record of His Performances in First-class Matches*, London, 1916

Lodge, Derek, *W. G. Grace: His Record Innings by Innings*, Famous Cricketers Series No.15, Nottingham, n.d.

Waring, Arthur J., '*W.G.*'; *or, The Champion's Career*, London, 1896

Weston, Neville G., *W. G. Grace, The Great Cricketer: A Statistical Record of His Performances in Minor Cricket*, Wymondham, Norfolk, 1973

CRICKET: General

Bailey, Philip and Philip Thorn, Peter Wynne-Thomas, (eds), *Who's Who of Cricketers*, London, 1984 (new edn 1993)

Frindall, Bill (comp.), *The Wisden Book of Cricket Records*, London, 1986

– *The Wisden Book of Test Cricket 1876–77 to 1977–78*, London, 1979

Haygarth, Arthur and Frederick Lillywhite, *Cricket Scores and Biographies*, 15 vols, London, 1877–1925

James Lillywhite's Cricketers' Annual

John Lillywhite's Cricketer's Companion (*John & James Lillywhite's Cricketers' Companion; James Lillywhite's Companion*)

John Wisden's Cricketers' Almanack

Lillywhite, Frederick (ed.), *The Guide to Cricketers*

King, Percival (ed.), *Scottish Cricketers' Annual and Guide*

Padwick, E. W. (comp.), *A Bibliography of Cricket*, London, 1977 (revised edn 1984); vol. II ed. Stephen Eley and Peter Griffiths, 1991

Swanton, E. W. (gen. ed.), *The World of Cricket*, London, 1966 (revised edn 1980)

HISTORICAL BACKGROUND

Arrowsmith's Dictionary of Bristol, Bristol, 1906

Cook, Chris and John Stevenson (eds), *The Longman Handbook of Modern British History, 1714–1995*, London, revised edn, 1996

Dictionary of National Biography

Metcalf, C., *England at a Glance Compiled from the Latest Authorities*, London, 1835

Palmer, Alan and Veronica (eds), *The Pimlico Chronology of British History*, London, revised edn 1996

Books and articles

The Hero of Cricket: an Appreciation of Mr W. G. Grace Together with some Remarkable Records, London, 1895

Leighton House, Westbury, Wiltshire, The Regular Commissions Board, n.d.

The Third Australian Team in England: A Complete Record of All the Matches, London, 1882 (rpt, Cambridge, 1989)

Alcock, C. W., *Famous Cricketers and Cricket Grounds 1895,* London, 1895

Allen, David Rayvern (ed.), *Cricket With Grace: An Illustrated Anthology on 'W.G.',* London, 1990

Altham, H. S., *A History of Cricket, Volume 1: From the Beginnings to the First World War,* London, 1962

Anthony, Edwyn, *Herefordshire Cricket,* Hereford, 1903

Arlott, John, *Rothmans Jubilee History of Cricket 1890–1965,* London, 1965

– (ed.), *Cricket: The Great Ones,* London 1967

Arrowsmith, R. L and B. J. W. Hill, *The History of I Zingari,* London, 1982

Ashley-Cooper, F. S., *Edward Mills Grace,* London, 1916

Bantock, Anton, *The Last Smyths of Ashton Court,* Part I 1802–1880, Bristol, 1990

Barker, Ralph and Irving Rosenwater, *England v. Australia: A Compendium of Test Cricket Between the Countries 1877–1968,* London, 1969

Bax, Clifford, *W. G. Grace,* London, 1952

Beldam, George W. and Charles B. Fry, *Great Batsmen: Their Methods at a Glance,* London, 1905

Bolland, William, *Cricket Notes, with a Letter Containing Practical Hints by William Clarke, Slow Bowler, and Secretary of the All England Eleven,* London, 1851

Bone, D. D., *Fifty Years' Reminiscences of Scottish Cricket,* Glasgow, 1898

Booker, Frank, *The Great Western Railway: A New History,* Newton Abbot, 1977

Bowen, Roland, *Cricket: A History of its Growth and Development Throughout the World,* London, 1970

Bradfield, Donald, *The Lansdown Story: A History of Lansdown Cricket Club,* Bath, 1971

Brodribb, Gerald, *The Croucher: A Biography of Gilbert Jessop,* London, 1974

– *Hit for Six,* London, 1960

Brodrick, the Hon. George C. (completed and revised by J. K. Fotheringham), *The History of England from Addington's Administration to the Close of William IV's Reign (1801–1837),* London, 1906

Brooke, Robert, *A History of the County Cricket Championship,* London, 1991

– 'The Tragedy of W. R. Gilbert', *Cricket Statistician,* March 1982, pp. 10–13

Browne, E., *A Short History of Nottinghamshire Cricket,* Nottingham, 1887

Brownlee, Methven, *W. G. Grace: A Biography,* London, 1887

Campbell, Ian Maxwell, *Reminiscences of a Vintner,* London, 1950

Cardus, Neville, *Cricket All the Year,* London, 1952

– *English Cricket,* London, 1947

– 'William Gilbert Grace 1848–1915' in *The Great Victorians,* vol. 1, Harmondsworth, 1932 (rpt 1937)

Carling, E. Rock and Purvis Stewart (eds), *The Westminster Hospital Reports,* vol. XVlll, 1911–12, London, 1913

Cashman, Richard, *The 'Demon' Spofforth,* Sydney, 1990

Chignell, W. R., *A History of Worcestershire County Cricket Club 1844–1950,* Worcester, 1951

Christen, Richard, *Some Grounds for Appeal,* Parramatta (NSW), 1995

Coldham, James P., *F. S. Jackson: A Cricketing Biography,* Marlborough, 1989

– *Lord Hawke: A Cricketing Biography,* Marlborough, 1990

Conan Doyle, Sir Arthur, *Memories and Adventures,* London, 1924 (rpt 1989)

Cotter, Gerry, *The Ashes Captains,* Marlborough, 1989

'Cover-Point' (T. Broadbent Trowsdale), *A Complete History of the Test Matches Between*

England and Australia (1877–1905), London, 1905

Cowell, George, FRCS, 'An Introductory Address Delivered on Wednesday, October 1, 1873, the Occasion of The Opening of the Session 1873–74 of the Westminster Hospital Medical School', London, 1873

Daft, Richard, A Cricketer's Yarns, ed. F. S. Ashley-Cooper, London, 1926

– Kings of Cricket, Bristol, 1893

Darling, K. D., Test Tussles On and Off the Field, Hobart, 1970

Darwin, Bernard, W. G. Grace, London, 1934 (rpt 1948)

Derriman, Philip, The Grand Old Ground: A History of the Sydney Cricket Ground, Sydney, 1981

Dunstan, Keith, The Paddock That Grew: The Story of the Melbourne Cricket Club, Surrey Hills (NSW), 1988

Ellmann, Richard, Oscar Wilde, London, 1987 (rpt 1988)

Engel, Matthew and Andrew Radd, The History of Northamptonshire County Cricket Club, London, 1993

Fitzgerald, R. A., Wickets in the West; or, The Twelve in America, London, 1873

– 'Quid', Jerks in from Short-Leg, London, 1866

Frith, David, By His Own Hand: A Study of Cricket's Suicides, London, 1991

– England versus Australia: A Pictorial History of the Test Matches since 1877, Guildford, 1989

– 'My Dear Victorious Stod' – A Biography of A. E. Stoddart, New Malden, 1970

Fry, C. B., The Book of Cricket: A New Gallery of Famous Players, London, 1899

– A Life Worth Living: Some Phases of an Englishman, London, 1939

Gale, Frederick, Echoes from Old Cricket Fields, London, 1871

Gardiner, Alfred George, 'Alpha of the Plough', Pebbles on the Shore, London, 1916

Gibson, Alan, Jackson's Year: the Test Matches of 1905, London, 1965

Giffen, George, With Bat and Ball, London, 1898

Gordon, Sir Home, Background of Cricket, London, 1939

– with Lord Hawke and Lord Harris (eds), The Memorial Biography of Dr W. G. Grace, London, 1919

Grace, W. G., Cricket, Bristol, 1891

– The History of a Hundred Centuries, London, 1895

– 'W.G.' Cricketing Reminiscences and Personal Recollections, London, 1899

– W.G.'s Little Book, London, 1909

Green, Benny, A History of Cricket, London, 1988

– (ed.) Wisden Anthology 1900–1940, London, 1988

– (ed.) The Wisden Papers 1888–1946, London, 1989

Gregory, Kenneth (ed.), In Celebration of Cricket, London, 1978

Hadfield, John, A Wisden Century 1850–1950, London, 1950

Hannam-Clark, Theodore, W. G. Grace and Gloucester (typescript, n.d.)

Harris, Lord, A Few Short Runs, London, 1921

– The History of Kent County Cricket, London, 1907

Harte, Chris, SACA: The History of the South Australian Cricket Association, Adelaide, n.d.

Hobbs, Jack, My Life Story, London, 1935

Hodgson, Randolph L., Cricket Memories by a Country Vicar, London, 1930

Honan, Park, Matthew Arnold, A Life, London, 1981

Horan, T. P. 'Felix', Cradle Days of Australian Cricket: An Anthology of the Writings of Felix, ed. Brian Crowley and Pat Mullins, Melbourne, 1989

Hudson, Roger, The Jubilee Years, London, 1996

Hughes, Thomas, Tom Brown's Schooldays, London, 1857 (2nd edn)

Humble, J. G. and Peter Hansell, Westminster Hospital 1716–1966, London, 1966

Hunt, Violet and Ford Madox Hueffer, *Zeppelin Nights: A London Entertainment*, London, 1916

James, Alfred, *The 2nd Australian XI's Tour of Australia, Britain and New Zealand in 1880–81*, Wahroonga (NSW), 1994

James, C. L. R., *Beyond a Boundary*, London, 1963

Jessop, G. L., *A Cricketer's Log*, London, 1922

Jones, Peris, *Gentlemen and Players*, Bristol, 1989

Kynaston, David, *Archie's Last Stand*, London, 1984

– *Bobby Abel, Professional Batsman 1857–1936*, London, 1982

– *W.G.'s Birthday Party*, London, 1990 (rpt 1992)

Leavitt, Judith Walzer, *Typhoid Mary*, Boston, 1996

Lemmon, David and Mike Marshall, *Essex County Cricket Club – The Official History*, London, 1987

Lewis, Tony, *Double Century: The Story of MCC and Cricket*, London, 1987

Lillywhite, Frederick, *The English Cricketers' Trip to Canada and the United States*, London, 1860

Lincoln, Bob, *Reminiscences of Sport in Grimsby*, Grimsby, 1912

Lorimer, Malcolm and Don Ambrose, *Cricket Grounds of Lancashire*, Nottingham, 1992

Low, Robert, *W.G.*, London, 1997

Lubbock, Alfred, *Memories of Eton and Etonians*, London, 1899

Lyttelton, H. H., W. J. Ford, C. B. Fry and G. Giffen, *Giants of the Game*, 1899 (rpt, Newton Abbot, 1974)

McGlynn, Frank, *Stanley: Sorcerer's Apprentice*, London, 1991

Martin-Jenkins, Christopher (ed.), *The Spirit of Cricket: A Personal Anthology*, London, 1994 (rpt 1995)

Mason, Ronald, *Jack Hobbs*, London, 1960

Meredith, Anthony, *The Demon and the Lobster*, London, 1987

Midwinter, Eric, *The Illustrated History of County Cricket*, London, 1992

– *W. G. Grace: His Life and Times*, London, 1981

Morrah, Patrick, *The Golden Age of Cricket*, London, 1967

Mullins, Pat and Philip Derriman, *Bat & Pad: Writings on Australian Cricket 1804–1984*, Melbourne, 1984

Moyes, A. G., *A Century of Cricketers*, London, 1950

Nevill, Barry St-John, *Life at the Court of Queen Victoria (1861–1901), with Selections from the Journals of Queen Victoria*, Exeter, 1984

Nicole, Christopher, *West Indian Cricket*, London, 1957

Nyren, John, *The Cricketer's Guide*, ed. Charles Cowden Clarke, London, 1833 (rpt in *Chronicles of Cricket*, 1888)

'An Occasional Visitor', *Cursory Observations on the Churches of Bristol*, 2nd edn, Bristol, 1843

Parker, Eric, *The History of Cricket*, London, 1950

Parker, Grahame, *Gloucestershire Road: A History of Gloucestershire County Cricket Club*, London, 1983

Peache, Nora, *Manuscript Diary 1875–8*

Pocock, George, *The Aeropleustic Art, or Navigation in the Air by Use of Kites, or Buoyant Sails*, London, 1827

– with J. Pyer and S. Smith, 'A Statement of Facts Connected with the Ejectment of Certain Ministers from the Society of Wesleyan Methodists in the City of Bristol, in February and March, 1820', Bristol, 1820

– with J. Pyer and S. Smith, 'The Facts without a Veil: or, A Further Account of the Circumstances Connected with the Ejectment of Certain Ministers from the Society of Wesleyan Methodists in this City; in reply to a pamphlet published by order of the

Methodist Leaders' Meeting and improperly entitled, "A Correct Statement of the Facts"', Bristol, 1820

Pocock, George junior and John Pocock, 'The Methodist Pill', Bristol, 1820

Pollard, Jack, *The Formative Years of Australian Cricket 1803–93*, London, 1987

– *The Turbulent Years of Australian Cricket 1893–1917*, London, 1987

Porritt, Arthur, *The Best I Remember*, London, 1922

Powell, A. G. and S. Canynge Caple, *The Graces: E.M., W.G., and G.F.*, London, 1948

Power, Sir D'Arcy and H. J. Waring, *A Short History of St Bartholomew's Hospital, 1123–1923*, London, 1923

Ralph, Elizabeth, 'People Matter: George Pocock', *St Stephen's Review*, Bristol, 1961–2

Ranjitsinhji, K. S., *The Jubilee Book of Cricket*, London, 1897

Robertson-Glasgow, R. C., *46 Not Out*, London, 1954

Rosenwater, Irving, *W. G. Grace: A Leviathan Was He*, privately printed from the *Journal of the Cricket Society*, autumn 1997

Sale, Charles, *Korty, The Legend Explained: The Story of Charles Kortright*, Hornchurch, 1986

Scott, Lord George, 'The Cricket of W. G. Grace', *National Review*, vol. 109, no. 654, August 1937

Sewell, E. H. D., *Overthrows*, London, 1946

Sharpham, Peter, *Trumper: The Definitive Biography*, Sydney, 1985

Sheen, Steven, *F. R. Spofforth*, Famous Cricketers Series No. 24, Nottingham, 1994

Sissons, Ric, *George Lohmann, the Beau Ideal*, Liechhardt (NSW), 1991

– *The Players: A Social History of the Professional Cricketer*, London, 1988

Small, E. Milton, *The Canterbury Cricket Week, Its Origin, Career, and Jubilee*, Canterbury, 1892

Smith, G. Munro, *A History of the Bristol Royal Infirmary*, Bristol, 1917

Smith, Rick, *ABC Guide to Australian Cricketers*, Sydney 1993

– and Ron Williams, *W. G. Down Under: Grace in Australia 1873–74 and 1891–92*, Tasmania, 1994

Southerton, James, Manuscript Diary of Australian Tour 1873–4, Nottinghamshire Cricket Club, Trent Bridge

Spencer, W. G., *Westminster Hospital: An Outline of its History*, London, 1924

Sulloway, Frank J., *Born To Rebel: Birth Order, Family Dynamics, and Creative Lives*, London, 1996

Taylor, Alfred D., *Annals of Lord's and History of the M.C.C.*, Bristol, 1903

Tennyson, Charles, *Life's All A Fragment*, London, 1953

Tennyson, Lionel, *From Verse to Worse*, London, 1933

Thesiger, Sir Frederick QC, *Smyth versus Smyth: A Narrative of This Extraordinary Trial*, London, 1869

Thomson, A. A., *The Great Cricketer*, London, 1957 (new edn 1968)

Toghill, P. J., MD, FRCP, 'Dr W. G. Grace: Medical Truant', *Journal of the Royal College of Physicians of London*, vol. 31, no. 1, Jan/Feb 1997

Trollope, Anthony (ed.), *British Sports and Pastimes*, London, 1868

Troup, Major Walter, *Sporting Memories: My Life as a Gloucestershire County Cricketer, Rugby and Hockey Player, and Member of Indian Police Service*, London, 1924

Trumble, Robert, *The Golden Age of Cricket*, Melbourne, 1968

Wakley, B. J., *Classic Centuries in the Test Matches between England and Australia*, London, 1964

Warne, F. G., *Dr. W. G. Grace: The King of Cricket*, London, 1899

Warner, Sir Pelham, *Gentlemen v. Players 1806–1949*, London, 1950

– *Long Innings*, London, 1951

– *Lord's 1787–1945*, London, 1946
Webb, Geoff, *They All Played at Lord's*, London, 1991
Webber, Roy, *The County Cricket Championship*, London, 1957
West, Derek G., *The Elevens of England*, London, 1988
– *Twelve Days of Grace*, London, 1989
– *Six More Days of Grace*, London, 1992
Westminster Hospital Reports, vol. XVIII, 1913
Whimpress, Bernard, 'Amazing Grace and the Colonial Response to "W.G."'s Two Australian
    Tours of 1873–4 and 1891–2', unpublished thesis, Flinders University of South Australia, 1991
– *W. G. Grace at Kadina: Champion Cricketer or Scoundrel?*, Adelaide, 1994
Wild, Roland, *'Ranji'*, London, 1934
Wilde, Simon, *Ranji: A Genius Rich and Strange*, London, 1990
– *Ranjitsinhji*, Famous Cricketers Series No.12, Nottingham, n.d.
Williams, Marcus (ed.), *Double Century: Cricket in* The Times, vol. I 1785–1935, London,
    1985 (rpt 1989)
Woods, S. M. J., *My Reminiscences*, London, 1925
Woodward, Sir Llewellyn, *The Age of Reform 1815–1870*, Oxford, 1962
Wye, Acton, *Dr W. G. Grace*, London, 1901
Wynne-Thomas, Peter, *England On Tour*, London, 1982
– *The History of Cricket*, London, 1997

Magazines, newspapers and journals

Aberdeen Journal, Adelaide Observer, Age (Melbourne), *Album, Argus* (Melbourne),
*Australasian, Bailey's Magazine of Sports and Pastimes, Ballarat Courier, Bell's Life in London
and Sporting Chronicle, Bendigo Advertiser, Bristol Mercury, Bristol Mirror, British Medical
Journal, Castlemaine Representative, Cricket: A Weekly Record of the Game, Cricketer, Cricket
Field, Cricket Lore, Daily Telegraph, Devizes and Wiltshire Gazette, Eltham and District Times,
Essex Times, Grimsby Herald and Lincolnshire Advertiser, Guardian, Hull News, Launceston
Examiner* (Tasmania), *Manchester Courier, Manchester Guardian, National Review,
Northampton Herald, Sheffield and Rotherham Independent, South Australian Register,
Sporting Life, Sportsman, Sydney Mail, Sydney Morning Herald, The Times, The Times
Literary Supplement, Wallaroo Times, Weekly Sun, Western Daily Press.*

Archives, private collections, sale catalogues

Public Record Office, Kew; Clydesdale Cricket Club papers, Mitchell Library, Glasgow; the
Davis Sporting Collection, the Albert Gregory collection *Cricketers*, and the E. S. Marks Sporting
Collection – all in the Mitchell Library, State Library of New South Wales, Sydney; Malcolm
Lorimer Collection; David Frith Collection; Roger Mann Collection; J. J. Davis Collection; Rick
Smith Collection (includes George Arthur Scrapbook); Bearne's Catalogue for sale of W. G.
Grace's books, 1996; Roy David's Catalogue of Manuscripts and Literary Portraits; archives of
Lord's, the Oval, Trent Bridge, Old Trafford and the County Ground, Bristol.

Video, audio-cassette

Frith, David and John Arlott, *Golden Greats of Cricket: Batsmen from the 19th Century to
    Modern Times*, Benson and Hedges, n.d.
Swanton, E. W., *The Golden Age*, BBC Radio Collection, 1996

NOTES

PREFACE

1 Thomson, *The Great Cricketer* (1957; new edn 1968), p. xiii.
2 Thomson, 'W. G. Grace', in Arlott (ed), *Cricket: The Great Ones* (1967), p. 16.
3 Fry, *A Life Worth Living* (1939), p. 214.
4 Green, *A History of Cricket* (1988), p. 69.
5 Gordon et al, *The Memorial Biography* (1919), p. 312.
6 *Wisden*, 1916, p. 88.
7 *Guardian*, 31 January, 1998.

ONE

1 Quoted in Bantock, *The Last Smyths of Ashton Court*, Part I (1990), p. 137.
2 Ibid., p. 161.
3 *The Times*, 9 August 1853.
4 Grace, *Cricket* (1891), pp. 61–2.
5 Quoted in Jones, *Gentlemen and Players* (1989), p. 12.
6 Elizabeth Ralph, 'People Matter: George Pocock' in *St Stephen's Review* (1961–2).
7 Metcalf, 'Bristol' in *England at a Glance* (1835).
8 George Pocock et al, 'A Statement of Facts' (1820), p. 13.
9 George Pocock junior and John Pocock, 'The Methodist Pill' (1820), p. 22.
10 George Pocock et al, 'The Facts without a Veil' (1820), p. 49.
11 George Pocock, *The Aeropleustic Art* (1827), pp. 10–12.
12 Letter from the Deputy Registrar, Royal Archives, 29 October 1996.
13 *The Times*, 2 November 1831.
14 *Bristol Mercury*, 1 November 1831.
15 'An Occasional Visitor', *Observations on the Churches of Bristol* (2nd edn, 1843), p. 150.

TWO

1 Grace, *Cricket*, p. 62.
2 Estate agent's poster, Roger Mann Collection.
3 *The Times*, 26 August 1836.
4 Ibid.
5 Quoted in Jones, *Gentlemen and Players*, p. 16.
6 Ibid., p. 14
7 Grace, *Cricket*, p. 71.
8 Supplement to *The Album*, 1 July 1895, p. 2.
9 Ibid.
10 Grace, *Cricket*, p. 71.

11 Grace, *Reminiscences* (1899), pp. 1–2.
12 Ibid., pp. 7–8.
13 Ibid., p. 7.
14 Darwin, *W. G. Grace* (1934, rpt 1948), p. 23.
15 Grace, *Cricket*, pp. 64, 72.
16 Ibid., p. 73.
17 Ibid., p. 71
18 Horan, *Cradle Days* (1989), p. 148.
19 Brownlee, *W. G. Grace*, (1887), p. 21.
20 Ibid., p. 20

THREE

1 Bolland, *Cricket Notes, with . . . Practical Hints by William Clarke* (1851), pp. 154–5.
2 Quoted in West, *The Elevens of England* (1988), p. 23.
3 Daft, *Kings of Cricket* (1893), p. 76.
4 Grace, *Reminiscences*, p. 4.
5 Ibid.
6 Daft, *Kings of Cricket*, p. 204.
7 Grace, *W.G.'s Little Book* (1909), p. 94.
8 Bowen, *Cricket: A History* (1970), p. 81.
9 Grace, *Reminiscences*, p. 5.
10 Ibid., p. 6.
11 Ibid., pp. 5–6.
12 Quoted in Darwin, *W. G. Grace*, p. 14.
13 Grace, *Cricket*, p. 43.
14 Bolland, *Cricket Notes*, p. 143.
15 Ibid., p. 142.
16 Ibid., p. 150.
17 Ibid., p. 35.
18 Ibid., p. 30.
19 Ibid., p. 44.

FOUR

1 Grace, *Cricket*, p. 68.
2 Ibid., pp. 69–70.
3 Ibid., p. 78.
4 *Western Daily Press*, 29 July 1858.
5 Grace, *Reminiscences*, p. 8.
6 *Western Daily Press*, 20 July 1860.
7 Grace, *Cricket*, p. 76.
8 Grace, *Reminiscences*, p. 8.
9 Quoted in Bradfield, *The Lansdown Story* (1971), p. 30.
10 Grace, *Cricket*, pp. 75, 76.
11 Ibid., p. 78.
12 Ibid., p. 81.
13 Ashley-Cooper, *Edward Mills Grace* (1916), p. 41.
14 Ibid.
15 Powell and Canynge Caple, *The Graces* (1948), p. 110.

16 Ashley-Cooper, *Edward Mills Grace*, p. 35.
17 Quoted in ibid., p. 21.
18 Lord Harris (ed), *The History of Kent County Cricket* (1907), p. 61.
19 Ibid., p. 62.
20 Sulloway, *Born to Rebel* (1996), p. 69.
21 Brownlee, *W. G. Grace*, p.26.
22 Ibid.

FIVE

 1 Grace, *Reminiscences*, p. 9.
 2 Grace, *Cricket*, p. 78.
 3 Powell and Canynge Caple, *The Graces*, p. 40.
 4 Quoted in ibid., p. 55.
 5 Grace, *Cricket*, pp. 385–6.
 6 Grace, *Reminiscences*, p.13
 7 Ibid., pp. 13, 14.
 8 Quoted in Gregory (ed.), *In Celebration of Cricket* (1978), pp. 15–16.
 9 Ashley-Cooper, *Edward Mills Grace*, p. 40.
10 Warner, *Lord's 1787–1945* (1946), p. 52.
11 Lubbock, *Memories of Eton and Etonians* (1899), p. 271.
12 Quoted in Kynaston, *Bobby Abel* (1982), p. 19.
13 Trollope (ed), *British Sports and Pastimes* (1868), p. 5.
14 Harris, *A Few Short Runs* (1921), p. 116.
15 Fitzgerald ('Quid'), *Jerks in from Short-Leg* (1866), p. 47.
16 Harris, *A Few Short Runs*, pp. 160–1.
17 Grace, *Reminiscences*, pp. 25, 26.
18 Altham, *A History of Cricket*, vol. I (1962), p. 36.
19 Sissons, *The Players* (1988), p. 5.
20 James, *Beyond a Boundary* (1963), pp. 150–1.
21 Harris, *A Few Short Runs*, p. 161.
22 Trollope, *British Sports and Pastimes*, preface and p. 307.
23 Fitzgerald ('Quid'), *Jerks in from Short Leg*, p. 9.
24 Ibid., p. 21.
25 Ibid., pp. 136–7.
26 Ashley-Cooper, *Edward Mills Grace*, p. 83.
27 Ibid., pp. 70–71.
28 Ibid., p. 93.
29 Ibid., p. 84.
30 Ibid., p. 119.
31 Ibid., p. 65.
32 Grace, *Reminiscences*, p. 15.
33 Grace, *Cricket*, p. 87.
34 Ibid.
35 C. G. Lyttelton (8th Viscount Cobham) quoted in Darwin, *W. G. Grace*, p. 33.
36 Grace, *Cricket*, p. 88.
37 *John Lillywhite's Cricketer's Companion*, 1865, pp. 92–3.
38 Lubbock, *Memories of Eton*, p. 280.
39 Grace, *W.G.'s Little Book*, p. 10.
40 Taylor, *Annals of Lord's* (1903), p. 108.

41 Ibid, p. 101.
42 Grace, *Reminiscences*, pp. 22, 23.
43 Quoted in Warner, *Lord's*, p. 60.
44 Lubbock, *Memories of Eton*, p. 227.
45 Taylor, *Annals*, p. 92.
46 *The Times*, 22 July 1864.
47 *Memorial Biography*, pp. 212, 213.
48 Grace, *Cricket*, p. 89.
49 *John Lillywhite's Companion*, 1866, p. 116; 1867, p. 159; 1868, p. 140; 1869, p. 134;
   1870, p. 142.
50 *Scores and Biographies*, vol. IX, pp. 13, 14.
51 Grace, *Cricket*, p. 100.
52 Ibid., p. 92.

SIX

 1 Bradfield, *The Lansdown Story*, p. 40.
 2 Grace, *Cricket*, p. 108.
 3 Bailey et al, *Who's Who of Cricketers* (1984, new edn 1993), p. 87.
 4 Grace, *Cricket*, p. 106.
 5 *Scores and Biographies*, vol. IX, p. 102.
 6 Ibid.
 7 *Memorial Biography*, p. 67.
 8 Grace, *Cricket*, p. 121.
 9 *Wisden*, 1948, p. 69.
10 Hannam-Clark, *W. G. Grace and Gloucestershire* (typescript, n.d.), p. 4.
11 C. G. Lyttelton, quoted in Powell and Canynge Caple, *The Graces*, pp. 55, 56.
12 Ashley-Cooper, *Edward Mills Grace*, p. 47.
13 Ibid., p. 52.
14 *Memorial Biography*, p. 37.
15 *Sheffield and Rotherham Independent*, 6 June 1866.
16 Grace, *Cricket*, p. 117.
17 Quoted in Frith, 'My Dear Victorious Stod' (1970), p. 48.
18 *Sheffield and Rotherham Independent*, 28 May 1866.
19 Grace, *Cricket*, p. 117.
20 Grace, *Reminiscences*, p. 30.
21 Grace, *Cricket*, p. 93.
22 Grace, *Reminiscences*, pp. 10, 11.
23 Thomson, *The Great Cricketer*, pp. 111, 173.
24 Details of this match from *Scores and Biographies*, vol. XI, p. 529.
25 Grace, *History of a Hundred Centuries* (1895), p. 12.
26 Grace, *Cricket*, p. 114.
27 Powell and Canynge Caple, *The Graces*, p. 48.
28 Interview, *Strand Magazine*, 1895, quoted in Allen (ed), *Cricket with Grace* (1990), p. 37.
29 Ibid.
30 *Memorial Biography*, p. 42.
31 Ibid, p. 68.
32 *Scores and Biographies*, vol. VIII, pp. 416, 417.
33 Grace, *Cricket*, p. 90.
34 Small, *Canterbury Cricket Week* (1892), p. 71.

35 Material from Anthony, *Herefordshire Cricket* (1903), p. 88.
36 Warner, *Lord's*, p. 45.
37 *Sporting Life*, 20 November 1867, quoted in Weston, *W. G. Grace, A Statistical Record* (1973), p. 24.
38 Lubbock, *Memories of Eton*, p. 286.
39 Grace, *Cricket*, p. 123.
40 *Wisden,* 1916, p. 121.
41 Grace, *Cricket*, p. 124.
42 Ibid, p. 125.
43 *Memorial Biography*, p. 68.
44 Ibid, pp. 67, 68.
45 Green, *A History*, pp. 79–80.
46 Lewis, *Double Century* (1987), p. 117.
47 Gale, *Echoes from Old Cricket Fields* (1871), pp. 107, 103.
48 Grace, *Reminiscences*, pp. 26–7.
49 Grace, *History of a Hundred Centuries*, p. 17.
50 Grace, *Reminiscences*, p. 34.
51 Quoted in Brownlee, *W. G. Grace*, p. 38.
52 Grace, *Reminiscences*, p. 37.
53 C. B. Fry, 'Now and Then', *Cricketer Annual*, 1946–7, p. 11.
54 James, *Beyond a Boundary*, pp. 44–5.
55 Grace, *Reminiscences*, pp. 283, 286, 292.
56 George Arthur Scrapbook, p. 38.
57 Arlott, *Rothmans History of Cricket* (1965), p. 13.
58 Quoted in Altham, *History of Cricket*, p. 123.
59 Arlott, *Rothmans History of Cricket*, p. 13.
60 Sewell, *Overthrows* (1946), p. 11.
61 Neville Cardus, 'Cardus Says . . .', *The Cricketer*, May 1967, p. 5.
62 Grace, *Reminiscences*, p. 293.
63 Ibid., p. 287.
64 *Wisden,* 1916, p. 87.
65 Ibid., p. 70.
66 Quoted in Powell and Canynge Caple, *The Graces*, pp. 87–8.
67 *Memorial Biography*, p. 208.
68 *Scores and Biographies*, vol. VIII, p. 416.
69 Quoted in *Memorial Biography*, p. 49.

SEVEN

1 *Scores and Biographies*, vol. XI, p. 273.
2 *The Times*, 21 May 1870.
3 Ibid., 17 May 1870.
4 Grace, *Cricket*, p. 129.
5 *Scores and Biographies*, vol. X, p. 368.
6 *The Times*, 23 May 1870.
7 Ibid., 28 May 1870.
8 *Scores and Biographies*, vol. XI, p. 274.
9 Grace, *Reminiscences*, pp. 339, 340.
10 Warner, *Lord's*, p. 65.
11 *Memorial Biography*, p. 69.

12 Ibid., p. 58.
13 Grace, *Cricket*, pp. 132, 133.
14 *The Times*, 14 June 1870.
15 Grace, *Reminiscences*, p. 113.
16 Grace, *Cricket*, p. 131.
17 Grace, *Reminiscences*, p. 109.
18 Grace, *Cricket*, p. 131.
19 West, *Elevens of England*, p. 150.
20 Grace, *Reminiscences*, p. 109.
21 *The Times*, 22 June 1870.
22 Ibid., 23 June 1870.
23 Grace, *Reminiscences*, p. 121.
24 *Scores and Biographies*, vol. XI, p. 477.
25 Grace, *Reminiscences*, p. 131.
26 Ibid., p. 114.
27 *Scores and Biographies*, vol. XI, p. 534.
28 *Memorial Biography*, p. 59.
29 Grace, *Cricket*, p. 135.
30 Ibid., pp .135–6.
31 Ibid., p. 136.
32 Ibid.
33 Lewis, *Double Century*, p. 117.
34 Quoted in Altham, *History of Cricket*, p. 126.
35 *Scores and Biographies*, vol. XII, p. 214.
36 Grace, *History of a Hundred Centuries*, p. 39.
37 Browne, *A Short History of Nottinghamshire Cricket* (1887), p. 19.
38 Taylor, *Annals*, p. 149.
39 Quoted in Honan, *Matthew Arnold* (1981), p .62.

EIGHT

1 Bone, *Fifty Years of Scottish Cricket* (1898), p. 90.
2 Clydesdale CC Minutes Book 1891–1900, Mitchell Library Glasgow, ref. TD 940/1/1.
3 Brownlee, *W. G. Grace*, p. 47.
4 Bone, *Fifty Years of Scottish Cricket*, p. 90.
5 Brownlee, *W. G. Grace*, p. 48.
6 *Scores and Biographies*, vol XII, p. 363.
7 Lubbock, *Memories of Eton*, pp. 304, 305.
8 Brownlee, *W. G. Grace*, p. 47.
9 Grace, *Reminiscences*, p. 120.
10 *The Times*, 5 August 1872.
11 Quoted in Booker, *The Great Western Railway* (1977), p. 80.
12 *The Times*, 5 August 1872.

NINE

1 Estate Duty Valuation, ref. I.R. 59/459 30979.
2 Grace, *Reminiscences*, p. 50.
3 *Scores and Biographies*, vol. XII p. 562.
4 Fitzgerald, *Wickets in the West* (1873), p. 11.

5 Quoted in ibid., p. 64.
6 Harris, *A Few Short Runs*, p. 35.
7 Fitzgerald, *Wickets in the West*, pp. 14–15.
8 Harris, *A Few Short Runs*, p. 51.
9 Grace, *Reminiscences*, pp. 37–8.
10 *The Times*, 27 August 1872.
11 Fitzgerald, *Wickets in the West*, p. 18.
12 Ibid., pp. 17–18.
13 Ibid., p. 19.
14 Grace, *Reminiscences*, p. 38.
15 Fitzgerald, *Wickets in the West*, p. 22.
16 Grace, *Reminiscences*, p. 38.
17 Fitzgerald, *Wickets in the West*, pp. 26–7.
18 Ibid., p. 35.
19 Grace, *Reminiscences*, pp. 39–40.
20 Fitzgerald, *Wickets in the West*, p. 43.
21 Ibid., p. 47.
22 Grace, *Reminiscences*, p. 42.
23 Fitzgerald, *Wickets in the West*, p. 48.
24 Ibid., pp. 49–50.
25 Ibid., p. 52.
26 Quoted in Grace, *Reminiscences*, p. 43.
27 Lubbock, *Memories of Eton*, pp. 310–11.
28 Grace, *Reminiscences*, p. 45.
29 Fitzgerald, *Wickets in the West*, p. 72.
30 Brownlee, *W. G. Grace*, p. 55.
31 Grace, *Reminiscences*, p. 46.
32 Fitzgerald, *Wickets in the West*, p. 83.
33 Grace, *Reminiscences*, p. 46.
34 Fitzgerald, *Wickets in the West*, p. 86.
35 Ibid., p. 94.
36 Ibid., p. 96.
37 Ibid., p. 99.
38 Ibid., p. 97.
39 Darwin, *W. G. Grace*, p. 53.
40 Fitzgerald, *Wickets in the West*, p. 98.
41 Ibid., p. 100.
42 Quoted in ibid., p. 108.
43 Ibid., p. 122.
44 Ibid., p. 118.
45 Ibid., p. 132.
46 Grace, *Reminiscences*, p. 49.
47 Quoted Wynne-Thomas, *England on Tour* (1982), p. 14.
48 Fitzgerald, *Wickets in the West*, pp. 146–7.
49 Ibid., p. 145.
50 Ibid., p. 147.
51 Ibid., p. 158.
52 Ibid., p. 156.
53 Ibid., p. 160.
54 Ibid., p. 167.

55 Ibid., pp. 168–9.
56 Grace, *Reminiscences*, pp. 51–2.
57 Fitzgerald, *Wickets in the West*, pp. 192–3.
58 Grace, *Reminiscences*, p. 52.
59 Fitzgerald, *Wickets in the West*, p. 228.
60 Ibid., p. 210.
61 Grace, *Reminiscences*, p. 54.
62 Quoted in Fitzgerald, *Wickets in the West*, p. 218.
63 Grace, *Reminiscences*, p. 55.
64 Fitzgerald, *Wickets in the West*, pp. 231–2.
65 Ibid., p. 239.
66 Grace, *Reminiscences*, p. 54.
67 Fitzgerald, *Wickets in the West*, p. 255.
68 Grace, *Reminiscences*, pp. 57–8.
69 Ibid., p. 59.
70 Harris, *A Few Short Runs*, p. 181.
71 Grace, *Reminiscences*, p. 61.
72 Fitzgerald, *Wickets in the West*, pp. 288–9.
73 Grace, *Reminiscences*, pp. 62–3.
74 Fitzgerald, *Wickets in the West*, p. 301.
75 Ibid., p. 319.
76 Ibid., p. 322.
77 Ibid., pp. 324–5.
78 Ibid., p. 331.
79 Information from Peggy Gruber.

TEN

1 *Lillywhite's Companion*, 1874, p. 15.
2 Quoted in *The Cricketer*, March 1970, p. 28
3 Gloucestershire CC Committee Minutes Book, 1873, County Ground, Bristol.
4 *Scores and Biographies*, vol. XII, p. 634.
5 Lewis, *Double Century*, p. 134.
6 *Lillywhite's Companion*, 1874, p. 9.
7 *Scores and Biographies*, vol. XII, p. 660.
8 *The Times*, 7 June 1873.
9 *Scores and Biographies*, vol. XII pp. 767–8.
10 Ibid., p. 789.
11 Ibid., p. 726.
12 West, *Elevens of England*, p. 136.
13 *The Times*, 1 July 1873.
14 Grace, *History of a Hundred Centuries*, p. 55.
15 *Memorial Biography*, p. 97.
16 Grace, *Reminiscences*, p. 133.
17 *The Times*, 5 August 1873.
18 *Sporting Life*, 6 August 1873.
19 Ibid., 9 August 1873.
20 Grace, *History of a Hundred Centuries*, p. 56.
21 Grace, *Reminiscences*, p. 131.
22 *Scores and Biographies*, vol. XII, p. 953.

23 *Aberdeen Journal*, 17 September 1873.
24 *Northampton Herald*, 20 September 1873.
25 Details from article in *Northampton Independent*, quoted in Engel and Radd, *The History of Northamptonshire Cricket Club* (1993), p. 29.
26 Weston, *W. G. Grace, A Statistical Record*, pp. 40, 41; *Lillywhite's Companion,* 1874, pp. 82, 83.
27 *Lillywhite's Companion,* 1874, p. 14.

ELEVEN

1 Taylor, *Annals*, p. 151.
2 Harte, *SACA*, pp. 31, 33.
3 Grace, *Reminiscences*, p. 64.
4 Ibid. p. 65.
5 Roger Mann Collection.
6 Quoted in Allen (ed.), *Cricket with Grace*, p. 16.
7 *The Times*, 11 October, 1873.
8 Grace, *Reminiscences*, p. 65.
9 *Lillywhite's Companion,* 1875, p. 18.
10 Brownlee, *W. G. Grace*, p. 65.
11 Grace, *Reminiscences*, p. 66.
12 Diary extracts from Brownlee, *W. G. Grace*, p. 65.
13 Grace, *Reminiscences*, p. 67.
14 Brownlee, *W. G. Grace*, pp. 66–7.
15 Ibid., p. 66.
16 Grace, *Reminiscences*, p. 67.

TWELVE

1 Grace, *Reminiscences*, p. 68.
2 *Age*, 15 December 1873.
3 *Sydney Mail*, 27 December 1873.
4 *Australasian*, 20 December 1873.
5 George Arthur Scrapbook, p. 4.
6 Report dated 10 September, printed in *The Times*, 29 October 1873.
7 Grace, *Reminiscences*, p. 71.
8 *Memorial Biography*, p. 104.
9 Cashman, *The 'Demon' Spofforth* (1990), p. 52.
10 George Arthur Scrapbook, p. 1
11 *Sydney Mail*, 3 January 1874.
12 Ibid.
13 Report dated 2 January, printed in *The Times*, 19 February 1874.
14 Quoted in the *Guardian*, 20 December 1997.
15 Southerton, Diary, 26 December 1873.
16 *Lillywhite's Companion,* 1875, p. 20.
17 *Sydney Mail*, 3 January 1874.
18 Brownlee, *W. G. Grace*, p. 68.
19 George Arthur Scrapbook, p. 11.
20 Ibid., p. 10.
21 *Sydney Morning Herald*, 5 January 1874.

22 Report dated 2 January, printed in *The Times*, 19 February 1874.
23 George Arthur Scrapbook, p. 64.
24 Ibid., pp. 15, 16.
25 Ibid., p. 42
26 Ibid., p. 7.
27 *Sydney Mail*, 3 January 1874.
28 Grace, *Reminiscences*, p. 74.
29 *Ballarat Courier*, 5 January 1874.
30 Grace, *Reminiscences*, p. 74
31 *Argus*, 5 January 1874.
32 *Ballarat Courier*, 5 January 1874.
33 Grace, *Reminiscences*, p. 75.
34 Ibid.
35 Ibid., pp. 76, 77.
36 *Lillywhite's Companion*, 1875, p. 21.
37 Grace, *Reminiscences*, p. 77.
38 George Arthur Scrapbook, p. 24.
39 Brownlee, *W. G. Grace*, p. 71.
40 Grace, *Reminiscences*, p. 79.
41 George Arthur Scrapbook, p. 25.
42 Grace, *Reminiscences*, p. 80.
43 Ibid., p. 81.
44 Ibid., p. 82.
45 *Lillywhite's Companion*, 1875, p. 22.
46 George Arthur Scrapbook, p. 25.
47 Ibid., p. 66.
48 Ibid., p. 42.
49 Grace, *Reminiscences*, p. 83.
50 Interview, *Pall Mall Budget*, 1886, in Mullins and Derriman (eds), *Bat & Pad*, p. 19.
51 Grace, *Reminiscences*, pp. 84, 85.
52 George Arthur Scrapbook, p. 29.
53 *The Empire*, undated cutting, George Arthur Scrapbook, p. 38.
54 Grace, *Reminiscences*, p. 87.
55 *Sydney Mail*, 14 February 1874.
56 Ibid.
57 Grace, *Reminiscences*, p. 90.
58 *Sydney Mail*, 14 February, 1874.
59 Ibid.
60 Ibid., 21 February 1874.
61 *The Australasian*, 14 February, 1874.
62 Grace, *Reminiscences*, p. 92.
63 *Bendigo Advertiser*, 14 February 1874.
64 *Castlemaine Representative*, 14 February 1874.
65 *James Lillywhite's Cricketers' Annual*, 1875, p. 27.
66 *Argus*, 17 February 1874
67 *Lillywhite's Companion*, 1875, p. 23.
68 Grace, *Reminiscences*, p. 87.
69 George Arthur Scrapbook, p. 38.
70 Ibid., p. 41.
71 Ibid.

72 Grace, *Reminiscences*, p. 95.
73 George Arthur Scrapbook, p. 45.
74 Grace, *Reminiscences*, p. 97.
75 *Lillywhite's Companion*, 1875, p. 24.
76 *Argus*, quoted in the *Sydney Mail* of 21 March 1874.
77 *Age*, 16 March 1874.
78 Quoted in Smith and Williams, *W.G. Down Under* (1994), pp. 55, 56.
79 *Argus*, 14 March 1874.
80 Ibid., 16 March 1874.

THIRTEEN

 1 *Wallaroo Times*, 7 March 1874.
 2 Whimpress, *W. G. Grace at Kadina* (1994), p. 3.
 3 *South Australian Register*, 27 January 1874.
 4 *Wallaroo Times*, 18 February 1874.
 5 Ibid., 11 February 1874.
 6 Ibid., 21 March 1874.
 7 Southerton's Diary, quoted in Smith and Williams, *W.G. Down Under*, pp. 59, 60.
 8 Whimpress, *W. G. Grace at Kadina*, pp. 7–8.
 9 *Wallaroo Times*, 25 March 1874.
10 Ibid., 21 March 1874.
11 Grace, *Reminiscences*, p. 99.
12 Grace's diary, quoted in Brownlee, *W. G. Grace*, p. 75.
13 George Arthur Scrapbook, p. 62.
14 Grace, *Reminiscences*, p. 99.
15 *Wallaroo Times*, 25 March 1874.
16 Ibid., 4 April 1874.
17 Ibid., 28 March 1874.
18 *South Australian Register*, 26 March 1874.
19 Harte, *SACA*, p. 43.
20 Grace, *Reminiscences*, p. 102.
21 *Wallaroo Times*, 28 March 1874.
22 Ibid., 1 April 1874.
23 *Adelaide Observer*, 28 March 1874.
24 George Arthur Scrapbook, p. 66.
25 Harte, *SACA*, p. 43.
26 Grace, *Reminiscences*, pp. 102, 103.
27 Giffen, *With Bat and Ball* (1898), pp. 3, 5.
28 Ibid., p. 3.
29 *Adelaide Observer*, 4 April 1874.
30 Grace, *Reminiscences*, p. 103.
31 *Lillywhite's Companion*, 1875, p. 25.
32 Ibid.
33 Brownlee, *W. G. Grace*, p. 76.
34 Ibid., p. 77.
35 *Sydney Mail*, 21 March 1874.
36 *Lillywhite's Companion*, 1875, p. 18.
37 Mullins and Derriman (eds), *Bat & Pad*, pp. 23, 24.
38 Grace, *Reminiscences*, pp. 103, 105.

FOURTEEN

1 Lodge, *W. G. Grace: His Record*, p. 21.
2 Warner, *Gentlemen v. Players* (1950), p. 148.
3 Quoted in ibid.
4 Darwin, *W. G. Grace*, p. 58.
5 Cardus, 'William Gilbert Grace', in *The Great Victorians*, p. 21.
6 Brownlee, *W. G. Grace*, p. 97.
7 *Memorial Biography*, p. 68.
8 *Wisden*, 1916, p. 71.
9 *Memorial Biography*, p. 259.
10 Quoted in Midwinter, *History of County Cricket* (1992), p. 32.
11 Grace, *Cricket*, p. 146.
12 Power and Waring, *A Short History of St Bartholomew's Hospital* (1923), p. 103.
13 *Memorial Biography*, p. 163.
14 Grace, *Cricket*, p. 146.
15 Ibid., p. 141.
16 Lubbock, *Memories of Eton*, p. 317.
17 *Memorial Biography*, p. 141.
18 Grace, *Cricket*, p. 147.
19 Rosenwater, *W. G. Grace: A Leviathan Was He*, pp. 1, 2.
20 Grace, *Cricket*, p. 147.
21 Hughes, *Tom Brown's Schooldays* (1857), pp. 3–4.
22 Quoted in Brownlee, *W. G. Grace*, pp. 127,128.
23 Nora Peache, Diary, 9 April 1876
24 Ibid., 23 April 1876.

FIFTEEN

1 Grace, *Reminiscences*, p.147.
2 Lincoln, *Sport in Grimsby* (1912), p. 116.
3 Ibid.
4 Ibid., p. 117.
5 *Grimsby Herald and Lincolnshire Advertiser*, 15 July 1876.
6 *Hull News*, 5 August 1876.
7 Ibid.
8 Grace, *History of a Hundred Centuries*, p. 76.
9 Ibid.
10 *Hull News*, 5 August 1876
11 *Memorial Biography*, p. 118.
12 Grace, *Reminiscences*, p. 148.
13 Ibid.
14 Footnote in Grace, *History of a Hundred Centuries*, p. 77.
15 Gregory (ed.), *In Celebration of Cricket*, p. 23.
16 *The Times*, 14 August 1876.
17 Grace, *History of a Hundred Centuries*, p. 79.
18 Quoted in Thomson, *The Great Cricketer*, p. 49.
19 Quoted in Warne, *Dr W. G. Grace: The King of Cricket* (1899), pp. 24, 25.
20 Quoted in ibid., pp. 30, 32.
21 Grace, *Reminiscences*, p. 152.

SIXTEEN

1 Cowell, 'Introductory Address' (1873), p. 14.
2 Humble and Hansell, *Westminster Hospital* (1966), p. 86.
3 Quoted in Spencer, *Westminster Hospital: An Outline of its History* (1924), p. 112.
4 *Westminster Hospital Reports*, XVIII (1913), p. 2.
5 David Frith Collection.
6 Grace, *Reminiscences*, p. 156.
7 Quoted in Warner, *Gentlemen v. Players*, p. 158.
8 Grace, *Reminiscences*, p. 154.
9 Grace, *History of a Hundred Centuries*, p. 83.
10 Grace, *W.G.'s Little Book*, p. 86.
11 Quotations from *Memorial Biography*, pp. 346, 347.
12 Ibid., p. 126.
13 Darwin, *W. G. Grace*, p. 61.
14 Grace, *Cricket*, p. 156.
15 Grace, *Reminiscences*, p. 159.
16 *Memorial Biography*, p. 129.
17 Horan, *Cradle Days*, p. 11.
18 Ibid., p. 12.
19 Quoted in Grahame Parker, 'The Midwinter File', *Wisden*, 1971, p. 147.
20 Horan, *Cradle Days*, p.12.
21 Grace, *Reminiscences*, p. 160.
22 Quoted in *Wisden*, 1971, p. 148.
23 *Manchester Guardian*, 26 July 1878.
24 Ibid., 27 July 1878.
25 Ibid.
26 Ibid., 28 July 1878.
27 Ibid.
28 Ibid., 29 July 1878.
29 *Lillywhite's Companion*, 1879, p. 10.
30 Quoted in Warner, *Lord's*, p. 76.
31 *Lillywhite's Companion*, 1879, pp. 7–8.

SEVENTEEN

1 Grace, *Reminiscences*, pp. 164–5.
2 Quoted in *The Times*, 14 January 1879.
3 Ibid.
4 *Lillywhite's Companion*, 1880, pp.7–8.
5 Ibid., p. 5.
6 Grace, *History of a Hundred Centuries*, p. 85.
7 Information given in letter from the Library Secretary, Royal College of Surgeons of England, 28 August 1997.
8 *The Times*, 23 July 1879.
9 *Memorial Biography*, p. 136.
10 Ibid.
11 Quoted in Thomson, *The Great Cricketer*, pp. 57–8.
12 *The Times*, 23 July 1879.
13 Grace, *History of a Hundred Centuries*, p. 87.
14 *Lillywhite's Companion*, 1880, p. 126.

EIGHTEEN

1 Quoted in James, *The 2nd Australian XI's Tour, 1880–81* (1994), p. iv.
2 Grace, *Reminiscences*, p. 170.
3 *Lillywhite's Companion*, 1881, p. 112.
4 Gordon, *Background of Cricket* (1939), p. 60.
5 Ibid., p. 29.
6 *Memorial Biography*, p. 154.
7 From an article in the *Sydney Mail*, quoted by James, *The 2nd Australian XI's Tour*, p. 111.
8 Gordon, *Background*, p. 28.
9 James, *The 2nd Australian XI's Tour*, p. 126.
10 Grace, *History of a Hundred Centuries*, p. 89.
11 James, *The 2nd Australian XI's Tour*, p. 127.
12 Grace, *History of a Hundred Centuries*, p. 89.

NINETEEN

1 Details from King (ed.), *Scottish Cricketers' Annual and Guide*, no. X, 1880–1, p. 11.
2 *Lillywhite's Companion*, 1881, p. 15.
3 *The Times*, 23 September 1880.
4 Grace, *Reminiscences*, p. 173.
5 Ibid., p. 172.
6 I am indebted to Ken and Anne Clarke for details of Harriet Fowler's life.
7 Details from the Gloucestershire CCC Committee Minutes, 1881.
8 Grace, *Reminiscences*, p. 174.
9 Quoted in Midwinter, *History of County Cricket*, p. 34.
10 Quoted in Warner, *Gentlemen v. Players*, p. 172.
11 Grace, *History of a Hundred Centuries*, p. 91.
12 *Memorial Biography*, p. 152.

TWENTY

1 Gloucestershire CCC Committee Minutes, 10 November 1881.
2 Horan, *Cradle Days*, pp. 21, 22.
3 Giffen, *With Bat and Ball*, p. 57.
4 Ibid., pp. 60, 61.
5 Horan, *Cradle Days*, p. 40.
6 West, *Elevens of England*, p. 138.
7 Grace, *Reminiscences*, p. 175.
8 Horan, *Cradle Days*, p. 45.
9 Ibid., p. 47.
10 Ibid., p. 49.
11 Ibid., p. 51.
12 Ibid., pp 52–3.
13 Ibid., p. 52
14 Ibid., p. 53.
15 R. J. A. Massie, letter, 30 October 1956, Lord's Collection.
16 Horan, *Cradle Days*, p. 53.
17 Ibid., p. 54.
18 R. J. A. Massie, letter, 30 October 1956, Lord's Collection.
19 *Bulletin*, 28 October 1882, quoted in Cashman, *Spofforth*, p. 124.

20 R. J. A. Massie, letter, 8 September 1956, Lord's Collection.
21 Newspaper cutting, 18 January,1933, Massie papers, in E. S. Marks Sporting Collection, Mitchell Library, State Library of New South Wales, Sydney.
22 Horan, *Cradle Days*, p. 45.
23 John Masefield, 'Eight-five to Win', quoted in Mullins and Derriman (eds), *Bat & Pad*, p. 108.
24 West, *Twelve Days of Grace*, p. 196.
25 Newspaper cutting, *Evening News* (Sydney?), 13 August 1930, Massie papers, E. S. Marks Sporting Collection, Mitchell Library, NSW.
26 Giffen, *With Bat and Ball*, p. 107.
27 Horan, *Cradle Days*, pp. 55–6.
28 Ibid., p. 56.
29 Ibid., p. 57.
30 *Lillywhite's Companion*, 1883, p. 8.
31 Quoted in Cashman, *Spofforth*, p. 129.
32 Quoted in West, *Twelve Days of Grace* (1989), p. 196.
33 *Memorial Biography*, p. 132.

TWENTY-ONE

1 Grace, *Reminiscences*, p. 179.
2 Gloucestershire CCC Committee Minutes Book, 1883.
3 *Memorial Biography*, pp. 148, 149.
4 Quoted in West, *Twelve Days of Grace*, pp. 198–9.
5 Grace, *Cricket*, p. 317.
6 Quoted in Allen (ed.), *Cricket with Grace*, p. 49.
7 Gloucestershire CCC Committee Minutes, 1884.
8 Giffen, *With Bat and Ball*, p. 70.
9 Ibid., p. 72.
10 Horan, *Cradle Days*, p. 109.
11 *Lillywhite's Companion*, 1885, p.35.
12 H. H. Spielmann MS, Lord's Collection.
13 *Lillywhite's Companion*, 1885, p. 41.
14 *Manchester Guardian*, 14 July 1884.
15 Quoted in Warner, *Lord's*, p. 82.
16 *Lillywhite's Companion*, 1885, p. 47.
17 Warner, *Lord's*, p. 82.
18 *Manchester Guardian*, 26 July 1885.
19 Giffen, *With Bat and Ball*, p. 72.
20 Quoted in ibid., p 76.
21 Grace, *Reminiscences*, p. 271.
22 Ibid., p. 375.
23 Ibid., p. 184.
24 Spielmann MS, Lord's
25 *Memorial Biography*, p. 142.

TWENTY-TWO

1 Grace, *Reminiscences*, p. 187.
2 Grace, *History of a Hundred Centuries*, p. 98.

3 *Memorial Biography*, p. 179.
4 Ibid., p 177.
5 Grace, *History of a Hundred Centuries*, p. 101.
6 Gloucestershire CCC Committee Minutes, 1885.
7 Ibid., 1886
8 Details of the Gilbert case from Robert Brooke, 'The Tragedy of W. R. Gilbert' in *Cricket Statistician*, March 1982, pp. 10–13.
9 Horan, *Cradle Days*, p. 106.
10 Wakley, *Classic Centuries*, p. 32.
11 Grace, *History of a Hundred Centuries*, p. 105.
12 Quoted in Wye, *Dr W. G. Grace* (1901), p. 66.
13 Giffen, *With Bat and Ball*, p. 81.
14 All quotations for the Oxford University match taken from Lord George Scott's account in the *National Review*, vol. 109, August 1937, pp. 229–31.
15 Grace, *Reminiscences*, p. 192.
16 *Memorial Biography*, p. 185.
17 Quoted in Warne, *Dr. W. G. Grace*, p. 48.
18 Grace, *Reminiscences*, p. 191.

TWENTY-THREE

1 Agustus Hare, quoted in Hudson, *The Jubilee Years* (1996), p. 20.
2 Taylor, *Annals*, p. 176.
3 Entry for 23 June 1887, Queen Victoria's diary, Nevill, *Life at the Court of Queen Victoria* (1984), p. 132.
4 Grace, *History of a Hundred Centuries*, p. 108.
5 *Manchester Guardian*, 22 July 1887.
6 Ibid., 23 July 1887.
7 Thomson, *The Great Cricketer*, p. 147.
8 *Memorial Biography*, p. 226.
9 *Manchester Guardian*, 23 July, 1887.
10 *Manchester Courier*, 23 July 1887.
11 Gloucestershire CCC Committee Minutes, 1887.
12 Grace, *Reminiscences*, p. 345.
13 Peter Hartland, 'The Misers' in *Cricket Lore*, vol. 3, issue 1, May 1997, p. 4.
14 Smith, *ABC Guide to Australian Test Cricketers* (1993), p. 265.
15 *Memorial Biography*, p. 193.
16 Ibid.
17 Frindall, *Wisden Book of Test Cricket*, p. 40.
18 Grace, *History of a Hundred Centuries*, p. 115.
19 Ibid., p. 116.
20 *Memorial Biography*, p. 194.
21 Gloucestershire CCC Committee Minutes, 1888.
22 Green (ed.), *Wisden Papers*, p. 135.

TWENTY-FOUR

1 Facsimile reproduced in Bradfield, *The Lansdown Story*.
2 Powell and Canynge Caple, *The Graces*, p. 118.
3 Quoted in *The Cricketer Spring Annual* (1967), p. 40.

4 Brownlee, *W. G. Grace*, p. 135.

5 Quoted in Warne, *Dr W. G. Grace*, p. 50.

6 Parker, *Gloucestershire Road* (1983), pp. 52–3.

7 Gloucestershire CCC Collection, County Ground, Bristol.

8 Grace, *Reminiscences*, p. 205.

9 Gordon, *Background of Cricket*, p. 319.

10 Grace, *History of a Hundred Centuries*, p. 117.

11 *Memorial Biography*, p.202.

12 Ibid.

13 Grace, *History of a Hundred Centuries*, p. 119.

14 *Memorial Biography*, p. 202.

15 Ibid., p. 201.

16 Grace, *Reminiscences*, pp. 183, 184.

17 Quoted in Warne, *Dr W. G. Grace*, p. 28.

18 *Memorial Biography*, p. 211.

19 Ibid., p. 210.

20 Gloucestershire CCC Committee Minutes, 1890.

21 Green (ed), *The Wisden Papers*, p. 38.

22 Gloucestershire CCC Committee Minutes, 1891.

23 Grace, *Reminiscences*, p. 216.

24 All correspondence concerning Cricket from Gloucestershire CCC Collection, Bristol.

25 Grace, *Cricket*, pp.253–4.

26 *Memorial Biography*, p. 214.

TWENTY-FIVE

1 Pollard, *The Formative Years* (1987), p. 305.

2 Sissons, *The Players*, p. 156.

3 Quoted in Pollard, *The Formative Years*, p. 306.

4 Quoted in Kynaston, *W.G.'s Birthday Party*, pp. 31,32.

5 Scrapbook cutting, Davis Sporting Collection, Mitchell Library, NSW.

6 Frith, *'My Dear Victorious Stod'*, p. 50.

7 Press cutting, Neville Weston scrapbook, Lorimer collection.

8 *Bulletin*, 28 November 1891.

9 Giffen, *With Bat and Ball*, p. 4.

10 Horan, *Cradle Days*, p. 82.

11 Quoted in Smith and Williams, *W.G. Down Under*, p. 92.

12 Horan, *Cradle Days*, p. 121.

13 Smith and Williams, *W.G. Down Under*, p. 97.

14 *Bulletin*, 5 December 1891.

15 Ibid., 28 November 1891.

16 Ibid., 6 February 1892.

17 Quoted in Smith and Williams, *W.G. Down Under*, p. 103.

18 *Ballarat Courier*, 31 December 1891.

19 Giffen, *With Bat and Ball*, pp. 121, 122.

20 *Wisden*, 1893, p. 337.

21 Giffen, *With Bat and Ball*, p.123.

22 Ibid.

23 'Australian Notes by W. G. Grace' in *The Cricket Field*, 28 May 1892.

24 *Australasian*, 9 January 1892.

25 *Bulletin*, 16 January, 1892.
26 Quoted in Smith and Williams, *W.G. Down Under*, p. 136.
27 Davis Sporting Collection, Mitchell Library, NSW.
28 *Wisden*, 1893, p. 342.
29 Giffen, *With Bat and Ball*, p.127.
30 Quoted in Gibson, *Jackson's Year* (1965), p. 52.
31 Quoted in Kynaston, *Bobby Abel*, p. 63.
32 Giffen, *With Bat and Ball*, p. 127.
33 *Wisden*, 1893, p. 242.
34 From an article in the *Argus*, quoted in Pollard, *Formative Years*, p. 312.
35 Quoted in ibid., p. 309.
36 *Australasian*, 2 April, 1892.
37 Smith and Williams, *W.G. Down Under*, p. 157.
38 *The Cricket Field*, 28 May 1892.
39 Quoted in Derriman, *The Grand Old Ground* (1981), p. 62.
40 *The Cricket Field*, 28 May 1892.
41 Quoted in Smith and Williams, *W.G. Down Under*, pp. 176–7.
42 Quoted in ibid., p. 179.
43 *Australasian*, 2 April 1892.

TWENTY-SIX

1 *Memorial Biography*, p. 257.
2 Grace, *Reminiscences*, p. 220.
3 *The Cricket Field*, 28 May 1892.
4 Grace, *Reminiscences*, p. 219.
5 *Wisden*, 1893, p. 330.
6 *The Cricket Field*, 7 May 1892.
7 *Memorial Biography*, p. 224.
8 Grace, *Reminiscences*, p. 223.
9 *Memorial Biography*, p.225.
10 Ibid.
11 Cotter, *The Ashes Captains* (1989), p. 52.
12 Press cutting, Davis Sporting Collection, Mitchell Library, NSW.
13 Smith, *ABC Guide to Australian Test Cricketers*, p. 42.
14 Press cutting, Davis Sporting Collection, Mitchell Library, NSW.
15 *Lillywhite's Annual*, 1895, p. 75.
16 Gloucestershire CCC Committee Minutes, 26 January 1893.
17 Quoted in *Memorial Biography*, p. 258.
18 Grace, *History of a Hundred Centuries*, p. 125.
19 Ibid.
20 *Memorial Biography*, p. 195.
21 Jessop, *A Cricketer's Log* (1922), p. 20.
22 Woods, *My Reminiscences* (1925), pp. 154, 155.
23 Grace, *History of a Hundred Centuries*, p. 126.

TWENTY-SEVEN

1 Grace, *Reminiscences*, p. 239.
2 Quoted in Midwinter, *W. G. Grace*, p.93.

3 *Lillywhite's Annual*, 1896, p. 61.
4 Quoted in Robertson-Glasgow, *46 Not Out* (1954), p. 130.
5 *Memorial Biography*, p. 250.
6 Quoted in Morrah, *The Golden Age of Cricket* (1967), p. 43.
7 Grace, *History of a Hundred Centuries*, p. 130.
8 Arlott, *Rothmans History of Cricket*, p. 34.
9 Grace, *History of a Hundred Centuries*, p. 131.
10 *The Sportsman*, 27 May 1895.
11 *Wisden*, 1949, p. 101.
12 Ellman, *Oscar Wilde* (1987, rpt 1988), pp. 448–9.
13 *The Times*, 31 May 1895.
14 Ibid.
15 Grace, *Reminiscences*, p. 239.
16 *The Hero of Cricket* (1895), p. 14.
17 Facsimile in Grace, *Reminiscences*, opp. p. 221.
18 Green (ed.), *The Wisden Papers*, p. 69.
19 Ibid., p 66.
20 *Lillywhite's Annual*, 1896, p. 63.
21 Ibid.
22 *Memorial Biography*, p. 72.
23 Warner, *Gentlemen v. Players*, p. 224.
24 *The Times*, 21 June 1895.
25 Jessop, *A Cricketer's Log*, p. 21.
26 Ibid., p. 28.
27 Albert Gregory Collection, *Cricketers*, Mitchell Library, NSW.
28 *Lillywhite's Annual*, 1896, 261.
29 *Memorial Biography*, p. 257.
30 Grace, *Reminiscences*, p. 240.
31 Warne, *Dr W. G. Grace*, p. 37.
32 Supplement to *The Album*, 1 July–14 October 1895, p. 14.
33 Quoted in Warne, *Dr W. G. Grace*, p. 37.
34 Quoted in Robertson-Glasgow, *46 Not Out*, pp. 130–1.
35 Quoted in *Memorial Biography*, p. 255.

TWENTY-EIGHT

1 Brownlee, *W. G. Grace*, p.10.
2 *Cricket*, 27 February 1896.
3 Waring, 'W.G.', p.11.
4 Fry, *A Life Worth Living*, pp. 205–6.
5 Quoted in B. G. Whitfield, 'Jonah and the Beard', in *The Cricketer Winter Annual*, 1956–7.
6 *Memorial Biography*, pp. 263, 264.
7 Giffen, Lyttelton et al., *Giants of the Game* (1899, rpt 1974), p. 184.
8 Quoted in Green, *History of Cricket*, p. 164.
9 *The Times*, 20 July 1896.
10 Wild, 'Ranji' (1934), p. 37.
11 Wilde, *Ranji: A Genius Rich and Strange* (1990), pp. 64, 65.
12 *Memorial Biography*, pp. 281–2.
13 Quoted in Sissons, *George Lohmann* (1991), p. 54.
14 Ibid.

15 Quoted in Kynaston, *Bobby Abel*, p. 142.
16 Ibid.
17 *The Weekly Sun*, 9 August 1896.
18 Grace, *Reminiscences*, p. 248.
19 Green (ed.), *The Wisden Papers*, p. 77.
20 Quoted in Kynaston, *Bobby Abel*, p. 144.
21 Quoted in Arrowsmith and Hill, *The History of I Zingari*, p. 108.
22 Ibid.
23 *Lillywhite's Annual*, 1897, p. 57.
24 *Memorial Biography*, p. 263.
25 *Lillywhite's Annual*, 1897, p. 96.
26 *Memorial Biography*, p. 261.
27 Grace, *Reminiscences*, p. 246.

TWENTY-NINE

1 Quoted in *Memorial Biography*, p. 264.
2 Fry, *The Book of Cricket: A New Gallery of Famous Players* (1899), p. 194.
3 Grace, *Reminiscences*, p. 251.
4 Ibid., p. 250.
5 Details from Brodribb, *The Croucher* (1974), pp. 60, 61.
6 *Memorial Biography*, p. 266.
7 Ibid., p. 267.
8 Warner, *Gentlemen v. Players*, p. 236.
9 Ranjitsinhji, *The Jubilee Book of Cricket* (1897), pp. 467–8.
10 Details of this match from Sale, *Korty, The Legend Explained* (1986), pp. 91–6.
11 *Memorial Biography*, p. 276.
12 Jessop, *A Cricketer's Log*, p. 41.
13 Ibid.
14 *Memorial Biography*, p. 73.
15 Kynaston, *W.G.'s Birthday Party*, p. 80. Kynaston is the main source for this section of the chapter.
16 Quoted in Warne, *Dr W. G. Grace*, p. 41.
17 Quoted in Kynaston, *W.G.'s Birthday Party*, p. 105.
18 Ibid.
19 *Memorial Biography*, p. 277.
20 Ibid.

THIRTY

1 Both letters courtesy David Kynaston.
2 *Memorial Biography*, p. 353.
3 Troup, *Sporting Memories* (1924), p. 57.
4 Brownlee, *W. G. Grace*, p. 133.
5 Interview with Dr Richard Bernard.
6 Jones, *Gentlemen and Players*, p. 54.
7 *Arrowsmith's Dictionary of Bristol* (1906), pp. 325–6.
8 Valuation for Estate Duty, Public Record Office, I.R. 59/459 30979.
9 Quoted in Kynaston, *W.G.'s Birthday Party*, p. 5.
10 Campbell, *Reminiscences of a Vintner* (1950), p. 49.

11 Porritt, *The Best I Remember* (1922), pp. 31–2.
12 Ibid., p. 32.
13 Ibid., p. 33.
14 Ibid., p. 34.
15 Warne, *Dr W. G. Grace*, p. 45.
16 Item 26, Roy David's Catalogue of Manuscripts and Literary Portraits.
17 Warner, *Long Innings* (1951), p. 36.
18 Leavitt, *Typhoid Mary* (1996), p. 27.
19 Quoted in Allen (ed.), *Cricket with Grace*, p. 57.
20 Alfred D. Taylor, 'The London County CC: Its Rise and Fall', in *Cricket*, 22 December 1904, p. 468.
21 *The Times*, 8 May 1899.
22 Quoted in Sharpham, *Trumper* (1985), pp. 35, 36.
23 *The Times*, 11 May, 1899.
24 Ibid.
25 Ibid., 26 May 1899.
26 Quoted in Thomson, *The Great Cricketer*, p. 114.
27 Troup, *Sporting Memories*, p. 94.
28 Quoted in Thomson, *The Great Cricketer*, p. 115.
29 Fry, *A Life Worth Living*, p. 202.
30 Ibid., p. 205.
31 *The Times*, 2 June 1899.
32 Sharpham, *Trumper*, p. 40.
33 *Cricket*, 8 June 1899.
34 *The Times*, 3 June, 1899.
35 Ibid.
36 Fry, *A Life Worth Living*, p. 207.
37 *Cricket*, 8 June 1899.
38 *The Times*, 5 June 1899.
39 Ibid.
40 Sharpham, *Trumper*, p. 41.
41 Grace, *Reminiscences*, pp. 368–9.
42 Coldham, *F. S. Jackson* (1989), p. 131.
43 *Memorial Biography*, p. 282.
44 Letter from A. S. Horley, author's collection.
45 Fry, *A Life Worth Living*, p. 206.
46 Wakley, *Classic Centuries*, p. 299.
47 Fry, *A Life Worth Living*, p. 207.
48 Hodgson, *Cricket Memories by a Country Vicar* (1930), p. 84.
49 Coldham, *Lord Hawke* (1990), p. 149.
50 *The Times*, 12 June 1899.
51 *The Sportsman*, 2 June 1899.
52 *The Times*, 16 June 1899.
53 Quoted in Sharpham, *Trumper*, p. 44.
54 *The Times*, 17 June 1899.
55 Altham, *History of Cricket*, p. 219.
56 Sharpham, *Trumper*, p 42.
57 *Memorial Biography*, p.282.
58 Grace, *W.G.'s Little Book*, p. 90.
59 Quoted in Meredith, *The Demon and the Lobster* (1987), p. 137.

60 Morrah, *The Golden Age of Cricket*, p. 98.

THIRTY-ONE

1 Bax, *W. G. Grace* (1952), p. 50.
2 *Memorial Biography*, p. 308.
3 Woods, *My Reminiscences*, p. 40.
4 Bax, *W. G. Grace*, pp. 8–9.
5 *Memorial Biography*, p. 311.
6 Quoted Lodge, *W. G. Grace: His Record*, pp. 98, 99.
7 Conan Doyle, *Memories and Adventures* (1924, new edn 1989), p. 282.
8 Ibid., p 283.
9 *Memorial Biography*, pp. 302, 311.
10 *The Times*, 12 June 1900.
11 *Wisden*, 1977, p. 138.
12 Ibid.
13 *The Times*, 12 June 1900.
14 Ibid., 14 June 1900.
15 James, *Beyond a Boundary*, p. 106.
16 *Memorial Biography*, p. 295.
17 Cutting from *The Referee*, Davis Sporting Collection, Mitchell Library, NSW.
18 *Cricket*, 14 June 1900.
19 Campbell, *Reminiscences*, p. 61.
20 *Cricket*, 22 December 1904.
21 *Memorial Biography*, p. 297.
22 Hobbs, *My Life Story* (1935), p. 60.
23 Gibson, *Jackson's Year*, p. 113.
24 *Memorial Biography*, p. 299.
25 Quoted in ibid.
26 Grace, *W.G.'s Little Book*, pp. 31, 32.
27 Quoted in Neville Weston, *W. G. Grace, The Great Cricketer*, p. 134.
28 Campbell, *Reminiscences*, p. 67.
29 Newspaper cutting, Gloucestershire CC Collection, County Ground, Bristol.
30 Grace, *W.G.'s Little Book*, p. 90.
31 *Cricket*, 29 October 1908.

THIRTY-TWO

1 I am indebted to Donald Trelford's article in the *Daily Telegraph* (20 January 1998) for this story.
2 Porritt, *The Best I Remember*, p. 33.
3 Quoted in Martin-Jenkins (ed.), *The Spirit of Cricket* (1994), p. 6.
4 Fry, *A Life Worth Living*, p. 55.
5 *Memorial Biography*, p. 298.
6 Kynaston, *W.G.'s Birthday Party*, p. 127.
7 Information supplied by Colonel G. F. Grace.
8 Personal communication from Robert Gretton.
9 James, *Beyond a Boundary*, p. 163.
10 *The Times*, 11 November 1903.
11 *Wisden*, 1908, pp. 30–31.

12 *Times Literary Supplement*, 3 June 1909.
13 Letters, Lord's Collection.
14 *Memorial Biography*, pp. 343, 344.
15 Ibid., p. 340.
16 *Daily Telegraph*, 24 January 1905.
17 Jessop, *A Cricketer's Log*, pp. 48–9.
18 Darwin, *W. G. Grace*, pp. 109–10.
19 *Memorial Biography*, p. 330.
20 Ibid., p. 336.
21 Roger Mann Collection.
22 *Memorial Biography*, p. 336.
23 Roger Mann Collection.
24 Public Record Office, ref. I.R. 59/459 30979.
25 12 October 1910, Lord's Collection.
26 Ashley-Cooper, *Edward Mills Grace*, p. 137.
27 Lord's Collection.
28 Information supplied by Colonel G. F. Grace.
29 *Wisden*, 1912, p. 168.
30 *The Times*, 22 May 1911.
31 Quoted in Bax, *W. G. Grace*, p. 51.
32 Lord's Collection.
33 David Frith Collection.
34 *Wisden*, 1914, p. 125.
35 Quoted in Thomson, *The Great Cricketer*, p. 125.
36 *Eltham and District Times*, 31 July 1914.
37 *The Sportsman*, 4 August 1914.
38 Tennyson, *From Verse to Worse* (1933), pp. 126, 127.
39 *The Sportsman*, 27 August 1914.
40 Ibid., 29 August 1914.
41 A. J. Batchelder, 'Playing the Greater Game: The Melbourne Cricket Club and Its Ground in World War I' (work in progress on behalf of the Melbourne Cricket Club Library).
42 Correspondence in the Lord's Collection.
43 Quoted in Darwin, *W. G. Grace*, p. 121.
44 *The Times*, 6 April 1915.
45 Quoted in Weston, *W. G. Grace, The Great Cricketer*, pp. 152, 153.
46 Quoted in Midwinter, *W. G. Grace*, p. 148.
47 Hunt and Hueffer (Ford), *Zeppelin Nights* (1916), p. 4.
48 Conan Doyle, *Memories*, p. 349.
49 12 October 1915, Lord's Collection.
50 Gardiner, *Pebbles on the Shore* (by 'Alpha of the Plough'; 1916), pp. 27–8.
51 *The Times*, 27 October 1915.
52 Information supplied by Colonel G. F. Grace.
53 Figures from the Valuation for Estate Duty in the Estate of Dr W. G. Grace (9 November 1915), Public Record Office, ref. I.R. 59/459 30979.
54 Quoted in Mason, *Jack Hobbs* (1960), p. 5.

INDEX

547